3/20

AP®
Psychology
Prep Plus
2020 & 2021

Withdrawn

D1608943

Editor:

M. Dominic Eggert

Special thanks to the following for their contributions to this text: Kathleen Alto, Elizabeth Babcock-Atkinson, Steve Bartley, Jimmy Carney, Olivia Cortellini, Brandon Deason, Monique Diderich, Tim Eich, Elizabeth Flagge, Paul Forn, Ashley Gifford, Joanna Graham, Adam Grey, Allison Harm, Katy Haynicz-Smith, Peter Haynicz-Smith, Samee Kirk, Rebecca Knauer, William Kochen, Laura Krivicich, Jennifer Land, Charlotte Larson, Liz Laub, Mandy Luk, Maureen McMahon, Jenn Moore, Iain Morton, Kristin Murner, Monica Ostolaza, Jose Pamintuan, Aishwarya Pillai, Dominique Polfliet, Maria Pomponio, Andrea Quinn, Mary Jo Rhodes, Jason Selzer, Noah Silva, Vaishnavi Tata, Rebecca Truong, Oscar Velazquez, Lee Weiss, Robert Verini, Veena Veeravalli, Bonnie Wang, Shayna Webb-Dray, Dan Wittich, MJ Wu, Jessica Yee, Amy Zarkos, and Nina Zhang.

Published by Kaplan Publishing, a division of Kaplan, Inc.
750 Third Avenue
New York, NY 10017

10 9 8 7 6 5 4 3 2 1

Retail ISBN: 978-1-5062-5977-2
Course ISBN: 978-1-5062-5979-6

Kaplan Publishing print books are available at special quantity discounts to use for sales promotions, employee premiums, or educational purposes. For more information or to purchase books, please call the Simon & Schuster special sales department at 866-506-1949.

TABLE OF CONTENTS

Additional resources available at www.kaptest.com/moreonline

Table of Contents

PART 4: PRACTICE EXAMS

PART 1

Getting Started

CHAPTER 1

What You Need to Know about the AP Psychology Exam

EXAM STRUCTURE

The AP Psychology exam is divided into two sections. Section I gives you 70 minutes to answer 100 multiple-choice questions covering a variety of topics from introductory psychology. Each question contains five possible answer choices, with only one correct response. The nine official AP Psychology course units, along with the frequency of questions on each topic, are as follows:

Unit 1: Scientific Foundations of Psychology (10–14%)

Unit 2: Biological Bases of Behavior (8–10%)

Unit 3: Sensation and Perception (6–8%)

Unit 4: Learning (7–9%)

Unit 5: Cognitive Psychology (13–17%)

Unit 6: Developmental Psychology (7–9%)

Unit 7: Motivation, Emotion, and Personality (11–15%)

Unit 8: Clinical Psychology (12–16%)

Unit 9: Social Psychology (8–10%)

Section II gives you 50 minutes to answer two free-response questions. These questions can involve any of the content tested in the multiple-choice section, but will require you to make connections across a variety of theories and ideas that relate to each question's theme. To receive full credit on one of these questions, you'll need to write a brief essay that discusses a number of specified concepts or completes a number of particular tasks, often listed as bullet points in the prompt.

EXAM SCORING

Section I is worth 100 points (one point per question), two-thirds of the total points on the exam. The questions in Section II are each worth 7 raw points. These raw points are then multiplied by a constant term ($\frac{25}{7}$, or about 3.57) in order to yield a weighted score out of 25 points for each of the two questions. Altogether, the 50 points available in Section II constitute one-third of the exam total.

✔ **AP Expert Note**

The Power of Guessing

Each correct multiple-choice question is worth one point, but no points are deducted from your score for answering a question incorrectly. So be sure to fill in an answer for every question! Even a blind guess has a 20% chance of being correct.

Multiple-choice scores are calculated by machine, but free-response questions are graded by actual human beings. Thus, you should make sure to write legibly. While it's essential to address every task specified in the prompt, it's not enough to just list ideas. You'll need to write sentences and paragraphs that form a coherent essay.

After your total score out of 150 points is calculated, your results are converted to a scaled score from 1 to 5. The range of points for each scaled score varies depending on the difficulty of the exam in a particular year, but the significance of each value is constant from year to year. According to the College Board, AP scores should be interpreted as follows:

5 = Extremely well qualified

4 = Very well qualified

3 = Qualified

2 = Possibly qualified

1 = No recommendation

Colleges will generally not award credit for any score below a 3, with more selective schools requiring a 4 or 5. Note that some schools will not award college credit regardless of score. Be sure to research schools that you plan to apply to, so you can determine the score you need to aim for on the AP Psychology exam.

Registration and Fees

To register for the exam, contact your school guidance counselor or AP Coordinator. If your school does not administer the AP exam, contact the College Board for a listing of schools that do.

There is a fee for taking AP exams, the current value of which can be found at the official exam website listed below. For students with acute financial need, the College Board offers a fee reduction equal to about one-third of the cost of the exam. In addition, most states offer exam subsidies to cover all or part of the remaining cost for eligible students. To learn about other sources of financial aid, contact your AP Coordinator.

For more information on all things AP, contact the Advanced Placement Program:

Phone: (888) 225-5427 or (212) 632-1780
Email: apstudents@info.collegeboard.org
Website: https://apstudent.collegeboard.org/home

CHAPTER 2

How to Get the Score You Need

HOW TO GET THE MOST OUT OF THIS BOOK

Kaplan's *AP Psychology Prep Plus* contains precisely what you'll need to get the score you want in the time you have to study. The unique format of this book allows you to customize your prep experience to make the most of your time. Start by going to https://www.kaptest.com/moreonline to register your book and get a glimpse of the additional online resources available to you.

Book Features

Specific AP Psychology Strategies

Later in this chapter (in "Question Strategies") and in the following chapter ("How to Answer Free-Response Questions"), you'll find a discussion of test-taking strategies tailored specifically to the AP Psychology exam. You'll learn how best to prepare for and answer each of the types of questions the exam contains: multiple-choice and free-response.

Customizable Study Plans

We recognize that every student is a unique individual and that there's no single recipe for success that works for everyone. To give you the best chance to succeed, we have developed three customizable study plans, each offering guidance on how to make the most of your study time, based on how many weeks you have to prepare. In addition, each of the Rapid Review and Practice chapters contains assessments that will help you to determine your strengths and weaknesses, along with specific recommendations on how to use that knowledge to better organize your studying. To begin the process, start with the section that follows entitled "Choosing the Best Study Plan for You."

Rapid Review and Practice

If you browsed the table of contents, you may have noticed that every topic covered on the test actually appears in two chapters: one labeled "Rapid Review and Practice" and the other labeled "Comprehensive Review." The Rapid Review and Practice chapters (4–12) each follow a deliberate pattern that enables you to make optimal choices about how to study. After introducing the chapter's Learning Objectives, each begins with a "Test What You Already Know" section containing a quiz and a checklist of key terms, so you can see how you stand with the content before you even begin studying it. In the middle, the section entitled "Rapid Review" contains a summary of key takeaways on the topic and a complete list of definitions for all of the key terms. Finally, the "Test What You Learned" section contains another quiz and another checklist, so you can see how you're doing after some studying. For both the pre-quiz and post-quiz, there are recommended "Next Steps," which will give you prep advice and instructions based on your performance. In short, the Rapid Review and Practice chapters will allow you to figure out exactly how much you need to study each topic and precisely what to do to study that topic effectively.

Comprehensive Review

Chapters 13–21 are the Comprehensive Review chapters. These chapters are like an abbreviated version of the textbook you used in your class. They review everything you need to know for the exam and highlight key terms (theories, concepts, historic experiments, etc.) in bold. In fact, these bold terms are the very same ones that appear in the Rapid Review and Practice checklists, and they follow the exact same order to make it easier for you to navigate between Comprehensive and Rapid Review chapters. The most commonly tested subtopics in these chapters are denoted with High Yield icons to help you recognize when information is absolutely essential to know.

Online Quizzes

While this book contains nearly 800 test-like questions, distributed across the pre-quizzes, post-quizzes, and full-length practice exams, you may still find yourself wanting additional practice on particular topics. That's what the online quizzes are for, with one additional quiz for each of the topic areas, for a total of 225 additional questions. Go to kaptest.com/moreonline to find them all.

Full-Length Practice Exams

In addition to all of the practice questions featured in quizzes, this book contains six full-length practice exams. These practice exams precisely mimic the real test; both multiple-choice and free-response sections are included, and the frequency of questions on different topics are exactly what you can expect when you take the real thing. Taking a practice AP exam gives you an idea of what it's like to answer psychology questions for two hours. Granted, that's not exactly a fun experience, but it is a helpful one. And the best part is that it doesn't count! Mistakes you make on our practice exams are mistakes you won't make on your real exam. See the study plan bookmarks for guidance on when to take these practice exams. To score your exams and see what number out of 5 you would achieve for a similar performance on the real thing, check out the score calculators in your online resources.

CHOOSING THE BEST STUDY PLAN FOR YOU

The tear-out sheet in the front of the book consists of three separable bookmarks, each of which covers a specific customizable study plan. You can use one of these bookmarks both to hold your place in the book and to keep track of your progress in completing one of these study plans. But how do you choose the study plan that's right for you?

Fortunately, all you need to know to make this decision is how much time you have to prep. If you have two months or more with plenty of time to study, then you should use the Two Months Plan. If you only have about a month, or more than a month but with less time to focus on AP Psychology, choose the One Month Plan. Finally, if you have less than a month to prep, your best bet is the Two Weeks Plan.

Regardless of the plan you choose, you have flexibility in how you follow the instructions. You can stick to the order and timing that the plan recommends or tailor those recommendations to your particular study schedule. For example, if you have six weeks before your exam, you could use the One Month Plan, but spread out the recommended activities for Week 1 across the first two weeks of your studying. Use the guidelines in the Rapid Review and Practice chapters, and your performance on those quizzes and key term identifications, to further customize how you study.

QUESTION STRATEGIES

The AP Psychology exam can be challenging, but with the right strategic mindset, you can get yourself on track for earning the 3, 4, or 5 that you need to qualify for college credit or advanced placement. Below and in the following chapter are strategies to aid you on each section of the exam. These section-specific strategies and the factual information reviewed in the chapters that follow are the one-two punch that'll make your performance on Test Day a knock-out!

Multiple-Choice Questions

Terminology

AP Psychology multiple-choice questions tend to be pretty straightforward in what they ask. Usually, they revolve around particular key terms, including major theories and concepts, historical experiments and studies, and noteworthy psychologists and thinkers. The vast majority of questions will ask you to either (1) identify one of these terms based on a description or (2) give you the term and ask you to define or apply it. Thus, the number-one tip for succeeding on the multiple-choice section is this: *Know your terminology!* Free-response questions (as you'll see below) also heavily rely on knowledge of terminology, so learning these terms and practicing with them by answering sample questions is hands-down the best way to prepare for the AP Psychology exam.

When studying terminology, it's crucial to learn both the definitions of terms and the connections they have to other terms. For example, for specific theoretical approaches, you should know what theories and concepts they include, as well as which psychologists belong to each approach. For specific psychologists, you should know what theories or concepts they are responsible for, as well as any major experiments they may have conducted. As you'll review in Chapter 17 on cognitive psychology, organizing the information in your mind in a more interconnected way will make it easier to recall when you take the exam.

Pacing

The questions on the AP Psychology exam are numbered, but that doesn't mean you have to answer them in the order presented. Keep in mind that with 70 minutes to answer 100 questions, you only have 42 seconds on average to answer each question. So if you spend minutes puzzling over a tough question, you lose time that you might spend more effectively answering other questions. Every question, regardless of how hard or easy it seems, is worth the same amount. That means you should feel free to answer the questions in an order that plays to your strengths and minimizes your weaknesses. Always be willing to skip over a tough question and come back to it later.

Process of Elimination and Educated Guessing

A blind guess on the AP Psychology exam gives you a 1-in-5 (20%) chance of getting the correct answer. But every wrong answer you can confidently eliminate increases those odds: eliminate one and you're at 25%, two and you're at 33%, three and you're at 50%. And if you eliminate all four incorrect answers, you just got the question right! So, whenever the correct answer isn't immediately clear, start eliminating and see where it gets you.

Free-Response Questions

While the free-response questions in Section II of the exam test the same content as the multiple-choice questions in Section I, the strategies involved in answering these questions are different enough to merit a separate chapter. See Chapter 3, "How to Answer Free-Response Questions," for everything you need to know to maximize your score.

COUNTDOWN TO THE EXAM

Three Days Before the Exam

Take a full-length practice exam under timed conditions. Use the techniques and strategies you've learned in this book. Approach the exam strategically, actively, and confidently.

> ✔ **AP Expert Note**
>
> Do NOT take a full-length practice exam if you have fewer than 48 hours left before your real exam. Doing so will probably exhaust you and may hurt your score on the actual test.

Two Days Before the Exam

Go over the results of your last practice exam. Don't worry too much about your score or whether you got a specific question right or wrong. Instead, examine your overall performance on the different topics, choose a few of the topics where you struggled the most, and brush up on them one final time.

The Night Before the Exam

DO NOT STUDY. Get together an "AP Psychology Exam Kit" containing the following items:

- A watch (as long as it doesn't have internet access, have an alarm, or make noise)
- A few No. 2 pencils (pencils with slightly dull points fill the ovals better; mechanical pencils are NOT permitted)
- A pen with black or dark blue ink (for the free-response questions)
- Erasers
- Your 6-digit school code (home-schooled students will be provided with their state's or country's home-school code at the time of the exam)
- Photo ID card
- Your AP Student Pack
- If applicable, your Student Accommodation Letter, which verifies that you have been approved for a testing accommodation such as braille or large-type exams

Know exactly where you're going, how you're getting there, and how long it takes to get there. It's probably a good idea to visit your test center sometime before the day of your exam so that you know what to expect—what the rooms are like, how the desks are set up, and so on.

Relax the night before the exam. Read a good book, take a long, hot shower, watch something you'll enjoy. Get a good night's sleep. Go to bed early and leave yourself extra time in the morning.

The Morning of the Exam

First, wake up on time. Then:

- Eat breakfast. Make it something substantial, but nothing too heavy or greasy.
- Don't drink a lot of coffee if you're not used to it. Bathroom breaks cut into your time, and too much caffeine is a bad idea.
- Dress in layers so that you can adjust to the temperature of the testing room.
- Read something. Warm up your brain with a newspaper or a magazine. You shouldn't let the exam be the first thing you read that day.
- Be sure to get there early. Allow yourself extra time for traffic, mass transit delays, and/or detours.

During the Exam

Don't be shaken. If you find your confidence slipping, remind yourself how well you've prepared. You know the structure of the exam; you know the instructions; you've had practice with—and have learned strategies for—every question type.

If something goes really wrong, don't panic. If you accidentally misgrid your answer page or put the answers in the wrong section, raise your hand and tell the proctor. He or she may be able to arrange for you to regrid your exam after it's over, when it won't cost you any time.

After the Exam

You might walk out of the AP Psychology exam thinking that you blew it. This is a normal reaction. Lots of people—even the highest scorers—feel that way. You tend to remember the questions that stumped you, not the ones that you knew. We're positive that you will have performed well and scored your best on the exam because you followed the Kaplan strategies outlined in this and the next chapter and reviewed all the content provided in the other chapters. Be confident in your preparation, and celebrate the fact that the AP Psychology exam is soon to be a distant memory!

CHAPTER 3

How to Answer Free-Response Questions

FREE-RESPONSE QUESTION STRATEGY

Overview

A full third of the available points on the AP Psychology exam come in the second and final section, Free Response. To achieve your goal score on Test Day, it's essential to go into Section II prepared. This chapter covers everything you need to know to expertly answer free-response questions (FRQs).

Your AP Psychology exam will actually include two free-response questions: a Concept Application question and a Research Design question. The Concept Application question typically provides a story or other scenario and a bulleted list of seven terms that you will be asked to define and apply to the given scenario. The Research Design question will describe an experiment and ask questions about it. The questions following the Research Design scenario tend to be a little more varied than those you'll see in the Concept Application question. Some Research Design questions will ask you simply to apply psychology content as in the first type, but others may ask you to describe features or flaws of the experiment, and still others could ask you to conduct some data analysis or reach conclusions based on provided results.

Complete the Tasks

Free-response questions on the AP Psychology exam require you to do some writing, but like the multiple-choice questions, they are relatively explicit about what you need to do to get the points. Both Concept Application and Research Design prompts will begin with a paragraph that describes the context for the question, perhaps providing the details of an experiment or describing the situation of an individual facing some life challenge. This is always followed by instructions on a task or set of tasks that you need to complete (multiple tasks are labeled Part A, Part B, etc.), with each task often further divided into bullet points that specify key concepts or distinct subtasks. The bullet points will list exactly what you need to write about, while the task(s) will indicate how you should discuss those ideas. The number of parts may vary, but there will always be a total of 7 raw points available for each question (which will then be multiplied to yield a score out of 25, as explained in Chapter 1).

To get all 7 of those raw points, you must complete all the specified tasks and subtasks. The types of tasks that the exam requires are relatively limited in number. Some of the most common are below.

- A task that uses the verb *identify* generally requires you only to name a particular relevant concept and connect it to the prompt.

- A task that says to *give an example* requires you to provide an appropriate example of the concept that's relevant to the prompt.

- A task that instructs you to *describe*, *show*, or *illustrate* a concept or theory requires you to define the term and apply it to the prompt.

- A task that uses *discuss*, *relate*, or *explain* requires you to go into greater depth about a particular concept or theory, possibly making connections to other ideas in your response.

Generally speaking, regardless of the task, simply identifying or defining a term will be insufficient; you'll need to apply that theory or concept to the specific situation in the prompt.

> **✔ AP Expert Note**
>
> You can only earn points for the tasks you attempt! Give it your best shot when you're not sure about a bullet point, because you may still end up saying enough to earn you the point. Just try not to contradict anything you say elsewhere in your response, and avoid common misconceptions, which can cause you to lose a point that you'd otherwise gain.

Plan Your Response

Now that you have a sense of *what* you need to do to earn those points, let's consider *how* you do it. You have 50 minutes for all of Section II, which leaves you only 25 minutes per question. Begin with whichever FRQ seems easier to you and aim to finish it in less than 25 minutes, so you have more time for the harder question.

Don't just begin writing; first, take three to five minutes to construct a plan for your response. You can generally follow the order provided by the list of tasks and subtasks, but you don't have to. Sometimes listed terms can be regrouped out of order and discussed together, so it can be helpful to jot down a brief outline on scratch paper to work out how you will complete each subtask successfully. Once you've laid out a plan of attack on paper or in your head, you're ready to begin writing.

> **✔ AP Expert Note**
>
> **Regrouping Subtasks**
>
> For an example of regrouping subtasks to better organize terms with similar meanings, see the Concept Application sample question later in this chapter.

Write Simply and Clearly

When composing your response, it's essential to recognize the difference between answering an AP Psychology FRQ and writing an essay. The grader of your response is given explicit instructions regarding how to award points. These instructions designate the content that is required for each point. Nowhere in the rubric are graders instructed to award points based on characteristics like style or word choice, so your focus while writing should be to answer the questions posed as directly as possible. This means that separate introductory and conclusion paragraphs are unnecessary. This is not to say that you should write FRQ responses as a set of bullet points—in fact, the exam explicitly discourages you from merely listing facts. Rather, you should introduce topics briefly (with no more than a sentence or two) and group related concepts together in paragraphs to make for easier reading. For examples of how to do this, see the sample responses in the next section.

Once you're ready to start writing, be sure to follow the plan you laid out earlier—there's a reason you invested a few minutes in planning. If you're unsure how to break up your response into paragraphs, consider using the existing structure of the question to guide you. For example, a three-part question could be written as three paragraphs, or you might split up one of the longer parts into separate paragraphs for each of the question's bullet points. Your paragraphs don't need to be masterful works of prose; you just need to put ideas into complete sentences that address all the bullet points and are clear enough for a grader to follow.

> ✔ **AP Expert Note**
>
> **Write Legibly**
>
> It doesn't matter how eloquent or effective your response is if the grader can't read it. If you have a tendency to produce indecipherable script, slow down a bit and try to write more neatly. Your score might depend on it!

SAMPLE QUESTIONS AND RESPONSES

The remainder of this chapter consists of two sample FRQs that you can use for practice. These are distinct from the FRQs contained in the six practice exams later in this book. Although each question is followed by an example response that would earn all the available points, we encourage you to try writing your own response on scratch paper first, before viewing ours. You can then compare what you wrote to what we did, and figure out how many points you would have scored with a similar question on Test Day.

Question 1: Concept Application

A dog's owners buy a new bowl that automatically dispenses food. The first time the dog approaches the bowl, a car backfires outside, making a loud noise. The dog, frightened, runs away from the bowl and refuses to approach it. Later that day the dog is hungry enough that it timidly eats from the bowl. Over the next few days, the dog stops showing distress and begins to eat from the bowl without displaying fear.

Explain how each of the following concepts relates to the scenario.

- Amygdala
- Drive-reduction theory
- Conditioned stimulus
- Approach-avoidance conflict
- Accidental conditioning
- Adrenal glands
- Extinction

> ✔ **AP Expert Note**
>
> **Responses to this kind of prompt need to both define the terms and describe how they apply to the given situation.**

Question 2: Research Design

Researchers interested in the effects of artificially induced stress hypothesize that such artificial stress has the same effect on performance as natural physiological arousal. The researchers conduct a study in which participants are asked to toss bean bags at a target from a distance of 10 meters. Trials consist of a practice phase followed by a testing phase, during which each participant is allowed five tosses. Average distance from the center of the target is measured during the testing phase. Several conditions are utilized: in the Practice condition, participants are given 30 minutes to practice; in the No Practice condition, subjects only participate in the testing phase. Additionally, some participants are given an injection of adrenaline, which induces a moderate amount of physiological stress, prior to the testing phase. The groups are numbered as shown in the table below:

	Practice	No Practice
Adrenaline Injection	Group 1	Group 3
No Injection	Group 2	Group 4

Part A

Identify each of the following in this study.

- Two independent variables
- The dependent variable

Part B

- Explain how the Yerkes-Dodson Law of Arousal applies to the study.

- Describe a change that would need to be made to the procedure for Group 4 to make it an appropriate control group.

Part C

Using the blank graph below, construct the following:

- A bar chart of results for each group that would help to support the researchers' hypothesis

- Appropriate labels for the graph's axes

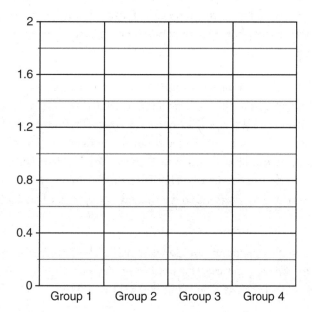

ANSWERS AND EXPLANATIONS

Question 1: Concept Application

This question is worth 7 points, 1 point for addressing each bullet. The following is a sample student response that would receive full credit, with indications of where points would be awarded in parentheses:

> This situation provides examples of several principles of classical conditioning. The fear response to the bowl is an example of accidental conditioning because the dog's approach to the bowl and the loud noise outside were unrelated, but were paired by the dog because they occurred at the same time. **(1 POINT)** The dog's bowl is a conditioned stimulus because it has been paired with an unconditioned stimulus, the loud noise, to produce a conditioned response, fear. **(1 POINT)** The dog became less afraid of the bowl over time because the loud noise did not recur. This is an example of extinction, which is the loss of a conditioned response over time when the unconditioned stimulus is no longer paired with the conditioned stimulus. **(1 POINT)**
>
> The learning that occurs is a direct result of specific biological processes. The amygdala is the structure in the brain that is associated with feelings of fear and is responsible for the dog's fear response to the loud noise. **(1 POINT)** The adrenal glands are responsible for releasing hormones like epinephrine and norepinephrine, which caused the dog's fight-or-flight response. **(1 POINT)** The dog's return to the bowl later that day can be explained by drive-reduction theory. According to this theory, physiological needs motivate behaviors to satisfy those needs. The dog's need to reduce hunger led him to use the bowl despite his fear. **(1 POINT)**
>
> The dog experiences an approach-avoidance conflict when eating from the bowl at the end of the first day because using the bowl is both appealing (to satisfy his hunger) and unappealing (a cause of fear) at the same time. **(1 POINT)**

Question 2: Research Design

This question is worth 7 points: 3 for Part A, 2 for Part B, and 2 for Part C. The following is a sample student response that would receive full credit, with indications of where points would be awarded in parentheses:

> The experiment contains three variables. The two independent variables are the amount of practice and the amount of artificially induced stress. **(2 POINTS)** The dependent variable is the average distance measured from the target. **(1 POINT)**
>
> The Yerkes-Dodson Law says that a moderate amount of arousal is helpful both when a task is well-practiced and when a task is not well-practiced. High levels of arousal are associated with a decrease in performance at low levels of practice only. The researchers are artificially inducing arousal and noting its effects on performance after differing amounts of practice. **(1 POINT)**

In order to make Group 4 an appropriate control group, the members of Group 4 could be made to perform a neutral, no-practice activity 30 minutes prior to testing to prevent introducing the confounding variable of amount of time spent in the lab. They could also receive a neutral saline injection to prevent introducing the potential confounding variable of stress caused by receiving an injection. **(1 POINT)**

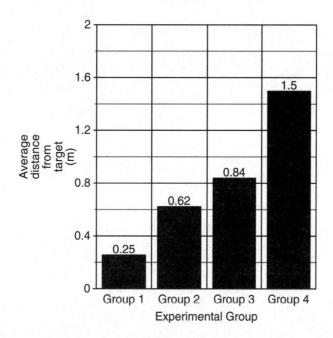

One potential response to Part C is shown above. The levels of the bars may vary and still earn credit, but Group 1 must perform better than Group 2, and Group 3 must perform better than Group 4. **(1 POINT)** Exact wording may vary, but the *x*-axis needs to identify that the groups are from the experiment, and the *y*-axis needs to include units for the distance. **(1 POINT)**

PART 2

Rapid Review and Practice

CHAPTER 4

Scientific Foundations of Psychology

LEARNING OBJECTIVES

After studying this chapter, you will be able to:

- Describe philosophical and physiological ideas leading to the foundation of psychology

- Compare and contrast distinct theoretical approaches throughout psychology's history

- Explain strengths and weaknesses of explaining behavior with psychological theories

- Distinguish between different domains in psychology

- Recognize important historical contributors to psychology

- Inventory the purpose, strengths, and weaknesses of various types of research

- Explain the effect of research design on research conclusions

- Differentiate among independent, dependent, confounding, and control variables in experiments

- Compare the uses of randomness in experimental conditions and in survey participant selection

- Evaluate the impact of research design quality on behavioral explanation validity

- Explain the importance of operational definitions and measurements to behavioral research

- Recognize the distinct purposes of descriptive and inferential statistics

- Apply basic principles of descriptive statistics

- Evaluate the impact of moral imperatives and legal guidelines on research practices

TEST WHAT YOU ALREADY KNOW

4

Part A: Quiz

1. A teacher wants to determine the impact of teaching style on quiz scores. To do this, she divides a class into two groups and teaches one group using one style and the other group using a second, different style. She then administers each group the same set of quizzes and compares results. The independent variable here is

   (A) group 1

   (B) group 2

   (C) teaching style

   (D) score on quizzes

   (E) the teacher

2. Which of the following psychologists started the first psychology lab in Germany?

   (A) William James

   (B) Wilhelm Wundt

   (C) John B. Watson

   (D) Ivan Pavlov

   (E) Sigmund Freud

3. A researcher decides to study how students in a classroom respond to positive feedback from their teacher by watching the classroom via a one-way mirror. This method of unobtrusive viewing of behavior in its usual setting is referred to as

   (A) a longitudinal study

   (B) a case study

   (C) a controlled experiment

   (D) remote viewing

   (E) naturalistic observation

4. Which philosopher is best known for his mind-body dualism?

   (A) Socrates

   (B) Aristotle

   (C) Descartes

   (D) Locke

   (E) Hume

5. If a teacher gives a test in two different classes and the scores in the second class have a larger standard deviation, which of the following MUST be true?

   (A) The scores in both classes have the same mean.

   (B) The scores in the first class have a larger mean.

   (C) The scores in the second class have a larger mean.

   (D) The scores in the first class are closer to the mean.

   (E) The scores in the second class are closer to the mean.

6. Which of the following would likely NOT be allowed based on current ethical principles for doing psychological research?

    (A) Participants give informed consent and are debriefed.

    (B) Participants give informed consent but are deceived before being debriefed.

    (C) Participants do not give informed consent but are debriefed after the study.

    (D) Participants are given full disclosure but are not able to tell the independent from the dependent variable.

    (E) Participants are not told exactly what to expect but give informed consent and are debriefed.

7. Which of the following would a social psychologist be most likely to investigate?

    (A) The amygdala's role in the fight-or-flight response

    (B) The effects of giving monetary rewards on academic success

    (C) Why humans often make irrational financial decisions

    (D) How the size of a group influences decisions made by group members

    (E) How unresolved internal conflicts affect one's personality

8. Suppose a researcher finds the correlation between two variables to be −0.98. Which of the following would then be an accurate statement?

    (A) There is a very weak relationship between the variables.

    (B) There is a very strong relationship between the variables.

    (C) Because the number is negative, there is almost no relationship between the variables.

    (D) Because the number is so close to −1, it is safe to conclude that one variable causes the other variable.

    (E) One of the variables must be a dependent variable and the other an independent variable.

9. Which of the following is a valid use for inferential statistics?

    (A) Establishing the strength of a relationship between variables

    (B) Establishing cause and effect between variables

    (C) Generalizing about a population

    (D) Describing a data set

    (E) Formulating hypotheses

10. To limit bias, a researcher decides which subjects are assigned to the experimental and control groups by drawing names out of a hat. This is an example of

    (A) random sampling

    (B) representative sampling

    (C) stratified sampling

    (D) random assignment

    (E) group matching

Part B: Key Terms

The following is a list of the major ideas and people for the AP Psychology topic of Scientific Foundations of Psychology. You will likely see many of these on the AP Psychology exam.

For each key term, ask yourself the following questions:

- Can I describe this key term?
- Can I discuss this key term in relation to other psychological ideas and specific psychologists?
- Could I correctly answer a multiple-choice question about this key term?
- Could I correctly answer a free-response question about this key term?

Check off the key terms if you can answer "yes" to at least three of these questions.

Precursors to Psychology

☐ René Descartes   ☐ Empiricism   ☐ Evolution

☐ Mind-body dualism   ☐ David Hume   ☐ Phrenology

☐ John Locke   ☐ Principles of association   ☐ Psychophysics

Theoretical Approaches

☐ Introspection   ☐ Behaviorism   ☐ Humanistic psychology

☐ Structuralism   ☐ Gestalt psychology   ☐ Cognitive revolution

☐ Functionalism   ☐ Psychoanalysis   ☐ Sociocultural approach

☐ Biological approach   ☐ Psychodynamic psychology

☐ Eugenics

Psychological Domains

☐ Biological psychology/ neuropsychology   ☐ Environmental psychology   ☐ Industrial and organizational psychology

☐ Clinical psychology   ☐ Experimental psychology   ☐ Personality psychology

☐ Cognitive psychology   ☐ Evolutionary psychology   ☐ Psycholinguistics

☐ Community psychology   ☐ Forensic psychology   ☐ Psychometrics

☐ Counseling psychology   ☐ Gerontological psychology/gerontology   ☐ Rehabilitation psychology

☐ Developmental psychology   ☐ Health psychology   ☐ School psychology

☐ Educational psychology   ☐ Human factors psychology   ☐ Social psychology

☐ Sport psychology

Important Contributors

- ☐ Alfred Adler
- ☐ Jerome S. Bruner
- ☐ Mary Whiton Calkins
- ☐ Noam Chomsky
- ☐ Charles Darwin
- ☐ Dorothea Dix
- ☐ Gustav Fechner
- ☐ Leon Festinger
- ☐ Sigmund Freud

- ☐ Franz Joseph Gall
- ☐ G. Stanley Hall
- ☐ Hermann von Helmholtz
- ☐ William James
- ☐ Carl Jung
- ☐ Abraham Maslow
- ☐ Ivan Pavlov
- ☐ Jean Piaget
- ☐ Carl Rogers

- ☐ B.F. Skinner
- ☐ Edward Titchener
- ☐ Lev S. Vygotsky
- ☐ Margaret Floy Washburn
- ☐ John B. Watson
- ☐ Ernst H. Weber
- ☐ Max Wertheimer
- ☐ Wilhelm Wundt

Types of Psychological Research

- ☐ Quantitative research
- ☐ Qualitative research
- ☐ Correlation coefficient
- ☐ Positive correlation
- ☐ Negative correlation
- ☐ Naturalistic observation
- ☐ Structured observation
- ☐ Coding

- ☐ Inter-rater reliability
- ☐ Participant observation
- ☐ Hawthorne effect
- ☐ Longitudinal study
- ☐ Cross-sectional study
- ☐ Case study
- ☐ Survey
- ☐ Nonresponse bias

- ☐ Surveyor bias
- ☐ Experiments
- ☐ Hypothesis
- ☐ Controlled experiment
- ☐ Field experiment
- ☐ Natural experiment/ quasi-experiment

Research Design

- ☐ Independent variables
- ☐ Dependent variables
- ☐ Control variables
- ☐ Confounding variables
- ☐ Control group
- ☐ Experimental group
- ☐ Placebo effect

- ☐ Placebo
- ☐ Single-blind experiment
- ☐ Double-blind experiment
- ☐ Sample
- ☐ Population
- ☐ Random sampling
- ☐ Representative sample

- ☐ Random assignment
- ☐ Internal validity
- ☐ External validity
- ☐ Demand characteristics
- ☐ Observer-expectancy effect
- ☐ Operational definition

4

Statistics

☐ Descriptive statistics   ☐ Type I error   ☐ Mean

☐ Inferential statistics   ☐ Type II error   ☐ Median

☐ Parameters   ☐ Line graphs   ☐ Mode

☐ Confidence intervals   ☐ Bar graphs   ☐ Outliers

☐ Null hypothesis   ☐ Histograms   ☐ Measures of dispersion

☐ Alternative hypothesis   ☐ Scatterplots   ☐ Range

☐ p-value   ☐ Line of best fit   ☐ Variance

☐ Significance level   ☐ Measures of central tendency   ☐ Standard deviation

☐ Statistically significant

Ethical and Legal Issues

☐ Informed consent   ☐ Confidentiality   ☐ Institutional review boards (IRBs)

☐ Debriefing

Next Steps

Step 1: Tally your correct answers from Part A and review the quiz explanations at the end of this chapter.

1. C   6. C

2. B   7. D

3. E   8. B

4. C   9. C

5. D   10. D

_____ out of 10 questions

Step 2: Count the number of key terms you checked off in Part B.

_____ out of 140 key terms

Step 3: Read the Rapid Review Key Takeaways in this chapter.

Step 4: Consult the table below and follow the instructions based on your performance.

If You Got . . .	Do This
80% or more of the Test What You Already Know assessment correct (8 or more questions from Part A and 112 or more key terms from Part B)	• Read definitions in this chapter for all the key terms you didn't check off. • Complete the Test What You Learned assessment in this chapter.
50% or less of the Test What You Already Know assessment correct (5 or fewer questions from Part A and 70 or fewer key terms from Part B)	• Read the comprehensive review for this topic in Chapter 13. ◦ If you are short on time, read only the High-Yield sections. • Read through all of the key term definitions in this chapter. • Complete the Test What You Learned assessment in this chapter.
Any other result	• Read the High-Yield sections of the comprehensive review of this topic in Chapter 13. • Read definitions in this chapter for all the key terms you didn't check off. • Complete the Test What You Learned assessment in this chapter.

RAPID REVIEW

Key Takeaways

1. The science of psychology is widely recognized as beginning in 1879 with Wilhelm Wundt's founding of the first psychology lab, but it has a long prehistory in philosophy and physiology.

2. A wide variety of theoretical orientations have emerged throughout psychology's history, each of which represents a distinctive approach to investigating behavior and mental processes.

3. Contemporary psychology consists of numerous specialized domains; today, there are many different types of psychologists.

4. Psychology would not be the science that it is today without the contributions of many talented men and women.

5. The study of psychology relies on a diverse array of qualitative and quantitative research methods, including observations, case studies, surveys, and controlled experiments.

6. Psychological research is carefully designed so that researchers can be confident about using results to draw conclusions about real-life phenomena. This is done by controlling variables, creating representative samples, controlling for internal and external validity, and operationalizing definitions and measurements.

7. Researchers use statistics to analyze and make sense of the data gathered in a research study. This involves the use of descriptive statistics like measures of central tendency and dispersion, as well as inferential statistics for making generalizations based on the data.

8. Because psychological study often involves the participation of human subjects, researchers must abide by established ethical principles and practices as well as by legal guidelines while conducting research.

Key Terms: Definitions

Precursors to Psychology

René Descartes: A French philosopher and mathematician well known for his endorsement of mind-body dualism.

Mind-body dualism: Maintains that the mind and the body are distinct substances, each operating according to its own set of principles.

John Locke: An English philosopher and empiricist who believed that every human mind begins as a *tabula rasa*, or blank slate, which is shaped by individual experiences to become a unique person.

Empiricism: The idea that all knowledge comes from experience; embraced by philosophers such as Locke and Hume, it also remains influential in contemporary psychology and other experimental sciences.

David Hume: A Scottish empiricist and member of the Associationist School who proposed several principles of association.

Principles of association: Rules that govern the ways in which the mind connects one idea to another and constructs complex ideas out of simpler ones.

Evolution: The idea, developed by Darwin, that species change over time, adapting to their environments in order to maximize survival and reproductive success by means of natural selection.

Phrenology: The idea developed by German physiologists Gall and Spurzheim that personal traits could be revealed by measuring the size and location of bumps on a person's skull; thoroughly discredited by subsequent research.

Psychophysics: A subfield of physiology created by the German scientists Weber and Fechner and concerned with the relationship between physical stimuli and the sensations they cause.

Theoretical Approaches

Introspection: A technique used by early scientific psychologists consisting of precise examination and description of an individual's conscious experience, typically in response to stimuli presented by the researcher.

Structuralism: The theoretical approach developed in the late nineteenth century by Wundt and Titchener, which seeks to uncover the structures of consciousness through detailed descriptions of experience in laboratory settings.

Functionalism: Developed by William James in response to structuralism, an approach that emphasized the functions of the mind over its structures and focused on how aspects of consciousness allowed human beings to adapt to their environments.

Biological approach: An approach that maintains that all psychological phenomena have a biological basis; emphasizes neuroscience, genetics, and evolution in its explanations.

Eugenics: The controversial and discredited idea that the human species can be improved through selective breeding.

Behaviorism: A theoretical approach founded on the belief that psychology should only study observable and measurable behavior; behaviorists emphasize the impact of learning and other environmental forces on human and animal behavior.

Gestalt psychology: A response to structuralism developed by Max Wertheimer and others in the early twentieth century that sought to discover principles that organized the whole of perceptual experience.

Psychoanalysis: The therapeutic approach invented by Freud, premised on the idea that some symptoms are the results of conflicts and other problems in the unconscious mind.

Psychodynamic psychology: The collective term used to describe the approaches of Freud, Jung, Adler, Horney, and similar thinkers, which tend to rely on ideas about the unconscious; influential in the early development of clinical psychology.

Humanistic psychology: Developed in the mid-twentieth century by Maslow, Rogers, and others, an approach that emphasizes human freedom and self-development.

Cognitive revolution: The ascendance of the cognitive approach in psychology, which sought to investigate a wide variety of cognitive processes, including language, memory, and attention.

Sociocultural approach: A perspective that emphasizes how social and cultural contexts influence the development of human cognition and behavior.

Psychological Domains

Biological psychology/neuropsychology: Biological psychologists and neuropsychologists investigate how the brain and nervous system cause behavior.

Clinical psychology: Clinical psychologists specialize in helping people who suffer from psychological disorders.

Cognitive psychology: Cognitive psychologists are interested in thinking and other cognitive processes, such as perception, memory, language use, reasoning, and decision making.

Community psychology: Community psychologists help build collaborative relationships among community members, organizations, and other groups to solve social problems. They study how individuals relate to their communities and the effect those communities have on the individual.

Counseling psychology: Though similar in some respects to clinical psychologists, counseling psychologists tend to assist individuals with less severe problems. They often help people looking for guidance in navigating through ordinary difficulties in life.

Developmental psychology: Developmental psychologists focus on human development throughout the course of life.

Educational psychology: Educational psychologists investigate how a variety of factors, such as ability, motivation, and classroom setting, affect students.

Environmental psychology: Environmental psychologists study the interactions between people and the natural environment and explore issues such as the impact of environmental stress on psychological health and productivity.

Experimental psychology: Experimental psychologists design and oversee empirical research projects to gain insights into psychological processes.

Evolutionary psychology: Evolutionary psychologists understand behavior and cognition through the lens of fitness, adaptation, and other evolutionary concepts.

Forensic psychology: Forensic psychologists are usually trained in both psychology and the law; they can provide valuable expertise within the judicial system, assessing defendants and inmates, advising judges, and conducting research on issues relevant to the justice system, such as jury behavior and eyewitness testimony.

Gerontological psychology/gerontology: Gerontology is the study of aging and the elderly; gerontological psychologists assess cognitive functioning in older people and assist in determining how much assistance an older person needs on a daily basis, as well as conduct research and teaching.

Health psychology: Health psychologists examine health and illness in the context of biological, psychological, and social factors.

Human factors psychology: Human factors specialists, also known as engineering psychologists, typically investigate how human beings can work safely and effectively with machines.

Industrial and organizational psychology: Industrial and organizational psychologists apply psychological principles and research methods to the workplace and are interested in improving productivity, health, and the quality of work life.

Personality psychology: Personality psychologists investigate how our personalities develop and how they affect the ways in which we think, feel, and act.

Psycholinguistics: Psycholinguists study language acquisition and other psychological processes that involve language.

Psychometrics: Psychometricians study the theories and techniques of psychological measurement. Some design tests that measure intelligence, attitudes, personality traits, and other psychological characteristics.

Rehabilitation psychology: Rehabilitation psychologists work with people affected by injuries, disabilities, and other medical conditions, helping clients adapt to their new situations, including adjusting to work and pain management.

School psychology: The majority of school psychologists work for school systems and provide a wide range of services, such as diagnosis, assessment, intervention, prevention, health promotion, and program development.

Social psychology: Social psychologists study group behavior, as well as the impact of other people on the behavior of individuals.

Sport psychology: Sport psychologists are generally knowledgeable in the areas of psychology, physiology, and kinesiology. These specialists focus on optimizing the performance of athletes.

Important Contributors

Alfred Adler: Austrian medical doctor and psychotherapist who was one of the first practitioners of family counseling and an advocate of the psychodynamic approach.

Jerome S. Bruner: American cognitive psychologist who developed a theory of cognitive growth; influential in educational psychology.

Mary Whiton Calkins: Student of William James best known for self-psychology, an introspective psychology that understands the self as a conscious organism that functions and has experiences and drives.

Noam Chomsky: Linguist and cognitive psychologist who views language acquisition as an innate human characteristic and argues for a universal grammar underlying all language.

Charles Darwin: British naturalist whose scientific theory of evolution by natural selection became the foundation of modern evolutionary studies. He influenced both the early functionalists and more contemporary evolutionary psychologists.

Dorothea Dix: Best known for investigating and exposing the atrocious conditions suffered by the mentally ill in state institutions and spearheading a reform movement for the humane treatment of mental patients.

Gustav Fechner: One of the founders of psychophysics, he examined quantitative relations between sensations and the stimuli producing them.

Leon Festinger: American social psychologist best known for cognitive dissonance theory and other work in social psychology.

Sigmund Freud: Austrian founder of psychoanalysis, a form of therapy that focuses on the unconscious. He also developed the structural model of personality that distinguishes between id, ego, and superego, and a stage theory of psychosexual development.

Franz Joseph Gall: Founder of phrenology who maintained that different functions were localized in different parts of the brain.

G. Stanley Hall: First president of the American Psychological Association and student of William James; also influential in the study of child development.

Hermann von Helmholtz: Conducted research on the nervous system, eye, and ear; advanced the trichromatic theory of color vision; and was the first to measure the speed of a nerve impulse.

William James: A founder of functionalism known for the James-Lange theory of emotion. He established one of the first psychological laboratories in the United States and wrote the first psychology textbook, *The Principles of Psychology* (1890).

Carl Jung: Psychodynamic thinker best known for developing the theory of archetypes and the collective unconscious, as well as the distinction between introverted and extraverted personalities.

Abraham Maslow: Humanistic psychologist best known for his hierarchy of needs.

Ivan Pavlov: Russian physiologist most famous for his work on classical conditioning, who influenced the behaviorists.

Jean Piaget: Swiss psychologist best known for his stage theory of cognitive development.

Carl Rogers: Humanistic psychologist who developed client-centered therapy.

B.F. Skinner: American behaviorist best known for operant conditioning theory and the "Skinner box," an apparatus used in learning experiments.

Edward Titchener: Student of Wundt, credited with bringing structuralism to the United States; instrumental in the establishment of experimental psychology.

Lev S. Vygotsky: Russian psychologist who advocated for the sociocultural approach and is known for the zone of proximal development and other ideas about cognitive development.

Margaret Floy Washburn: First woman to receive a Ph.D. in psychology; best known for her book *The Animal Mind* (1908), which advocated for the scientific study of mental phenomena (contrary to the behaviorists).

John B. Watson: Founder of behaviorism, known for his contributions to classical conditioning theory and his Little Albert experiment.

Ernst H. Weber: One of the founders of psychophysics, he is known for the concept of the just-noticeable difference.

Max Wertheimer: Founder of Gestalt psychology, who emphasized the study of perception as a whole.

Wilhelm Wundt: German structuralist who founded the first psychological laboratory; widely recognized as the "father of psychology."

Types of Psychological Research

Quantitative research: Research that uses operational measurements and statistical techniques to reach conclusions on the basis of numerical data, such as correlational studies and experiments.

Qualitative research: Research that does not rely on numerical representations of data, such as naturalistic observations, unstructured interviews, and case studies.

Correlation coefficient: A number (symbolized by r) between -1 and $+1$, which represents the strength and direction of the correlation between two variables. The closer the coefficient is to -1 or $+1$, the stronger the correlation between the variables.

Positive correlation: An r value above 0, which indicates that two variables have a direct relationship: when one variable increases, the other also increases.

Negative correlation: An r value below 0, which indicates that two variables have an inverse relationship: when one variable increases, the other decreases.

Naturalistic observation: A research method, typically qualitative in nature and usually covert and undisclosed, that attempts to document behavior as it spontaneously occurs in a real-world setting.

Structured observation: A type of observational research typically conducted in a laboratory setting, where the researcher can control some aspects of the environment.

Coding: The classification of behaviors into discrete categories, used especially in structured observations to achieve a level of consistency in recording and describing observations.

Inter-rater reliability: A statistical measure of the degree of agreement between different codings of the same phenomena.

Participant observation: A mostly qualitative research method in which the researcher becomes a member of a studied group, either overtly or covertly.

Hawthorne effect: A phenomenon in which research subjects tend to alter their behavior in response to knowledge of being observed.

Longitudinal study: A research design that examines how individuals develop by studying the same sample over a long period of time.

Cross-sectional study: A research design conducted at a single point in time, comparing groups of differing ages to arrive at conclusions about development.

Case study: A research design involving an in-depth and detailed examination of a single subject, or case, usually an individual or a small group.

Survey: A mostly quantitative research method involving a list of questions filled out by a group of people to assess attitudes or opinions.

Nonresponse bias: A distortion of data that can occur in surveys with a low response rate.

Surveyor bias: A distortion of data that can occur when survey questions are written in a way that prompts respondents to answer a certain way.

Experiments: Deliberately designed procedures used to test research hypotheses.

Hypothesis: A proposed, testable explanation for a phenomenon, often constructed in the form of a statement about the relationship between two or more variables.

Controlled experiment: A research design for testing a causal hypothesis, in which all aspects of the study are deliberately controlled and only independent variables are manipulated to isolate their effects on dependent variables.

Field experiment: Experiments conducted out in the real world, with fewer controls than would be found in a lab.

Natural experiment/quasi-experiment: An experiment that does not involve the direct manipulation of variables, in which researchers rely on natural variations and advanced statistics to draw conclusions.

Research Design

Independent variables: Factors manipulated in an experiment to test their effects on one or more dependent variables.

Dependent variables: The factors measured as outcomes or results in an experiment.

Control variables: Those factors present in an experiment that are kept constant between control and experimental groups.

Confounding variables: Factors other than the independent variable(s) that influence dependent variables or that alter the effects of independent variables on dependent variables.

Control group: A group of participants in an experiment that represents a standard to which experimental groups are compared.

Experimental group: A group of participants in an experiment that is exposed to some variation of the independent variable (other than the control value).

Placebo effect: A psychological phenomenon in which a person's mere belief that he or she is receiving a treatment causes the treatment to work.

Placebo: An inactive imitation of a treatment, such as a sugar pill.

Single-blind experiment: An experiment in which the researchers know whether participants are in a control group or an experimental group, but the participants themselves lack this information.

Double-blind experiment: An experiment in which neither the researchers nor the participants know who belongs to the control and experimental groups.

Sample: All the individuals participating in a research study.

Population: The larger, total set of individuals from which the sample is selected.

Random sampling: The process of selecting individuals at random from a population to form a more representative sample.

Representative sample: A set of individuals with a range of characteristics that match that of the larger population.

Random assignment: The process of giving every participant an equal chance of being assigned to any particular group.

Internal validity: A measure of the extent to which an experiment investigates what it is supposed to; that is, the causal influence of independent variables on dependent variables.

External validity: The extent to which the results of an experiment reflects and can be generalized to real people, situations, and life outside the lab.

Demand characteristics: Factors that influence a study's participants to change their behavior (consciously or not) to fit what they believe to be the experiment's purpose.

Observer-expectancy effect: A phenomenon in which experimenters communicate (often unintentionally) their expectations of what the results of a study will be and thereby influence the behavior of participants.

Operational definition: A specification of how a particular variable will be quantified and measured.

Statistics

Descriptive statistics: Numerical values that describe basic patterns and characteristics in a set of data; includes measures of central tendency and measures of dispersion.

Inferential statistics: Statistics used to make larger generalizations, or inferences, about a population based on sets of data.

Parameter: A measurable characteristic of a population, such as average height. Parameters are contrasted with *statistics*, which are the measurable characteristics of *samples*.

Confidence interval: A range of likely values for a parameter based on statistics calculated from the sample.

Null hypothesis: The assertion that no relationship exists between the independent and dependent variables.

Alternative hypothesis: The assertion that there is a relationship (generally a causal relationship) between the independent and dependent variables.

p-value: A measure that indicates the probability that the null hypothesis is true, based on the results of the study. A lower *p*-value indicates a greater probability that the alternative hypothesis is true.

Significance level: The set percentage (usually 0.05 or 0.01) that the *p*-value must be below in order to conclude that the alternative hypothesis is supported.

Statistically significant: When the *p*-value for the null hypothesis falls below the designated significance level.

Type I error: The improper rejection of a true null hypothesis and the incorrect assumption that a relationship exists between variables (a false positive).

Type II error: The improper affirmation of a false null hypothesis and the incorrect assumption that no relationship exists between variables (a false negative).

Line graph: A graph that represents the relationship between two variables, typically with the independent variable plotted on the *x*-axis and the dependent variable plotted on the *y*-axis.

Bar graph: A graph that uses the heights or lengths of rectangular bars to represent numerical data.

Histogram: A bar graph that represents the frequency of particular data points.

Scatterplot: A graph that represents all the data points collected in a study, typically using discrete dots to represent individual data points.

Line of best fit: A straight line drawn in a scatterplot to approximate the relationship between two variables.

Measures of central tendency: Statistics that describe the middle of a distribution of data, including mean, median, and mode.

Mean: The average of a data set, equal to the sum of the data divided by the total number of data points.

Median: The value in the middle of a data set when the data is arranged in increasing or decreasing order.

Mode: The most frequently occurring value in a data set.

Outliers: Points that have extreme values relative to the rest of the data in a set.

Measures of dispersion: Statistics that describe the distribution of data in a set, including range, variance, and standard deviation.

Range: The difference between the highest value and the lowest value in a data set.

Variance: A numerical value used to show how widely individual data points differ from the mean.

Standard deviation: A measure of the average difference between any given data point and the mean.

Ethical and Legal Issues

Informed consent: The practice of obtaining consent when disclosing to subjects specific details about the research prior to participation, including its purpose, the procedures involved, the expected benefits and risks, and the participants' rights.

Debriefing: The process of disclosing important information to participants after a study concludes, including why information was concealed or distorted, the actual purpose and procedures of the study, and the results of the study.

Confidentiality: A commitment to controlling access to personal information and maintaining privacy for all research participants.

Institutional review boards (IRBs): Committees that review and approve or reject proposals for human subjects research projects based on ethical principles.

TEST WHAT YOU LEARNED

Part A: Quiz

1. Suppose a psychologist wants to study the effect of caffeine on happiness. Which of the following would be the MOST appropriate operational definition for happiness?

   (A) The number of times a subject smiles during the experiment

   (B) Whether or not the subject seems happy during the experiment

   (C) The amount of caffeine a subject consumes during the experiment

   (D) The number of times a subject smiles before the experiment

   (E) Whether or not the subject seems happy before the experiment

2. Which of the following reviews research proposals to determine whether an experiment is ethically sound?

   (A) An institutional review board (IRB)

   (B) The American Psychological Association (APA)

   (C) The researchers themselves

   (D) A review panel made up of former participants

   (E) A peer review board

3. Which of the following approaches focuses on free will and personal growth?

   (A) Biological

   (B) Cognitive

   (C) Sociocultural

   (D) Psychodynamic

   (E) Humanistic

4. Which of the following is a measure of dispersion?

   (A) Correlation

   (B) Mean

   (C) Median

   (D) Standard deviation

   (E) p-value

5. A negative correlation typically means that

   (A) variables are inversely related

   (B) variables are directly related

   (C) variables are unrelated

   (D) variables are weakly related

   (E) variables are strongly related

6. Which of the following research designs utilizes the most control?

   (A) Correlational study

   (B) Field experiment

   (C) Naturalistic observation

   (D) Participant observation

   (E) Operationalization

7. A scientist wants to study the effects of exercise on dopamine levels in rats. In such an experiment, the dependent variable would be

   (A) the group of rats made to exercise

   (B) the group of rats not made to exercise

   (C) amount of exercise

   (D) dopamine levels

   (E) the number of rats in the study

8. The psychologist who is most responsible for developing the school of thought called *functionalism* is

    (A) James

    (B) Wundt

    (C) Titchener

    (D) Watson

    (E) Skinner

9. A researcher pays a student to sort subjects into two groups and store the information in a secure document, without informing subjects of the group that they are in. After the experiment begins, one of the subjects reacts adversely, forcing the researcher to read the document. As a result, the experiment became a

    (A) single-blind experiment

    (B) placebo

    (C) case study

    (D) double-blind experiment

    (E) correlational study

10. Even though he knows it is against hospital policy, a new doctor gives his boss his username and password for the hospital's online database. When questioned about it later, the doctor said that while he knew it was wrong, he had a hard time disobeying an order from an authority figure at the hospital. Whose classic experiment does this scenario best reflect the results of?

    (A) Philip Zimbardo

    (B) Stanley Milgram

    (C) Thomas Young

    (D) Jean Piaget

    (E) Robert Rosenthal

Part B: Key Terms

This key terms list is the same as the list in the Test What You Already Know section earlier in this chapter. Based on what you have now learned, again ask yourself the following questions:

- Can I describe this key term?
- Can I discuss this key term in relation to other psychological ideas and specific psychologists?
- Could I correctly answer a multiple-choice question about this key term?
- Could I correctly answer a free-response question about this key term?

Check off the key terms if you can answer "yes" to at least three of these questions.

Precursors to Psychology

☐ René Descartes
☐ Mind-body dualism
☐ John Locke

☐ Empiricism
☐ David Hume
☐ Principles of association

☐ Evolution
☐ Phrenology
☐ Psychophysics

Theoretical Approaches

☐ Introspection
☐ Structuralism
☐ Functionalism
☐ Biological approach
☐ Eugenics

☐ Behaviorism
☐ Gestalt psychology
☐ Psychoanalysis
☐ Psychodynamic psychology

☐ Humanistic psychology
☐ Cognitive revolution
☐ Sociocultural approach

Psychological Domains

☐ Biological psychology/ neuropsychology
☐ Clinical psychology
☐ Cognitive psychology
☐ Community psychology
☐ Counseling psychology
☐ Developmental psychology
☐ Educational psychology

☐ Environmental psychology
☐ Experimental psychology
☐ Evolutionary psychology
☐ Forensic psychology
☐ Gerontological psychology/gerontology
☐ Health psychology
☐ Human factors psychology

☐ Industrial and organizational psychology
☐ Personality psychology
☐ Psycholinguistics
☐ Psychometrics
☐ Rehabilitation psychology
☐ School psychology
☐ Social psychology
☐ Sport psychology

Important Contributors

- ☐ Alfred Adler
- ☐ Jerome S. Bruner
- ☐ Mary Whiton Calkins
- ☐ Noam Chomsky
- ☐ Charles Darwin
- ☐ Dorothea Dix
- ☐ Gustav Fechner
- ☐ Leon Festinger
- ☐ Sigmund Freud

- ☐ Franz Joseph Gall
- ☐ G. Stanley Hall
- ☐ Hermann von Helmholtz
- ☐ William James
- ☐ Carl Jung
- ☐ Abraham Maslow
- ☐ Ivan Pavlov
- ☐ Jean Piaget
- ☐ Carl Rogers

- ☐ B.F. Skinner
- ☐ Edward Titchener
- ☐ Lev S. Vygotsky
- ☐ Margaret Floy Washburn
- ☐ John B. Watson
- ☐ Ernst H. Weber
- ☐ Max Wertheimer
- ☐ Wilhelm Wundt

Types of Psychological Research

- ☐ Quantitative research
- ☐ Qualitative research
- ☐ Correlation coefficient
- ☐ Positive correlation
- ☐ Negative correlation
- ☐ Naturalistic observation
- ☐ Controlled observation
- ☐ Coding

- ☐ Inter-rater reliability
- ☐ Participant observation
- ☐ Hawthorne effect
- ☐ Longitudinal study
- ☐ Cross-sectional study
- ☐ Case study
- ☐ Survey
- ☐ Nonresponse bias

- ☐ Surveyor bias
- ☐ Experiments
- ☐ Hypothesis
- ☐ Controlled experiment
- ☐ Field experiment
- ☐ Natural experiment/ quasi-experiment

Research Design

- ☐ Independent variables
- ☐ Dependent variables
- ☐ Control variables
- ☐ Confounding variables
- ☐ Control group
- ☐ Experimental group
- ☐ Placebo effect

- ☐ Placebo
- ☐ Single-blind experiment
- ☐ Double-blind experiment
- ☐ Sample
- ☐ Population
- ☐ Random sampling
- ☐ Representative sample

- ☐ Random assignment
- ☐ Internal validity
- ☐ External validity
- ☐ Demand characteristics
- ☐ Observer-expectancy effect
- ☐ Operational definition

Statistics

- ☐ Descriptive statistics
- ☐ Inferential statistics

- ☐ Parameters
- ☐ Confidence intervals

- ☐ Null hypothesis
- ☐ Alternative hypothesis

4

☐ *p*-value   ☐ Histograms   ☐ Mode

☐ Significance level   ☐ Scatterplots   ☐ Outliers

☐ Statistically significant   ☐ Line of best fit   ☐ Measures of dispersion

☐ Type I error   ☐ Measures of central tendency   ☐ Range

☐ Type II error   ☐ Mean   ☐ Variance

☐ Line graphs   ☐ Median   ☐ Standard deviation

☐ Bar graphs

Ethical and Legal Issues

☐ Informed consent   ☐ Confidentiality   ☐ Institutional review boards (IRBs)

☐ Debriefing

Next Steps

Step 1: Tally your correct answers from Part A and review the quiz explanations at the end of this chapter.

1. **A**   6. **B**

2. **A**   7. **D**

3. **E**   8. **A**

4. **D**   9. **A**

5. **A**   10. **B**

_____ out of 10 questions

Step 2: Count the number of key terms you checked off in Part B.

_____ out of 140 key terms

Step 3: Compare your Test What You Already Know results to these Test What You Learned results to see how exam-ready you are for this topic.

If you need to study this topic further:

• Read (or reread) the comprehensive review for this topic in Chapter 13.

• Go to kaptest.com to complete the online quiz questions for Scientific Foundations of Psychology.

    ○ Haven't registered your book yet? Go to kaptest.com/moreonline to begin.

ANSWERS AND EXPLANATIONS

Test What You Already Know

1. C

In an experiment, the independent variable is controlled and altered to test its effect on a dependent variable. In this case, the teacher changes her teaching style to see its effect on quiz scores, so teaching style is the independent variable; **(C)** is correct. Although the groups are controlled, they are not manipulated and measured as a variable; (A) and (B) are incorrect. (D) is also incorrect; the quiz scores are the dependent variable because their results are dependent on changes in teaching style. The teacher is the researcher conducting the study, so (E) is incorrect.

2. B

Wundt, **(B)**, is credited by most scholars as starting the first lab in psychology in 1879 at the University of Leipzig, when he began training his first graduate student. James, (A), worked exclusively in the United States, although he did found an early psychology lab there. Watson, (C), was a later behaviorist who worked in the U.S. largely after Wundt's time. Pavlov, (D), was a Russian physiologist; and Freud, (E), was an Austrian who focused primarily on therapy and the development of the psychoanalytic school.

3. E

This method is an example of naturalistic observation, making **(E)** correct. In naturalistic observation, researchers observe participants in a natural environment, typically without the participants being aware. (A) is incorrect; a longitudinal study is a research design that examines variables or participants over time. A case study is an in-depth, detailed examination of an individual or small group, so (B) is incorrect. (C) is also incorrect; a controlled experiment is a research design that manipulates variables to study cause and effect. Remote viewing is a term associated with psychic abilities, not scientific research; (D) is incorrect.

4. C

René Descartes, **(C)**, is best known for believing that the mind and the body were separate substances, a position known as mind-body dualism. None of the other choices advocated this position.

5. D

Standard deviation is a measure of how far data spreads out from the mean (average) of the data. The smaller the standard deviation, the closer the data is to the mean, and vice versa. Because the scores in the second class have a larger standard deviation, the scores deviate more from the mean; **(D)** must be correct, and (E) is incorrect. Without additional information, it's impossible to know whether both classes share the same mean score or whether the mean is larger in one of the classes; (A), (B), and (C) are incorrect.

6. C

Unless given explicit permission from an IRB, an experiment should not be performed without informed consent; **(C)** is correct. Deception is possible as long as there is informed consent and a full debriefing afterward; thus (A) and (B) are incorrect. Researchers are not required to tell participants exactly what they should expect, and participants do not need to know the variables being tested; (D) and (E) are incorrect.

7. D

Social psychologists largely concern themselves with group behavior, as well as with how groups influence individuals. Thus, a study on how group size influences individual decisions is very likely to be conducted by a social psychologist, making **(D)** correct. (A), (B), (C), and (E) would be studied by other types of psychologists.

8. B

A correlation coefficient is a way to indicate both the strength of the relationship between two variables and whether that relationship is direct ($+$) or inverse ($-$). The closer the coefficient is to 1 or -1, the stronger the relationship is. A correlation of -0.98 is a very strong relationship, so **(B)** is correct and (A) is incorrect. A negative number indicates an inverse correlation between variables, not strength or weakness; (C) is incorrect. Be careful not to assume that because two variables have a strong relationship, one variable causes the other; correlation does not equal causation. Therefore, (D) and (E) are incorrect.

9. C

Inferential statistics techniques are used to make generalizations, or inferences, based on data; **(C)** is correct. Inferential statistics are not directly used to determine the strength of a relationship (as with a correlation coefficient) or establish cause and effect between variables; (A) and (B) are incorrect. Descriptive statistics (e.g., mean, mode, standard deviation, etc.) are used to describe a data set, making (D) incorrect. Inferential statistics can be used to test hypotheses by calculating a p-value, but inferential statistics is not used when formulating hypotheses; (E) is incorrect.

10. D

Random assignment is the process of assigning participants to experimental and control groups by chance, as with drawing names out of a hat; **(D)** is correct. Random sampling, (A), involves choosing participants from a larger population in a random manner that allows each member of the population to have an equal chance of being chosen. Representative sampling, (B), involves choosing a sample from a larger population that accurately represents the various unique and diverse aspects of that population. Stratified sampling, (C), involves dividing the population into subpopulations, or strata, before pulling samples from each stratum. In group matching, (E), researchers categorize subjects by demographic characteristics before dividing them into control and experimental groups, to ensure that both groups have similar compositions.

Test What You Learned

1. A

In order to be used as a variable in an experiment, an abstract concept like happiness needs an operational definition, that is, an objective way of measuring it. The best operational definition among the options provided is **(A)**; a smile is easily observed and is a good indicator of happiness. Whether a subject "seems" happy could be difficult to measure and highly subjective, depending on the observer's interpretation of happiness; (B) and (E) are incorrect. (C) is incorrect because the amount of caffeine is the independent variable in the experiment; it is controlled by the researcher, not measured as an indicator for happiness. (D) is incorrect because the number of smiles before the experiment is irrelevant to the study.

2. A

While the APA sets the ethical guidelines that researchers must follow when using humans as participants, it is the job of local institutional review boards to determine whether research proposals can be approved; **(A)** is correct and (B) is incorrect. (C) is incorrect; researchers would be unable to provide an unbiased evaluation of their own proposed study. Former participants are not involved in the ethical review process, and a peer review board determines whether an academic paper is suitable for publishing; (D) and (E) are incorrect.

3. E

Humanistic psychologists focus on personal growth and freedom. **(E)** is correct. Only humanistic psychologists acknowledge freedom of the will; the approaches in choices (A) through (D) offer a variety of other causal explanations for human behavior.

4. D

Standard deviation, which represents the average distance between any given data point and the mean of a data set, is a commonly used measure of dispersion; **(D)** is correct. Correlation, a measure of the relationship between variables, is not a measure of dispersion, so (A) is incorrect. (B) and (C) are incorrect; mean and median are statistical measures of central tendency. The p-value is a statistical measure used in hypothesis testing; (E) is incorrect.

5. A

A negative correlation is one in which the variables move in opposite directions. As one variable increases in value, the other decreases, creating an inverse relationship; **(A)** is correct, and thus (B) and (C) are incorrect. The strength of a correlation is indicated by the absolute value of the correlation coefficient (how close it is to -1 or $+1$), not whether it is positive or negative; (D) and (E) are incorrect.

6. B

In an experiment of any kind, researchers are able to exercise the most control over variables and groups of participants; **(B)** is correct. Correlational studies feature very little control and no manipulation of variables, so (A) is incorrect. Strict observational studies, whether naturalistic or participatory, exercise very little control; (C) and (D) are incorrect. Operationalization is not a research design; (E) is incorrect.

7. D

The dependent variable is the variable that is measured in the experiment. In this case, the dependent variable is dopamine levels, making **(D)** correct. (A) and (B) are incorrect because they are not variables, but rather the experimental group and control group, respectively. Amount of exercise is the independent variable, since it is manipulated in the experiment to determine its effects on dopamine levels; (C) is incorrect. (E) is also incorrect; the number of rats in the study represents the sample, not a variable.

8. A

William James emphasized the investigation of the functions of consciousness over its structure and is largely recognized as the first functionalist in psychology; **(A)** is correct. (B) and (C) are incorrect because Wundt and Titchener were structuralists, who focused on studying the structures that constitute consciousness. (D) and (E) are incorrect because Watson and Skinner were behavioral psychologists, who avoided the investigation of consciousness altogether, focusing only on observable behavior.

9. A

A single-blind experiment is one in which the subjects do not know which group they are in, while the researcher does. Though this experiment started out as double-blind, (D), where neither the researcher nor the participants knew who was assigned to each group, once the researcher looked at the document and saw where each subject was assigned, the experiment became single-blind, making **(A)** correct. A placebo, (B), is a substance or treatment with no actual therapeutic effect that is used to make members of the control group think they are in the experimental group. Since the study described in the question stem is an experiment consisting of multiple subjects, (C) is incorrect. A correlational study, (E), is used to determine the level of association between two or more characteristics of interest.

10. B

Stanley Milgram's controversial experiment demonstrated the tendency of people to obey authority figures, even when doing so is contrary to how they would normally act. Since the new doctor gave his supervisor his information even though he knew he shouldn't, **(B)** is correct. Philip Zimbardo, (A), is well-known for his Stanford prison experiment, through which he studied how social roles influence people's behavior. Thomas Young, (C), is known for contributing to the trichromatic theory of color vision. Jean Piaget, (D), is known for his studies on cognitive development in children. Robert Rosenthal, (E), is known for studying the effects of self-fulfilling prophecies, such as the Pygmalion effect.

CHAPTER 5

Biological Bases of Behavior

LEARNING OBJECTIVES

After studying this chapter, you will be able to:

- Describe basic neural processes and systems forming the biological bases of behavior

- Explain how drugs influence neurotransmitters

- Inventory the nervous system's subdivisions and their functions

- Describe neuroplasticity's impact on brain trauma

- Describe the endocrine system's effect on behavior

- Identify research strategies and technologies in biopsychology

- Explain psychology's continuing interest in the interactivity of heredity, environment, and evolution in the shaping of behavior

- Predict the adaptive value of evolved traits and behaviors

- Contrast various conscious states in terms of their influence on behavior

- Identify significant characteristics of sleep and dreaming

- Outline and categorize major psychoactive drugs

- Define and elaborate upon the concepts of drug dependency, tolerance, addiction, and withdrawal

- Recognize important contributors to biopsychology

TEST WHAT YOU ALREADY KNOW

Part A: Quiz

1. The area of the brain responsible for controlling voluntary movement is the
   (A) hindbrain
   (B) temporal lobe
   (C) frontal lobe
   (D) midbrain
   (E) occipital lobe

2. Which of the following technologies uses an injected radioactive dye to reveal brain functioning?
   (A) PET
   (B) MRI
   (C) CT
   (D) EEG
   (E) fMRI

3. The endocrine system is ultimately regulated by the
   (A) amygdala
   (B) thyroid gland
   (C) parietal lobe
   (D) hypothalamus
   (E) thalamus

4. REM sleep is called paradoxical sleep because
   (A) our brains are active even as our muscles are paralyzed
   (B) sometimes we wake up from sleep feeling more tired than before
   (C) our blood pressure and body temperature are lowest when we wake up
   (D) our brains shut down and relax even though we are actively dreaming
   (E) our muscle tone increases during dreams as our brain activity decreases

5. The electrical signal that travels down the axon of a neuron is a(n)
   (A) action potential
   (B) neurotransmitter
   (C) hormone
   (D) electroencephalograph
   (E) agonist

6. The region of the brain responsible for speech comprehension is named after
   (A) Alois Alzheimer
   (B) Paul Broca
   (C) Francis Galton
   (D) Roger Sperry
   (E) Carl Wernicke

7. Compared to an axon without myelin, a myelinated axon will

   (A) cause an action potential to travel more slowly

   (B) cause an action potential to travel more quickly

   (C) release fewer neurotransmitters with each action potential

   (D) release more neurotransmitters with each action potential

   (E) be less electrically insulated

8. Which branch of the nervous system is activated specifically in response to a stressful situation?

   (A) Central nervous system

   (B) Peripheral nervous system

   (C) Sympathetic nervous system

   (D) Parasympathetic nervous system

   (E) Somatic nervous system

9. Which of the following ideas is NOT a part of Charles Darwin's theory of evolution?

   (A) Traits and their variations are inherited from one generation to the next.

   (B) The traits of an organism are completely determined by its genes.

   (C) Fitter organisms survive more successfully and produce more offspring.

   (D) Members of a species vary with respect to their traits.

   (E) Some variations of a trait are more adaptive in an environment than others.

10. Dave has trouble staying asleep because several times during the night, he stops breathing and wakes up for a short time. Dave likely suffers from

    (A) sleep apnea

    (B) insomnia

    (C) selective attention

    (D) narcolepsy

    (E) cataplexy

Part B: Key Terms

The following is a list of the major ideas and people for the AP Psychology topic of Biological Bases of Behavior. You will likely see many of these on the AP Psychology exam.

For each key term, ask yourself the following questions:

- Can I describe this key term?
- Can I discuss this key term in relation to other psychological ideas and specific psychologists?
- Could I correctly answer a multiple-choice question about this key term?
- Could I correctly answer a free-response question about this key term?

Check off the key terms if you can answer "yes" to at least three of these questions.

Neurons

- ☐ Neurons
- ☐ Soma/cell body
- ☐ Dendrites
- ☐ Axon
- ☐ Myelin sheath
- ☐ Terminal buttons
- ☐ Synapse
- ☐ Action potential

- ☐ Neurotransmitter
- ☐ Excitatory
- ☐ Inhibitory
- ☐ Acetylcholine
- ☐ Dopamine
- ☐ Serotonin
- ☐ Gamma amino butyric acid (GABA)

- ☐ Norepinephrine
- ☐ Glutamate
- ☐ Agonists
- ☐ Antagonists
- ☐ Reuptake inhibitors
- ☐ Selective serotonin reuptake inhibitors (SSRIs)

The Nervous System

- ☐ Nervous system
- ☐ Nerves
- ☐ Brain
- ☐ Central nervous system (CNS)
- ☐ Hindbrain
- ☐ Cerebellum
- ☐ Medulla
- ☐ Pons
- ☐ Reticular formation
- ☐ Midbrain

- ☐ Forebrain
- ☐ Thalamus
- ☐ Hypothalamus
- ☐ Amygdala
- ☐ Hippocampus
- ☐ Limbic system
- ☐ Cerebrum
- ☐ Cerebral cortex
- ☐ Lobes
- ☐ Frontal lobe
- ☐ Parietal lobe

- ☐ Temporal lobe
- ☐ Occipital lobe
- ☐ Hemisphere
- ☐ Lateralization
- ☐ Wernicke's area
- ☐ Broca's area
- ☐ Spinal cord
- ☐ Reflex
- ☐ Peripheral nervous system (PNS)
- ☐ Somatic nervous system

□ Autonomic nervous system

□ Sympathetic nervous system

□ Parasympathetic nervous system

□ Neuroplasticity

□ Synaptic plasticity

□ Neurogenesis

The Endocrine System

□ Endocrine system

□ Homeostasis

□ Hormones

□ Glands

□ Pituitary gland

□ Thyroid gland

□ Adrenal glands

□ Ovaries

□ Testes

Biopsychological Research

□ Electroencephalograph (EEG)

□ MRI

□ Functional MRI (fMRI)

□ PET scan

□ CT scan

□ Traumatic brain injury (TBI)

□ Corpus callosum

□ Split-brain patients

□ Contralateral organization

□ Twin study

Heredity, Environment, and Evolution

□ Variation

□ Inheritance

□ Fitness

□ Natural selection

□ Adaptations

□ Sexual selection

Types of Conscious States

□ Consciousness

□ State of consciousness

□ Altered state of consciousness

□ Conscious level

□ Nonconscious level

□ Preconscious level

□ Unconscious level

□ Subconscious level

□ Priming

□ Mere-exposure effect

Sleep and Dreaming

□ Non-rapid eye movement (NREM) sleep

□ Rapid eye movement (REM) sleep

□ Hypnagogic hallucinations

□ Sleep spindles

□ Slow wave sleep

□ Paradoxical sleep

□ Manifest content

□ Latent content

□ Activation-synthesis hypothesis

□ Information-processing theory

□ Night terrors

□ Insomnia

□ Sleep apnea

□ Narcolepsy

□ Somnambulism

Psychoactive Drugs

□ Psychoactive drugs

□ Depressants

□ Narcotics

□ Stimulants

□ Hallucinogens

Important Contributors

- ☐ Alois Alzheimer
- ☐ Thomas Bouchard
- ☐ Paul Broca
- ☐ Charles Darwin

- ☐ Sigmund Freud
- ☐ Francis Galton
- ☐ Michael Gazzaniga
- ☐ William James

- ☐ Roger Sperry
- ☐ Carl Wernicke
- ☐ Wilhelm Wundt

Next Steps

Step 1: Tally your correct answers from Part A and review the quiz explanations at the end of this chapter.

1. C
2. A
3. D
4. A
5. A

6. E
7. B
8. C
9. B
10. A

_____ out of 10 questions

Step 2: Count the number of key terms you checked off in Part B.

_____ out of 124 key terms

Step 3: Read the Rapid Review Key Takeaways in this chapter.

Step 4: Consult the table below and follow the instructions based on your performance.

If You Got . . .	Do This
80% or more of the Test What You Already Know assessment correct (8 or more questions from Part A and 100 or more key terms from Part B)	• Read definitions in this chapter for all the key terms you didn't check off. • Complete the Test What You Learned assessment in this chapter.
50% or less of the Test What You Already Know assessment correct (5 or fewer questions from Part A and 62 or fewer key terms from Part B)	• Read the comprehensive review for this topic in Chapter 14. ○ If you are short on time, read only the High-Yield sections. • Read through all of the key term definitions in this chapter. • Complete the Test What You Learned assessment in this chapter.
Any other result	• Read the High-Yield sections of the comprehensive review of this topic in Chapter 14. • Read definitions in this chapter for all the key terms you didn't check off. • Complete the Test What You Learned assessment in this chapter.

RAPID REVIEW

Key Takeaways

1. All human (and animal) behavior is a product of biological structures and processes, highly organized on multiple interconnected levels. Understanding these biological precursors of behavior can lead to treatments for psychological disorders, such as drugs that influence neurotransmitter function.

2. The nervous system is highly specialized and hierarchical in its structure, but neuroplasticity gives the brain some flexibility to adapt its structure and function.

3. Though interconnected with and regulated by the nervous system, the endocrine system produces effects on behavior in a distinct way: endocrine glands secrete hormones into the bloodstream, allowing hormones to reach and interact directly with target organs.

4. Biopsychological researchers use a variety of imaging technologies to view the structure and function of the brain, along with specialized research strategies that allow them to learn more about the brain's organization and the origin of psychological traits.

5. While many behaviors are learned as a result of experience within a particular environment, the very capacity to learn such behaviors has a genetic basis, and such capacities only persist because they contribute to the fitness of organisms.

6. Since the late nineteenth century, psychologists have investigated consciousness, including the awareness of one's self and environment, the ways consciousness can be altered, and the various levels and states of consciousness.

7. Sleep cycles through multiple stages that vary in levels of neural activity, muscle control, biological functions, and dreaming; sleep disorders cause disruptions to these processes.

8. Psychoactive drugs, including depressants, narcotics, stimulants, and hallucinogens, affect brain chemistry to alter the perceptions and behavior of users; some psychoactive drugs are used medicinally and/or recreationally, and some have a high potential for abuse.

Key Terms: Definitions

Neurons

Neurons: The basic functional units of the nervous system; cells which contain specialized structures to communicate signals.

Soma/cell body: The part of a neuron that contains its nucleus and other standard cellular structures.

Dendrites: The multiple thin, treelike fibers that branch off from a neuron's soma and contain receptors to accept incoming signals from other neurons.

Axon: A long, tubular structure in a neuron that transmits action potentials.

Myelin sheath: A fatty substance that coats an axon, insulating it and enhancing its ability to transmit action potentials.

Terminal buttons: The branching structures at the ends of axons that release neurotransmitters.

Synapse: The small gap between the axon of a presynaptic neuron and the dendrites of a postsynaptic neuron.

Action potential: The electrical impulse sent along an axon when the dendrites of a neuron are sufficiently excited.

Neurotransmitter: A specialized chemical messenger that sends signals between neurons.

Excitatory: Describes a neurotransmitter that causes a postsynaptic neuron to propagate more action potentials.

Inhibitory: Describes a neurotransmitter that causes a postsynaptic neuron to propagate fewer action potentials.

Acetylcholine: A neurotransmitter involved in learning, memory, and muscle contraction.

Dopamine: A neurotransmitter involved in mood, movement, attention, and learning.

Serotonin: A neurotransmitter that regulates sleep, mood, appetite, and body temperature.

Gamma amino butyric acid (**GABA**): The primary inhibitory neurotransmitter in the nervous system.

Norepinephrine: A neurotransmitter important in controlling alertness, wakefulness, mood, and attention.

Glutamate: The main excitatory neurotransmitter in the central nervous system; important for learning and memory.

Agonists: Drugs that mimic a particular neurotransmitter, activating the same receptors that it does.

Antagonists: Drugs that block a particular neurotransmitter from activating its receptors.

Reuptake inhibitors: Drugs that prevent a neurotransmitter from being reabsorbed by presynaptic axons, causing greater activation of postsynaptic receptors.

Selective serotonin reuptake inhibitors (**SSRIs**): Drugs that prevent the reabsorption of serotonin, leading to greater activation of serotonin receptors.

The Nervous System

Nervous system: The organ system that governs the reception, processing, and transmission of information throughout the body.

Nerves: Fibrous bundles of neurons.

Brain: The primary organ in the nervous system, which oversees most of its operations.

Central nervous system (**CNS**): The brain and spinal cord.

Hindbrain: The lowest segment of the brain, primarily involved in the regulation of basic bodily functions and consisting of the cerebellum, medulla, pons, and reticular formation.

Cerebellum: Regulates motor coordination.

Medulla: Controls autonomic responses, including breathing, heart rate, and blood pressure.

Pons: Transfers information between the cerebellum and other parts of the brain.

Reticular formation: Contributes to attention and conscious state by filtering incoming stimuli and selectively relaying information.

Midbrain: The middle segment of the brain, involved with motor control, vision, hearing, arousal, sleep, temperature regulation, and the transmission of sensory information.

Forebrain: The highest segment of the brain, consisting of the thalamus, hypothalamus, hippocampus, amygdala, and cerebrum.

Thalamus: Relays signals from other parts of the brain to the cerebral cortex and regulates sleep, consciousness, appetite, and alertness.

Hypothalamus: Regulates a variety of drives, including hunger, thirst, sexual arousal, and temperature; the master regulator in the endocrine system.

Amygdala: Involved with fear, aggression, and other emotions, as well as memory consolidation.

Hippocampus: Involved in the formation of long-term memories.

Limbic system: Regulates emotions and drives; consists of the thalamus, hypothalamus, amygdala, hippocampus, and other structures.

Cerebrum: The largest part of the human brain; contains the cerebral cortex.

Cerebral cortex: The wrinkled surface of the cerebrum, divided into four lobes and two hemispheres.

Lobes: Four specialized regions in the cerebral cortex.

Frontal lobe: Controls voluntary movement and higher-order cognitive processes; at the front of the brain.

Parietal lobe: Integrates perceptions from different senses; at the top of the brain.

Temporal lobe: Controls hearing and language; at both sides of the brain.

Occipital lobe: Controls vision; at the back of the brain.

Hemisphere: One of two symmetrical halves (left and right) of the brain, specialized for particular functions.

Lateralization: The localization of some functions in one of the two hemispheres.

Wernicke's area: The region in the temporal lobe of a person's dominant hemisphere that controls speech comprehension.

Broca's area: The region in the frontal lobe of a person's dominant hemisphere that controls speech production.

Spinal cord: The long tube of nerves that connects the brain to most of the rest of the body; protected by the vertebral column.

Reflex: An automatic, involuntary response to a particular stimulus.

Peripheral nervous system (**PNS**): All nerves outside of the brain and spinal cord.

Somatic nervous system: Part of the PNS that controls skeletal muscles and their voluntary movements.

Autonomic nervous system: Part of the PNS that controls involuntary bodily functions.

Sympathetic nervous system: Part of the autonomic nervous system activated during the "fight or flight" response to stress.

Parasympathetic nervous system: Part of the autonomic nervous system activated during the "rest and digest" response to non-stressful situations.

Neuroplasticity: The capacity of the brain to reorganize itself at a high level, such as might happen in response to traumatic injury; it decreases with age.

Synaptic plasticity: The ability for certain neural connections to be strengthened or weakened over time, a process essential for memory and learning.

Neurogenesis: The processes that create new neurons.

The Endocrine System

Endocrine system: The system of glands that secrete hormones into the bloodstream in order to maintain the body's homeostasis.

Homeostasis: A dynamic state of internal equilibrium within a changing external environment.

5

Hormones: Chemical messengers that travel through the bloodstream, interacting with organs to stimulate or inhibit various biological processes.

Glands: Endocrine organs that produce and secrete hormones.

Pituitary gland: The primary gland in the endocrine system, regulated by the hypothalamus; produces hormones that interact with the other endocrine glands.

Thyroid gland: Produces and secretes hormones that regulate metabolism; found in the neck.

Adrenal glands: Produce and secrete stress hormones like cortisol and epinephrine (adrenaline); found directly above the kidneys.

Ovaries: Female gonads (sex glands) that secrete hormones like estrogen and progesterone, which regulate the menstrual cycle and pregnancy.

Testes: Male gonads (sex glands) that secrete androgens (male sex hormones) like testosterone, which regulates sexual development and sexual desire.

Biopsychological Research

Electroencephalograph (**EEG**): A device that uses electrodes on the scalp to detect and record brain waves.

MRI: Stands for "magnetic resonance imaging"; a technique that uses magnetic fields and radio waves to produce high-resolution images of brain structure.

Functional MRI (**fMRI**): An imaging technique similar to MRI, which measures blood oxygen levels to determine brain function.

PET scan: A technique that uses a radioactive dye injected into the bloodstream to detect neurological activity.

CT scan: A technique that uses X-rays to create 3-D images of brain structure.

Traumatic brain injury (**TBI**): Damage to some part of the brain caused by an external force; may impede cognitive, emotional, or behavioral functions.

Corpus callosum: The bundle of nerves that serves as the primary connection between the left and right cerebral hemispheres.

Split-brain patients: Individuals with a severed corpus callosum; used in studies of brain lateralization.

Contralateral organization: The tendency of the left cerebral hemisphere to control and perceive from the right side of the body, and vice versa.

Twin study: A research design that investigates the traits of identical and fraternal twins to determine the extent to which traits are genetically or environmentally controlled.

Heredity, Environment, and Evolution

Variation: The natural range of differences found among the traits of members of a species.

Inheritance: The transmission of various traits from one generation to the next. (Genes are the units of inheritance.)

Fitness: The tendency of a trait or organism to be well-suited to a particular environment.

Natural selection: The process by which fitter organisms are able to genetically outcompete others of their species by living longer and having more offspring.

Adaptations: Evolved traits that are well-suited to a particular environment.

Sexual selection: The process by which organisms with more attractive traits are able to genetically outcompete others of their species by having more offspring.

Types of Conscious States

Consciousness: A state of being awake and aware of external stimuli and one's own mental activity.

State of consciousness: The features of consciousness experienced by an individual at a particular point in time.

Altered state of consciousness: A temporary state that differs significantly from a normal waking state; includes sleep, meditation, a coma, hypnosis, or the influence of drugs.

Conscious level: All of the things within one's awareness at the present moment, including information about one's self and current environment.

Nonconscious level: The body's automatic biological processes, like breathing and heartbeat, which are controlled by the brain but are generally outside of one's active awareness.

Preconscious level: In Freud's psychoanalytic theory, all of the unrepressed stored memories, thoughts, and information that can be recalled and moved from the unconscious to the conscious level in a matter of seconds.

Unconscious level: In Freud's psychoanalytic theory, the unconscious mind represents the thoughts, desires, and urges that are actively repressed from consciousness and that affect mental activity outside of active awareness.

Subconscious level: Information beyond a person's conscious awareness that affects mental processes.

Priming: When exposure to a stimulus beneath conscious awareness influences a response to other stimuli.

Mere-exposure effect: The preference for familiar stimuli over new stimuli, even when exposure to the stimuli does not occur on a conscious level.

Sleep and Dreaming

Non-rapid eye movement (NREM) sleep: A period of dreamless sleep divided into four distinct, continuous stages.

Rapid eye movement (REM) sleep: The period of sleep that is most associated with dreaming.

Hypnagogic hallucinations: Sensory phenomena, like visions and sounds, that a sleeper perceives in the transition between wakefulness and sleep.

Sleep spindles: Bursts of neural activity that take place in stage 2 of NREM sleep and may be important for memory consolidation.

Slow wave sleep: Stages 3 and 4 of NREM sleep, the deepest stages of sleep, when neural activity and brain waves are slowest.

Paradoxical sleep: Another name for REM sleep, due to the contradictory way in which the brain is active but the body is at rest.

Manifest content: The actual events and imagery within a dream that, according to Freud, serves to mask the unconscious thoughts and desires of the dreamer.

Latent content: In Freudian terms, the unconscious thoughts and desires underlying the manifest content of dreams.

Activation-synthesis hypothesis: The theory that maintains dreams are the brain's interpretations of neural activity during REM sleep.

Information-processing theory: The theory that maintains dreaming is a way for the brain to deal with stress.

Night terrors: A sleep disorder that causes the sleeper to wake from NREM sleep suddenly with feelings of extreme fear, agitation, or dread.

Insomnia: A sleep disorder marked by difficulty falling or staying asleep.

Sleep apnea: A sleep disorder caused by breathing interruptions during sleep.

Narcolepsy: A neurological sleep disorder characterized by irregular sleep patterns and the inability to control and regulate sleep and wakefulness.

Somnambulism: A sleep disorder also known as sleepwalking that occurs during slow wave sleep and results in walking or performing other behaviors while asleep.

Psychoactive Drugs

Psychoactive drugs: Drugs that affect the chemical and physical functioning of the brain, altering the perception and behavior of the user.

Depressants: Drugs that slow down neural activity.

Narcotics: Drugs that dull the senses and relieve pain, also called opioids.

Stimulants: Drugs that excite neural activity and speed up body functions, including heart and respiration rates; often used to relieve fatigue and increase alertness.

Hallucinogens: Drugs that alter mood, distort perceptions, and evoke sensory images in the absence of sensory input.

Important Contributors

Alois Alzheimer: Discovered Alzheimer's disease, named after him, when he performed an autopsy on the brain of a 55-year-old woman who had died after many years of progressive mental decline.

Thomas Bouchard: American psychologist best known for studying identical twins separated at birth to determine the effects of genetics and environment on a variety of traits.

Paul Broca: A French scientist who investigated speech disorders. The region of the cerebrum responsible for speech production was named after him (Broca's area), as was an associated speech disorder (Broca's aphasia, also known as expressive aphasia).

Charles Darwin: Developed the idea of evolution through natural selection, which he used to explain the origin of species.

Sigmund Freud: The founder of psychoanalysis. His approach to therapy included dream interpretation, which Freud believed could reveal insights about the unconscious mind.

Francis Galton: An English scientist who founded the field of behavioral genetics, popularized the phrase "nature versus nurture," and was the first to apply statistical methods to study heredity and intelligence.

Michael Gazzaniga: An American cognitive neuroscientist, best known for his research with Sperry on split-brain patients.

William James: Founder of functionalism who maintained that psychology should aim to understand how consciousness helps organisms adapt to their environments.

Roger Sperry: An American neuropsychologist who conducted groundbreaking research with Gazzaniga on split-brain patients, which helped to improve understanding of brain lateralization.

Carl Wernicke: A German scientist who studied speech disorders. The region of the cerebrum responsible for speech comprehension was named after him (Wernicke's area), as was an associated speech disorder (Wernicke's aphasia, also known as receptive aphasia).

Wilhelm Wundt: Founder of structuralism; used the technique of introspection to investigate structures of consciousness.

TEST WHAT YOU LEARNED

Part A: Quiz

1. The chemical messengers that cross synapses to send signals from one neuron to the next are called

   (A) action potentials

   (B) glands

   (C) neurotransmitters

   (D) genes

   (E) hormones

2. To determine how much of a trait is due to environmental influences using a twin study, it would be most directly revealing to compare

   (A) fraternal twins raised together with fraternal twins raised apart

   (B) identical twins raised apart with fraternal twins raised apart

   (C) identical twins raised together with fraternal twins raised apart

   (D) identical twins raised together with fraternal twins raised together

   (E) identical twins raised together with identical twins raised apart

3. Which of the following is NOT a structure in the limbic system?

   (A) Hippocampus

   (B) Medulla

   (C) Amygdala

   (D) Hypothalamus

   (E) Thalamus

4. "Long ago, it was more dangerous for our ancestors to be active when it was dark, so sleeping at night became an advantage for their survival." Which theoretical approach would be MOST supportive of this theory about sleep?

   (A) Psychoanalytic

   (B) Evolutionary

   (C) Cognitive

   (D) Behavioral

   (E) Biological

5. Which of the following technologies does NOT produce an image of the structure or functioning of the brain?

   (A) CT

   (B) MRI

   (C) PET

   (D) EEG

   (E) fMRI

6. Which of the following glands releases hormones with the primary function of regulating metabolism?

   (A) Adrenals

   (B) Thyroid

   (C) Pituitary

   (D) Ovaries

   (E) Testes

5

7. Which of the following psychologists conducted split-brain studies with Roger Sperry?

    (A) Thomas Bouchard

    (B) Alois Alzheimer

    (C) Michael Gazzaniga

    (D) Carl Wernicke

    (E) Paul Broca

8. Which of the following hormones regulates sexual development in males?

    (A) Testosterone

    (B) Progesterone

    (C) Epinephrine

    (D) Cortisol

    (E) Estrogen

9. Little Tommy is having trouble sleeping. Almost immediately after falling asleep, he wakes up screaming and crying uncontrollably, and his heart is racing. Tommy is probably suffering from

    (A) enuresis

    (B) nightmares

    (C) cataplexy

    (D) night terrors

    (E) sleep apnea

10. The part of a neuron that can receive information from neighboring cells is the

    (A) vesicle

    (B) axon

    (C) nucleus

    (D) terminal button

    (E) dendrite

Part B: Key Terms

This key terms list is the same as the list in the Test What You Already Know section earlier in this chapter. Based on what you have now learned, again ask yourself the following questions:

- Can I describe this key term?

- Can I discuss this key term in relation to other psychological ideas and specific psychologists?

- Could I correctly answer a multiple-choice question about this key term?

- Could I correctly answer a free-response question about this key term?

Check off the key terms if you can answer "yes" to at least three of these questions.

Neurons

- ☐ Neurons
- ☐ Soma/cell body
- ☐ Dendrites
- ☐ Axon
- ☐ Myelin sheath
- ☐ Terminal buttons
- ☐ Synapse
- ☐ Action potential

- ☐ Neurotransmitter
- ☐ Excitatory
- ☐ Inhibitory
- ☐ Acetylcholine
- ☐ Dopamine
- ☐ Serotonin
- ☐ Gamma amino butyric acid (GABA)

- ☐ Norepinephrine
- ☐ Glutamate
- ☐ Agonists
- ☐ Antagonists
- ☐ Reuptake inhibitors
- ☐ Selective serotonin reuptake inhibitors (SSRIs)

The Nervous System

- ☐ Nervous system
- ☐ Nerves
- ☐ Brain
- ☐ Central nervous system (CNS)
- ☐ Hindbrain
- ☐ Cerebellum
- ☐ Medulla
- ☐ Pons
- ☐ Reticular formation
- ☐ Midbrain

- ☐ Forebrain
- ☐ Thalamus
- ☐ Hypothalamus
- ☐ Amygdala
- ☐ Hippocampus
- ☐ Limbic system
- ☐ Cerebrum
- ☐ Cerebral cortex
- ☐ Lobes
- ☐ Frontal lobe
- ☐ Parietal lobe

- ☐ Temporal lobe
- ☐ Occipital lobe
- ☐ Hemisphere
- ☐ Lateralization
- ☐ Wernicke's area
- ☐ Broca's area
- ☐ Spinal cord
- ☐ Reflex
- ☐ Peripheral nervous system (PNS)
- ☐ Somatic nervous system

- ☐ Autonomic nervous system
- ☐ Sympathetic nervous system
- ☐ Parasympathetic nervous system
- ☐ Neuroplasticity
- ☐ Synaptic plasticity
- ☐ Neurogenesis

The Endocrine System

- ☐ Endocrine system
- ☐ Homeostasis
- ☐ Hormones
- ☐ Glands
- ☐ Pituitary gland
- ☐ Thyroid gland
- ☐ Adrenal glands
- ☐ Ovaries
- ☐ Testes

Biopsychological Research

- ☐ Electroencephalograph (EEG)
- ☐ MRI
- ☐ Functional MRI (fMRI)
- ☐ PET scan
- ☐ CT scan
- ☐ Traumatic brain injury (TBI)
- ☐ Corpus callosum
- ☐ Split-brain patients
- ☐ Contralateral organization
- ☐ Twin study

Heredity, Environment, and Evolution

- ☐ Variation
- ☐ Inheritance
- ☐ Fitness
- ☐ Natural selection
- ☐ Adaptations
- ☐ Sexual selection

Types of Conscious States

- ☐ Consciousness
- ☐ State of consciousness
- ☐ Altered state of consciousness
- ☐ Conscious level
- ☐ Nonconscious level
- ☐ Preconscious level
- ☐ Unconscious level
- ☐ Subconscious level
- ☐ Priming
- ☐ Mere-exposure effect

Sleep and Dreaming

- ☐ Non-rapid eye movement (NREM) sleep
- ☐ Rapid eye movement (REM) sleep
- ☐ Hypnagogic hallucinations
- ☐ Sleep spindles
- ☐ Slow wave sleep
- ☐ Paradoxical sleep
- ☐ Manifest content
- ☐ Latent content
- ☐ Activation-synthesis hypothesis
- ☐ Information-processing theory
- ☐ Night terrors
- ☐ Insomnia
- ☐ Sleep apnea
- ☐ Narcolepsy
- ☐ Somnambulism

Psychoactive Drugs

☐ Psychoactive drugs ☐ Narcotics ☐ Hallucinogens

☐ Depressants ☐ Stimulants

Important Contributors

☐ Alois Alzheimer ☐ Sigmund Freud ☐ Roger Sperry

☐ Thomas Bouchard ☐ Francis Galton ☐ Carl Wernicke

☐ Paul Broca ☐ Michael Gazzaniga ☐ Wilhelm Wundt

☐ Charles Darwin ☐ William James

Next Steps

Step 1: Tally your correct answers from Part A and review the quiz explanations at the end of this chapter.

1.	C	6.	B
2.	E	7.	C
3.	B	8.	A
4.	B	9.	D
5.	D	10.	E

_____ out of 10 questions

Step 2: Count the number of key terms you checked off in Part B.

_____ out of 124 key terms

Step 3: Compare your Test What You Already Know results to these Test What You Learned results to see how exam-ready you are for this topic.

If you need to study this topic further:

• Read (or reread) the comprehensive review for this topic in Chapter 14.

• Go to kaptest.com to complete the online quiz questions for Biological Bases of Behavior.

 ◦ Haven't registered your book yet? Go to kaptest.com/moreonline to begin.

ANSWERS AND EXPLANATIONS

Test What You Already Know

1. C

The frontal lobe controls voluntary motion and higher-order cognitive functions, so **(C)** is correct. (A) is incorrect because the hindbrain regulates basic bodily functions. (B) is incorrect because the temporal lobe controls hearing and language. (D) is incorrect because the midbrain transmits sensory information, among other tasks. (E) is incorrect because the occipital lobe processes vision.

2. A

Positron emission tomography, or PET, involves the injection of a radioactive dye into the bloodstream, which can be used to detect which brain areas are more active (are receiving more blood), thereby providing a picture of brain functioning. **(A)** is therefore correct. (B) and (C) are incorrect because the MRI and CT only reveal brain structure. (D) is incorrect because the EEG uses electrodes (not a dye) and only detects brain waves. (E) is incorrect because the fMRI uses magnetic fields and radiofrequency pulses, not a dye, to detect brain functioning.

3. D

The hypothalamus regulates the pituitary gland, which in turn serves as the master gland of the endocrine system. **(D)** is thus correct. (A) is incorrect because the amygdala is involved in emotion and memory consolidation. (B) is incorrect because the thyroid is an endocrine gland that regulates metabolism. (C) is incorrect because the parietal lobe controls sensory perception and integration. (E) is incorrect because the thalamus relays signals from other parts of the brain to the cerebral cortex.

4. A

In a paradox, one thing is in contradiction to something else. REM sleep is marked by a very active brain and a very inactive body—a paradoxical situation. **(A)** is correct. While (B) and (C) are sometimes true, they are incorrect because they are not the reason REM sleep is called paradoxical sleep. The brain remains active during REM sleep and dreaming, while muscle tone decreases; both (D) and (E) are incorrect.

5. A

An action potential is the electrical signal fired by a neuron when it is sufficiently activated, traveling down the axon and leading to neurotransmitter release from the terminal buttons. **(A)** is correct. (B) is incorrect because a neurotransmitter is a chemical signal released from the terminal button of an axon. (C) is incorrect because a hormone is a chemical messenger that travels through the bloodstream. (D) is incorrect because the electroencephalograph, or EEG, is a device that records brain waves. (E) is incorrect because an agonist is a drug that mimics a neurotransmitter.

6. E

Wernicke's area, named after a German physician who studied speech disorders involving that region of the brain, controls language comprehension. **(E)** is correct. (A) is incorrect because Alzheimer first described the disease that would be named after him. (B) is incorrect because Broca's area manages speech production, not speech comprehension. (C) is incorrect because Galton founded behavioral genetics. (D) is incorrect because Roger Sperry studied split-brain patients.

7. B

Myelin insulates axons and speeds up the transmission of an action potential as it jumps from one unmyelinated segment (known as a node of Ranvier) to the next. **(B)** is thus correct. (A) states the opposite. (C) and (D) are incorrect because myelination does not affect the amount of neurotransmitter release. (E) is incorrect because myelination leads to greater insulation.

8. C

During a "fight or flight" response to a perceived threat, the sympathetic nervous system is activated, preparing the body for aggressive or evasive behavior. **(C)** is correct. (D) is incorrect because the parasympathetic nervous system is activated during "rest and digest" responses to nonthreatening situations. The other choices are incorrect because they are not specifically activated depending on stress levels.

9. B

A number of ideas make up Darwin's theory of evolution, but not genetic determinism, the idea that traits are completely determined by genes. **(B)** is thus correct. The remaining choices present elements of Darwin's theory: (A) describes inheritance, (C) describes natural selection, (D) describes variation, and (E) describes fitness.

10. A

Sleep apnea is a common sleep disorder caused by breathing interruptions during sleep. Many people who suffer from this disorder don't know that they have it, yet they may wake up frequently in the night or feel drowsy the next day; **(A)** is correct. Insomnia is a general sleep disorder characterized by difficulty falling or staying asleep, but it is not associated with breathing difficulties, so (B) is incorrect. Selective attention refers to attention and focus and is not related to sleep, making (C) incorrect. Narcolepsy is a sleep disorder characterized by excessive sleepiness and involuntary sleep during normal waking hours, and cataplexy, often associated with narcolepsy, refers to strong, uncontrollable muscle spasms and paralysis; both (D) and (E) are incorrect.

Test What You Learned

1. C

Neurotransmitters are the chemical messengers that cross the synapse to send signals between neurons, making **(C)** correct. (A) is incorrect because an action potential is the electrical impulse that travels down an axon. (B) is incorrect because glands are endocrine organs that produce and secrete hormones. (D) is incorrect because genes are the units of heredity found in the nucleus of every cell. (E) is incorrect because hormones are chemical messengers that travel through the bloodstream, not between neurons.

2. E

Identical twins share 100% of their genes, while fraternal twins share only about 50% of theirs. Twins raised together grow up in largely the same environment, while twins raised apart grow up in largely different environments. Thus, to determine the influence of the environment, compare twins raised apart with those raised together, but to ensure that genetic differences aren't interfering, use identical twins for both groups. Therefore, comparing identical twins raised together with those raised apart, **(E)**, will give the best indication of environmental influences on a trait. The other choices include fraternal twins, who differ in their genetics and would make it harder to isolate only the environmental influences.

3. B

The limbic system includes the hippocampus, (A), the amygdala, (C), the hypothalamus, (D), and the thalamus, (E). Only **(B)** is not part of the limbic system; the medulla is the part of the hindbrain that controls breathing, heart rate, and other autonomic functions.

4. B

Evolutionary theorists, who view human behaviors as the result of natural selection and survival instincts, argue that nighttime sleep became important for survival because it was dangerous to be active at night. According to this view, early humans who slept at night had an evolutionary advantage over those who did not; **(B)** is correct. Psychoanalytic theory, pioneered by Freud, focuses on the unconscious aspects of sleep and dreams; (A) is incorrect. Both cognitive and biological theorists would likely examine the internal processes and brain mechanisms associated with sleep, making (C) and (E) incorrect. Behavioral theory would likely look at sleep from a framework of conditioning, reinforcement, and punishment; (D) is also incorrect.

5. D

The electroencephalograph (or EEG) only detects and records brain waves; it does not produce actual images of the brain. **(D)** is correct. (A) and (B) are incorrect because CT and MRI produce images of brain structure. (C) and (E) are incorrect because PET and fMRI produce images of brain functioning.

6. B

The thyroid glands release thyroid hormones that primarily influence metabolism. **(B)** is correct. (A) is incorrect because the adrenals secrete stress hormones. (C) is incorrect because the pituitary is the master gland that regulates other endocrine glands. (D) and (E) are incorrect because the ovaries and testes are the female and male gonads, respectively, which release sex hormones.

5

7. C

Michael Gazzaniga was Sperry's graduate student and collaborated in his research on split-brain patients. **(C)** is correct. (A) is incorrect because Bouchard conducted twin studies. (B) is incorrect because Alzheimer studied what came to be called Alzheimer's disease. (D) and (E) are incorrect because Wernicke and Broca studied speech disorders.

8. A

Androgens like testosterone regulate male sexual development. **(A)** is correct. (B) and (E) are incorrect because estrogen and progesterone are female sex hormones that regulate pregnancy and the menstrual cycle. (C) and (D) are incorrect because epinephrine and cortisol are stress hormones secreted by the adrenals.

9. D

Because the disturbance occurs soon after falling asleep, most likely during NREM sleep, Tommy is most likely suffering from night terrors, making **(D)** correct. Night terrors are not dreams, but rather intense feelings of dread that can occur in the early stages of NREM sleep, most commonly in children. (A) is incorrect, although enuresis, or bed-wetting, sometimes occurs alongside night terrors. Nightmares are frightening dreams that occur during REM sleep, so (B) is incorrect. Cataplexy is involuntary muscle spasms or paralysis caused by an REM sleep disorder; (C) is incorrect. Sleep apnea is a sleep disorder caused by breathing difficulties; (E) is also incorrect.

10. E

The dendrites of a neuron contain receptors to which neurotransmitters from neighboring neurons can bind and send a signal. **(E)** is correct. (A) is incorrect because a vesicle is a small compartment isolated by its own membrane, used in neurons to transport and release neurotransmitters. (B) is incorrect because the axon of a neuron carries the action potential and releases neurotransmitters. (C) is incorrect because the nucleus is the control center of the cell, containing the genetic material. (D) is incorrect because the terminal buttons are at the end of the axon and release neurotransmitters.

CHAPTER 6

Sensation and Perception

LEARNING OBJECTIVES

After studying this chapter, you will be able to:

- Describe basic principles of sensory transduction
- Identify sensory processes and structures for each of the senses
- Recognize common sensory disorders
- Evaluate general principles of sensory organization and integration
- Discuss how top-down processing produces vulnerability to illusion
- Explain the impact of culture and experience on perception
- Evaluate the role that attention plays in behavior
- Debunk popular parapsychological beliefs
- Recognize important contributors to sensation and perception research

TEST WHAT YOU ALREADY KNOW

Part A: Quiz

1. Which of the following is NOT one of the basic tastes?

   (A) Salty

   (B) Savory

   (C) Bitter

   (D) Spicy

   (E) Sour

2. The process of receiving information from the environment is known as

   (A) perception

   (B) comprehension

   (C) transduction

   (D) sensation

   (E) top-down processing

3. The minimum change between two stimuli required to determine that they are distinct is known as

   (A) Weber's law

   (B) the absolute threshold

   (C) the just-noticeable difference

   (D) perceptual set

   (E) sensory adaptation

4. John is so focused on his exam that he fails to notice the ant crawling on his desk. Not seeing the ant is an example of

   (A) a just-noticeable difference

   (B) selective attention

   (C) the cocktail party effect

   (D) inattentional blindness

   (E) perceptual set

5. The part of the brain responsible for processing visual information is the

   (A) temporal lobe

   (B) somatosensory cortex

   (C) hypothalamus

   (D) occipital lobe

   (E) frontal lobe

6. The structure in the eye that is specialized for sensing color is the

   (A) rod

   (B) iris

   (C) cone

   (D) retina

   (E) sclera

7. The conversion of mechanical energy into neural impulses is known as

    (A) reception

    (B) transduction

    (C) perception

    (D) sensation

    (E) induction

8. The structure that contains auditory receptor cells is the

    (A) semicircular canal

    (B) tympanic membrane

    (C) pinna

    (D) malleus

    (E) cochlea

9. The structure that contains receptors for the vestibular sense is the

    (A) semicircular canals

    (B) papillae

    (C) cochlea

    (D) eustachian tube

    (E) sclera

10. After bumping his arm on a counter, Mike begins to rub it and the pain starts to subside. This can best be explained by which of the following theories?

    (A) Signal-detection theory

    (B) Temporal theory

    (C) Gate-control theory

    (D) Trichromatic theory

    (E) Opponent-process theory

6

Part B: Key Terms

The following is a list of the major ideas and people for the AP Psychology topic of Sensation and Perception. You will likely see many of these on the AP Psychology exam.

For each key term, ask yourself the following questions:

- Can I describe this key term?
- Can I discuss this key term in relation to other psychological ideas and specific psychologists?
- Could I correctly answer a multiple-choice question about this key term?
- Could I correctly answer a free-response question about this key term?

Check off the key terms if you can answer "yes" to at least three of these questions.

Sensory Processes and Disorders

- ☐ Sensation
- ☐ Transduction
- ☐ Receptors
- ☐ Absolute threshold
- ☐ Just-noticeable difference (JND)
- ☐ Weber's law
- ☐ Signal-detection theory (SDT)
- ☐ Cornea
- ☐ Iris
- ☐ Pupil
- ☐ Lens
- ☐ Accommodation
- ☐ Sclera
- ☐ Retina
- ☐ Photoreceptors
- ☐ Rods
- ☐ Cones
- ☐ Fovea

- ☐ Visual acuity
- ☐ Optic nerve
- ☐ Blind spot
- ☐ Visual cortex
- ☐ Feature detectors
- ☐ Trichromatic theory
- ☐ Opponent-process theory
- ☐ Afterimages
- ☐ Color blindness
- ☐ Audition
- ☐ Pinna
- ☐ Auditory canal
- ☐ Tympanic membrane
- ☐ Middle ear
- ☐ Malleus
- ☐ Incus
- ☐ Stapes
- ☐ Inner ear
- ☐ Oval window

- ☐ Cochlea
- ☐ Place theory
- ☐ Temporal theory
- ☐ Volley theory
- ☐ Cochlear implant
- ☐ Mechanical senses
- ☐ Chemical senses
- ☐ Gustation
- ☐ Olfaction
- ☐ Taste buds
- ☐ Papillae
- ☐ Olfactory bulb
- ☐ Tactile sensations
- ☐ Proprioception
- ☐ Kinesthesis
- ☐ Vestibular sense
- ☐ Semicircular canals
- ☐ Nociceptors
- ☐ Gate-control theory

Perceptual Processes

- ☐ Perception
- ☐ Gestalt psychology
- ☐ Depth perception

- ☐ Convergence
- ☐ Retinal disparity
- ☐ Stroboscopic motion

- ☐ Bottom-up processing
- ☐ Top-down processing
- ☐ Müller-Lyer illusion

Attention

- ☐ Attention
- ☐ Selective attention
- ☐ Cocktail party effect

Debunking Parapsychology

- ☐ Parapsychology
- ☐ Extrasensory perception (ESP)

Important Contributors

- ☐ Gustav Fechner
- ☐ Hermann von Helmholtz

- ☐ Ewald Hering
- ☐ David Hubel and Torsten Wiesel

- ☐ Ernst Weber

Next Steps

Step 1: Tally your correct answers from Part A and review the quiz explanations at the end of this chapter.

1. D
2. D
3. C
4. D
5. D
6. C
7. B
8. E
9. A
10. C

_____ out of 10 questions

Step 2: Count the number of key terms you checked off in Part B.

_____ out of 75 key terms

Step 3: Read the Rapid Review Key Takeaways in this chapter.

Step 4: Consult the table below and follow the instructions based on your performance.

If You Got . . .	Do This
80% or more of the Test What You Already Know assessment correct (8 or more questions from Part A and 60 or more key terms from Part B)	• Read definitions in this chapter for all the key terms you didn't check off. • Complete the Test What You Learned assessment in this chapter.
50% or less of the Test What You Already Know assessment correct (5 or fewer questions from Part A and 37 or fewer key terms from Part B)	• Read the comprehensive review for this topic in Chapter 15. ◦ If you are short on time, read only the High-Yield sections. • Read through all of the key term definitions in this chapter. • Complete the Test What You Learned assessment in this chapter.
Any other result	• Read the High-Yield sections of the comprehensive review of this topic in Chapter 15. • Read definitions in this chapter for all the key terms you didn't check off. • Complete the Test What You Learned assessment in this chapter.

RAPID REVIEW

Key Takeaways

1. Understanding the specialized nature of each sensory system enables researchers to generate theories about how information is transmitted and develop treatments for disorders that result when these systems are impaired.

2. After sensory information is transmitted to the brain, it must undergo additional processing to create perception. A variety of factors influence perception, including specific features of the information itself, the individual's biological dispositions and past experience, and even cultural influences.

3. The brain uses selective attention and other processes to manage the wide variety of stimuli it continually perceives and focus only on information deemed important.

4. Many people believe in "paranormal" phenomena, such as extrasensory perception, but psychological research demonstrates that there is no empirical basis to parapsychological claims.

Key Terms: Definitions

Sensory Processes and Disorders

Sensation: The process by which sensory receptors receive information from the environment; includes vision, hearing, smell, taste, touch, and the vestibular and kinesthetic senses.

Transduction: Conversion of one form of energy into another, as when environmental stimuli are transformed into neural signals.

Receptors: Specialized structures that detect specific types of environmental stimuli and transduce them into neural signals.

Absolute threshold: The minimum stimulation required for a particular stimulus to be detected 50% of the time.

Just-noticeable difference (**JND**): The smallest change in stimulation that a person can detect 50% of the time.

Weber's law: States that the size of the JND is directly proportional to the strength of the original stimulus.

Signal-detection theory (**SDT**): A theory that explains how individuals distinguish between meaningful sensory signals and random noise.

Cornea: The transparent, protective outer layer of the eye that bends light waves to assist in proper focus.

Iris: A piece of muscle tissue that sits behind the cornea and helps the eye adjust how much light enters. It gives the eye its color.

Pupil: A small, adjustable opening that is constricted or dilated by the iris. Constriction decreases the amount of light entering while dilation increases the amount of light entering.

Lens: A transparent structure that sits behind the pupil and can adjust its shape to bend light for proper focus (working with the cornea).

Accommodation: The process by which the lens changes shape to focus on near or far objects by adjusting how light hits the retina.

Sclera: The white part of the eye that provides structural support and contains blood vessels.

6

Retina: The light-sensitive inner surface of the eye containing a vast network of photoreceptors.

Photoreceptors: Specialized light-sensitive neurons in the retina that convert light into neural impulses; includes rods and cones.

Rod: A type of photoreceptor that processes black, white, and gray light; clustered in the retina's periphery.

Cone: A type of photoreceptor that distinguishes colors and detects fine details in well-lit conditions; clustered in the fovea.

Fovea: A small indentation at the center of the retina that contains the highest concentration of cones.

Visual acuity: The ability to see fine details.

Optic nerve: A bundle of retinal ganglion axons that carries information from the eye to the thalamus.

Blind spot: The location where the optic nerve exits the eye, preventing vision.

Visual cortex: The structure in the occipital lobe that integrates visual information and produces vision.

Feature detectors: Specialized nerve cells in the visual cortex that respond to particular elements like shape, movement, edges, and angles.

Trichromatic theory: Developed by Helmholtz and Young and also known as three-color theory, it suggests that the retina has three color receptors that are sensitive to red, green, and blue light.

Opponent-process theory: Developed by Hering, it suggests that the retina has receptors for three opposing pairs of colors: white–black, red–green, and yellow–blue.

Afterimages: Images that remain visible after viewing an object. A negative afterimage reverses the colors in the original image.

Color blindness: A diminished capacity to see differences in color; also called color vision deficiency.

Audition: The process of transducing acoustic energy into perceivable sound; also known as hearing.

Pinna: The outermost part of the ear that funnels sound waves into the ear's auditory canal.

Auditory canal: Focuses sound waves collected by the pinna and funnels them toward the eardrum.

Tympanic membrane: A tight, thin membrane that vibrates when hit by sound waves; also known as the eardrum.

Middle ear: Composed of three ossicles, or small bones, that work together to concentrate sound from the tympanic membrane and transmit it to the inner ear.

Malleus: One of the three ossicles; also known as the hammer.

Incus: One of the three ossicles; also known as the anvil.

Stapes: One of the three ossicles; also known as the stirrup.

Inner ear: The innermost part of the ear, containing the cochlea, auditory nerve, semicircular canals, and vestibular sacs.

Oval window: A membrane that transmits vibrations from the ossicles in the middle ear to the cochlea in the inner ear.

Cochlea: A fluid-filled snail-shaped tube in the inner ear that transmits vibrations from the oval window to receptor hair cells in the basilar membrane, where they are converted into neural impulses.

Place theory: Maintains that pitch is perceived through activation of neurons at different locations on the cochlea.

Temporal theory: Maintains that pitch is perceived through the frequency at which neurons in the cochlea fire; also called frequency theory.

Volley theory: A supplement to the temporal theory that maintains higher frequencies are encoded through the firing of multiple, out-of-sync neurons.

Cochlear implant: An electronic device that directly stimulates the auditory nerve to provide a sense of hearing to a hearing-impaired individual.

Mechanical senses: Senses such as hearing and touch that respond to pressure, bending, or other physical distortions of a receptor.

Chemical senses: Senses such as taste and smell that arise from the interactions of specific chemical compounds and receptors.

Gustation: The process by which specific compounds are detected after coming into contact with receptors on the tongue; also known as taste.

Olfaction: The process by which airborne compounds are detected after coming into contact with receptors in the nose; also known as smell.

Taste buds: Specialized receptors in the mouth that detect specific types of chemicals; they detect flavors including salty, sweet, bitter, sour, and umami.

Papillae: Protrusions on the tongue that contain taste buds.

Olfactory bulb: The smell center of the brain, which receives and processes chemical information from the olfactory nerve.

Tactile sensations: Touch, pain, temperature and other bodily sensations detected by receptors just inside the skin.

Proprioception: A somatic sense of the position of your body in space.

Kinesthesis: A somatic sense of the movement of your body in space.

Vestibular sense: The somatic sense that allows an individual to coordinate movement and maintain balance.

Semicircular canals: Fluid-filled structures in the inner ear that help to maintain balance.

Nociceptors: Pain receptors found under the skin. They respond to stimuli such as intense pressures, extreme temperatures, and caustic chemicals.

Gate-control theory: Theory suggesting that the spinal cord acts like a neurological gate that can open or close to manage whether pain signals travel to the brain.

Perceptual Processes

Perception: The process of integrating and interpreting sensory data.

Gestalt psychology: A subfield of psychology that suggests that the brain forms a perceptual whole that is greater than the sum of its parts.

Depth perception: The ability to see three-dimensional objects and judge distance, even though the images that strike the retina are two-dimensional.

Convergence: The slight inward rotation of the eyes that occurs when viewing closer objects, which can be used to gauge distance.

Retinal disparity: The difference between the images seen by each eye, which can be used to gauge distance.

Stroboscopic motion: The illusion of apparent movement caused by viewing a continuous series of slightly differing images.

Bottom-up processing: The perceptual process of starting with basic sensory data and integrating them into a more complex whole.

Top-down processing: The perceptual process in which memories, expectations, and other factors give organization to the whole of perception.

Müller-Lyer illusion: An optical illusion consisting of two line segments, one with arrows pointing inward and one with arrows pointing outward. Though both lines are of equal length, the line with the inward-pointing arrows is typically perceived to be longer.

Attention

Attention: The focus of awareness on particular aspects of perception.

Selective attention: Allows individuals to focus their awareness on a specific stimulus while ignoring all other stimuli.

Cocktail party effect: Describes an individual's ability to attend to only one voice even with extensive and varied background noise.

Debunking Parapsychology

Parapsychology: The study of paranormal phenomena such as extrasensory perception and psychokinesis.

Extrasensory perception (ESP): The purported ability to perceive something without any sensory input; debunked by scientific research.

Important Contributors

Gustav Fechner: With Weber, founder of psychophysics who studied the relations between physical changes and perceived changes in stimuli.

Hermann von Helmholtz: Developed the trichromatic theory of color vision, building on the work of Thomas Young.

Ewald Hering: Proposed the opponent-process theory of color vision.

David Hubel and **Torsten Wiesel**: Demonstrated how specialized cells in the brain respond to visual information.

Ernst Weber: A founder of psychophysics who investigated the just-noticeable difference and proposed Weber's law.

TEST WHAT YOU LEARNED

Part A: Quiz

1. The part of the eye responsible for receiving photons of light and translating them into neural messages is the

   (A) sclera

   (B) lens

   (C) cornea

   (D) pupil

   (E) retina

2. Which of the following terms refers to the minimum intensity of a stimulus that must be present in order for an individual to detect it?

   (A) Absolute threshold

   (B) Just-noticeable difference

   (C) Perceptual set

   (D) Weber's law

   (E) Sensory adaptation

3. The part of the brain responsible for processing auditory information is the

   (A) temporal lobe

   (B) occipital lobe

   (C) somatosensory cortex

   (D) frontal lobe

   (E) hypothalamus

4. Which of the following explains why we perceive cartoons as fluidly moving even though they are actually a series of static images?

   (A) Gestalt psychology

   (B) Convergence

   (C) Retinal disparity

   (D) Stroboscopic motion

   (E) Müller-Lyer illusion

5. Which of the following is an example of a somatic sense?

   (A) A teenager spits out milk after realizing it has gone bad.

   (B) A baby cries when she sees her mother enter the room.

   (C) A man feels himself lose his balance when he misses a step.

   (D) A woman smells a burnt odor after cooking a dish for too long.

   (E) A child hears his mother calling for him to come home.

6. The process of organizing and interpreting sensory data received from the external environment is known as

   (A) perception

   (B) comprehension

   (C) detection

   (D) sensation

   (E) transduction

6

7. Which of the following is the correct pathway through which sound travels to the temporal lobe of the brain?

   (A) Tympanic membrane → malleus → incus → stapes → cochlea → oval window → pinna

   (B) Pinna → tympanic membrane → ossicles → oval window → cochlea

   (C) Pinna → oval membrane → malleus → ossicles → tympanic membrane → cochlea

   (D) Tympanic membrane → pinna → ossicles → oval window → cochlea

   (E) Auditory canal → pinna → tympanic membrane → malleus → incus → stapes → cochlea

8. Suppose that Mark is able to detect when a 2-pound weight is added to the 30-pound dumbbells he lifts, but he cannot detect any smaller addition. If Mark were instead lifting 60-pound dumbbells, the smallest weight he would notice being added would be

   (A) 1 pound

   (B) 2 pounds

   (C) 4 pounds

   (D) 10 pounds

   (E) 30 pounds

9. Artists working on flat surfaces use all of the following environmental cues in their art to indicate depth except

   (A) height in the visual field

   (B) focus

   (C) light and shadow

   (D) relative positioning of objects

   (E) convergence

10. Farah views the neighborhood dog as threatening because she was bitten by a dog when she was younger. This is an example of

   (A) top-down processing

   (B) Gestalt psychology

   (C) gate-control theory

   (D) bottom-up processing

   (E) opponent-process theory

Part B: Key Terms

This key terms list is the same as the list in the Test What You Already Know section earlier in this chapter. Based on what you have now learned, again ask yourself the following questions:

- Can I describe this key term?

- Can I discuss this key term in relation to other psychological ideas and specific psychologists?

- Could I correctly answer a multiple-choice question about this key term?

- Could I correctly answer a free-response question about this key term?

Check off the key terms if you can answer "yes" to at least three of these questions.

Sensory Processes and Disorders

- ☐ Sensation
- ☐ Transduction
- ☐ Receptors
- ☐ Absolute threshold
- ☐ Just-noticeable difference (JND)
- ☐ Weber's law
- ☐ Signal-detection theory (SDT)
- ☐ Cornea
- ☐ Iris
- ☐ Pupil
- ☐ Lens
- ☐ Accommodation
- ☐ Sclera
- ☐ Retina
- ☐ Photoreceptors
- ☐ Rods
- ☐ Cones
- ☐ Fovea

- ☐ Visual acuity
- ☐ Optic nerve
- ☐ Blind spot
- ☐ Visual cortex
- ☐ Feature detectors
- ☐ Trichromatic theory
- ☐ Opponent-process theory
- ☐ Afterimages
- ☐ Color blindness
- ☐ Audition
- ☐ Pinna
- ☐ Auditory canal
- ☐ Tympanic membrane
- ☐ Middle ear
- ☐ Malleus
- ☐ Incus
- ☐ Stapes
- ☐ Inner ear
- ☐ Oval window

- ☐ Cochlea
- ☐ Place theory
- ☐ Temporal theory
- ☐ Volley theory
- ☐ Cochlear implant
- ☐ Mechanical senses
- ☐ Chemical senses
- ☐ Gustation
- ☐ Olfaction
- ☐ Taste buds
- ☐ Papillae
- ☐ Olfactory bulb
- ☐ Tactile sensations
- ☐ Proprioception
- ☐ Kinesthesis
- ☐ Vestibular sense
- ☐ Semicircular canals
- ☐ Nociceptors
- ☐ Gate-control theory

Perceptual Processes

☐ Perception   ☐ Convergence   ☐ Bottom-up processing

☐ Gestalt psychology   ☐ Binocular disparity   ☐ Top-down processing

☐ Depth perception   ☐ Stroboscopic motion   ☐ Müller-Lyer illusion

Attention

☐ Attention   ☐ Selective attention   ☐ Cocktail party effect

Debunking Parapsychology

☐ Parapsychology   ☐ Extrasensory perception (ESP)

Important Contributors

☐ Gustav Fechner   ☐ Ewald Hering   ☐ Ernst Weber

☐ Hermann von Helmholtz   ☐ David Hubel and Torsten Wiesel

Next Steps

Step 1: Tally your correct answers from Part A and review the quiz explanations at the end of this chapter.

1. E   6. A

2. A   7. B

3. A   8. C

4. D   9. E

5. C   10. A

_____ out of 10 questions

Step 2: Count the number of key terms you checked off in Part B.

_____ out of 75 key terms

Step 3: Compare your Test What You Already Know results to these Test What You Learned results to see how exam-ready you are for this topic.

If you need to study this topic further:

- Read (or reread) the comprehensive review for this topic in Chapter 15.

- Go to kaptest.com to complete the online quiz questions for Sensation and Perception.

  ○ Haven't registered your book yet? Go to kaptest.com/moreonline to begin.

ANSWERS AND EXPLANATIONS

Test What You Already Know

1. D

The five basic tastes detected by human taste buds are salty, sweet, bitter, sour, and savory (or umami), so (A), (B), (C), and (E) can be eliminated. Spiciness is not classified as a basic taste because it does not result from the activation of taste buds; compounds like capsaicin directly stimulate nerves to cause the sensation of spiciness. **(D)** is correct.

2. D

Sensation is the process by which sensory receptors receive information from the environment. Thus, **(D)** is correct. Perception, (A), is the processing of sensory data into meaningful information. Comprehension, (B), is the process of understanding something. Transduction, (C), is the conversion of one form of energy into another. Top-down processing, (E), is a type of perceptual processing.

3. C

The just-noticeable difference is the smallest amount by which two sensory stimuli can differ in order for them to be perceived as different. Thus, **(C)** is correct. Weber's law, (A), states that the size of the just-noticeable difference is directly proportional to the strength of the original stimulus. The absolute threshold, (B), is the minimum stimulation required for a particular stimulus to be detected. Perceptual set, (D), is the predisposition to perceive things in a certain way based on schemata, which are mental representations of how the world is expected to be, based on past experiences. Sensory adaptation, (E), refers to an individual's decreasing response to a stimulus as a result of constant, prolonged stimulation.

4. D

Inattentional blindness occurs when a person fails to see visible objects because his or her attention is focused elsewhere. Since John does not notice the ant because he is so focused on his test, **(D)** is correct. (A) is incorrect because a just-noticeable difference refers to the minimum detectable difference between two similar stimuli. Selective attention, (B), allows individuals to focus their conscious awareness on a specific stimulus while ignoring all other stimuli. While John is selectively paying attention to his test, the fact that he does not notice the ant is indicative of inattentional blindness. The cocktail party effect, (C), is a type of selective attention that describes an individual's ability to attend to only one voice amid a mixture of conversations and background noises. Perceptual set, (E), is the predisposition to perceive things in a certain way based on schemata, which are mental representations of how the world is expected to be based on past experiences.

5. D

The occipital lobe contains the visual cortex and processes visual information, making **(D)** correct. The temporal lobe, (A), processes auditory information and plays an important role in language comprehension. The somatosensory cortex, (B), produces the awareness of the different parts of the body in space. The hypothalamus, (C), regulates the endocrine system. The frontal lobe, (E), is important for higher-level cognitive functioning.

6. C

Cones are photoreceptors that detect fine detail and distinguish colors; thus, **(C)** is correct. Rods, (A), are photoreceptors that process black, white, and gray. The iris, (B), is a piece of muscle that helps the eye adjust how much light enters. The retina, (D), is the light-sensitive inner surface of the eye that contains both rods and cones. The sclera, (E), is the outer casing also known as the white of the eye.

7. B

Transduction is the conversion of one form of energy into another. Thus, the conversion of mechanical energy into neural impulses, which constitute a type of electrical energy, is an example of transduction, making **(B)** correct. Reception, (A), is the process of taking in energy prior to transduction. Perception, (C), refers to how information is interpreted, which occurs after transduction. Sensation, (D), is the process by which sensory receptors detect stimuli from the environment. Induction, (E), is a method of logical reasoning.

8. E

The cochlea is a fluid-filled snail-shaped tube in the inner ear that transmits vibrations to the receptor hair cells in the basilar membrane, where they are then converted into neural impulses. Thus, **(E)** is correct. A semicircular canal, (A), is one of three fluid-filled structures in the inner ear that transmit neural impulses to the cerebellum to coordinate movement and balance. The tympanic membrane, (B), vibrates when hit by sound waves and transmits the vibrational energy to the middle ear. The pinna, (C), is the outermost part of the ear, visible on the side of the head, which funnels sound waves into the ear's auditory canal. The malleus, (D), is one of the ossicles in the middle ear that concentrates sound from the tympanic membrane and transmits it to the inner ear.

9. A

The vestibular sense is primarily responsible for helping individuals maintain their balance. When your head moves, the liquid inside your semicircular canals moves as well, triggering tiny hairs in the canals. This motion is then converted into electrical signals and transmitted to your brain to relay information about your body's orientation in space. Thus, **(A)** is correct. Papillae are small buds on the tongue that contain taste buds. They are important for the sense of taste, eliminating (B). The cochlea is a snail-shaped structure in the inner ear that contains fluid which transmits vibrations from the oval window to receptor hair cells in the basilar membrane, where they are then converted into neural impulses. Though the mechanism of action is similar to the semicircular canals, which are, in fact, attached to the cochlea, the cochlea is used primarily for the sense of hearing, eliminating (C). (D) is incorrect because the eustachian tube is a tube between the middle ear and the throat that allows the pressure on both sides of the eardrum to be equalized. The sclera is the white part of the eye, which provides structural support and contains blood vessels, eliminating (E).

10. C

Gate-control theory posits that the spinal cord acts like a neurological gate that opens when pain is detected, allowing those signals to travel to the brain. The gate opens when pain signals travel up small nerve fibers and is closed by signals traveling up larger fibers. So, when Mike rubbed his arm, non-nociceptive touch signals would be transmitted through the large nerve fibers, closing the gate. Thus, **(C)** is correct. Signal-detection theory, (A), explains how individuals distinguish between meaningful sensory signals and random noise. Temporal theory, (B), maintains that pitch is perceived through the frequency at which neurons in the cochlea fire. Trichromatic theory, (D), also known as the three-color theory, states that the retina has three types of receptors that are sensitive to red, green, and blue light. (E) is incorrect because the opponent-process theory of vision maintains that retinal cells are turned on or off by opposing colors (red-green, yellow-blue, white-black), allowing us to see color.

Test What You Learned

1. E

The retina is the light-sensitive inner surface of the eye containing a vast network of photoreceptors that translate photons of inbound light into neural impulses, which are then transmitted to the brain. Thus, **(E)** is correct. The sclera, (A), is the white part of the eye that provides structural support and contains the blood vessels that supply the eye. The lens, (B), adjusts how light hits the retina by changing its shape in order to focus on objects as they move closer or farther away. The cornea, (C), is the transparent, protective outer layer of the eye that bends the light waves so the image can be focused properly. The pupil, (D), constricts and dilates to control how much light enters the eye.

2. A

The absolute threshold is the minimum stimulation required for a particular stimulus to be detected 50% of the time; thus, **(A)** is correct. The just-noticeable difference, (B), is the smallest amount by which two sensory stimuli can differ in order for them to be perceived as different. Perceptual set, (C), is the predisposition to perceive things in a certain way based on schemata, which are mental representations of how the world is expected to be, based on past experiences. Weber's law, (D), states that the size of the just-noticeable difference is directly proportional to the strength of the original stimulus. Sensory adaptation, (E), refers to an individual's decreasing response to a stimulus as a result of constant, prolonged stimulation.

3. A

The temporal lobe is involved in auditory perception, making **(A)** correct. The occipital lobe, (B), contains the visual cortex and processes visual information. The somatosensory cortex, (C), receives and processes somatosensory information. The frontal lobe, (D), is important for higher-level cognitive functioning. The hypothalamus, (E), regulates the endocrine system.

4. D

Stroboscopic motion is the illusion of apparent movement caused by a constant, continuous series of slightly different static images; the images change so rapidly that they are perceived as moving. Thus, **(D)** is correct. Gestalt psychology, (A), is a subfield of psychology that suggests that the brain forms a perceptual whole that is more complex than the sum of its parts. Convergence, (B), refers to the slight inward rotation of the eyes that allows an image to strike both retinas simultaneously. Retinal disparity, (C), refers to the difference between the images seen by both eyes that allows the brain to compute the distance of the object. The Müller-Lyer illusion, (E), is a common optical illusion.

5. C

The somatic (or bodily) senses include touch, pressure, pain, and temperature, in addition to proprioception, kinesthetic sense, and vestibular sense. The vestibular sense helps people coordinate movement and maintain their balance. Since the man is able to process that he is losing his balance, he is using his vestibular sense, making **(C)** correct. (A) is an example of the chemical sense of taste. (B) is an example of the sense of vision. (D) is an example of the chemical sense of smell. (E) is an example of the mechanical sense of hearing.

6. A

Perception is the process of integrating sensory data from the environment into meaningful information. Thus, **(A)** is correct. Comprehension, (B), is the act of understanding something. Detection, (C), is the process of noticing or identifying something. Sensation, (D), is the process by which sensory receptors receive information from the environment. Transduction, (E), is the conversion of one form of energy into another.

7. B

The external, visible part of the ear is known as the pinna. It collects and concentrates sound waves into the auditory canal toward the tympanic membrane, which is a tight, thin membrane that vibrates in response to sound waves. The vibrations of the tympanic membrane are transmitted through the ossicles (the malleus, incus, and stapes) to the oval window, finally reaching the cochlea. The cochlea contains auditory receptors, which then send information to the brain. Thus, **(B)** is correct. The other choices rearrange the order.

8. C

According to Weber's law, the just noticeable difference is proportional to the intensity of the stimulus. This means that two stimuli must differ by a minimum percentage (rather than by a fixed value) in order to be perceived as different. Thus, in this case, since the stimulus (the weights) is being doubled, the change in stimulus would need to be doubled as well for the difference to be detectable. Since the original value of the added weight was 2 pounds, the new weight must be 4 pounds, making **(C)** correct. The remaining choices do not reflect Weber's law.

9. E

(A), (B), (C), and (D) are all examples of monocular cues, which are light cues that only depend on one eye. Height in the visual field, (A), is defined as the relative height of an object with respect to the rest of the visual field. Focus, (B), can be visualized as farther away objects appearing hazy and closer objects appearing to be sharp and clear. Light and shadow, (C), suggests that light-colored objects seem closer and darker objects seem farther away. When one object overlaps another, the overlapped object is perceived as being farther away, eliminating (D). Convergence is a binocular cue that uses the extent to which the eyes converge inward when looking at an object to determine distance. Because convergence depends on the actual distance of a feature (rather than the apparent distance), this cue cannot be utilized by artists working on a flat surface in which all features are at approximately the same distance from the observer, making **(E)** correct.

10. A

Farah is using a past experience to arrive at her perception that the neighborhood dog is unfriendly. Thus, since her interpretation of new sensory information is shaped by past experience, she is using top-down processing, making **(A)** correct. Gestalt psychology, (B), is a subfield of psychology that suggests that the brain forms a complex perceptual whole that is greater than the sum of its parts. Gate-control theory, (C), posits that the spinal cord acts like a neurological gate that opens when pain is detected, allowing those signals to travel to the brain. Bottom-up processing, (D), describes the perceptual process of starting with basic sensory data and integrating them into a more complex whole. Opponent-process theory, (E), states that the retina has receptors for three opposing pairs of colors.

CHAPTER 7

Learning

LEARNING OBJECTIVES

After studying this chapter, you will be able to:

- Contrast the principles of classical conditioning, operant conditioning, and observational learning

- List and explain fundamentals of classical conditioning

- Forecast operant conditioning's effects

- Explain the effect on learning of practice, reinforcement schedules, and motivational support

- Employ graphs to interpret learning experiment results

- Offer examples of learning predispositions resulting from biological constraints

- Define and contrast insight, latent, and social learning

- Explain emotional learning, taste aversion, superstitious behavior, and learned helplessness in terms of learning principles

- List means of addressing behavioral problems through behavior modification, biofeedback, coping strategies, and self-control

- Recognize important contributors to the psychology of learning

TEST WHAT YOU ALREADY KNOW

Part A: Quiz

1. Rochelle wants to quit smoking cigarettes. Which of the following techniques would be most likely to help Rochelle achieve this goal?

   (A) Biofeedback

   (B) Positive reinforcement

   (C) Aversion therapy

   (D) Modeling

   (E) Systematic desensitization

2. A participant in an experiment hears a tone right before an apparatus blows a puff of air into her eye, which causes her to blink. After this is repeated several times, the participant blinks immediately upon hearing the tone. The blinking caused by the puff of air is called

   (A) the unconditioned stimulus

   (B) the unconditioned response

   (C) the conditioned stimulus

   (D) the conditioned response

   (E) the neutral stimulus

3. Tammy is interested in helping her daughter learn table manners. Each time her daughter does something that is close to appropriate, Tammy provides her with a small reward. Eventually, her daughter does learn her manners. This process is an example of

   (A) higher order conditioning

   (B) observational learning

   (C) priming

   (D) generalization

   (E) shaping

4. If a rat receives food after every 10 bar presses, the schedule of reinforcement is

   (A) continuous

   (B) fixed ratio

   (C) variable ratio

   (D) fixed interval

   (E) variable interval

5. Which type of learning was demonstrated in Bandura's Bobo doll experiment?

   (A) Classical conditioning

   (B) Latent learning

   (C) Insight learning

   (D) Cognitive learning

   (E) Social learning

6. According to Skinner, punishment is effective only under very specific conditions. Which of the following is one of these conditions?

   (A) The punishment is mild.

   (B) The punishment is delayed.

   (C) The punishment is threatened but not given.

   (D) The punishment immediately follows the behavior.

   (E) The punishment occurs on a variable schedule.

7. The person most responsible for developing the framework for classical conditioning was

   (A) Ivan Pavlov

   (B) John Watson

   (C) B.F. Skinner

   (D) Albert Bandura

   (E) Erik Erikson

8. One evening after a meal of veal parmigiana, Phoebe came down with a nasty case of the flu that left her feeling nauseous for days. Afterwards, she could no longer eat veal without becoming sick. This is an example of

   (A) superstitious behavior

   (B) shaping

   (C) learned helplessness

   (D) taste aversion

   (E) flashbulb memories

9. Classical conditioning is a means of changing

   (A) a neutral stimulus into a conditioned stimulus

   (B) a conditioned stimulus into a neutral stimulus

   (C) an unconditioned stimulus into a conditioned stimulus

   (D) a neutral response into a conditioned response

   (E) a conditioned response into an unconditioned response

10. Which of the following provides the best example of a superstition as defined by a behaviorist?

    (A) Alex fell into a pool when he was five and nearly drowned, so he has a fear of water and does not like going to the beach.

    (B) Billie believes that the number thirteen is unlucky, and avoids going outside on Friday the thirteenth.

    (C) Cameron ate some cheese dip and got sick shortly afterwards. He finds that he no longer has an appetite for cheese dip.

    (D) Devin practiced a great deal for a piano recital and did very well. She resolves to practice as much or more for all future recitals.

    (E) Emery wore a certain pair of socks the day she got a perfect score on a math test, so she wears that pair of socks for every subsequent test.

7

Part B: Key Terms

The following is a list of the major ideas and people for the AP Psychology topic of Learning. You will likely see many of these on the AP Psychology exam.

For each key term, ask yourself the following questions:

- Can I describe this key term?
- Can I discuss this key term in relation to other psychological ideas and specific psychologists?
- Could I correctly answer a multiple-choice question about this key term?
- Could I correctly answer a free-response question about this key term?

Check off the key terms if you can answer "yes" to at least three of these questions.

Principles of Learning

- ☐ Learning
- ☐ Classical conditioning
- ☐ Operant conditioning
- ☐ Observational learning/ social learning

Classical Conditioning

- ☐ Unconditioned stimulus (UCS)
- ☐ Unconditioned response (UCR)
- ☐ Neutral stimulus (NS)
- ☐ Conditioned stimulus (CS)
- ☐ Conditioned response (CR)
- ☐ Acquisition
- ☐ Higher order conditioning
- ☐ Expectancy
- ☐ Stimulus generalization
- ☐ Stimulus discrimination
- ☐ Extinction
- ☐ Spontaneous recovery

Operant Conditioning

- ☐ Law of effect
- ☐ Skinner box
- ☐ Operant
- ☐ Reinforcer
- ☐ Positive reinforcer
- ☐ Negative reinforcer
- ☐ Escape conditioning
- ☐ Avoidance conditioning
- ☐ Punishment
- ☐ Discriminative stimulus
- ☐ Shaping
- ☐ Primary reinforcer
- ☐ Secondary reinforcer
- ☐ Token reinforcer
- ☐ Token economy
- ☐ Continuous reinforcement
- ☐ Partial reinforcement
- ☐ Schedule of reinforcement
- ☐ Fixed ratio (FR)
- ☐ Variable ratio (VR)
- ☐ Fixed interval (FI)
- ☐ Variable interval (VI)
- ☐ Partial reinforcement extinction effect

Other Types of Learning

- ☐ Cognitive learning
- ☐ Cognitive map
- ☐ Latent learning
- ☐ Bobo doll experiment
- ☐ Self-efficacy
- ☐ Insight learning

Applications of Learning

- ☐ Emotional learning
- ☐ Little Albert experiment
- ☐ Taste aversion
- ☐ Superstitious behavior
- ☐ Accidental conditioning
- ☐ Learned helplessness

Solutions to Behavioral Problems

- ☐ Behavior modification
- ☐ Systematic desensitization
- ☐ Aversion therapy
- ☐ Biofeedback
- ☐ Coping

Important Contributors

- ☐ Albert Bandura
- ☐ John Garcia
- ☐ Ivan Pavlov
- ☐ Robert Rescorla
- ☐ Martin Seligman
- ☐ B.F. Skinner
- ☐ Edward Thorndike
- ☐ Edward Tolman
- ☐ John Watson

7

Next Steps

Step 1: Tally your correct answers from Part A and review the quiz explanations at the end of this chapter.

1. C
2. B
3. E
4. B
5. E

6. D
7. A
8. D
9. A
10. E

_____ out of 10 questions

Step 2: Count the number of key terms you checked off in Part B.

_____ out of 65 key terms

Step 3: Read the Rapid Review Key Takeaways in this chapter.

Step 4: Consult the table below and follow the instructions based on your performance.

If You Got . . .	Do This
80% or more of the Test What You Already Know assessment correct (8 or more questions from Part A and 52 or more key terms from Part B)	• Read definitions in this chapter for all the key terms you didn't check off. • Complete the Test What You Learned assessment in this chapter.
50% or less of the Test What You Already Know assessment correct (5 or fewer questions from Part A and 32 or fewer key terms from Part B)	• Read the comprehensive review for this topic in Chapter 16. ○ If you are short on time, read only the High-Yield sections. • Read through all of the key term definitions in this chapter. • Complete the Test What You Learned assessment in this chapter.
Any other result	• Read the High-Yield sections of the comprehensive review of this topic in Chapter 16. • Read definitions in this chapter for all the key terms you didn't check off. • Complete the Test What You Learned assessment in this chapter.

7

RAPID REVIEW

Key Takeaways

1. Learning is the changing of behavior in response to experience and comes in a number of forms, each of which operates according to distinct principles.

2. Classical conditioning is the process of repeatedly pairing an original (unconditioned) stimulus, which naturally produces a reflexive (unconditioned) response, with a new (neutral) stimulus, such that the new stimulus produces the same response.

3. Operant conditioning theory is based on the idea that human behavior is influenced by "operants" in the environment. These include positive and negative reinforcement, which encourage behavior, as well as punishment, which suppresses behavior.

4. According to cognitive psychologists, complex higher-level mental processes are at work during the learning process, as can be seen in cognitive maps, latent learning, insight learning, and observational learning.

5. Learning theories can explain phenomena like emotional learning, taste aversion, superstitious behavior, and learned helplessness.

6. One practical application of learning theories is finding solutions to behavioral problems via techniques such as behavior modification, biofeedback, coping strategies, and self-control.

Key Terms: Definitions

Principles of Learning

Learning: A relatively permanent change in behavior based on experience.

Classical conditioning: A method of learning that creates new associations between neutral stimuli and reflex-causing stimuli.

Operant conditioning: A method of learning that alters the frequency of a behavior by manipulating its consequences through reinforcement or punishment.

Observational learning/social learning: A form of learning that occurs by watching the behaviors of others.

Classical Conditioning

Unconditioned stimulus (UCS): A stimulus capable of reflexively evoking a response.

Unconditioned response (UCR): A reflexive response produced by an unconditioned stimulus.

Neutral stimulus (NS): A stimulus that does not produce a reflexive response.

Conditioned stimulus (CS): A stimulus that produces a response because it has been repeatedly paired with an unconditioned stimulus.

Conditioned response (CR): A learned response produced by a conditioned stimulus.

Acquisition: When a behavior, such as a conditioned response, has been learned.

Higher order conditioning: A form of classical conditioning in which a previously conditioned stimulus is used to produce further learning.

Expectancy: The anticipation of future events or relationships based on past experience.

7

Stimulus generalization: The tendency to respond to another stimulus that is similar but not identical to the original conditioned stimulus.

Stimulus discrimination: The ability to distinguish between similar but nonidentical stimuli.

Extinction: The cessation of a learned response, usually resulting from an end to conditioning.

Spontaneous recovery: The reappearance of a learned response after its apparent extinction.

Operant Conditioning

Law of effect: The idea that responses that lead to positive effects are repeated, while responses that lead to negative effects are not repeated.

Skinner box: A laboratory apparatus used to study operant conditioning in animals, which typically contains a lever that animals can press to dispense food as reinforcement.

Operant: A behavior that has some effect on the environment.

Reinforcer: A stimulus that increases the likelihood that a specific behavior will occur.

Positive reinforcer: Any pleasant stimulus rewarded after a desired behavior.

Negative reinforcer: Anything that counteracts an unpleasant stimulus.

Escape conditioning: Conditioning with a negative reinforcer that reduces or removes the unpleasantness of something that already exists.

Avoidance conditioning: Conditioning with a negative reinforcer that prevents the unpleasantness of something that has yet to occur.

Punishment: The use of a negative stimulus or the withdrawal of a positive stimulus in order to suppress an undesirable behavior.

Discriminative stimulus: A stimulus that signals whether a behavior or response will lead to reinforcement.

Shaping: The process of gradually molding behavior to get a final desired response by reinforcing successive approximations to the desired behavior.

Primary reinforcer: A stimulus that is intrinsically pleasant, often because it satisfies a basic need.

Secondary reinforcer: A stimulus that individuals have been conditioned to desire through association with a primary reinforcer.

Token reinforcer: Any secondary reinforcer that is tangible, such as money or gold stars given by a teacher.

Token economy: A system in which token reinforcers are used to reward positive behaviors and can be traded for other reinforcers.

Continuous reinforcement: The use of reinforcement after each and every instance of a desired response.

Partial reinforcement: The use of reinforcement after a desired response only part of the time.

Schedule of reinforcement: A rule or plan for determining how often behaviors will be reinforced.

Fixed ratio (FR): A schedule in which reinforcement follows a constant number of responses.

Variable ratio (VR): A schedule in which reinforcement follows a varied number of responses.

Fixed interval (FI): A schedule in which reinforcement for a desired response is only available after a set amount of time.

Variable interval (VI): A schedule in which reinforcement for a desired response is only available after a varying amount of time.

Partial reinforcement extinction effect: Behaviors learned on a partial reinforcement schedule are more difficult to extinguish than behaviors learned on a continuous reinforcement schedule.

Other Types of Learning

Cognitive learning: High-level learning that involves thinking, anticipating, and other complex mental processes.

Cognitive map: A mental representation of an environment or concept that facilitates understanding.

Latent learning: Learning that occurs without any obvious reinforcement and remains unexpressed until reinforcement is provided.

Bobo doll experiment: A classic study by Albert Bandura in which children viewed a film of an adult violently hitting an inflatable "Bobo" doll and then were allowed to play with the doll. The children showed aggression toward the doll, demonstrating the power of observational learning.

Self-efficacy: The extent to which a person believes him- or herself capable of success in a particular situation.

Insight learning: A type of learning that occurs by suddenly understanding how to solve a problem rather than solving it by trial and error.

Applications of Learning

Emotional learning: How emotions and emotional state affect cognitive processes, including memory formation and retrieval.

Little Albert experiment: John Watson conditioned an 11-month-old boy to have a fear of white rats using classical conditioning.

Taste aversion: An active dislike for a particular food, developed through conditioning.

Superstitious behavior: Behavior that is learned through an accidental reinforcement process, creating a false link between cause and effect.

Accidental conditioning: Conditioning that occurs when a good or bad outcome happens to follow a particular behavior for unconnected reasons, thus promoting superstitious behavior.

Learned helplessness: The learned inability to overcome obstacles or avoid punishment.

Solutions to Behavioral Problems

Behavior modification: The process and techniques used to change a particular behavior.

Systematic desensitization: A behavior modification technique that attempts to treat phobias through planned exposure to fearful stimuli.

Aversion therapy: A process of behavior modification that works by associating an undesirable habitual behavior with an unpleasant stimulus.

Biofeedback: The electronic monitoring of autonomic functions (like heart rate, blood pressure, or stress responses) for the purpose of bringing those functions under partially voluntary control.

Coping: The behavioral and cognitive strategies used to manage stress.

Important Contributors

Albert Bandura: Conducted the Bobo doll experiment, which demonstrated that aggression is learned by observing and modeling others.

John Garcia: Discovered taste aversion when looking at the impact of radiation on rats. Rats became nauseous from the radiation, but since the taste of water from a plastic bottle was accidentally paired with this radiation, the rats developed an aversion for this water.

Ivan Pavlov: Conditioned dogs to salivate at the sound of a bell after repeated pairings with food, thereby discovering classical conditioning.

Robert Rescorla: Studied cognitive processes in classical conditioning and maintained that an unconditioned stimulus is more effective if it surprises the learner.

Martin Seligman: Developed the concept of learned helplessness after conducting experiments on dogs that were unable to escape an unpleasant situation.

B.F. Skinner: The behaviorist most responsible for developing operant conditioning theory.

Edward Thorndike: A behaviorist known for the law of effect, which served as the foundation for Skinner's operant conditioning theory.

Edward Tolman: A behaviorist who developed the idea of latent learning by conducting experiments in which rats learned to run mazes even when reinforcement was withheld.

John Watson: Founder of the behaviorist school who believed that psychology could only scientifically examine behavior, and not unobservable mental processes. Watson conducted the Little Albert experiment.

TEST WHAT YOU LEARNED

Part A: Quiz

1. Which of the following is an example of a fixed interval schedule of reinforcement?

   (A) Getting a treat every time for sitting on command

   (B) Receiving a reward for good behavior once in a while

   (C) Earning a free coffee after five purchases

   (D) Collecting a paycheck once a week on Fridays

   (E) Winning money at a slot machine

2. In Edward Tolman's experiments with rats in mazes, the rats who were able to learn the layout of the maze without having food placed at the exit demonstrated

   (A) latent learning

   (B) cognitive learning

   (C) social learning

   (D) observational learning

   (E) insight learning

3. Classical conditioning and operant conditioning differ in that

   (A) classical conditioning relies on reinforcement and punishment

   (B) classical conditioning includes shaping

   (C) classical conditioning deals exclusively with reflexive behavior

   (D) operant conditioning deals exclusively with reflexive behavior

   (E) operant conditioning is ineffective in most situations

4. Phobic behavior can most effectively be eliminated through

   (A) aversion therapy

   (B) punishment

   (C) modeling

   (D) reinforcement

   (E) systematic desensitization

5. A dog has been conditioned to bark at the sound of a bell. However, the dog has also started to bark at the sound of a whistle. This is an example of

   (A) shaping

   (B) generalization

   (C) extinction

   (D) discrimination

   (E) desensitization

6. One of the biggest differences between negative reinforcement and punishment is that

   (A) negative reinforcement involves aversive stimuli

   (B) punishment involves aversive stimuli

   (C) negative reinforcement increases the likelihood of a desired behavior

   (D) punishment increases the likelihood of a desired behavior

   (E) negative reinforcement decreases the likelihood of a desired behavior

7. Accidental reinforcement is most likely to cause

   (A) superstitious behavior

   (B) extinction

   (C) stimulus generalization

   (D) spontaneous recovery

   (E) stimulus discrimination

8. The person most responsible for developing the framework for operant conditioning was

   (A) Ivan Pavlov

   (B) B.F. Skinner

   (C) John Watson

   (D) Albert Bandura

   (E) Sigmund Freud

9. A mother wants to use candy to reinforce her child's positive behaviors in public. Which of the following would result in a decrease in the strength of the reinforcement?

   (A) Giving the child three pieces of candy instead of just one

   (B) Avoiding the use of candy to reward good grades in school

   (C) Waiting until returning home to give the child candy

   (D) Avoiding giving the child candy as a routine snack

   (E) Providing candy after some instances of the behavior and not others

10. A night security guard performs rounds every fifteen minutes because he knows he will be reprimanded if he does not, since his actions can be observed via a system of security cameras in the building. One week the guard learns that the camera system is down, and starts performing rounds less often. In this scenario, the cameras are an example of a

    (A) primary reinforcer

    (B) secondary reinforcer

    (C) token reinforcer

    (D) discriminatory stimulus

    (E) Skinner box

Part B: Key Terms

This key terms list is the same as the list in the Test What You Already Know section earlier in this chapter. Based on what you have now learned, again ask yourself the following questions:

- Can I describe this key term?

- Can I discuss this key term in relation to other psychological ideas and specific psychologists?

- Could I correctly answer a multiple-choice question about this key term?

- Could I correctly answer a free-response question about this key term?

Check off the key terms if you can answer "yes" to at least three of these questions.

Principles of Learning

- ☐ Learning
- ☐ Classical conditioning
- ☐ Operant conditioning
- ☐ Observational learning/ social learning

Classical Conditioning

- ☐ Unconditioned stimulus (UCS)
- ☐ Unconditioned response (UCR)
- ☐ Neutral stimulus (NS)
- ☐ Conditioned stimulus (CS)
- ☐ Conditioned response (CR)
- ☐ Acquisition
- ☐ Higher order conditioning
- ☐ Expectancy
- ☐ Stimulus generalization
- ☐ Stimulus discrimination
- ☐ Extinction
- ☐ Spontaneous recovery

Operant Conditioning

- ☐ Law of effect
- ☐ Skinner box
- ☐ Operant
- ☐ Reinforcer
- ☐ Positive reinforcer
- ☐ Negative reinforcer
- ☐ Escape conditioning
- ☐ Avoidance conditioning
- ☐ Punishment
- ☐ Discriminative stimulus
- ☐ Shaping
- ☐ Primary reinforcer
- ☐ Secondary reinforcer
- ☐ Token reinforcer
- ☐ Token economy
- ☐ Continuous reinforcement
- ☐ Partial reinforcement
- ☐ Schedule of reinforcement
- ☐ Fixed ratio (FR)
- ☐ Variable ratio (VR)
- ☐ Fixed interval (FI)
- ☐ Variable interval (VI)
- ☐ Partial reinforcement extinction effect

Other Types of Learning

☐ Cognitive learning   ☐ Latent learning   ☐ Self-efficacy

☐ Cognitive map   ☐ Bobo doll experiment   ☐ Insight learning

Applications of Learning

☐ Emotional learning   ☐ Taste aversion   ☐ Accidental conditioning

☐ Little Albert experiment   ☐ Superstitious behavior   ☐ Learned helplessness

Solutions to Behavioral Problems

☐ Behavior modification   ☐ Aversion therapy   ☐ Coping

☐ Systematic desensitization   ☐ Biofeedback

Important Contributors

☐ Albert Bandura   ☐ Robert Rescorla   ☐ Edward Thorndike

☐ John Garcia   ☐ Martin Seligman   ☐ Edward Tolman

☐ Ivan Pavlov   ☐ B.F. Skinner   ☐ John Watson

Next Steps

Step 1: Tally your correct answers from Part A and review the quiz explanations at the end of this chapter.

1. D   6. C

2. A   7. A

3. C   8. B

4. E   9. C

5. B   10. D

_____ out of 10 questions

Step 2: Count the number of key terms you checked off in Part B.

_____ out of 65 key terms

Step 3: Compare your Test What You Already Know results to these Test What You Learned results to see how exam-ready you are for this topic.

If you need to study this topic further:

- Read (or reread) the comprehensive review for this topic in Chapter 16.

- Go to kaptest.com to complete the online quiz questions for Learning.

  - Haven't registered your book yet? Go to kaptest.com/moreonline to begin.

ANSWERS AND EXPLANATIONS

Test What You Already Know

1. C

Aversion therapy is a therapeutic technique in which a patient pairs an undesired behavior, such as smoking, with an unpleasant stimulus, such as a drug that induces nausea. Thus, Rochelle would have the best chance of quitting smoking by using aversion therapy, **(C)**. (A) is incorrect because biofeedback is a technique used to bring autonomic functions like heart rate under partially voluntary control. (B) is incorrect because positive reinforcement increases the frequency of a behavior, but Rochelle wants to decrease her smoking behavior. (D) is incorrect because modeling is a technique in which a therapist demonstrates desired behavior for a patient, but simply watching her therapist refrain from smoking is unlikely to put an end to Rochelle's addiction to cigarettes. (E) is incorrect because systematic desensitization is used primarily to treat phobias.

2. B

An unconditioned response is an instinctual response that happens automatically after exposure to a specific stimulus. This describes the blinking caused by the puff of air, making **(B)** correct. The puff of air is the unconditioned stimulus, so (A) is incorrect. (C) and (E) are incorrect because the tone is initially a neutral stimulus, which then becomes a conditioned stimulus after repeated association with the puff of air. (D) is incorrect because the blinking is only a conditioned response when it happens as a result of the tone.

3. E

Shaping specifically refers to developing a behavior by reinforcing successive approximations to the target behavior, which is what Tammy is doing; **(E)** is correct. (A) is incorrect; in classical conditioning, higher order conditioning means using a previously conditioned stimulus to produce further learning, but the question stem presents a type of operant conditioning. Observational learning occurs by watching the behavior of others, which does not describe how Tammy's daughter learns, so (B) is incorrect. Priming refers to changes in cognition or behavior caused by presentations of stimuli beneath the level of awareness, making (C) incorrect. (D) is also

incorrect; generalization refers to responding to a stimulus that is similar but not identical to the original stimulus.

4. B

Since the rat receives food after following a fixed number of responses (10 bar presses), the reinforcement schedule is a fixed ratio; **(B)** is correct. In a continuous reinforcement schedule, the rat would receive food after every bar press, so (A) is incorrect. A variable ratio would mean the number of bar presses needed to produce food would vary (e.g., the rat would receive food after 7–10 bar presses); therefore, (C) is incorrect. In a fixed interval schedule of reinforcement, the rat would receive food after a set time period, and in a variable interval schedule, the time period would vary; both (D) and (E) are incorrect.

5. E

In Bandura's Bobo doll experiment, children learned to act aggressively toward a clown doll after observing adults in a film hit the doll. This was an example of observational or social learning; **(E)** is correct. (A) is incorrect because classical conditioning depends upon instinctual responses, which were not relied upon in the Bobo doll experiment. (B) is incorrect because latent learning is learning that occurs without reinforcement but begins to be expressed when reinforcement is provided, which does not describe the experiment. (C) is incorrect because insight learning involves solving a problem upon a sudden flash of realization, but no insight was required to hit Bobo. (D) is incorrect because cognitive learning involves higher-order mental processes, but these were not employed in the experiment.

6. D

Skinner believed that punishment is effective only if it immediately follows a behavior, so **(D)** is correct and (B) is incorrect. Also, in order for punishment to be effective, it should be applied consistently and be severe enough to influence behavior. Therefore, (A), (C), and (E) are incorrect.

7. A

Ivan Pavlov developed the framework for classical conditioning through his famous experiments on dogs; **(A)** is correct. Although John Watson was a behaviorist who conducted classical conditioning experiments like the Little Albert experiment, he built on the framework that Pavlov constructed, so (B) is incorrect. B.F. Skinner is known for developing operant conditioning, not classical conditioning, so (C) is incorrect. Albert Bandura studied observational learning in his Bobo doll experiments; (D) is incorrect. Erik Erikson studied psychosocial development in children and was not even a behaviorist, making (E) incorrect.

8. D

A taste aversion is a learned dislike for a particular food, which can result when a person experiences intense nausea after eating the food. This precisely describes Phoebe's situation, making **(D)** correct. (A) is incorrect because there is no evidence that Phoebe is acting superstitiously; her body is reacting automatically to the taste of veal. (B) is incorrect because shaping is a technique of reinforcing approximations of a desired behavior. (C) is incorrect because learned helplessness is a learned incapacity to escape an unpleasant situation that results from repeated frustrations. (E) is incorrect because flashbulb memories are vivid, emotionally laden memories.

9. A

Classical conditioning is a process of associating an unconditioned stimulus (such as the meat in Pavlov's experiment) with a neutral stimulus that does not normally create a response (such as the bell). As a result, both the unconditioned stimulus and the neutral stimulus will generate the same response, at which point the neutral stimulus becomes a conditioned stimulus; **(A)** is correct. (B) gets the order wrong, and (C) is incorrect because the unconditioned stimulus does not become the conditioned stimulus (i.e., the meat does not turn into the bell). There is no such thing as a neutral response, so (D) is incorrect. Finally, (E), like (B), gets the order wrong because classical conditioning turns an unconditioned response into a conditioned response.

10. E

To a behaviorist, a superstition is a behavior that results from an association of cause and effect between two things that are not actually related. The story in **(E)** is an example of this; it is much more likely that it was a coincidence than that Emery's socks actually improved her performance on the test. (A) is not superstition because fear of water as a result of almost drowning is rational.

(B) is a classic example of what is commonly referred to as a superstition, but there is no mention of a supposed causal relationship, so (B) does not fit the learning definition of superstition. (C) is an example of taste aversion, and is not a superstition because the cheese dip could actually have caused Cameron to feel unwell. (D) is incorrect for the same reason; it is not unreasonable to suspect that increased practice causes increased skill.

Test What You Learned

1. D

Getting paid for work every Friday is an example of a fixed interval schedule of reinforcement, in which reinforcement is provided consistently after a set amount of time; **(D)** is correct. (A) is incorrect because receiving reinforcement (a treat) after every response (sitting on command) is a continuous schedule of reinforcement. Getting rewarded once in a while for good behavior represents a variable interval schedule, so (B) is incorrect. (C) is incorrect; earning a free coffee after five purchases is an example of a fixed ratio schedule. Winning money at a slot machine is an example of a variable ratio schedule; (E) is incorrect.

2. A

In Tolman's famous experiments, he showed that rats could learn to navigate mazes even without immediate reinforcement, a type of learning known as latent learning. **(A)** is correct. (B) is incorrect because cognitive learning involves higher-order cognitive processes that rats are generally incapable of. (C) and (D) are incorrect because social or observational learning involves watching others behave, but the rats in the second group could not see the rats in the first group. (E) is incorrect because the rats did not solve the maze through a sudden flash of insight, but through repeated exposure.

3. C

Classical conditioning always begins with an unconditioned stimulus (e.g., food) that produces a reflexive (automatically occurring), unconditioned response (e.g., salivation). Thus, **(C)** is correct. In contrast, operant conditioning deals most often with voluntary behavior, making (D) incorrect. (A) and (B) are also incorrect, since reinforcement, punishment, and shaping are all components of operant conditioning. Both operant and classical conditioning are effective at changing behavior in many situations, so (E) is incorrect.

4. E

Joseph Wolpe developed systematic desensitization as a therapeutic technique for treating phobias by gradually exposing patients to stimuli they feared while in a relaxed environment. **(E)** is thus correct. (A) is incorrect because aversion therapy is used to give up bad habits. (B) is incorrect because punishment would simply involve adding another aversive stimulus to the fearful stimulus, which would be unlikely to reduce phobic behavior. (C) is incorrect because modeling is more effective at treating phobias only when it is combined with other techniques that involve direct patient involvement, such as systematic desensitization. (D) is incorrect because reinforcement is used to increase instances of a behavior, so it could not decrease phobic behavior.

5. B

Stimulus generalization occurs when a new stimulus (a whistle) that is similar but not identical to the original conditioned stimulus (a bell) causes the conditioned response (barking); **(B)** is correct. The opposite of generalization is discrimination, the ability to distinguish between two similar stimuli, so (D) is incorrect. Shaping refers to the reinforcing of successive approximations to reach a target behavior; (A) is incorrect. (C) is also incorrect; extinction is the weakening or stopping of a conditioned response over time. Desensitization refers to a behavior modification technique for reducing fear and anxiety through gradual exposure to aversive stimuli; (E) is incorrect.

6. C

Unlike punishment, which is used to decrease a behavior, negative reinforcement is always used to increase a desired behavior. The desired behavior (e.g., taking a daily vitamin) is encouraged because it lessens or removes the possibility of an aversive stimulus (e.g., getting sick). Therefore **(C)** is correct, while (D) and (E) are incorrect. Both negative reinforcement and punishment can involve aversive stimuli, so (A) and (B) are also incorrect.

7. A

Accidental reinforcement is a type of accidental conditioning that occurs when a behavior is coincidentally, but not causally, connected to a positive outcome that follows

it. The lack of a genuine causal connection is likely to lead to superstitious behavior; **(A)** is correct. The remaining answer choices are incorrect because they can occur with any kind of reinforcement; accidental reinforcement is not more likely to cause them.

8. B

Through his study of reinforcement and punishment, Skinner played a major role in developing operant conditioning theory; **(B)** is correct. Pavlov is known for his work in the development of classical conditioning, so (A) is incorrect. (C) is also incorrect; Watson established the psychological school of behaviorism. Bandura is known for his work on observational learning; (D) is incorrect. Freud, though an important figure in the field of psychoanalysis, was not involved in learning theory, so (E) is incorrect.

9. C

There are many factors that contribute to the strength of a reinforcement. Size, immediacy, contingency, satiation, and the schedule of reinforcement all make a difference. **(C)** violates the principle of immediacy, which maintains that the sooner the reward is given, the stronger the reinforcement. Waiting until returning home, therefore, would decrease the strength of the reinforcement, making **(C)** correct. (A) can be eliminated because it increases the size of the reward. (B) ensures contingency, as it prevents using the same reward for other behaviors. (D) ensures satiety, as the strength of the reward increases when the subject is usually deprived of the reward. Finally, (E) puts the reinforcement on a variable ratio schedule, which is the schedule that produces the highest rates of response.

10. D

Much like a dog not barking for food when its owner is not home, this security guard knows that he will not be punished for inaction in the absence of cameras, and so he decreases his patrolling behavior. Stimuli that signal the possibility of a reward or punishment are called discriminatory stimuli, so **(D)** is correct. The cameras themselves are not a reward or punishment, so (A), (B), and (C) can all be eliminated. Finally, a Skinner box, (E), is a tool, the inner mechanisms of which can be manipulated to perform different experiments on operant conditioning, but such a tool is not present in this scenario.

CHAPTER 8

Cognitive Psychology

LEARNING OBJECTIVES

After studying this chapter, you will be able to:

- Differentiate among important cognitive processes

- Compare and contrast psychological and physiological memory systems

- Organize underlying principles of memory encoding, storage, and construction

- Identify memory improvement strategies

- Explain the interrelationship of biological, cognitive, and cultural factors in advancing language acquisition, development, and use

- Describe and evaluate effective problem-solving strategies

- Identify characteristics of creative thinking

- Summarize the meaning of intelligence and processes by which it is measured

- Discuss culture's influence on definitions of intelligence

- Distinguish among intelligence theories

- Outline the design and evaluation of psychological tests

- Employ a normal curve to interpret test scores and such labels as "gifted" and "cognitively disabled"

- Identify cultural and other controversies associated with intelligence testing

- Recognize important contributors to cognitive psychology

TEST WHAT YOU ALREADY KNOW

Part A: Quiz

1. The aspect of Sternberg's triarchic theory of intelligence that is typically measured by traditional IQ tests is

    (A) verbal-linguistic intelligence

    (B) creative intelligence

    (C) emotional intelligence

    (D) practical intelligence

    (E) analytical intelligence

2. Which of the following terms refers to the smallest unit of sound in a language?

    (A) Semantics

    (B) Lexicon

    (C) Morpheme

    (D) Phoneme

    (E) Syntax

3. The process of placing new information into short-term memory is called

    (A) transduction

    (B) retrieval

    (C) encoding

    (D) sensation

    (E) perception

4. Alfred Binet worked for the French government to create an intelligence test that would

    (A) avoid all cultural biases while measuring intelligence

    (B) evaluate analytical and creative intelligence in separate subtests

    (C) determine intelligence without reliance on verbal measures

    (D) evaluate abilities of public school teachers

    (E) determine which students would benefit the most from extra services

5. Ernie has to list all past presidents of the United States in chronological order for an upcoming history quiz. Using what he learned in AP Psychology, he broke the past presidents down into groups of four, so that instead of remembering 44 names, he just learned 11 groups. This method of grouping items together to make them easier to remember is known as

    (A) chunking

    (B) the spacing effect

    (C) the method of loci

    (D) retrieval

    (E) cramming

8

6. The briefest form of memory, in which detailed images can be lost quickly if not transferred to other forms of memory, is called

    (A) short-term memory

    (B) long-term memory

    (C) déjà vu

    (D) sensory memory

    (E) working memory

7. Suppose you want to memorize all of the countries of the world and decide to make up a song to help you. When you do this, you are using what psychologists call

    (A) a mnemonic

    (B) state-dependent learning

    (C) the self-reference effect

    (D) context-dependent learning

    (E) acoustic encoding

8. Ms. Dorsey asks the other psychology teachers at her school to look over her final exam to ensure it fairly represents the material covered during the semester. Ms. Dorsey is having others assist her in evaluating her exam for

    (A) split-half reliability

    (B) equivalent-form reliability

    (C) test-retest reliability

    (D) content validity

    (E) criterion-related validity

9. Individuals who are considered to be mildly intellectually disabled are capable of reaching the level of a grade 6 education and can often live independently. The IQ range of an individual with a mild intellectual disability is

    (A) 10 to 25

    (B) 25 to 40

    (C) 40 to 55

    (D) 55 to 70

    (E) 70 to 85

10. Research suggests that the capacity of short-term memory is

    (A) 2±3 items

    (B) 5±1 items

    (C) 3±2 items

    (D) 9±2 items

    (E) 7±2 items

8

Part B: Key Terms

The following is a list of the major ideas and people for the AP Psychology topic of Cognitive Psychology. You will likely see many of these on the AP Psychology exam.

For each key term, ask yourself the following questions:

- Can I describe this key term?
- Can I discuss this key term in relation to other psychological ideas and specific psychologists?
- Could I correctly answer a multiple-choice question about this key term?
- Could I correctly answer a free-response question about this key term?

Check off the key terms if you can answer "yes" to at least three of these questions.

Cognitive Processes

- ☐ Cognition
- ☐ Automatic processing
- ☐ Effortful processing
- ☐ Shallow processing
- ☐ Deep processing
- ☐ Attention
- ☐ Focused attention
- ☐ Divided attention

Memory

- ☐ Memory
- ☐ Encoding
- ☐ Acoustic codes
- ☐ Visual codes
- ☐ Semantic codes
- ☐ Imagery
- ☐ Self-reference effect
- ☐ Sensory memory
- ☐ Iconic memory
- ☐ Echoic memory
- ☐ Short-term memory
- ☐ Maintenance rehearsal
- ☐ Working memory
- ☐ Elaborative rehearsal
- ☐ Implicit memory/ procedural memory
- ☐ Explicit memory/ declarative memory
- ☐ Semantic memory
- ☐ Episodic memory
- ☐ Spacing effect
- ☐ Recency effect
- ☐ Primacy effect
- ☐ Serial position effect
- ☐ Mnemonic
- ☐ Method of loci
- ☐ Chunking
- ☐ Retrieval
- ☐ Recall
- ☐ Recognition
- ☐ Relearning
- ☐ Priming
- ☐ Mood-congruent memory
- ☐ Déjà vu
- ☐ Misinformation effect
- ☐ Source amnesia
- ☐ Memory decay
- ☐ Amnesia
- ☐ Anterograde amnesia
- ☐ Retrograde amnesia
- ☐ Interference
- ☐ Retroactive interference
- ☐ Proactive interference
- ☐ Repression
- ☐ Suppression
- ☐ Flashbulb memory

Language

- ☐ Language
- ☐ Phonology
- ☐ Phoneme
- ☐ Morphology
- ☐ Morpheme
- ☐ Semantics
- ☐ Syntax
- ☐ Grammar
- ☐ Pragmatics
- ☐ Babbling
- ☐ One-word stage
- ☐ Two-word stage
- ☐ Language acquisition device
- ☐ Universal grammar

Problem-Solving Strategies

- ☐ Trial-and-error
- ☐ Algorithm
- ☐ Heuristic
- ☐ Availability heuristic
- ☐ Representativeness heuristic
- ☐ Insight

Creative Thinking

- ☐ Creativity
- ☐ Convergent thinking
- ☐ Divergent thinking
- ☐ Overconfidence
- ☐ Belief bias
- ☐ Belief perseverance
- ☐ Confirmation bias
- ☐ Fixation
- ☐ Mental set
- ☐ Functional fixedness

What Is Intelligence?

- ☐ Intelligence
- ☐ Aptitude tests
- ☐ Achievement tests
- ☐ Speed tests
- ☐ Power tests
- ☐ Verbal tests
- ☐ Abstract tests

Intelligence Theories

- ☐ Factor analysis
- ☐ g factor
- ☐ Crystallized intelligence
- ☐ Fluid intelligence
- ☐ Savant syndrome
- ☐ Multiple intelligence theory
- ☐ Triarchic theory of intelligence
- ☐ Analytical intelligence
- ☐ Creative intelligence
- ☐ Practical intelligence
- ☐ Emotional intelligence

8

Intelligence Tests

- ☐ Mental age
- ☐ Stanford-Binet IQ Test
- ☐ Intelligence Quotient (IQ)
- ☐ Wechsler Intelligence Scale for Children (WISC)
- ☐ Wechsler Adult Intelligence Scale (WAIS)
- ☐ Validity

- ☐ Reliability
- ☐ Content validity
- ☐ Face validity
- ☐ Criterion-related validity
- ☐ Concurrent validity
- ☐ Predictive validity
- ☐ Split-half reliability
- ☐ Equivalent-form reliability

- ☐ Test-retest reliability
- ☐ Standardization
- ☐ Norms
- ☐ Flynn effect
- ☐ Normal curve
- ☐ Gifted
- ☐ Intellectual disability
- ☐ Cultural bias

Important Contributors

- ☐ Alfred Binet
- ☐ Noam Chomsky
- ☐ Hermann Ebbinghaus
- ☐ Francis Galton
- ☐ Howard Gardner
- ☐ Daniel Goleman

- ☐ Wolfgang Köhler
- ☐ Elizabeth Loftus
- ☐ George A. Miller
- ☐ Charles Spearman
- ☐ Robert Sternberg
- ☐ Lewis Terman

- ☐ L.L. Thurstone
- ☐ Lev Vygotsky
- ☐ David Wechsler

Next Steps

Step 1: Tally your correct answers from Part A and review the quiz explanations at the end of this chapter.

1. E
2. D
3. C
4. E
5. A

6. D
7. A
8. D
9. D
10. E

_____ out of 10 questions

Step 2: Count the number of key terms you checked off in Part B.

_____ out of 137 key terms

Step 3: Read the Rapid Review Key Takeaways in this chapter.

Step 4: Consult the table below and follow the instructions based on your performance.

If You Got . . .	Do This
80% or more of the Test What You Already Know assessment correct (8 or more questions from Part A and 110 or more key terms from Part B)	• Read definitions in this chapter for all the key terms you didn't check off. • Complete the Test What You Learned assessment in this chapter.
50% or less of the Test What You Already Know assessment correct (5 or fewer questions from Part A and 68 or fewer key terms from Part B)	• Read the comprehensive review for this topic in Chapter 17. ○ If you are short on time, read only the High-Yield sections. • Read through all of the key term definitions in this chapter. • Complete the Test What You Learned assessment in this chapter.
Any other result	• Read the High-Yield sections of the comprehensive review of this topic in Chapter 17. • Read definitions in this chapter for all the key terms you didn't check off. • Complete the Test What You Learned assessment in this chapter.

8

RAPID REVIEW

Key Takeaways

1. Cognitive processes vary along several dimensions, including effortful versus automatic processing, deep versus shallow processing, and focused versus divided attention.

2. Several distinct types of memory exist, with memories encoded, stored, transformed, and retrieved by a variety of processes. Memory can be improved using mnemonics and other strategies.

3. Language contains a number of distinct aspects including phonology, morphology, semantics, syntax, and pragmatics. A variety of biological, cognitive, and cultural factors affect how we acquire, develop, and use language.

4. Humans use a variety of methods to solve problems, including trial-and-error, algorithms, heuristics, and insight.

5. A number of processes govern creative thinking, which enables human beings to discover new ideas and novel solutions to problems.

6. Intelligence refers to general cognitive ability and is assessed by a number of different kinds of tests. Intelligence research and testing remains controversial because of disagreements about the meaning of intelligence.

7. Different theories present a range of definitions of intelligence. Early theories posited a single general intelligence that applied to all mental abilities. More recent theories have suggested there are multiple kinds of intelligence.

8. IQ tests were originally developed for children and measured abstract verbal abilities as a way to assess intelligence. Modern IQ tests employ both verbal and non-verbal questions to assess intelligence. When developing intelligence tests, researchers strive for high measures of validity and reliability.

9. Cultures place importance on the type of intelligence that is most applicable to their societies.

Key Terms: Definitions

Cognitive Processes

Cognition: The process of thinking or mentally processing information such as concepts, language, and images.

Automatic processing: The unconscious processing of incidental or well-learned information.

Effortful processing: Active processing of information that requires sustained effort.

Shallow processing: Processing information based on its surface characteristics.

Deep processing: Processing information with respect to its meaning.

Attention: The brain's ability to focus on stimuli.

Focused attention: The ability to concentrate on a single target stimulus.

Divided attention: The ability to focus on two or more stimuli simultaneously; colloquially known as multitasking.

Memory

Memory: Learning that has persisted over time and information that has been stored and can be retrieved.

Encoding: The process of putting new information into memory.

Acoustic codes: The encoding of information as sequences of sounds.

Visual codes: The encoding of information as pictures.

Semantic codes: The encoding of information with respect to its meaning.

Imagery: A set of mental pictures that serves as an aid to effortful processing.

Self-reference effect: The tendency to recall information best when it is put into a personal context.

Sensory memory: The stage of memory that holds an exact copy of incoming information for just a few seconds.

Iconic memory: Visual sensory memory.

Echoic memory: Auditory sensory memory.

Short-term memory: The memory system that holds small amounts of information for brief periods of time.

Maintenance rehearsal: Repetition of a piece of information to keep it within your active short-term memory.

Working memory: Type of memory that enables you to keep a few different pieces of information in your consciousness at the same time and to actively process that information.

Elaborative rehearsal: Type of rehearsal that links new information with existing memories and knowledge.

Implicit memory/procedural memory: The long-term memory of conditioned responses and learned skills.

Explicit memory/declarative memory: Memories that require conscious recall.

Semantic memory: Explicit memory of facts.

Episodic memory: Explicit memory of experiences.

Spacing effect: The tendency for distributed study to result in better, longer-term retention than other methods.

Recency effect: Enhanced memory of items at the end of a list.

Primacy effect: Enhanced memory of items at the start of a list.

Serial position effect: The tendency to most effectively recall the first and last several items in a list.

Mnemonic: A memory aid, especially a technique that uses imagery and organizational devices.

Method of loci: A mnemonic technique that works by placing an image of each item to be remembered at particular points along an imaginary journey through a location.

Chunking: A memory trick that involves taking individual elements of a large list and grouping them together into elements with related meaning.

Retrieval: The process of demonstrating that something learned has been retained.

Recall: The ability to retrieve information with minimal external cues.

Recognition: The ability to correctly identify previously learned information.

Relearning: Memorization of information that was previously learned and forgotten, which is faster than initial learning.

Priming: The activation, often unconsciously, of particular associations that helps with memory retrieval.

Mood-congruent memory: Occurs when one's current mood cues memories that were formed during the same mood.

Déjà vu: The feeling that a new experience, such as visiting an unfamiliar place, has actually happened to you before.

Misinformation effect: A phenomenon in which memories are altered by misleading information provided at the point of encoding or recall.

Source amnesia: A memory construction error in which a person remembers the details of an event, but confuses the context under which those details were gained.

Memory decay: The natural loss of memories over time.

Amnesia: The inability to store and/or retrieve memories.

Anterograde amnesia: The inability to encode new memories.

Retrograde amnesia: The inability to recall previously formed memories, usually those memories prior to a brain injury.

Interference: A retrieval error caused by the existence of other similar information.

Retroactive interference: The disruptive effect of new learning on the retrieval of old information.

Proactive interference: The disruptive effect of old learning on the retrieval of new information.

Repression: A basic defense mechanism in which a person unconsciously pushes unwanted, anxiety-producing memories out of awareness.

Suppression: A basic defense mechanism in which a person actively tries to push a memory out of mind.

Flashbulb memory: Images that seem locked in the memory at a time of personal trauma, an accident, or some other emotionally significant event.

Language

Language: Words or symbols and the rules for combining them meaningfully.

Phonology: The actual sound of language.

Phoneme: The smallest unit of sound in a language.

Morphology: The structure of words.

Morpheme: The smallest unit of meaning in a language.

Semantics: The set of rules that we use to derive meaning from words and sentences.

Syntax: The way in which words are put together to form sentences.

Grammar: The set of rules for combining language units into meaningful speech or writing.

Pragmatics: The dependence of language on context and preexisting knowledge.

Babbling: The repetition of syllables that represent an infant's first attempt at speech.

One-word stage: The stage of language development during which children tend to use one word at a time.

Two-word stage: The stage of language development during which children tend to use two-word phrases.

Language acquisition device: A theoretical pathway in the brain that allows infants to process and absorb language rules.

Universal grammar: A theoretical common set of rules that apply to all languages.

Problem-Solving Strategies

Trial-and-error: A less sophisticated type of problem-solving approach in which different solutions are tried until the correct one is found.

Algorithm: A step-by-step procedure that guarantees a solution to a problem.

Heuristic: A simple thinking strategy or technique that allows one to make judgments efficiently.

Availability heuristic: A mental shortcut through which judgments are based on the information that is most easily brought to mind.

8

Representativeness heuristic: A mental shortcut that involves judging whether something belongs in a given class on the basis of its similarity to other members of that class.

Insight: A sudden and often completely new realization of the solution to a problem.

Creative Thinking

Creativity: The ability to create ideas that are new.

Convergent thinking: Thinking that is directed to the discovery of a single right solution.

Divergent thinking: Thinking that produces many alternatives and promotes open-ended thought.

Overconfidence: The tendency to overestimate the correctness of your beliefs and judgments.

Belief bias: Making illogical conclusions in order to confirm your preexisting beliefs.

Belief perseverance: The tendency to maintain a belief even after the evidence you used to form the belief is proven wrong.

Confirmation bias: The tendency to search for information that supports your existing beliefs and to ignore evidence that contradicts what you think is true.

Fixation: The tendency to repeat wrong solutions as a result of becoming blind to alternatives.

Mental set: The tendency to use old patterns to solve new problems.

Functional fixedness: The tendency to think about familiar objects only in familiar ways.

What Is Intelligence?

Intelligence: The ability to solve problems, learn from experience, and use knowledge to adapt to novel situations.

Aptitude tests: Tests designed to predict future performance in an ability.

Achievement tests: Tests designed to assess current performance in an ability.

Speed tests: Tests that assess quickness of problem solving by offering many questions in limited time.

Power tests: Tests with questions of increasing difficulty, used to assess the highest-difficulty problem a person can solve.

Verbal tests: Tests that use word problems to assess abilities.

Abstract tests: Tests that use non-verbal measures to assess abilities.

Intelligence Theories

Factor analysis: A statistical method that identifies common causes of variance in different tests.

g factor: The general intelligence factor, which accounts for a large amount of the variability in IQ scores.

Crystallized intelligence: The ability to apply previously learned knowledge to solve a new task.

Fluid intelligence: The ability to solve new tasks for which there is no prior knowledge.

Savant syndrome: A condition in which someone shows exceptional ability in a single skill but limited general mental ability.

Multiple intelligence theory: Gardner's theory that proposes eight different intelligences: musical-rhythmic, visual-spatial, verbal-linguistic, logical-mathematical, bodily-kinesthetic, interpersonal, intrapersonal, and naturalistic.

Triarchic theory of intelligence: Sternberg's theory that proposes three distinct intelligences (analytical, creative, and practical), which work together to make up your overall intelligence.

Analytical intelligence: The ability to solve traditional academic problems, as measured by early IQ tests.

Creative intelligence: The ability to apply knowledge to new situations.

Practical intelligence: The ability to apply life experiences to problem-solving tasks.

Emotional intelligence: The ability to perceive, understand, manage, and correctly utilize emotion in everyday life.

Intelligence Tests

Mental age: Based on the average level of performance for a particular chronological age, mental age represents a child's level of cognitive ability.

Stanford-Binet IQ Test: An early IQ test created by Terman that originally measured intelligence by dividing mental age by chronological age and multiplying by 100.

Intelligence Quotient (IQ): A standardized scale used to measure intellectual abilities.

Wechsler Intelligence Scale for Children (WISC): An IQ test that measures intelligence using both verbal and non-verbal tasks.

Wechsler Adult Intelligence Scale (WAIS): The first commonly used intelligence test specifically designed for adults, which measures intelligence using both verbal and non-verbal tasks.

Validity: A measure of the extent to which a test actually assesses what it claims.

Reliability: A measure of consistency in test results.

Content validity: The extent to which a test accurately assesses the entire range of abilities it is designed to measure.

Face validity: A superficial measure of validity based only on a brief examination; does not require the use of statistical analysis.

Criterion-related validity: The extent to which a test correlates with current or future performance in the area it purports to measure.

Concurrent validity: The extent to which a test correlates with current performance in the area it purports to measure.

Predictive validity: The extent to which a test correctly predicts future performance in the area it purports to measure.

Split-half reliability: A measure of reliability that involves splitting items on a test into random halves and scoring each separately.

Equivalent-form reliability: A measure of reliability that compares scores on two versions of the same test administered at separate times.

Test-retest reliability: A measure of reliability that compares scores on the same test by the same test-takers at two different times.

Standardization: A process by which scores for a population are placed into set intervals to allow for easy analysis of test results.

Norms: In testing, average scores after standardization for a population.

Flynn effect: The ongoing increase in average IQ scores over time, which requires IQ tests to be renormed periodically.

Normal curve: A bell-shaped pattern that is formed when plotting population norms for a large number of natural abilities.

Gifted: A label for individuals who have an IQ above 130.

Intellectual disability: A condition of varying severity found in individuals with IQ scores below 70.

Cultural bias: The allegation that IQ tests give unfair advantages or disadvantages to members of particular cultures.

Important Contributors

Alfred Binet: Pioneer in intelligence testing who created a standardized test to identify children requiring extra attention in school.

Noam Chomsky: One of the founders of modern linguistics, whose theory of language acquisition emphasizes universal grammar and maintains that humans have a built-in readiness to learn language.

Hermann Ebbinghaus: Ebbinghaus's memory experiments demonstrated that meaningless stimuli are more difficult to memorize and recall than meaningful stimuli, that learning is more effective when spaced out over time, and that forgetting happens most rapidly right after learning occurs and slows down over time.

Francis Galton: Founded psychometrics, developed the idea of nature versus nurture, and believed genetics was the most important factor in intelligence.

Howard Gardner: Developed the theory of multiple intelligences to expand upon traditional conceptions of intelligence.

Daniel Goleman: Proponent of the importance of emotional intelligence.

Wolfgang Köhler: Conducted research on chimpanzees, who used insight to solve the problem of obtaining out-of-reach food using poles and stackable boxes.

Elizabeth Loftus: Known for her work in the study of false memory formation and the misinformation effect, Loftus's experiments revealed that the memories of eyewitnesses can often be altered after exposing them to incorrect information about an event, demonstrating the malleability of memory.

George A. Miller: One of the founders of cognitive psychology, Miller discovered that human short-term memory is usually limited to holding between five and nine pieces of information at a time.

Charles Spearman: Believed all intelligence could be traced to a single underlying general mental ability known as *g*.

Robert Sternberg: Created the triarchic theory of intelligence, which maintains that analytical, creative, and practical abilities come together to create intelligence.

Lewis Terman: Expanded Binet's system to create the concept of IQ and early IQ tests, which used mental and chronological age to calculate IQ.

L.L. Thurstone: Critic of Spearman who believed intelligence was made up of seven separate mental abilities.

Lev Vygotsky: A prominent educational psychologist who argued that culture was the most important force in cognitive development, including the development of language.

David Wechsler: Developed modern IQ tests for children and adults with subscores for different mental abilities.

8

TEST WHAT YOU LEARNED

Part A: Quiz

1. Which of the following is an example of episodic memory?

   (A) Recalling how to tie your shoes

   (B) Recollecting a time you visited a theme park

   (C) Remembering your locker combination

   (D) Visualizing the layout of your childhood home

   (E) Knowing the seven wonders of the ancient world

2. Given that IQ tests are based on a normal distribution in which 100 is the average and the standard deviation is 15, approximately what percentage of IQ scores fall between 70 and 130?

   (A) 34

   (B) 50

   (C) 68

   (D) 95

   (E) 100

3. The two-word stage of language acquisition is the first time a child uses which of the following linguistic concepts?

   (A) Phonemes

   (B) Morphemes

   (C) Semantics

   (D) Syntax

   (E) Pragmatics

4. The SAT is designed to predict success in college, which makes the SAT a(n)

   (A) emotional intelligence test

   (B) culture-biased test

   (C) achievement test

   (D) aptitude test

   (E) interpersonal intelligence test

5. Which of the following events is most likely to be remembered as a flashbulb memory?

   (A) An afternoon of reading

   (B) What you ate for lunch last Tuesday

   (C) Hearing your favorite song on the radio

   (D) Seeing an array of ten words briefly displayed on a screen

   (E) Being involved in a car crash

6. A psychologist looking to support a particular hypothesis reads a number of research papers. He pays attention only to those results that support his hypothesis and discards the papers that contradict his ideas. This is most clearly an example of

   (A) fixation

   (B) belief perseverence

   (C) functional fixedness

   (D) overconfidence

   (E) confirmation bias

7. Suppose that a teacher tells you the due date for a paper, but you cannot immediately write it down. If you repeat the date to yourself over and over while you look for a pencil, which of the following memory processes are you using?

   (A) Maintenance rehearsal

   (B) Elaborative rehearsal

   (C) A mnemonic

   (D) Semantic memory

   (E) The recency effect

8. Principal Scott created a math readiness test to give to eighth graders prior to entering high school. He chose a representative group of students to give the test to and compared each student's scores on odd versus even questions. He found a strong positive correlation between the odd and even scores, which gave him evidence that the test he made had high

   (A) content validity

   (B) construct validity

   (C) equivalent-form reliability

   (D) test-retest reliability

   (E) split-half reliability

9. A student closes his eyes and listens to his teacher read a poem. He is struck by the rhythm of each line and the clever way the poet uses rhyme. What memory process is this student primarily using?

   (A) Explicit memory

   (B) Implicit memory

   (C) Visual encoding

   (D) Acoustic encoding

   (E) Semantic encoding

10. The original formula for determining IQ scores utilized by Terman was

   (A) chronological age ÷ mental age × percentile rank

   (B) mental age ÷ chronological age × z score × 100

   (C) chronological age ÷ mental age × z score × 100

   (D) chronological age ÷ mental age × 100

   (E) mental age ÷ chronological age × 100

Part B: Key Terms

This key terms list is the same as the list in the Test What You Already Know section earlier in this chapter. Based on what you have now learned, again ask yourself the following questions:

- Can I describe this key term?
- Can I discuss this key term in relation to other psychological ideas and specific psychologists?
- Could I correctly answer a multiple-choice question about this key term?
- Could I correctly answer a free-response question about this key term?

Check off the key terms if you can answer "yes" to at least three of these questions.

Cognitive Processes

- ☐ Cognition
- ☐ Automatic processing
- ☐ Effortful processing

- ☐ Shallow processing
- ☐ Deep processing
- ☐ Attention

- ☐ Focused attention
- ☐ Divided attention

Memory

- ☐ Memory
- ☐ Encoding
- ☐ Acoustic codes
- ☐ Visual codes
- ☐ Semantic codes
- ☐ Imagery
- ☐ Self-reference effect
- ☐ Sensory memory
- ☐ Iconic memory
- ☐ Echoic memory
- ☐ Short-term memory
- ☐ Maintenance rehearsal
- ☐ Working memory
- ☐ Elaborative rehearsal
- ☐ Implicit memory/ procedural memory

- ☐ Explicit memory/ declarative memory
- ☐ Semantic memory
- ☐ Episodic memory
- ☐ Spacing effect
- ☐ Recency effect
- ☐ Primacy effect
- ☐ Serial position effect
- ☐ Mnemonic
- ☐ Method of loci
- ☐ Chunking
- ☐ Retrieval
- ☐ Recall
- ☐ Recognition
- ☐ Relearning
- ☐ Priming

- ☐ Mood-congruent memory
- ☐ Déjà vu
- ☐ Misinformation effect
- ☐ Source amnesia
- ☐ Memory decay
- ☐ Amnesia
- ☐ Anterograde amnesia
- ☐ Retrograde amnesia
- ☐ Interference
- ☐ Retroactive interference
- ☐ Proactive interference
- ☐ Repression
- ☐ Suppression
- ☐ Flashbulb memory

8

Language

- ☐ Language
- ☐ Phonology
- ☐ Phoneme
- ☐ Morphology
- ☐ Morpheme

- ☐ Semantics
- ☐ Syntax
- ☐ Grammar
- ☐ Pragmatics
- ☐ Babbling

- ☐ One-word stage
- ☐ Two-word stage
- ☐ Language acquisition device
- ☐ Universal grammar

Problem-Solving Strategies

- ☐ Trial-and-error
- ☐ Algorithm

- ☐ Heuristic
- ☐ Availability heuristic

- ☐ Representativeness heuristic
- ☐ Insight

Creative Thinking

- ☐ Creativity
- ☐ Convergent thinking
- ☐ Divergent thinking
- ☐ Overconfidence

- ☐ Belief bias
- ☐ Belief perseverance
- ☐ Confirmation bias
- ☐ Fixation

- ☐ Mental set
- ☐ Functional fixedness

What Is Intelligence?

- ☐ Intelligence
- ☐ Aptitude tests
- ☐ Achievement tests

- ☐ Speed tests
- ☐ Power tests
- ☐ Verbal tests

- ☐ Abstract tests

Intelligence Theories

- ☐ Factor analysis
- ☐ g factor
- ☐ Crystallized intelligence
- ☐ Fluid intelligence

- ☐ Savant syndrome
- ☐ Multiple intelligence theory
- ☐ Triarchic theory of intelligence

- ☐ Analytical intelligence
- ☐ Creative intelligence
- ☐ Practical intelligence
- ☐ Emotional intelligence

8

Intelligence Tests

- ☐ Mental age
- ☐ Stanford-Binet IQ Test
- ☐ Intelligence Quotient (IQ)
- ☐ Wechsler Intelligence Scale for Children (WISC)
- ☐ Wechsler Adult Intelligence Scale (WAIS)
- ☐ Validity

- ☐ Reliability
- ☐ Content validity
- ☐ Face validity
- ☐ Criterion-related validity
- ☐ Concurrent validity
- ☐ Predictive validity
- ☐ Split-half reliability
- ☐ Equivalent-form reliability

- ☐ Test-retest reliability
- ☐ Standardization
- ☐ Norms
- ☐ Flynn effect
- ☐ Normal curve
- ☐ Gifted
- ☐ Intellectual disability
- ☐ Cultural bias

Important Contributors

- ☐ Alfred Binet
- ☐ Noam Chomsky
- ☐ Hermann Ebbinghaus
- ☐ Francis Galton
- ☐ Howard Gardner

- ☐ Daniel Goleman
- ☐ Wolfgang Köhler
- ☐ Elizabeth Loftus
- ☐ George A. Miller
- ☐ Charles Spearman

- ☐ Robert Sternberg
- ☐ Lewis Terman
- ☐ L.L. Thurstone
- ☐ Lev Vygotsky
- ☐ David Wechsler

Next Steps

Step 1: Tally your correct answers from Part A and review the quiz explanations at the end of this chapter.

1. B
2. D
3. D
4. D
5. E
6. E
7. A
8. E
9. D
10. E

_____ out of 10 questions

Step 2: Count the number of key terms you checked off in Part B.

_____ out of 137 key terms

Step 3: Compare your Test What You Already Know results to these Test What You Learned results to see how exam-ready you are for this topic.

If you need to study this topic further:

- Read (or reread) the comprehensive review for this topic in Chapter 17.

- Go to kaptest.com to complete the online quiz questions for Cognitive Psychology.

  ○ Haven't registered your book yet? Go to kaptest.com/moreonline to begin.

ANSWERS AND EXPLANATIONS

Test What You Already Know

1. E

Analytical intelligence, **(E)**, the ability to solve problems and reason, is typically measured on traditional IQ tests. Verbal-linguistic intelligence, (A), is part of Howard Gardner's multiple intelligences theory. Creative intelligence, (B), is Sternberg's concept of intelligence that involves the capacity to generate novel solutions and new ideas. Emotional intelligence, (C), is the capacity to understand emotions. Practical intelligence, (D), is Sternberg's concept of intelligence that includes the ability to apply knowledge in daily life.

2. D

Phonemes are the smallest units of sound in a language. **(D)** is thus correct. Semantics, (A), are the rules that provide meaning. The lexicon, (B), is the set of words in a language. A morpheme, (C), is the smallest unit of meaning (not sound). Syntax, (E), concerns how words are organized to form sentences.

3. C

Encoding, **(C)**, is the process of getting information into short-term memory, making it correct. Transduction, (A), is the transformation of energy into a different form, such as occurs in sensation. Retrieval, (B), is the process of taking information from memory. Sensation, (D), and perception, (E), refer to the processes of taking in sensory information and giving it a meaningful structure.

4. E

Binet worked on an intelligence test to identify students who could benefit from supplemental services to improve their performance in school. **(E)** is thus correct. Binet's test did not address issues related to cultural bias, (A), or evaluate Sternberg's concepts of analytical and creative intelligences, (B). Binet's test relied solely on verbal measures, contrary to (C). It was not designed to determine teacher effectiveness, (D).

5. A

Chunking is the memory technique of combining individual items to be memorized into groups and memorizing each group as whole, consolidating the information into fewer total pieces. This describes Ernie's process, so **(A)** is correct. The spacing effect, (B), is the mnemonic technique of studying over a longer period of time, relearning the information multiple times to store it more faithfully. The method of loci, (C), involves taking a mental walk through a location and associating each of the items to be memorized with specific points in the walk. Retrieval, (D), is simply recalling information from memory, and cramming, (E), involves attempting to memorize a vast amount of information in a short period of time (which is often ineffective).

6. D

The briefest type of memory is sensory memory, **(D)**, which holds an exact copy of incoming information for just a few seconds. Short-term memory, (A), despite its name actually lasts longer than sensory memory. (B) is incorrect because long-term memory is the longest-lasting type of memory. Déjà vu, (C), is the feeling that a new experience, such as visiting an unfamiliar place, has actually happened to you before; it is a retrieval error, not a type of memory. Working memory, (E), is a form of short-term memory that allows you to keep a few pieces of information in mind at a time and manipulate them, as when doing mental math; it also lasts longer than sensory memory.

7. A

If you use some kind of trick to store information into long-term memory, you are using a mnemonic, or memory aid, so **(A)** is correct. State-based learning, (B), refers to the phenomenon of recall being easier when a person is in the same mood or state of consciousness as when the information was learned, just as context-dependent learning, (D), draws upon the physical location the person was in. The self-reference effect, (C), is the idea that things are easier to memorize when they are related to something personal. (E) might sound tempting; after all, you are using a song, which can be considered acoustic. However, acoustic encoding refers to the way you process incoming information (hearing the sound of it versus remembering the way it looked or the meaning behind it). Since this only applies to the way you *receive* the information and not how you *memorize* it, this choice is incorrect.

8. D

The test was being evaluated to determine if it included items that were reasonably representative of the content of the course, which is **(D)**, content validity. Split-half reliability, (A), is a tool for determining if the test is consistent by comparing scores on two halves of the same test. Equivalent-form reliability, (B), involves evaluating tests for consistency by comparing the results of the same individuals who took two different versions of the test. Test-retest reliability, (C), is used to check consistency in a test by having the same individuals take the same assessment on two different occasions. Criterion-related validity, (E), involves evaluating a test for accuracy in terms of how well the results match up to another measure or how well they predict future success.

9. D

Mildly intellectually disabled individuals generally fall within the IQ range of 55–70, **(D)**. Individuals with IQ scores in the range of 10–25, (A), are considered profoundly intellectually disabled and need full-time care. IQs in the range of 25–40, (B), are categorized as severely intellectually disabled, while scores ranging from 40–55, (C), are moderately intellectually disabled. IQ scores from 70–85, (E), do not represent an intellectual disability, although they are below the average IQ score of 100.

10. E

The capacity of short-term memory is approximately five to nine items, or seven plus or minus two. **(E)** is correct. The other choices do not represent the capacity demonstrated by several studies, most notably by Miller in 1956.

Test What You Learned

1. B

Episodic memory is specifically the recollection of your experiences. Of these choices, only **(B)** is a memory of an experienced event. (A) is an example of implicit memory because it involves a learned skill. (C) could be either a semantic memory if you just remember the list of numbers or an implicit memory if you remember the movement of your fingers when opening the locker. (D) is an example of visual memory. (E) is an example of semantic memory because it's a fact.

2. D

Scores between 70 and 130 are within two standard deviations of the mean, which in a normal distribution encompasses 95% of the population, **(D)**. (A) is the percentage above or below one standard deviation, while (B) is the percentage above or below the mean. (C) is the percentage scoring within one standard deviation of the mean. (E) is all test takers.

3. D

An infant is using phonemes, or sounds, in the babbling stage, and morphemes, or units of meaning, in the one-word stage, so (A) and (B) are incorrect. By changing inflection, young children can change the semantic meaning of their words (for example, stating that a toy is present versus asking for one), even in the one-word stage; (C) is incorrect. The two-word stage is the first time that word order (governed by rules of syntax) matters, so **(D)** is correct. (E) is incorrect because pragmatics, or using different words depending on social context, is highly unlikely to be present as early as the two-word stage, but develops much later.

4. D

The SAT is considered an aptitude test, **(D)**, because it is intended to predict how successful a person will be in college. Emotional intelligence tests, (A), are designed to evaluate people's capacity to understand emotions in themselves and others. Culture-biased tests, (B), are flawed assessments that provide an advantage to members of some cultural groups over others. Achievement tests, (C), evaluate how well an individual has mastered a particular subject. Interpersonal intelligence is one of the multiple intelligences articulated in Gardner's theory, but the SAT does not measure interpersonal abilities, making (E) incorrect.

5. E

Flashbulb memories are significant life events, positive or negative, that are locked into memory when they happen. **(E)** is the most likely to be such an event, as (A), (B), and (C) are mundane as presented. (D) might represent an example of iconic memory, in which visual information is encoded and lost very quickly, but this is not what is meant by flashbulb memory.

6. E

When we seek information that supports our existing beliefs and ignore contrary evidence, we are engaging in confirmation bias, **(E)**. Fixation, (A), is the tendency to repeat wrong solutions as a result of becoming blind to alternatives, but this researcher might not be wrong. Belief perseverance, (B), refers to our tendency to maintain a belief even after the evidence we used to form the belief is proven wrong; since the researcher could find supporting evidence, this is incorrect. Functional fixedness, (C), is the tendency to think about familiar objects in familiar ways. Overconfidence, (D), is the tendency to overestimate the correctness of our beliefs and judgments; this researcher may very well be overconfident, but his actions go further.

7. A

The repetition of information to temporarily keep it in the forefront of short-term memory is known as maintenance rehearsal, **(A)**. (B) is incorrect because elaborative rehearsal requires making connections with other information, but you are merely repeating the same date in your head. (C) is incorrect because you are not using any memory aid besides mere repetition. (D) is incorrect because semantic memory is a type of long-term memory, but you are using short-term memory. (E) is incorrect because the recency effect is the tendency to remember items at the end of a list better than other items in the list.

8. E

This is an example of evaluating a test for split-half reliability, **(E)**, a measure of consistency within the same test. Content validity, (A), refers to how well a test measures the total meaning of the concept and whether it includes a reasonable representation of the material it is evaluating. Construct validity, (B), refers to a test's ability to measure an abstract idea. Equivalent-form reliability, (C), involves evaluating consistency by having people take two versions of the same test. Test-retest reliability, (D), involves having individuals retake the same test and then comparing the scores.

9. D

Because the student's focus is on how the words sound, the information is being acoustically encoded. **(D)** is correct. (A) and (B) are incorrect because explicit and implicit memories are part of long-term memory. There is no image, so visual encoding, (C), cannot be correct. Semantic encoding, (E), is incorrect because he is paying attention to the sounds, not to their meanings.

10. E

To calculate IQ scores, Terman initially divided mental age by chronological age and multiplied by 100, making **(E)** correct. The other formulas have never been used to calculate IQ.

8

CHAPTER 9

Developmental Psychology

LEARNING OBJECTIVES

After studying this chapter, you will be able to:

- Explain ways in which nature and nurture interact to influence behavior

- Describe conception and gestation's impact on fetal development

- Explain how motor skills develop

- Summarize the impact of temperament and other social characteristics on attachment and appropriate socialization

- Evaluate intimacy-related decisions in the course of maturation

- Describe the impact of parenting styles on development

- Outline processes by which cognitive abilities develop

- Evaluate moral development theories

- Outline processes of socialization and the development of personality

- Recognize sex and gender's impact on development and socialization

- Summarize challenges, especially family challenges, to maturing in adolescence

- Explain physical and cognitive changes caused by aging and evaluate potential remedies

- Recognize important contributors to developmental psychology

TEST WHAT YOU ALREADY KNOW

Part A: Quiz

1. According to Vygotsky, the gap between the skills that children have the ability to do alone and those that they are incapable of doing is

   (A) assimilation

   (B) the zone of proximal development

   (C) object permanence

   (D) a more knowledgeable other

   (E) accommodation

2. Sandy complained there were more meatballs on his brother's plate than on his, but his mother explained that they each had the same number, only Sandy's were closer together. According to Piaget, Sandy would be in which stage of cognitive development?

   (A) Sensorimotor

   (B) Preoperational

   (C) Concrete operational

   (D) Formal operational

   (E) Pre-conventional

3. The process of culling neuronal connections to improve the efficiency of brain activity is called

   (A) pruning

   (B) trimming

   (C) filling

   (D) scoring

   (E) firing

4. Which of the following refers to the reflex that causes infants to outstretch their arms and legs in response to a loud noise or other sudden change in the environment?

   (A) Rooting reflex

   (B) Sucking reflex

   (C) Grasping reflex

   (D) Babinski reflex

   (E) Moro reflex

5. In Ainsworth's Strange Situation, an infant consistently becomes distressed when his primary caregiver leaves the room and is not soothed when his primary caregiver returns. The infant is demonstrating

   (A) secure attachment

   (B) avoidant attachment

   (C) ambivalent attachment

   (D) disorganized attachment

   (E) anxious-preoccupied attachment

6. Ali tells a friend that cheating in his favorite board game is wrong because the rules clearly state that no cheating is allowed. According to Kohlberg, Ali most likely reasons at which stage of moral development?

   (A) Pre-conventional

   (B) Conventional

   (C) Post-conventional

   (D) Formal operational

   (E) Concrete operational

9

7. Susan spends a few months trying to join a soccer team, then a few more months hanging out with kids from the art club, before finally finding a sense of belonging in her school's math club. According to Erikson, Susan has been facing which of the following conflicts?

    (A) Intimacy vs. isolation
    (B) Initiative vs. guilt
    (C) Identity vs. role confusion
    (D) Industry vs. inferiority
    (E) Ego integrity vs. despair

8. Which of the following is a primary sex characteristic that develops during puberty?

    (A) Onset of menstruation
    (B) Growth of breasts
    (C) Widening of hips
    (D) Development of facial hair
    (E) Enlargement of the larynx

9. Which of the following presents two of the most common teratogens?

    (A) LSD and marijuana
    (B) Epinephrine and norepinephrine
    (C) Serotonin and dopamine
    (D) Alcohol and tobacco
    (E) Phonemes and morphemes

10. Which psychologist proposed the Electra complex?

    (A) Sigmund Freud
    (B) Mary Ainsworth
    (C) Albert Bandura
    (D) Jean Piaget
    (E) Carl Jung

Part B: Key Terms

The following is a list of the major ideas and people for the AP Psychology topic of Developmental Psychology. You will likely see many of these on the AP Psychology exam.

For each key term, ask yourself the following questions:

- Can I describe this key term?
- Can I discuss this key term in relation to other psychological ideas and specific psychologists?
- Could I correctly answer a multiple-choice question about this key term?
- Could I correctly answer a free-response question about this key term?

Check off the key terms if you can answer "yes" to at least three of these questions.

Nature and Nurture

☐ Nature   ☐ Nurture   ☐ Range of reaction

Gestation

☐ Gestation/prenatal development ☐ Germinal stage ☐ Teratogens

☐ Conception ☐ Embryonic stage ☐ Fetal alcohol syndrome

  ☐ Fetal stage

Motor Skill Development

☐ Motor development ☐ Moro reflex ☐ Cephalocaudal rule

☐ Reflexes ☐ Grasping reflex ☐ Proximodistal rule

☐ Rooting reflex ☐ Babinski reflex

☐ Sucking reflex ☐ Plantar reflex

Temperament and Attachment

☐ Attachments ☐ Secure attachment ☐ Disorganized attachment

☐ Internal working model of attachment ☐ Avoidant attachment ☐ Temperament

  ☐ Ambivalent attachment

Parenting Styles

☐ Demandingness ☐ Authoritative parenting ☐ Authoritarian parenting

☐ Responsiveness ☐ Permissive parenting ☐ Neglectful parenting

Cognitive Development

- ☐ Cognitive development
- ☐ Sensorimotor stage
- ☐ Schemata
- ☐ Assimilation
- ☐ Accommodation
- ☐ Object permanence
- ☐ Preoperational stage
- ☐ Egocentrism
- ☐ Theory of mind
- ☐ Concrete operational stage
- ☐ Conservation
- ☐ Formal operational stage
- ☐ Zone of proximal development (ZPD)
- ☐ More knowledgeable other (MKO)

Moral Development

- ☐ Pre-conventional stage
- ☐ Conventional stage
- ☐ Post-conventional stage
- ☐ Ethics of care
- ☐ Moral intuitionist perspective

Socialization

- ☐ Psychosexual stages
- ☐ Erotogenic zone
- ☐ Libido
- ☐ Fixation
- ☐ Oral stage
- ☐ Anal stage
- ☐ Phallic stage
- ☐ Oedipus complex
- ☐ Electra complex
- ☐ Latency stage
- ☐ Genital stage
- ☐ Trust vs. mistrust
- ☐ Autonomy vs. shame and doubt
- ☐ Initiative vs. guilt
- ☐ Industry vs. inferiority
- ☐ Identity vs. role confusion
- ☐ Intimacy vs. isolation
- ☐ Generativity vs. stagnation
- ☐ Ego integrity vs. despair

Sex and Gender

- ☐ Biological sex
- ☐ Intersex
- ☐ Gender identity
- ☐ Gender expression
- ☐ Transgender
- ☐ Gender role

Adolescence

- ☐ Adolescence
- ☐ Puberty
- ☐ Primary sex characteristics
- ☐ Secondary sex characteristics
- ☐ Synaptic pruning

Aging

- ☐ Socioemotional selectivity theory

Important Contributors

- ☐ Mary Ainsworth
- ☐ Albert Bandura
- ☐ Diana Baumrind
- ☐ John Bowlby
- ☐ Erik Erikson
- ☐ Sigmund Freud
- ☐ Harry Harlow
- ☐ Lawrence Kohlberg
- ☐ Konrad Lorenz
- ☐ Jean Piaget
- ☐ Lev Vygotsky

Next Steps

Step 1: Tally your correct answers from Part A and review the quiz explanations at the end of this chapter.

1. B
2. B
3. A
4. E
5. C

6. B
7. C
8. A
9. D
10. E

_____ out of 10 questions

Step 2: Count the number of key terms you checked off in Part B.

_____ out of 94 key terms

Step 3: Read the Rapid Review Key Takeaways in this chapter.

Step 4: Consult the table below and follow the instructions based on your performance.

If You Got . . .	Do This
80% or more of the Test What You Already Know assessment correct (8 or more questions from Part A and 76 or more key terms from Part B)	• Read definitions in this chapter for all the key terms you didn't check off. • Complete the Test What You Learned assessment in this chapter.
50% or less of the Test What You Already Know assessment correct (5 or fewer questions from Part A and 47 or fewer key terms from Part B)	• Read the comprehensive review for this topic in Chapter 18. ○ If you are short on time, read only the High-Yield sections. • Read through all of the key term definitions in this chapter. • Complete the Test What You Learned assessment in this chapter.
Any other result	• Read the High-Yield sections of the comprehensive review of this topic in Chapter 18. • Read definitions in this chapter for all the key terms you didn't check off. • Complete the Test What You Learned assessment in this chapter.

RAPID REVIEW

Key Takeaways

1. There are a variety of factors that contribute to an individual's physical, social, and cognitive development. Most psychologists agree that both nature and nurture play a role in development.

2. Infants are born with a variety of reflexes and tend to develop motor skills in a particular order and according to certain rules.

3. Infants are born with temperaments, characteristic ways of reacting emotionally that influence how infants become attached to their caregivers, which in turn influences how they form attachments as adults.

4. Piaget maintained that cognitive development occurred in a series of four stages, while Vygotsky focused on sociocultural influences on cognitive development and argued that children need the assistance of others to learn new abilities.

5. Kohlberg argued that moral reasoning occurs at three distinct stages, while his critics contend that behaviors are often not confined to a single stage and that his model ignored feminist values like empathy.

6. People achieve significant developmental milestones as they age and pass through adolescence, adulthood, and older adulthood. Freud and Erikson use stage theories to describe these changes.

Key Terms: Definitions

Nature and Nurture

Nature: Innate biological factors that influence development and personality.

Nurture: External and environmental factors, including learning, that influence development and personality.

Range of reaction: The upper and lower boundaries of a characteristic set by an individual's genes. Environmental factors determine where within that range the characteristic will fall.

Gestation

Gestation/prenatal development: The process of development from conception to birth.

Conception: Fusion of two gametes: one male sex cell (the sperm) and one female sex cell (the egg).

Germinal stage: The first stage of gestation, which lasts about 2 weeks, in which the zygote migrates from the Fallopian tube to implant itself in the uterine wall.

Embryonic stage: The second stage of gestation, which lasts about 6 weeks, in which cells begin to differentiate and organs begin to develop.

Fetal stage: The final stage of gestation, which lasts about 7 months, in which the fetus gains increased mobility and develops rapidly.

Teratogens: Substances that damage the process of fetal development such as tobacco and alcohol.

Fetal alcohol syndrome: A developmental disorder caused by a mother's heavy alcohol use during pregnancy.

Motor Skill Development

Motor development: The emergence of the ability to execute physical actions such as walking, crawling, reaching, and rolling.

Reflexes: Innate motor responses that are triggered by specific patterns of sensory stimulation.

Rooting reflex: The tendency for an infant to move its mouth toward any object that touches its cheek.

Sucking reflex: The tendency for an infant to suck any object that enters its mouth.

Moro reflex: The outstretching of the arms and legs in response to a loud noise or a sudden change in the environment.

Grasping reflex: The vigorous grasping of an object that touches the palm.

Babinski reflex: The projection of the big toe and the fanning of the other toes when the sole of the foot is touched, found only in infants.

Plantar reflex: The curling of the toes when the sole of the foot is touched, developed after infancy.

Cephalocaudal rule: The tendency for motor skills to emerge in sequence from the head to the feet, also known as the "top-to-bottom" rule.

Proximodistal rule: The tendency for motor skills to emerge in sequence from the center to the periphery, also known as the "inside to outside" rule.

Temperament and Attachment

Attachments: Strong emotional bonds to other people.

Internal working model of attachment: A set of expectations an infant forms about how its primary caregiver will respond to it.

Secure attachment: Attachment style for an infant who feels safe in the presence of its caregiver, becomes distressed when its caregiver leaves, and is soothed when its caregiver returns.

Avoidant attachment: Attachment style for an infant who shows little emotion toward its caregiver and appears to be unconcerned if its caregiver stays or leaves.

Ambivalent attachment: Attachment style for an infant who is distressed when its caregiver leaves but isn't soothed when its caregiver returns, ignoring or rebuffing its caregiver's attempts to calm it.

Disorganized attachment: Attachment style for an infant who shows no consistent pattern of response when its caregiver is present or absent.

Temperament: An individual's characteristic pattern of emotional reactivity.

Parenting Styles

Demandingness: The extent to which parents control their children's behavior or demand their maturity.

Responsiveness: The degree to which parents are accepting and sensitive to their children's emotional and developmental needs.

Authoritative parenting: Parents have high expectations for their children but are able to adjust their expectations with understanding and support.

Permissive parenting: Parents are responsive, but not demanding, and may establish inconsistent rules for their children in an attempt to avoid confrontation; also called indulgent parenting.

Authoritarian parenting: Parents are demanding and cold, tend to have very high expectations of their children but typically fail to show positive affirmation, even when their children succeed; also called strict parenting.

Neglectful parenting: Parents are cold and unresponsive to their children, tend not to establish rules for them, and are often indifferent to how they behave.

Cognitive Development

Cognitive development: The emergence of intellectual abilities, as well as the study of this process.

Sensorimotor stage: A Piagetian stage in which infants (ages 0–2) learn about the world through movement and senses, develop schemata, and begin to show evidence of object permanence.

Schemata: Theories or models about how the world works; plural of *schema*.

Assimilation: The application of a schema to a novel situation.

Accommodation: The revision of a schema when presented with new information.

Object permanence: The understanding that objects continue to exist even when they are no longer visible.

Preoperational stage: A Piagetian stage in which young children (ages 2–6) lack understanding of conservation and initially think egocentrically but eventually develop theory of mind.

Egocentrism: A self-centered perspective that arises from the failure to understand that the world appears differently to different people.

Theory of mind: The understanding that human behavior is guided by mental representations of the world, and that the world appears differently to different people.

Concrete operational stage: A Piagetian stage in which children (ages 6–11) can think logically about physical objects and understand the conservation of physical properties.

Conservation: The understanding that quantities remain constant even when outward appearances change.

Formal operational stage: The Piagetian stage in which children and adolescents (age 11+) gain a deeper understanding of their own and others' minds and begin to reason abstractly.

Zone of proximal development (**ZPD**): According to Vygotsky, a set of skills that children are not yet able to do independently, but that they can do with the assistance of a more knowledgeable other.

More knowledgable other (**MKO**): According to Vygotsky, someone who has a better understanding of a task compared to the learner.

Moral Development

Pre-conventional stage: The first stage of Kohlberg's moral development theory, in which the morality of an action is determined by the consequences for the actor.

Conventional stage: The second stage of Kohlberg's moral development theory, in which the morality of an action is determined by the extent to which it conforms with rules and norms.

Post-conventional stage: The third stage of Kohlberg's moral development theory, in which the morality of an action is determined by general principles and core values.

Ethics of care: Carol Gilligan's feminist approach to moral development that emphasizes values like empathy and benevolence over abstract duties and obligations.

Moral intuitionist perspective: The idea that humans evolved to react emotionally to events that are particularly relevant to our survival and reproduction, and that these emotional responses dictate how we respond in moral dilemmas.

9

Socialization

Psychosexual stages: Freud's distinct developmental stages that focus on pleasures and behaviors associated with particular parts of the body.

Erotogenic zone: The part of the body that the child's libido is fixated on in a given psychosexual stage.

Libido: A psychic energy that is part of an individual's id, encompassing all drives that an individual possesses.

Fixation: According to Freud, fixation occurs when a person's libido becomes arrested at a particular psychosexual stage, which may have long-term implications for one's personality.

Oral stage: An infant focuses on the pleasures and frustrations associated with the mouth, sucking, and being fed.

Anal stage: A child experiences pleasures and frustrations associated with the anus, retention and excretion of feces and urine, and toilet training.

Phallic stage: The child's experience is dominated by pleasures, conflicts, and frustrations associated with the genital region.

Oedipus complex: A developmental episode during the phallic stage in which a boy develops sexual feelings for his mother, initial jealousy of his father, and eventually, in an effort to resolve this conflict, identifies with his father.

Electra complex: A developmental episode during the phallic stage in which a girl develops sexual feelings for her father and identifies with her mother to resolve this conflict.

Latency stage: When the child does not experience a major conflict and instead focuses on the development of creative, intellectual, athletic, and interpersonal skills.

Genital stage: Freud's final psychosexual stage, in which the individual develops a full adult personality with the capacity to work, love, and relate to others.

Trust vs. mistrust: Erikson's first stage, which lasts from birth to 18 months, in which an infant develops a sense of trust when its caregiver provides reliable care and protection, or mistrust when deprived of a stable relationship with its caregiver.

Autonomy vs. shame and doubt: Erikson's second stage, which lasts from 18 months to 3 years, in which a child strives to develop a sense of personal independence, experiencing shame and doubt if he is unable to do tasks independently.

Initiative vs. guilt: Erikson's third stage, which lasts from 3 to 6, in which a child either begins leading her peers and develops initiative, or develops guilt if she fails to have positive peer interactions.

Industry vs. inferiority: Erikson's fourth stage, which lasts from 6 to 12, in which a child attempts to learn skills that have social value, but can develop feelings of inferiority if she fails to learn these skills.

Identity vs. role confusion: Erikson's fifth stage, which occurs during adolescence, in which individuals try out multiple roles before deciding what role they want to occupy in society, with the risk of developing role confusion if a stable role isn't found.

Intimacy vs. isolation: Erikson's sixth stage, which occurs during young adulthood, in which individuals share themselves more intimately with others, but can develop feelings of isolation.

Generativity vs. stagnation: Erikson's seventh stage, which occurs in middle age, in which older adults reflect on how they're giving back to society, and may develop a sense of stagnation if they feel their contributions are inadequate.

9

Ego integrity vs. despair: Erikson's eighth and final stage, which occurs during old age, in which seniors look back on their lives and contemplate their accomplishments, potentially developing feelings of despair if they are dissatisfied with the course their lives ran.

Sex and Gender

Biological sex: The set of physiological characteristics, including chromosomal composition, hormones, and genitalia, that individuals are born with that determine if they are male, female, or intersex.

Intersex: A broad classification that describes anyone whose physiological characteristics are neither clearly male nor clearly female.

Gender identity: The psychological identification as male, female, something in between, or neither.

Gender expression: How someone outwardly expresses their gender identity through fashion, pronoun preference, and physical appearance.

Transgender: Individuals whose gender identity does not align with their sex at birth.

Gender role: A set of social expectations for behaviors that are deemed appropriate based on a person's gender.

Adolescence

Adolescence: The period of development that begins with the onset of sexual maturity and lasts until the beginning of adulthood.

Puberty: A period of bodily changes associated with sexual maturity.

Primary sex characteristics: Bodily structures or processes directly involved with reproduction.

Secondary sex characteristics: Bodily structures or processes that are not directly involved with reproduction but that change dramatically during puberty.

Synaptic pruning: A process by which neural synapses that are not frequently used are targeted for elimination.

Aging

Socioemotional selectivity theory: A theory stating that young adults tend to focus on useful information, while older adults tend to focus on information that brings emotional satisfaction.

Important Contributors

Mary Ainsworth: Developed the Strange Situation and attachment theory.

Albert Bandura: Known for his contribution to the field of observational learning, including his famous Bobo doll experiment on aggression.

Diana Baumrind: Known for her research on four types of parenting styles.

John Bowlby: Contributed to attachment theory and developed the idea of an internal working model of attachment.

Erik Erikson: A psychoanalyst known for identifying psychosocial developmental stages.

Sigmund Freud: The founder of psychoanalysis, who created a theory of psychosexual developmental stages.

Harry Harlow: Conducted research on rhesus monkeys, discovering they prefer contact to food acquisition, which was influential for attachment theory.

Lawrence Kohlberg: Developed a theory of moral development involving three distinct stages of moral reasoning.

Konrad Lorenz: Conducted naturalistic observations of geese and other animals and discovered a simple form of attachment known as imprinting.

Jean Piaget: Developed a well-known stage theory of cognitive development, involving a progression of four distinct stages.

Lev Vygotsky: A proponent of sociocultural theory who introduced the concepts of zone of proximal development (ZPD) and more knowledgeable other (MKO).

TEST WHAT YOU LEARNED

Part A: Quiz

1. An infant with an avoidant attachment style will most likely respond to his primary caregiver leaving the room by

    (A) crying and become distressed

    (B) becoming calmer and playing with his toys

    (C) attempting to follow his caregiver out of the room

    (D) showing no apparent concern about his caregiver's absence

    (E) playing with the stranger instead

2. During which stage of prenatal development does the differentiation of cells begin?

    (A) Conception

    (B) Germinal stage

    (C) Embryonic stage

    (D) Fetal stage

    (E) Birth

3. The cephalocaudal rule states that

    (A) motor skills tend to emerge in sequence from head to feet

    (B) motor skills tend to emerge earlier for males than they do for females

    (C) gross motor skills tend to emerge before fine motor skills

    (D) motor skills tend to emerge in sequence from the center to the periphery

    (E) involuntary motor skills tend to develop before voluntary motor skills

4. According to Kohlberg, an individual who states that cheating on the AP Psychology exam is wrong because "you would not earn college credit if you got caught" probably reasons at which stage of moral development?

    (A) Pre-conventional

    (B) Conventional

    (C) Post-conventional

    (D) Concrete operational

    (E) Sensorimotor

5. A child refers to her puppy as "doggie." She then sees a kitten for the first time and calls out "doggie!" This is an example of

    (A) object permanence

    (B) conservation

    (C) spreading activation

    (D) accommodation

    (E) assimilation

6. Suppose a child who used to call all pets "doggie" has just learned that dogs and cats are different creatures, and can now discriminate between the two. This process is referred to as

    (A) object permanence

    (B) conservation

    (C) spreading activation

    (D) accommodation

    (E) assimilation

9

7. According to Freud, an individual who becomes obsessively neat is fixated at which psychosexual stage?

   (A) Oral

   (B) Anal

   (C) Phallic

   (D) Latency

   (E) Genital

8. Which of the following is NOT a change associated with aging?

   (A) Decreased muscle mass and increased fat storage

   (B) Increased asymmetrical activation of lobes in the brain

   (C) Decreased sensory abilities

   (D) A shift from focusing on useful information to satisfying information

   (E) Reduction in size of social circles

9. Baby Andy moves her mouth toward a cookie after her brother Abel brushes it against her cheek gently. Andy is most likely displaying the

   (A) rooting reflex

   (B) Moro reflex

   (C) grasping reflex

   (D) Babinski reflex

   (E) sucking reflex

10. Which of the following correctly orders the stages of prenatal development?

   (A) embryonic, germinal, fetal

   (B) germinal, embryonic, fetal

   (C) germinal, fetal, embryonic

   (D) embryonic, fetal, germinal

   (E) fetal, embryonic, germinal

Part B: Key Terms

This key terms list is the same as the list in the Test What You Already Know section earlier in this chapter. Based on what you have now learned, again ask yourself the following questions:

- Can I describe this key term?

- Can I discuss this key term in relation to other psychological ideas and specific psychologists?

- Could I correctly answer a multiple-choice question about this key term?

- Could I correctly answer a free-response question about this key term?

Check off the key terms if you can answer "yes" to at least three of these questions.

Nature and Nurture

☐ Nature   ☐ Nurture   ☐ Range of reaction

Gestation

☐ Gestation/prenatal development   ☐ Germinal stage   ☐ Teratogens

☐ Embryonic stage   ☐ Fetal alcohol syndrome

☐ Conception   ☐ Fetal stage

Motor Skill Development

☐ Motor development   ☐ Moro reflex   ☐ Cephalocaudal rule

☐ Reflexes   ☐ Grasping reflex   ☐ Proximodistal rule

☐ Rooting reflex   ☐ Babinski reflex

☐ Sucking reflex   ☐ Plantar reflex

Temperament and Attachment

☐ Attachments   ☐ Secure attachment   ☐ Disorganized attachment

☐ Internal working model of attachment   ☐ Avoidant attachment   ☐ Temperament

☐ Ambivalent attachment

Parenting Styles

☐ Demandingness   ☐ Authoritative parenting   ☐ Authoritarian parenting

☐ Responsiveness   ☐ Permissive parenting   ☐ Neglectful parenting

Cognitive Development

☐ Cognitive development   ☐ Schemata   ☐ Accommodation

☐ Sensorimotor stage   ☐ Assimilation   ☐ Object permanence

9

- ☐ Preoperational stage
- ☐ Egocentrism
- ☐ Theory of mind
- ☐ Concrete operational stage
- ☐ Conservation
- ☐ Formal operational stage
- ☐ Zone of proximal development (ZPD)
- ☐ More knowledgeable other (MKO)

Moral Development

- ☐ Pre-conventional stage
- ☐ Conventional stage
- ☐ Post-conventional stage
- ☐ Ethics of care
- ☐ Moral intuitionist perspective

Socialization

- ☐ Psychosexual stages
- ☐ Erotogenic zone
- ☐ Libido
- ☐ Fixation
- ☐ Oral stage
- ☐ Anal stage
- ☐ Phallic stage
- ☐ Oedipus complex
- ☐ Electra complex
- ☐ Latency stage
- ☐ Genital stage
- ☐ Trust vs. mistrust
- ☐ Autonomy vs. shame and doubt
- ☐ Initiative vs. guilt
- ☐ Industry vs. inferiority
- ☐ Identity vs. role confusion
- ☐ Intimacy vs. isolation
- ☐ Generativity vs. stagnation
- ☐ Ego integrity vs. despair

Sex and Gender

- ☐ Biological sex
- ☐ Intersex
- ☐ Gender identity
- ☐ Gender expression
- ☐ Transgender
- ☐ Gender role

Adolescence

- ☐ Adolescence
- ☐ Puberty
- ☐ Primary sex characteristics
- ☐ Secondary sex characteristics
- ☐ Synaptic pruning

Aging

- ☐ Socioemotional selectivity theory

Important Contributors

- ☐ Mary Ainsworth
- ☐ Albert Bandura
- ☐ Diana Baumrind
- ☐ John Bowlby
- ☐ Erik Erikson
- ☐ Sigmund Freud
- ☐ Harry Harlow
- ☐ Lawrence Kohlberg
- ☐ Konrad Lorenz
- ☐ Jean Piaget
- ☐ Lev Vygotsky

9

Next Steps

Step 1: Tally your correct answers from Part A and review the quiz explanations at the end of this chapter.

1.	D	6.	D
2.	C	7.	B
3.	A	8.	B
4.	A	9.	A
5.	E	10.	B

_____ out of 10 questions

Step 2: Count the number of key terms you checked off in Part B.

_____ out of 94 key terms

Step 3: Compare your Test What You Already Know results to these Test What You Learned results to see how exam-ready you are for this topic.

If you need to study this topic further:

- Read (or reread) the comprehensive review for this topic in Chapter 18.

- Go to kaptest.com to complete the online quiz questions for Developmental Psychology.

  ○ Haven't registered your book yet? Go to kaptest.com/moreonline to begin.

ANSWERS AND EXPLANATIONS

Test What You Already Know

1. B

In between abilities that children can do alone and those they cannot do are abilities that children can do with support. This area is known by Vygotsky as the zone of proximal development (or ZPD), making **(B)** correct. (A), (C), and (E) are incorrect because they are Piagetian concepts. (D) is incorrect because a more knowledgeable other is someone who helps a child to learn skills in her ZPD.

2. B

Sandy is unable to grasp the concept of conservation, so meatballs that are more spaced out on the other plate will appear to be more numerous to him. This finding describes a child in the preoperational stage of cognitive development, **(B)**. A child in the sensorimotor stage, (A), also does not understand conservation, but would be too young to articulate that. (C) and (D) are incorrect because children in the concrete and formal operational stages have already mastered conservation. (E) is a stage from Kohlberg's theory of moral development.

3. A

Pruning, **(A)**, is the process of culling neuronal connections to improve the efficiency of brain activity. The other choices are not terms used by developmental psychologists.

4. E

The Moro reflex, **(E)**, describes the reaction outlined in the question stem. The rooting reflex, (A), is the tendency for an infant to move its mouth toward any object that touches its cheek. The sucking reflex, (B), is the tendency for an infant to suck any object that enters its mouth. The grasping reflex, (C), is the vigorous grasping of an object that touches the palm. The Babinski reflex, (D), is the projection of the big toe and the fanning of the other toes when the sole of the foot is touched.

5. C

Infants who show distress when their primary caregiver leaves but fail to be soothed when they return are said to have an ambivalent attachment style, **(C)**. In the Strange Situation, an infant with a secure attachment, (A), would be distressed when her caregiver leaves and soothed when the caregiver returns; an infant with an avoidant attachment, (B), would appear unconcerned regardless of his caregiver's presence; and an infant with a disorganized attachment, (D), would show no consistent pattern of responses. (E) is incorrect because anxious-preoccupied is an adult attachment style.

6. B

An individual who bases the morality of an action on either rules or laws is said to be in the conventional stage of moral reasoning; **(B)** is correct. (A) is incorrect because the pre-conventional stage describes an individual who is motivated by punishments and rewards. (C) is incorrect because the post-conventional stage describes individuals who use internal sets of core values to guide their moral reasoning. Formal operational, (D), and concrete operational, (E), are two of Piaget's stages of cognitive development.

7. C

Susan is "trying on" various identities before deciding which one fits her best. Erikson called the conflict at this stage of development identity vs. role confusion; **(C)** is correct. Intimacy vs. isolation, (A), describes young adults learning to form more intimate relationships. Initiative vs. guilt, (B), describes children learning to be leaders among their peers or concluding that their presence is a nuisance to others. Industry vs. inferiority, (D), refers to the stage in which children are trying to learn new skills that have social value. Ego integrity vs. despair, (E), describes seniors who are looking back on their lives and considering whether they are satisfied with their legacy.

9

8. A

Only **(A)** correctly describes a primary sex characteristic, one which directly affects structures or processes related to reproduction; the menstrual cycle is essential for female reproduction. All of the other choices describe secondary sex characteristics: (B) and (C) develop in girls and (D) and (E) in boys.

9. D

Teratogens are substances that hinder prenatal development, potentially leading to birth defects. Alcohol and tobacco are among the most common teratogens, so **(D)** is correct. (A) is incorrect because neither LSD nor marijuana have been shown to have detrimental effects on prenatal development. Epinephrine and norepinephrine, (B), and serotonin and dopamine, (C), are all neurotransmitters. Phonemes and morphemes, (E), are units of language in linguistics.

10. E

The Electra complex describes a a girl's psychosexual competition with her mother for her father, which occurs during the phallic stage of development. Although the Electra complex simply extends Sigmund Freud's Oedipus complex to girls, it was actually named and proposed by his associate Carl Jung. **(E)** is correct and (A) is incorrect. Mary Ainsworth, (B), is recognized for her theory of attachment styles in infants. Albert Bandura, (C), is well known for his contributions to observational learning. Jean Piaget, (D), is best known for his stage theory of cognitive development.

Test What You Learned

1. D

In Mary Ainsworth's Strange Situation, infants with an avoidant attachment style will show no concern when their caregiver leaves the room and will not acknowledge their caregiver when he or she returns; **(D)** is correct. (A) describes how securely attached and ambivalently attached infants might respond. (B) describes how a securely attached infant responds when his caregiver returns. (C) and (E) describe behaviors not typically seen in the Strange Situation.

2. C

The differentiation of cells begins in the embryonic stage, so **(C)** is correct. Conception, (A), is the fusion of two gametes. The division of cells begins during the germinal stage, (B). In the fetal stage, (D), the fetus further develops muscles and a skeletal system and undergoes rapid brain growth. (E) is incorrect because birth is not a stage of prenatal development, which literally means development *before* birth.

3. A

The cephalocaudal rule, also known as the "top-to-bottom" rule, describes the tendency for motor skills to emerge in sequence from the head to the feet. **(A)** is correct. (D) describes the proximodistal rule. (B), (C), and (E) are not tendencies commonly identified in development.

4. A

Deciding on the morality of an action based on its consequences for the actor is reasoning in the pre-conventional stage, **(A)**. (B) and (C) are incorrect because conventional reasoning is based upon following rules, laws, and norms, while post-conventional reasoning is based upon internal sets of core values. (D) and (E) are Piagetian stages of cognitive development.

5. E

Assimilation is the process of fitting experiences into existing schemata, such as calling any small pet a "doggie." **(E)** is correct. Object permanence, (A), is the recognition that objects persist when out of sight. (B), conservation, is the recognition that quantities remain constant after superficial changes. Spreading activation, (C), is a memory process in cognitive psychology. Accommodation, (D), refers to revising old schemata and developing new ones.

6. D

The process described involves the revision of existing schemata, which makes it accommodation, **(D)**. (A), object permanence, is the recognition that objects persist when out of sight. Conservation, (B), is the recognition that quantities remain constant after superficial changes. Spreading activation, (C), is a memory process in cognitive psychology. (E), assimilation, is the application of existing schemata to new experiences.

7. B

According to Freud, an anal fixation leads to individuals becoming anal retentive, meaning they have an obsession with being neat and clean. **(B)** is thus correct. (A) is incorrect because individuals with oral fixations are prone to smoking and overeating. (C) is incorrect because individuals with phallic fixations suffer some kind of sexual dysfunction or deviancy. (D) and (E) are incorrect because fixations do not occur in these stages, according to Freud.

8. B

Older individuals tend to show an increase in activation across both lobes when completing a variety of tasks when compared to younger adults. Researchers believe that older individuals do this to compensate for diminished performance in specific brain regions. Thus, **(B)** is the opposite of what is expected with aging. All of the other choices describe known effects of aging.

9. A

The tendency for an infant to move her mouth toward an object that brushes her cheek is referred to as the rooting reflex. **(A)** is correct. The Moro reflex, (B), refers to an infant's tendency to outstretch arms and legs in response to a loud noise or a sudden change in the environment. The grasping reflex, (C), refers to an infant's tendency to grasp any object placed in hand. The Babinski reflex, (D), is the projection of the big toe and the fanning of the other toes when the sole of the foot is touched. The sucking reflex, (E), is the tendency for an infant to suck any object that enters the mouth.

10. B

Prenatal development begins with the germinal stage, which lasts for the first two weeks after conception, is followed by the embryonic stage, which lasts through the eighth week, and concludes with the fetal stage, which lasts until birth. **(B)** is correct. The other choices arrange the stages incorrectly.

9

CHAPTER 10

Motivation, Emotion, and Personality

LEARNING OBJECTIVES

After studying this chapter, you will be able to:

- Apply fundamental motivational concepts to explain human and animal behavior

- Describe needs, drives, homeostasis, and other biological aspects of motivation

- Cite similarities and differences among important theories of motivation

- Summarize classic research on major motivational systems

- Explain stress theories and stress's effect on well being

- Distinguish among major theories of emotion

- Identify the influences of culture on emotional expression

- Distinguish among major personality theories

- Contrast personality psychology research methods

- List, and evaluate for reliability and validity, common personality assessments

- Explain the possible influence of cultural context on self-concept and other aspects of personality development

- Recognize important contributors to the psychology of motivation, emotion, and personality

TEST WHAT YOU ALREADY KNOW

Part A: Quiz

1. Which of the following is an example of a humanistic personality theorist?

   (A) Margaret Mead

   (B) Alfred Adler

   (C) B.F. Skinner

   (D) Carl Rogers

   (E) William Sheldon

2. Even though Dmitri hates the company he works for, he refuses to quit. When a friend asks him why he does not look for other work, he says it is because he makes good money. This is an example of

   (A) intrinsic motivation

   (B) punishment

   (C) groupthink

   (D) extrinsic motivation

   (E) negative reinforcement

3. Which of the following would someone from a collectivist culture be LEAST likely to value?

   (A) Honesty

   (B) Family

   (C) Generosity

   (D) Unity

   (E) Assertiveness

4. Which of the following would most weaken the James-Lange theory of emotion?

   (A) A patient with a spinal cord injury continues to exhibit the same level of emotion after her injuries as before.

   (B) A teenager reasons that she is sad after she begins to cry.

   (C) A patient experiences pain after being pricked by a needle, which causes a feeling of sadness.

   (D) A child is unable to differentiate between fear when she sees a mean dog barking next door and enjoyment when she sees an animated dog barking on TV.

   (E) A patient with a spinal cord injury exhibits a diminished level of emotion after her injuries compared to before.

5. Emily walks through the mall food court and sees a new cafe offering an Indian food buffet. As she gets closer, she can't help but notice that the food smells delicious. The smell of the food is referred to as a(n)

   (A) need

   (B) drive

   (C) instinct

   (D) incentive

   (E) intrinsic motivation

6. Which of the following provides the best example of eustress?

    (A) A soccer player goes through physical therapy after rupturing her Achilles tendon during a game.

    (B) A recent college graduate has trouble adjusting to life on his own.

    (C) A marathon runner is confident she will beat her personal record as she completes her fifth marathon.

    (D) A student studies anxiously for a make-up exam in a class that he previously failed.

    (E) A teenager nervously and excitedly researches and purchases her first car.

7. Each of the following is an example of an objective personality assessment EXCEPT the

    (A) Beck Depressive Inventory

    (B) Minnesota Multiphasic Personality Inventory

    (C) Thematic Apperception Test

    (D) Myers-Briggs Type Indicator

    (E) Keirsey Temperament Sorter

8. Which of the following is often compared to a thermostat because of the role it plays in regulating bodily functions to maintain equilibrium?

    (A) Instinct

    (B) Homeostasis

    (C) Need

    (D) Incentive

    (E) Extrinsic motivation

9. A decrease in blood pressure triggers the renin-angiotensin system, which stimulates thirst. This mechanism is most relevant to which of the following theories of motivation?

    (A) Arousal theory

    (B) Incentive theory

    (C) Drive-reduction theory

    (D) General adaptation syndrome

    (E) Instinct theory

10. Suppose you have three friends: the first is bossy and always urging you to do random things, the second constantly judges you and pesters you to be a good person, and the third tries to help mediate between the other two. Your friends are, respectively, like the Freudian unconscious structures of

    (A) id, superego, and ego

    (B) id, ego, and superego

    (C) ego, superego, and id

    (D) superego, id, and ego

    (E) superego, ego, and id

10

Part B: Key Terms

The following is a list of the major ideas and people for the AP Psychology topic of Motivation, Emotion, and Personality. You will likely see many of these on the AP Psychology exam.

For each key term, ask yourself the following questions:

- Can I describe this key term?
- Can I discuss this key term in relation to other psychological ideas and specific psychologists?
- Could I correctly answer a multiple-choice question about this key term?
- Could I correctly answer a free-response question about this key term?

Check off the key terms if you can answer "yes" to at least three of these questions.

Motivation

- ☐ Motivation
- ☐ Extrinsic motivation
- ☐ Intrinsic motivation
- ☐ Approach-approach conflicts
- ☐ Avoidance-avoidance conflicts
- ☐ Approach-avoidance conflicts

- ☐ Instincts
- ☐ Instinct theory
- ☐ Drive
- ☐ Primary drives
- ☐ Homeostasis
- ☐ Secondary drives
- ☐ Drive-reduction theory
- ☐ Arousal
- ☐ Arousal theory

- ☐ Yerkes-Dodson law
- ☐ Incentive theory
- ☐ Need
- ☐ Maslow's hierarchy of needs
- ☐ Self-actualization
- ☐ Obesity
- ☐ Sex drive
- ☐ Sexual orientation

Stress

- ☐ Stress
- ☐ Stressors
- ☐ Distress

- ☐ Eustress
- ☐ Stress reactions
- ☐ Cognitive appraisal

- ☐ General adaptation syndrome (GAS)

Emotion

- ☐ Emotion
- ☐ James-Lange theory

- ☐ Cannon-Bard theory
- ☐ Two-factor theory

- ☐ Appraisal theory of emotion

Personality Theories

- ☐ Personality
- ☐ Type theory

- ☐ Trait theory
- ☐ Type-A

- ☐ Type-B
- ☐ PEN model

- ☐ Psychoticism
- ☐ Extraversion
- ☐ Neuroticism
- ☐ Big Five
- ☐ Openness to experience
- ☐ Conscientiousness
- ☐ Agreeableness
- ☐ Biopsychological approach
- ☐ Behaviorist approach
- ☐ Social cognitive perspective
- ☐ Reciprocal determinism
- ☐ Psychoanalytic/ psychodynamic perspective
- ☐ Structural model
- ☐ Id

- ☐ Pleasure principle
- ☐ Primary process
- ☐ Wish fulfillment
- ☐ Superego
- ☐ Conscience
- ☐ Ego-ideal
- ☐ Ego
- ☐ Reality principle
- ☐ Secondary process
- ☐ Defense mechanism
- ☐ Repression
- ☐ Suppression
- ☐ Regression
- ☐ Reaction formation
- ☐ Projection
- ☐ Rationalization
- ☐ Displacement

- ☐ Sublimation
- ☐ Personal unconscious
- ☐ Collective unconscious
- ☐ Archetype
- ☐ Persona
- ☐ Shadow
- ☐ Anima
- ☐ Animus
- ☐ Inferiority complex
- ☐ Basic anxiety
- ☐ Basic hostility
- ☐ Moving toward
- ☐ Moving against
- ☐ Moving away
- ☐ Humanistic perspective
- ☐ Peak experience

Personality Research and Assessments

- ☐ Objective test
- ☐ Myers-Briggs Type Indicator (MBTI)

- ☐ Keirsey Temperament Sorter
- ☐ Minnesota Multiphasic Personality Inventory (MMPI-2)

- ☐ Projective test
- ☐ Rorschach inkblot test
- ☐ Thematic Apperception Test

Personality and Culture

- ☐ Individualistic culture
- ☐ Collectivist culture

Important Contributors

- ☐ Alfred Adler
- ☐ Gordon Allport
- ☐ Albert Bandura
- ☐ Paul Costa and Robert McCrae
- ☐ Hans and Sybil Eysenck

- ☐ Sigmund Freud
- ☐ Karen Horney
- ☐ William James
- ☐ Carl Jung
- ☐ Alfred Kinsey
- ☐ Abraham Maslow

- ☐ William Masters and Virginia Johnson
- ☐ Margaret Mead
- ☐ Stanley Schachter
- ☐ Hans Selye
- ☐ William Sheldon

10

Next Steps

Step 1: Tally your correct answers from Part A and review the quiz explanations at the end of this chapter.

1.	D	6.	E
2.	D	7.	C
3.	E	8.	B
4.	A	9.	C
5.	D	10.	A

_____ out of 10 questions

Step 2: Count the number of key terms you checked off in Part B.

_____ out of 113 key terms

Step 3: Read the Rapid Review Key Takeaways in this chapter.

Step 4: Consult the table below and follow the instructions based on your performance.

If You Got . . .	Do This
80% or more of the Test What You Already Know assessment correct (8 or more questions from Part A and 91 or more key terms from Part B)	• Read definitions in this chapter for all the key terms you didn't check off. • Complete the Test What You Learned assessment in this chapter.
50% or less of the Test What You Already Know assessment correct (5 or fewer questions from Part A and 56 or fewer key terms from Part B)	• Read the comprehensive review for this topic in Chapter 19. ◦ If you are short on time, read only the High-Yield sections. • Read through all of the key term definitions in this chapter. • Complete the Test What You Learned assessment in this chapter.
Any other result	• Read the High-Yield sections of the comprehensive review of this topic in Chapter 19. • Read definitions in this chapter for all the key terms you didn't check off. • Complete the Test What You Learned assessment in this chapter.

RAPID REVIEW

Key Takeaways

1. Various theories of motivation strive to explain why people behave in certain ways by exploring the roles of instincts, internal and external rewards, the desire to maintain a certain level of arousal, the drive to reduce uncomfortable states, and the urge to fulfill physiological and psychological needs.

2. Some types of motivation, like hunger and sex, have been the subject of extensive psychological research, which has sometimes produced controversial findings.

3. Stress comes in a variety of forms, which can be either positive (eustress) or negative (distress), depending on the characteristics of individuals, their circumstances, and their coping abilities.

4. Emotions consist of physiological, behavioral, and cognitive components. Psychologists primarily rely on three key theories to explain emotional responses.

5. Personality theories are ways of describing the qualities of people that make them unique individuals. Type and trait theories seek to classify people or specific parts of their personality. The behavioral perspective says that people are a product of their environment, while the biopsychological perspective says that people are a product of their genes. The social cognitive perspective says that personality and environment influence each other, and the humanistic perspective focuses on the positive and healthy aspects of personality.

6. The psychoanalytic perspective is a controversial theory of personality that has evolved over time. Psychoanalysts use unconscious instincts and desires to explain thoughts, feelings, and behaviors.

7. Psychologists use objective and projective tests to study personality. Objective tests are questionnaires that reveal personality traits, but care must be taken to ensure their internal and external validity. Projective tests seek to reveal unconscious thoughts through the use of ambiguous images, but critics feel these tests reveal more about recent experiences or conscious thoughts than unconscious feelings.

8. Culture has an impact on the way personality develops. In particular, collectivist and individualistic cultures differently affect personal thoughts, behaviors, and values.

Key Terms: Defined

Motivation

Motivation: Processes that initiate, direct, and sustain behavior.

Extrinsic motivation: Motivation driven by an external reward or punishment.

Intrinsic motivation: Motivation driven by internal factors such as enjoyment and satisfaction.

Approach-approach conflicts: Conflicts in which you must decide between desirable options.

Avoidance-avoidance conflicts: Conflicts in which you must decide between undesirable options.

Approach-avoidance conflicts: Conflicts in which you must decide between options with both desirable and undesirable features.

Instincts: Inborn, fixed patterns of behavior that present in response to certain stimuli and are often species-specific.

Instinct theory: A theory, based on the work of Darwin, stating that people perform certain behaviors due to instincts developed through generations of evolution.

Drive: A state of unrest or irritation that energizes particular behaviors to alleviate that state.

Primary drives: Innate needs that are found in all humans and animals and are vital to survival, such as the needs for food, water, and warmth.

Homeostasis: A dynamic state of equilibrium maintained by fulfilling drives and regulating internal conditions such as body temperature and blood pressure.

Secondary drives: Needs, such as money and social approval, that are learned through experience.

Drive-reduction theory: A theory stating that imbalances to your body's internal environment generate drives that cause you to act in ways that restore homeostasis.

Arousal: The physiological and psychological state of being active and alert, as reflected by factors such as heart rate, muscle tone, brain activity, and blood pressure.

Arousal theory: A theory stating that individuals are motivated to perform behaviors in order to maintain an optimal arousal level, typically a moderate level.

Yerkes-Dodson law: A moderate level of arousal allows for optimal performance, though this optimal level can vary based on the individual and the nature of the task.

Incentive theory: A theory of motivation stating that behaviors are motivated by the desire to attain rewards and avoid punishments.

Need: An internal desire or deficiency that can motivate behavior.

Maslow's hierarchy of needs: A theory that classifies needs into five categories, ranked by priority from lowest to highest: physiological, safety, love, esteem, and self-actualization.

Self-actualization: The last level in Maslow's hierarchy, this need is met when individuals accept themselves and attain their full potential.

Obesity: A medical condition characterized by a body mass index of greater than 30 and associated with various health problems, such as an increased risk of heart disease and diabetes.

Sex drive: An example of a primary drive, it describes how motivated an individual is to partake in sexual behavior.

Sexual orientation: A person's identity in relation to the group or gender to which they are attracted; most commonly homosexual, heterosexual, bisexual, or asexual.

Stress

Stress: The physiological and emotional state that an individual experiences in response to challenging environmental demands.

Stressors: Objects or circumstances that cause individuals to experience stress.

Distress: Stress caused by a negative stressor that can have adverse effects, such as making you sick or keeping you from reaching a goal.

Eustress: Stress caused by a positive stressor that can have beneficial effects, such as energizing you or helping you reach a goal.

Stress reactions: Physiological, psychological, and behavioral responses to stress, such as fatigue, anxiety, and nausea.

Cognitive appraisal: An individual's subjective evaluation of a stress-inducing situation.

General adaptation syndrome (GAS): Developed by Selye to explain the body's response to stress, it consists of three phases: alarm, resistance, and exhaustion.

Emotion

Emotion: A psychological and physiological response characterized by pleasure, pain, and/or other feelings.

James-Lange theory: A theory stating that emotional responses occur as a result of physiological arousal.

Cannon-Bard theory: A theory stating that physiological arousal and an emotional experience in response to a stimulus occur simultaneously.

Two-factor theory: Also known as the Schachter–Singer theory, it states that both physiological arousal and proper cognitive labeling of that arousal are necessary for an individual to experience emotions.

Appraisal theory of emotion: A theory stating that cognition precedes both physiological arousal and emotional experience. Primary appraisal is the determination of the meaning of the stimulus and secondary appraisal is the determination of the ability to cope with the stimulus.

Personality Theories

Personality: The set of thoughts, feelings, traits, and behaviors that are characteristic of a person and consistent over time and in different situations.

Type theory: A kind of personality theory that organizes people into different sorts of individuals.

Trait theory: A kind of personality theory that lists classifiable characteristics that add together in different combinations and to different degrees to make a unique personality.

Type-A: An ambitious and competitive personality, according to one type theory.

Type-B: A laid-back and relaxed personality, according to one type theory.

PEN model: Trait theory that focuses on placing people on a continuum for each of three personality traits: psychoticism, extraversion, and neuroticism.

Psychoticism: PEN trait that corresponds to aggression and non-conformity.

Extraversion: PEN trait that corresponds to thriving on external stimulation; also a member of the Big Five.

Neuroticism: PEN trait that corresponds to anxiety and fight-or-flight stress response; also a member of the Big Five.

Big Five: Trait theory that reorganizes and builds on the PEN traits, keeping extraversion and neuroticism, and adding openness to experience, conscientiousness, and agreeableness. Can be remembered using the mnemonic OCEAN.

Openness to experience: Big Five trait that corresponds to curiosity vs. caution.

Conscientiousness: Big Five trait that corresponds to organization vs. carelessness.

Agreeableness: Big Five trait that corresponds to friendliness vs. detachment.

Biopsychological approach: Theory that maintains that personality is heavily influenced by genes.

Behaviorist approach: Theory that maintains that personality is heavily influenced by environment and experience.

Social cognitive perspective: Theory that maintains personality both shapes and is shaped by environment.

Reciprocal determinism: The idea from the social cognitive perspective that thoughts, feelings, beliefs, and environment all influence each other in determining a person's actions in a given situation.

10

Psychoanalytic/psychodynamic perspective: Personality theory that explains behaviors by looking at unconscious drives and feelings.

Structural model: Divides the conscious and unconscious mind into the id, ego, and superego.

Id: The part of the personality that consists of all of the basic, primal urges and instincts to survive and reproduce.

Pleasure principle: The drive for instant gratification and catharsis (the relief of pent-up tension).

Primary process: The style of thought generated by the id that is simple, primal, and aimed at seeking pleasure and avoiding pain.

Wish fulfillment: The use of fantasy to imagine satisfying an urge that would be unacceptable to act out.

Superego: The part of the personality that is focused on creating the ideal self.

Conscience: The part of the superego that causes feelings of guilt when you succumb to the urges of the id.

Ego-ideal: The part of the superego that responds with feelings of pride when you overcome the urges of the id.

Ego: The part of the personality that suppresses the needs of the id and superego.

Reality principle: The ego's drive to put off instant gratification and fulfill desires in socially acceptable ways.

Secondary process: The style of thought generated by the ego that seeks to relieve the tension caused by delaying gratification.

Defense mechanism: The ego's means of denying, distorting, or falsifying reality to reduce the anxiety caused by the clash between the id and the superego.

Repression: Defense mechanism marked by pushing an unwanted or socially unacceptable feeling out of conscious awareness.

Suppression: Defense mechanism marked by consciously setting aside thoughts or feelings that would be unhelpful in the current situation.

Regression: Defense mechanism marked by reverting to an earlier stage of emotional or mental development in response to stress.

Reaction formation: Defense mechanism marked by turning an unwanted thought or feeling into its opposite.

Projection: Defense mechanism marked by attributing your own unwanted feelings to others.

Rationalization: Defense mechanism marked by justifying unacceptable behaviors to make them more acceptable to yourself or others and to hide your true motivations.

Displacement: Defense mechanism marked by redirecting an unwanted feeling from one target to another.

Sublimation: Defense mechanism marked by transforming an undesirable feeling or drive into a socially acceptable one.

Personal unconscious: Any part of the personality or memory that is not currently conscious because it has been forgotten or repressed.

Collective unconscious: The instincts and emotionally-charged symbols shared among all people due to our common ancestry, according to Jung.

Archetype: One of the emotional instincts or symbols that make up a person's personality.

Persona: Archetype that represents the part of the personality that people present to the outside world.

Shadow: Archetype that represents the part of the personality that is socially unacceptable and hidden away.

10

Anima: Archetype that represents a man's feminine qualities.

Animus: Archetype that represents a woman's masculine qualities.

Inferiority complex: A person's feelings of incompleteness or imperfection that lead to striving for superiority.

Basic anxiety: Feelings of anxiety or helplessness caused by inadequate parenting.

Basic hostility: Anger caused by parental neglect or rejection.

Moving toward: Strategy to overcome basic anxiety or hostility marked by attempts to gain others' good will.

Moving against: Strategy to overcome basic anxiety or hostility marked by attempts to gain the upper hand on others.

Moving away: Strategy to overcome basic anxiety or hostility marked by attempts to withdraw from others.

Humanistic perspective: Personality theory that focuses on the positive aspects of personality and the ways in which healthy people strive toward self-realization.

Peak experience: Deeply moving events in a person's life that have important and long-lasting effects on the individual.

Personality Research and Assessments

Objective test: Self-report questionnaires that tend to focus on types or traits.

Myers-Briggs Type Indicator (MBTI): Objective test that sorts people into personality types based on four continua: Extraversion (E) versus Introversion (I), Sensing (S) versus Intuition (N), Thinking (T) versus Feeling (F), and Judging (J) versus Perceiving (P).

Keirsey Temperament Sorter: Objective test that uses metrics similar to the MBTI but provides names and descriptions for each of the personality types.

Minnesota Multiphasic Personality Inventory (MMPI-2): Objective test used to assess both personality traits and the presence of psychological disorders.

Projective test: Personality test based on the idea that people will interpret ambiguous stimuli in ways that reflect their unconscious thoughts and feelings.

Rorschach inkblot test: Projective test that asks participants to describe what they see in abstract designs.

Thematic Apperception Test: Projective test that presents participants with a series of images and asks them to tell a story about what is happening.

Personality and Culture

Individualistic culture: A culture that places an emphasis on individual goals and personal achievement.

Collectivist culture: A culture that sees people primarily as members of a family or larger social group.

Important Contributors

Alfred Adler: Psychoanalyst who disagreed with Freud over the importance of sexual drives in personality; originated the concept of the inferiority complex.

Gordon Allport: Trait theorist who identified three kinds of traits—cardinal, central, and secondary—that carry different weights in making up an individual's personality.

Albert Bandura: Social cognitive theorist who proposed reciprocal determinism, the idea that thoughts, beliefs, and environment all interact with and change each other.

Paul Costa and **Robert McCrae**: Expanded and reorganized the PEN trait model into the Big Five or OCEAN model of personality traits.

Hans and **Sybil Eysenck**: Trait theorists who originated the PEN model of personality.

Sigmund Freud: Founder of psychoanalysis who developed the structural model, which states that the mind is made up of the id, ego, and superego.

Karen Horney: Sought to move psychoanalysis away from sexuality- and male-focused ideas; maintained that inadequate parenting can lead to basic anxiety or basic hostility.

William James: Developed the James-Lange theory of emotion, along with Carl Lange, which proposes that emotions occur because of physiological reactions to events.

Carl Jung: Psychoanalyst who stated that the unconscious mind can be divided into the personal and collective unconscious, the latter of which contains archetypes.

Alfred Kinsey: Known for his systematic, scientific study of sexual behavior, he developed the Kinsey Scale to describe sexual orientation.

Abraham Maslow: Developed a theory of motivation called the hierarchy of needs, made up of five levels of needs, and claimed that lower-level needs must be satisfied before higher-level needs.

William Masters and **Virginia Johnson**: Researched sexual arousal and proposed a four-stage human sexual response cycle.

Margaret Mead: Cultural anthropologist who studied children and adolescents in Samoa and other island nations to demonstrate the relationship between culture and personality.

Stanley Schachter: Developed the two-factor theory of emotion, along with Jerome Singer, which states that emotional experience requires conscious interpretation of one's physiological arousal.

Hans Selye: Developed the general adaptation syndrome model to explain how the body responds and adapts to stress.

William Sheldon: Type theorist who created the concept of somatotypes and attempted to correlate body type to personality.

TEST WHAT YOU LEARNED

Part A: Quiz

1. Which of the following provides the best example of distress?

   (A) A young man decides to lose weight by training for a triathalon.

   (B) A man chooses to move in with his mother as she recovers from knee surgery.

   (C) After failing an entrance exam, a student chooses to take a gap year and reapply.

   (D) A recently unemployed woman confidently searches for a new job.

   (E) An anxious student grabs the wrong set of notecards on the day of her final presentation.

2. A person is presented with an image of a young boy looking sadly at a violin and is asked to tell a story about the boy. This person is most likely taking

   (A) the Rorschach test

   (B) the Keirsey Temperament Sorter

   (C) the Thematic Apperception Test

   (D) a word association test

   (E) an intelligence test

3. A study shows that rats display different emotional responses to identical stimuli depending on their prior states and environments. This supports which of the following theories of emotion?

   (A) James-Lange theory

   (B) Gate-control theory

   (C) Cannon-Bard theory

   (D) Three-factor theory

   (E) Schachter-Singer theory

4. A woman who is very frustrated with her boss's behavior spends her entire commute home yelling at other drivers on the road. According to the psychoanalytic perspective of personality, which of the following defense mechanisms is this woman employing?

   (A) Displacement

   (B) Projection

   (C) Repression

   (D) Suppression

   (E) Sublimation

5. A young woman decides to leave medical school in order to pursue her dream of becoming a Hollywood actress. How could her risk-taking behavior be explained by drive-reduction theory?

   (A) Since her low-priority needs are met, she can focus on fulfilling her needs for esteem and self-actualization.

   (B) She was driven to change careers in order to fulfill her mother's dream of being an actress.

   (C) She feels excited when she is performing and she is motivated to maintain this level of arousal.

   (D) She has feelings of anxiety due to her untested potential, which create an internal tension that she is motivated to relieve despite the risk.

   (E) She is driven by the desire to reduce her debt by achieving fame and fortune.

10

6. Suppose the statement "I find it easy to trust and cooperate with others" were an item on an objective personality inventory. Which of the following traits would this item most likely be used to evaluate?

   (A) Openness to experience

   (B) Conscientiousness

   (C) Extraversion

   (D) Agreeableness

   (E) Neuroticism

7. According to Maslow's hierarchy of needs, before focusing on improving his or her sense of belonging, an individual must first fulfill the need for

   (A) self-acceptance

   (B) admiration from others

   (C) self-fulfillment

   (D) compassion

   (E) secure housing

8. "An adult who lives in a city with a high population and few social ties is more likely to develop impatience and rudeness as personality traits." Which of the following personality theorists would be most likely to make this statement?

   (A) Karen Horney

   (B) Hans and Sybil Eysenck

   (C) Carl Jung

   (D) B.F. Skinner

   (E) Margaret Mead

9. Which of the following statements is most likely to have been made by someone who comes from an individualistic culture?

   (A) "My own achievements ultimately reflect on my parents and grandparents."

   (B) "A person should always try to be honest and trustworthy."

   (C) "No act is more virtuous than giving to charity."

   (D) "I feel a deep connection to the other people who live in my town."

   (E) "My goal is to work hard so that I can support myself."

10. After learning that her robotics team made it to the final round of competition, Zara jumped up on the table to do a victory dance. Which of the following theories or concepts could NOT provide a plausible explanation for her actions?

    (A) Incentive theory

    (B) Arousal theory

    (C) Instinct theory

    (D) Hierarchy of needs

    (E) Extrinsic motivation

Part B: Key Terms

This key terms list is the same as the list in the Test What You Already Know section earlier in this chapter. Based on what you have now learned, again ask yourself the following questions:

- Can I describe this key term?

- Can I discuss this key term in relation to other psychological ideas and specific psychologists?

- Could I correctly answer a multiple-choice question about this key term?

- Could I correctly answer a free-response question about this key term?

Check off the key terms if you can answer "yes" to at least three of these questions.

Motivation

- ☐ Motivation
- ☐ Extrinsic motivation
- ☐ Intrinsic motivation
- ☐ Approach-approach conflicts
- ☐ Avoidance-avoidance conflicts
- ☐ Approach-avoidance conflicts

- ☐ Instincts
- ☐ Instinct theory
- ☐ Drive
- ☐ Primary drives
- ☐ Homeostasis
- ☐ Secondary drives
- ☐ Drive-reduction theory
- ☐ Arousal
- ☐ Arousal theory

- ☐ Yerkes-Dodson law
- ☐ Incentive theory
- ☐ Need
- ☐ Maslow's hierarchy of needs
- ☐ Self-actualization
- ☐ Obesity
- ☐ Sex drive
- ☐ Sexual orientation

Stress

- ☐ Stress
- ☐ Stressors
- ☐ Distress

- ☐ Eustress
- ☐ Stress reactions
- ☐ Cognitive appraisal

- ☐ General adaptation syndrome (GAS)

Emotion

- ☐ Emotion
- ☐ James-Lange theory

- ☐ Cannon-Bard theory
- ☐ Two-factor theory

- ☐ Appraisal theory of emotion

Personality Theories

- ☐ Personality
- ☐ Type theory
- ☐ Trait theory

- ☐ Type-A
- ☐ Type-B
- ☐ PEN model

- ☐ Psychoticism
- ☐ Extraversion
- ☐ Neuroticism

10

- ☐ Big Five
- ☐ Openness to experience
- ☐ Conscientiousness
- ☐ Agreeableness
- ☐ Biopsychological approach
- ☐ Behaviorist approach
- ☐ Social cognitive perspective
- ☐ Reciprocal determinism
- ☐ Psychoanalytic/ psychodynamic perspective
- ☐ Structural model
- ☐ Id
- ☐ Pleasure principle
- ☐ Primary process

- ☐ Wish fulfillment
- ☐ Superego
- ☐ Conscience
- ☐ Ego-ideal
- ☐ Ego
- ☐ Reality principle
- ☐ Secondary process
- ☐ Defense mechanism
- ☐ Repression
- ☐ Suppression
- ☐ Regression
- ☐ Reaction formation
- ☐ Projection
- ☐ Rationalization
- ☐ Displacement
- ☐ Sublimation

- ☐ Personal unconscious
- ☐ Collective unconscious
- ☐ Archetype
- ☐ Persona
- ☐ Shadow
- ☐ Anima
- ☐ Animus
- ☐ Inferiority complex
- ☐ Basic anxiety
- ☐ Basic hostility
- ☐ Moving toward
- ☐ Moving against
- ☐ Moving away
- ☐ Humanistic perspective
- ☐ Peak experience

Personality Research and Assessments

- ☐ Objective test
- ☐ Myers-Briggs Type Indicator (MBTI)

- ☐ Keirsey Temperament Sorter
- ☐ Minnesota Multiphasic Personality Inventory (MMPI-2)

- ☐ Projective test
- ☐ Rorschach inkblot test
- ☐ Thematic Apperception Test

Personality and Culture

- ☐ Individualistic culture
- ☐ Collectivist culture

Important Contributors

- ☐ Alfred Adler
- ☐ Gordon Allport
- ☐ Albert Bandura
- ☐ Paul Costa and Robert McCrae
- ☐ Hans and Sybil Eysenck

- ☐ Sigmund Freud
- ☐ Karen Horney
- ☐ William James
- ☐ Carl Jung
- ☐ Alfred Kinsey
- ☐ Abraham Maslow

- ☐ William Masters and Virginia Johnson
- ☐ Margaret Mead
- ☐ Stanley Schachter
- ☐ Hans Selye
- ☐ William Sheldon

Next Steps

Step 1: Tally your correct answers from Part A and review the quiz explanations at the end of this chapter.

1.	E	6.	D
2.	C	7.	E
3.	E	8.	D
4.	A	9.	E
5.	D	10.	C

_____ out of 10 questions

Step 2: Count the number of key terms you checked off in Part B.

_____ out of 113 key terms

Step 3: Compare your Test What You Already Know results to these Test What You Learned results to see how exam-ready you are for this topic.

If you need to study this topic further:

- Read (or reread) the comprehensive review for this topic in Chapter 19.
- Go to kaptest.com to complete the online quiz questions for Motivation, Emotion, and Personality.
  - Haven't registered your book yet? Go to kaptest.com/moreonline to begin.

10

ANSWERS AND EXPLANATIONS

Test What You Already Know

1. D

Carl Rogers, **(D)**, was the champion of humanism in psychology. Mead, (A), was a cultural anthropologist who studied personality as it relates to culture. Adler, (B), was a proponent of the psychodynamic perspective. Skinner, (C), was a behaviorist, and Sheldon, (E), was a type theorist who proposed the idea of somatotypes.

2. D

Extrinsic motivation refers to behaviors that are driven by the desire to receive a reward or avoid punishment. Since Dmitri is motivated to remain at his job due to the financial reward he receives for working there, he is experiencing extrinsic motivation, making **(D)** correct. Intrinsic motivation refers to behaviors that are driven by internal rewards like enjoyment and satisfaction. Since Dmitri does not enjoy his job, (A) is incorrect. Punishment is an unpleasant stimulus that makes a behavior less likely to occur in the future, but since the question stem indicates that Dmitri is not likely to quit his job anytime soon, (B) is incorrect. Groupthink is a characteristic associated with certain types of cohesive groups, in which poor decisions are made due to a desire to promote harmony. Since the question stem does not indicate that Dmitri's behavior is the result of a group's decision, (C) is incorrect. (E) is incorrect because negative reinforcement is the removal of an unpleasant stimulus to increase the frequency of a behavior, which also does not apply.

3. E

For members of a collectivist culture, unity and group cohesiveness are highly important. As a result, qualities that set a person apart from others, such as **(E)**, assertiveness, are less important. The other choices are values that are perfectly compatible with a collectivist culture.

4. A

The James-Lange theory states that emotional responses occur as a result of physiological arousal. Thus, (B) and (C) are both examples that directly support the James-Lange theory. According to the James-Lange theory, patients with spinal cord injuries would be expected to exhibit diminished levels of emotion after their injuries; however, the theory was actually challenged when these patients were shown to experience the same level of emotion after their injuries as before. Thus, (E) can be eliminated and **(A)** must be correct. (D) would weaken the Schachter-Singer theory, which states that both physiological arousal (increased heart rate after hearing barking) and proper cognitive labeling of that arousal (the neighbor's dog is dangerous, the cartoon dog is funny) are necessary for an individual to experience emotions.

5. D

Incentives are external stimuli like rewards or punishments that motivate behaviors. Since the enticing aroma hints at the delicious taste of the food, which could be characterized as a reward for eating it, **(D)** is correct. The remaining choices are incorrect because they describe internal states rather than external stimuli: needs, (A), are internal deficiencies that can motivate behaviors; drives, (B) are internal states of unrest that encourage actions to alleviate them; instincts, (C), are inborn, fixed patterns of behavior that present in response to certain stimuli; and intrinsic motivation, (E), comes from within, based on what we naturally enjoy doing.

6. E

Eustress is a positive stressor that can have beneficial effects like energizing an individual or helping someone reach a goal. An important characteristic of eustress is that an individual finds the stressor challenging but manageable. Though the teenager is nervous about purchasing a car, her excitement drives her forward, making **(E)** correct. While experiencing an injury and undergoing physical therapy can certainly be stressful, (A) is not example of eustress because an injury is not a positive life change. Similarly, while having trouble adjusting after a major life change can be stressful, (B) is incorrect because it appears that the graduate is unable to manage the situation. (C) is not an example of eustress because, for someone who has run a marathon four times before, it is unlikely that a fifth marathon would cause significant stress. While studying for an exam is stressful, (D) is incorrect because the stress the student is experiencing does not appear to be energizing him or having a positive impact on his studying.

10

7. C

(A), (B), (D), and (E) are all objective personality tests because they are questionnaires that focus on types and traits. The Thematic Apperception Test, **(C)**, is a projective test because it presumes that people will interpret presented images in ways that reflect unconscious thoughts and feelings.

8. B

Homeostasis is a dynamic state of equilibrium maintained by fulfilling drives and regulating internal conditions such as body temperature and blood pressure. Thus, like a thermostat, maintaining homeostasis requires constant adjustments to achieve desired performance, making **(B)** correct. Instincts, (A), are complex, inborn fixed patterns of behavior that present in response to certain stimuli. Needs, (C), are internal desires or deficiencies that can motivate behaviors. Incentives, (D), are external stimuli like rewards or punishments that motivate behaviors. Extrinsic motivation, (E), refers to behaviors that are driven by the desire to receive a reward or avoid punishment.

9. C

Drive-reduction theory states that physiological needs lead to uncomfortable states that motivate behaviors intended to satisfy those needs. In this case, the physiological need for increased blood pressure aroused the individual's thirst in order to motivate the consumption of fluids, thereby fulfilling the thirst. Thus, **(C)** is correct. Arousal theory, (A), states that individuals are motivated to perform behaviors in order to maintain an optimal arousal level. Incentive theory, (B), states that behaviors are motivated by the desire to attain rewards and avoid negative stimuli. General adaptation syndrome, (D), is a theory stating that the body's response to stress consists of three phases—alarm, resistance, and exhaustion. Instinct theory, (E), states that people perform certain behaviors due to inborn, evolutionary-based instincts.

10. A

The order would be id, superego, and ego, as in **(A)**. The id is the part of the personality that is always demanding immediate gratification, the superego is like your conscience, and the ego is the mediator between the other two. The remaining choices scramble the order.

Test What You Learned

1. E

Distress is an unpleasant stressor that can have adverse effects like making you sick or keeping you from reaching a goal. Since the final presentation is already making the student anxious, grabbing the wrong set of notecards will definitely serve as an adverse stressor, making **(E)** correct. Losing weight by training to achieve a goal is more likely to be an example of eustress, making (A) incorrect. Similarly, since the man is willingly choosing to move in with and help his mother, it is unlikely he is experiencing distress, eliminating (B). Even though failing an entrance exam is stressful, the student seems to have taken it in stride and is not letting his results distract him from his goal, so (C) is not an example of distress. Though losing a job can be stressful, the unemployed woman is able to manage the situation and remain positive, making it likely that she is experiencing eustress. Thus, (D) is incorrect.

2. C

The Thematic Apperception Test, **(C)**, presents participants with a series of images and asks them to tell a story about what is happening. The Rorschach test uses ambiguous inkblots for the same purpose, so (A) can be eliminated. The Keirsey Temperament Sorter is an objective test based on the Myers-Briggs Type Indicator, so (B) is not correct either. Neither (D) nor (E) utilize this task, so both are likewise incorrect.

3. E

The Schachter-Singer theory accounts for the role of context in emotion. It specifically states that both physiological arousal and proper cognitive labeling of that arousal are necessary for an individual to experience emotions. Since this study shows the role of both arousal and context, **(E)** is correct. The James-Lange theory, (A), does not account for the role of context in experiencing emotion, instead stating that emotional responses occur only as a result of physiological arousal. Gate-control theory, (B), is a theory of pain, not emotion. The Cannon-Bard theory, (C), does not account for the role of context in experiencing emotion, instead stating that physiological arousal and emotion occur simultaneously. The Schachter-Singer theory is also known as the two-factor theory, not the three-factor theory, making (D) incorrect.

10

4. A

This woman is directing her anger with her boss at the more socially acceptable targets in the cars around her. This is therefore an example of **(A)**, displacement. Projection would occur if the woman imagined that her boss was frustrated with her rather than the other way around, so (B) is incorrect. Since the woman isn't burying her feelings consciously or unconsciously, (C) and (D) can be eliminated. (E) would be correct if the woman were redirecting her anger into a more positive outlet.

5. D

Drive-reduction theory states that physiological needs lead to aroused states that motivate behaviors to reduce the needs and restore homeostasis. Thus, because it provides an example of a physiological need (her anxiety) resulting in an aroused state (her desire to test her potential as an actress) that motivates a behavior (leaving medical school to be an actress), **(D)** is correct. (A) is more characteristic of Maslow's hierarchy of needs, which maintains that an individual must meet his or her lowest level of unmet needs before moving on to higher-level needs. (B) is an example of incentive theory, since fulfilling her mother's dream would allow the young woman to receive the external reward of her mother's happiness. (C) is characteristic of arousal theory, which states that individuals are motivated to perform behaviors in order to maintain an optimal arousal level. (E) is also characteristic of incentive theory since wealth and recognition are examples of external rewards.

6. D

The trait of agreeableness, **(D)**, is a measure of friendliness, trust, sympathy, and empathy, which is exactly what this inventory item is asking about. The other choices are the other members of the Big Five. (C), extraversion, also has to do with interactions with others, but concerns preferences for spending time alone versus spending time with others, rather than willingness to trust others.

7. E

Maslow's hierarchy of needs suggests that an individual cannot attend to a need at a particular level until they have fulfilled all other lower-priority needs. The five classifications of needs in order of priority are physiological needs, safety needs, needs for love and belonging, esteem needs, and self-actualization needs. Thus, before focusing on needs for love and belonging, an individual must first address his or her safety needs, such as the need for secure housing. As a result, **(E)** is correct. (A), (C), and (D) are all examples of self-actualization needs, while (B) is an example of an esteem need.

8. D

The statement reflects the belief that a specific environment has an effect on personality traits, which means that the theorist in question most likely comes from the behavioral or social cognitive perspective. Of the choices, only **(D)** is a match. (A) and (C) are incorrect because Horney and Jung were psychoanalysts who believed that personality is a result of unconscious urges. The Eysencks, (B), were interested in personality traits, but trait theorists are not interested in where traits come from. Mead, (E), focused on the ways in which culture affected personality development in children, but the question stem specifies an adult.

9. E

(A), (B), (C), and (D) all focus attention on interpersonal relationships and the good of the group. These are all therefore more likely to have been made by someone in a collectivist culture. **(E)**, on the other hand, focuses on independence, which is a quality that is favored in individualistic cultures, and is therefore correct.

10. C

Since it is unlikely that Zara's enthusiasm is an unlearned, innate, fixed pattern of behavior that presents in response to certain stimuli, instinct theory does not explain her actions, making **(C)** correct. (A) and (E) can be eliminated because it is possible that Zara has experienced incentives in the past in response to her extraverted actions and, as a result, she is motivated to continue these behaviors. Similarly, (B) can be eliminated because it is possible that staying the center of attention allows Zara to maintain an optimum level of arousal. (D) can be eliminated because Zara may be using dancing on the table as a way to fulfill her need for love and belongingness by gaining the appreciation of her peers and increasing her social standing.

CHAPTER 11

Clinical Psychology

LEARNING OBJECTIVES

After studying this chapter, you will be able to:

- Summarize past and present conceptions of psychological disorders

- Assess the strengths and weaknesses of various theoretical perspectives on psychological disorders

- Recognize the American Psychiatric Association's *Diagnostic and Statistical Manual of Mental Disorders* (DSM) as the main basis of diagnostic judgments

- Identify the major diagnostic categories of psychological disorders and their corresponding symptoms

- List the pros and cons of assigning diagnostic labels

- Describe the interaction of psychology and the judicial system

- Summarize psychological treatment's primary characteristics

- Identify major treatment orientations and formats and their influence on treatment

- Assess particular treatments' effects on particular psychological disorders

- Explain the impact of cultural and ethnic context on the selection and outcome of treatment

- List tactics designed to promote resilience and competence

- Recognize important contributors to clinical psychology

TEST WHAT YOU ALREADY KNOW

Part A: Quiz

1. Dan has an inflated sense of his self-worth, believing himself to be the most important man in the world, and yet withers in response to even mild criticisms. Which of the following person-ality disorders would be the most appropriate diagnosis for Dan?

    (A) Narcissistic

    (B) Antisocial

    (C) Dependent

    (D) Paranoid

    (E) Borderline

2. A patient who suffers from a phobia would likely find an effective treatment with

    (A) psychoanalytic therapy

    (B) drug therapy

    (C) systematic desensitization

    (D) cognitive restructuring

    (E) client-centered therapy

3. Which of the following would NOT justify a breach of confidentiality?

    (A) A depressed patient insists repeatedly throughout the course of a therapy session that she's going to kill herself

    (B) A patient with antisocial personality disorder describes in detail how he intends to assault a neighbor he dislikes

    (C) A clinical psychologist conducts a case study that pioneers a revolutionary treat-ment for a patient with a rare disorder

    (D) A psychiatrist is called as an expert witness when one of her patients pleads insanity in court

    (E) A schizophrenic patient discusses his attempts to construct a bomb and blow up a municipal building

4. Which of the following contributes the most to the early termination rates of psychotherapy patients from marginalized groups?

    (A) Multicultural competence

    (B) Eurocentric treatments

    (C) Psychopharmacology

    (D) Unconditional positive regard

    (E) Active listening

11

5. Ricardo is having trouble moving his hip, but doctors can find nothing wrong with it. As a track star, Ricardo is preparing for the biggest race of the year, but his hip problem will probably keep him from competing. Ricardo most likely suffers from

   (A) schizophrenia

   (B) conversion disorder

   (C) dysthymia

   (D) acrophobia

   (E) seasonal affective disorder

6. Which of the following studies yielded results that called into question the value of diagnostic labels?

   (A) The Milgram experiment

   (B) The Stanford prison experiment

   (C) The Rosenhan experiment

   (D) The Little Albert experiment

   (E) The Bobo doll experiment

7. While in class, Jolene suddenly finds herself overwhelmed with anxiety. Her heart pounds, her breathing quickens, and she feels jittery. Jolene is probably experiencing a(n)

   (A) manic episode

   (B) depressive episode

   (C) psychotic episode

   (D) heart attack

   (E) panic attack

8. The concept most associated with Rogerian or client-centered therapy is

   (A) dream interpretation

   (B) free association

   (C) unconditional positive regard

   (D) positive reinforcement

   (E) punishment

9. The DSM-5 is used to

   (A) establish best practices for treating disorders

   (B) provide patients with information about support groups

   (C) document case studies of patients with severe disorders

   (D) set guidelines for diagnosing psychological disorders

   (E) educate patients about confidentiality and other legal rights

10. Which of the following is NOT a component of evidence-based practice?

    (A) The patient's specific context

    (B) The patient's culture

    (C) The therapist's clinical expertise

    (D) The therapist's favorite therapy

    (E) The best available research evidence

Part B: Key Terms

The following is a list of the major ideas and people for the AP Psychology topic of Clinical Psychology. You will likely see many of these on the AP Psychology exam.

For each key term, ask yourself the following questions:

- Can I describe this key term?
- Can I discuss this key term in relation to other psychological ideas and specific psychologists?
- Could I correctly answer a multiple-choice question about this key term?
- Could I correctly answer a free-response question about this key term?

Check off the key terms if you can answer "yes" to at least three of these questions.

What Are Psychological Disorders?

- ☐ Abnormal behavior
- ☐ Deinstitutionalization
- ☐ Medical model
- ☐ Psychoanalytic model
- ☐ Humanistic model
- ☐ Cognitive model
- ☐ Biological model
- ☐ Sociocultural model
- ☐ Behavioral model

Diagnostic Categories

- ☐ *Diagnostic and Statistical Manual of Mental Disorders* (DSM)
- ☐ Anxiety disorders
- ☐ Fear
- ☐ Anxiety
- ☐ Generalized anxiety disorder
- ☐ Specific phobias
- ☐ Panic disorder
- ☐ Panic attacks
- ☐ Social anxiety disorder
- ☐ Dissociative disorders
- ☐ Depersonalization/derealization disorder
- ☐ Dissociative amnesia
- ☐ Dissociative fugue

- ☐ Dissociative identity disorder (DID)
- ☐ Feeding and eating disorders
- ☐ Anorexia nervosa
- ☐ Bulimia nervosa
- ☐ Binge eating disorder
- ☐ Somatic symptom and related disorders
- ☐ Somatic symptom disorder
- ☐ Conversion disorder
- ☐ Illness anxiety disorder
- ☐ Obsessive-compulsive and related disorders
- ☐ Obsessive-compulsive disorder (OCD)

- ☐ Obsessions
- ☐ Compulsions
- ☐ Body dysmorphic disorder
- ☐ Depressive disorders
- ☐ Major depressive disorder
- ☐ Dysthymia
- ☐ Seasonal affective disorder (SAD)
- ☐ Bright light therapy
- ☐ Bipolar and related disorders
- ☐ Depressive episodes
- ☐ Manic episodes
- ☐ Bipolar I disorder
- ☐ Bipolar II disorder
- ☐ Cyclothymic disorder

11

- ☐ Personality disorders
- ☐ Cluster A
- ☐ Paranoid personality disorder
- ☐ Schizotypal personality disorder
- ☐ Schizoid personality disorder
- ☐ Cluster B
- ☐ Antisocial personality disorder
- ☐ Borderline personality disorder
- ☐ Histrionic personality disorder

- ☐ Narcissistic personality disorder
- ☐ Cluster C
- ☐ Avoidant personality disorder
- ☐ Dependent personality disorder
- ☐ Obsessive-compulsive personality disorder (OCPD)
- ☐ Psychotic disorders
- ☐ Positive symptoms
- ☐ Negative symptoms
- ☐ Schizophrenia
- ☐ Neurodevelopmental disorders

- ☐ Attention deficit hyperactivity disorder (ADHD)
- ☐ Autism spectrum disorder
- ☐ Specific learning disorder
- ☐ Intellectual disability/ intellectual developmental disorder
- ☐ Trauma- and stressor-related disorders
- ☐ Posttraumatic stress disorder (PTSD)
- ☐ Neurocognitive disorders
- ☐ Alzheimer's disease
- ☐ Parkinson's disease

Diagnostic Labels

- ☐ Diagnostic labels
- ☐ Rosenhan experiment

Psychology and the Law

- ☐ Confidentiality
- ☐ Insanity

What Is Psychological Treatment?

- ☐ Mental health professionals
- ☐ Psychotherapy
- ☐ Pharmacological treatment

Treatment Orientations and Formats

- ☐ Theoretical orientation
- ☐ Dream interpretation
- ☐ Free association
- ☐ Transference
- ☐ Self-actualization
- ☐ Client-centered therapy
- ☐ Unconditional positive regard

- ☐ Active listening
- ☐ Gestalt therapy
- ☐ Existential therapy
- ☐ Learned helplessness
- ☐ Applied behavioral analysis (ABA)
- ☐ Token economies
- ☐ Systematic desensitization

- ☐ Aversion therapy
- ☐ Rational-emotive behavior therapy
- ☐ Cognitive distortions
- ☐ Core belief
- ☐ Thought log
- ☐ Socratic questioning
- ☐ Cognitive restructuring

11

- [ ] Cognitive behavioral therapy (CBT)
- [ ] Third wave cognitive therapies
- [ ] Mindfulness
- [ ] Psychopharmacology
- [ ] Tricyclic antidepressants (TCAs)

- [ ] Selective serotonin reuptake inhibitors (SSRIs)
- [ ] Benzodiazepines
- [ ] Lithium carbonate
- [ ] Atypical anti-psychotics
- [ ] Electroconvulsive therapy (ECT)
- [ ] Deep brain stimulation

- [ ] Psychosurgery
- [ ] Eclectic therapy
- [ ] Transtheoretical model
- [ ] Individual psychotherapy
- [ ] Group psychotherapy
- [ ] Couples psychotherapy
- [ ] Family psychotherapy
- [ ] Systemic therapy

How Effective Is Treatment?

- [ ] Meta-analysis studies
- [ ] Evidence-based practice (EBP)

- [ ] Evidence-based treatments (EBTs)

- [ ] Randomized controlled trial
- [ ] Common factors theory

Therapy and Culture

- [ ] Culture
- [ ] Worldview
- [ ] Culture-bound syndrome

- [ ] Eurocentric
- [ ] Multiculturalism
- [ ] Multicultural competence

- [ ] Social justice therapy
- [ ] Afrocentric therapy

Prevention Strategies

- [ ] Prevention

- [ ] Competence

- [ ] Resilience

Important Contributors

- [ ] Aaron T. Beck
- [ ] Mary Cover-Jones
- [ ] Dorothea Dix
- [ ] Albert Ellis

- [ ] Sigmund Freud
- [ ] Fritz Perls
- [ ] Frederick Phillips
- [ ] Carl Rogers

- [ ] B.F. Skinner
- [ ] Joseph Wolpe
- [ ] Irving Yalom

Next Steps

Step 1: Tally your correct answers from Part A and review the quiz explanations at the end of this chapter.

1.	A	6.	C
2.	C	7.	E
3.	C	8.	C
4.	B	9.	D
5.	B	10.	D

_____ out of 10 questions

Step 2: Count the number of key terms you checked off in Part B.

_____ out of 149 key terms

Step 3: Read the Rapid Review Key Takeaways in this chapter.

Step 4: Consult the table below and follow the instructions based on your performance.

If You Got . . .	Do This
80% or more of the Test What You Already Know assessment correct (8 or more questions from Part A and 120 or more key terms from Part B)	• Read definitions in this chapter for all the key terms you didn't check off. • Complete the Test What You Learned assessment in this chapter.
50% or less of the Test What You Already Know assessment correct (5 or fewer questions from Part A and 74 or fewer key terms from Part B)	• Read the comprehensive review for this topic in Chapter 20. ○ If you are short on time, read only the High-Yield sections. • Read through all of the key term definitions in this chapter. • Complete the Test What You Learned assessment in this chapter.
Any other result	• Read the High-Yield sections of the comprehensive review of this topic in Chapter 20. • Read definitions in this chapter for all the key terms you didn't check off. • Complete the Test What You Learned assessment in this chapter.

11

RAPID REVIEW

Key Takeaways

1. A variety of conceptions of the causes of psychological disorders have emerged throughout history. Those models that are still embraced by contemporary psychologists each possess distinctive strengths and weaknesses.

2. The DSM-5 is the diagnostic tool used by clinical practitioners to diagnose a wide assortment of recognized disorders. The DSM-5 organizes these disorders by categories and identifies them by clusters of symptoms.

3. The use of diagnostic labels carries advantages (like heightened consistency in diagnosis, treatment, and research) but also disadvantages (such as those revealed by the Rosenhan experiment).

4. The judicial system interacts with clinical psychology in a number of ways, including confidentiality regulations and the insanity defense.

5. Psychological treatment is provided by mental health professionals in a variety of settings. The two most common types of treatment are psychotherapy and pharmacological treatment.

6. Psychotherapies come in a variety of theoretical orientations and formats. The most common treatment orientations are psychodynamic, humanistic, behavioral, cognitive, biomedical, and integrated. The four main formats of psychotherapy are individual, group, couples, and family.

7. Research suggests that psychotherapy generally helps patients to make positive changes in their lives, but some types of treatment are more effective for particular conditions than others.

8. Culture influences a variety of factors important to treatment. Decreased access, racism, and Eurocentrism contribute to unequal outcomes for patients from marginalized groups, but measures such as multicultural competence may help to alleviate these inequalities.

9. Effective prevention programs reduce environmental risk factors for mental illness and build up strengths. Prevention efforts might focus on promoting health, increasing competence, or building resilience.

Key Terms: Definitions

What Are Psychological Disorders?

Abnormal behavior: Maladaptive actions or cognitive processes that defy social norms.

Deinstitutionalization: Late twentieth-century movement to release large numbers of asylum patients and reintegrate them into their communities.

Medical model: Maintains that abnormal behaviors are symptoms of an underlying disease.

Psychoanalytic model: Maintains that abnormal behaviors are caused by repressed memories of childhood trauma and unconscious conflicts.

Humanistic model: Views psychological disorders as temporary impediments to self-actualization that result from unsatisfied needs.

Cognitive model: Maintains that abnormal behaviors result from faulty beliefs and maladaptive emotional responses.

Biological model: Maintains that psychological disorders result from imbalances in brain chemistry and other biological causes, including heredity and evolution.

Sociocultural model: Maintains that psychological disorders are culturally specific and caused by a variety of social and cultural factors.

Behavioral model: Maintains that abnormal behaviors are the products of learning, just like any other behaviors.

Diagnostic Categories

Diagnostic and Statistical Manual of Mental Disorders (DSM): The diagnostic tool published by the American Psychiatric Association, used to categorize and diagnose psychological disorders.

Anxiety disorders: Disorders characterized by excessive fear and anxiety.

Fear: An emotional response to a real or perceived threat that activates the sympathetic nervous system.

Anxiety: The expectation of a threat, which results in hypervigilance, evasive behaviors, and bodily tension.

Generalized anxiety disorder: A disorder characterized by excessive worry about numerous aspects of life.

Specific phobias: Irrational and excessive fears of particular stimuli, such as heights (acrophobia), spiders (arachnophobia), or crowds (agoraphobia).

Panic disorder: A disorder characterized by repeat, unexpected panic attacks.

Panic attacks: Episodes of acute fear that involve intense autonomic arousal.

Social anxiety disorder: A disorder characterized by anxiety in response to social or performance situations.

Dissociative disorders: Disorders characterized by a disconnection from one's identity.

Depersonalization/derealization disorder: A disorder characterized by feelings of detachment from oneself and/or one's environment.

Dissociative amnesia: A disorder characterized by extensive gaps in memory that result from emotional, rather than physiological, trauma.

Dissociative fugue: A subtype of dissociative amnesia in which patients construct new identities and personal histories for themselves.

Dissociative identity disorder (**DID**): A disorder characterized by the presence of two or more distinct personalities that alternate in their control of a patient's behavior; formerly known as multiple personality disorder.

Feeding and eating disorders: Disorders characterized by obsessive and unhealthy eating habits.

Anorexia nervosa: A disorder characterized by a strong desire to lose weight, a low BMI, and habitually restrictive eating.

Bulimia nervosa: A disorder characterized by bingeing and purging behavior and a normal BMI.

Binge eating disorder: A disorder characterized by a tendency to consume large quantities of food and an inability to regulate consumption.

Somatic symptom and related disorders: Disorders characterized by a pattern of physical symptoms that result in stress and impaired functioning.

Somatic symptom disorder: A disorder characterized by the presence of bodily symptoms that lack physiological causes.

Conversion disorder: A disorder characterized by the unexplained inhibition of voluntary functions.

11

Illness anxiety disorder: A disorder characterized by constant, invasive thoughts about suffering from severe medical conditions.

Obsessive-compulsive and related disorders: Disorders characterized by obsessions and compulsions.

Obsessive-compulsive disorder (OCD): A disorder characterized by the presence of stress-inducing obsessions and stress-relieving compulsions.

Obsessions: Intrusive, recurring impulses that are a source of stress.

Compulsions: Repetitive behaviors that reduce the stress of obsessions.

Body dysmorphic disorder: A disorder characterized by a distorted and negative perception of one's physical appearance.

Depressive disorders: Disorders characterized by extreme sadness without the presence of manic episodes.

Major depressive disorder: A disorder characterized by depressed mood and anhedonia over extended periods of time.

Dysthymia: A less severe form of depression.

Seasonal affective disorder (SAD): A depressive disorder that follows a seasonal pattern, typically most prevalent in winter.

Bright light therapy: Used to treat patients with SAD, whose depressed mood may be influenced by diminished light levels during winter months.

Bipolar and related disorders: Disorders characterized by oscillation between manic and depressive episodes.

Depressive episodes: Periods of diminished mood, inactivity, inhibition, and feelings of helplessness.

Manic episodes: Periods of heightened mood, frenetic activity, and inflated self-esteem.

Bipolar I disorder: A disorder characterized by severe manic episodes and psychotic episodes; may include depressive episodes.

Bipolar II disorder: A disorder characterized by hypomanic episodes and at least one major depressive episode.

Cyclothymic disorder: A disorder characterized by hypomanic and dysthymic episodes.

Personality disorders: Disorders characterized by rigid, maladjusted, dysfunctional behavior without recognition of the behavior as problematic.

Cluster A: Personality disorders characterized by odd or eccentric behavior.

Paranoid personality disorder: A disorder characterized by mistrust and suspicion of others.

Schizotypal personality disorder: A disorder characterized by extreme superstitions and other strange patterns of thinking.

Schizoid personality disorder: A disorder characterized by emotional detachment and poor social skills.

Cluster B: Personality disorders characterized by dramatic or erratic behavior.

Antisocial personality disorder: A disorder characterized by extreme disregard for others and a lack of remorse.

Borderline personality disorder: A disorder characterized by unstable mood, disturbed identity, and fear of abandonment.

Histrionic personality disorder: A disorder characterized by extreme extraversion and attention-seeking behavior.

Narcissistic personality disorder: A disorder characterized by self-entitlement, self-importance, and vulnerable self-esteem.

Cluster C: Personality disorders characterized by anxious or fearful behavior.

Avoidant personality disorder: A disorder characterized by extreme shyness and intense fear of rejection.

Dependent personality disorder: A disorder characterized by excessive dependence and self-doubt.

Obsessive-compulsive personality disorder (OCPD): A disorder characterized by stubbornness and perfectionist tendencies.

Psychotic disorders: Disorders characterized by positive and negative psychotic symptoms.

Positive symptoms: Additions to normal behavior, including delusions and hallucinations.

Negative symptoms: Subtractions from normal behavior, including avolition and disturbed affect.

Schizophrenia: A disorder characterized by a break with reality and symptoms such as delusions, hallucinations, disorganized speech, catatonic behavior, and negative symptoms.

Neurodevelopmental disorders: Disorders characterized by developmental impairments that may be specific or general.

Attention deficit hyperactivity disorder (ADHD): A disorder characterized by inattention, disorganization, and impulsivity.

Autism spectrum disorder: A disorder characterized by restricted behaviors, communication deficits, and social impairment.

Specific learning disorder: A disorder characterized by a developmental deficiency in a particular area.

Intellectual disability/intellectual developmental disorder: A disorder characterized by general deficiencies in higher cognitive functions.

Trauma- and stressor-related disorders: Disorders characterized by stress reactions that result from a traumatic incident.

Posttraumatic stress disorder (PTSD): A disorder characterized by disturbing memories, flashbacks, or nightmares of a traumatic incident.

Neurocognitive disorders: Disorders characterized by cognitive decline and loss of independence.

Alzheimer's disease: A disease characterized by progressive memory loss, disorientation, and neurological degeneration.

Parkinson's disease: A disease characterized by tremors, slurred speech, movement difficulties, and dementia.

Diagnostic Labels

Diagnostic labels: The categories of disorders recognized by the DSM, used to diagnose patients.

Rosenhan experiment: Experiment underscoring the way that diagnostic labels can bias people's perceptions of patients; hospital staff did not recognize that pseudopatients with a diagnosis of mental illness were in fact healthy.

Psychology and the Law

Confidentiality: The obligation not to disclose particular kinds of information, including mental health information, except in limited cases. Mandated in the U.S. by HIPAA.

Insanity: Immunity from legal responsibility due to an inability to tell the difference between right and wrong; a legal category, not a psychiatric one.

What Is Psychological Treatment?

Mental health professionals: Psychologists, medical doctors and nurses, social workers, and licensed counselors who provide psychological treatment.

11

Psychotherapy: An ongoing relationship between a patient and a therapist, in which the two discuss the patient's experiences and symptoms.

Pharmacological treatment: When a mental health professional prescribes a drug for a patient to alleviate psychological distress.

Treatment Orientations and Formats

Theoretical orientation: A therapist's belief system about the cause and nature of psychological distress and the appropriate treatment, which influences the therapist's choice of techniques and treatment goals.

Dream interpretation: A psychodynamic therapy technique that analyzes the meaning of symbols from dreams to help access the unconscious.

Free association: A psychodynamic therapy technique in which the patient is instructed to "think out loud" to help access the unconscious.

Transference: A term from psychodynamic therapy to describe when feelings directed at one person become redirected to another person, often the therapist.

Self-actualization: A term from humanistic therapy that refers to an individual's ability to live up to his or her full human potential.

Client-centered therapy: The most popular humanistic therapy, which views patients as "clients" and focuses on authenticity and healthy self-concept; created by Carl Rogers.

Unconditional positive regard: A client-centered technique in which the therapist communicates positive feelings and acceptance to the client, regardless of what the client says or does.

Active listening: A client-centered technique in which the therapist verbally and non-verbally communicates interest in what the client is saying in order to encourage openness.

Gestalt therapy: A humanistic therapy that maintains that psychological distress occurs when patients focus on what could be, rather than on the present moment; developed by Fritz Perls.

Existential therapy: A humanistic therapy based on the theory that psychological distress occurs when life lacks meaning; popularized by Irving Yalom.

Learned helplessness: A phenomenon described by behaviorists in which an individual, frustrated by failed attempts to escape an adverse situation, gives up all efforts to escape it.

Applied behavioral analysis (ABA): A behavioral therapy technique used to identify factors in the environment that are reinforcing or punishing certain behaviors.

Token economies: A technique used in behavioral therapy to reinforce positive behaviors with tokens, which can be exchanged for other rewards.

Systematic desensitization: A behavioral therapy used to treat phobias by gradually associating feared stimuli with relaxing stimuli; created by Joseph Wolpe.

Aversion therapy: A behavioral therapy used to decrease the frequency of a habitual behavior by pairing it with an aversive stimulus.

Rational-emotive behavior therapy: A cognitive therapy that focuses on the rational analysis of thought; created by Albert Ellis.

Cognitive distortions: Automatic and irrational perceptions of the world that contribute to feelings of anxiety or depression.

Core belief: A deeply held belief that guides an individual's thoughts.

Thought log: A type of homework in cognitive therapy in which the patient writes down his or her automatic thoughts throughout the day.

Socratic questioning: A cognitive therapy technique that helps patients identify cognitive distortions and core beliefs by asking critical questions.

Cognitive restructuring: A cognitive therapy technique that requires patients to challenge irrational beliefs and replace them with more realistic ones.

Cognitive behavioral therapy (CBT): A popular evidence based treatment that combines both cognitive and behavioral techniques to identify solutions for patients' concerns; created by Aaron Beck.

Third wave cognitive therapies: A collection of recent cognitive therapies that focus on values and techniques like mindfulness to manage psychological distress.

Mindfulness: Strategies to cultivate a state of conscious awareness, often used in third wave cognitive therapies.

Psychopharmacology: The most common biomedical treatment, which uses psychotropic drugs to treat mental illness.

Tricyclic antidepressants (TCAs): One of the earliest psychotropic medications used to treat depression.

Selective serotonin reuptake inhibitors (SSRIs): A class of psychotropic medications, such as Prozac, used to treat depression and other mood disorders.

Benzodiazepines: Common psychotropic medications used to treat anxiety.

Lithium carbonate: A psychotropic medication used to treat bipolar disorders; also called lithium salts or lithium.

Atypical anti-psychotics: A class of psychotropic medications used to treat schizophrenia.

Electroconvulsive therapy (ECT): A biomedical treatment for depression that delivers small electric currents to the brain to deliberately cause a seizure.

Deep brain stimulation: An invasive biomedical treatment that delivers electric shocks to the brain directly through an implanted electrode; sometimes used for severe OCD.

Psychosurgery: A medical technique in which part of the brain is removed or deliberately damaged.

Eclectic therapy: A common type of therapy in which the therapist intentionally draws from a variety of treatment approaches.

Transtheoretical model: An integrative approach to behavior change in therapy that focuses on patients' readiness to make changes in their lives; it can be applied to any psychotherapy treatment.

Individual psychotherapy: A format in which a patient and mental health professional meet one-on-one.

Group psychotherapy: A format in which multiple patients meet with one or two therapists at the same time.

Couples therapy: A format in in which a therapist provides psychological treatment to romantic partners.

Family psychotherapy: A format in which a therapist provides psychological treatment to a family unit.

Systemic therapy: A commonly used treatment approach in couples and family therapy that examines how people are influenced by complex family systems.

How Effective Is Treatment?

Meta-analysis study: A type of study that analyzes the results of many studies at once.

Evidence-based practice (EBP): The effective integration of three components in psychotherapy: the patient's specific context, including culture, preferences, and characteristics; the therapist's clinical expertise; and the best research evidence available.

Evidence-based treatments (EBTs): Treatments that research has demonstrated are effective at reducing psychological distress.

Randomized control trial: An experiment that randomly assigns participants to receive either a psychological treatment or a placebo treatment; used to determine what is an EBT.

Common factors theory: A theory challenging the assumption that a specific psychotherapy approach is superior to another, instead focusing on what is effective across different therapies.

Therapy and Culture

Culture: A collection of experiences, language, values, attitudes, and beliefs that are shared by a group in a specific place and time.

Worldview: Based in culture, this is how an individual interprets and understands the world.

Culture-bound syndrome: A psychological disorder that occurs only in a specific cultural context.

Eurocentric: A term that describes approaches derived from a European worldview and value system.

Multiculturalism: The integration, acceptance, and embrace of cultural differences.

Multicultural competence: A therapist's ability to work with patients from different cultures; includes awareness, knowledge of cultural context, and the use of culturally sensitive treatments.

Social justice therapy: A multiculturally sensitive therapy that recognizes many patients face structural and institutional challenges that influence their psychological well being.

Afrocentric therapy: A multiculturally sensitive therapy that is rooted in African, rather than Eurocentric, values.

Prevention Strategies

Prevention: An attempt to reduce the incidence of psychological disorders by addressing the causes that give rise to them.

Competence: The ability to navigate appropriate social, emotional, cognitive, and behavioral tasks at different developmental stages.

Resilience: The ability to thrive, develop, and succeed despite adverse circumstances, or the ability to turn a high-risk situation into a positive outcome.

Important Contributors

Aaron T. Beck: Created the popular cognitive behavioral therapy (CBT).

Mary Cover-Jones: One of the first people to apply classical conditioning techniques to psychological treatment; successfully treated a child's rabbit phobia by pairing rabbits with a positive stimulus.

Dorthea Dix: An advocate for the creation of state institutions to treat people with mental illness who helped bring moral treatment, a more humane approach to psychological treatment, to the United States.

Albert Ellis: An early pioneer of cognitive therapy who created rational-emotive behavioral therapy.

Sigmund Freud: The founder of psychoanalytic therapy, the first "talking cure."

Fritz Perls: Creator of Gestalt therapy, a type of humanistic therapy.

Frederick Phillips: Creator of Afrocentric therapy, a multiculturally sensitive psychotherapy.

Carl Rogers: Creator of client-centered therapy, the most popular humanistic psychotherapy.

B.F. Skinner: A behaviorist who believed that application of learning principles could help patients improve their functioning.

Joseph Wolpe: Created systematic desensitization, now used to treat phobias.

Irving Yalom: Popularized existential therapy, a humanistic psychotherapy.

TEST WHAT YOU LEARNED

Part A: Quiz

1. Client-centered therapy was originally developed by

   (A) Joseph Wolpe

   (B) Carl Rogers

   (C) Sigmund Freud

   (D) Wilhelm Wundt

   (E) B.F. Skinner

2. Which of the following perspectives maintains that psychological disorders can vary based on time and place and are caused by a variety of interpersonal factors?

   (A) Biological model

   (B) Psychoanalytic model

   (C) Sociocultural model

   (D) Behavioral model

   (E) Medical model

3. Fred has no regard for the well being of others and consistently violates others' rights with no remorse. Fred would most likely be diagnosed with

   (A) dissociative identity disorder

   (B) dissociative amnesia

   (C) major depressive disorder

   (D) antisocial personality disorder

   (E) obsessive-compulsive personality disorder

4. What is the gold standard for determining whether a treatment is evidence-based?

   (A) A randomized controlled trial

   (B) Multicultural competence

   (C) Psychopharmacology

   (D) Clinical expertise

   (E) A patient's preferences

5. Which of the following is NOT an advantage of the use of diagnostic labels?

   (A) Diagnoses are more consistent between clinicians.

   (B) Treatments can be targeted to particular disorders.

   (C) Disorders are more easily operationalized in research.

   (D) Patients can be empowered by naming their problems.

   (E) A label is a useful lens for understanding all patient behavior.

6. Which of the following would be considered a negative symptom in a diagnosis of schizophrenia?

   (A) Delusions

   (B) Disorganized speech

   (C) Avolition

   (D) Catatonia

   (E) Hallucinations

11

7. Which of the following symptoms is NOT associated with bulimia nervosa?

    (A) Vomiting after meals

    (B) Excessive use of laxatives

    (C) Binge eating

    (D) Obsession with weight loss

    (E) Low body mass index

8. A school program is designed to enhance resilience in children. Which of the following is most likely to be a goal of the program?

    (A) Increasing intelligence

    (B) Decreasing substance use

    (C) Building self-esteem

    (D) Improving math scores

    (E) Stopping bullying

9. Which of the following techniques is NOT used by psychodynamic approaches?

    (A) Dream interpretation

    (B) Transference

    (C) Cognitive restructuring

    (D) Free association

    (E) Resolving unconscious conflicts

10. Which of the following conceptions of the causes of abnormal behavior is neither psychogenic nor somatogenic?

    (A) Demonic possession

    (B) Humoral imbalance

    (C) Unconscious conflict

    (D) Physiological disease

    (E) Unsatisfied needs

11

Part B: Key Terms

This key terms list is the same as the list in the Test What You Already Know section earlier in this chapter. Based on what you have now learned, again ask yourself the following questions:

- Can I describe this key term?

- Can I discuss this key term in relation to other psychological ideas and specific psychologists?

- Could I correctly answer a multiple-choice question about this key term?

- Could I correctly answer a free-response question about this key term?

Check off the key terms if you can answer "yes" to at least three of these questions.

What Are Psychological Disorders?

- ☐ Abnormal behavior
- ☐ Psychoanalytic model
- ☐ Biological model
- ☐ Deinstitutionalization
- ☐ Humanistic model
- ☐ Sociocultural model
- ☐ Medical model
- ☐ Cognitive model
- ☐ Behavioral model

Diagnostic Categories

- ☐ *Diagnostic and Statistical Manual of Mental Disorders* (DSM)
- ☐ Anxiety disorders
- ☐ Fear
- ☐ Anxiety
- ☐ Generalized anxiety disorder
- ☐ Specific phobias
- ☐ Panic disorder
- ☐ Panic attacks
- ☐ Social anxiety disorder
- ☐ Dissociative disorders
- ☐ Depersonalization/ derealization disorder
- ☐ Dissociative amnesia
- ☐ Dissociative fugue

- ☐ Dissociative identity disorder (DID)
- ☐ Feeding and eating disorders
- ☐ Anorexia nervosa
- ☐ Bulimia nervosa
- ☐ Binge eating disorder
- ☐ Somatic symptom and related disorders
- ☐ Somatic symptom disorder
- ☐ Conversion disorder
- ☐ Illness anxiety disorder
- ☐ Obsessive-compulsive and related disorders
- ☐ Obsessive-compulsive disorder (OCD)
- ☐ Obsessions

- ☐ Compulsions
- ☐ Body dysmorphic disorder
- ☐ Depressive disorders
- ☐ Major depressive disorder
- ☐ Dysthymia
- ☐ Seasonal affective disorder (SAD)
- ☐ Bright light therapy
- ☐ Bipolar and related disorders
- ☐ Depressive episodes
- ☐ Manic episodes
- ☐ Bipolar I disorder
- ☐ Bipolar II disorder
- ☐ Cyclothymic disorder
- ☐ Personality disorders
- ☐ Cluster A

- ☐ Paranoid personality disorder
- ☐ Schizotypal personality disorder
- ☐ Schizoid personality disorder
- ☐ Cluster B
- ☐ Antisocial personality disorder
- ☐ Borderline personality disorder
- ☐ Histrionic personality disorder
- ☐ Narcissistic personality disorder

- ☐ Cluster C
- ☐ Avoidant personality disorder
- ☐ Dependent personality disorder
- ☐ Obsessive-compulsive personality disorder (OCPD)
- ☐ Psychotic disorders
- ☐ Positive symptoms
- ☐ Negative symptoms
- ☐ Schizophrenia
- ☐ Neurodevelopmental disorders

- ☐ Attention deficit hyperactivity disorder (ADHD)
- ☐ Autism spectrum disorder
- ☐ Specific learning disorder
- ☐ Intellectual disability/ intellectual developmental disorder
- ☐ Trauma- and stressor- related disorders
- ☐ Posttraumatic stress disorder (PTSD)
- ☐ Neurocognitive disorders
- ☐ Alzheimer's disease
- ☐ Parkinson's disease

Diagnostic Labels

- ☐ Diagnostic labels
- ☐ Rosenhan experiment

Psychology and the Law

- ☐ Confidentiality
- ☐ Insanity

What Is Psychological Treatment?

- ☐ Mental health professionals
- ☐ Psychotherapy
- ☐ Pharmacological treatment

Treatment Orientations and Formats

- ☐ Theoretical orientation
- ☐ Dream interpretation
- ☐ Free association
- ☐ Transference
- ☐ Self-actualization
- ☐ Client-centered therapy
- ☐ Unconditional positive regard

- ☐ Active listening
- ☐ Gestalt therapy
- ☐ Existential therapy
- ☐ Learned helplessness
- ☐ Applied behavioral analysis (ABA)
- ☐ Token economies
- ☐ Systematic desensitization

- ☐ Aversion therapy
- ☐ Rational-emotive behavior therapy
- ☐ Cognitive distortions
- ☐ Core belief
- ☐ Thought log
- ☐ Socratic questioning
- ☐ Cognitive restructuring

11

- ☐ Cognitive behavioral therapy (CBT)
- ☐ Third wave cognitive therapies
- ☐ Mindfulness
- ☐ Psychopharmacology
- ☐ Tricyclic antidepressants (TCAs)

- ☐ Selective serotonin reuptake inhibitors (SSRIs)
- ☐ Benzodiazepines
- ☐ Lithium carbonate
- ☐ Atypical anti-psychotics
- ☐ Electroconvulsive therapy (ECT)
- ☐ Deep brain stimulation

- ☐ Psychosurgery
- ☐ Eclectic therapy
- ☐ Transtheoretical model
- ☐ Individual psychotherapy
- ☐ Group psychotherapy
- ☐ Couples psychotherapy
- ☐ Family psychotherapy
- ☐ Systemic therapy

How Effective Is Treatment?

- ☐ Meta-analysis studies
- ☐ Evidence-based practice (EBP)

- ☐ Evidence-based treatments (EBTs)

- ☐ Randomized controlled trial
- ☐ Common factors theory

Therapy and Culture

- ☐ Culture
- ☐ Worldview
- ☐ Culture-bound syndrome

- ☐ Eurocentric
- ☐ Multiculturalism
- ☐ Multicultural competence

- ☐ Social justice therapy
- ☐ Afrocentric therapy

Prevention Strategies

- ☐ Prevention

- ☐ Competence

- ☐ Resilience

Important Contributors

- ☐ Aaron T. Beck
- ☐ Mary Cover-Jones
- ☐ Dorothea Dix
- ☐ Albert Ellis

- ☐ Sigmund Freud
- ☐ Fritz Perls
- ☐ Frederick Phillips
- ☐ Carl Rogers

- ☐ B.F. Skinner
- ☐ Joseph Wolpe
- ☐ Irving Yalom

11

Next Steps

Step 1: Tally your correct answers from Part A and review the quiz explanations at the end of this chapter.

1.	B	6.	C
2.	C	7.	E
3.	D	8.	C
4.	A	9.	C
5.	E	10.	A

_____ out of 10 questions

Step 2: Count the number of key terms you checked off in Part B.

_____ out of 149 key terms

Step 3: Compare your Test What You Already Know results to these Test What You Learned results to see how exam-ready you are for this topic.

If you need to study this topic further:

- Read (or reread) the comprehensive review for this topic in Chapter 20.
- Go to kaptest.com to complete the online quiz questions for Clinical Psychology.
  - Haven't registered your book yet? Go to kaptest.com/moreonline to begin.

ANSWERS AND EXPLANATIONS

Test What You Already Know

1. A

Narcissistic personality disorder is characterized by feelings of entitlement, delusions about one's success and importance, a need for admiration, and vulnerable self-esteem. This describes Dan's behavior perfectly, so **(A)** is correct. (B) is incorrect because antisocial personality disorder involves extreme disregard for others and violation of their rights. (C) is incorrect because dependent personality disorder involves extreme dependence on another individual and self-doubt. (D) is incorrect because paranoid personality disorder involves mistrust and suspicion of other people. (E) is incorrect because borderline personality disorder involves unstable behavior and a fear of abandonment.

2. C

Systematic desensitization, in which patients are gradually exposed to their fears in a controlled way, is the type of behavioral therapy most often utilized with success for treating phobic disorders. **(C)** is correct. (A), (B), and (E) are incorrect because psychoanalytic, drug, and client-centered therapy are not commonly used to treat phobias. Cognitive restructuring is a cognitive therapy technique and is not commonly used to treat phobias either, making (D) incorrect.

3. C

Breaches of confidentiality are only justified in rare circumstances, such as when a patient credibly threatens to harm him- or herself or other people—making (A), (B), and (E) incorrect—or when a patient is attempting an insanity plea and therapists are called as expert witnesses, as in (D). **(C)** is correct because even groundbreaking research does not justify breaches of confidentiality.

4. B

Racism and the use of Eurocentric treatments, which adopt attitudes and assumptions traditionally associated with predominantly white European and North American cultures, contribute to early termination rates for non-white patients. **(B)** is thus correct. (A) refers to a therapist's ability to work with different types of people, which should actually reduce early termination rates in these

patients. (C) is treatment of mental disorders with medication, which has not been shown to deter these patients from continuing treatment. (D) and (E) are techniques of client-centered therapy, which also has no known impact on the willingness of these patients to continue treatment.

5. B

A conversion disorder involves the conversion of psychological stress into physiological symptoms, such as the impairments to movement that Ricardo is experiencing, which may be brought about by his stress about the big race. **(B)** is correct. (A) is incorrect because schizophrenia is a psychotic disorder characterized by positive and negative symptoms. (C) is incorrect because dysthymia is a less extreme form of depression. (D) is incorrect because acrophobia is an irrational fear of heights. (E) is incorrect because seasonal affective disorder is a depressive disorder with a seasonal pattern.

6. C

The Rosenhan study is best known for revealing biases against patients diagnosed with psychological conditions, calling into question the value of diagnostic labels. **(C)** is correct. (A) is incorrect because the Milgram experiment investigated obedience to authority. (B) is incorrect because the Stanford prison experiment studied the effects of social roles on behavior. (D) is incorrect because the Little Albert experiment investigated classical conditioning. (E) is incorrect because the Bobo doll experiment investigated observational learning.

7. E

A panic attack involves an acute onset of intense anxiety and a number of physiological symptoms, such as hyperventilation, heart palpitations, and shaking. Because this accurately describes Jolene's symptoms, **(E)** is correct. (A) is incorrect because a manic episode is a period of heightened mood and activity. (B) is incorrect because a depressive episode is a period of diminished mood and desire. (C) is incorrect because a psychotic episode involves a break with reality and symptoms associated with schizophrenia. (D) is incorrect because a heart attack is a physiological disorder caused by insufficient blood flow to cardiac muscles.

8. C

Client-centered therapy, developed by Carl Rogers, includes among its techniques unconditional positive regard, in which the therapist responds to the client with a consistent attitude of acceptance and warmth, regardless of what the client says. **(C)** is correct. (A) and (B) are incorrect because dream interpretation and free association are techniques used in psychoanalysis. (D) and (E) are incorrect because punishment and positive reinforcement are aspects of operant conditioning that might be used in behavioral therapy.

9. D

The *Diagnostic and Statistical Manual of Mental Disorders*, fifth edition (DSM-5) was created by the American Psychiatric Association to provide criteria for diagnosing psychological disorders. **(D)** is thus correct. The other choices provide worthy objectives, but not ones that the DSM is well suited to accomplish.

10. D

Evidence-based practice involves the integration of the patient's context, (A), including the patient's culture, (B), preferences, and characteristics, along with the therapist's clinical expertise, (C), and the best research evidence available, (E). The therapist's preferences, including his or her favorite type of therapy, are not included, making **(D)** correct.

Test What You Learned

1. B

Carl Rogers developed client-centered therapy, a type of humanistic therapy. **(B)** is thus correct. (A) was the creator of systematic desensitization, (C) was the founder of psychoanalysis, (D) was the first experimental psychologist, and (E) influenced the development of behaviorism and behavioral therapy.

2. C

The sociocultural model maintains that disorders are specific to particular cultures and that a wide array of social forces contribute to the development of disorders. **(C)** is thus correct. (A) attributes psychological disorders to neurochemical imbalances. (B) suggests that disorders emerge from unconscious mental processes. (D) sees abnormal behavior as the product of learning. (E) treats psychological disorders as diseases.

3. D

Antisocial personality disorder is characterized by disregard for others and a lack of remorse; **(D)** is correct. (A) involves the presence of multiple distinct personalities. (B) involves significant gaps in memory. (C) involves diminished mood and anhedonia. (E) involves stubbornness and perfectionism.

4. A

Randomized controlled trials are used to identify which treatments provide positive outcomes compared to a placebo. Treatments that show significantly improved outcomes compared to a placebo are considered evidence-based treatments. **(A)** is thus correct. (B) is the ability to work successfully with diverse patients. (C) is a type of psychological treatment. (D) and (E) are two components of evidence-based practice, but they are not used to determine what counts as evidence-based treatment.

5. E

The Rosenhan experiment revealed the dangers of interpreting behaviors in light of a diagnostic label. Consequently, attempting to understand all of a patient's behaviors by recourse to his or her diagnostic label would do a serious disservice to that patient. Thus, **(E)** is not an advantage of diagnostic labels, making it correct. The other choices do present advantages.

6. C

Positive symptoms of schizophrenia include delusions, (A), disorganized speech, (B), catatonia, (D), and hallucinations, (E). Negative symptoms include decreased motivation, otherwise known as avolition, and disturbed affect. **(C)** is correct.

7. E

Bulimia nervosa is characterized by binge eating, purging through vomiting or the use of laxatives, an obsession with weight loss, and a normal body mass index. Thus, (A), (B), (C), and (D) are incorrect. A low body mass index is actually associated with the eating disorder anorexia nervosa. **(E)** is correct.

8. C

Resilience refers to the ability to thrive, develop, and succeed despite adverse circumstances. Self-esteem, self-reliance, self-reflection, problem-solving abilities, and social skills are considered to be characteristic of resilience. **(C)** is thus correct. None of the other choices directly involve building resilience.

9. C

Psychodynamic approaches use techniques such as dream interpretation, transference, free association, and the resolution of unconscious conflicts to treat psychological disorders, making (A), (B), (D), and (E) incorrect. **(C)** is correct because cognitive restructuring is a technique used in cognitive therapy to challenge faulty, disempowering beliefs and replace them with more realistic, empowering ones.

10. A

Somatogenic perspectives maintain that abnormal behaviors have physiological causes, such as a disease (as in the medical model) or an imbalance in the four humors (as in Hippocrates' view). (B) and (D) are incorrect. Psychogenic perspectives maintain that abnormal behaviors have psychological causes, such as unconscious conflicts (as in the psychoanalytic model) or unsatisfied needs (as in the humanistic model). (C) and (E) are incorrect. Demonic possession, in contrast, assumes an external supernatural force is responsible for abnormal behavior, so it is neither somatogenic nor psychogenic. **(A)** is correct.

CHAPTER 12

Social Psychology

LEARNING OBJECTIVES

After studying this chapter, you will be able to:

- Describe attitude formation and change

- Explain motives through the use of attribution theory

- Discuss factors contributing to attraction, altruism, and aggression

- Anticipate the effect of others' presence on individuals' behavior

- Describe individuals' responses to others' expectations

- Predict ways in which behavior can affect a self-fulfilling prophecy

- Summarize specific types of group behavior in terms of structure and function

- Describe the influence of gender, race, and ethnicity on self-concept and interpersonal relations

- List factors tending to create stereotypes, prejudice, and discrimination among members of groups

- Recognize important contributors to social psychology

TEST WHAT YOU ALREADY KNOW

Part A: Quiz

1. Which of the following is an example of the "foot-in-the-door" technique?

    (A) You buy a car because your brother does.

    (B) You wear a shirt because your friend bought it for you.

    (C) You face the front of the elevator because everyone else is facing front.

    (D) You buy expensive perfume because the salesperson gives you a small gift.

    (E) You stand while everyone else is saying the Pledge of Allegiance.

2. The fact that people are not likely to help someone if they are in a large group is called

    (A) the foot-in-the-door technique

    (B) the bystander effect

    (C) social facilitation

    (D) the door-in-the-face technique

    (E) groupthink

3. Social loafing typically occurs when

    (A) one is alone

    (B) one is in a small group

    (C) one is in a large group

    (D) a project is past its deadline

    (E) members of a crowd fail to help someone

4. When someone consistently and automatically assumes that a person behaved the way he did because of internal causes, this is called

    (A) the fundamental attribution error

    (B) the bystander effect

    (C) self-serving bias

    (D) stereotyping

    (E) a self-fulfilling prophecy

5. The results of Milgram's famous experiment on obedience suggested that participants

    (A) were obedient because they were men

    (B) were obedient because of the situation

    (C) possessed sadistic tendencies

    (D) always did what they thought was right

    (E) never listened to authority figures

6. Which of the following provides the best example of conformity?

    (A) Your friend says, "Let's go to the mall," and you do.

    (B) You stop at a stop sign.

    (C) You sing the national anthem because everyone else is singing.

    (D) You arrive home when you are told to do so by your parents.

    (E) You lend a classmate money when asked.

12

7. Which of the following describes the tendency for people to perform certain tasks better when in front of an audience?

   (A) Social loafing

   (B) Groupthink

   (C) Conformity

   (D) Obedience

   (E) Social facilitation

8. The tendency for someone to commit aggressive acts while in a group because of a loss of identity is called

   (A) groupthink

   (B) social loafing

   (C) deindividuation

   (D) obedience

   (E) social facilitation

9. Being convinced by a logical argument is an example of the

   (A) central route to persuasion

   (B) peripheral route to persuasion

   (C) door-in-the-face technique

   (D) foot-in-the-door technique

   (E) mere-exposure effect

10. Kathleen's teacher believes she does not care about chemistry because Kathleen always fails to turn in her chemistry assignments. According to Harold Kelley, what kind of cue is Kathleen's teacher using to make this attribution?

    (A) Consensus

    (B) Distinctiveness

    (C) Consistency

    (D) Situational

    (E) Dispositional

12

Part B: Key Terms

The following is a list of the major ideas and people for the AP Psychology topic of Social Psychology. You will likely see many of these on the AP Psychology exam.

For each key term, ask yourself the following questions:

- Can I describe this key term?
- Can I discuss this key term in relation to other psychological ideas and specific psychologists?
- Could I correctly answer a multiple-choice question about this key term?
- Could I correctly answer a free-response question about this key term?

Check off the key terms if you can answer "yes" to at least three of these questions.

Intrapersonal Social Phenomena

- ☐ Attitudes
- ☐ Central route to persuasion
- ☐ Peripheral route to persuasion
- ☐ Mere-exposure effect
- ☐ Foot-in-the-door technique
- ☐ Door-in-the-face technique
- ☐ Cognitive dissonance
- ☐ Attribution theory
- ☐ Dispositional attribution

- ☐ Situational attribution
- ☐ Stable attribution
- ☐ Unstable attribution
- ☐ Fundamental attribution error
- ☐ Self-serving bias
- ☐ Just-world hypothesis
- ☐ Attraction
- ☐ Physical attractiveness
- ☐ Matching hypothesis
- ☐ Proximity

- ☐ Similarity
- ☐ Reciprocal liking
- ☐ Altruism
- ☐ Kin selection
- ☐ Reciprocity
- ☐ Sexual selection
- ☐ Aggression
- ☐ Instrumental aggression
- ☐ Hostile aggression
- ☐ Frustration-aggression model

Group Psychology

- ☐ Group
- ☐ Norms
- ☐ Roles
- ☐ Relations
- ☐ Social facilitation

- ☐ Kitty Genovese
- ☐ Bystander effect
- ☐ Diffusion of responsibility
- ☐ Social loafing
- ☐ Groupthink

- ☐ Conformity
- ☐ Asch conformity experiment
- ☐ Obedience
- ☐ Compliance

☐ Authority

☐ Milgram experiment

☐ Self-fulfilling prophecy

☐ Pygmalion effect

☐ Deindividuation

☐ Stanford prison experiment

☐ Group polarization

☐ Social trap

Society and Diversity

☐ Social and cultural categories

☐ Self-concept

☐ Gender identity

☐ Sexual orientation

☐ Ethnic identity

☐ In-group

☐ Out-group

☐ Stereotypes

☐ Prejudice

☐ Discrimination

☐ Racism

☐ Sexism

☐ Ethnocentrism

☐ Stereotype threat

☐ Individual discrimination

☐ Institutional discrimination

☐ Superordinate goals

☐ Robbers Cave experiment

Important Contributors

☐ Solomon Asch

☐ Albert Bandura

☐ Leon Festinger

☐ Irving Janis

☐ Harold Kelley

☐ Stanley Milgram

☐ Muzafer Sherif

☐ Philip Zimbardo

Next Steps

Step 1: Tally your correct answers from Part A and review the quiz explanations at the end of this chapter.

1. D

2. B

3. C

4. A

5. B

6. C

7. E

8. C

9. A

10. C

_____ out of 10 questions

Step 2: Count the number of key terms you checked off in Part B.

_____ out of 77 key terms

Step 3: Read the Rapid Review Key Takeaways in this chapter.

Step 4: Consult the table below and follow the instructions based on your performance.

If You Got . . .	Do This
80% or more of the Test What You Already Know assessment correct (8 or more questions from Part A and 62 or more key terms from Part B)	• Read definitions in this chapter for all the key terms you didn't check off. • Complete the Test What You Learned assessment in this chapter.
50% or less of the Test What You Already Know assessment correct (5 or fewer questions from Part A and 38 or fewer key terms from Part B)	• Read the comprehensive review for this topic in Chapter 21. ◦ If you are short on time, read only the High-Yield sections. • Read through all of the key term definitions in this chapter. • Complete the Test What You Learned assessment in this chapter.
Any other result	• Read the High-Yield sections of the comprehensive review of this topic in Chapter 21. • Read definitions in this chapter for all the key terms you didn't check off. • Complete the Test What You Learned assessment in this chapter.

RAPID REVIEW

Key Takeaways

1. Social phenomena can affect individuals in a variety of ways, including in the attitudes they form, the attributions they make, the people they find attractive, and the prosocial and anti-social behaviors they perform.

2. Being in a group influences members' behavior in a variety of ways that are caused by the presence of other group members, expectations within the group, and the tendency for groups to be more extreme than their individual members.

3. Social and cultural categories such as gender, race, and ethnicity play important psychological roles, both for individuals and groups.

4. Human beings often distinguish between in-groups and out-groups, which can lead to the development of stereotypes, prejudice, and discrimination. One technique for counteracting these is the adoption of superordinate goals.

Key Terms: Definitions

Intrapersonal Social Phenomena

Attitudes: Beliefs and feelings that predispose people to respond in particular ways to situations and other people.

Central route to persuasion: A method of persuasion in which you are convinced by the content of the message.

Peripheral route to persuasion: A method of persuasion in which you are convinced by something other than the message's content.

Mere-exposure effect: The tendency to like new stimuli more when you encounter them more frequently.

Foot-in-the-door technique: A persuasive technique that begins with a small request to encourage compliance with a larger request.

Door-in-the-face technique: A persuasive technique that begins with an outrageous request in order to increase the likelihood that a second, more reasonable request is granted.

Cognitive dissonance: An uncomfortable state of mind arising when you recognize inconsistencies in your beliefs and/or behaviors.

Attribution theory: A theory that describes how people explain their own and others' behavior.

Dispositional attribution: A type of attribution in which you assign responsibility for an event or action to the person involved.

Situational attribution: A type of attribution in which you assign responsibility for an event or action to the circumstances of the situation.

Stable attribution: An attribution in which you believe a cause to be consistent and relatively constant over time.

Unstable attribution: An attribution that credits a one-time source as the cause of an event.

Fundamental attribution error: The tendency to make dispositional attributions instead of situational attributions for other people's behavior.

12

Self-serving bias: The tendency to make dispositional attributions about your successes and situational attributions about your failures.

Just-world hypothesis: The belief that good things happen to good people and bad things happen to bad people.

Attraction: The ways in which you take interest in and feel positively towards others (romantically or platonically).

Physical attractiveness: The possession of outward physiological characteristics deemed to be appealing.

Matching hypothesis: The tendency for people to pick partners who are roughly equal in level of attractiveness to themselves.

Proximity: The tendency to like people geographically close to you.

Similarity: The tendency to be attracted to people who share characteristics with you.

Reciprocal liking: The tendency to like people who like you.

Altruism: Prosocial behaviors that benefit other people at a cost to yourself.

Kin selection: An evolutionary explanation for altruism proposing that people are altruistic to family members to ensure the continuation of their genes.

Reciprocity: The tendency to help people who help you; a theory that may explain altruistic behavior towards non-family members.

Sexual selection: The tendency for genes that increase reproductive fitness to perpetuate. Altruism may be sexually selected because people find kindness attractive.

Aggression: Any type of behavior, physical or verbal, that is intended to harm or destroy.

Instrumental aggression: "Cold" aggressive behaviors that are carried out to attain a certain goal.

Hostile aggression: "Hot" aggressive behaviors that aim to inflict pain or harm.

Frustration-aggression model: Proposes that, when a desired goal is unmet, a person becomes frustrated, which can lead to aggressive behaviors.

Group Psychology

Group: Two or more people who interact in some way. Members of groups may share a common worldview, purpose, or identity, or simply a common location.

Norms: Expectations about how group members behave.

Roles: Specific positions within a group governed by particular norms, including privileges or responsibilities.

Relations: Specific patterns of interactions between group members.

Social facilitation: The tendency for people to perform simple tasks and tasks they've extensively practiced better in front of an audience.

Kitty Genovese: A young woman who was brutally murdered outside of her New York City apartment in 1964. Due to inaccurate initial reports, her murder is used as an example of the bystander effect.

Bystander effect: The tendency not to intervene while in a crowd, related to diffusion of responsibility.

Diffusion of responsibility: Tendency for members of a crowd to assume less responsibility for taking action, due to the assumption that others will do something.

Social loafing: Tendency for some members of a group with a common goal to avoid doing their fair share of work to accomplish the goal.

12

Groupthink: Named by Irving Janis, the tendency of particular groups to make poor decisions as a result of members' desire to maintain harmony.

Conformity: Tendency for people to follow implicit social norms and mimic the attitudes or behaviors of a group's majority.

Asch conformity experiment: A famous study conducted by Solomon Asch in which participants would generally conform with the group, even when group members gave obviously wrong answers.

Obedience: When individuals follow the explicit directives of an authority figure.

Compliance: When individuals follow explicit requests from peers.

Authority: An individual in a position of social power.

Milgram experiment: Experiment by Stanley Milgram in which participants demonstrated obedience to authority, administering dangerous shocks (or so they thought) when told to do so by researchers.

Self-fulfilling prophecy: A set of expectations about a social situation that causes that situation to come into being.

Pygmalion effect: Robert Rosenthal described this type of self-fulfilling prophecy in which higher expectations lead to improved educational performance.

Deindividuation: The loss of self-identity within a group, often accompanied by uncharacteristic behavior.

Stanford prison experiment: Experiment conducted by Philip Zimbardo in which deindividuation of participants roleplaying as prison guards led to uncharacteristic aggression.

Group polarization: Tendency for groups to adopt more extreme positions and make more extreme decisions than the members of the group would individually.

Social trap: A situation in which individuals within a group act in their own short-term self-interest to the overall long-term detriment of the group.

Society and Diversity

Social and cultural categories: Categories like gender, race, and ethnicity that play important psychological roles for individuals and groups.

Self-concept: The collection of ways you define yourself.

Gender identity: A component of self-concept based on whether you identify as masculine, feminine, androgynous, gender-fluid, or undifferentiated.

Sexual orientation: A component of self-concept based on the type of people to whom you are romantically or sexually attracted; orientations include heterosexual, homosexual, bisexual, and asexual.

Ethnic identity: A component of self-concept based on belonging to one or more ethnic groups in which members share a common ancestry, cultural heritage, and language.

In-group: A group you belong to.

Out-group: A group you don't belong to.

Stereotypes: Cognitive beliefs about characteristics that define a group, typically based on limited and superficial information.

Prejudice: A negative emotional response toward a particular group, often formed prior to extensive contact with the group.

Discrimination: Differential treatment of members of different groups.

12

Racism: Stereotyping, prejudice, or discrimination directed against members of marginalized racial or ethnic groups.

Sexism: Discrimination based on sex or gender, typically directed against women.

Ethnocentrism: Judging other cultures on the basis of the values of your own culture.

Stereotype threat: When a member of a stereotyped group performs worse due to fear of confirming a stereotype about his or her group.

Individual discrimination: When one person discriminates against a group.

Institutional discrimination: Discriminatory treatment by social, cultural, or governmental organizations.

Superordinate goals: Shared objectives that require cooperation between groups to accomplish.

Robbers Cave experiment: An experiment conducted by Muzafer Sherif in which two groups of boys at a summer camp overcame prejudices against each other by focusing on superordinate goals.

Important Contributors

Solomon Asch: Known for his conformity experiments.

Albert Bandura: His Bobo doll experiment suggested that observational learning plays a key role in the development of aggression.

Leon Festinger: Introduced the concept of cognitive dissonance.

Irving Janis: Developed the theory of groupthink and coined the term.

Harold Kelley: Contributed to attribution theory by identifying three types of cues that influence attributions.

Stanley Milgram: Best known for his experiments investigating obedience, involving the seeming administration of electric shocks.

Muzafer Sherif: Known for the Robbers Cave experiment, which showed both how prejudices can be learned and counteracted.

Philip Zimbardo: Most famous for his Stanford prison experiment.

TEST WHAT YOU LEARNED

Part A: Quiz

1. Prosocial behavior that imposes costs on yourself but benefits others is

   (A) the bystander effect

   (B) altruism

   (C) social loafing

   (D) deindividuation

   (E) obedience

2. The attribution of our successes to internal causes and our failures to external causes is called

   (A) the fundamental attribution error

   (B) the just-world hypothesis

   (C) self-serving bias

   (D) groupthink

   (E) a self-fulfilling prophecy

3. The tendency to change behavior to fit that of a peer group is known as

   (A) reciprocity

   (B) obedience

   (C) the bystander effect

   (D) conformity

   (E) altruism

4. The act of doing something that you do not want to do simply because you are told to do so by someone more powerful is

   (A) conformity

   (B) obedience

   (C) social facilitation

   (D) compliance

   (E) persuasion

5. The fundamental attribution error occurs when someone attributes causes to

   (A) the environment

   (B) the person

   (C) the group

   (D) society

   (E) luck

6. In a classic study, it was demonstrated that children who were labeled as potential high achievers outdistanced those labeled as low achievers, even though there was no difference between the groups prior to the study. This is an example of

   (A) a self-fulfilling prophecy

   (B) the bystander effect

   (C) the fundamental attribution error

   (D) prejudice

   (E) self-serving bias

7. The tendency for groups to adopt more extreme positions and decisions than their members would individually is known as

   (A) deindividuation

   (B) group polarization

   (C) groupthink

   (D) social loafing

   (E) conformity

8. Suppose your friend agrees to help you with a homework assignment, and later you agree to give her a ride to the airport, even though you are very busy. This would be an example of

   (A) social loafing

   (B) deindividuation

   (C) obedience

   (D) conformity

   (E) reciprocity

9. The Robbers Cave experiment demonstrated that prejudice can be combated with

   (A) stereotypes

   (B) altruism

   (C) discrimination

   (D) superordinate goals

   (E) obedience

10. Research shows that many people are drawn to individuals who are roughly equal in attractiveness to themselves. This tendency is referred to as

   (A) proximity

   (B) similarity

   (C) reciprocal liking

   (D) the matching hypothesis

   (E) kin selection

Part B: Key Terms

This key terms list is the same as the list in the Test What You Already Know section earlier in this chapter. Based on what you have now learned, again ask yourself the following questions:

- Can I describe this key term?
- Can I discuss this key term in relation to other psychological ideas and specific psychologists?
- Could I correctly answer a multiple-choice question about this key term?
- Could I correctly answer a free-response question about this key term?

Check off the key terms if you can answer "yes" to at least three of these questions.

Intrapersonal Social Phenomena

☐ Attitudes

☐ Central route to persuasion

☐ Peripheral route to persuasion

☐ Mere-exposure effect

☐ Foot-in-the-door technique

☐ Door-in-the-face technique

☐ Cognitive dissonance

☐ Attribution theory

☐ Dispositional attribution

☐ Situational attribution

☐ Stable attribution

☐ Unstable attribution

☐ Fundamental attribution error

☐ Self-serving bias

☐ Just-world hypothesis

☐ Attraction

☐ Physical attractiveness

☐ Matching hypothesis

☐ Proximity

☐ Similarity

☐ Reciprocal liking

☐ Altruism

☐ Kin selection

☐ Reciprocity

☐ Sexual selection

☐ Aggression

☐ Instrumental aggression

☐ Hostile aggression

☐ Frustration-aggression model

Group Psychology

☐ Group

☐ Norms

☐ Roles

☐ Relations

☐ Social facilitation

☐ Kitty Genovese

☐ Bystander effect

☐ Diffusion of responsibility

☐ Social loafing

☐ Groupthink

☐ Conformity

☐ Asch conformity experiment

☐ Obedience

☐ Compliance

☐ Authority

☐ Milgram experiment

☐ Self-fulfilling prophecy

☐ Pygmalion effect

☐ Deindividuation

☐ Stanford prison experiment

☐ Group polarization

☐ Social trap

12

Society and Diversity

- ☐ Social and cultural categories
- ☐ Self-concept
- ☐ Gender identity
- ☐ Sexual orientation
- ☐ Ethnic identity
- ☐ In-group
- ☐ Out-group
- ☐ Stereotypes
- ☐ Prejudice
- ☐ Discrimination
- ☐ Racism
- ☐ Sexism
- ☐ Ethnocentrism
- ☐ Stereotype threat
- ☐ Individual discrimination
- ☐ Institutional discrimination
- ☐ Superordinate goals
- ☐ Robbers Cave experiment

Important Contributors

- ☐ Solomon Asch
- ☐ Albert Bandura
- ☐ Leon Festinger
- ☐ Irving Janis
- ☐ Harold Kelley
- ☐ Stanley Milgram
- ☐ Muzafer Sherif
- ☐ Philip Zimbardo

Next Steps

Step 1: Tally your correct answers from Part A and review the quiz explanations at the end of this chapter.

1. B	6. A
2. C	7. B
3. D	8. E
4. B	9. D
5. B	10. D

_____ out of 10 questions

Step 2: Count the number of key terms you checked off in Part B.

_____ out of 77 key terms

Step 3: Compare your Test What You Already Know results to these Test What You Learned results to see how exam-ready you are for this topic.

If you need to study this topic further:

- Read (or reread) the comprehensive review for this topic in Chapter 21.
- Go to kaptest.com to complete the online quiz questions for Social Psychology.
  - Haven't registered your book yet? Go to kaptest.com/moreonline to begin.

ANSWERS AND EXPLANATIONS

Test What You Already Know

1. D

According to the foot-in-the-door technique, you are more likely to comply with a larger request (buying perfume) when you have already complied with a smaller request (accepting a gift). **(D)** is correct. All of the other choices are examples of conformity.

2. B

According to the bystander effect, a person will be less likely to help when in a large crowd of people. **(B)** is thus correct. (A) and (D) are techniques for establishing compliance. (C) is the tendency for people to perform certain tasks better when in front of an audience. (E) is the tendency to make poor decisions in a cohesive group as a result of members trying to maintain harmony.

3. C

Social loafing is more likely to occur in larger groups. A person is likely to coast when there is less of a chance of being forced to take responsibility. **(C)** is correct, and (A) and (B) are incorrect. (D) is incorrect because members of a group are more likely to step up when a project is past its deadline because of heightened social pressure. (E) describes the bystander effect, a distinct phenomenon.

4. A

The fundamental attribution error is the tendency to favor dispositional attributions over situational attributions, especially when evaluating others. **(A)** is correct. (B) occurs when someone doesn't help because of membership in a large crowd, (C) occurs when we attribute our failures to external causes and our successes to internal causes, (D) is a cognitive bias against a group, and (E) occurs when people's behavior changes as a result of others' expectations.

5. B

The results of Milgram's study suggested that people were obedient due to the situation they were in, in which an apparent authority figure (a scientist in a lab coat) was telling them what to do. **(B)** is correct. (A) is incorrect because the results never suggested that only men were obedient. (C) is incorrect because sadism was not a characteristic Milgram observed in participants; many were distraught about potentially harming the confederate. (D) is incorrect because the results suggested some people would act in ways they may not have believed to be right when commanded by an authority. (E) is incorrect because many of the participants in the experiment obeyed.

6. C

Conformity is the tendency for people to follow social norms, such as engaging in the same activity that most others in the group are doing. Singing along when everyone else is singing, as in **(C)**, is one example of conformity. (A) and (E) are examples of compliance, submitting to the requests of peers. (B) and (D) are examples of obedience, submitting to the commands of authorities.

7. E

Social facilitation is the tendency for people to perform simple tasks and tasks they've extensively practiced better in front of an audience. **(E)** is thus correct. (A) is the tendency for people to avoid work in a large group due to the assumption that others will pick up the slack. (B), (C), and (D) are all examples of the influence of group expectations, not simply the influence of the presence of others.

8. C

Deindividuation refers to the loss of self-identity within a group, often accompanied by uncharacteristic behavior. **(C)** is correct. (A) is when a group makes poor decisions to preserve harmony, (B) is when members of a large group do less work, (D) is when people follow orders from authority figures, and (E) is when people perform some tasks better in front of an audience.

9. A

The central route to persuasion occurs when a person is persuaded on the basis of the content of a message, such as a logical argument that it contains. **(A)** is correct. (B) is persuasion on the basis of something other than the message. (C) and (D) are manipulative techniques that use preliminary requests to increase compliance. (E) is the tendency to like something just because you've encountered it frequently.

12

10. C

(C) is correct because consistency cues concern how an individual behaves in the same situation over time; in this case, Kathleen consistently fails to turn in chemistry assignments, leading her teacher to view an inherent lack of interest in the subject as responsible. According to Kelley, (A) is based on how other people behave and (B) is based on how an individual behaves in distinct situations. (D) and (E) are incorrect because situational and dispositional are types of attributions, not cues that lead to attributions.

Test What You Learned

1. B

Altruism is prosocial behavior that benefits others at your own expense. **(B)** is correct. The bystander effect, (A), refers to the tendency for people not to help in a crowd. Social loafing, (C), occurs when a member of a large group lets other people pick up the slack. Deindividuation, (D), occurs when people lose their sense of self-identity within a group. Obedience, (E), is submitting to commands from authorities.

2. C

Self-serving bias is the tendency to make dispositional attributions about our successes and situational attributions about our failures; **(C)** is correct. The fundamental attribution error, (A), occurs when we attribute other people's behavior to internal characteristics. The just-world hypothesis, (B), is the idea that good things happen to good people and bad things happen to bad people. Groupthink, (D), occurs when groups make poor decisions while trying to maintain harmony, and a self-fulfilling prophecy, (E), occurs when expectations of an outcome lead to that outcome.

3. D

Conformity is the tendency to mimic peers and follow other social norms. **(D)** is correct. (A) is incorrect because reciprocity refers to the tendency to help people who help us. (B) is incorrect because obedience is following commands from authority figures. (C) is incorrect because the bystander effect is the tendency not to help out in a crowd. (E) is incorrect because altruism is prosocial behavior that benefits others.

4. B

Obedience is the tendency to do something because an authority figure commands it; **(B)** is correct. (A) is incorrect because conformity is action in accordance with group norms. (C) is incorrect because social facilitation is the tendency to perform some tasks better in front of an audience. (D) is incorrect because compliance is agreeing to requests made by peers, not by people who are more powerful. (E) is incorrect because persuasion involves being convinced by the content or other characteristics of a message.

5. B

The fundamental attribution error is the tendency to make dispositional or personal attributions. **(B)** is correct. The other choices present external factors that would be considered situational attributions, not dispositional.

6. A

The study mentioned, conducted by Rosenthal, demonstrated the Pygmalion effect, the tendency for high expectations to lead to high performance, which is a type of self-fulfilling prophecy, **(A)**. (B) is incorrect because the bystander effect is the tendency to stand by and do nothing while in a crowd. (C) is incorrect because the fundamental attribution error is the tendency to make dispositional attributions about other people. (D) is incorrect because a prejudice is an irrational, negative emotional response to a group. (E) is incorrect because self-serving bias is the tendency to make dispositional attributions for our successes and situational attributions for our failures.

7. B

Group polarization, **(B)**, is the tendency for groups to be more extreme than their members, and to push members to adopt more extreme positions themselves. (A) is incorrect because deindividuation happens to an individual who loses his or her sense of self when in a group. (C) is incorrect because groupthink refers to the tendency of groups to make poor decisions in an effort to preserve cohesion. (D) is incorrect because social loafing is the tendency to slack off in large groups. (E) is incorrect because conformity is behavior in accordance with the norms of a group.

12

8. E

Reciprocity is the tendency to help other people who have helped (or will help) us. This describes the situation in the question stem, making **(E)** correct. (A) is the tendency to slack off in a group. (B) is the loss of self-identity in a group. (C) is following the orders of authorities. (D) is the act of following group norms.

9. D

In the Robbers Cave experiment, researchers were able to diminish prejudice between groups by having the groups cooperate on achieving common objectives known as superordinate goals. **(D)** is correct. (A) and (C) are incorrect because stereotypes and discrimination are complementary to prejudice and often accompany it.

(B) is incorrect because altruism is prosocial behavior done to benefit others; while it may help combat prejudice, it was not something demonstrated in the Robbers Cave experiment. (E) is incorrect because the researchers did not try to command members of the groups to be less prejudiced.

10. D

The matching hypothesis maintains that people tend to be attracted to others who roughly match them in attractiveness; **(D)** is correct. (A) refers to the tendency to pick partners who are nearby, (B) refers to the tendency to pick partners based on shared characteristics, (C) refers to the tendency to like people who like you, and (E) is an explanation for altruism.

PART 3

Comprehensive Review

CHAPTER 13

Scientific Foundations of Psychology

Psychology has two different but complementary foundations that support it. As a field of study, it is built upon the thinkers and perspectives that have shaped it historically; as a science, it is built upon the scientific method, the principles of good research design, and a variety of statistical techniques. In this chapter, we'll take a look at the way people thought about brain and behavior before modern psychology as well as the modern frameworks through which we view these ideas. We'll also discuss the ways we use research and experimentation to learn more about how humans and other animals think and act.

PRECURSORS TO PSYCHOLOGY

LEARNING OBJECTIVE

- Describe philosophical and physiological ideas leading to the foundation of psychology

Unlike philosophy, mathematics, chemistry, biology, and other disciplines that have been around for hundreds or even thousands of years, psychology is a relatively new field. In fact, the science of psychology is widely recognized as beginning in 1879 with the work of German medical doctor and sensation researcher Wilhelm Wundt. Wundt is generally regarded as "the father of psychology" because he set up the first psychology laboratory, which he founded at the University of Leipzig.

Ancient and Medieval Influences

Of course, the study of psychology didn't start from scratch in 1879. Throughout history, people have often posed psychological questions, asking how the mind works; why human beings think, feel, and act in the ways they do; and what makes individuals differ so much from one another. The roots of psychology can be traced back as early as Greek antiquity, to the era of Socrates, Plato, and Aristotle. Understanding these origins and psychology's subsequent historical development can help you to appreciate how psychology came to be the science that it is today.

The philosopher Socrates believed in the perfectibility of the soul as the key to happiness. Using what later came to be called "the Socratic method," Socrates would bombard prominent Athenian citizens (politicians, priests, poets, philosophers) with questions, urging them to examine their lives, their actions, and their beliefs, all for the sake of bettering their souls. Indeed, this kind of *logos* (Greek for "rational discourse") of the *psyche* (Greek for "soul") is precisely what the word "psychology" originally meant.

Ancient Greek thinkers after Socrates also played a role in psychology's history. For instance, Plato and Aristotle debated about the location where thinking occurs in the human body. While Plato believed that thoughts originated in the brain, Aristotle maintained that the heart was the source of mental processes. Though we now take it for granted that Plato was correct, it's important to note that Aristotle's view is not as far-fetched as it may seem. Indeed, the nervous system extends throughout the entire body, and people often experience strong emotional states as localized in parts outside of the brain, as recognized in expressions such as "being heartbroken" and "having butterflies in your stomach."

Even though he was wrong about the heart's role in mental processes, Aristotle did develop a number of ideas about psychology that remained highly influential for many centuries. His treatise *On the Soul* (sometimes known by its Latin title, *De Anima*) maintained that there were three levels of psyches or souls. The nutritive soul, possessed by all living things (even organisms as simple as plants), regulates nutrition, growth, and reproduction. The sensible soul is shared by all animals, including human beings, and enables perception and emotion. The rational soul, found only in humans, allows for higher cognitive processes like language use and reasoning. Thus, for Aristotle, understanding human psychology required appreciation of all three types of souls, because human beings are not merely rational, but also possess nutritive and sensible capacities shared with other organisms.

Long after the Greeks, other intellectual traditions made significant contributions to psychology's foundation. For instance, during the Islamic Golden Age, a prominent scholar by the name of Hasan Ibn al-Haytham conducted experiments on vision and composed a seven-volume treatise on optics. Although many believed at the time in the emission theory of vision, which held that the eyes send out rays of light in order to see, Ibn al-Haytham's extensive studies of the eye's structure and function revealed that sight actually depends upon light striking the eye from outside. His discovery is largely regarded as the first psychological conclusion based on systematic research, though it occurred several hundred years before Wundt founded his psychological laboratory.

Modern Influences

Early modern European philosophy also had an impact on psychology's development. French philosopher **René Descartes** tried to establish a new foundation for human knowledge by systematically doubting everything he could. After clearing away any belief that could be doubted, he arrived at what he regarded as a certain truth, often articulated as *cogito ergo sum* ("I think, therefore I am"). In other words, even if he was wrong about everything else, even if he didn't actually possess a physical body but was merely deceived into believing he had one, he could not be wrong about the fact that he existed as a thinking thing, a doubting thing, a mind. This distinction between the mind, about which we can be certain, and the body, about which our knowledge can be doubted, formed the basis of **mind-body dualism**, the idea that mind and body are separate substances that operate according to distinct principles. While this division between mind and body has been strongly questioned by later thinkers, it undoubtedly had an influence on psychology by suggesting that the mind functions according to its own set of rules that could theoretically be discovered by specialized scientists of the mind—psychologists.

English philosopher **John Locke** sought to do exactly that—to discover how the mind worked by studying its contents. Contrary to the views of many previous thinkers, who maintained that some ideas are innate (that people are born with them), Locke believed that all knowledge derives from experience, a view known as **empiricism**. According to Locke, all the contents of the mind (which he referred to broadly as "ideas," but which included perceptions, memories, imaginings, feelings, and reflections) can be traced to sense experience. Indeed, he conceived of the human mind as a *tabula rasa* (a blank slate) upon which experience would write, shaping each mind to become a unique person. Although twentieth-century behaviorists such as John Watson and B.F. Skinner had little interest in "the mind," they agreed with Locke that human beings could be molded to become just about anything, simply based on the experiences to which they were exposed.

Eighteenth- and nineteenth-century British philosophers built upon Locke's empirical approach to develop more systematic accounts of how the mind worked. A number of thinkers in the "Associationist School" attempted to explain the mind's operation through the association of ideas. According to this view, even the most complex thoughts and feelings that we find in our minds are ultimately built up from simple impressions, combined in particular ways according to principles of association. Scottish philosopher **David Hume** suggested a number of distinct **principles of association**, including similarity, contiguity in space and time, and cause and effect. Throughout his work, Hume used an empirical approach to explain a wide variety of mental phenomena, and these explanations had a lasting impact on how early scientific psychologists, such as structuralists like Titchener, understood the mind.

Of course, philosophers were not the only figures whose work served as precursors to the science of psychology. Though typically regarded as a biologist, Charles Darwin also contributed to psychology's foundation. His accounts of the origin of species and of **evolution** through natural selection implied a continuity between humans and nonhuman animals, suggesting that the mental lives of human beings must not be so different from those of other animals. Indeed, Darwin identified a number of "human" qualities in the behavior of animals, including pride, jealousy, shame, courage, and devotion. Conversely, some of the "primitive" dispositions of nonhuman animals, such as the "fight or flight" response, can be found in human beings. But, more than just noting points of similarity, Darwin could explain both the similarities and the differences among humans and other animals. The similarities resulted from the common ancestry shared by all animals, while the differences arose from evolved adaptations to the distinctive environmental challenges humans and other species faced in their struggle to survive and reproduce. Darwin's theory of evolution has been hugely influential in psychology, particularly for functionalism in the late nineteenth century and for contemporary evolutionary psychology.

Much early work in physiology was also instrumental to the establishment of psychology. For instance, German scientists Franz Joseph Gall and Johann Spurzheim formulated a controversial approach known as **phrenology**. Gall and Spurzheim claimed to have identified 35 distinct mental faculties, each of which corresponded to a specific location in the brain. Advocates of phrenology maintained that simply measuring the bumps on a person's skull could reveal how developed these faculties were and how likely that person would be to engage in particular behaviors. The claims of phrenology have been thoroughly debunked, but contemporary psychologists widely agree that there is a strong connection between the physiology of the brain and human behavior—it's just far more complex than Gall and Spurzheim originally believed.

Other German scientists, such as Ernst Weber and Gustav Fechner, focused on a field that Fechner dubbed "**psychophysics**," which examined the relationship between incoming physical stimuli and the sensations these stimuli produce. Psychophysics led to the development of a number of concepts still accepted by contemporary psychologists of sensation, including the absolute threshold and the just-noticeable difference (JND), both of which are discussed in Chapter 15 on Sensation and Perception.

Hermann von Helmholtz was another influential German physiologist, who conducted research on vision, hearing, and nerve impulses. Helmholtz invented a device called the ophthalmoscope to observe the retina, and made other significant contributions in the study of color vision and depth perception. As an accomplished pianist, he brought his musical training to bear in discovering how the ear detects and distinguishes between pitches. In research on frogs, Helmholtz was able to detect and measure the speed of signal transmission through a nerve. Helmholtz's findings remain relevant for contemporary psychologists of sensation and perception.

As should now be clear, psychology had a long and illustrious prehistory, even if its history only spans less than a century and a half. Though many other ideas from a vast array of thinkers also influenced the early development of psychology, awareness of the philosophers and scientists discussed here should be more than adequate for the AP Psychology exam.

THEORETICAL APPROACHES

High-Yield

LEARNING OBJECTIVES

- Compare and contrast distinct theoretical approaches throughout psychology's history
- Explain strengths and weaknesses of explaining behavior with psychological theories

Now that you have a sense of the major roots of and precursors to psychology, we'll turn to the development of the science in the United States and Europe. We'll start with the founding fathers of psychology during the late nineteenth century and early twentieth century: the aforementioned Wilhelm Wundt, along with Edward Titchener and William James, laid a strong foundation for the discipline that developed into modern scientific psychology.

Structuralism and Functionalism

Wundt viewed psychology as the scientific study of immediate experience, that is, of human consciousness. He believed that psychologists could identify the structure of consciousness and answer the fundamental question: What are the components of experience or mind? To that end, he characterized sensations and feelings as structures of consciousness. In his laboratory, he presented subjects with various kinds of lights, textures, and sounds, and asked those subjects to report the intensity and quality of their sensations. In other words, he asked them to look within themselves, a practice known as **introspection**—the precise examination and description of conscious experience. Wundt then changed the stimuli, repeated the process, and documented the changes in people's reports. Like the philosophers Locke and Hume before him, Wundt embraced empiricism and attempted to learn about human psychology through direct, detailed observations of experience. Wundt's approach was named **structuralism** by his disciple Edward Titchener.

British-born psychologist Edward B. Titchener, perhaps the most famous of Wundt's students, emigrated to the United States in 1892, where he became a psychology professor at Cornell University and founded the first psychology laboratory in the U.S. In an effort to transplant the psychology of Wundt to the United States, Titchener created English translations of 11 German works by Wundt and other German scholars. Titchener is also known for his manuals on laboratory research, in which he outlined the procedures for qualitative and quantitative experiments, modeled after experiments in chemistry. He advocated a systematic experimental study of the adult mind and proposed a precise examination and description of conscious experience by means of introspection.

Around the time that Titchener was working in his lab, Harvard University's William James—originally a physiologist and philosopher—emphasized what the mind does, rather than what the mind is. Inspired by Charles Darwin, James believed that the goal of psychology is the study of how consciousness functions to aid human beings in adapting to their environment. Because of his focus on the functions of the mind, rather than its structures, James's new approach became known as **functionalism**. According to the functionalist approach, mental states are identified by what they do, rather than by what they are composed of.

In 1890, James published *The Principles of Psychology*, an encyclopedic work that served as the first psychological textbook; it covered a vast array of topics, including consciousness, emotions, habits, and the will. Unsurprisingly, James is widely recognized as the founder of American psychology. James was instrumental in promoting and developing Darwin's vision of human evolution and was adamant that the mind and consciousness itself would not exist if they did not serve some practical, adaptive purpose. This more biological orientation to psychology would see further development in subsequent thinkers.

Biological Approaches

The **biological approach** maintains that all psychological phenomena can be understood in terms of biological processes. In other words, for a biological psychologist, the mind can be reduced to the operation of the brain and nervous system. Biopsychologists often turn to physiology, especially neurology, to find the biological underpinnings of behavior, as well as to genetics and evolution to understand how the brain developed. Advocates of this approach may differ in focus, but all would agree that thoughts, feelings, and behaviors ultimately have biological causes.

Physiology is essential to the biological approach, because it helps to assess how the nervous and endocrine systems function and how changes in the structures of these systems can affect behavior. For example, psychologists who use a biological approach may examine how prescribed drugs that treat depression affect behavior through their interactions with specific neurotransmitters or hormones.

The study of genetics and inheritance patterns reveals information about what psychological characteristics are heritable. For example, many contemporary biological psychologists are interested in twin studies, discussed in Chapter 14 on the Biological Bases of Behavior. Studies of identical twins raised apart are particularly informative because such individuals have identical genetics but grew up in different environments, thus allowing a better gauge of whether nature (genetics) or nurture (environment) has a larger impact on the development of specific traits.

Of course, attempting to explain human psychology through genetics has significant downsides. For instance, early in psychology's history, some biological psychologists speculated that criminal behavior runs in families, and that it was largely due to the influence of genetics. Advocates of a now-discredited ideology called **eugenics** embraced this conclusion and further believed that the human species could be improved by weeding out criminality and other undesirable characteristics from the gene pool. Some eugenicists called for mandatory sterilization of criminals, the developmentally challenged, and other individuals deemed to have undesirable traits. While eugenics has now largely been rejected, such ideas caused a lot of turmoil and bloodshed, arguably even playing a role in leading to the bloodiest conflict in human history, World War II.

Behaviorism

In stark contrast to the focus of Wundt, Titchener, and James on consciousness, **behaviorism** maintains that the proper subject matter of psychology is observable and measurable behavior. Indeed, behaviorists liken the mind to a black box, believing it impossible to study scientifically. Early behaviorists studied animal learning, working with dogs, cats, rats, and other animals. Ivan Pavlov, a Russian physiologist, noticed that dogs in his lab would salivate as soon as they saw the lab worker who usually fed them. This observation led Pavlov to develop the theory of classical conditioning (discussed in Chapter 16 on Learning), a basic form of learning in which an organism learns to form a new association between two stimuli.

Inspired by Pavlov's studies, John B. Watson advocated for the controlled observation of behavior with the theoretical goal of prediction and control. Watson is perhaps most famous for his experiment with a nine-month-old infant, Little Albert, who learned to develop a fear of white rats and similar-looking objects. The Little Albert study (discussed in Chapter 16) became a classic example of the behaviorist approach to learning. Indeed, John Watson is widely recognized as the founder of behaviorism.

Burrhus Frederic (B.F.) Skinner further developed the behavioral approach to psychology with his theory of operant conditioning (also discussed in Chapter 16). With this type of learning, behavior can be shaped in novel ways by reinforcing desired behavior and punishing undesired behavior. For example, Skinner was able to use such shaping to train pigeons to make circles. Thanks to the influence of psychologists like Watson and Skinner, behaviorism was the dominant approach to psychology in the United States from the 1920s to the 1950s.

Gestalt and Psychodynamic Approaches

While psychologists in the United States came to consider behaviorism the only proper method for scientific psychology, native German-speaking scholars in Germany, Austria, and Switzerland followed different approaches. Some of these psychologists initially continued in the vein of Wilhelm Wundt, but ultimately rejected Wundt's focus on breaking down the structure of consciousness in favor of a more holistic approach that came to be known as the Gestalt, German for "shape" or "form."

Gestalt psychology, founded in the early twentieth century by Max Wertheimer and several of his colleagues, became a reaction to Wundt's structuralism. The Gestalt school maintained that the components of consciousness were not as important as its totality: they viewed the whole as more than just the sum of its parts. According to this view, the mind should be studied in all its complexity, rather than separated into discrete components. Perception, learning, behavior, and other aspects of psychology must be examined as structured wholes.

For example, Gestalt psychologists discovered that when two lights were flashed in succession under specific conditions, an illusion of continuous motion could be produced—this is the principle behind motion pictures, or movies. This and other experiments led Gestalt psychologists to conclude that the mind imposes its own patterns of organization on the stimuli it receives, rather than merely reproducing them. Though they rejected Wundt's approach to introspection, Gestalt psychologists did value a less structured form of introspection known as "phenomenology," which explored questions regarding individual perceptions of motion, size, and color.

Meanwhile in Vienna, Sigmund Freud, an Austrian physician specializing in neurological disorders, encountered patients in his medical practice who were suffering from physical symptoms for which he couldn't detect a biological cause. To address these symptoms, Freud developed the technique of free association, in which a patient is encouraged to talk freely, expressing ideas immediately as they come to mind, with the hope that this would eventually uncover the unconscious basis of the patient's problems.

According to Freud, people have many unconscious conflicts that cause them discomfort, sometimes manifesting as psychological or physiological symptoms. Freud speculated that these symptoms may be attributed to repressed early childhood memories and other conflicts buried deep in the unconscious. Freud's approach became known as **psychoanalysis**, and relied upon free association, hypnosis, and dream analysis as tools for uncovering patients' repressed conflicts.

Carl Jung, a Swiss psychiatrist and associate of Freud, also focused on the unconscious but developed a different perspective. Jung was interested in symbolism, mythology, and spirituality, believing that people seek spiritual meaning during the course of life. He expanded on Freud's concept of the unconscious by proposing the existence of a collective unconscious, a repository of instincts and symbols supposedly shared by all human beings.

Alfred Adler, an Austrian colleague of Freud, also developed a different outlook and placed an emphasis on an individual's need for belonging, the desire to be a part of a community or other social group. Unlike Freud, he wanted to create a sense of equality between a patient and his or her therapist. Because of his focus on social interests and on improving community health by means of public education, Adler is known for being the first real community psychologist.

Though each differed in their perspectives, the approaches of Freud, Jung, Adler, and other thinkers like Karen Horney and Erik Erikson are collectively known as **psychodynamic psychology**. Psychodynamics was particularly influential in early clinical psychology, especially in the treatment of patients through talk therapy.

Humanistic Approach

Humanistic psychology evolved in the 1950s and 1960s as a reaction not only to the psychodynamic approach of Freud and his disciples, but also to the behaviorism of Watson and Skinner. Humanists rejected both the pessimistic view of human nature implicit in psychoanalysis and behaviorism's denial of human agency and reduction of human beings to stimulus-response machines. Instead, the humanistic approach celebrated people's innate potential and insisted that human beings have the power to shape their own destinies. The ultimate goal of the humanistic psychologist is to aid individuals in realizing their full potential. Two major figures were particularly influential to this approach: Maslow and Rogers.

Abraham Maslow is best known for outlining a hierarchy of needs that defines what human beings require to live a fulfilling life. These needs are hierarchical, according to Maslow, because lower-level needs must be satisfied before those at higher levels. At the very top of this hierarchy is the need for self-actualization, the full realization of one's potential. See Chapter 19 on Motivation, Emotion, and Personality for more on self-actualization and Maslow's hierarchy.

The other major contributor to humanistic psychology was Carl Rogers, who advocated the client-centered approach to psychotherapy. Client-centered therapists seek to facilitate self-acceptance and self-understanding by conveying empathy, warmth, and the unconditional belief that, no matter what the client says or does, he or she is still a valuable person. See Chapter 20 on Clinical Psychology for more on Rogers' approach.

Cognitive Approach

While the humanists were critical of behaviorism for denying free will, another group of psychologists came to lodge a different criticism, rejecting behaviorism's insistence that the mind is a "black box" not susceptible to scientific study. These psychologists came to embrace the "**cognitive revolution**," a radical shift in the approach to psychology that sought to understand the cognitive processes that underlie behavior. Cognitive psychologists revisited many of the areas that originally interested the structuralists and functionalists, but sought to understand both the structures and functions of cognition, as well as the relations between cognition and behavior. The cognitive revolution spawned research into a wide array of cognitive processes, including memory, language, thought, and attention (all of which are discussed further in Chapter 17 on Cognitive Psychology).

Cognitive research on memory revealed characteristics that influenced people's ability to store and recall information, such as the importance of semantic relatedness—relatedness on the basis of meaning. For example, it was found that study participants have an easier time recalling words that are semantically related than those that are not. Other studies of memory revealed phenomena such as the primacy effect, in which people more easily recall items presented at the beginning of a list; and the recency effect, in which people are better able to remember items presented at the end of a list (the most recent information).

The psychology of language, or psycholinguistics, became another important area of study for cognitive psychologists, due in large part to the work of Noam Chomsky. Chomsky argued that there is a universal grammar—that all languages possess a similar underlying logic. He maintained that the human capacity for language is innate, rather than learned, based on observations that children are exposed to only a small subset of words and expressions when they learn their first language, and yet come to acquire a nearly unlimited ability to say anything that comes to mind.

Other psychologists who adopted this approach focused on other aspects of cognition. Jerome Bruner studied individuals' responses to stimuli and their internal interpretations of those stimuli. He proposed that intellectual ability develops in stages from infancy to adulthood and was particularly influential in the field of education. Leon Festinger, a cognitive psychologist and social psychologist introduced the theory of cognitive dissonance, which describes how people manage conflicting beliefs about themselves, their behavior, and the world around them. Festinger maintained that the discomfort that arises when people experience cognitive dissonance can actually motivate them to change their beliefs. See Chapter 21 on Social Psychology for more on cognitive dissonance.

Sociocultural Approach

Many of the psychological approaches already discussed emphasize the psychology of the individual, or the interactions between an individual and the physical world around him or her. In contrast, sociocultural psychologists seek to understand how social and cultural contexts influence human behavior and cognition, resulting in the great diversity of individuals that we find in the world today.

Russian psychologist Lev Vygotsky is generally regarded as the pioneer of the **sociocultural approach**. Vygotsky became interested in developmental psychology and studied the ways children learn within in a given cultural context. Children interact with not just a physical but also an interpersonal environment, and those interactions influence their cognitive development. Vygotsky recognized that parents, teachers, older siblings, and others can shape instructional methods, acknowledging three distinct approaches: imitative learning, instructional learning, and collaborative learning. The types of learning methods preferred, and the subsequent cognitive skills that arise, are largely specific to the child's culture. See Chapter 18 on Developmental Psychology for more on Vygotsky.

Modern Approaches

The cognitive approach is popular today in many areas of psychology, including social, developmental, personality, and clinical psychology. The overriding idea is that to understand the individual, one must understand the way that people think, remember, process information, and reason about the world. Contemporary cognitive psychology has broadened its focus to acknowledge sociocultural influences on cognitive development.

Evolutionary theory has also made a resurgence in recent years, leading to the development of evolutionary psychology. For example, the concept of kin selection (the idea that enhancing the survival and reproductive fitness of close kin is an indirect way of propagating one's genes) has been used as way to explain altruistic behavior, which might otherwise seem at odds with evolutionary theory (see Chapter 21). Evolutionary psychology seeks to explain a wide range of human behaviors by describing how they enhance fitness.

The wide array of approaches that emerged during psychology's history have afforded contemporary psychologists greater flexibility in studying the subject matter that interests them. For example, a psychologist who seeks to understand the effects of traumatic brain injuries is more likely to take a biological approach, a researcher interested in attitude formation and change would be more likely to ground his or her research in cognitive psychology and theories of persuasion, and a scholar who wants to study cultural differences in some trait would be most likely to adopt a sociocultural approach. Indeed, students of psychology are encouraged to be pluralistic in their initial studies, understanding the whole panoply of perspectives that makes psychology the rich discipline it has become today.

Strengths and Weaknesses of Psychological Theories

Throughout psychology's history, a great number of theories have arisen to explain different aspects of human behavior and cognition. But can any theory be fully adequate to explain the richness and diversity of human psychology? In addition to requiring knowledge of specific psychological theories, the AP Psychology exam also expects you to recognize the benefits and limitations of using theories to explain human psychology.

Let's start by considering some of the advantages of using theories. Theories can be powerful explanatory tools, not only helping us to make sense of why we think and act in the ways that we do, but perhaps also even allowing us to make predictions about how people will behave in the future. This ability to predict responses can be used to take control of the circumstances of our lives, to use characteristics of our psychology to grow as people, and to bring about positive change in the world more effectively.

Theories are also valuable in experimental sciences like psychology because they can help researchers to understand their experimental results better and to design new experiments to test novel hypotheses derived from those theories. Moreover, theories can be refined in light of the empirical data, with unexpected results leading to amendments, exceptions, or even entirely new theories. The interplay between theory and data can lead to a fuller, richer understanding of human psychology.

Of course, the strengths of these theories can lead to negative outcomes in some circumstances. The ability to predict and control can be used for self-interested or even malicious purposes, while an enhanced understanding of how the human mind works might undermine people's beliefs in free will and personal responsibility. Indeed, if all behavior results from genetic predispositions, conditioning from the environment, or some combination of the two, it's hard to see how human beings can possess any real sense of freedom. Similar criticisms have often been leveled against biological and behaviorist theories.

In addition, there are other limitations inherent to theoretical explanations. A single theory will never be able to explain everything, but can only explain certain specific aspects of human behavior. Many theories that purport to explain human nature as a whole will, in fact, only account for a limited subset of human experience, perhaps confined only to a single culture or demographic group. This kind of bias can lead advocates of a theory to dismiss the experience of individuals who fall outside of the theory's field of application.

Psychological theories may also have difficulty addressing aspects of the human mind that cannot be easily measured, quantified, or observed from an outside perspective, such as consciousness and creativity. Or, if a theory does attempt to address some of the less quantifiable aspects of psychology, it may not be susceptible to any kind of empirical verification, making it little better than idle speculation. Indeed, many psychodynamic and humanistic theories have been critiqued for being insufficiently rigorous in this respect.

Theories can also contribute to promoting dangerous ideologies, as has been seen in psychology's history with respect to phrenology, eugenics, and other now-discredited ideas. A theory might present an overly pessimistic view of human nature, something Freudian psychoanalysis is often criticized for, or an overly optimistic one, as in humanistic psychology. Indeed, just about any theory can be taken too far if it is accepted as a universal principle that explains everything.

Despite all of these limitations and disadvantages, theories will remain an essential part of psychology for the foreseeable future, just as they remain essential for any natural or social science. The key is to recognize that theories are always partial explanations, and to allow them to enhance our understanding of the world without letting any single one of them dominate our worldview.

PSYCHOLOGICAL DOMAINS

LEARNING OBJECTIVE

- Distinguish between different domains in psychology

Since its birth in 1879 with Wilhelm Wundt's laboratory in Germany, psychology has grown like a tree. Though some of its branches have been pruned over the years (such as structuralism and behaviorism), other branches have sprouted and flourished. Now that you have reviewed the roots of psychology, its nineteenth- and twentieth-century history as well as its millennia of prehistory,

13

you should also be aware of its shoots, the wide variety of psychological specialties practiced today in the twenty-first century.

A comprehensive list of psychological domains can be found in the Rapid Review section of Chapter 4. You should aim to have at least a basic idea of what each domain involves for the exam.

IMPORTANT CONTRIBUTORS

LEARNING OBJECTIVE

- Recognize important historical contributors to psychology

The AP Psychology exam tests your familiarity not only with psychology's history and a wide variety of its theories and domains, but also with individual psychologists who have made significant contributions to their fields. See the list of important contributors in the Rapid Review section of Chapter 4.

TYPES OF PSYCHOLOGICAL RESEARCH

LEARNING OBJECTIVE

- Inventory the purpose, strengths, and weaknesses of various types of research

Earlier in this chapter, you encountered some examples of types of research, such as the method of introspection used by the structuralists and the conditioning experiments of the behaviorists. Now, we'll look more systematically at the research methods that psychologists use, starting with a discussion of the different types of research. You'll review how each method works, when and why it is used, and its strengths and limitations.

Quantitative vs. Qualitative Research

Before looking at particular types of studies, it is important to make a basic distinction between quantitative and qualitative research methods. The simplest way to distinguish between them is as follows: **quantitative research** involves numerical data, while **qualitative research** does not. Quantitative research includes correlational studies like structured observations and surveys, as well as most experiments. Qualitative research, in contrast, includes many naturalistic observations, unstructured interviews, and some case studies. Some types of research mix both methods, so quantitative versus qualitative should be considered as more of a spectrum than a simple binary division.

Quantitative research is used whenever psychologists are seeking to make generalizations about behavior and cognition. Quantitative methods can establish correlations between variables, test hypotheses, and support or challenge existing psychological theories. The data in quantitative studies are more objective and less subject to interpretation than qualitative data. In addition, quantitative data can be statistically analyzed to yield higher-quality generalizations. And unlike qualitative studies, many quantitative studies can easily be replicated. On the other hand, quantitative studies are limited insofar as they generally do not take place in natural environments, so they may only reflect what occurs in more controlled settings. In addition, quantitative studies ignore any data gathered that cannot be quantified. This has the potential of leaving out important information.

In contrast, qualitative research is used when researchers want to try to understand psychological phenomena from the perspective of research participants in a more natural setting. Qualitative research can explain how and why phenomena occur within a particular context, though it cannot make generalizations or properly test hypotheses. Qualitative data can be subjected to limited analysis, such as when behaviors are coded and collated in naturalistic observations. The great strength of qualitative research is that it yields a greater depth of insight into particular phenomena within a specific context. Qualitative research is limited, though, because it does not allow robust generalizations, it is not properly replicable, and it can be quite costly and time-consuming (so it generally investigates a smaller number of participants than quantitative research). Qualitative research is also limited both in terms of its validity and its reliability.

Correlational Studies

Correlational studies constitute a broad category of quantitative research that includes surveys, some observational studies, and some case studies. The common thread in all correlational studies is that they can determine correlations between variables but can offer no conclusions about causality.

A correlation is a particular type of relationship between variables, typically expressed by the **correlation coefficient**, r. The value of r ranges from -1 to $+1$. A **positive correlation** (an r value above zero) indicates that two variables are directly related, meaning they follow the same pattern: when one variable increases, the other also increases; when one decreases, the other also decreases. For example, height and weight are positively correlated: taller people tend to weigh more than shorter people. A **negative correlation** (an r value below zero) indicates the opposite, an inverse relationship: when one variable increases, the other decreases. For example, weight and levels of physical activity are negatively correlated: more physically active people tend to weigh less. An r value of exactly zero indicates no correlation; the two variables vary completely independently of each other. As a general rule, the higher the absolute value of r (the closer it is to either -1 or $+1$), the stronger the relationship between the two variables.

The biggest limitation of correlational studies is that they reveal nothing about causality. Even if two variables, A and B, are found to have a correlation coefficient of 1, there is no way of knowing (without conducting controlled experiments) whether A causes B, B causes A, or some third variable, C, causes both of them. Despite this significant limitation, correlational studies can be quite valuable, especially in situations in which controlled experiments are not feasible. They tend to be less expensive, less time-consuming, and easier to conduct than experiments. Learning about the relationships between variables can still be informative and can lay the groundwork for future experimentation.

13

Observational Studies

Observational research methods come in a wide variety of forms and are adapted to fit the goals and constraints of specific research projects. Unlike experiments, in which researchers create an artificial and highly controlled set of circumstances, observational studies generally seek to investigate phenomena as they actually occur in the real world. For the purposes of the AP Psychology exam, you should be familiar with three broad types of observational studies: naturalistic, structured, and participant.

Naturalistic observation is used when researchers want to document behavior as it naturally happens in a real-world setting. Such observation is conducted outside of a laboratory in the natural environment where the behavior spontaneously occurs. As such, it is typically a qualitative research method, though some steps can be taken to make it more quantitative, such as the use of larger sample sizes or coding. Because the researcher him- or herself can influence the way that people or nonhuman animals behave, naturalistic observation is typically conducted in a manner that is covert (meaning that subjects are unable to detect the presence of observers) and undisclosed (meaning that subjects are not informed that they are being watched). Such covert observation, however, can be ethically problematic because it may violate the privacy of individuals who are unaware that they are being watched.

In contrast to naturalistic observation, **structured observation** is typically conducted in a laboratory setting. This type of observation is usually disclosed, but the presence of researchers may be made unobtrusive to minimize their influence on the situation. While structured observations may have some impact on the behavior of the subjects being observed, the impact is likely to be less extensive than other methods of research, such as interviews, which are based on self-reports of behavior (which may be inaccurate for a number of reasons, especially if the behavior carries a social stigma) rather than on subjects actually engaging in the behavior under investigation.

Often when conducting structured observations, and sometimes during other types of observations, researchers attempt to achieve some level of consistency in describing their observations by using a system of **coding**, in which particular behaviors are classified into a number of discrete categories. This allows for a more quantitative approach and easier replication by other researchers. Coding, however, does bring with it some additional concerns. For example, multiple coders may not be consistent in how they're classifying behaviors. Such discrepancies diminish the **inter-rater reliability**, a measure of concordance between different classifications of the same phenomena. The greater the inter-rater reliability, the more confident that researchers can be in their conclusions.

A third type of observation is **participant observation**, in which researchers deliberately enter into interactions with observed subjects, integrating themselves into the group being investigated. Like naturalistic observation, this research method tends to be more qualitative. Participant observation may be overt, in which case researchers identify themselves as outsiders to the group who are interested in studying it, or covert, in which case researchers conceal their motives and take on false identities, attempting to join the group like any other member. Overt participant observations face the same problems as other types of overt observation, such as possibly influencing the behavior of group members due to the presence of an outsider. On the other hand, covert participant observation comes with its own set of issues, including the ethical concerns involved in deceiving a group, as well as the possibility that researchers may come to identify with the group being studied, which can cause bias in their reporting. With covert observation, it may also be difficult to report observations accurately; researchers may have to rely on memory if they are unable to take notes or electronically record interactions out of fear of blowing their cover. Relying on memory introduces the possibility of recall bias, in which researchers emphasize more memorable details while neglecting what is less memorable.

Generally speaking, observations carry a number of limitations, some of which have already been noted. In addition to the ethical dilemmas involved in hiding from or deceiving study subjects, the types of conclusions that can be drawn from observations are limited. Unlike controlled experiments, in which researchers can make cause and effect attributions, the conclusions of observations are at best correlational (when they are quantitative). Nevertheless, observations are often a good choice for pilot studies because they allow researchers to gain a sense of the phenomena that they're investigating before they design and conduct controlled experiments.

One prominent example of a common limitation in observational studies is the **Hawthorne effect**. Named after the Hawthorne Works, a factory in a suburb of Chicago where research was conducted in the late 1920s, the Hawthorne effect refers to the tendency of subjects to change their behavior simply by virtue of knowing that they are being watched. The research that revealed this effect attempted to investigate the productivity of workers in response to changes in the work environment, such as increases in ambient illumination. Although employees increased their productivity during the course of the research, these gains proved to be short-lived, disappearing after the research was concluded. Subsequent interpreters concluded that the increased attention on the workers, as well as the novelty of being research participants, was the actual cause of the changes in productivity, not the increased lighting and other modifications to the factory environment. The Hawthorne effect is relevant whenever observations are overt and/or disclosed to subjects.

✔ **AP Expert Note**

Longitudinal versus Cross-Sectional Studies

When developmental psychologists are interested in observing how cognition, behavior, or other traits change over the course of the lifespan, they have two basic research strategies they can adopt. In a **longitudinal study**, researchers follow the same set of participants over time, sometimes long stretches of time, to see how they change with age. In contrast, a **cross-sectional study** is conducted at a single point in time, comparing groups of differing ages to arrive at conclusions about development. While longitudinal studies provide a more complete picture of how individuals actually change over time, cross-sectional studies are much easier to conduct since they don't require years of commitment.

Case Studies

A **case study** is an in-depth and detailed examination of a specific subject, or case. The case in psychological research is often a single individual, though it could also be an organization or other social group. Like observational studies, case studies typically involve less manipulation of the case and surrounding environment, reporting instead on a case as it exists in the real world. Thus, case studies are typically qualitative, though some involve limited quantitative methods. Case studies are especially useful in clinical research, where researchers can gain a greater understanding of a psychological disorder by investigating all the ways in which the symptoms manifest in a particular patient and how they interact with the patient's environment and life circumstances. Both Sigmund Freud and Carl Rogers used the results of numerous clinical case studies (from their own therapeutic practice) as a basis for the development of their distinctive theoretical approaches.

While case studies can yield great insight into specific cases by examining them in depth, they carry a number of limitations. Most notably, cases being investigated (which are usually limited to only one or a handful of subjects) may not be representative, meaning that their results are difficult to generalize. Because most case studies are qualitative—and even those with quantitative aspects often have ambiguity in their data, which makes it more difficult to collate data across case studies—they simply cannot produce robust generalizations about human or animal psychology, even when drawing upon the results of multiple case studies. And like observational studies, case studies cannot generate conclusions about cause and effect since they lack experimental manipulations, and are also similarly subject to bias.

Surveys

A **survey** is typically a list of questions filled out by a group of people to assess attitudes or opinions. Surveys are administered in a wide variety of ways: in person, by mail, by phone, or even over the internet. Many surveys contain closed-ended questions with fixed responses (such as yes/no or a 1 to 5 scale that indicates levels of agreement), but some are open-ended, allowing respondents to provide their own answers. Some open-ended surveys may be qualitative, but most surveys feature primarily quantitative research methods.

When conducting survey research, psychologists can either construct their own surveys to fit their particular research needs or draw on existing databases (known as secondary datasets or archival research). Many such databases are now available for researchers to draw on. While it may be more difficult in some cases to find the data a researcher needs, using an existing dataset generally saves time and money.

Surveys are especially useful for studying what cannot be observed directly, such as attitudes and beliefs. They can be administered to large numbers of participants, allowing for larger sample sizes and more generalizable results. Because they are standardized (each participant answers the same questions), they often carry high reliability. In addition, surveys tend to be less expensive than other types of research and can be administered in a wide array of formats.

Survey research does carry limitations. Like other correlational research, surveys cannot be used to draw conclusions about cause and effect. Moreover, there is no guarantee that respondents carefully consider their answers or even answer truthfully. When surveys are administered by a human being, either in person or over the phone, respondents may give socially desirable answers rather than saying what they truly feel. Another potential limitation is the response rate. When only a small percentage of subjects complete the survey, the results may be less representative and even biased (a phenomenon known as **nonresponse bias**). In addition, there is the possibility of **surveyor bias**, which results from questions that are written in a way that steers respondents to particular answers. Researchers can often avoid such bias by carefully wording their questions, but this is not always easy. Finally, surveys can be inflexible because they cannot be changed during the data collection period without distorting the results.

Experiments

Experiments are deliberately designed procedures used to test research hypotheses. Typically, a **hypothesis** is a statement about a relationship between two or more variables. Hypotheses are often derived from developed psychological theories, so an experiment can sometimes serve as a test of a particular theory. While the results of an experiment do not outright *prove* the truth or falsity of the hypothesis they test, they do provide support either in favor of or against the hypothesis, making the truth or falsity of that hypothesis more probable.

The gold standard in experimentation is the controlled experiment. A **controlled experiment** carefully manipulates the experimental circumstances, using controls and other precautions to ensure that the hypothesis can be tested precisely. As noted in the discussion of correlational studies previously, only controlled experiments are capable of supporting or challenging statements about cause and effect. Controlled experiments usually take place in a laboratory setting, where this level of control is more feasible. Details on the design of controlled experiments are discussed later in the chapter.

In contrast to a controlled experiment, a **field experiment** is conducted outside of the lab in the real world. Field experiments still involve experimental manipulations, but there are greater limitations on how many variables can be controlled, so researchers must rely upon more advanced statistical techniques to isolate variables of interest. Field experiments are often used when dealing with phenomena that cannot be replicated in a lab, such as complex, large-scale social behavior. The real-world setting is both an asset and a liability: results may be more generalizable since they are not obtained in an artificial environment like a lab, but there is a greater possibility of external factors confounding those results. Consequently, conclusions in field experiments are often more correlational than causal.

In addition to controlled and field experiments, there are also natural experiments. A **natural experiment** or **quasi-experiment** does not involve direct manipulations of variables, but instead relies upon natural variations in the variables of interest. Natural experiments are particularly valuable in cases where it is impossible or highly unethical to manipulate the variables. For instance, if a researcher wanted to study the effect of being orphaned on cognitive development, he or she must rely upon already-orphaned children, since creating new orphans is not an ethical option. Though natural experiments allow the study of phenomena that could otherwise not be investigated experimentally, they are subject to the same limitations as field experiments, including susceptibility to confounding variables. If anything, these limitations are more pronounced in quasi-experiments, since researchers are unable to manipulate any variables directly.

Generally speaking, the greatest strength of experimentation is its ability to offer insights into cause and effect relationships. As noted, controlled experiments are particularly useful for this, but well-designed field and natural experiments can also offer some insight into causality, though with less

13

confidence. But, as can be seen in the contrast between controlled experiments and other types of experiments, experimentation faces a trade-off between confidence and generalizability. The more artificially controlled the circumstances, the more confident researchers can be about the results, but the less generalizable those results will be since the real world does not typically carry such artificial constraints. In addition, experiments tend to be more expensive, time-consuming, and difficult to conduct than other types of quantitative research.

RESEARCH DESIGN

 High-Yield

LEARNING OBJECTIVES

- Explain the effect of research design on research conclusions

- Differentiate among independent, dependent, confounding, and control variables in experiments

- Compare the uses of randomness in experimental conditions and in survey participant selection

- Evaluate the impact of research design quality on behavioral explanation validity

- Explain the importance of operational definitions and measurements to behavioral research

The scientific method is able to enhance our knowledge about the world only by carefully isolating, manipulating, and measuring specific aspects of experience. The key to doing this is sound research design: the better the design of an experiment or other type of research, the more confident researchers can be about their conclusions. But particular research designs can be limited in the types of questions they answer, so researchers must know what kind of conclusion (causal, correlational, etc.) they seek before designing a study.

So what does good research design require? This section will explore that question in all its richness and depth.

Types of Variables in Experiments

Before we can understand what good research design involves, it's essential to understand some basic terminology. As has been noted, research reveals relationships between variables, and experimental research in particular can provide evidence of causal relationships between variables. To test a causal hypothesis, a researcher will identify one or more **independent variables** to be manipulated in the experiment, and one or more **dependent variables** to be measured in the experiment. All other factors should be held constant; these constants in an experiment are known as **control variables**. If a researcher fails to hold all other factors constant, he or she runs the risk of introducing **confounding variables**, factors other than the independent and dependent variables that influence experimental results. Successfully controlling confounding factors allows a researcher to conclude with confidence that any change measured in a dependent variable is caused by a manipulation made to an independent variable.

Independent Variables vs. Dependent Variables

While these terms sound similar, they have very distinctive meanings that you need to keep straight for the exam. To remember that independent variables are the suspected causes in a research hypothesis and dependent variables are the suspected effects, think about the one-way nature of cause and effect: Cause → Effect. Effects *depend* upon causes, not the other way around. Thus, *dependent* variables *depend* upon independent variables.

For example, a sleep researcher might design an experiment to test the hypothesis "administration of the hormone melatonin prior to bedtime causes people to sleep longer." In this case, the independent variable in her experiment is melatonin administration and the dependent variable is the amount of time asleep. To test this hypothesis, she must obtain a pool of research subjects and divide participants into at least two groups. In controlled experiments, researchers need at least one control group and at least one experimental group. A **control group** is effectively the default, a reflection of circumstances without the influence of the independent variable. In this example, a good control group might be a number of participants who receive no melatonin supplement. An **experimental group**, in contrast, is exposed to the independent variable in some way. In this case, the researcher might create two experimental groups, one that receives a smaller amount of melatonin and one that receives a larger amount. Ideally, the only difference between a control group and an experimental group is the absence or presence of the independent variable. If all other variables are controlled, the researcher can confidently conclude that any change in the dependent variable was caused by changing the independent variable—here, that giving people melatonin did (or did not, depending on the results) cause them to sleep longer.

In psychology, researchers take extra precautions to control for confounding variables because human beings (along with nonhuman animals) can be affected by many circumstances in an experimental setting. For example, in the melatonin experiment, simply taking a pill—any pill—prior to bedtime could cause the expectation of better sleep, and that expectation alone could be sufficient to cause a person to sleep longer. This is a phenomenon known as the **placebo effect**. To control for this, researchers in experiments that involve the administration of drugs or other treatments will often supply control groups with a **placebo**, an inactive imitation of the treatment, such as a sugar pill. If the sleep researcher gave her control group sugar pill placebos that looked exactly like the melatonin pills given to the experimental groups, then she could be more confident that any increase in sleep time relative to the control group is caused by the melatonin.

Actually controlling for the placebo effect requires the use of at least a single-blind design. In a **single-blind experiment**, research participants do not know (are "blind" to) whether they are in a control group or an experimental group. Placebos tend to lose their effectiveness if participants realize they are given a placebo—although this is not true entirely, as the results of some surprising research have shown! Thus, to ensure more controlled conditions, everyone in a single-blind experiment believes they are being given the treatment. Double-blind research takes this even further. In a **double-blind experiment**, neither the participants nor the researchers conducting the experiment know who is assigned to which group. This prevents the researchers from treating control group members differently from experimental group members, a condition which has been shown to distort experimental results in the past. Knowledge of the control and experimental groups is kept hidden and not revealed until the data has been collected and is ready for analysis. A double-blind setup is the gold standard for research like the melatonin experiment.

In addition to the complications introduced by social expectations that are controlled through double-blind design, there are other difficulties inherent in research on human subjects. The control and experimental groups are supposed to be as similar as possible, with the only differences being found in the independent variable(s). But, almost always, these groups will be composed of distinct individuals who could vary widely as a result of differences in life experiences, biological traits, and sociocultural characteristics. True control of the variables would seem to require testing the same individuals both with and without the presence of the independent variable. While this can be done in some experiments by subjecting participants to both control and experimental conditions at two different times, more often researchers draw upon techniques like random assignment to ensure as much similarity as possible between control and experimental groups.

Randomness in Research

Psychologists seek to make general conclusions about large populations (sometimes as large as the entire human species), but research can generally only involve a small subset of individuals. To ensure that research results are more robust, researchers use elements of randomness in a variety of ways.

For example, in survey research, to ensure that a **sample** (the individuals who participate in a study) is representative of the larger **population** (the entire set of all individuals being investigated), researchers use **random sampling**. By selecting individuals at random from the population, a researcher is more likely to create a **representative sample**, that is, a set of individuals with a range of characteristics that mirror the diversity found within the population. Ideally, everyone in the population being studied should have an equal chance of being selected in order to provide the best chances of a sample being representative. In reality, even if the sample is initially selected this way, there's no guarantee that the people who actually respond to the survey will be representative, and the possibility of nonresponse bias, discussed earlier, remains.

Researchers also need to be mindful of using representative samples in experiments, but because participation in experiments tends to be far more demanding, achieving representativeness can be a challenge. Nevertheless, randomness is used in other ways in experimental design for the sake of producing more robust results. Most notably, when determining the membership of control and experimental groups, experimenters typically use **random assignment**, giving every individual in the pool of participants an equal chance of belonging to any particular group. As long as the sample used in the experiment is large enough, there will be a decent chance that there are no systematic differences between experimental and control groups. Random assignment thus reduces the possibility of introducing confounding variables.

Validity

The term "validity" has a number of distinct meanings in psychology, but two are particularly relevant in the context of research design: internal and external. **Internal validity** is a measure of the extent to which the experiment investigates what it is supposed to, that is, the causal influence of independent variables on dependent variables. An experiment has high internal validity if differences in the independent variable are in fact the only significant differences between the control and experimental groups. The presence of one or more confounding variables will consequently lower internal validity. In contrast, **external validity** is a measure of how true to life or generalizable the results of a study are. If an experiment has high external validity, then it presents an accurate reflection of how things work in the real world.

Research design has a clear impact on internal validity. Internal validity can be threatened by **demand characteristics**, the tendency for experimental participants to change their behavior (whether deliberately or not) to fit what they believe to be the purpose of the experiment. While it may be impossible to eliminate them entirely, the use of techniques like single-blind or double-blind design and placebos can reduce demand characteristics. The **observer-expectancy effect**, in which experimenters communicate (often unintentionally) their expectations of what the results will be and thereby influence the behavior of participants, is another threat to internal validity. This effect can be avoided specifically through the use of a double-blind design: if the experimenters don't know what to expect from any given participant, then they have no expectations of results that they could communicate. Besides these specific threats to internal validity, researchers must generally take care to ensure that there are no relevant, significant differences between control and experimental groups in their experiments. Internal validity is maximized when the only differences between groups are differences in the independent variable(s). Random assignment is one way to make this result more likely.

External validity is also influenced by research design, though in different ways. For example, results are more generalizable if a sample is representative, such as is more likely to occur when the sample is randomly selected. Moreover, experimental conditions that depart too far from real-world circumstances can reduce external validity. Of course, this brings about a potential conflict with measures taken to improve internal validity. Exerting a greater degree of control over the experimental circumstances can reduce the possibility of confounding variables, but it also has the possibility of making the experiment less true to life. Thus, researchers must strive to find a balance between controlling extraneous variables and making experiments feel more natural.

Different types of research find this balance differently. Controlled experiments are often more internally valid than externally valid, which is why phenomena that have been well-established in laboratory settings don't always figure prominently in our day-to-day lives. In contrast, studies like field experiments, natural experiments, and naturalistic observations often have low internal validity (indeed, correlational research doesn't even contain anything that could properly be considered an independent variable) but high external validity. Results observed in these studies can more confidently be generalized to the real world, but it is much more difficult to know what is causing changes observed in any measured quantities.

✔ **AP Expert Note**

Internal validity and external validity are not the only types of validity that are relevant to psychology. Learn about more types of validity in Chapter 17 on Cognitive Psychology.

Operational Definitions and Measurements

As noted earlier in this chapter, experiments and correlational studies are types of quantitative research because they rely upon numerical data. But unlike natural sciences such as physics and chemistry, in which quantities like length, mass, temperature, and concentration are easily measurable, psychology contains fewer obvious natural quantities. Thus, psychological researchers must take an additional step when designing and conducting research: they must operationalize their variables.

An **operational definition** is a specification of how a particular variable will be quantified and measured. Often, operationalization involves taking an abstract or vague concept that cannot be measured directly and finding some measurable quantity that serves as an indirect indication of it. For example, the nebulous quality we call intelligence is usually operationally defined in psychological experiments as the results on a standardized IQ test. While an IQ score is not the same thing as intelligence, it is an objective quantity that reflects (albeit imperfectly) the underlying quality of intelligence. A high level of intelligence causes (or at least strongly correlates with) high performance on IQ tests, so it is generally acceptable to use IQ score as an operational definition of intelligence. (See Chapter 17 for more on IQ.)

Operational definitions make correlational and experimental research possible in psychology because they allow for objective measurement of otherwise immeasurable qualities. The type of measurement introduced by an operational definition may vary among four different levels or scales, first identified by psychologist Stanley Smith Stevens. In *nominal measurement*, qualities are assigned arbitrary numerical values. For instance, gender could be designated as (1) for female, (2) for male, and (3) for other, with these quantities having no real meaning except as a way of distinguishing between categories. In *ordinal measurement*, numbers indicate a ranking order, such as might be found in a list of preferences. In *interval measurement*, differences between numerical values have a fixed meaning in the scale. For example, temperature in degrees Fahrenheit uses an interval scale: a difference of ten degrees always means the same thing, regardless of whether you're comparing 10° to 20° or 80° to 90°. In *ratio measurement*, both intervals and ratios between numbers are meaningful. So, for instance, on the Kelvin scale (a type of ratio scale), 200° is twice as hot as 100°, which is not true for an interval scale like Fahrenheit. Ratio measurements are possible because they assign zero to a non-arbitrary value (so, in the Kelvin scale, absolute zero, the complete absence of heat, is defined as 0°).

Interval and ratio scales generally allow for the most robust conclusions, but any type of measurement can help to quantify data and allow for statistical analysis of research results. What these statistical analyses involve and how they are used in psychology is the subject of the next section.

STATISTICS

LEARNING OBJECTIVES

- Recognize the distinct purposes of descriptive and inferential statistics
- Apply basic principles of descriptive statistics

Two Kinds of Statistics

Experiments and other quantitative studies yield a lot of raw numerical data. Researchers use statistics to analyze and help make sense of these data. In psychology, two different types of statistics are employed: descriptive and inferential. Each involves distinctive techniques and is used for specific purposes.

Descriptive statistics describe patterns in data. They have nothing to say about whether a research conclusion is valid or a hypothesis is confirmed, but they do say a lot about what the raw data looks like. Descriptive statistics answer questions like: What value is most frequent in the data? What value is in the middle? How spread apart are the data points? How does one particular value compare to the rest of the data? Psychologists use descriptive statistics to answer these questions and to provide summaries of other patterns in their data. Because the exam expects you to know how to apply a few specific descriptive statistical techniques, these are discussed more in depth below.

In contrast, **inferential statistics** concern larger generalizations, or inferences, that can be made from the data. For the purposes of the AP Psychology exam, these inferences are of two kinds: approximations of parameters and tests of hypotheses.

Earlier in the chapter, samples were distinguished from populations as being subsets of populations used for research purposes. **Parameters** refer to the characteristics of populations (parameters are often contrasted with "statistics," which in this sense refers to the characteristics of samples). For instance, you can distinguish between average height as a parameter of the population (which could only be calculated precisely if every single person were measured) and average height as a statistic of a sample (which can be calculated using only the data collected in a study). Depending on how representative the sample is, the statistic may or may not be a good indication of the parameter. Thus, one kind of inferential statistics concerns how to generalize from the statistics of samples to the parameters of populations. In psychology, parameter approximations include measures such as **confidence intervals**, which offer ranges of likely values for a parameter based on statistics calculated from the sample. For instance, the 95% confidence interval for a particular variable is the range of values in which the true parameter would fall in 95 out of 100 cases.

The other major technique in inferential statistics besides parameter approximation is hypothesis testing. As noted earlier in the chapter, experiments and other types of research are ways of putting particular hypotheses to the test. The actual testing, though, involves the use of statistics, as in the following example, which assumes a simple experiment with a single independent variable and a single dependent variable, along with one control group and one experimental group. (Other

13

statistical techniques besides those discussed below are sometimes used in hypothesis testing, but you don't need to know them for the exam.)

First, a researcher formulates a **null hypothesis**, which asserts that there is no relationship between the independent variable and the dependent variable. Then, the researcher constructs an **alternative hypothesis**, which states that there is a particular kind of relationship between the two variables, such as that the independent variable exerts a causal influence on the dependent variable. (This alternative hypothesis is typically the research hypothesis that the researcher initially adopted when designing the experiment.) The researcher will then compare the results of the control group and experimental group and calculate a **p-value**, a statistic that indicates the probability that the null hypothesis is true, based on those results. In other words, when the results of an experiment seem to indicate a relationship between a pair of variables, the p-value is the probability that this result occurred due to random chance. Because this is a measure of how likely it is that there's no relationship between the variables, lower values of p indicate a greater probability of a relationship. If the calculated p-value is below a set **significance level**, usually 5% (0.05) or 1% (0.01), then the null hypothesis is rejected and the alternative hypothesis is confirmed. When this occurs, the results are said to be **statistically significant**.

> ✔ **AP Expert Note**
>
> ### Types of Error
>
> In addition to the concepts discussed in the text above, you may also see references on the exam to types of error in inferential statistics. **Type I error**, also known as a false positive, is the improper rejection of a correct null hypothesis. In other words, it's assuming that there's a relationship between the variables that isn't really there. Type I error can generally be reduced by using a stricter significance level (such as 0.01 instead of 0.05). In contrast, **type II error**, or a false negative, is the improper affirmation of an incorrect null hypothesis. In other words, it's assuming that there's no relationship between the variables when there really is one.

Descriptive Statistics

As explained above, descriptive statistics describe patterns in numerical data. The AP Psychology exam expects you to have familiarity with three basic skills in descriptive statistics: working with graphs, calculating measures of central tendency, and calculating or estimating measures of dispersion.

Graphs

As you likely already know from studying mathematics and natural sciences, graphs are visual representations of data. The AP Psychology exam expects you to be able both to interpret the data presented in graphs and to construct simple graphs from given data. The most common types of graphs you'll encounter in AP Psychology are line graphs, bar graphs, and scatterplots.

Line graphs are graphs that represent relations between two variables. In most line graphs of experimental results, the independent variable is plotted on the horizontal x-axis and the dependent variable is plotted on the vertical y-axis. In line graphs, the data points are connected by a line or curve. A line with a positive slope (one that increases as you move from left to right) indicates a positive correlation between variables, while a line with a negative slope (decreasing from left to right) indicates a negative correlation. A flat line (with a slope of zero) indicates no correlation.

Bar graphs use the heights or lengths of rectangles to represent numerical data. Similar to bar graphs are **histograms**, which are representations of the frequency of particular data points. For example, in a histogram of test scores, the highest rectangular bar represents the mode, while two bars with the same height would indicate that equal numbers of students received those scores.

Scatterplots are graphs that represent all the data points collected in a study. Unlike line graphs, in which all the points are connected, scatterplots typically just represent each data point with a discrete dot or other symbol. Sometimes a scatterplot features a **line of best fit**, a line that passes through the middle of the data points. A line of best fit represents the correlation between the variables, just as in a line graph.

> ✔ **AP Expert Note**
>
> **Learning Graphs**
>
> Learning graphs are a special kind of graph that you should also be able to interpret for the exam. See Chapter 16 on Learning for more on these distinctive graphs.

Measures of Central Tendency

Measures of central tendency are statistics that describe the middle of a distribution of data. There are three such measures to know for the exam. The **mean**, or average, is equal to the sum of the data divided by the number of data points. The **median** is the value in the middle of the data when it is arranged in increasing or decreasing order. (When there is an even number of data points, it is equal to the average of the two points in the middle.) The **mode** is the most frequently occurring value in the set of data.

For example, consider the following five data points, which could be measurements of a single dependent variable like number of words recalled or seconds required to respond to a prompt: 4, 1, 7, 2, 1. The mean of this data is 3, which is calculated as follows:

$$\text{mean} = \frac{\text{sum of data}}{\text{number of points}} = \frac{4+1+7+2+1}{5} = \frac{15}{5} = 3$$

The median of the data is 2, the number that appears in the middle when the data are arranged in order: 1, 1, 2, 4, 7. The mode is 1 because it appears twice, more often than any other value.

In some distributions of data, such as the normal curve (discussed in Chapter 17 on Cognitive Psychology), the mean, median, and mode all correspond to the same value. In other cases, the three values may be widely divergent, such as when data contains a lot of **outliers**, that is, points that have extreme values relative to the rest of the data. For example, in the distribution of household incomes in the United States, there are a relatively small number of multimillionaires and billionaires that raise the mean (which is more than $70,000 in recent data) far higher than the median (which is less than $60,000). In such skewed data, the median often serves as a better indication of where the "true middle" is (so, in this case, it would give a better idea of who belongs to the middle class). As a result, while the mean is the measure of central tendency that is usually used to analyze a data set, the median is often used in cases when the data set is heavily skewed. The mode is the least used measure of central tendency, but is helpful in describing nominal data; that is, data that falls into non-ordered categories. For example, psychologists might collect data on hair color, presence or absence of a certain gene, or participants' selection from several options. In these cases where taking an average doesn't make much sense, the mode answers the question "which result was the most common?"

Measures of Dispersion

Measures of dispersion (also known as measures of variation or measures of spread) are descriptive statistics that describe the distribution of data, or how spread out it is. The most common measures of dispersion are range, variance, and standard deviation.

The **range** is the difference between the highest value and the lowest value in the set of data. In the set of data from before, the highest value was 7 and the lowest value was 1, so the range would be: $7 - 1 = 6$. The range is useful because it gives a sense of the entire spectrum of the data, though it does not reveal anything about how points are dispersed within that spectrum, as do variance and standard deviation.

The **variance** is calculated by (1) determining the difference between each data point and the mean, (2) squaring those differences, (3) adding those squares together, and finally (4) dividing by the number of points minus one. So, for the set {4, 1, 7, 2, 1} from before, recall that the mean was 3. The variance can be calculated as follows:

1. Subtract the mean from each value: $4 - 3 = 1$, $1 - 3 = -2$, $7 - 3 = 4$, $2 - 3 = -1$, and $1 - 3 = -2$

2. Square those differences: $1^2 = 1$, $(-2)^2 = 4$, $4^2 = 16$, $(-1)^2 = 1$, and $(-2)^2 = 4$

3. Sum up those squares: $1 + 4 + 16 + 1 + 4 = 26$

4. Divide by the number of points – 1: $\dfrac{26}{5-1} = \dfrac{26}{4} = 6.5$

Thus, the variance of the data is 6.5.

The **standard deviation** is simply the square root of the variance. It offers an approximation of the average difference between any given data point and the mean. The higher the value of the standard deviation, the more spread out the data points are. Continuing with the data from before, the standard deviation would be calculated as: $\sqrt{6.5} \approx 2.55$. The standard deviation is perhaps the most commonly employed measure of dispersion and is the one that most often appears on the AP Psychology exam.

ETHICAL AND LEGAL ISSUES

LEARNING OBJECTIVE

- Evaluate the impact of moral imperatives and legal guidelines on research practices

Basic Ethical Principles

In the nineteenth century and much of the twentieth century, many ethically questionable experiments and other studies were conducted on human subjects. For example, the infamous Tuskegee syphilis study, overseen by the U.S. Public Health Service from 1932 to 1972, allowed hundreds of African American men with syphilis to go undiagnosed and untreated, in the supposed interest of studying the progression of the disease. In response to the Tuskegee study and other morally suspect research, the U.S. government commissioned the Belmont Report in the late 1970s. The Belmont Report outlined three fundamental ethical imperatives that govern any use of human subjects in research:

- *Respect for persons*: Human subjects research must respect individuals and their autonomy (their capacity to act freely). Researchers should always stress that participation is voluntary and should receive informed consent from participants before conducting research. Individuals with limited autonomy (such as children, the mentally disabled, and the incarcerated) should receive additional protections.

- *Beneficence*: Researchers must do no lasting or severe harm to their subjects. They must minimize risks and maximize benefits for research participants. In addition, research should provide net social benefits, contributing to the betterment of society in some way.

- *Justice*: The burdens and benefits of research must be distributed fairly. The burdens involved in research participation should be equal for all participants and researchers must take care not to rely excessively on disadvantaged populations as research subjects. By the same token, benefits should also be distributed equally among participants, and larger social benefits that result from the research should be widely available. Unequal distribution is only permissible when done for compelling reasons, such as differences in individual need or effort.

These three principles inspired a lot of subsequent legislation and other organizational guidelines on human subjects research. The ethical practices discussed below are ultimately based on one or more of these principles, so they remain relevant today.

Informed Consent

Among the suggestions of the Belmont Report was the requirement for informed consent in human subjects research. **Informed consent** refers to the practice of disclosing to subjects specific details about the research prior to participation. These details should include the purpose(s) of the research, the procedure(s) it involves, expected benefits and risks of participation, and any other factors that may influence an individual's desire to participate. Prospective participants should also be informed of their rights, including the right to leave the study at any time, and be given the opportunity to ask and receive answers to questions. The practice of informed consent follows directly from the principle of respect for persons because it allows participation in research to be more truly voluntary: it is impossible to freely agree to do something unless you actually know what that thing is.

Of course, fully informed consent has the potential to invalidate results in some cases. For example, in the experiment described earlier in this chapter testing the effect of melatonin on sleep duration, revealing to subjects whether the pills they take contain melatonin or a placebo could have an effect on how long they sleep. Consequently, researchers are selectively allowed to conceal information or even temporarily deceive subjects when absolutely necessary for the experiment. However, in such cases, researchers must still provide as much accurate information as they can prior to the study, must still allow participants to leave the study when they want, and must debrief participants after the study has concluded. This **debriefing** should explain to participants why information was concealed or distorted, what the actual purpose(s) and procedure(s) of the study were, the results the study obtained, and any other relevant information. (Note that debriefing should be a standard procedure, even when participants are fully informed beforehand.)

Other Obligations

In addition to the provision of informed consent, the principle of respect for persons requires respect for personal privacy as well. **Confidentiality** should be maintained for all research participants, with access to personally-identifying information restricted as much as is feasible to conduct the research.

On top of general obligations like informed consent and confidentiality, governments and other institutions impose and enforce a variety of regulations on human subject research. In the United States, for example, the Department of Health and Human Services and its Office for Human Research Protections oversee a system of institutional review boards. **Institutional review boards** (**IRBs**) are committees that review and approve or reject proposals for human subjects research projects. IRBs apply the principles outlined in the Belmont Report to ensure that research is conducted ethically. Any human subjects research that lacks IRB approval is illegal in the U.S., with a small number of limited exceptions.

There are distinct guidelines for research involving nonhuman animals, who obviously cannot sign informed consent forms. While researchers face fewer restrictions when working with animals, they still face ethical and legal guidelines. In addition to governmental regulations on animal research, colleges and universities maintain laboratory animal care committees to review proposed animal research in an effort to ensure that animals are treated humanely and that any discomfort is kept to a minimum. Researchers are encouraged to explore alternative research designs to avoid potentially painful procedures whenever possible. Moreover, both the American Psychological Association and the Society for Neuroscience have published guidelines for the proper use of animals in research, including that animals be properly fed and that their cages be kept clean.

Unethical Research from History

The history of psychology is full of fascinating but ethically questionable research studies. While these studies sometimes produced astonishing findings and led to startling conclusions, researchers who tried anything similar today would never get approval from an IRB. The following table summarizes a few of the most noteworthy psychological studies that could never be conducted now, in addition to the aforementioned Tuskegee experiments.

Famous Unethical Psychological Studies	
The Little Albert Experiment	John B. Watson conditioned nine-month-old infant Albert to have a fear of furry animals by startling him with loud sounds when he was exposed to a white rat.
The Milgram Experiment	Stanley Milgram investigated participants' obedience to authority, deceiving them into thinking they were administering increasingly strong electric shocks to another participant (an actor). Requests to continue from a man in a lab coat led 65% to administer up to the highest level of 450 volts, even after the actor stopped responding to prompts.
The Stanford Prison Experiment	Phillip Zimbardo set up a mock prison and assigned informed volunteers roles as guards or prisoners, intending to investigate the psychological effects of imbalances in power. The experiment had to be concluded early, after only six days, due to the cruel behavior that "guards" were inflicting on "prisoners."

NEXT STEP: PRACTICE

Go to Rapid Review and Practice Chapter 4 or to your online quizzes at kaptest.com for exam-like practice on this topic.

Haven't registered your book yet? Go to kaptest.com/moreonline to begin.

CHAPTER 14

Biological Bases of Behavior

To understand how biology affects behavior, it is important first to understand the workings of two major bodily systems: the nervous system and the endocrine system. The nervous system oversees and directs biological functions and is made up of the brain, spinal cord, and all the nerve fibers throughout the body. The endocrine system is made up of glands that work to regulate the body by secreting special chemicals called hormones into the bloodstream. In addition to focusing on these systems, this chapter will also look at the tools and techniques involved in biopsychological research; the influences of heredity, environment, and evolution; the biological factors that affect different states of consciousness, including sleep and dreaming; and important contributors to biological psychology.

NEURONS

LEARNING OBJECTIVES

- Describe basic neural processes and systems forming the biological bases of behavior

- Explain how drugs influence neurotransmitters

The nervous system is made up of a vast network of nerve cells called **neurons**. As you can see in the following figure, a neuron contains several parts. First, there is a **soma** or **cell body**. Like other cells, the neuron's cell body has a nucleus, mitochondria, a Golgi apparatus, ribosomes, and an outer membrane. These substructures either build molecules for use in other parts of the cell or serve metabolic functions. Neurons also contain unique, specialized structures called dendrites and axons. Each neuron possesses many tiny fibers called **dendrites**, which extend outward from the cell body's membrane. These thin, branching, treelike fibers contain receptors to accept signals from other nearby neurons. Most neurons have only one **axon**, whose job is to transmit the information from the cell body to other neurons.

> **✔ AP Expert Note**
>
> To keep dendrites and axons straight, just remember: *d*endrites *detect* incoming messages while *a*xons send messages *away* from the neuron.

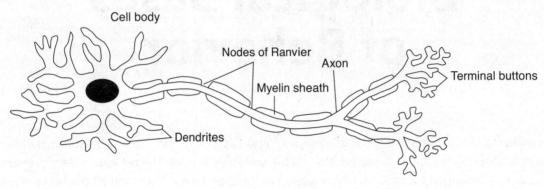

Neuron Structure

The neuron's **myelin sheath** is a protective covering that surrounds the axon. The primary functions of myelin are to insulate the axon and to speed up the transmission of nerve impulses. At the end, or terminus, of the axon, there are branch-like structures called **terminal buttons** (also known as synaptic knobs and axon terminals). These tip-like end pieces facilitate the communication between neurons. Between the terminal buttons of the sending (or presynaptic) neuron and the dendrites of the receiving (or postsynaptic) neuron is a tiny gap called the **synapse**. Communication between neurons, in the form of chemical messages, flows across synaptic gaps, from presynaptic neurons to postsynaptic neurons.

How does neural communication take place? When the dendrites of a neuron are excited enough to reach a set threshold, an electrical impulse is generated that travels down the axon. This brief impulse is called an **action potential**. (Note that action potentials are all-or-nothing: if the threshold is reached, the resulting impulse will always have the same strength.) As the action potential travels to the end of the axon, a chemical called a **neurotransmitter** is released from the terminal buttons. Acting as messengers, neurotransmitters are dispersed from tiny bags called vesicles, flow across the synaptic gap, and activate receptors on the dendrites of a postsynaptic neuron. After being released by those postsynaptic receptors, the remaining neurotransmitters will then be removed from the synapse in one of a few ways: being taken back up by the axon of the presynaptic neuron, being degraded by enzymes in the synapse, or diffusing out of the synaptic gap into the surrounding area.

Neurotransmitters can be **excitatory**, in which case they cause postsynaptic neurons to fire more action potentials, or **inhibitory**, in which case they decrease the frequency of postsynaptic action potentials. The nature of a neurotransmitter as excitatory or inhibitory is dependent upon the behavior of the receptors for that neurotransmitter. As such, some neurotransmitters are able to act as excitatory signals in some synapses, and inhibitory signals in others. The most common excitatory neurotransmitter is glutamate. The most common inhibitory neurotransmitter is gamma amino butyric acid, or GABA. Each of the major neurotransmitters is further described in the following table.

A Few Common Neurotransmitters	
Acetylecholine	Important for its role in neurological arousal, learning, memory, and muscle contraction
Dopamine	Involved in mood, movement, attention, cognition, and learning
Serotonin	Helps regulate sleep, mood, appetite, cognition, memory, and body temperature
Gamma amino butyric acid (GABA)	An inhibitory neurotransmitter that reduces neuron and brain activity
Norepinephrine	Important in controlling alertness, wakefulness, mood, and attention; enhances memory of emotional events
Glutamate	Main excitatory transmitter in the central nervous system; important for memory and learning

Drugs and Neurotransmitters

In the last 60 to 70 years, one of the most promising areas of medical research has been in the field of psychopharmacology—the study of how drugs impact the mind and behavior. One way that drugs influence the brain is through their interactions with neurotransmitters or their receptors. In fact, nearly everything that a psychopharmaceutical drug does involves adjusting neural activity in this way. The three most commonly tested categories of these drugs are agonists, antagonists, and reuptake inhibitors.

Drugs that mimic neurotransmitters and make postsynaptic neurons fire are called **agonists**. An agonist binds to receptors on dendrites and causes them to activate, usually because the agonist has a structure that's similar enough to the neurotransmitter that it's mimicking. With enough activation, the dendrites then prompt the neuron to fire an action potential (unless the drug is an agonist of an inhibitory neurotransmitter like GABA, in which case binding to the receptors leads to fewer action potentials).

Drugs that prevent receptors from activating are called **antagonists**. These drugs bind to the receptor sites of postsynaptic neurons without causing them to activate, thereby preventing the neurotransmitters from activating the receptors. For example, dopamine antagonists block the neurotransmitter dopamine from binding to its receptors. Dopamine helps regulate movement and cognitive functions. Too little dopamine can result in disorders like Parkinson's disease (with symptoms like movement impairment and dementia), while too much dopamine can result in schizophrenia, bipolar disorder, and other psychological disorders. Because it lowers dopamine activation, a dopamine antagonist can be used to treat bipolar disorder or schizophrenia, but there is the danger of Parkinson's-like side effects if the dosage is too high.

A third class of psychopharmaceuticals are called **reuptake inhibitors**. This kind of drug attaches to the axon's terminal buttons and doesn't allow the axon to reabsorb excess neurotransmitters left in the synapses. For example, consider the class of medications known as **selective serotonin reuptake inhibitors**, or **SSRIs**, commonly used to treat depression. Serotonin is a neurotransmitter that affects mood, cognition, and memory processing. When serotonin levels are too low, depression and other mood disorders can result. SSRIs make more serotonin available by slowing the "reuptake" process (when serotonin is taken back up by the presynaptic neuron after activating postsynaptic receptors). By slowing reuptake of serotonin by presynaptic neurons, serotonin builds up in the synapses, causing more postsynaptic receptor activations, which in turn lead to more action potentials fired. This increased activation can result in a mood-lifting effect, although scientists don't completely understand the mechanism by which this occurs.

THE NERVOUS SYSTEM

LEARNING OBJECTIVES

- Inventory the nervous system's subdivisions and their functions
- Describe neuroplasticity's impact on brain trauma

The **nervous system** is a vast communications network of **nerves** (bundles of neurons) that spans the entire body and receives, processes, and transmits information. The nervous system consists of two primary subsystems: the central nervous system (CNS) and the peripheral nervous system (PNS).

The Brain

Weighing about three pounds (or about 1.4 kilograms), the **brain** is a soft, wrinkled organ with two hemispheres that is encased within the cranial cavity and protected by the skull. The brain and the spinal cord form the **central nervous system** (**CNS**), where information is received, processed, and transmitted. The brain controls mental functions such as consciousness, decision-making, memory, and movement. It also controls physiological functions such as heart rate, breathing, blood pressure, and digestion. The human brain is divided into three regions: hindbrain, midbrain, and forebrain.

The Hindbrain

The **hindbrain** is a continuation of the spinal cord, found below the other regions of the brain. The hindbrain consists of the cerebellum, the medulla, the pons, and the reticular formation. Much of what happens in the hindbrain involves the regulation of normal bodily functions. The following table summarizes the structures and functions of the hindbrain that you should know for the exam.

Important Parts of the Hindbrain	
Cerebellum	Extending from the brainstem, the cerebellum (Latin for "little brain") is responsible for motor coordination (e.g., walking and keeping your balance).
Medulla	Located at the top of the brainstem, the medulla controls some autonomic responses, such as breathing, heart rate, and blood pressure.
Pons	The pons is a bulge-like structure at the front of the brainstem. It transfers information from other parts of the brain to the cerebellum and helps with breathing, swallowing, sleeping, emotion, motor coordination, and cognition.
Reticular formation	Inside the brainstem, the reticular formation filters incoming stimuli and relays information to other parts of the brain. The reticular formation is also partly located in the midbrain.

The Midbrain

The **midbrain**, a small region located above the hindbrain, is associated with motor control, vision, hearing, arousal, sleep, and temperature regulation. One of the midbrain's most important functions is to transmit information through its sensory pathways to other parts of the brain.

The Forebrain

The **forebrain** is made up of the thalamus, hypothalamus, hippocampus, amygdala, and cerebrum.

The **thalamus** is located between the midbrain and the cerebral cortex. One of its main functions is to relay signals to various parts of the cerebral cortex. It also helps regulate sleep and wakefulness, consciousness, appetite, and alertness.

Located just below the thalamus, the **hypothalamus** is important for regulating hunger, thirst, temperature, and sexual arousal. It is also responsible for control and regulation of the endocrine system, discussed later in this chapter.

The **amygdala**, consisting of two bean-shaped neural clusters, is a center of emotion and memory consolidation. It is particularly associated with emotions such as fear and aggression. The amygdala combines different types of sensory information in memory. Such memories are usually easier to recall when they are accompanied by a strong emotional response.

The **hippocampus** helps to consolidate short-term memories into long-term memories. As you study for an exam, your hippocampus is working to help you remember all of the facts, dates, and events that you are trying to "cram" into your brain. Damage to this region of the brain can result in the inability to form new memories.

Together, the thalamus, hypothalamus, amygdala, hippocampus, and a few other structures make up the **limbic system**. This system regulates emotions and drives (such as hunger, thirst, and sex).

The **cerebrum** is the largest part of the brain. The cerebrum's surface is an intricate layer of gray matter called the **cerebral cortex**. The cerebral cortex is likely what you picture in your mind when you think about what the brain looks like—the folded, wrinkled surface. The cerebral cortex is made up of four **lobes** called the frontal, parietal, temporal, and occipital lobes. The cerebrum has many functions, including the control of higher brain functions like logic, language, creativity, and decision making.

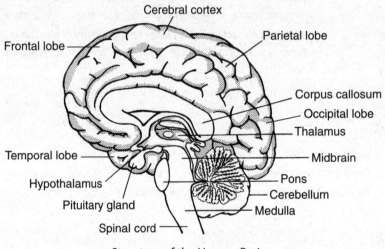

Structure of the Human Brain

The Four Lobes of the Brain
The **frontal lobe** is located in the front of your brain and is responsible for voluntary movement (specifically within the primary motor cortex) and many higher-order cognitive processes, such as memory, problem solving, and impulse control.
The **parietal lobe,** on the top of your brain, integrates perceptions from the different senses and contains the somatosensory cortex, which is responsible for proprioception (awareness of the parts of your body in space).
The **temporal lobe** is located on the sides of your brain (in both hemispheres) and is responsible for processing auditory information as well as language comprehension.
The **occipital lobe** is located at the rear of the cerebral cortex (the back of your brain) and is responsible for vision.

In addition to being divided into four lobes, the cerebrum (and each of its lobes) is divided into a left and a right **hemisphere**. The two hemispheres look roughly symmetrical, but the cerebrum exhibits a characteristic known as **lateralization**, in which some functions are localized to particular hemispheres. One of the two hemispheres is dominant, and in most people this tends to be the left hemisphere. The dominant hemisphere (whether left or right) contains two particularly important regions associated with language. **Wernicke's area**, a region in the temporal lobe near the auditory cortex, is associated with speech comprehension, while **Broca's area**, a region in the frontal lobe, is associated with speech production.

The Spinal Cord

Together, the brain and spinal cord make up the central nervous system. The **spinal cord** is an information pathway connecting the brain to the peripheral nervous system. Beginning at the medulla on the brainstem, the spinal cord runs down the back, terminating in the lumbar (lower) region of the back. The spinal cord is a delicate structure, but it is protected by the vertebral column.

Neural fibers in the spinal cord send sensory information to the brain, and the brain sends back motor-control information. One very common transmission through the spinal cord involves pain. For example, if you accidentally twist your ankle while at the gym, pain signals will travel through your nerves, up your spinal cord, and to your brain. As such, the spinal cord acts like a neurological "highway" to the brain. In addition to conveying information from the brain to the rest of the body, the spinal cord is responsible for many of the automatic responses called reflexes. A **reflex** is an involuntary action and almost instantaneous movement in response to a stimulus. For example, if your doctor taps your knee to check your "knee-jerk reflex," the reflex that your knee makes is due to neurons firing from your spinal cord.

The Peripheral Nervous System

The **peripheral nervous system** (**PNS**) has two subsystems: the somatic and autonomic nervous systems. The only function of the **somatic nervous system** is the voluntary control of skeletal muscles. The **autonomic nervous system**, on the other hand, controls many of the involuntary functions of the body, regulating activities such as digestion, breathing, and heartbeat.

The autonomic system in turn is divided into two parts: the sympathetic and parasympathetic nervous systems. The **sympathetic nervous system** controls the "fight or flight" response, causing physiological arousal in response to stress. For example, when in a dangerous situation, your sympathetic nervous system increases your breathing and heart rate, slows your digestion, increases your blood sugar, and heightens your alertness and readiness to act. In contrast, the **parasympathetic nervous system** manages the "rest and digest" response, reversing the arousal caused by the sympathetic nervous system, lowering breathing and heart rate and speeding up digestion, among other effects. Together, the sympathetic and parasympathetic nervous systems work to protect you from environmental threats and to keep your internal biology in a well-balanced state.

✔ AP Expert Note

Divisions of the Nervous System

The following diagram summarizes the divisions of the nervous system that you should know for the exam.

14

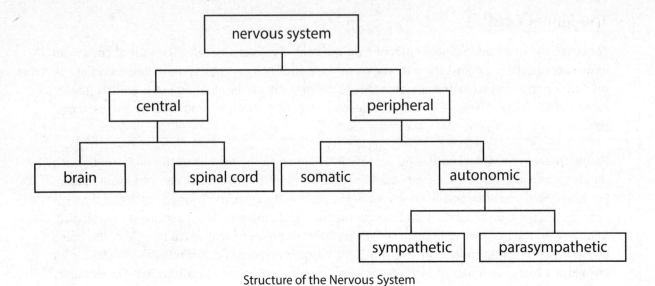

Structure of the Nervous System

Neuroplasticity

The central nervous system possesses an important property called **neuroplasticity**. This refers to the CNS's ability to adapt: to change its connections and functioning in response to environmental stimuli or trauma. Neuroplasticity, which describes changes to the larger-scale organization of the CNS, can be contrasted with **synaptic plasticity**, which refers to the strengthening or weakening of particular synapses over time, a process that is essential for learning and memory.

Neuroplasticity diminishes with age, being at a maximum in infancy and childhood, when the brain is still developing. Nevertheless, even older adults retain some neuroplasticity in their central nervous systems. The effects of neuroplasticity are most pronounced in response to traumatic brain injuries. Even if entire brain structures are destroyed (even whole hemispheres of the cerebrum), the brain of a child can reorganize itself, rerouting numerous connections to use alternative structures to accomplish the functions originally performed by the damaged areas. Adult brains, with their diminished neuroplasticity, can do this only to a far more limited extent, and may never recover certain lost functions.

Other ways in which neuroplasticity manifests can be seen in the loss of senses. Individuals who go deaf often develop enhanced visual acuity as parts of the brain that normally control hearing are retasked with contributing to vision. Similar enhancements happen to the senses of touch and hearing in those who go blind. Again, these changes are more pronounced when the loss of a sense occurs at a young age.

Of course, the CNS's ability to adapt to trauma is limited, especially in adults. Damage from spinal cord injuries, stroke, Alzheimer's disease, and Parkinson's disease is often irreversible. Medical researchers have been investigating **neurogenesis**, the process of creating new neurons, in an effort to reverse such damage, but there is a still a lot of progress yet to be made. For now, most individuals who suffer from traumatic brain injuries must make do with the natural neuroplasticity of their brains and learn to work around the limitations caused by the loss of functions that cannot be naturally restored.

THE ENDOCRINE SYSTEM

LEARNING OBJECTIVE

- Describe the endocrine system's effect on behavior

Another biological basis for behavior is the endocrine system. The main function of the **endocrine system** is to maintain the body's **homeostasis** (its internal equilibrium within a changing external environment) by releasing hormones into the bloodstream. **Hormones** are specialized chemicals that stimulate or inhibit different kinds of activity in receiving cells. Produced by endocrine organs called **glands**, hormones are similar to neurotransmitters in the sense that both convey information in the form of chemical messages. However, unlike the rapid transmission of neurotransmitters, hormones tend to take longer to work and produce longer-lasting effects. If a person has hormonal imbalances, he or she may behave irregularly over extended periods of time.

While there are many types of hormones in the body, each hormone acts in a unique way to affect tissues, organs, and organ systems. Though the endocrine system is distinct from the nervous system, the two systems work together very closely—and it will come as no surprise that the brain is in charge of the endocrine system. The brain controls and directs the glands that release hormones, and the brain itself is actually the target of many hormones.

The most influential gland in the endocrine system is the **pituitary gland**. This gland is a tiny structure located in the brain's core and controlled by the hypothalamus, discussed in the previous section. The pituitary gland releases hormones that promote growth and development. The pituitary gland's hormones also activate and direct other glands throughout the body. You can think of the pituitary gland as being the master gland of the endocrine system, though it is itself regulated by the hypothalamus.

One important gland directly controlled by the pituitary gland is the **thyroid gland**. Located in the front, center part of the neck, the thyroid secretes hormones that control metabolism in the body. (Metabolism refers to the rate at which the body converts food into usable energy.) Insufficient levels of thyroid hormones can make individuals feel sluggish or depressed and gain weight, while excessive levels can cause nervousness, irritability, and weight loss.

As discussed in the previous section, when faced with a frightening or dangerous situation, your sympathetic nervous system goes into action. Atop your kidneys are endocrine organs called **adrenal glands**. These glands secrete hormones that activate the fight or flight response, thereby giving you a sharp increase in energy so that you can handle a stressful situation. Indeed, the secretion of the stress hormones cortisol and adrenaline (also known as epinephrine) prepares our muscles to act, allowing us to use physical force or to run away as needed.

Two other important endocrine glands are the ovaries and the testes, collectively known as gonads. In females, the **ovaries**, located in the pelvic area, secrete female hormones called estrogen and progesterone. Both hormones play essential roles in the menstrual cycle and pregnancy. In males, the **testes**, located in the scrotum, secrete male sex hormones called androgens. The most common androgen is testosterone, which directs the growth of sex organs, causes puberty, and creates sexual desire.

BIOPSYCHOLOGICAL RESEARCH

LEARNING OBJECTIVE

- Identify research strategies and technologies in biopsychology

One of the most challenging hurdles for biopsychological researchers is actually "seeing" the brain and its activity. Given the brain's location, encased within the skull, scientists have had to develop imaging tools and techniques so that they can peer inside. These high-tech devices have allowed researchers to gain greater insight into the brain's anatomy (structure) and physiology (function). In addition, researchers employ a number of well-established research strategies to learn more about the organization of the brain and the heredity of psychological traits.

Research Technologies

One of the earliest-developed tools for researching the brain is the **electroencephalograph** (**EEG**). After multiple electrodes are placed on the subject's scalp, the EEG detects and records electrical brain activity, or brain waves. The results of EEGs can help doctors identify changes in behavior. EEGs are convenient because they are noninvasive, but they can only detect large-scale brain activity, not the functioning of localized areas of the brain.

The **MRI** (MRI stands for "magnetic resonance imaging") is an imaging technique that measures the radiofrequency waves of the brain after exposing it to a magnetic field. The result is a detailed, high-resolution image of brain structure. MRIs can help researchers map the brain regions associated with different behaviors, as well as study specific brain injuries.

A related technology is the **functional MRI**, or **fMRI**. The fMRI reveals changes in blood oxygen and blood flow, enabling researchers to detect ongoing changes in neural activity. One example of what the fMRI can show is the activity of the visual cortex, located in the occipital lobe. When a patient in the fMRI machine is given a photo to look at, for example, colors in the fMRI image change, particularly in the visual cortex, indicating increased activity. When the patient stops looking at the photo, the colors change again to indicate diminished activity. With such a technique, researchers can "see" what the brain is doing during certain behaviors. Thus, while MRIs reveal brain structure, fMRIs reveal brain function (hence the name, functional MRI).

Another technology is the **PET scan** (PET stands for "positron emission tomography"). This imaging device works by first injecting a special radioactive dye in the bloodstream. Then, as the dye is absorbed by the brain, the PET scan locates and records brain activity. PET scans can help doctors diagnose neurological disorders. By performing an imaging study, the doctor can infer the presence of areas of neuron depletion, which may indicate Alzheimer's disease or some other type of dementia. In patients who have epilepsy, doctors can use PET scans to pinpoint the exact areas of the brain that are causing seizures.

Another sophisticated imaging device is the **CT scan** (CT stands for "computed tomography"). Using X-ray technology, a CT scan is able to produce a highly detailed, three-dimensional image of the brain's anatomy. Unlike a PET scan, a CT scan does not reveal much about the brain's physiology or functioning. While a PET scan may reveal details about the activity of a tumor, for example, a CT scan would show the structure of the tumor.

Research Strategies

Researchers use the technologies discussed above in conjunction with particular types of research designs in order to learn more about the anatomy and physiology of the brain, as well as the heritability of psychological traits. Three strategies worth knowing in particular are brain injury studies, split-brain studies, and twin studies.

Brain Injury Studies

Studies of **traumatic brain injury** (**TBI**) can be useful for determining the functions of different structures in the brain. As noted earlier in this chapter, children who suffer these types of injuries often have enough neuroplasticity for their brains to reorganize and compensate for the functions of the lost structures. Thus, the patients most typically studied in this type of research are adults, though there are separate benefits to studying children who have experienced TBI (such as learning more about neuroplasticity).

In such studies, patients are given different kinds of tasks to perform—involving memory, problem solving, language use, motor control, or whatever other functions the researchers are interested in investigating—and researchers evaluate their performance in comparison to controls. Because specific traumatic brain injuries can be rare, these are often case studies, although sometimes larger studies are conducted when multiple people with the same injury can be located. The differences revealed by comparison to controls give researchers a better idea of the specific functions controlled by the damaged or missing areas of the brain.

In related studies involving nonhuman animals, researchers can sometimes even perform controlled experiments by creating lesions in specific parts of animal brains in the experimental group. This more controlled approach (though unethical to perform on humans) can reveal even more about the functioning of specific structures. However, differences between animal and human brains mean that conclusions cannot always be generalized from the nonhuman case to the human one.

Split-Brain Studies

Another way in which researchers have gained understanding of brain structure and function is by doing split-brain studies. A thick bundle of nerves called the **corpus callosum** connects the two hemispheres of the brain, serving as their primary means of communicating with one another. Research on patients with epilepsy has revealed that severing the corpus callosum can reduce the frequency and severity of epileptic seizures, so some epileptic patients elect to have this procedure done to treat their condition. Such patients, along with others who have damage to the corpus callosum for other reasons, are known as **split-brain patients**, because the two hemispheres of their cerebrum are separated, with much less communication between the two. (The corpus callosum is the primary connector between the hemispheres, but not the only one, so limited communication remains.)

To conduct research on such patients, researchers including Roger Sperry and Michael Gazzaniga have devised several novel techniques. The brain has what is known as a **contralateral organization**, meaning that the left hemisphere of the cerebrum receives information from and controls the right side of the body, and vice versa. That means, for example, that the left hemisphere controls the right hand while the right hemisphere controls the left hand. Researchers can thus test the different capacities of the two hemispheres in split-brain patients by having them use each hand separately. To ensure that communicated information only reaches one side of the brain, researchers will flash words or images in the left half of the visual field (which is processed by the right hemisphere) or the right half (which is processed by the left).

Through such studies, Sperry, Gazzaniga, and other researchers have uncovered a number of interesting lateralized functions. Most notably, they've gained a better sense of the cerebrum's lateralization and the specializations of the two hemispheres. Setting aside individual differences due to neuroplasticity, the right hemisphere typically manages tasks such as spatial perception and creative thinking, while the left hemisphere usually manages reasoning, problem solving, and language tasks.

Twin Studies

One final research strategy in biological psychology does not focus primarily on the brain, but more broadly on an assortment of physiological and psychological traits: the twin study. A **twin study** examines differences between monozygotic and dizygotic twins in an effort to determine the extent to which traits are genetically determined. Genetics and heredity are discussed more fully in the next section, but what's relevant here is that identical (monozygotic) twins share 100% of their genes, while fraternal (dizygotic) twins only share about 50% of their genes (just like any pair of siblings born at different times). Through careful comparisons (most often, identical twins vs. fraternal twins, and identical twins raised together vs. identical twins separated at birth and raised by separate families), researchers can gauge how much of a particular trait is due to genetics and how much is due to environmental factors.

Psychologist Thomas Bouchard and colleagues at the University of Minnesota conducted one of the first studies that compared identical twins raised together and those raised separately. The results showed that genetics played a powerful role in shaping behavior, personality, and even intelligence, but that environment still played a considerable role. While correlations in traits such as IQ are higher between identical twins than between fraternal twins (demonstrating the genetic influence), identical twins raised together have higher correlations in traits than those raised apart (demonstrating the environmental influence).

HEREDITY, ENVIRONMENT, AND EVOLUTION

LEARNING OBJECTIVES

- Explain psychology's continuing interest in the interactivity of heredity, environment, and evolution in the shaping of behavior

- Predict the adaptive value of evolved traits and behaviors

The study of the nervous and endocrine systems can help to reveal how human behaviors occur, but alone they cannot explain why humans behave in the ways they do. For that, it is essential to draw on areas of biology beyond neuroscience, to the study of evolution, heredity, and genetics. In the science of psychology, two relevant subfields overlap with these areas of biology: behavioral genetics, which examines the genetic contribution to behavior, and evolutionary psychology, which investigates the adaptive value of behavior—the ways in which specific types of behavior promoted fitness in human ancestors. Both of these subfields draw heavily on Charles Darwin's theory of evolution by natural selection.

Darwin's theory of evolution depends on a few key ideas: (1) **variation**, the observation that individual organisms of the same species differ in their traits; (2) **inheritance**, the recognition that these variations in traits can be passed on from one generation to the next; (3) **fitness**, the tendency of some variations to be better suited to the organism's environment than others; and (4) **natural selection**, the process by which organisms with fitter traits outcompete less fit organisms by living longer and having more offspring. Thus, even though new variations are constantly emerging, only those that promote fitness will be inherited in the long run. Evolved traits are sometimes called **adaptations**, reflecting the fact that the characteristics of species change over time to better adapt to their environments.

Beyond Nature versus Nurture

A common misunderstanding of biology is that psychological and physiological traits are *either* the result of innate biological characteristics such as genetics (so-called "nature") *or* a product of parenting, socialization, learning, and other environmental factors (so-called "nurture"). But there is typically not simple "gene for X" when X is some complex trait like a pattern of behavior or a psychological disposition, and the environment can only shape organisms to develop capacities that they already have the potential for. Thus, the nature versus nurture debate is premised on a misconception. Rather than either/or, the relationship should be considered both/and: nature and nurture work together to shape human behavior.

When evolutionary psychologists ask about the adaptive value of a particular behavior, they need not assume that the behavior is genetically determined and instinctual. Rather, what they are really asking is, why do we have the capacity to engage in such a behavior? How did the development of that capacity contribute to the fitness of human ancestors? Some human traits and behaviors are adaptive because they promote the satisfaction of physiological needs, but others are adaptive simply because they make an individual more attractive to members of the opposite sex. Traits of the

14

latter sort could be said to be the products of **sexual selection**, a concept also originally developed by Darwin. While natural selection and sexual selection are often complementary, sometimes they work at cross purposes, as can be seen in the development of traits that increase attractiveness but endanger survival. To consider an obvious nonhuman example, a peacock's elaborate tail feathers won't help it to escape from any predators (and likely make such an escape more difficult), but they will catch the eyes of any peahens in his environment.

Behavioral geneticists have a similar interest in the ways that genetics and environment interact, although they tend to concern themselves more with figuring out the relative contributions of each and which plays a bigger role in any particular behavior. (They do this through the use of techniques such as twin studies, discussed earlier in this chapter.) The insights of both subfields of psychology are useful for developing a richer understanding of why humans behave in the ways we do.

TYPES OF CONSCIOUS STATES

LEARNING OBJECTIVE

- Contrast various conscious states in terms of their influence on behavior

Consciousness is a topic that has fascinated psychologists since the beginning of experimental psychology in the late nineteenth century. In fact, the earliest writings in psychology focused on the concept of consciousness. Wilhelm Wundt and William James, both notable founders of psychology, were fascinated with consciousness, both from the perspective of how it was organized (Wundt) and how it worked (James). Today, researchers continue to explore what consciousness is, how we are to understand it, and what it means to be in a "state of consciousness."

Consciousness refers to the active processing of information in the brain. It is your awareness of yourself and your environment. As you sit there, what are you thinking about? This book? Your day? What you are going to have for dinner? All of those thoughts would be part of your consciousness. The features of your consciousness at any given point in time are referred to as your **state of consciousness**. While in a normal state of consciousness, you are awake and alert. In an **altered state of consciousness**, however, you experience a disruption to your normal state—such as falling asleep or drifting off into a daydream. Other altered states of consciousness include being under the influence of drugs, in a meditative state, in a coma, or under hypnosis.

While you are quite certain that you are conscious right now—reading this book and studying for your exam—you may not have realized that you experience different states of consciousness throughout each day. Researchers generally agree that we can classify these various states of consciousness into different levels of awareness.

The **conscious level** represents all of the things about you and your current environment that you are actively aware of. For example, you are aware of reading this book and studying for your exam right now. Later, if you talk to a friend or family member, you will be consciously aware of your conversation. But you are likely not actively aware of your breathing, heartbeat, and other biological functions. These body processes, which are being controlled by your brain, are happening on a **nonconscious level**.

According to psychoanalytic theory, all of the memories that you have stored and could actively start thinking about, if prompted, represent the **preconscious level**. For example, who was your favorite childhood friend? Or what did you have for breakfast this morning? You could probably transfer those memories from the preconscious level to the conscious level in just a few seconds.

According to Sigmund Freud, each person possesses desires and urges— especially those that may be socially unacceptable—that are actively repressed from his or her consciousness. Freud said that these desires and urges affect your mental activity on an **unconscious level**, meaning that these desires and urges are outside your awareness. While many psychologists today doubt Freud's claims about the unconscious, they generally agree that people are affected by information that they are not aware of consciously. This information is acting on a **subconscious level**. Two examples that illustrate subconscious processing are *priming* and the *mere-exposure effect*.

Priming refers to the processing of information from stimuli that are outside of conscious awareness. For example, studies show that people can correctly answer questions that they have seen previously—even when they do not remember seeing the questions. This can be very useful for exam takers! When you are testing, even if you cannot actively recall everything you studied previously, your brain may be "primed" to find the correct answer. The **mere-exposure effect** happens when a person prefers stimuli he or she has seen previously over new stimuli—even when the person does not remember the old stimuli. Both priming and the mere-exposure effect represent mental activities that occur on a subconscious level.

SLEEP AND DREAMING

`High-Yield`

LEARNING OBJECTIVE

- Identify significant characteristics of sleep and dreaming

The most common altered state of consciousness—and one that we all normally experience on a daily basis—is sleep. In fact, you will spend approximately one-third of your life asleep! Sleep is a complex process that occurs for reasons that are not totally understood, but researchers have made some progress in understanding it. We know there are mechanisms in the brain that cause us to fall asleep, such as the operations of the suprachiasmatic nucleus at the base of the brain, which controls circadian rhythms of sleep and wakefulness. In addition, we believe that there are a number of benefits to sleep: it saves energy, it allows the brain an opportunity for restorative functions that couldn't be performed while awake, and it limits our exposure to the unique dangers that nighttime darkness poses.

14

Through the careful study of sleep, using devices such as the electroencephalogram (EEG) to measure brain waves, researchers have been able to classify sleep into different categories and stages. There are two general categories of sleep: **non-rapid eye movement (NREM) sleep** and **rapid eye movement (REM) sleep**. NREM sleep is further divided into four distinct, continuous stages referred to as stages 1, 2, 3, and 4. Each category and stage has its own unique characteristics, including differences in brain wave patterns, eye movements, and muscle tone. Every 90 minutes or so, you will cycle through stages of NREM and REM sleep. If you sleep eight hours per night, then you will typically complete about five sleep cycles before waking.

NREM Sleep

Stage 1

Unless you have a sleep disorder such as narcolepsy (see below), when you first go to sleep, you enter stage 1 sleep. In this stage, your brain waves are similar to those when you are awake—when quite a bit of activity occurs. This activity sometimes includes **hypnagogic hallucinations**, the experience of sights, sounds, and other sensations that occurs in the transition between wakefulness and sleep. In stage 1 sleep, you are barely asleep and can be awakened easily. For example, an individual at this stage may be awakened by a hypnagogic jerk, a rapid, spontaneous twitch of the legs or other muscles, sometimes accompanied by the sensation of falling. Early in the sleep period, stage 1 only lasts about 6–8 minutes. While present in the first sleep cycle of the night, stage 1 often disappears from later sleep cycles.

Stage 2

In stage 2, your brain waves slow down significantly, your pulse and breathing also slow, and you slip into a deeper stage of sleep. Bursts of neural activity—called **sleep spindles**—take place. Researchers hypothesize that sleep spindles are important for memory consolidation. While in this stage, you are not easily awakened. Stage 2 sleep constitutes approximately 50 percent of the total sleep period in normal healthy adults.

Stage 3

This is the first stage of what is called **slow wave sleep**. Brain activity and, hence, brain waves are very slow. Pulse and breathing rate are also slower than in previous stages. While in this stage, you sleep more deeply and are difficult to wake up. This stage only makes up about eight percent of the sleep period in normal healthy adults.

Stage 4

This is the deepest stage of sleep, and the second part of slow wave sleep. During this stage, the brain waves are the slowest. In this stage, if you tried to shut off a ringing alarm, you would likely feel groggy and move slowly because you have to "speed up" your brain activity to engage in that conscious action. Stage 4 sleep makes up about 15 percent of the sleep period in normal healthy adults.

REM Sleep

Stages 1–4 constitute non-rapid eye movement (NREM) sleep. Distinct from NREM is rapid eye movement sleep, or REM sleep. REM sleep is the period of sleep when dreaming most commonly occurs. During REM sleep, brain waves resemble those of stage 1, when activity is almost as high as during waking hours. However, during REM sleep, muscle tone and control are diminished, effectively paralyzing the body to ensure that dreamers don't act out the dreams or nightmares they experience. REM sleep is often called **paradoxical sleep** because of this tendency of the brain to behave almost as it does while waking, even though the body remains inert. Periods of REM sleep tend to lengthen over the course of a night, even as the total length of sleep cycles remains roughly constant.

✔ **AP Expert Note**

Sleep Cycles

While sleep is likely to begin by progressing through all 4 stages of NREM, the subsequent order of the stages is somewhat irregular. Typically, after completing stages 1–4 in order, sleepers will return to stage 3, and then stage 2, before experiencing their first REM sleep. After the first REM period, the pattern is typically 2–3–4–3–2–REM, with each of these cycles lasting about 90 minutes. As sleep goes on, stages 3 and 4 decrease in length (with stage 4 eventually disappearing entirely), while periods of stage 2 and REM sleep become longer.

Dreaming

Have you ever been awakened while you were dreaming? If so, you were likely in a period of REM sleep. In fact, most dreams take place in REM sleep. Dreams have been of interest to humans for all of recorded history. At one time, they were considered to be messages from other people or from spirits. Although those beliefs are discounted by the modern scientific community, the challenge of "accessing" dreams still makes it difficult to validate theories about dreaming.

Sigmund Freud is the most notable early researcher to take up the study of dreams. According to Freud, our dreams indirectly communicate our unconscious desires, so dream analysis is a major part of psychoanalytic therapy: proper interpretation of dreams can reveal information that can aid in treatment. In Freudian terms, **manifest content** consists of the parts of our dreams that we remember. Underlying the manifest content are our unconscious thoughts and desires, which Freud called the **latent content**.

There is no scientific consensus on dream interpretation; there is insufficient supporting evidence for the Freudian/Jungian claim that dreams can be interpreted to any degree of precision. Hobson and McCarley have argued that dreams are simply the brain's attempt to make sense of the large amount of neural activity that occurs during REM sleep. When you dream, your brain is as active as it is while you are awake, and you experience images, memories, etc. that your brain synthesizes into dreams. This is called the **activation-synthesis hypothesis**.

In contrast to the Freudian and activation-synthesis theories, proponents of **information-processing theory** argue that more stress throughout the day increases the likelihood and intensity of dreams. Dreaming is, therefore, the brain's way of dealing with daily stress.

> ✔ **AP Expert Note**
>
> **Night Terrors**
>
> **Night terrors** are not actually nightmares or scary dreams, but a distinctive phenomenon that usually occurs during slow wave sleep (NREM stages 3 and 4). Night terrors typically involve intense feelings of fear, rapid breathing and heart rate, sweating, and sometimes even flailing of the limbs and screaming upon waking. While more common in children, about 3% of adults report suffering from night terrors.

Sleep Deprivation

Sleep plays an important role in promoting health and well being throughout your life. Getting enough sleep protects your physical and mental health as well as your quality of life. In children and teens, sleep also supports healthy growth and development. Research indicates that sleep improves learning, problem-solving skills, creativity, and decision-making ability.

The negative effects of sleep deprivation can occur in an instant. For example, a lot of automobile accidents result from a lack of sleep. Being chronically sleep deficient is also associated with many negative health effects. While asleep, your body works to heal cells, tissues, and blood vessels. Ongoing sleep deficiency is linked to an increased risk of heart disease, high blood pressure, diabetes, and obesity. Further, adequate sleep is associated with a healthy immune system, which works to protect you from getting sick. If you are sleep deprived, you could have trouble fighting off an infection. Sleep deprivation can also make it more difficult to learn or remember; studies have shown that learning is impaired on the day following a night of inadequate sleep.

Sleep Disorders

Sleep disorders are conditions that prevent a person from getting quality sleep and can therefore cause daytime sleepiness and dysfunction. Though there are many different sleep disorders, the most commonly studied include insomnia, sleep apnea, narcolepsy, and somnambulism.

Insomnia

Insomnia is a sleep disorder in which a person has difficulty falling or staying asleep. He or she may wake up often during the night and have trouble going back to sleep, or may wake up too early in the morning and not feel refreshed. An insomniac could experience daytime sleepiness, fatigue, mood shifts, and trouble concentrating. There is also an increased risk for accidents, making insomnia potentially very dangerous to one's well being. Insomnia can be a short- or long-term disorder. Insomnia is classified as chronic when a person has insomnia at least three nights a week for a month or longer.

Sleep Apnea

Sleep apnea is a disorder that occurs when a person experiences breathing interruptions during sleep. Without medical treatment, a person with sleep apnea can stop breathing several times during his or her sleep.

Sleep apnea can be caused by a blockage of the airway, usually when the soft tissue in the back of the throat collapses during sleep. It can also be caused by the brain failing to tell the body to breathe. Medical treatment, such as the use of special breathing masks worn during sleep, can manage the symptoms of sleep apnea successfully in most cases. Prevention methods include weight loss and the avoidance of alcohol and tranquilizers.

Narcolepsy

Narcolepsy is a neurological sleep disorder characterized by irregular sleep patterns and the inability to control and regulate sleep and wakefulness. A person with narcolepsy often experiences excessive daytime sleepiness and periodic, uncontrollable episodes of falling asleep during the daytime. These sudden sleep episodes may occur during any time of the day, even when the person is actively engaged with a task. For some with narcolepsy, laughter or other intense emotions can trigger a sudden sleep attack. While narcolepsy usually begins between the ages of 15 and 25, it can present at any age. It is believed to be associated with reduced levels of orexin, a neuropeptide that helps to keep the brain awake.

Somnambulism

Somnambulism, better known as sleepwalking, is a sleep disorder that occurs during sleep stages 3 or 4 and results in walking or performing other behaviors while asleep. Somnambulism is more common in children than adults, and it is more likely to occur if a person is sleep deprived. Because a sleepwalker is in either stage 3 or 4—periods of deep sleep—he or she may be difficult to awaken and will probably not remember sleepwalking. It is a common myth that a sleepwalker should not be awakened; in fact, it could be dangerous to leave a sleepwalker asleep.

Sleep talking, also known as somniloquy, may accompany somnambulism, but may also occur independently. Somniloquy can encompass a wide range of verbal expression: brief mumbling, prolonged rambling, even loud shouting. It typically occurs during stages 3 or 4, but can also happen at other points during the sleep cycle, including dreaming.

PSYCHOACTIVE DRUGS

LEARNING OBJECTIVES

- Outline and categorize major psychoactive drugs

- Define and elaborate upon the concepts of drug dependency, tolerance, addiction, and withdrawal

Psychoactive drugs affect the chemical and physical functioning of the brain. Often called "mind-altering" drugs, psychoactive drugs alter the behavior and perceptions of the user. Major groups of psychoactive drugs include depressants, narcotics, stimulants, and hallucinogens. All psychoactive drugs have some level of impact on consciousness.

Depressants

Depressants are psychoactive drugs that include alcohol, barbiturates (e.g., phenobarbital and Pentothal), and benzodiazepines (e.g., Xanax, Valium, and Ativan). These drugs can put users to sleep, relieve anxiety, alter mood, alleviate muscle spasms, and prevent seizures. Some types of depressants, such as benzodiazepines, can be effective treatments when used under a doctor's supervision. When depressants are abused, however, the results can be serious or even fatal. Long-term use of depressants produces psychological dependence and tolerance. Some of the negative side effects include loss of motor function, blurred vision, slurred speech, nausea, and cardio-respiratory issues. In the long-term, depressant abuse can cause permanent organ damage. Unlike with other types of drugs, withdrawal from depressants can be life threatening, and the user should be under the care of a trained medical expert to effectively end the addiction.

The most commonly used depressant is alcohol. Consuming alcohol slows a person's brain processes, thereby slowing down his or her reactions and impairing his or her judgment. Alcohol consumption also interferes with sleep and can contribute to the effects of sleep deprivation. Because alcohol consumption and alcoholism are so prevalent in today's society, alcohol remains the most researched type of depressant.

Narcotics

Also known as "opioids," **narcotics** are a group of drugs that dull the senses and relieve pain. Examples of narcotics include opium, heroin, morphine, and OxyContin. Some narcotics have valuable medical uses and are commonly prescribed by doctors to treat patients suffering from chronic pain and other medical complications. For example, surgical patients are often treated with morphine, and cancer patients with OxyContin.

Repeated use of narcotics can create psychological dependence. Long after the medical need for the drug has passed, the addict may continue to feel a need for the drug. Stopping the use of certain narcotics is challenging for many users and, without treatment, relapse is quite common.

Effects of narcotics depend heavily on the dosage, how they are taken, and previous exposure to the drugs. Users commonly experience slowed physical activity, slowed breathing, and nausea. Physical dependence becomes stronger with increased usage over time, and withdrawal symptoms occur when drug use is discontinued. In withdrawal, users can experience irritability, loss of appetite, restlessness, tremors, changes in heart rate, drug cravings, and depression. Overdoses on narcotics are common; in fact, the U.S. Centers for Disease Control and Prevention (the CDC) reports that fatalities due to opioid overuse have quadrupled in the past 15 years.

Stimulants

Stimulants are drugs that excite neural activity and speed up body functions, including heart and respiration rates. Stimulants are often used to relieve fatigue and increase alertness. Users of stimulants typically build up tolerance, which means they have to take increasingly larger amounts in order to maintain the desired effects. The most widely used stimulants are nicotine (found in tobacco products such as cigarettes) and caffeine (found in coffee).

The abuse of more potent stimulants such as amphetamines, methamphetamines, and cocaine has been especially problematic, particularly in North America. Users take these stimulants in an attempt to enhance self-esteem, improve physical and mental performance, and produce a sense of exhilaration. With increased use often comes agitation, panic, aggression, hostility, and paranoia. Common side effects include tremors, headaches, chest pain, nausea, and dizziness. The abuse of any stimulant in large amounts can be detrimental and even fatal. More potent stimulants, especially methamphetamines, have proved to be especially deadly—abusers have died from heart attack, stroke, and organ failure.

Hallucinogens

Hallucinogens, also called psychedelic drugs, are drugs that alter mood, distort perceptions, and evoke sensory images in the absence of sensory input. Among the oldest known drugs, hallucinogens are found in plants and fungi, as well as being synthetically produced in laboratories. Physiological effects include increased heart rate and blood pressure. Common hallucinogens include LSD (lysergic acid diethylamide) and MDMA (better known as Ecstasy). Hallucinogens are usually taken orally or smoked. Overdoses of these drugs can result in respiratory impairment, coma, seizures, and in some cases death. Most hallucinogens are illegal substances in the United States.

While LSD and MDMA are considered strong hallucinogens, the drug called THC (tetrahydrocannabinol), which is found in cannabis (marijuana), has a milder hallucinogenic effect. THC can cause euphoria, induce relaxation, and increase certain sensitivities to tastes and sounds. The detrimental effects of marijuana include disrupted memory, slowed reaction time, impaired judgment, lung or breathing issues, and hormonal disruptions. In some U.S. states, cannabis is legal for medicinal and/or recreational uses, but it remains illegal on the federal level.

14

IMPORTANT CONTRIBUTORS

LEARNING OBJECTIVE

- Recognize important contributors to biopsychology

See the list of important contributors to biological psychology in the Rapid Review section of Chapter 5.

 ## NEXT STEP: PRACTICE

Go to Rapid Review and Practice Chapter 5 or to your online quizzes at kaptest.com for exam-like practice on this topic.

Haven't registered your book yet? Go to kaptest.com/moreonline to begin.

CHAPTER 15

Sensation and Perception

Animal behavior is largely a response to the physical environment, so the processes that enable humans and other animals to sense and perceive the world around them are fundamental to psychology. In this chapter, we'll discuss the sensory, perceptive, and cognitive systems that allow us to do just that. We'll also briefly examine parapsychology, a pseudoscience that empirical research has largely discredited.

SENSORY PROCESSES AND DISORDERS

LEARNING OBJECTIVES

- Describe basic principles of sensory transduction
- Identify sensory processes and structures for each of the senses
- Recognize common sensory disorders

Sensation is the process of receiving information from the environment. Vision, hearing, smell, touch, and taste are the five classic examples of sensation, but we also have other senses recognized by psychologists, such as the awareness of our bodies in space and our sense of balance (proprioception, kinesthesis, and vestibular sense, discussed later in this section).

Each sense has a system that allows for the reception and transformation of incoming sensory information. The sense organs receive information mechanically or chemically and then pass along the information for further processing. In other words, each of the senses transforms information from outside the nervous system into neural activity.

How Sensory Systems Work

When the senses detect stimuli from the environment, they translate the stimuli into neural activity. This conversion process of changing incoming stimuli to neural activity is called **transduction**. Transduction starts in specialized neurons called **receptors**, located in sensory organs. Receptors code the physical properties of stimuli into patterns of neural activity sent to the brain. For the five classic senses (excluding smell), these pathways lead to the brain's thalamus, which does its own processing before sending the data to the cerebral cortex. The cortex produces what you experience as sensation and perception.

Psychophysics is a branch of psychology devoted to investigating the connection between physical stimuli and the sensations they produce. A key concept in psychophysics is the **absolute threshold**, the lowest amount of stimulus energy (e.g., from light, touch, or sound) that an individual can detect at least 50 percent of the time. Absolute threshold represents the quietest sound that you can consistently hear or the softest touch you can feel, the point at which a stimulus goes from undetectable to consistently detectable to your senses. Another important concept is the **just-noticeable difference** (**JND**), the amount of physical change required in a stimulus in order for the senses to detect a change in that stimulus.

Weber's Law

Weber's law states that the size of the JND varies in a constant ratio with the strength of the original stimulus. To see how this works, imagine that you are closing your eyes and holding a two-pound weight in your hand, and then your friend places a one-pound weight on top of it. You would surely feel the additional weight. But what if you were originally holding a ten-pound weight or a twenty-pound one? With larger starting weights, it's less likely you'd notice the extra pound. What Weber's law underscores is that our psychological experience of differences in sensation is relative, requiring changes of large enough size for us to notice. For example, if the JND were 10%, you'd barely notice the addition of a one-pound weight to a ten-pound one, but you likely wouldn't notice adding that one-pound weight to a twenty-pound one.

Signal-Detection Theory

An alternative model of how individuals respond to stimuli is called **signal-detection theory** (**SDT**). Because we do not encounter stimuli in isolation, but instead find ourselves in complex environments with many competing stimuli, reaching the absolute threshold might not be sufficient for a particular stimulus to be detectable. Instead, our brains must process sensory information to discern between *signal* (meaningful information) and *noise* (random information). Thus, according to SDT, there is a cognitive component to sensation, which explains why the exact same stimulus might be sensed in one situation but not in another. Our responses to stimuli can vary based on our environments and mental states.

Visual System

Vision begins with the eye, the sensory organ that contains receptors for light. As you can see from the diagram that follows, the eye is made up of several distinct parts.

The eye's outer protective layer is called the **cornea**. The cornea is a curved, transparent structure through which light waves enter the eye. The cornea then bends those light waves, which is

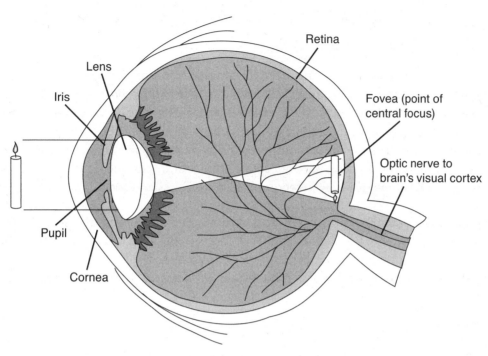

Structure of the Eye

necessary for image focusing. In fact, a popular type of laser eye surgery works by reshaping the cornea to allow for the proper bending of light into the eye.

Just behind the cornea is a piece of muscle tissue called the **iris**, which gives the eye its color and helps to adjust the amount of light that enters. Once light enters the eye, it passes through the **pupil**, a small adjustable opening surrounded by the iris. The iris reduces the amount of incoming light by constricting (making smaller) the pupil, or increases the amount of light by dilating (making larger) the pupil.

Just behind the pupil lies the **lens**, a transparent structure that works in conjunction with the cornea to bend light to reach the retina. The area between the lens and the cornea is filled with aqueous humour, also known as intraocular fluid. The lens works by changing shape to adjust the focus for objects at different distances, a process called **accommodation**. If the lens were to become damaged, light could not be "accommodated" properly.

The white part of the eye is called the **sclera**. The sclera provides structure to the eye and contains blood vessels that supply it with nutrients. Within the sclera is the vitreous humour, a clear fluid that fills the space between the lens and the retina and makes up most of the volume of the eye.

Stretching across the back of the eye is the **retina**. This multilayered structure contains a vast network of **photoreceptors**, specialized neurons that convert light into neural activity. The two main types of photoreceptors are rods and cones. **Rods**, clustered in the retina's periphery, are very sensitive to light. The rods process black, white, and gray, making them essential for seeing in dim conditions. While not as sensitive to light as the rods, the **cones** detect fine detail and distinguish colors. The cones are clustered in the center of the retina in an area called the **fovea**. Having the right concentration of cones in the fovea is one of several important components of **visual acuity**, the ability to see details.

Before sending visual information to the brain, the retina sharpens the images. Visual data is transferred from the rods and cones to bipolar cells on the surface of the retina, which process the data and then activate another network of cells called ganglion cells. The axons of the ganglion cells merge to form the **optic nerve**, a bundle of fibers that sends visual data to the brain. The point where the optic nerve exits the eye is called the **blind spot**. At the blind spot, you cannot actually see anything because there are no photoreceptors present at this location (though other parts of visual processing fill in the gap, so you tend not to notice your blind spot without effort).

The optic nerve carries information to the brain's thalamus. From the thalamus, visual data is sent to the **visual cortex**, located at the back of the brain in the occipital lobe. In the visual cortex there are specialized cells called **feature detectors** that respond to the specific features of an object, such as its shape, movement, edges, and angles. It is ultimately in the visual cortex that sight is produced.

Color and Vision

Color is created through the combination of light waves associated with three primary colors: blue, red, and green. The **trichromatic theory** (or the three-color theory) maintains that the retina has three color receptors—one for each of the primary colors. When these receptors are stimulated, the pattern of the stimulation produces the perception of a specific color. The trichromatic theory is also known as the Young-Helmholtz theory because it was developed in the 1800s by Hermann von Helmholtz, who furthered the color vision research of English scientist Thomas Young.

> ✔ **AP Expert Note**
>
> Recent data has indicated that some individuals are in fact tetrachromatic, possessing a fourth color receptor. However, this variation only impacts a small proportion of the world population.

Shortly after the introduction of the trichromatic theory, a researcher named Ewald Hering wondered why people with missing color receptors could still see other colors, such as yellow. According to Hering, the Young-Helmholtz theory did not completely account for color vision. His work led to the **opponent-process theory**, which holds that there are opposing visual processes that allow for color vision. When light enters our visual system, we analyze it in terms of three sets of opponent colors: white-black, red-green, and yellow-blue. Cells in the retina and thalamus are either turned on or off. For example, some cells are turned on by green and off by red, while others are turned on by red and off by green. You can see evidence of this theory directly yourself by observing **afterimages**: for example, after staring intently at a blue object, you'll see a yellow afterimage for a few seconds after you close your eyes.

Though distinct, these theories may nevertheless be somewhat compatible. It is quite possible that color vision is a two-stage process: the retina's blue, red, and green receptors respond to color stimuli (as the trichromatic theory suggests), and then the neural signals are processed by the visual system's opponent-process cells while on the pathway to the visual cortex.

Color Blindness

Color blindness, also known as color vision deficiency, is one of the most common deficiencies in vision and the one most frequently tested on the AP Psychology exam. In dichromatic color blindness, individuals are capable of seeing two of the three sets of colors from opponent-process theory, lacking the capacity to distinguish either between red and green or between yellow and blue. Those with monochromatic color blindness are only capable of seeing in shades of gray. Color blindness is usually present from birth as the result of a genetic condition.

> ✔ **AP Expert Note**
>
> **Men are more likely to be color blind than women because the genes most associated with color vision are found on the X chromosome. Men have only one copy of the X chromosome, so if they possess a deficient copy of a color vision gene, they don't have the potential for a functional back-up, as women do with their two X chromosomes.**

Hearing

The function of **audition** (hearing) is to transduce acoustic energy into perceptible sound. This is accomplished by passing sound waves through the ears until they reach specialized cells that transform the waves into neural impulses, which your brain then decodes and interprets.

The outermost structure in the auditory system is the **pinna**, the external part of the ear that you see. The pinna, composed of cartilage and fat deposits, collects and funnels sound waves into the ear's **auditory canal**, which is approximately 2.5 centimeters in length. Its purpose is to focus the sound waves toward the eardrum, which is also called the tympanic membrane. The **tympanic membrane** is a tight, thin membrane that vibrates in response to sound waves.

After the sound waves cause the tympanic membrane to vibrate, the vibrations are carried further into the **middle ear** via three ossicles (or small bones): the **malleus** (hammer), the **incus** (anvil), and the **stapes** (stirrup). These are the three smallest bones in the human body; they work together to move the sound from the tympanic membrane through the middle ear and into the **inner ear**. The sounds pass into the inner ear through a membrane, called the **oval window**, and reach the cochlea. The **cochlea** is a snail-shell-shaped, fluid-filled structure that contains auditory receptors. These auditory receptors operate as follows:

- In the middle of the cochlea is the basilar membrane, which floats in the cochlea's fluid.

- The stapes (stirrup) presses against the fluid in the cochlea and causes waves to flow through the fluid.

- The waves cause the basilar membrane to vibrate. The vibrations stimulate receptor cells on the basilar membrane.

- The patterns of stimulation are transmitted along the basilar membrane and then along the auditory nerve to the auditory cortex, in the temporal lobe on both sides of the brain.

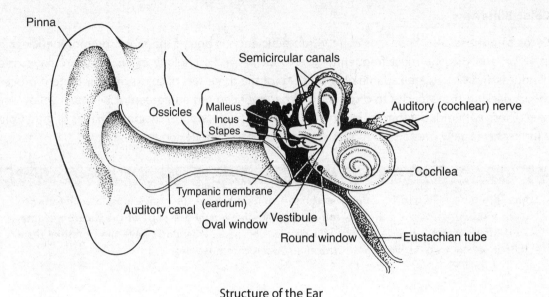

Structure of the Ear

Pitch Perception

A number of theories attempt to explain the capacity to differentiate between pitches. According to **place theory**, different tones activate distinct locations on the cochlea. In contrast, the **temporal theory**, also known as frequency theory, maintains that pitch is encoded in the frequency at which specialized neurons in the cochlea fire. The **volley theory** is a supplement to the temporal theory that maintains that higher frequencies (ones that exceed the rate at which action potentials can fire) are encoded through the firing of multiple neurons out of phase, that combine to produce a higher rate of firing than a single neuron alone. All of these theories may be complementary, accounting for the perception of pitch at different frequency ranges.

Hearing Loss

Tiny hair cells (stereocilia) line the surface of the inner ear. As stimuli enter the inner ear, these hair cells bend and move, which triggers neural impulses in the neurons that form the auditory nerve. One reason why people suffer from hearing loss is because of damage to these hair cells. Another reason for hearing loss is a malfunctioning auditory nerve. Damage to the auditory nerve or cochlea as a result of birth defects, medical conditions, or trauma can also lead to deafness. While there is no ideal fix for nerve deafness, scientists have created an electronic device called a **cochlear implant**. Cochlear implants are literally wired into the nervous system and can send sound information directly to the brain.

Structural damage to the eardrum is another major cause of hearing loss. If the eardrum is punctured or if the tiny ossicles inside the ear are damaged, the ear can no longer properly vibrate in response to sound waves. Another cause of hearing loss is prolonged exposure to high-intensity sounds at a close range, which can happen when regularly listening to extremely loud music through headphones.

Taste and Smell

In contrast to **mechanical senses** like hearing that convert mechanical energy into neural signals, the senses related to taste and smell are referred to as **chemical senses** because they arise from the interaction of specific chemical compounds and receptors. **Gustation**, or the sense of taste, detects specific types of chemicals that come into contact with receptors on the tongue. With **olfaction**, or the sense of smell, you detect airborne compounds that come into contact with receptors in your nose. These two senses—gustation and olfaction—work very closely together, as you likely know quite well from the wide array of flavors and scents you experience while eating.

Gustation operates in the following way. As chemicals enter into the mouth, they are detected by receptor cells in **taste buds**, located on protrusions called **papillae**. While every human tongue contains thousands of taste buds, we can detect only a few basic types of taste sensations, including the four classic types: salty, sweet, bitter, and sour. A fifth taste sensation called *umami* (a Japanese word meaning "delicious," but which corresponds to what people experience as a "savory" taste) detects proteins in meat. When the taste bud receptors are triggered, they send messages to the brain's temporal lobe for final processing.

Olfaction involves a similar but distinct set of processes. As airborne odors waft through your nose, odoriferous compounds pass through your mucous membrane and bind to receptors on olfactory neurons. A bundle of olfactory neurons forms the olfactory nerve. From there, messages travel to the brain's **olfactory bulb**, which further processes the chemical messages before sending them to the brain's amygdala. As mentioned in the previous chapter, the amygdala is a specialized structure associated with emotions and memory formation. This helps to explain why memories, along with the strong feelings that accompany them, can often be triggered merely by smelling a distinctive odor.

Somatic senses

The skin, the largest organ in the body, detects **tactile sensations**, such as touch, pain, and temperature. Just inside the skin are receptors that collect tactile signals and translate them into messages sent to your brain. The location of the receptors tells your brain where the sensation is occurring, while the frequency of signals communicates the intensity of the stimulus: more action potentials firing translates into a more intense sensation. For example, touching a hot stove triggers a rapid firing of neurons that quickly results in you pulling your hand away.

In addition to the sensations commonly associated with the sense of touch, there are also other somatic senses. Important sensors in your skeletal structure (bones, joints, tendons, etc.) and skin enable you to sense the position and movement of your body. The sense of body position is referred to as **proprioception**, and the sense of movement is **kinesthesis**. Closely related is the **vestibular sense**, which helps you to maintain your balance. The vestibular sense relies upon structures in the inner ear, such as the fluid-filled **semicircular canals**. The motion of fluid in these canals (which are oriented at right angles to detect motion in all directions) is converted into signals sent to the cerebellum, which helps to coordinate movement and balance.

Pain

When the intensity of a tactile sensation increases sufficiently, it may result in the feeling of pain. Pain informs your body about potential threats and prompts you to withdraw and seek a safe space to recover. Intense stimuli are received by pain receptors called **nociceptors**, which are found at the ends of nerves that extend from the spinal cord to the skin. Once a pain signal is detected by these nociceptors, it travels to the spinal cord and then to the brain. The nervous system has various types of pain neurons that are activated by different stimuli, such as pressure, temperature, or caustic chemicals.

One interesting feature about the spinal cord is that it contains millions of tiny nerve fibers that conduct pain signals, along with large fibers that control other sensory signals. Because of this structure, some theorists believe that the spinal cord acts like a neurological "gate." When your sensory organs detect pain, the tiny fibers fire, which opens the gate for the pain signals to travel to the brain. The gate can then be closed by the activation of the large fibers. This is known as the **gate-control theory**.

Gate-control theory may explain differences in how people experience pain. If the pain signal is sufficiently strong, the gate opens—because the pain is a high-priority event. But for a minor pain, the gate does not open and you hardly even perceive it. According to the gate-control theory, pain-relieving medicines, along with the body's natural endorphins, work by closing the gate. The pain is still present to the extent that a stimulus is triggering nociceptors in the body, but the brain does not perceive it because the pain messages are blocked by the spinal cord.

PERCEPTUAL PROCESSES   `High-Yield`

LEARNING OBJECTIVES

- Evaluate general principles of sensory organization and integration
- Discuss how top-down processing produces vulnerability to illusion
- Explain the impact of culture and experience on perception

From Sensations to Perceptions

Perception is the process of integrating the sensations from your environment and giving them meaning. When you encounter a busy environment, such as your school's hallway, your perceptual abilities prioritize certain sounds, objects, or other parts of the environment. The features that you emphasize are called *figures*. For example, maybe you spot your best friend in a crowd, or maybe you hear the voice of your favorite teacher over all other voices. By doing so, you have separated these figures from the less important part of the environment, which is called the *ground*.

Psychologists of perception seek to understand how the brain determines what is figure and what is ground. As it turns out, a number of factors, including an object's size, shape, color, motion, edges, and sound, help you to make such determinations in conjunction with the input from other parts of the brain, such as relevant memories.

Gestalt Psychology

Human beings make perceptual determinations by automatically grouping certain stimuli together. The subfield known as **Gestalt psychology** puts forth several principles that describe how people organize their perception of wholes. The Gestalt principles include proximity, similarity, continuity, and closure, summarized in the following table.

Gestalt Principles of Perception	
Proximity	We tend to perceive objects that are close to each other as forming a group.
Similarity	We tend to group objects that are similar in some way, such as color, shape, or size.
Continuity	We tend to group objects if they follow a continuous pattern, such as a line or shape.
Closure	We tend to fill in gaps in recognizable patterns, perceiving discontinuous figures as wholes (see figure below).

Gestalt Principle of Closure

Depth Perception

Depth perception is the ability to see the world in three dimensions and to judge distance. Although you receive two-dimensional retinal images, you can perceive depth due to environmental cues and important properties of your visual system. Environmental cues include height in the visual field, clarity, light and shadow, and relative positioning of objects.

Particular features of visual anatomy known as *binocular cues* also aid in depth perception. The two most important binocular cues are convergence and retinal disparity. **Convergence** refers to the way in which the eyes must rotate inwards (or converge) to perceive objects that are closer (and rotate outwards to perceive objects farther away). The precise amount of rotation gives the brain information about how close the object is. **Retinal disparity**, also known as stereopsis, refers to the difference between images received on each retina due to the different location of each eye in space. The larger the disparity in images, the closer the object is.

Motion Perception

Your brain is able to perceive constant, continuous motion in a rapid series of slightly different stationary images. This is called **stroboscopic motion**. One entertaining way you've likely experienced stroboscopic motion is by watching movies and television shows, which are really just rapid slide shows of static images. Because these motionless images succeed one another so rapidly, you perceive the images themselves as moving.

Bottom-Up Processing vs. Top-Down Processing

Perceptual processing can occur in two ways. In **bottom-up processing**, incoming data from the environment is received by sensory receptors, then transmitted to the brain, where it is processed, organized, and interpreted. Specialized neurons in the brain respond to particular perceptual cues, such as lines, shapes, edges, and spatial orientations. Other parts of the brain then integrate these responses into a complete perception. In short, bottom-up processing starts with the particular details and builds up to a complex perceptual whole.

In contrast to bottom-up processing, **top-down processing** begins with organized wholes, such as memories, expectations, and preconceived beliefs, and uses them to fill in the details. While top-down processing can allow us to make more sense of our perceptions, it also carries the danger of distorting what we perceive. This can be seen in the discussion of perceptual constancy below.

Top-down and bottom-up processing work together to provide us information about our environment. While bottom-up processing allows us to have accurate representations of the small details, top-down processing enables us to make more sense of the overarching experience. Together, these processes create the relatively seamless perceptual wholes that we experience every day.

Perceptual Constancy

Perceptual constancy is the ability to see objects as unchanging—constant in color, shape, size, and other properties—even when retinal images change due to distance or lighting. An object's size, for example, is perceived as approximately the same regardless of changes in the size of retinal images. As the brain discerns the distance of an object, it uses top-down processing to adjust the perception of its size, so that perceived size remains constant even as the image changes. Consequently, if you see your friend at the other end of a hallway walking toward you, you perceive him or her to remain the same size, even though the retinal image of your friend grows as he or she approaches.

The top-down processes that create perceptual constancy carry some unexpected side effects in the form of susceptibility to optical illusions. For example, you normally perceive the color and brightness of an object to be constant, even if the ambient lighting changes and cause alterations to the images your retinas receive. However, your perceptual system does this by comparing the brightness of surrounding images. Consequently, the exact same wavelength and intensity of light can seem to be different colors when appearing in different contexts. An example of this can be seen in the figure below. The rectangle in the middle possesses a consistent shade of gray throughout (as can be seen by covering up the rest of the figure), but appears lighter on the left and darker on the right due to the gradient in the background.

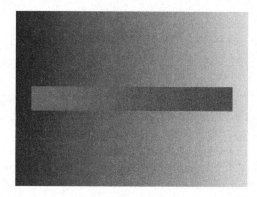

Brightness Illusion

Culture and Experience

As discussed previously, a person's experience plays a significant role in how he or she perceives the world. Nearly all of our perceptual capabilities are influenced by our previous sensory experiences—or by the lack of previous experience. One of the greatest influences on your experience is the culture that you grow up in. In addition to impacting the way you think about the world, culture can also affect the ways in which you perceive it.

Consider one of the most famous optical illusions, the **Müller-Lyer illusion**, depicted below. This optical illusion consists of two line segments, capped on both sides by arrows that point in opposite directions. When looking at the illusion, it may at first appear that the bottom line with the inward-pointing arrows is longer. However, both lines are actually of equal size (as can be seen in the comparison image below the illusion).

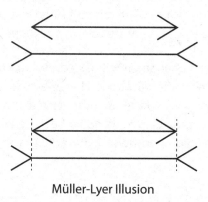

Müller-Lyer Illusion

But not everyone perceives this illusion in the same way. According to cross-cultural studies conducted with peoples from Africa, India, East Asia, and Oceania, some people don't perceive a difference in length. Individuals from Western cultures (e.g., North America and Western Europe) tend to fall for the illusion at a higher rate than individuals from elsewhere. People from some parts of Africa, for example, tend to see no difference in the lengths of the lines and are perplexed by the idea that anyone might see them differently. Studies such as these illustrate that what we learn growing up in a particular culture can literally change the way we see the world.

ATTENTION

LEARNING OBJECTIVE

- Evaluate the role that attention plays in behavior

Attention is the focus of awareness on particular aspects of perception. As someone who probably studies for classes and exams regularly, you know that you can improve your understanding of material by concentrating on it while avoiding distractions. You also know that studying takes effort, just like all instances of paying attention. Finally, you know there are limits to attention; you can only pay attention to the same thing for so long without getting tired.

> ✔ **AP Expert Note**
>
> **Studying and Attention**
>
> If you've been studying for a long time, you realize that your attention is limited. So instead of studying for hours and hours without a break, try taking short breaks. The period of rest will improve your focus when you return to the material, which will make your studying more effective.

Selective attention is the capacity to concentrate on particular information in your environment while ignoring all else. For example, when you study, you use selective attention to focus on the material in front of you and ignore distractions such as other people talking, sounds from a television, or incoming social media messages. The failure to notice a particular stimulus, such as can occur when using selective attention, is referred to as *inattentional blindness*.

One noteworthy attention-related phenomenon is called the **cocktail party effect**. Have you ever been in conversation with a friend while surrounded by other talking people? Your ability to isolate your friend's voice and simultaneously ignore the other talkers is an example of the cocktail party effect. This type of auditory attention gained its name because when people are at a party, they generally ignore surrounding background noise, but perk up and pay attention when they hear someone say their name.

DEBUNKING PARAPSYCHOLOGY

LEARNING OBJECTIVE

- Debunk popular parapsychological beliefs

The sensory and perceptual processes discussed in this chapter were once considered mysteries, but scientific research has revealed much about how they actually work. Nevertheless, people still report mysterious perceptual phenomena that defies what we normally experience. The study of these "paranormal" phenomena is sometimes referred to as **parapsychology**, but this study has yielded few, if any, empirically verifiable results.

Amazingly, surveys estimate that nearly half of Americans believe that there are people capable of **extrasensory perception** (**ESP**). If a person had the power of ESP, he or she would be able to perceive something without input from the senses. Three distinct types of ESP are often distinguished: *precognition* is the purported ability to perceive the future, *clairvoyance* is the purported ability to perceive events happening in other locations, and *telepathy* is the purported ability to communicate thoughts directly between minds.

While ESP is not the only phenomenon studied in the "field" of parapsychology (there are others, such as astrological prediction, psychic healing, communicating with the dead, out-of-body experiences, and psychokinesis, the ability to move objects directly with the mind), it is perhaps the one that has been most thoroughly investigated by actual experimental scientists. In hundreds of experiments, ESP has repeatedly been debunked. Nevertheless, because many people continue to believe in the paranormal, more research will likely be conducted in the future, though it's questionable whether it will ever convince any true believer.

IMPORTANT CONTRIBUTORS

LEARNING OBJECTIVE

- Recognize important contributors to sensation and perception research

See the list of important contributors to sensation and perception research in the Rapid Review section of Chapter 6.

 # NEXT STEP: PRACTICE

Go to Rapid Review and Practice Chapter 6 or to your online quizzes at kaptest.com for exam-like practice on this topic.

Haven't registered your book yet? Go to kaptest.com/moreonline to begin.

CHAPTER 16

Learning

As it's commonly used, the word "learning" means gaining new knowledge. For example, you are in the process of learning (or relearning) the information you need to know to succeed on the AP Psychology exam. But to a psychologist, "learning" refers specifically to the establishment of new *behaviors*. In this chapter, we'll examine the ways in which new behaviors are acquired and how they might be lost. We'll also look at how these principles can be applied, including how they're used to help people solve behavioral problems.

PRINCIPLES OF LEARNING

LEARNING OBJECTIVE

- Contrast the principles of classical conditioning, operant conditioning, and observational learning

Most of the activities you perform on a daily basis are not things you knew how to do when you were born—rather, they are products of learning. **Learning** refers to a relatively permanent change in behavior based on experience. One of the keywords in this definition is "permanent." Temporary changes in behavior don't actually count. For instance, shifts in behavior due to being tired, hurt, or sick would not translate into *learning*. While there are many types of learning, classical conditioning, operant conditioning, and observational learning are among the most researched. Each operates according to distinct principles.

Classical conditioning is a method of learning that creates new associations between stimuli by preceding a reflex-causing stimulus with a neutral stimulus. After sufficient repetition of this pairing, the new stimulus will eventually cause the reflexive behavior itself. In other words, classical conditioning depends on what happens before a particular behavior.

Operant conditioning is a method of learning that increases or decreases the frequency of a behavior by manipulating its consequences: reinforcements cause the frequency of the behavior to increase, while punishments cause the frequency to decrease. In short, operant conditioning depends on what happens after a particular behavior.

Observational learning (or **social learning**) is a form of learning that occurs when learners watch the behavior of others. Typically, this results in the learner simply mimicking the observed behavior, but sometimes observational learners will avoid a particular behavior if they saw it lead to negative consequences. Social learning is especially important for children.

CLASSICAL CONDITIONING

LEARNING OBJECTIVE

- List and explain fundamentals of classical conditioning

In this section, we will discuss the famous experiments by Ivan Pavlov that gave rise to the theory of classical conditioning and its further study by behaviorist John Watson and numerous other researchers. The basic principles of classical conditioning include acquisition, higher order conditioning, expectancy, generalization and discrimination, extinction, and spontaneous recovery.

Pavlov and Classical Conditioning

The theory of classical conditioning largely stems from the work done by Russian physiologist Ivan Pavlov, including his famous experiments on the behavior of dogs at feeding time. Pavlov believed that humans learn patterns of behavior in the same basic way as did the dogs in his research.

In the classic version of Pavlov's experiment, he noticed that a dog would *salivate* (secrete watery fluid in the mouth) when presented with food. Pavlov experimented and found that if he paired the food with a neutral stimulus, such as the sound of a bell, enough times, then the ringing of the bell would eventually elicit the salivation by itself. Ordinarily, the sound of a ring would not elicit salivation but, according to Pavlov, the animal learned to associate the ring with the food and, thus, salivated.

Psychologists use special terms to describe this event. The food served as the **unconditioned stimulus (UCS)**, which is a stimulus that causes a natural response, or reflex. The salivation is called the **unconditioned response (UCR)**, which is the naturally occurring response. Before the dog associates the bell with the food, the bell is considered a **neutral stimulus (NS)**, a stimulus that does not produce a response.

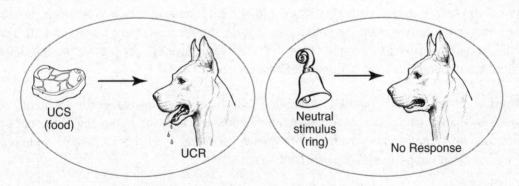

Before Conditioning

Once the bell is associated with the food, the bell becomes the conditioned stimulus. A **conditioned stimulus (CS)** is a stimulus that produces a response because it has been repeatedly paired with an unconditioned stimulus. Finally, the salivation in response to the bell is called the conditioned response. A **conditioned response (CR)** is a learned response evoked by a conditioned stimulus. The behavior that constitutes the CR is the same as the UCR (salivation); the only difference is that it is triggered by a different stimulus.

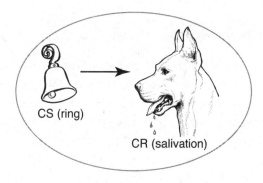

CS (ring)

CR (salivation)

After Conditioning

Principles of Classical Conditioning

Acquisition and Higher Order Conditioning

During his experiment, Pavlov trained the dogs to respond to the bell. The training period is referred to as the acquisition period, the time period during which a response is learned. **Acquisition** occurs when the conditioned stimulus (e.g., the bell) is followed by, or paired with, the unconditioned stimulus (e.g., the food). The conditioning process will typically occur most quickly when the unconditioned stimulus immediately (i.e., within a second or two) follows the conditioned stimulus.

Let's say that you are replicating Pavlov's dog experiment, but you want to go further with the conditioning. Once the dogs are trained to salivate at the sound of the bell, you start clapping your hands before you ring the bell. After you practice this a few times with the dogs, you notice that they eventually start salivating when you clap your hands. The dogs have learned to associate your hand clapping with getting food. This process is known as higher order conditioning. **Higher order conditioning** is a form of classical conditioning in which a conditioned stimulus is used to produce further learning. In other words, higher order conditioning extends the learning one or more steps beyond the original conditioned stimulus.

Expectancy, Generalization, and Discrimination

Classical conditioning ultimately works by altering a person or an animal's expectancy. An **expectancy** is an anticipation about future events or relationships. Because the bell is reliably sounded before the food is presented, the dogs develop an expectancy and, as a result, the conditioned stimulus (bell) *predicts* the unconditioned stimulus (food).

Suppose you are replicating Pavlov's experiment at your house and one day your phone rings. As you answer it, you notice the dogs are salivating again, even though it's still hours from feeding time. What happened? Well, this would be an example of stimulus generalization. **Stimulus generalization** is the tendency of a learner to respond to another stimulus that is similar to the original conditioned stimulus. If the dogs eventually figure out that your ringtone is not followed by food, then they will have learned to discriminate between the two stimuli, the bell and the ringtone. This is referred to as **stimulus discrimination**.

Extinction and Spontaneous Recovery

But what if the food stops coming after the bell sounds? Would the dogs keep salivating on future rings? If the unconditioned stimulus stops being paired with the conditioned stimulus, eventually the learned behavior (conditioned response) will stop as well. This process is referred to as **extinction**. For example, it may take several episodes of ringing the bell without providing food in order to stop the dogs from salivating. The more ingrained the learning is, the longer it will take to extinguish the behavior. If, however, following an apparent extinction of the behavior, the dogs suddenly start salivating again when they hear the bell, this is called spontaneous recovery. **Spontaneous recovery** is the reappearance of a learned response after its supposed extinction.

From Pavlov to Watson

Pavlov's groundbreaking work on classical conditioning paved the way for John Watson and his theory of behaviorism. Watson did not believe that mental processes—such as thoughts, motives, and feelings—were related to learning. Instead, for Watson, learning was all about how people and animals responded to stimuli in their environments. According to behaviorism, psychology should only investigate observable behavior. While many modern psychologists disagree with Watson, most accept that classical conditioning is a common process that animals use to learn from their environments.

OPERANT CONDITIONING `High-Yield`

LEARNING OBJECTIVES

- Forecast operant conditioning's effects
- Explain the effect on learning of practice, reinforcement schedules, and motivational support
- Employ graphs to interpret learning experiment results

Classical conditioning is often described as passive learning; it just sort of happens to a person or animal as an unconditioned stimulus follows a conditioned stimulus. Operant conditioning, by contrast, is a more active type of learning, in which behavioral consequences influence how learners behave in the future. The underlying basis of operant learning is simple: actions that are reinforced tend to be repeated and actions that are punished tend not to be repeated.

Basic Principles of Operant Conditioning

One of the fundamental principles of operant conditioning is called the law of effect. The **law of effect** states that responses that lead to positive effects are repeated, while responses that lead to negative effects are not repeated.

American psychologist Edward Thorndike conducted much of the early research on the consequences of behavior. In one well-known experiment, Thorndike put a cat in a specially designed box. To get out of the box, the cat had to press a pedal, which unlocked and opened the door. At first, the cat didn't know to step on the pedal, but in time it accidentally stumbled onto the pedal and the door opened. After many trials, the cat was eventually able to escape quickly by pressing the pedal immediately after being closed in the box. According to Thorndike, the cat's behavior illustrated learning based on the law of effect. The response of pressing down on the pedal led to the positive effect of the door opening, so the cat repeated this behavior.

Nearly three decades after Thorndike's original research, B.F. Skinner furthered his work and coined the term "operant conditioning." Skinner said that an animal, such as the cat in Thorndike's experiment, learns how to respond by operating on the environment. To study operant conditioning, Skinner designed his own special box, which came to be known as the **Skinner box**.

In a Skinner box, a rat or other animal could press a lever to get a food pellet. Skinner devised the box so that he and his research team could do different experiments testing particular responses and consequences. He found that a lot of the principles of classical conditioning (such as extinction, stimulus generalization and discrimination, and spontaneous recovery) are principles of operant conditioning too. But he also found additional principles that related specifically to operant conditioning, including concepts known as operants, reinforcers, discriminative stimuli, and shaping.

Operants

In Pavlov's dog experiment, the response of the dogs salivating did not have an effect on the bell or the delivery of the food. In contrast, if a dog were to bark when it was hungry and then its owner promptly presented food (and this happened each time the dog was hungry), then the response of barking is an operant response. The dog's barking "operates" on the environment and influences when food is delivered by its owner. An **operant** is a response that has some effect on the environment.

Reinforcers

If the owner's delivery of the food quickly followed the barking, then the food would serve as a reinforcer. A **reinforcer** is a stimulus that increases the likelihood that the behavior immediately preceding it will occur again. In other words, when the dog learns that barking results in food, the dog will be more likely to bark the next time it gets hungry.

Reinforcers are either positive or negative. A **positive reinforcer** is a pleasant stimulus rewarded after a desired behavior. Food, money, and compliments are common stimuli that are used as positive reinforcers. A **negative reinforcer**, in contrast, counteracts an unpleasant stimulus. For example, the pain relief caused by aspirin serves as a negative reinforcer that increases the likelihood someone will take aspirin in response to a headache.

> ✔ **AP Expert Note**
>
> **Escape versus Avoidance**
>
> Conditioning using negative reinforcers can be subdivided into escape conditioning and avoidance conditioning, which differ in the timing of the unpleasant stimulus.
>
> - In **escape conditioning**, the negative reinforcer reduces or removes the unpleasantness of something that already exists.
> - In **avoidance conditioning**, the negative reinforcer prevents the unpleasantness of something that has yet to occur.

The effectiveness of reinforcement is also influenced by certain properties of the reinforcer, including size, immediacy, contingency, and satiation. These are summarized in the following table.

Principles of Effectiveness	
Size	The bigger the reinforcement, the more likely behavior will occur.
Immediacy	The quicker the reinforcement is delivered, the more likely behavior will occur.
Contingency	A reinforcer is most effective when it is only ever received by the desired behavior (i.e., no other action will result in the same reward).
Satiation	The more an organism is deprived of a reinforcer, the more effective it becomes, because the desire becomes stronger.

Punishment

Positive and negative reinforcers increase the likelihood and frequency of a response. However, such reinforcers are not the only way operant conditioning can take place. There is also **punishment**, the presentation of a negative stimulus or the withdrawal of a positive stimulus following undesirable behavior. Simply put, punishment is the process of suppressing a particular behavior.

Suppose your puppy has developed a bad habit of chewing on your shoes, so each time you see it chewing on them, you lock it in the bathroom for five minutes. Eventually, the bad behavior may extinguish when the puppy learns to associate chewing on shoes with being locked up. But punishment can bring negative consequences not seen with reinforcement conditioning. For example, your puppy may learn to fear you because you lock it in the bathroom. Moreover, if the punishment does not result soon after the bad behavior, then it could be ineffective. For example, if you locked your puppy in the bathroom ten minutes after the chewing episode, it may not appreciate the nature of the consequence. Finally, while punishment reduces the frequency of a behavior, it may not entirely extinguish it. In fact, studies show that people or animals often continue to repeat the bad behavior when they believe they will not get caught.

Discriminative Stimuli

Another characteristic of operant conditioning is called discriminative stimuli. A **discriminative stimulus** is a stimulus that signals whether reinforcement is available for a particular response. For example, when a dog gets hungry, it knows to bark. But the dog will likely figure out that the barking only results in food if its owner is at home. If the dog does not bark—despite being hungry—when the owner has gone to work, then the dog has learned stimulus discrimination. The ability to discriminate among stimuli can be influenced by positive and negative reinforcement, as well as by punishment.

Shaping

Sometimes a considerable amount of time is needed before a subject learns how to respond. For example, let's say that there's a rat in a Skinner box, and it hasn't figured out how to press the lever. Instead of just waiting around for hours or even days, the researcher can coax or nudge the rat in the right direction. The researcher may give the rat rewards as it gets closer and closer to pressing the lever. This process of gradually molding behavior to get a final desired response is called **shaping**. Shaping works based on rewarding or reinforcing successive approximations to the desired behavior. This type of procedure can be used to reinforce complicated behaviors that would not manifest spontaneously: maybe after rewarding the rat for pressing the lever, the researcher begins only rewarding the rat for pressing the lever with its left paw. Then perhaps only after pressing the lever with its left paw following a three hundred and sixty degree turn. With enough time, shaping could be used to train the rat to perform an intricate dance to get a treat.

Primary, Secondary, and Token Reinforcement

There are different types of reinforcers. A **primary reinforcer** is a stimulus that is inherently pleasant, usually because it satisfies a basic survival need. Examples include food, water, and sex. Every time you eat breakfast, for instance, your behavior reflects primary reinforcement. A **secondary reinforcer** is a learned reinforcer, one that has come to be associated with a primary reinforcer. Praise, approval, money, and good grades are all secondary reinforcers. For example, money works as a secondary reinforcer because it can be used to purchase meals and other necessities.

A particular type of secondary reinforcer is called a token reinforcer. A **token reinforcer** is any secondary reinforcer that is tangible, such as money or gold stars given by a teacher. For example, suppose that an elementary school teacher gives a student a gold star each time he or she earns an A on homework assignments. And the teacher has a rule: when a student collects five gold stars, he or she gets a piece of candy. Token reinforcement like this can be especially effective, not only because the candy serves as primary reinforcement, but also because the students will eventually be conditioned to find the gold star tokens rewarding by themselves. Systems like these, in which token reinforcers can be traded for other rewards, are called **token economies**.

Schedules of Reinforcement

Suppose you are training your puppy to sit at your command—and when it sits, you give it a treat. Early in the training, you would likely give the treat to your puppy after each and every instance of obeying. This is known as **continuous reinforcement**. After a while, you may decide that giving your puppy treats after every sitting is excessive. At this point, you might switch to **partial reinforcement**, an approach to operant conditioning in which desired responses are reinforced only part of the time. In deciding how often to reward your puppy, you choose a **schedule of reinforcement**, a rule or plan for determining how often behaviors will be reinforced. The table below summarizes the different types of reinforcement schedules (the last four types are all partial reinforcement schedules).

Schedules of Reinforcement	
Continuous	A continuous schedule provides reinforcement after every response. For example, you give your puppy a treat every time it sits.
Fixed ratio (FR)	An FR schedule provides reinforcement following a fixed number of responses. For example, you give your puppy a treat after every four instances of sitting.
Variable ratio (VR)	A VR schedule also provides reinforcement after a certain number of responses, but that number varies. For example, you give your puppy a treat after every three to five instances of sitting.
Fixed interval (FI)	An FI schedule gives reinforcement only when a correct response is made after a set amount of time has passed since the last reinforcement. For example, you give your puppy a treat the first time it sits after four hours have elapsed since its last treat.
Variable interval (VI)	A VI schedule provides reinforcement only when a correct response is made after a varied amount of time has passed since the last reinforcement. For example, you give your puppy a treat the first time it sits after three to five hours have elapsed since its last treat.

Fixed ratio and variable ratio schedules have proven to be especially effective for learning. Why? The learner figures out that after so many responses, a desired stimulus will come. For example, if the puppy figures out that after three instances of sitting, it will get a treat, it may sit more often. While both ratio schedules are effective, variable ratio schedules tend to produce the highest rates of response, which may help to explain the appeal of slot machines and other types of gambling.

A fixed interval schedule is generally less effective than a variable interval schedule, as can be seen in the following example. Suppose that your psychology teacher gives a quiz every Friday. So, once a week, you have the opportunity to earn a reward (a good grade) for studying the material. Once you figure this out, you may be tempted not to study during the week and postpone all your quiz preparation to Thursday night. (This tendency to respond only immediately before the fixed interval has elapsed is common, as can be seen in the learning graph that follows.) But what if your teacher instead gives unannounced "pop quizzes"? You could get it on Monday or Thursday or any other day of the week. In that case, you'd be more likely to study consistently throughout the week, right? Of course, as you'll see in Chapter 17 on Cognitive Psychology, spacing out your studying throughout the week is a more effective way to remember information, so that pop-quiz-loving teacher might actually be doing you a favor by using a variable interval schedule.

Different reinforcement schedules vary in their susceptibility to extinction. Responses that are reinforced under a partial schedule take more time to learn initially, but once learned are far more difficult to extinguish than behavior learned on a continuous schedule. This is known as the **partial reinforcement extinction effect**. If you were to give your puppy a treat every time it sat down, the puppy would develop a very strong expectation for the treat, so it would likely stop sitting soon after it stopped receiving rewards. But if you used a variable interval schedule, the puppy would be more likely to continue sitting after you stopped. Although a treat may not be presented, the puppy still expects that a treat is possible.

Interpreting Graphs

The results of conditioning are often presented in graphs, which you should be able to interpret for the AP Psychology exam. For example, the graph below contrasts the effectiveness of the different schedules of partial reinforcement. Each of the small line segments represents a reinforcement, while the steepness of the larger line indicates how frequently the desired response occurs. As you can see, the variable ratio schedule produces the greatest frequency of responses, while the fixed ratio schedule produces more of a staircase pattern, with longer pauses after a reward is administered. Variable interval schedules produce more sustained responses, as do variable ratio schedules, but with less frequent responses overall (and thus a shallower slope). Finally, fixed interval schedules tend to produce a scalloped curve, in which responses only tend to occur in spurts immediately before the fixed interval has elapsed.

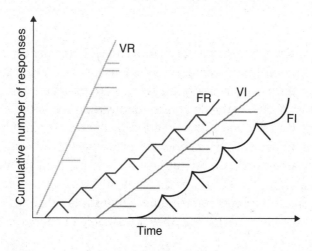

Schedules of Reinforcement

OTHER TYPES OF LEARNING

LEARNING OBJECTIVES

- Offer examples of learning predispositions resulting from biological constraints
- Define and contrast insight, latent, and social learning

Cognitive Processes in Learning

Cognitive learning is a more sophisticated type of learning that involves thinking, anticipating, and other higher-order mental processes. Behaviorists such as Watson and Skinner denied that learning could be studied without observable behavior, but later cognitive psychologists argued that even classical and operant conditioning involved cognitive processes, such as the expectancy (a type of belief) formed in classical conditioning. Other types of cognitive learning include the construction of cognitive maps, latent learning, social learning, and insight.

Cognitive Maps

How do you know how to navigate your school's campus? When you are inside, most likely you know exactly where your classrooms are, where the cafeteria, library, and gym are, and where the entrances and exits are. This understanding has developed through your experience of navigating the school and is referred to as a cognitive map. A **cognitive map** is a mental image or representation of an area (e.g., your home, a school campus, a castle in a video game) that gives you the ability to navigate that particular environment. In addition to mapping real or virtual spatial locations, cognitive maps can also represent concepts or subject matters. For example, you've been developing a cognitive map of the different topics and concepts in psychology as you read this book and prepare for your exam.

Latent Learning

Latent learning is learning that occurs without any obvious reinforcement and remains unexpressed until reinforcement is provided. Latent learning was demonstrated by American psychologist Edward Tolman in a series of experiments involving rats learning to navigate mazes. Tolman placed two groups of rats in separate mazes. In the first maze, food was placed at the exit, so rats released in this maze were motivated to find the path to the exit by hunger. The second maze had no food, so the rats in this group tended to wander about for quite a while before stumbling upon the exit. However, after approximately 10 trials, food was finally placed for the first time in the second maze. The result? Performance on the tenth trial was the same for both groups, with the non-food group exhibiting a sudden increase in speed. Tolman thus demonstrated that rats can learn in ways that aren't immediately reflected in behavior, that they are capable of cognitive learning.

Observational or Social Learning

Observational (or social) learning is a form of learning by watching the behaviors of others. In social learning, the learner observes the behavior of another individual or individuals (and sometimes also the consequences of that behavior) and then adjusts his or her own behavior accordingly, often modeling the observed behavior.

The power of modeling was illustrated in the classic **Bobo doll experiment**, first performed by Albert Bandura. Bandura showed a group of children a film that featured an adult punching and kicking a large, inflatable doll named Bobo. The ending of the film varied, with one group seeing the adult labeled a "champion," another group seeing the adult called a "bad person," and a third group seeing a neutral ending with no label. After the film, the children were allowed to play with the Bobo doll. The children who saw the "champion" ending were the most violent toward the doll, but many children who saw the neutral ending also exhibited strong aggression. Even children who saw the "bad person" ending still showed aggression to a small degree.

> ✔ **AP Expert Note**
>
> ### Self-efficacy
>
> Bandura is also noted for his concept of **self-efficacy**, the extent to which a person believes him- or herself capable of success in a particular situation. Observational learning is more likely to be successful when a learner possesses a high degree of self-efficacy.

Learning by Insight

German psychologist Wolfgang Köhler is well known for his studies on insight learning using chimpanzees. **Insight learning** occurs when one suddenly realizes how to solve a problem. Köhler showed the power of insight learning by placing a piece of fruit above the reach of chimpanzees and observing how they attempted to acquire the food. In the room there were several boxes, none of which was high enough alone to enable the chimpanzees to reach the banana. Köhler found that the chimpanzees spent most of their time unproductively wandering around the room rather than working toward a solution. The chimps would run and jump until, all of a sudden, they would pile the boxes on top of each other, climb up, and grab the fruit. According to Köhler, the solution could not occur until the chimpanzees had a cognitive insight about how to solve the problem.

APPLICATIONS OF LEARNING

LEARNING OBJECTIVE

- Explain emotional learning, taste aversion, superstitious behavior, and learned helplessness in terms of learning principles

Emotional Learning

Emotional learning refers to how our emotions and emotional state affect our cognitive processes, including the formation and retrieval of memory. As a student, you no doubt know that your emotional state affects your ability to study effectively. If you are angry or worried, for instance, you may find it nearly impossible to comprehend what you are studying.

Research has shown that your emotional state at the time of an event impacts your ability to process information, as well as your ability to later recall a stored memory. You can often vividly recall events that occurred during moments of intense emotion. This is a phenomenon known as a flashbulb memory, and is discussed in greater depth in Chapter 17.

The Little Albert Experiment

Behaviorist John Watson did some of the most groundbreaking research on emotional learning. One of Watson's most famous experiments was the **Little Albert experiment**. Albert was a 9-month-old boy at the start of the experiment who, like most kids his age, was frightened by loud noises. But he was not afraid of white rats, or at least not at first. When Watson and his team showed Albert a white rat, he was fine. Then, they showed him the white rat again, but this time they made a loud noise that made Albert cry; in other words, they used classical conditioning principles to pair the stressful loud noise with the white rat. After repeating this sequence a few times, Albert would burst into tears whenever he saw the white rat—even before the noise. After a few days, Albert not only cried at the sight of the white rat, but also at the sight of similar animals such as a rabbit or a small dog, a clear example of stimulus generalization.

Taste Aversion

Taste aversion is an active dislike for a particular food that can be learned through classical conditioning. For example, if you eat a particular kind of fish and then become extremely ill not long afterwards, you may come to associate the taste or smell of that fish (a conditioned stimulus) with the feeling of nausea (a conditioned response)—and you would do this even if the original sick feeling was completely unconnected to the fish you ate! Any time thereafter that you attempted to eat that fish, you would feel nauseous. Often, only one such experience is sufficient to produce a taste aversion, and it may be permanent or take years to overcome. Many psychologists believe that we evolved this capacity for taste aversion for survival reasons. After all, it does help us to avoid food that makes us sick, even if it sometimes makes us averse to perfectly safe foods out of coincidence.

Superstitious Behavior

Some people believe that walking under a ladder can bring bad luck, so they go to great lengths to avoid walking under one. This is an example of a **superstitious behavior**, a behavior based on a mistaken causal connection. Superstitious behaviors are learned through an **accidental conditioning** process, in which a behavior happens to be followed by a good or bad outcome with some outside cause. In accidental conditioning, a learner infers a connection between cause and effect when there's really just a coincidence.

For example, suppose a baseball player receives a new bat as a gift and, in his first swing with it during a game, he hits a homerun. In his second at-bat, he almost strikes out but then hits a second homerun. After that, he starts calling it his "lucky bat" and clinging to it possessively in the dugout. In such a case, clearly there's nothing special about the bat that caused the two homeruns; only the timing of the good outcomes led the player to believe otherwise. Even if the player strikes out in his next five at-bats, an occasional homerun with the bat now and again would create a variable ratio reinforcement schedule that would likely only further cement the superstition in his mind. Indeed, as discussed earlier in this chapter, partial reinforcement schedules make behaviors harder to extinguish.

Learned Helplessness

When we behave in a certain way, we have expectations about what will result. But what happens when our behaviors have no impact on the outcome of a situation? If these circumstances continue long enough, we may develop what is referred to as learned helplessness. **Learned helplessness** is a learned *inability* to overcome obstacles or to avoid punishment. It is a process in which a person or animal stops trying to control a situation after experience suggests that control is not possible.

Some of the earliest research on learned helplessness was conducted by psychologist Martin Seligman. He and his colleagues strapped dogs in harnesses and subjected them to repeated shocks, with one group of dogs having no opportunity to avoid or escape them. In time, the dogs in that group became passive and visibly depressed. Later, the same dogs were placed in another situation where they could escape the punishment simply by leaping a hurdle, but the dogs did not even try to jump the hurdle and avoid the shocks.

SOLUTIONS TO BEHAVIORAL PROBLEMS

LEARNING OBJECTIVE

- List means of addressing behavioral problems through behavior modification, biofeedback, coping strategies, and self-control

Behaviorists maintain that behavioral problems are the results of conditioning and other types of learning. But if a behavior can be learned, then it can also be unlearned. Thus behavioral psychologists have developed a number of techniques to address a variety of problems. These techniques include behavior modification, biofeedback, coping strategies, and self-control.

Behavior Modification

Behavior modification refers to the techniques used to change a particular kind of behavior. Often, this is the primary method employed by parents to teach their children right from wrong. The parent's response to particular actions teaches the child what is appropriate and what is not. Behavior modification can also be used in therapy to treat abnormal behavior. Different methods of behavior modification include positive reinforcement, punishment, and modeling (each discussed earlier in this chapter), as well as systematic desensitization and aversion therapy.

Systematic Desensitization

Systematic desensitization is a behavior modification technique developed by Joseph Wolpe to treat phobias through planned exposure to fearful stimuli. Wolpe would have his patients visualize a series of anxiety-producing stimuli while remaining in a safe, relaxed environment. He showed in numerous patients that this process gradually weakens the learned association between the fear and the fear-producing object, allowing many to extinguish their phobic behaviors.

Aversion Therapy

Aversion therapy works by associating an undesirable habitual behavior with an aversive (uncomfortable or even painful) stimulus. This method largely relies on the principles of classical conditioning. For example, patients sometimes agree to be given an electric shock as they smoke cigarettes. After several trials, the shocks cause the smoking addict to develop a conditioned aversion to cigarettes. The more immediate or discomforting the shock is, the more likely the patient is to change the behavior. Aversion therapy has been used to cure alcoholism, smoking addiction, nail-biting, bed-wetting, gambling, and myriad other addictions and bad habits.

Biofeedback

Biofeedback refers to a technique of electronically monitoring autonomic functions (like heart rate, blood pressure, or stress responses) for the sake of bringing these functions under partially voluntary control. For example, a patient suffering from high blood pressure could use biofeedback as follows. First, the patient would be hooked up to a medical device that measures his blood pressure and displays it on a screen. The patient would then be encouraged to think peaceful thoughts, all the while receiving feedback about how these thoughts affected his blood pressure. As he discovers which patterns of thinking are most effective at lowering his blood pressure, he can then repeat and refine these patterns until he has proven personal methods for lowering his blood pressure. After being removed from the biofeedback machines, the patient can still use these methods on his own: he will have *learned* how to regulate his own blood pressure.

Coping Strategies

Coping refers to behavioral and cognitive efforts to manage stress. There are two major categories of coping strategies that psychologists have developed: problem-focused and emotion-focused. *Problem-focused coping strategies* are task-oriented and involve dealing directly with stressors. For example, if you are stressed out about not understanding a topic in math class and you decide to get help from your teacher or a tutor, then you have used a problem-focused strategy. *Emotion-focused coping strategies* attempt to deal with stress by avoiding the stressor or by attending to the emotional needs related to the stress. For example, if you are stressed out about your math class but you feel better about it after talking to a friend, then you're using an emotion-focused strategy.

Self-Control

The principles of operant conditioning can be used for *self-control*, the process of managing your own behavior. Learning principles can be used to break bad habits and to reinforce or strengthen good habits. Here is a summary of how some psychologists suggest we learn self-control:

- Identify a behavior that you would like to adjust.

- Monitor the number of desired or undesired responses related to that behavior.

- Create a realistic goal.

- Pick out some reinforcers. For example, if you meet your goal each day, you will give yourself something you enjoy. Increase the magnitude of the reward as you meet bigger and bigger goals (using the principle of shaping).

- Monitor and record your progress, and adjust your plan as you learn more about your behavior.

IMPORTANT CONTRIBUTORS

LEARNING OBJECTIVE

- Recognize important contributors to the psychology of learning

See the list of important contributors to the study of learning in the Rapid Review section of Chapter 7.

 ## NEXT STEP: PRACTICE

Go to Rapid Review and Practice Chapter 7 or to your online quizzes at kaptest.com for exam-like practice on this topic.

Haven't registered your book yet? Go to kaptest.com/moreonline to begin.

CHAPTER 17

Cognitive Psychology

Some of the most intriguing questions that psychologists ask are related to cognition. How do we think? How do we create art, literature, and science? How do we store and retrieve our memories? Create language? Solve problems? In this chapter, we will discuss cognitive processes related to memory, language, problem-solving strategies, creative thinking, and intelligence.

COGNITIVE PROCESSES

LEARNING OBJECTIVE

- Differentiate among important cognitive processes

Cognition refers, simply, to the process of thinking. While other branches of psychology are concerned with more automatic processes involved in behavior such as instincts, action potentials, or responses to classical conditioning, the study of cognition focuses on our ability to interpret the outside world, reason about it, and respond to it accordingly. Cognition is not a uniquely human trait, but no other species possesses our capacity for complex thought. We will begin by examining three ideas that describe the way we process information from our environment:

- Effortful versus automatic processing
- Deep versus shallow processing
- Focused versus divided attention

Automatic versus Effortful Processing

Much of the information that you take in is passively absorbed from the environment. As you walk down your school hallways, you are constantly bombarded with information: your classmates and teachers; the posters on the walls; the patterns in the tiles on the floor; the weather outside; the sounds of the buzzing of the lights and the air conditioning. All of this information is gained without much effort and typically discarded just as easily. This is **automatic processing**: the gaining of information without the need for attention. This kind of processing happens involuntarily and, often, without our awareness that it is occurring.

There are, however, times when you must actively work to gain information. In studying for the AP Psychology exam, for example, you might review the lists of key terms in this book to memorize details about the brain or concepts from social psychology. This active memorization is known as **effortful processing**. With practice, effortful processing can transform into automatic processing. For example, when people first learn how to drive, they typically have a hard time paying attention to all of the signs and signals on the road, the actions of all of the other drivers around them, and the functions of all of the controls needed to operate the vehicle. After some practice, though, most people are able to respond to the brake lights of the car in front of them by slowing down themselves, and can do simple tasks such as using their turn signal, all without much mental effort and while focusing on other things.

Shallow versus Deep Processing

Cognitive processing can be classified as either shallow or deep. The **shallow processing** of information occurs when you focus on the superficial aspects of information. You might, for instance, notice the color or font of a bit of text on a sign, or think about someone's tone of voice while speaking. When you instead take in the meaning of those words, **deep processing** occurs. The meaning may be analyzed in terms of other associations, images, or past experiences. With shallow processing, the new information will likely be quickly forgotten, but with deep processing the information is much longer-lasting. For example, suppose you are listening to your English teacher talk in class. As you take in your teacher's words, you are using shallow processing—you might notice that your teacher's voice is deep or nasal, quiet or energetic. But as you think about what your teacher is saying and ascribe meaning to it, you use deep processing.

Focused versus Divided Attention

Attention is your brain's ability to focus on stimuli or other information. Your attention span is your ability to keep your mind focused on something through careful observing or listening over time. Attention is often a prerequisite for other cognitive functions: you first must pay attention to something before you can process it for meaning and understanding. The brain uses different kinds of processing, depending on whether attention is trained on a single object (focused) or multiple objects (divided).

Focused attention is the ability to concentrate your attention on a target stimulus. When you use focused attention, you can pick out particular stimuli and concentrate on fine details and other relevant information. The target stimulus might be external sights and sounds, or it might be internal, as when you think about the way your body feels or your emotions. If you screen out all background stimuli and focus exclusively on the target, you're using a similar process known as selective attention (discussed in Chapter 15).

Divided attention is the ability to process two or more stimuli or to react to multiple demands simultaneously. As such, divided attention is often referred to as multitasking. It is not possible to apply focused attention to multiple tasks; some information is always lost from at least one of the tasks. If you have ever tried to navigate a busy hallway while texting, you have used divided attention, and you may have found yourself bumping into things or making more texting errors than usual.

MEMORY

LEARNING OBJECTIVES

- Compare and contrast psychological and physiological memory systems
- Organize underlying principles of memory encoding, storage, and construction
- Identify memory improvement strategies

While people often think of memory as a vast warehouse of facts and past experiences, memory is actually a more active process than you might suspect. **Memory** consists of learning that has persisted over time and information that has been stored and can be retrieved. Memory involves three distinct processes called *encoding*, *storage*, and *retrieval*. Incoming information is first encoded, or changed into a usable form. Next, the information is stored in your brain, so that it can later be retrieved and used. As you study for your AP Psychology exam, you are going to have to encode, store, and retrieve a lot of information about key terms, concepts, theories, and contributors to psychology.

Encoding

Encoding is the process of putting new information into memory. As discussed earlier in the chapter, you take in some types of information automatically and other types effortfully.

Your brain uses different types of *memory codes* to translate information from your senses into mental representations:

- **Acoustic codes** represent information as sequences of sounds.
- **Visual codes** represent information as pictures.
- **Semantic codes** represent the general meaning of experiences.

Suppose, for example, you see a poster that reads, "The school dance is next Friday." You might encode the sound of the words as if they had been spoken (acoustic coding), the image of the letters as they were arranged on the poster (visual coding), or the mental image or idea of what the school dance will be like (semantic coding). When using semantic encoding, the more vivid the context, the stronger the encoding. For example, you will be much less likely to forget there is a dance if upon seeing the poster you imagine yourself at the dance and think about what it will be like.

Both visual and semantic encoding are enhanced in situations with ample imagery. **Imagery** is a set of mental pictures that serves as an aid to effortful processing. Children, for example, are typically shown pictures that represent new words they are learning. In addition, we tend to recall information best when we can put it into the context of our own lives, a phenomenon called the **self-reference effect**.

Storage

After encoding, information must be stored if it is to be later recalled. Memory storage can be classified into several categories, including sensory, working, short-term, and long-term memory.

Sensory Memory

Sensory memory is the first stage of memory, which holds an exact copy of incoming information for just a few seconds. This is the most fleeting kind of memory storage, and consists most notably of visual and auditory memory, as well as memories for the other senses. Visual memory is referred to as **iconic memory**, and auditory memory is called **echoic memory**.

Short-Term Memory

Because sensory memory fades very quickly and could be lost altogether, it is essential to transfer important information into short-term memory. **Short-term memory** is a memory system that holds small amounts of information for brief periods of time. In other words, your short-term memory is limited in both capacity and duration. Not everything that you see or hear stays in your memory; your selective attention controls what information moves on to your short-term memory. Most of us can only retain about seven (plus or minus two) pieces of information at any given time; without rehearsal or chunking, this information can fade in under a minute.

Short-term memory can be prolonged through **maintenance rehearsal**, which is the repetition of a piece of information to prevent forgetting until it can be used. For example, if someone tells you their phone number, you might repeat it out loud or in your mind until you can find a pen to write it down.

Working Memory

Working memory is closely connected to short-term memory. **Working memory** enables you to keep a few different pieces of information in your consciousness at the same time and to actively process that information. You can think of working memory as a kind of "mental scratchpad." This is the form of memory that allows you to do simple math in your head.

Long-Term Memory

With enough rehearsal, information is consolidated from short-term into long-term memory, a seemingly limitless warehouse for knowledge that you are then able to recall on demand, sometimes for the rest of your life. One of the ways that information makes it into long-term memory is elaborative rehearsal. **Elaborative rehearsal**, closely tied to the self-reference effect noted earlier, is a type of rehearsal that links new information with existing memories and knowledge. Unlike maintenance rehearsal, which is simply a way of keeping the information at the forefront of consciousness, elaborative rehearsal is the association of the information with other knowledge already stored in long-term memory.

There are two basic types of long-term memory: implicit and explicit. **Implicit memory**, also referred to as **procedural memory**, is the long-term memory of conditioned responses and learned skills. The skills involved in riding a bike or typing on a keyboard are examples of implicit, procedural memories. **Explicit memory**, also known as **declarative memory**, consists of those memories that require conscious recall. Knowing that Paris is the capital of France or remembering the Pythagorean theorem are examples of explicit memories. Explicit memory can be further divided into **semantic memory** (the facts that you know) and **episodic memory** (your experiences).

Spacing Effect

Research has revealed that fast learning can result in quicker forgetting. You tend to retain information longer when you rehearse the information over time. This tendency for distributed study to result in better, longer-term retention is called the **spacing effect**. For example, as you prepare for your AP Psychology exam, you will retain more information if you spread out your study over multiple sessions for several weeks, as opposed to "cramming" at the last moment. As you'll see in the section on memory retrieval below, Hermann Ebbinghaus conducted foundational research demonstrating the effectiveness of this kind of spaced learning.

Serial Position Effect

One of the most common memory experiments involves giving someone a long list of words or names, letting the person read the list once or twice, and then asking him or her to recall from memory as many of the list's items as possible. It turns out that most people best recall the first and last few items on the list. Remembering the last few list items is referred to as the **recency effect**; the last items are still in the person's working memory. Remembering the first few items is called the **primacy effect**; it occurs because the learner has had more time to process the memory of the first items. The recency and primacy effects combine to produce something called the serial position effect. The **serial position effect** is the tendency to most effectively recall the first and last several items in a list.

Mnemonics

Mnemonic devices are a common way to store information, particularly lists. A **mnemonic** is a memory aid, especially a technique that uses imagery and organizational devices. For example, in your math class, you may have encountered the mnemonic "Please Excuse My Dear Aunt Sally" to memorize the order of operations rule known as *PEMDAS* (parentheses, exponents, multiplication, division, addition, subtraction). Such devices can be extremely useful, especially for students.

One especially powerful type of mnemonic device is called the method of loci (pronounced "LOW-sigh," *loci* is the plural for *locus*, meaning place or location). The **method of loci** is a mnemonic technique that works by placing an image of each item to be remembered at particular points along an imaginary journey through a location. The information can then be recalled in a specific order by retracing the same route through the location. To use this technique, first think about a familiar location, such as your home. Imagine that you walk through your front door, and then go into the living room, kitchen, and every other room. In each room, you imagine there is an item that you want to remember. The more vivid or unusual the image you construct, the more memorable that item will be. Later, when you wish to recall the list, simply take a mental walk through your home and recall the images you formed earlier.

Chunking

Chunking (sometimes referred to as *clustering*) is a memory trick that involves taking a large list and dividing its elements into meaningful subgroups. For example, consider the following list of 16 letters: E-M-O-S-E-W-A-O-S-S-I-H-C-Y-S-P. Memorizing the list in order might prove difficult until you realize that you can reverse the order and group the letters into meaningful chunks: PSYCH, IS, SO, AWESOME. Similarly, when you learn a phone number, you typically remember it as two groups of three numbers and a group of four numbers, rather than as ten numbers in a sequence.

Retrieval

Memories that are stored are of no further use unless you can pull them back out to use them. **Retrieval** is the process of demonstrating that something learned has been retained. Most people think about retrieval in terms of **recall**—the ability to reproduce memorized information with a minimum of external cues—but retrieval can be also be demonstrated by recognizing or quickly relearning information.

Recognition, the ability to correctly identify previously learned information, is often easier than recall. Police departments tend to believe in the high accuracy of recognition—which is why they frequently use "police lineups" to help identify potential criminals. Recognition ability is something that you can take advantage of in the multiple-choice section of the AP Psychology exam, as you need only to recognize the correct information presented among the choices. In the free-response section, however, you'll need to rely more upon your recall of unprompted information to answer completely, which requires studying of greater depth and detail.

Relearning is another way of demonstrating that information has been stored in long-term memory. In studying the memorization of lists, German researcher Hermann Ebbinghaus found that his recall of a list of short words he had learned the previous day was often quite poor. However, he was able to rememorize the list much more quickly the second time. Ebbinghaus interpreted this to mean that the information had been stored, even though it wasn't readily available for recall. Through additional research, he discovered that the longer the amount of time between sessions of relearning, the greater the retention of the information later on. Ebbinghaus called this phenomenon the *spacing effect* (defined earlier in this chapter).

After conducting several memorization experiments, Ebbinghaus noted what he called a "curve of forgetting." Within the first couple of days of memorizing a list of words, his recall dropped sharply. Then the forgetting leveled off, and he was able to retain 20–25 percent of the words over a long period of time, as can be seen in the following figure.

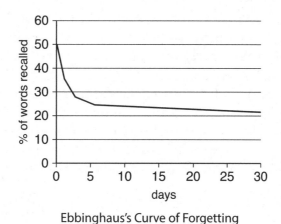

Ebbinghaus's Curve of Forgetting

Retrieval Cues

If you were to read this chapter twice, on your second read-through, your implicit memories (unintentional recollection from prior experience) stored during the first reading would help you read it faster the second time. This improvement of performance is referred to as priming. **Priming** is the activation, often unconscious, of particular associations that helps with memory retrieval.

Memories may also be evoked, or primed, by emotions. Emotions that accompany positive or negative events become retrieval cues. Because of this tendency, some memories can be described as mood-congruent. **Mood-congruent memory** occurs when your current mood cues memories that were formed during the same mood. For example, research has shown that people who learned a list of words while in a happy mood recalled them better when happy.

One of the most interesting memory phenomena is **déjà vu** (from the French for "already seen"), which is the feeling that a new experience, such as visiting an unfamiliar place, has actually happened to you before. How is it that your memory system produces such a feeling? Some researchers believe it is because the cues of the current situation retrieve a similar situation from an earlier time.

Memory Construction Errors

Unfortunately, memory construction is not without error. While there are multiple types of memory construction errors, two prominent errors include the misinformation effect and source amnesia.

Misinformation Effect

Memory can be faulty to the point where two people can recall the same event as occurring in completely different ways. Memories are influenced heavily by your thoughts, moods, and feelings both while the event is occurring and later during recall.

Cognitive psychologist Elizabeth Loftus has done some of the most notable research on the **misinformation effect**, a phenomenon in which memories are altered by misleading information provided at the point of encoding or recall. Loftus' studies show that when eyewitnesses to an event are later exposed to new and misleading information about it, their recollections often become distorted. In one example, participants viewed a simulated automobile accident at an intersection with a stop sign. After the viewing, half the participants received a suggestion that the traffic sign was a yield sign. When asked later what traffic sign they remembered seeing at the intersection, those who had been given the suggestion tended to claim that they had seen a yield sign. Those who had not received the false information were much more accurate in their recollection.

Source Amnesia

Source amnesia is another memory construction error involving confusion between semantic and episodic memory: a person remembers the details of an event, but confuses the context under which those details were gained. Source amnesia often manifests when a person hears a story of something that happened to someone else and later recalls the story as having happened to him- or herself.

Memory Loss and Forgetting

Memory—even long-term memory—is not always permanent. Several phenomena can result in the loss of memorized information. Memory loss is often associated with a loss of cognitive function or other types of brain disorders. And memories are simply lost naturally over time through a process of fading referred to as **memory decay**.

Amnesia

Amnesia is the inability to store and/or retrieve memories. **Anterograde amnesia** is the inability to encode new memories. Those suffering from this type of amnesia can usually recall events that are already in their memory. Anterograde amnesia often results from damage to the brain's hippocampus. **Retrograde amnesia**, on the other hand, is the inability to recall previously formed memories, usually those memories prior to a brain injury.

Interference

Forgetting can also be due to **interference**, which is a retrieval error caused by the existence of other (usually similar) information. Interference can be classified as either retroactive or proactive. **Retroactive interference** is the disruptive effect of new learning on the retrieval of old information. For example, if you took a French class last year, and a Spanish class this year, your new Spanish language skills may hinder your ability to recall the French you learned. In contrast, when you experience **proactive interference**, old information is interfering with new learning. Ebbinghaus found that with each successive list he learned, his recall for new lists decreased over time, an effect he attributed to interference caused by older lists.

17

Repression

According to Sigmund Freud and psychoanalytic theory, another way that we forget is through repression. **Repression** is a basic defense mechanism in which a person unconsciously pushes unwanted, anxiety-producing memories out of awareness. In this same theoretical framework, if a person actively tries to put something out of mind, then that is called **suppression**.

While some events are repressed, others seem to be frozen in your memory. The term **flashbulb memory** is used to describe images that seem to be locked in memory at a time of personal trauma, an accident, or some other emotionally significant event. For example, people who were old enough at the time of the moon landing, the fall of the Berlin Wall, or the September 11th terrorist attacks in the United States are often able to recall where they were when they learned about those events with tremendous clarity. Like photographs, flashbulb memories preserve particular experiences in great detail and are almost immediately available in your memory, due to the strong emotional connections (positive or negative) they possess.

Improving Memory

As a student, you are probably sometimes disappointed with your forgetfulness—especially during a really tough exam. Fortunately, there are a few strategies that can help you strengthen your memories:

- Use repetition. To learn something, study it over several study sessions. New memories will be weak, so you have to practice them.

- Make the information meaningful. By relating the information to your life or something you already know well, you will increase the number of retrieval cues.

- Self-assess your own knowledge by testing yourself. Then rehearse the information you were not able to recall.

- Mentally recreate the situation or mood you were in when you first learned the information. This can jog your memory.

- Use mnemonic devices, acronyms, and rhymes to build more memorable associations.

- Minimize interference by studying in a quiet environment.

- Health matters. Getting enough sleep and eating a healthy, well-balanced diet have shown to be key in memory construction.

17

LANGUAGE

LEARNING OBJECTIVE

- Explain the interrelationship of biological, cognitive, and cultural factors in advancing language acquisition, development, and use

Language consists of words or symbols and the rules for combining them meaningfully. Whether it is written, spoken, or signed, language is fundamental to both thinking and communicating with others. How language is structured is a key focus of this section.

Basic Components of Language

According to many linguists and psycholinguists, there are five basic components of language: phonology, morphology, semantics, syntax, and pragmatics.

Phonology

Phonology refers to the actual sound of language. There are about 40 speech sounds or phonemes in English, although many more exist in other languages. A **phoneme** is the smallest unit of sound in a language. Children must learn to produce and recognize the sounds of language, separating them from environmental noises and other human-created sounds, like coughing. For a child to learn to say the word *cat*, he or she must utter the phonemes *c*, *a*, and *t*.

Morphology

Morphology refers to the structure of words. Many words are composed of multiple building blocks called morphemes, each of which connotes a particular meaning. A **morpheme** is the smallest unit of meaning in a language. Small words, such as *dog* or *walk*, are morphemes. If you add the letter *s* to *dog*, you now have two morphemes: *dog(s)*. If you add *–ing* to *walk*, you also have two morphemes: *walk(ing)*. Many words are composed of a variety of morphemes combined to produce a unique meaning. Consider the word *circumscribed*, which can be broken into three morphemes: *circum–*, meaning "around"; *–scribe–*, the verb root meaning "to write"; and *–ed*, indicating an action in the past. Together, you can see that *circumscribed* describes an action in which someone "drew a circle around something."

> ✔ **AP Expert Note**
>
> *Phonemes* are the basic speech sounds of a language, and *morphemes* are the smallest meaningful units (e.g., syllables, words, prefixes, and suffixes) in a language.

Semantics and Syntax

Semantics refers to the set of rules that you use to derive meaning from words and sentences. A child must learn that certain combinations of phonemes represent certain physical objects or events, and that words may refer to entire categories, such as *women*, while others refer to specific members of categories, such as *mommy*. One can see this skill developing in young children as they may initially refer to all women as "mommy."

Syntax refers to how words are put together to form sentences. For example, "Eli has only four classes this semester" has a very different meaning than "Only Eli has four classes this semester."

Together, semantics and syntax form a language's grammar. **Grammar** is the set of rules for combining language units into meaningful speech or writing. Grammar allows for a language to be *productive*, to generate new thoughts or ideas. Words can be arranged to make a seemingly infinite number of sentences, providing a powerful tool for thinking.

Pragmatics

Finally, **pragmatics** refers to the dependence of language on context and preexisting knowledge. In other words, the manner in which you speak may differ depending on the audience and your relationship to that audience. Imagine asking to share a seat on a bus. Depending on whom you ask, you might word this request in wildly different ways. To a stranger, you might be more formal: "Pardon me, do you mind if I share this seat?" To a close friend, you may be less so: "Hey, move over!"

How We Learn Language

To effectively interact with their families and society, children must learn to communicate through language. An important precursor to language is babbling. **Babbling** is the repetition of syllables, forming the first sounds infants make that resemble speech. Almost without exception, children—including deaf children—spontaneously begin to babble during their first year. For hearing children, babbling reaches its highest frequency between nine and twelve months. For deaf children, verbal babbling ceases soon after it begins.

The timeline of language acquisition is fairly consistent among children. Around their first birthday, most children enter the **one-word stage**—the stage of language development during which children tend to use one word at a time. From 12 to 18 months, children typically integrate about one additional word into their lexicons per month.

Starting at around 18 months, an "explosion of language" begins in which the child quickly learns dozens of words, and uses each word with varying inflection and gestures to convey a desired meaning. For example, a child may ask, "Ball?," while pointing at a pile of various toys, in an effort to request a ball. The same child may also point to a toy car and ask, "Ball?," in an attempt to distinguish between a ball and a car. For children at this age, gestures, inflection, and context are essential for the parent or caregiver to identify the meaning. Between 18 and 20 months of age, children begin to combine words. By their second birthday, most have entered the **two-word stage**—the stage of language development during which children tend to use two-word statements. The child in the previous example may point at the ball and say "play ball" to tell a parent that she would like to play with the ball.

17

By the age of two-and-a-half to three years, children can usually speak in longer sentences. Vocabulary grows very rapidly. As a child creates longer sentences, grammatical errors increase as the child internalizes the complex rules of grammar. These include errors of growth in which a child applies a grammatical rule (often a morpheme) in a situation where it does not apply: *runned* instead of *ran*, or *funner* instead of *more fun*.

For the most part, language is substantially mastered by the age of five. The acquisition of language appears easy for most children, which has led to significant speculation on exactly how this occurs.

Language Acquisition Theories

Attempts to explain how humans acquire language have resulted in a number of theories. Two prominent theories come from behaviorism and from biological psychology.

Behaviorist Theory

The behaviorist theory on language, proposed by B.F. Skinner, explains language acquisition through operant conditioning. Young babies are capable of distinguishing between phonemes of all human languages. By six months of age, however, they show a strong preference for the phonemes in the language spoken by their parents.

> **✔ AP Expert Note**
>
> **See Chapter 16 on Learning for more on operant conditioning.**

Skinner suggested that children learn language by imitating the language of their parents and other adults. Successful attempts are rewarded (reinforced) through praise, and unsuccessful attempts are corrected or ignored. Just as learning principles can be used to teach animals various tasks (e.g., pressing levers and buttons), so too can these principles be used to teach children language.

While the behaviorist theory may account for the development of words and speech, many psycholinguists point out that this theory cannot fully explain the explosion in vocabulary that occurs during childhood. As such, some theorists consider biology as a factor in language development.

Nativist (Biological) Theory

Nativist theorists argue that children do not simply copy the language that they hear around them. Famed linguist Noam Chomsky has suggested that learning principles alone cannot account for the huge amount of language that children quickly learn.

Instead, children must deduce rules from what they hear, which they can then use to produce sentences that they have never even heard before. They are able to do this because, Chomsky argues, they are born with a language acquisition device. The **language acquisition device** is a theoretical pathway in the brain that allows infants to process and absorb language rules. As such, children are able to understand what Chomsky termed **universal grammar**, a common set of rules that apply to different languages.

One prominent rule of universal grammar concerns word order. A lot of languages have a basic subject-verb-object sentence structure (e.g., "My class went on a field trip"). A significant majority of the world's languages use either a subject-verb-object or a subject-object-verb structure. Other structures such as object-subject-verb are much less common. Chomsky says that children can change the word order around and still understand the sentence. For example, a preschooler may say, "My class on a field trip went" before adjusting to a more typical word order: "My class went on a field trip." Chomsky noted that children learn to make such transformations effortlessly. Nativists believe in a *critical period* for language acquisition between two years and puberty. If no language exposure occurs during this time, later training is largely ineffective.

Cultural Influences on Language Development

Cognitive development, including the development of language, is inextricably connected to culture, since your culture largely determines what you are expected to learn. Some cultures place a higher value on culture-specific knowledge, including cultural traditions and roles, while other cultures value academic knowledge. In addition, culture also influences the rate of cognitive development, since children might be treated differently from culture to culture.

Lev Vygotsky, a sociocultural psychologist, proposed that the engine driving cognitive development is the child's internalization of her culture, including interpersonal and societal rules, symbols, and language. According to Vygotsky, the child's mind grows through contact with other minds. The culture in which a person develops will have its own values, beliefs, and tools of intellectual adaptation. These all have an effect on cognitive functions, including language development.

Vygotsky suggested that language development is affected and shaped by cultural and social routines. In the United States, for example, those routines may involve eating at American restaurants, watching American movies, and playing American sports. In other cultures, social routines may be very different. Vygotsky emphasized how children learn to describe their daily routines, which in turn affects their level of knowledge and understanding of cognitive tasks.

The language of a culture also influences cognitive abilities. For example, languages differ in how they communicate numbers. In Korean math books, the different place values of numbers (e.g., ones, tens, hundreds) are associated with different colors. Some believe this gives Korean students an edge in developing number skills. Linguists suggest that in the Chinese language, the names of numbers are clearer than those of other languages. These are just two of many possible examples that illustrate how children's cognitive development and language acquisition are affected by the culture in which they live.

17

PROBLEM-SOLVING STRATEGIES

LEARNING OBJECTIVE

- Describe and evaluate effective problem-solving strategies

Do you ever feel like you have a lot of problems to solve? Actually, it turns out that you are faced with multiple problems every day. Many of these problems you solve without any real conscious thought about what is happening; their solutions seem automatic. Solving other problems involves a more active process. Different approaches to problem-solving include trial-and-error methods, algorithms, heuristics, and insight.

Trial and Error

Trial-and-error is a less sophisticated type of problem-solving approach in which different solutions are tried until the correct one is found. This type of problem-solving is usually only effective when there are relatively few possible solutions. For example, if you were taking a multiple-choice math test and were trying to find the solution to an equation, you could test out each of the answer choices to see which one solves the equation. The fewer the possible answer choices, the more efficient this method becomes.

Algorithms

An **algorithm** is a step-by-step procedure that guarantees a solution to a problem. An example of an algorithm that you learned years ago in your math class is the procedure for doing long division. At first, you probably had to think about each little step, and then you got faster and faster as you continued to practice the algorithm. Of course, your problem does not have to be as academic as solving a math question. You can use algorithms to describe ordinary activities in your everyday life. For instance, if you were baking a cake, you might need a recipe. The recipe would serve as your algorithm.

Heuristics

Decision making can be complicated, but we use a number of tools to speed up or simplify the process. One such tool is called a heuristic. A **heuristic** (pronounced "hyoo-ris-tik") is a simple thinking strategy or technique that allows one to make judgments efficiently. Heuristics are sometimes referred to as "rules of thumb."

One type of heuristic, the **availability heuristic**, is a mental shortcut through which judgments are based on the information that is most easily brought to mind. The availability heuristic often works acceptably well, but it can lead to incorrect or biased judgments. For example, during the summer, the news media frequently report on shark attacks and shark sightings, especially near popular beach areas. Based on those news reports, a person may think that shark attacks are common at those areas, while in reality shark attacks remain extremely uncommon. But the mental availability of the events (e.g., the news reports) does not match with the actual frequency of shark attacks.

17

Another type of heuristic, the **representativeness heuristic**, is a mental shortcut that involves judging whether something belongs in a given class on the basis of its similarity to other members of that class. For example, suppose you flip a coin five times and it lands on heads every time. What is the probability that it will land on heads the next flip? Mathematically, the probability must still be 50 percent, but most individuals will underestimate the probability based on the pattern that has been established. Hence, like the availability heuristic, the use of the representativeness heuristic can sometimes lead to error.

While heuristics aren't perfect, they are useful most of the time. They help you simplify your world and organize massive amounts of information, so that you can make decisions without being paralyzed by information overload. For example, medical doctors often have to make diagnoses based on limited information. A doctor will ask patients for their family history, run a number of tests and review their results, and then make decisions about diagnosis and treatment. The doctor won't know everything about a patient's medical history and can't run every possible test, but using heuristics derived from past experience can allow a doctor to focus on the most important information and reach justifiable medical conclusions.

Insight

Have you ever puzzled over a tough problem, and then suddenly the solution hits you? If so, you had a sudden flash of insight. An **insight** is a sudden and often completely new realization of the solution to a problem. The solution is found without using any type of conscious problem-solving strategy. Sometimes an insight is referred to as an "aha" or "eureka" (from the ancient Greek for "I have found it!") moment, due to the joyous surprise that often accompanies a sudden discovery.

> ✔ **AP Expert Note**
>
> See Chapter 16 for a discussion of Wolfgang Köhler and his research on insight in chimpanzees.

CREATIVE THINKING

LEARNING OBJECTIVE

- Identify characteristics of creative thinking

Creativity is the ability to create ideas that are new. Creativity is distinct from intelligence; people who score high on intelligence (IQ) tests are not always creative, and vice versa. In the areas of music, art, science, medicine, and technology, original ideas have changed the course of human history. Although creativity can be difficult to quantify, psychologists have learned a great deal about how creativity occurs and how to promote it.

Convergent and Divergent Thinking

In routine problem solving, there is typically one right answer—and the objective is to find it. Thinking that is directed to the discovery of a single right solution is referred to as **convergent thinking**. The steps of your problem solving method are supposed to *converge* on the right answer. **Divergent thinking**, on the other hand, is thinking that produces many alternatives and promotes open-ended thought. As such, divergent thinking is more closely related to creativity. Rather than repeating learned approaches, divergent thinking produces new solutions and ideas.

Characteristics of Creative Thinking

While there is no formula for becoming more creative, there are certain characteristics that tend to be associated with creativity. Below is a summary of five key traits.

- *Expertise*: having a solid base of knowledge to help furnish new ideas

- *Imaginative thinking*: having the ability to see things in new ways, to recognize patterns, and to make new connections

- *Adventuresome personality*: having the willingness to seek new experiences, to take risks, and to accept failure along the way to your goal

- *Intrinsic motivation*: being driven by personal motivation and challenging yourself rather than focusing on extrinsic motivators

- *A creative environment*: putting yourself in a place that sparks, supports, and promotes creative thinking

Obstacles to Creativity and Problem Solving

Overconfidence

If you don't approach decision making with an open mind, you may be unrealistically confident in your solutions. **Overconfidence** is the tendency to overestimate the correctness of your beliefs and judgments. Often, how confident you are in a judgment is not a good indicator of whether or not you are correct. Two concepts related to overconfidence are belief bias and belief perseverance. **Belief bias** happens when you make illogical conclusions in order to confirm your preexisting beliefs. **Belief perseverance** refers to the tendency to maintain a belief even after the evidence you used to form the belief is proven wrong.

Confirmation Bias

Another obstacle to successful problem solving is confirmation bias. **Confirmation bias** is a tendency to search for information that supports your existing beliefs and to ignore evidence that contradicts what you think is true. As a consequence, you may miss evidence important to finding the correct solution. In researching political issues, for example, it is important not to rely on just one source for all of your information. Comparing and contrasting information from a variety of sources may prevent your confirmation bias.

Fixation

Another obstacle to problem solving and creativity is referred to as **fixation**, the tendency to repeat wrong solutions as a result of becoming blind to alternatives. The end result is an inability to find a new perspective necessary to solve a problem. There are two examples of fixation: mental sets and functional fixedness. A **mental set** is the tendency to use old patterns to solve new problems, while **functional fixedness** is the tendency to think about familiar objects in familiar ways.

There is a well-known example of functional fixedness referred to as the *Duncker Candle Problem.* Imagine you walk into a room and there's no working light. Instead, you have a candle, some thumbtacks, and a box of matches. With only these three items, how would you mount the candle on the wall so that no wax will drip onto the floor? Pause to think about that before moving on to the solution in the next paragraph.

The key to the candle problem is to realize that the matchbox could serve as a candle holder (and not just as a storage container for matches). You can tack the box onto the wall and place the candle in the box. By using your creativity in problems such as this, you can overcome the obstacle of functional fixedness.

WHAT IS INTELLIGENCE?

LEARNING OBJECTIVES

- Summarize the meaning of intelligence and processes by which it is measured
- Discuss culture's influence on definitions of intelligence

The study of intelligence differs from other scientific pursuits due to the difficulty of operationalizing the concept of intelligence. Compared to a biological quantity like blood pressure, which is well understood and easily measurable with a medical device called a sphygmomanometer, intelligence is much harder to get at. Ultimately, how we measure intelligence depends on how we define it.

While we will encounter criticisms of this definition later in the chapter, for now consider **intelligence** to be broadly defined as the ability to solve problems, learn from experience, and use knowledge to adapt to novel situations. Psychological tests that have been developed to measure intelligence can examine a single factor of intelligence, such as learning from experience, or multiple factors together.

Psychometricians and other test makers have developed a wide range of measures to assess intelligence. **Aptitude tests** are designed to predict future performance, while **achievement tests** are designed to gauge mastery of material that has already been learned. **Speed tests** focus on solving as many problems as possible in a short amount of time, while **power tests** present problems in increasing difficulty to determine the highest-level problem a test-taker can solve. Finally, **verbal tests** focus on using word problems to assess intelligence, while **abstract tests** focus on reasoning problems that use shapes or other non-verbal measures.

These different methods of testing are often combined. For example, the SAT, which you are likely already familiar with, is a speed aptitude test with both verbal and abstract questions. It is an aptitude test, as opposed to an achievement test, because research has shown that SAT scores correlate with academic achievement in college, so many colleges use it to predict how well a particular student would do if admitted. IQ tests and other commonly used assessments of intelligence will be discussed later in this chapter.

The Effect of Culture

Which skill is more important: calculating the area of a circle or operating a dogsled alone in the winter to travel to a neighboring village? While most of us would probably say the former, for a Yupik Eskimo teenager living in Alaska, the answer is almost certainly the latter. Indeed, when psychologists compared Yupik students to students from American inner cities, they found that the Yupik students had substantially higher levels of practical knowledge (hunting, fishing, dogsledding, etc.) but lower levels of academic knowledge.

A distinct study performed in a small town in Kenya arrived at similar results for a very different culture. In this village, 95% of children suffer from parasitic illnesses, so most of the children medicate themselves or others on a weekly basis. Researchers administered both a traditional academic test and a test on the use of herbal medicines to these students, and found that the higher the children scored on the herbal medicines test, the lower they scored on the academic. Locals generally believed practical indigenous knowledge to be more important than what was taught in the Western-style school set up in their village.

Both of these examples illustrate that different cultures value different types of abilities. While citizens of Western cultures are more likely to view academic skill as the greatest hallmark of intelligence, members of some more traditional cultures (like the Yupik Eskimos and those Kenyan villagers) view practical mastery as the true measure of intelligence. While the psychological study of intelligence focuses primarily on the Western understanding of the concept, researchers try to be mindful of cultural differences such as these.

INTELLIGENCE THEORIES

High-Yield

LEARNING OBJECTIVE

- Distinguish among intelligence theories

The broad definition of intelligence introduced in the previous section is far from the final word on the meaning of the concept. Indeed, a number of theorists throughout the history of psychology have proposed alternative understandings of intelligence, extending the concept in new directions. While the list of theories discussed below is not exhaustive, it does cover the most influential theories, those most likely to be tested on the AP Psychology exam.

Spearman's General Intelligence

Charles Spearman believed that all intelligence could be traced to a single underlying general mental ability. Spearman came up with this hypothesis after noting that children who performed well in school tended to perform well regardless of subject. Spearman used **factor analysis**, a statistical method which identifies underlying factors that are responsible for trends, to search for this general ability.

Spearman found a common factor, which he called **g factor**, or general intelligence factor. Roughly 40–50% of the variability in intelligence scores can be attributed to the g factor. Furthermore, the g factor has been shown to be a predictor of future educational, economic, and social outcomes, making it one of the most universally predictive measures in psychology.

The g factor has two sub-components. **Crystallized intelligence** is the ability to apply previously learned knowledge to solve a new task. **Fluid intelligence** is skill at solving novel tasks for which you have no previous experience. Scores on these two factors are usually correlated with each other, but they can vary, and most modern intelligence tests attempt to measure both.

> ✔ **AP Expert Note**
>
> While many psychologists agreed with Spearman, L.L. Thurstone disagreed, proposing that there are 7 independent types of mental abilities, including perceptual speed and memory. However, upon further analysis, researchers found that scores in these 7 abilities were positively correlated, reinforcing the idea of general intelligence.

Gardner's Multiple Intelligences

Howard Gardner maintains that intelligence extends beyond the traditional abilities that have been included in intelligence theories. Gardner's views on intelligence came from his work with a group of people known as savants. **Savant syndrome** is a condition in which someone has limited general mental ability but exceptional ability in a single skill.

Kim Peek is an example of a savant. Kim was born with a brain condition known as macrocephaly, which caused abnormal brain development. While Kim was unable to walk until the age of four, he started demonstrating an incredible memory before his second birthday. Reading the left page of a book with his left eye and the right page with his right eye, Kim was able to speed read through a book in an hour and remember important information from that book for the rest of his life. It is estimated that, before he died, he memorized the content of 12,000 books, but never learned how to button his shirt correctly or solve reasoning problems.

17

Savants like Kim Peek suggested to Gardner that intelligence can exist in areas beyond traditional definitions of intelligence. So Gardner set forth a new conception of multiple intelligences, with a list of eight criteria that must be met for something to be considered an "intelligence." These criteria include scientific support, savant existence, and distinct developmental progression. This list allows new intelligences to be established as support for them grows. Gardner's **multiple intelligence theory** currently recognizes eight different intelligences, summarized in the table below.

Gardner's Multiple Intelligences	
Intelligence	**Related Abilities**
Musical-rhythmic	Appreciation of sound, rhythm, tone, and other musical qualities
Visual-spatial	Spatial judgment, navigation, and object visualization
Verbal-linguistic	Comprehension and production of language, writing, and story-telling
Logical-mathematical	Abstract reasoning, mathematical skill, and critical thinking
Bodily-kinesthetic	Object manipulation, reaction time, and body control
Interpersonal	Effective communication and empathizing with others
Intrapersonal	Personal growth and self-reflection
Naturalistic	Identifying plants, hunting, and cooking

✔ AP Expert Note

Despite Gardner's suggestion that each intelligence is distinct, subsequent research has shown that visual-spatial, logical-mathematical, and verbal-linguistic intelligence are positively correlated, once again suggesting the existence of an underlying general intelligence factor.

Sternberg's Three Intelligences

Robert Sternberg can be seen as a middle road between the theory of general intelligence and Gardner's eight separate intelligences. Sternberg proposed a **triarchic theory of intelligence**, in which there are three separate intelligences that work together to constitute your overall intelligence. The three intelligences in the triarchic theory are as follows:

- **Analytical intelligence** is the ability to solve traditional academic problems, such as logical reasoning and math problems.

- **Creative intelligence** is the ability to apply information to novel situations and is frequently seen to be high in inventors.

- **Practical intelligence** is the ability to apply knowledge to real-world situations and to influence one's environment. Practical intelligence is commonly known as "street smarts."

Emotional intelligence

In recent years, Daniel Goleman and other psychologists have promoted the concept of emotional intelligence. **Emotional intelligence** (sometimes referred to as EQ, or emotional quotient) is the ability to perceive, understand, manage, and utilize emotion in everyday life. Examples of emotional intelligence skills include emotional regulation, or the ability to avoid letting emotions like anger and sadness hinder achievement, and emotional sensitivity, or awareness of the feelings of others coupled with a capacity to respond to those feelings sympathetically. (Emotional intelligence is actually quite similar to two of Gardner's proposed intelligences: interpersonal and intrapersonal.) Studies from multiple countries have shown that those with a high degree of emotional intelligence have better job performance and more stable personal and professional relationships.

INTELLIGENCE TESTS

LEARNING OBJECTIVES

* Outline the design and evaluation of psychological tests

* Employ a normal curve to interpret test scores and such labels as "gifted" and "cognitively disabled"

* Identify cultural and other controversies associated with intelligence testing

Intelligence Quotient

Modern intelligence testing began in France in the early 1900s, when Alfred Binet was asked to create a test to determine which children needed extra attention in school. Binet came up with the theory of **mental age**, a measure of intelligence based on average performance for children of a given age. So, a typical 10-year-old has a mental age of 10, while a high-performing 10-year-old will have a mental age of 11 or higher. Binet determined mental age using a test designed to assess abstract, verbal, and quantitative reasoning.

Louis Terman, a professor at Stanford, took Binet's work a step further, creating what we now call the **Stanford-Binet IQ Test**. **Intelligence quotient** (**IQ**) is a scale that attempts to provide an objective measure of intelligence. It was originally computed by taking a person's mental age and dividing it by their chronological age (actual age), then multiplying the result by 100. For example, a 10-year-old child with the mental age of an 11-year-old would have an IQ of 110: $\frac{11}{10} \times 100 = 110$.

Since the initial efforts of Binet and Terman, IQ testing has evolved to provide more sophisticated measures of intelligence. David Wechsler created a series of tests for children and adults known as the Wechsler intelligence scales, which include the **Wechsler Intelligence Scale for Children (WISC)** and the **Wechsler Adult Intelligence Scale (WAIS)**. These tests contain traditional measures, such as assessments of verbal and abstract reasoning, but also non-verbal measures of intelligence: for example, test-takers may have to point out a missing detail in a picture or make an accurate copy of a complex symbol. IQ, as measured by the Wechsler scales and other modern tests, has generally been found to be stable over the course of a person's lifetime.

Validity and Reliability

In Chapter 13, we reviewed how the concepts of internal and external validity applied to the design of experiments and other psychological research. Similar concepts of validity and reliability are also relevant to the design of psychometric measures like IQ tests. In testing, **validity** refers to the extent to which a test accurately measures what it claims to, while **reliability** refers to the level of consistency in test results. Psychometricians often further distinguish between different kinds of validity and reliability.

Content validity is a way to measure if a test accurately assesses the entire range of abilities it is supposed to. For example, if a test is trying to assess arithmetic ability, it should cover all aspects of arithmetic. If it only tested addition and division, it would not be considered a valid test of all arithmetic skill (because it neglected topics like subtraction and multiplication) and would therefore have low content validity.

Face validity refers to a superficial measure of validity based only on a brief examination. Since face validity does not require any data to interpret, it is the easiest and often the first type of validity assessed for a test. Face validity is generally considered to be relatively weak as a measurement, but it is useful in the early stages of test design.

Criterion-related validity describes how well a test predicts performance in the abilities that it measures. Criterion-related validity is generally broken down into two categories. **Concurrent validity** refers to how well a test correlates with other current measures of performance. If an intelligence test administered to high school students had high concurrent validity, for example, then students who scored well on it would tend to have higher current grade point averages (GPAs) than students who scored poorly on it. In contrast, **predictive validity** indicates how well a test predicts future performance. An intelligence test with high predictive validity would see high school students who performed well on it earning higher GPAs later in college.

Split-half reliability is a measure of internal consistency within a test. To assess split-half reliability, researchers administer a test to a sample, split the items on the completed test into two groups at random, and then score each half separately. The closer the two scores for each half are, the higher the split-half reliability. This reliability requires that the test have a large number of questions—at least 100 is recommended.

Equivalent-form reliability measures the correlation between scores on two (or more) versions of the same test. It is similar to split-half reliability insofar as it requires splitting test items into multiple groups scored separately. It differs, however, in that the questions are administered at different times to the same sample of test-takers. The closer the scores for the different versions of the test are, the higher the equivalent-form reliability. In other words, tests with high equivalent-form reliability are consistent between different versions of the test. Like split-half reliability, equivalent-form reliability requires 100 or more questions in order to be assessed effectively.

Test-retest reliability is a measure of the correlation between two administrations of the same test. Generally, this involves giving the same set of questions to the same sample of individuals at different times. Assessing this type of validity can be a challenge for a number of reasons. Most notably, test-takers going through the exam a second time may remember the answers to questions from the first time, particularly if the time between administrations is relatively short. Thus, the second administration might be more of a test of memory than a test of the skills originally intended to be assessed.

Designing a test with sufficient levels of validity and reliability can take some time. But with each new administration of the test, researchers collect more data, allowing them to monitor the validity and reliability and potentially to make improvements to subsequent versions. This process of continuous revision has allowed modern intelligence tests (like the Stanford-Binet IQ test, the WISC, and the WAIS) to rate highly on each of these measures of validity and reliability.

Standardization and the Normal Curve

For common intelligence tests like the Stanford-Binet and the WAIS, the average score is always 100. To determine this score, large portions of the population are given a test and the resulting scores are shifted to an ordinal scale (discussed at the end of the Research Design section in Chapter 13) with a mean of 100. When designing a psychological test, this process of computing and working with population averages is known as **standardization**, while the average scores for a population are called the **norms**.

> ✔ **AP Expert Note**
>
> **The Flynn Effect**
>
> The average person now is more intelligent than the average person in the early 1900s, according to the results of IQ tests. This is thought to be due to a number of factors, including improved nutrition and increased access to education. This increase in intelligence test results over time is known as the **Flynn effect**. As a result of the Flynn effect, norms on IQ tests must continually be recalculated to account for the changing population.

When examining the norms for a test, the scores for a population generally fall into a common bell-shaped pattern known as a **normal curve**. This type of distribution can be found when studying many characteristics of a population, including weight, height, intelligence, and reaction time. As can be seen in the figure that follows, the majority of the population falls into the center of the curve, with high- and low-scoring individuals found on the tail ends. The mean and standard deviation of a test can vary depending on whether the test has been normalized, but the percentage of the population that falls in between standard deviations remains steady across tests.

17

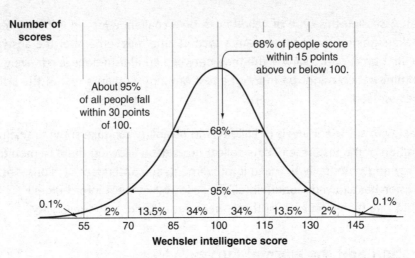

Normal Curve of IQ Scores

As can be seen from the graph, the mean score for the WAIS IQ test is 100, with a standard deviation of 15. (The same is true for the Stanford-Binet.) This means that 68% of the population has an IQ between 85 and 115, while approximately 95% of the population has an IQ between 70 and 130. Those who possess an IQ above 130 are labeled as **gifted**. Individuals with an IQ below 70 are considered to have an **intellectual disability**, also known as a cognitive disability. The severity of the disability depends on the IQ score, as indicated in the following table.

IQ Range	Level of Disability	Description
55–70	Mild	Individuals at this level generally progress academically to a sixth-grade level and are usually capable of having jobs and living independently.
40–55	Moderate	Individuals at this level generally progress academically to a second-grade level and are usually incapable of living independently.
25–40	Severe	Individuals possess the ability to complete some basic tasks but require considerable support to go about their daily lives.
25 or less	Profound	Individuals need assistance with even basic tasks and may have difficulty communicating.

Intelligence Testing Controversies

Despite a wealth of empirical evidence supporting the validity and reliability of intelligence tests, these assessments remain controversial. For example, critics like Howard Gardner have alleged that they only measure a narrow range of abilities but fail to assess other important aspects of intelligence. The most significant criticism of intelligence testing that you should be aware of for the AP Psychology exam is the allegation of **cultural bias**, the idea that these tests define and measure intelligence in ways that favor some cultures over others.

17

As evident in the examples of the Yupik Eskimos and the Kenyan villagers from earlier in the chapter, not all cultures value the same types of skills. Individuals from less academically-oriented cultures are likely to be at a significant disadvantage when taking a traditional intelligence test. Other unfair disadvantages may be present for minority groups within a particular culture. For example, research has suggested that some racial or ethnic groups tend to have higher average scores on intelligence tests than others. One possible explanation for this discrepancy is that the tests are biased in favor of members of the dominant culture and against members of minority groups.

IMPORTANT CONTRIBUTORS

LEARNING OBJECTIVE

- Recognize important contributors to cognitive psychology

See the list of important contributors to the study of cognitive psychology in the Rapid Review section of Chapter 8.

 ## NEXT STEP: PRACTICE

Go to Rapid Review and Practice Chapter 8 or to your online quizzes at kaptest.com for exam-like practice on this topic.

Haven't registered your book yet? Go to kaptest.com/moreonline to begin.

17

CHAPTER 18

Developmental Psychology

In the past few chapters, we've talked about your ability to sense, learn, and think, but not all of these abilities are fully formed when you are born. So how did you become the person you are today? Developmental psychology seeks to answer this question by investigating the processes that enable human beings to realize their potential. In this chapter, we'll examine the ways that people change physically, intellectually, morally, and socially, from conception to the time that they are fully realized adults.

NATURE AND NURTURE

LEARNING OBJECTIVE

- Explain ways in which nature and nurture interact to influence behavior

Two types of factors influence human development: innate biological factors (**nature**) and external environmental factors (**nurture**). While some more extremist views maintain that only one of these factors is important (like genetic determinists who maintain that genes are destiny or behaviorists who believe that all behavior is learned), most psychologists recognize that nature and nurture work together in human development.

As discussed in Chapter 16, many human behaviors are learned as a result of experience of an external environment. But human beings are only capable of learning because of distinctive biological structures like the brain. These structures are in turn the products of both genetic and environmental factors. Genes are often likened to blueprints, but you'll find no map of your brain encoded in your DNA. A better analogy is that your genes are a recipe for making you: they provide the basic instructions, but the end product depends on how the recipe gets followed. More specifically, your genes provide the boundaries that define the minimum and maximum values for many of your characteristics. For example, your genes set an upper and lower limit on how tall you will be when you're finished growing. The space between these boundaries is called the **range of reaction**. Your environment determines exactly where within this range you end up. So, for instance, suffering from malnutrition or serious illness during development often puts an individual at the lower edge of his or her range of reaction for height, while sound nutrition and good health typically push an individual higher. While human behavior is more complex than physiological traits like height, many psychological characteristics also have ranges of reaction, which explains why identical twins sometimes differ in personality or intelligence.

> ### ✔ AP Expert Note
>
> **Twin Studies**
>
> The twin study is a method that researchers use to determine the relative contributions of genetic and environmental factors to the development of particular traits. See Chapter 14 for more on this type of research.

GESTATION

LEARNING OBJECTIVE

- Describe conception and gestation's impact on fetal development

Conception

When you calculate your age, you likely mark the years that have passed since the day of your birth. But prior to birth, you underwent approximately nine months of significant development. The period known as **gestation** or **prenatal development** starts with conception and ends with birth. **Conception** is the fusion of two gametes, one male sex cell (a sperm) and one female sex cell (an egg).

Gestation

Gestation is divided into three stages. The first stage is the **germinal stage**, which is the two-week period following conception. The second stage is the **embryonic stage**, which lasts from the second week of development until about the eighth week. From the ninth week until birth, the developing fetus is in the **fetal stage**.

Stages of Gestation	
Germinal Stage	Division of the single-celled zygote begins. The zygote migrates from the Fallopian tube to implant itself in the uterine wall.
Embryonic Stage	Cell differentiation begins. The embryo begins sexual differentiation and starts to develop organs and other major body structures.
Fetal Stage	The fetus develops muscles and a skeletal system, which enable it to move around the uterus. Organs continue to develop. Rapid brain development occurs during the last 3 months of pregnancy.

During the fetal stage, brain cells begin to generate axons and dendrites, which allow for communication between cells. They also start to undergo myelination, the formation of a fatty sheath around axons, which provides insulation and speeds up signal conduction in neurons (see Chapter 14 for more). The process of myelination continues after birth and does not occur at a constant rate in all areas of the brain. Although the brain undergoes rapid growth during the fetal stage, a newborn's brain is only about 25% of its adult size, so much of the brain's development occurs after birth.

Influences on Prenatal Development

What a mother is exposed to during pregnancy has an impact on the health of her child, in large part because of their exchange of nutrients, wastes, and other compounds through the placenta. During the embryonic stage, the embryo is particularly vulnerable to **teratogens**, substances that hinder prenatal development and can lead to birth defects. One prominent teratogen is alcohol, which can lead to fetal alcohol syndrome if consumed during pregnancy. **Fetal alcohol syndrome** is a developmental disorder characterized by reduced brain size, cognitive disabilities, and distinctive facial features. Another teratogen is tobacco, which can cause lowered birth weight and perceptual and attentional deficits. Other teratogens include heavy metals like lead and mercury.

Birth defects can also be caused by other sources. Infections, exposure to radiation, and nutritional deficiencies can all hinder prenatal development. When it comes to nutrition, mothers who are malnourished due to famine or other reasons tend to give birth to children with marked physiological and psychological deficits. But even for well-fed mothers, deficiencies of specific essential nutrients, such as folate, iron, and zinc, can lead to birth defects or other developmental issues.

18

MOTOR SKILL DEVELOPMENT

LEARNING OBJECTIVE

- Explain how motor skills develop

Motor development is the emergence of the ability to execute physical actions such as walking, crawling, reaching, and rolling. Most infants begin life with specific innate reflexes and develop motor abilities in the same order around roughly the same age.

Reflexes

All neonates are born with a small set of **reflexes**, innate motor responses that are triggered by specific patterns of sensory stimulation. Many of the reflexes present at birth eventually disappear as the infant develops more advanced motor skills.

Two of the most notable infant reflexes are the rooting reflex and the sucking reflex. The **rooting reflex** is the tendency for an infant to move its mouth toward any object that touches its cheek. The **sucking reflex** is the tendency for an infant to suck any object that enters its mouth. Both of these reflexes allow a newborn to find its mother's nipple and begin feeding, which is absolutely crucial for the infant's survival.

Two other reflexes that are believed to help a newborn thrive are the Moro reflex and the grasping reflex. The **Moro reflex** is the outstretching of the arms and legs in response to a loud noise or a sudden change in the environment. The infant's body tenses; its arms are extended and then drawn in as if embracing. This reflex may have developed to help an infant cling to its mother. The **grasping reflex** is the vigorous grasping of an object that touches the palm. This reflex is believed to prepare an infant's hand muscles for developing voluntary grasping in the months to come.

Not all newborn reflexes have well-understood purposes. The **Babinski reflex** is the projection of the big toe and the fanning of the other toes when the sole of the foot is touched. Infants typically lose this reflex between the ages of 12 months and 2 years. After that point, children instead display the **plantar reflex**, in which the toes curl under when the sole of the foot is touched. Observing the Babinski reflex in adults is a sign of underlying pathology.

Motor Skills

Motor skills development tends to follow two general rules. The first is the **cephalocaudal rule** (also known as the "top-to-bottom" rule), which describes the tendency for motor skills to emerge in sequence from the head to the feet. An infant will first gain control of his head, then his trunk, and finally his feet. The second rule is the **proximodistal rule** (also known as the "inside to out-side" rule), which describes the tendency for motor skills to emerge in sequence from the center to the periphery. An infant first gains control of her trunk, then her elbows and knees, followed by her hands and feet.

TEMPERAMENT AND ATTACHMENT

LEARNING OBJECTIVES

- Summarize the impact of temperament and other social characteristics on attachment and appropriate socialization

- Evaluate intimacy-related decisions in the course of maturation

Human infants are unable to survive without their caregivers. Caregivers not only provide food, shelter, and safety—all of which are clearly critical for an infant's survival—they also provide something less tangible but no less important: an emotional bond. The attachment that an infant forms with its caregiver has a profound impact on its psychological development.

Harlow's Monkeys

During World War II, psychologists studied infants who were living in orphanages. Despite the fact that these children had shelter, warmth, safety, and food, many grew up to be physically and developmentally stunted. This finding led psychologist Harry Harlow to study social isolation in rhesus monkeys. Harlow found that when rhesus monkeys were socially isolated for the first six months of their lives, they developed a variety of abnormalities, such as difficulty communicating or learning from others. The females from the experiment who went on to become mothers ignored, rejected, and in some cases even attacked their own babies.

Another study conducted by Harlow placed the socially isolated rhesus monkeys inside a cage with two "artificial mothers." One mother was made of wire and dispensed food, while the other was made of soft cloth and dispensed no food. Harlow found that the rhesus monkeys spent the majority of their time clinging to the cloth mother, despite the fact that the wire mother was the one who provided food. Based on these results, Harlow concluded that the need for affection was perhaps even more essential than the need for food.

✔ **AP Expert Note**

Imprinting

Austrian biologist Konrad Lorenz also contributed to the study of attachment with his discovery of the process of "imprinting" in geese and other species. While conducting naturalistic observations of greylag geese, Lorenz noticed that goslings form an instinctive attachment to the first moving object they encounter within a critical period after hatching, following the object wherever it goes. While imprinting is not observed in human beings, it exemplifies a simple form of attachment found in some nonhuman animals.

Attachment Styles in Infants

Psychiatrist John Bowlby wanted to follow up on the findings of Harlow to understand how human infants formed attachments to their caregivers. Unlike the goslings studied by Lorenz, newborn humans are born without the ability to physically follow their caregivers. Because of this limitation, human babies have developed an alternative strategy: they cry, coo, gurgle, and smile. These actions cause most adults to reflexively move toward a baby.

Bowlby claimed that infants send these signals to individuals who are near them and keep a mental tally of who responds the most often and the most promptly. They then begin to target the majority of their signals to the best responder, also known as their primary caregiver. A baby may feel secure playing while its primary caregiver is in the room, but then cry and become distressed when its primary caregiver exits. Bowlby suggested that this happens because infants are predisposed to form **attachments**, or emotional bonds, with their primary caregivers.

Once an infant has established a primary caregiver, it keeps track of the caregiver's responsiveness and develops an **internal working model of attachment**, which is a set of expectations an infant forms about how its primary caregiver will respond to it. Infants develop different attachment styles on the basis of these models.

Psychologist Mary Ainsworth developed the Strange Situation test to determine what type of attachment an infant had. She observed the behavior of an infant in the following eight stages, each of which lasted three minutes:

- Primary caregiver, infant, and experimenter interact in a room.

- Experimenter leaves, caregiver and infant interact alone.

- A stranger joins the caregiver and infant.

- Caregiver leaves, infant and stranger remain.

- Caregiver returns and stranger leaves.

- Caregiver leaves, infant is now alone.

- Stranger returns.

- Caregiver returns and stranger leaves.

Ainsworth observed 3 different attachment styles: secure, ambivalent, and avoidant. A fourth attachment style (disorganized) was later identified by other researchers.

Secure Attachment

Among American infants, about 60% show a **secure attachment** style. In the Strange Situation, a securely attached infant is distressed when its primary caregiver leaves and then soothed when the caregiver returns. These infants believe that their caregiver will respond when they are in distress.

Avoidant Attachment

About 20% of American infants show an **avoidant attachment** style. In the Strange Situation, they are unconcerned when their primary caregiver leaves the room and generally do not acknowledge their return. These infants believe that their caregiver will not respond when they are in distress.

Ambivalent Attachment

Roughly 15% of American infants display an **ambivalent attachment** style. In the Strange Situation, such an infant will be distressed when its caregiver leaves the room. However, compared to an infant with a secure attachment style, an ambivalent infant will not be soothed when its primary caregiver returns. It may ignore its caregiver or rebuff its caregiver's attempts to calm it. These infants are uncertain about whether their caregiver will respond when they are in distress.

Disorganized Attachment

Very few American infants (less than 5%) have a **disorganized attachment** style. In the Strange Situation, such an infant will show no consistent pattern of responses when its caregiver leaves or returns. Infants with disorganized attachment appear to be confused about their caregivers, which some psychologists believe may be an indication of abuse.

18

Influences on Attachment Style

Research suggests that a child's attachment style may change over time. Additionally, countries vary slightly in which attachment styles are more prominent. Although a secure attachment style is the most common in every country that has ever been studied, other attachment styles vary. For example, in Japan (where it is more common for mothers to stay at home), children are more likely to have ambivalent attachment styles than they are to have avoidant attachment styles.

Compared to attachment, which is an interaction between two people, **temperament** describes an individual's characteristic pattern of emotional reactivity. Differences in temperament appear to arise from differences in biology. For example, between 10% and 15% of infants have overactive limbic systems. Such individuals tend to cry and become distressed as infants when shown a new toy or object, grow into children who avoid new people and situations, and become shy and cautious adults.

Three main types of infant temperament have been identified: easy, difficult, and slow-to-warm (see the table below). Research suggests that temperament tends to impact attachment style. For example, easy infants tend to have a secure attachment style, perhaps because primary caregivers find them less challenging to deal with and easier to show affection towards.

Temperament	Description
Easy	Displays a regular routine, adapts to novelty with positivity.
Difficult	Displays an irregular routine, is slow to adapt to novelty, and reacts to slightly negative situations with intense distress.
Slow-to-warm	Slow to adapt to novelty; however, over time can adapt positively to change. Tend to have a higher frequency of negative moods.

Attachment Styles in Adults

In the 1960s, attachment theory focused primarily on the attachment between an infant and its primary caregiver. In the late 1980s, however, Cindy Hazan and Phillip Shaver applied attachment theory to intimate relationships between adults. They found that there were many similarities between adult intimacy and caregiver-infant relationships. For example, adults desire to be close to each other, feel comforted when their partners show them care, and experience distress when they are ignored.

Hazan and Shaver proposed four attachment styles in adults. These attachment styles are loosely correlated with the attachment styles that Ainsworth initially proposed between infants and primary caregivers. The secure attachment style in adults corresponds to the secure attachment style in children. The anxious-preoccupied attachment style in adults corresponds to the ambivalent attachment style in children. However, the dismissive-avoidant and the fearful-avoidant attachment styles, which are distinct in adults, correspond to a single avoidant attachment style in children.

Secure

Securely attached adults tend to be able to form deep relationships with intimacy and commitment. They believe that they are worthy and capable of love. In addition to forming healthy relationships, individuals with a secure attachment style are comfortable with their independence and do not fear being alone. They tend to view themselves and their relationships with others positively.

Anxious-Preoccupied

Adults with anxious-preoccupied attachments tend to seek high levels of intimacy very quickly in relationships. Adults with this attachment style may constantly worry that the affection they feel for their partner is not reciprocated. These individuals tend to fear being alone and have a low sense of self-worth.

Dismissive-Avoidant

The dismissive-avoidant attachment style describes individuals who place a large value on their independence and self-sufficiency. They tend to avoid entering relationships or engaging in intimate situations. Many characterize these individuals as being defensive and unwilling to discuss their feelings.

Fearful-Avoidant

Individuals with the fearful-avoidant attachment style are often survivors of a traumatic event, such as abuse of some kind. They tend to desire close relationships, but also fear the potential negative implications of a relationship. They experience difficulty with trust and dependence on others.

PARENTING STYLES

LEARNING OBJECTIVE

- Describe the impact of parenting styles on development

Psychologist Diana Baumrind noted that preschoolers exhibited different types of behavior that correlated highly with how their parents treated them. Today, research has recognized four major parenting styles: authoritative, permissive, authoritarian, and neglectful. These parenting styles are based on two dimensions of parenting behavior. The first is **demandingness**, which refers to the extent that parents control their children's behavior or demand their maturity. The second dimension is **responsiveness**, which refers to the degree that parents are accepting and sensitive to their children's emotional and developmental needs. The four parenting styles are summarized in the table below.

	High Demandingness	**Low Demandingness**
High Responsiveness	Authoritative	Permissive
Low Responsiveness	Authoritarian	Neglectful

Authoritative Parenting

Authoritative parenting is a style of parenting in which parents have high expectations for their children but are able to adjust their expectations with understanding and support. This parenting style is often regarded as the most effective and beneficial style of parenting. These parents value their children's independence and are warm and responsive. They tend to raise children who are well-behaved with high self-esteem and superior social skills.

Permissive Parenting

Permissive parenting, which is also known as indulgent parenting, is a style of parenting in which parents are responsive, but not demanding. These parents may establish inconsistent rules with their children in an attempt to avoid confrontation. They tend to be very warm and responsive, but they easily give in to their children's wishes. These parents tend to raise children who are impulsive, egocentric, and have difficulty forming interpersonal relationships.

Authoritarian Parenting

Authoritarian parenting, which is also known as strict parenting, describes parents who are demanding and cold. These parents tend to have very high expectations of their children but typically fail to show positive affirmation, even when their children succeed. Children raised by authoritarian parents tend to grow up to have low self-esteem, low academic performance, and poor social skills.

Neglectful Parenting

Neglectful parenting is a style of parenting in which parents are cold and unresponsive to their children. Neglectful parents tend not to establish rules for their children and are often indifferent to how their children behave. They tend to raise children who are impulsive, depressed, and have an increased incidence of suicide.

18

COGNITIVE DEVELOPMENT

LEARNING OBJECTIVE

- Outline processes by which cognitive abilities develop

Cognitive development refers to the emergence of intellectual abilities, as well as the study of this process. While there are many theories of cognitive development, the two you really need to know for the AP Psychology exam are those developed by Swiss psychologist Jean Piaget and by Russian psychologist Lev Vygotsky.

Piaget's Stages of Cognitive Development

How do infants and children construct a mental model of the world? Piaget sought to answer this question by observing children's cognitive development, finding that when he presented children within the same age group with challenging problems, they tended to make the same mistakes. Based on these and other results, he concluded that children move through four sequential stages of cognitive development, summarized in the table below.

Piaget's Stages of Cognitive Development		
Stage	**Ages**	**Characteristics**
Sensorimotor	0–2	Infant learns more about the world through movement and senses. Infant develops schemata and begins to show evidence of object permanence.
Preoperational	2–6	Child begins stage by thinking egocentrically, but is eventually able to understand others' minds. Child lacks understanding of the conservation of physical properties.
Concrete Operational	6–11	Child can think logically about physical objects and understands the conservation of physical properties.
Formal Operational	11+	Child can think logically and abstractly and understand hypotheticals.

Sensiormotor Stage

The first of Piaget's stages is called the **sensorimotor stage**, which lasts from birth until about two years old. As the name suggests, children in this stage primarily rely on their abilities to sense and move in order to understand the world. As young children see things, touch things, and put things in their mouths, they develop **schemata** (singular: *schema*), which are models or theories about how the world works. For example, a child may adopt a schema in which she classifies all small, furry animals with pointy ears as "cats."

These schemata are subject to two distinct processes. The first is **assimilation**, the application of schemata to a novel situation. If a child learns that tugging her favorite toy can bring it closer, she can extend this knowledge to bring other objects closer to her, like cookies. Children soon learn that they occasionally need to revise their schemata when presented with new information. This process of revising your schemata is called **accommodation**. Consider what would happen if a child tugged on the tail of her family cat to try and bring it closer. Rather than coming closer, as the child may expect, the cat would probably run in the opposite direction. The child could then revise her schema to understand that tugging *inanimate* objects will bring them closer, but that the same isn't always true with *animate* ones.

As children reach the end of the sensorimotor stage, Piaget discovered, they develop a capacity known as object permanence. **Object permanence** is the understanding that objects continue to exist even when they are no longer visible. Consider a young boy whose favorite toy is hidden under a blanket. Prior to developing object permanence, the boy would believe his toy simply vanished, so he would not think to check under the blanket. After developing object permanence, however, he would most likely just pull back the blanket, knowing that his favorite toy was simply out of sight.

Preoperational Stage

Piaget's next stage is the **preoperational stage**, from ages 2 to 6. During this stage, children display **egocentrism**, a self-centered perspective that arises from the failure to understand that the world appears differently to different people. For example, imagine that you place a teddy bear on a table facing a four-year-old girl. On the opposite side of the table sits a boy, who faces the back of the teddy bear. If you ask the girl what she sees, she will describe the front of the teddy bear. But if you ask her what the boy sees, she will still describe the front of the bear, since she doesn't yet understand how the boy sees something different than she does.

As children progress toward the end of the preoperational stage, they start to develop theory of mind. **Theory of mind** refers to the understanding that human behavior is guided by mental representations of the world. This gives rise to the recognition that the world appears differently to different people; in other words, not everyone sees what you see. Developing a theory of mind is what allows children to overcome egocentrism. If the girl from the previous example had developed theory of mind, she would have understood that the boy across from her sees the back of the teddy bear, not the front of the teddy bear that she sees.

Concrete Operational Stage

Children in the preoperational stage have a preliminary understanding of the physical world but fail to understand how actions ("operations") transform objects. As children transition to the **concrete operational stage**, which generally lasts from ages 6 to 11, they learn how operations transform objects. In one study, Piaget showed preoperational children and concrete operational children a row of cups and asked them to place an egg in each cup. Both groups realized that the number of eggs remained the same after being placed in cups. Piaget then removed the eggs from the cups and spread the eggs out in a wider line than the line of cups. This time, children in the preoperational stage now incorrectly reported that there were more eggs than cups, while children in the concrete operational stage didn't make this mistake. The concrete operational children understood that quantity is a property that is not affected by spreading out the objects, which simply alters the objects' appearance. Piaget called this cognitive milestone **conservation**, the understanding that quantities remain constant even when outward appearances change.

Formal Operational Stage

Piaget's final stage is the **formal operational stage**. This stage begins roughly at age 11 and lasts through adulthood. Piaget described this stage as the time that children gain a deeper understanding of their own and others' minds and begin to reason abstractly. Older children can understand and apply complex concepts like *morality* and *freedom*, despite the fact that these concepts lack physical representations. Children also learn to think in hypothetical terms during this stage, gaining the ability to consider possibilities and counterfactual situations.

Vygotsky's Sociocultural View of Development

Lev Vygotsky believed that Piaget's theory failed to appreciate social and cultural influences on cognitive development. Vygotsky argued that children's cognitive development depended on specific cultural tools, such as language and mathematics, as well as on their interactions with other people.

Vygotsky is perhaps most famous for developing the concept of the **zone of proximal development (ZPD)**. All children have a range of skills they can do on their own, as well as a range of skills they're incapable of. In between these two ranges is the zone of proximal development, which encompasses a set of skills that children can do with the assistance of a more knowledgeable other. A **more knowledgeable other (MKO)** is someone who has a better understanding of a task when compared to the learner. Vygotsky maintained that learners gain new abilities by working on skills within their ZPD with the assistance of an MKO. For example, children learn how to ride bikes with the assistance of an MKO who already knows how to ride one.

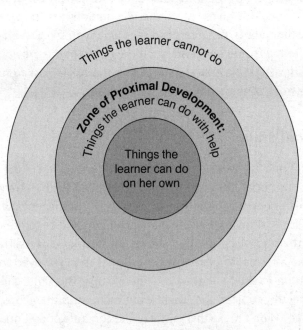

Zone of Proximal Development

MORAL DEVELOPMENT

High-Yield

LEARNING OBJECTIVE

- Evaluate moral development theories

As seen in the preceding discussion of Piaget's cognitive development theory, young children (specifically those in the sensorimotor and preoperational stages) tend to be egocentric, considering the world only from their own perspective. So how do children evolve beyond this selfish state of mind to appreciate the worth and dignity of other people? The study of moral development is the investigation of how this happens.

Kohlberg's Stage Theory of Moral Development

According to Lawrence Kohlberg, moral reasoning proceeds through three major stages, each of which can be further divided into two substages. These are summarized in the table below.

Kohlberg's Stages of Moral Development		
Stage	**Substage**	**Motivation**
Pre-Conventional	Obedience/Punishment	To avoid punishment
	Self-Interest	To gain rewards
Conventional	Conformity	To be seen as a good person by one's peers
	Authority	To follow the rules
Post-Conventional	Social Contract	To act in a way that makes life better for everyone
	Universal Principles	To follow one's own carefully developed moral code, which may differ from established social norms

✔ **AP Expert Note**

The Heinz Dilemma

Kohlberg worked out his theory by studying individual responses to a series of moral dilemmas. The most famous of these is the Heinz dilemma, in which a man is unable to afford a life-saving drug for his dying wife and must decide whether to steal the drug from the druggist who made it. Kohlberg would ask participants why the man should steal the drug (or why he shouldn't), using the type of reasoning they offered to classify their moral development.

Pre-Conventional Stage

In the **pre-conventional stage**, the morality of an action is determined by the consequences for the actor. Kohlberg found that most young children occupy this stage. An action is judged as immoral if it is punished or as moral if it is rewarded. When thinking through the Heinz dilemma, individuals in this stage may use reasoning such as "it would be bad if the man went to jail for stealing" or "it would be bad if the man was blamed for his wife's death."

Conventional Stage

Kohlberg suggested that older children and adults move to the conventional stage of reasoning. In the **conventional stage**, individuals judge the morality of an action by the extent to which it conforms with social rules. Individuals in this stage believe that people should follow laws and uphold the widely accepted norms of their culture. An individual in the conventional stage of reasoning could respond to the Heinz dilemma by saying that "the man should not steal the drug because stealing is against the law" or "the man should steal the drug because he has a duty to protect his wife."

Post-Conventional Stage

Kohlberg believed that some, but not all, adults progressed to the post-conventional stage of moral reasoning. In the **post-conventional stage**, the morality of an action is determined by a set of general principles that reflect core values, such as the promotion of liberty, the right to life, or the maximization of happiness. When an action violates one or more of these principles, it is immoral. In some cases, it is justified to defy social norms or even break laws if they come into conflict with the principles. An individual in the post-conventional stage may respond to the Heinz dilemma by saying, for example, that "the woman's life is more important than the druggist's profit, so stealing the drug is justified."

Criticisms of Kohlberg

While subsequent research has offered support for Kohlberg's theory, some evidence suggests that the stages are not as discrete as Kohlberg initially believed. For example, an individual might use pre-conventional reasoning in one situation but post-conventional in another. This suggests that, rather than stages, Kohlberg's classification scheme reveals a set of moral reasoning skills that individuals can acquire over time.

Psychologist Carol Gilligan also famously criticized Kohlberg's theory, contending that it was biased in favor of a masculine perspective of morality that prioritized abstractions like rights and justice. She maintained that Kohlberg's theory implied that boys and men were more morally advanced than girls and women. In response, Gilligan proposed an alternative theory known as the **ethics of care**, which adopted a more feminist perspective, emphasizing values such as empathy and benevolence over abstract duties and obligations.

Moral Intuitionist Perspective

In contrast to the reasoning-centered view of Kohlberg, the **moral intuitionist perspective** maintains that human ethical behavior is primarily a product of our emotional responses, which evolved to promote our survival and reproduction as a highly social species. Moral intuitionists contend that most ethical reasoning is just post-hoc rationalization used to justify our decisions after the fact.

Consider the following scenario, known as the trolley problem. You are standing on a bridge and see below you a runaway trolley hurtling down a track towards five people. You realize that you can save these people if you pull a lever that switches the trolley to a different track, but doing so would cause it to kill someone else on that track. Is it moral to divert the trolley, killing one person who otherwise would have survived but saving five lives in the process? What if, instead of pulling a lever, you could push a large man off the bridge into the path of the trolley, killing him but stopping the train from reaching the five people on the track?

If you are like most people, you would choose to pull the lever but not push the man off the bridge. Rationally speaking, though, there is no morally relevant difference between these two scenarios. The end result is the same: one person dies while five live. Your intention is the same: you cause the death of one person to save the lives of five people. The only difference is the proximity of the person whose death you cause. Moral intuitionists interpret this discrepancy to be the result of our revulsion at making physical contact to kill someone and our relative comfort with impersonally pulling a lever—in other words, we would *act* differently simply because we *feel* differently about the two situations.

SOCIALIZATION

LEARNING OBJECTIVE

- Outline processes of socialization and the development of personality

In addition to the other developmental stage theories covered in this chapter, you should also be familiar with the theories of Freud and Erikson, which concern the development of sexuality, personality, and social skills.

Freud's Psychosexual Stages

Austrian neurologist Sigmund Freud theorized that a person's basic personality is formed in childhood during a series of sensitive periods. Freud called these sensitive periods **psychosexual stages**, which are distinct developmental stages that focus on pleasures and behaviors associated with particular parts of the body. Each stage has a distinct **erotogenic zone** on which the child, specifically the child's libido, is fixated. Freud defined **libido** as the psychic energy intrinsic to an individual's id (see Chapter 19 for more on the id). While the word *libido* has sexual connotations today, Freud used the term to encompass all drives an individual possesses, including those not traditionally considered sexual.

Freud believed that problems and conflicts at any psychological stage will influence personality in adulthood. The conflict can result from either being deprived or overindulged at a given stage. This conflict could result in a **fixation**, in which a person's libido becomes arrested at a particular psychosexual stage. The stages are summarized in the table that follows.

Freud's Psychosexual Stages				
Stage	**Age**	**Focus**	**Development**	**Fixation(s)**
Oral	Birth to 18 months	Mouth: sucking, chewing, biting	Weaning	Smoking, overeating
Anal	18 months to 3 years	Anus: bowel and bladder control	Toilet training	Orderliness, messiness
Phallic	3 to 6 years	Genitals: coping with incestuous feelings	Resolving Oedipus or Electra Complex	Deviancy, sexual dysfunction
Latency	6 years to puberty	None: sexual feelings dormant	Developing defense mechanisms	None
Genital	puberty to adulthood	Genitals: maturation of sexual interest	Reaching full sexual maturity	None

Oral Stage

For the first year and a half, an infant occupies the **oral stage**, during which time she focuses on the pleasures and frustrations associated with the mouth, sucking, and being fed. Children that fixate on this stage may develop an impulse to constantly have things in their mouths, such as food or (later) cigarettes. Freud believed that an adult with an oral fixation may develop personality traits such as depression, lack of trust, envy, and demandingness.

Anal Stage

After the oral stage, the child moves on to the **anal stage**, in which she experiences pleasures and frustrations associated with the anus, retention and excretion of feces and urine, and toilet training. Freud argued that toddlers who experience significant issues with toilet training may become adults who are "anal retentive," or controlling and obsessively neat.

Phallic Stage

During the **phallic stage**, the child's experience is dominated by pleasures, conflicts, and frustrations associated with the genital region. Additionally, Freud argued that a child in this stage coped with powerful incestuous feelings of love, hate, and jealousy. Freud described a boy's experience in the phallic stage as an effort to resolve the **Oedipus complex**, a developmental episode in which a boy develops sexual feelings for his mother and, initially, jealousy of his father. In an effort to resolve this conflict, he will later come to identify with his father. Freud believed that fixation in this stage could lead to significant issues with intimate relationships later in life. Men with a phallic fixation may be jealous, competitive, and authoritarian.

Although Freud did not develop a specific account of what happens to girls in the phallic stage, his colleague Carl Jung proposed the **Electra complex**, in which a girl develops sexual feelings for her father and identifies with her mother to resolve this conflict. Jung believed that women fixated in the phallic stage would display flirtatiousness, seductiveness, and jealousy.

Latency Stage

During the **latency stage**, which lasts until the onset of puberty, the child does not experience a major conflict and instead focuses on the development of creative, intellectual, athletic, and interpersonal skills (as well as the development of the defense mechanisms discussed in Chapter 19). Freud believed that development in this stage had no major impact on an individual's personality.

Genital Stage

After puberty comes the final stage of psychosexual development. In the **genital stage**, the individual develops a full adult personality with the capacity to work, love, and relate to others. Freud suggested that individuals who are encumbered by unresolved conflicts from preceding stages may experience difficulty reaching the genital stage of development. He argued that an individual who successfully reached this stage would develop a healthy sexuality and become a well-adjusted adult.

Even though Freud's psychosexual stages are frequently referenced in popular culture, most contemporary psychologists do not take them seriously. The stages themselves are based on case studies, but Freud in particular is infamous for not taking notes until after completing interviews with patients. Thus, due to these issues with data collection and generalizability, Freud's theory is primarily studied in psychology only for its historical value.

Erikson's Psychosocial Stages

Erik Erikson was a German-American developmental psychologist who was heavily influenced by the work of Freud. He proposed eight developmental stages, each of which focused on a particular conflict. Similar to Freud, Erikson believed that resolving each stage's conflict would lead to successful development of particular abilities (which he called virtues), while failing to resolve a conflict could result in negative long-term consequences. These stages are summarized in the table below.

Erikson's Psychosocial Stages	
Age (years)	**Conflict**
0–1.5	**Trust vs. Mistrust**
1.5–3	**Autonomy vs. Shame and Doubt**
3–6	**Initiative vs. Guilt**
6–12	**Industry vs. Inferiority**
12–18	**Identity vs. Role Confusion**
18–40	**Intimacy vs. Isolation**
40–65	**Generativity vs. Stagnation**
65+	**Ego Integrity vs. Despair**

Trust vs. Mistrust

When an infant is first born, the world can be a scary and uncertain place. Infants look to their primary caregivers to provide stability and assurance. If the infant obtains consistent and supportive care from its caregiver, it will develop a sense of trust. The virtue that arises from this stage is hope, as the infant will feel confident that it can rely on others during difficult times. A lack of success in this stage can result in significant mistrust in relationships, which can go on to cause long-term difficulties with insecurity and intimacy.

Autonomy vs. Shame and Doubt

Between the ages of 18 months and 3 years, a child becomes more active and starts to explore the world around her. She makes choices about what to wear, what toys to play with, what to eat, and also learns new abilities like tying her shoes. This increase in decision making and skill acquisition can make a child feel independent. Erikson maintained that parents should allow their children to explore during this time, or else risk their children not developing a healthy independence. Moreover, if a child is overly critiqued in this stage, she can develop doubt about her abilities and avoid trying new things later in life. The virtue that arises from this stage is will, which enables the child to try new things with confidence.

Initiative vs. Guilt

Between the ages of 3 and 6, children often begin attending preschool for the first time, encountering many new people and new opportunities. Children in this age group often engage in pretend play with their peers, and Erikson suggested that this pretend play helps children learn that they can gain control over their environment. If children are successful in this stage, they develop initiative and feel confident in their ability to lead others and to make decisions. If a child does not have positive social interactions in this stage, either with his parents or his peers, then he may start to experience guilt over being a nuisance to others. This guilt can have long-term implications, as the child may grow up having difficulties establishing relationships with others. The virtue that arises from success in this stage is purpose.

Industry vs. Inferiority

During this stage, typically between the ages of 6 and 12, children are exposed to a variety of new tasks and rules as they enter primary school. Also, a child's peer group starts to have a larger influence in her life. Children tend to feel the need to gain approval from their peers by demonstrating certain competencies that have social value. For example, a girl may spend hours learning how to ride a bike because she believes mastering this skill will earn her approval from her peers and other people. Success in this stage will lead a child to feel self-confident and to have pride in her accomplishments. Failure in this stage can result in feelings of inferiority. The virtue of this stage is competence, which enables an individual to feel capable and proud of herself.

Identity vs. Role Confusion

This stage occurs during adolescence, between the ages of 12 and 18. Adolescents search for a sense of identity by adopting values and goals. They begin to think critically about what they want for the future (in terms of career, relationships, location, etc.) and become more independent. An adolescent will continuously question who he is and what roles he wants to play in society. Erikson believed that this questioning arises from the fact that adolescents go through a period of significant social, emotional, and physical changes. They need to try on many hats before discovering their true identities. Adolescents tend to experience difficulty during this stage if they receive external or internal pressure to fulfill an identity that is not right for them. The virtue of this stage is fidelity, a commitment to your sense of self.

Intimacy vs. Isolation

This stage occurs during young adulthood, from ages 18 to 40. During this time, young adults share themselves more intimately with others and develop long-term relationships with individuals who are not family members. Individuals who are successful in this stage are able to develop deep, meaningful relationships with others. These relationships are often romantic but can also extend to family and friends. Individuals who are not successful in this stage are prone to experience significant issues forming intimate relationships with others, which can lead to feelings of loneliness and frustration. The virtue of this stage is love.

Generativity vs. Stagnation

During middle adulthood, from 40 to 65, adults tend to settle into a career, maintain long-term relationships, and have families. Adults in this stage often want to give back to the community by raising children and being productive in their careers. Success in this stage leads to developing the virtue of care, the tendency to act benevolently toward other people and society at large. A feeling of stagnation can occur if an adult believes that he is not making significant contributions to society.

Ego Integrity vs. Despair

After the age of 65, individuals tend to slow down and take on fewer responsibilities. At this point, people generally look back over their lives and contemplate their accomplishments. If an individual feels proud of her accomplishments, she will develop ego integrity. If an individual feels regret, shame, or guilt about her past, she will likely develop despair, hopelessness, and depression. The virtue of this final stage is wisdom.

SEX AND GENDER

LEARNING OBJECTIVE

- Recognize sex and gender's impact on development and socialization

Biological Sex

Biological sex refers to the set of physiological characteristics, including chromosomal composition, hormone levels, and genitalia, that determine whether a person is male, female, or intersex. Being **intersex** is a broad classification that describes anyone whose physiological characteristics are neither clearly male nor clearly female.

When individuals enter puberty, their differences in biological sex become more pronounced through the development of primary and secondary sex characteristics (discussed in the following section on adolescence). Females tend to start and end puberty about 2 years before males do. Girls who reach puberty earlier than their peers are more likely to experience a variety of negative consequences ranging from distress to delinquency. Early-maturing girls do not have as much time as their peers to develop the skills needed to cope with adolescence, but because they look mature, others expect them to act like adults. Girls who mature earlier tend to receive more attention from older boys, which can lead to risky behaviors such as unprotected sexual intercourse and the use of alcohol and other drugs.

Gender

Gender is a broader and more complicated concept when compared to biological sex. **Gender identity** refers to one's psychological identification as male, female, something in between, or neither. A closely related concept is the idea of **gender expression**, which refers to how someone outwardly expresses their gender identity through fashion, pronoun preference, and physical appearance. Individuals whose gender identity does not align with their biological sex at birth are said to be **transgender**.

A **gender role** is a set of expectations about what is appropriate behavior for a particular gender. For example, female gender roles in some cultures may include nurturing, raising children, and communicating, while male gender roles may include providing for a family, suppressing emotional responses, and being competitive. A child's understanding of gender roles influences how he or she interacts with peers. Research suggests that children gain an understanding of gender roles around the age of 4. Unsurprisingly, the way that parents discuss gender roles with their children has a large impact on how their children understand gender. Children who are raised to see gender roles as inflexible tend to personally conform to their own gender roles to a greater degree than children who are raised to see gender roles as flexible.

Children with inflexible perceptions of gender roles also tend to extend their stringent gender expectations to their peers. A study by Carol Martin showed that cross-sex behavior is generally discouraged in both sexes, although more so in males. Gender roles place constraints upon what a child is allowed to do, based upon what their peers deem acceptable. Children also tend to prefer spending time with peers of the same gender until they are around the age of 16, which often only serves to reinforce gender roles.

ADOLESCENCE

LEARNING OBJECTIVE

- Summarize challenges, especially family challenges, to maturing in adolescence

Adolescence is the period of development that begins with the onset of sexual maturity (typically between ages 11 and 14) and lasts until the beginning of adulthood (between ages 18 and 21). This period of development includes significant physiological, emotional, and cognitive changes.

18

Physiological Changes

Over the course of 3 to 4 years, the average adolescent will gain 40 pounds and grow 10 inches. Girls tend to hit their growth spurt at age 10 and reach their maximum height around age 15. Boys tend to hit their growth spurt at age 12 and reach their maximum height around age 17. These growth spurts typically mark the onset of **puberty**, which is the set of bodily changes that are associated with sexual maturity. These changes include both development of **primary sex characteristics**, which are bodily structures and processes directly involved with reproduction (such as the onset of the menstrual cycle), and **secondary sex characteristics**, which are not directly involved with reproduction but that change dramatically during puberty based on sex (such as the development of male facial hair).

Emotional Changes

Adolescence is a time of transition between the carefree ease of childhood and the serious responsibilities of adulthood. Some theorists categorize adolescents as adults who have been denied a place in society and thus act out to try to prove they are mature. Adolescents may act out by having sex, consuming alcohol, or breaking laws.

The characterization of adolescents as moody teenagers may not be as accurate as popular media often portrays it to be. Research shows that adolescents are comparable to children in terms of mood stability and that their changes in hormonal levels have a relatively small impact on their overall moods.

Cognitive Changes

An infant's brain forms many more neural synapses than it actually needs. By the time an infant is 2 years old, she will have about 15,000 synapses per neuron, which is twice the number found in a grown adult. As an individual ages, she experiences **synaptic pruning**, a process through which synapses that are not frequently used are targeted for elimination. Although this process occurs throughout childhood, there is significant synaptic pruning in the prefrontal cortex during adolescence. This pruning roughly corresponds to the time that individuals enter the formal operational stage of cognitive development, as discussed earlier.

Sexuality

Almost all adolescents start to develop an interest in sex during puberty. A survey conducted in 2000 shows that over 65% of American women and 90% of American men report having sex before the age of 18. The United States has one of the highest incidences of teenage pregnancy of all modern industrialized nations. It is important to note that American adolescents are not having sex more than adolescents from other countries; they simply know less about how to practice safe sex.

18

Parents and Peers

Adolescents spend a lot of time trying to figure out what they want and what they believe. Young children tend to believe what their parents believe, but adolescents spend more time with peers and often begin to question who they are as people, separate from who their parents are. This marks a major distinction between children and adolescents: children define themselves by their relationships to their parents and siblings, while adolescents define themselves by their relationships with peers. Psychologist Erik Erikson, discussed earlier, suggested that the major task of adolescence is the development of an independent adult identity.

Developing this independent adult identity can be problematic for multiple reasons. The first is that there are a variety of social groups that adolescents can join. Peer groups can have a profound impact on the values, attitudes, and beliefs that adolescents develop. For example, if a teenage boy befriends a group with disdain for authority and hostility towards other peer groups, he will likely adopt those attitudes as well. Another complication is that parents often struggle with the newfound independence that adolescents seek out. Thus, relationships between parents and adolescents tend to involve less frequent interactions and more conflict.

AGING

LEARNING OBJECTIVE

- Explain physical and cognitive changes caused by aging and evaluate potential remedies

Cognitive abilities, health, and stamina tend to peak in human beings during your early 20s. As the brain and body continue to age past this point, slow and steady decline begins, which does not end until death. While that may sound bleak, it's not all bad news. Research suggests that individuals over the age of 65 tend to be happier than they were at any other point during their lifespans.

Physiological Changes

As human beings reach old age, they tend to experience significant physiological changes. Hair starts to thin, muscle mass decreases as fat steadily increases, bones weaken, skin becomes less elastic, sensory abilities decrease, and brain cells die more quickly. Of course, some of the physical deterioration of aging starts much earlier, just 10 to 15 years after puberty. Females tend to experience greater difficulties having children after age 32 and typically reach menopause between the ages of 45 and 55. Males experience a decrease in fertility after the age of 40, at which time their sperm quality decreases, though many men retain some fertility even into old age.

Cognitive Changes

After the age of about 65, the prefrontal cortex deteriorates more quickly than other areas of the brain. The prefrontal cortex is responsible for controlled processing, which means that the most notable cognitive decline occurs with tasks that require effort, initiative, or strategy. Older adults

18

tend to experience the greatest reduction to their working memory when compared to their long-term memory, episodic memory, and semantic memory.

Although cognitive changes are inevitable, research shows that individuals are often able to compensate by using other cognitive abilities more skillfully. How does this work? Across a variety of tasks, young adults tend to activate their right prefrontal cortex when working with spatial information and their left prefrontal cortex when working with verbal information. Older adults, however, tend to activate both right and left prefrontal cortices with either type of information. This more distributed activation can help to overcome natural neurological deterioration.

Although the deterioration of her prefrontal cortex is partially to blame, there is another reason that grandma can't find her car keys. According to the **socioemotional selectivity theory**, young adults tend to focus on acquiring information that will be useful to them in the future, such as recalling where they last left their keys, while older adults tend to focus on information that brings emotional satisfaction, such as thinking about their grandchildren.

Emotional and Social Changes

Research suggests that individuals are happiest after age 65. Older adults are not only less likely to remember negative information, they are also less likely to be affected by it. Younger adults show activation in the amygdala for both pleasant and unpleasant pictures, while older adults show much greater activation when looking at pleasant pictures.

The older we get, the smaller our social circles become. Older adults are more selective about who they spend time with, choosing to spend the majority of their time with family or with close friends. Research shows that older adults have just as many emotionally close partners as younger adults, but they tend to have fewer acquaintances.

18

IMPORTANT CONTRIBUTORS

LEARNING OBJECTIVE

- Recognize important contributors to developmental psychology

See the list of important contributors to developmental psychology in the Rapid Review section of Chapter 9.

 ## NEXT STEP: PRACTICE

Go to Rapid Review and Practice Chapter 9 or to your online quizzes at kaptest.com for exam-like practice on this topic.

Haven't registered your book yet? Go to kaptest.com/moreonline to begin.

CHAPTER 19

Motivation, Emotion, and Personality

This chapter is about the motives, stresses, emotions, and personality traits that underlie human behavior. Internal factors, external cues, learned expectations, and social and cultural factors all influence how we feel and what we want. We will look at the factors that influence motivation, the components of emotion, the causes of stress, and different aspects of personality. We will also look at theories used to explain these processes and associated behaviors, as well as methods used to assess personality characteristics.

MOTIVATION

LEARNING OBJECTIVES

- Apply fundamental motivational concepts to explain human and animal behavior
- Describe needs, drives, homeostasis, and other biological aspects of motivation
- Cite similarities and differences among important theories of motivation
- Summarize classic research on major motivational systems

Motivation consists of the internal processes that initiate, direct, and sustain activities. You can think of motivation as a process that *energizes* your behavior and *directs* it toward a goal. Your goal does not have to be as lofty as choosing a college major or a career; simple, everyday goals require motivation too. If you get hungry or thirsty after studying psychology for a while, you will be motivated to seek food and drink. If you exercise later, that too will require motivation. Avoiding pain can also be a motivating factor. For instance, brushing your teeth regularly will help you avoid the pain associated with bad teeth.

> ✔ **AP Expert Note**
>
> **Motivation can be directed toward minimizing pain, maximizing pleasure, or it can be rooted in a particular physical need such as eating, drinking, or sleeping.**

The factors that motivate people to act can be categorized as external or internal. External forces result in what's called **extrinsic motivation**, which is motivation based on rewards, obligations, and punishment. You might perform a desired behavior to earn a reward such as a good grade, pay, or praise. Or you might avoid certain other actions in order to avoid punishment. **Intrinsic motivation**, on the other hand, is motivation that comes from within, rather than from external factors. Often this is motivation that is based on personal enjoyment of a task or activity. If you participate in an activity because you find it fun, see it as a challenge, or want to improve some ability, then you are intrinsically motivated. Intrinsic motivation also concerns satisfying basic needs, such as hunger and thirst.

> ✔ **AP Expert Note**
>
> ### Conflicts in Motivation
>
> Sometimes motives conflict, generating one of a variety of conflicts. **Approach-approach conflicts** require deciding between desirable outcomes, while **avoidance-avoidance conflicts** require deciding between undesirable ones. **Approach-avoidance conflicts** occur when you must choose among options that have both desirable and undesirable features.

Theories of Motivation

There are multiple perspectives that psychologists have used to study and understand motivation. These include instincts that elicit natural behavior, the drive to reduce uncomfortable states, the desire to maintain optimal levels of arousal, the push and pull of incentives, and the goal of satisfying physiological and psychological needs.

Instinct Theory

Early attempts to understand the basis of motivation focused on **instincts**, which are inborn, fixed patterns of behavior in response to stimuli. Instincts tend to be rigidly patterned throughout a particular species. For example, many species of birds instinctively build nests, honeybees instinctively move toward food sources, and human infants instinctively suck their thumbs to soothe themselves in response to stress.

According to the **instinct theory** of motivation, individuals are driven to perform certain behaviors based on pre-programmed, evolutionary-based instincts. This theory was one of the first to describe motivation and was derived from Charles Darwin's theory of evolution. William James maintained that human behavior was driven by many instincts, possibly more than any other animal studied. James suggested that human actions are derived from 20 physical instincts, including suckling and locomotion, and 17 mental instincts, including curiosity and fearfulness. However, he said that many of these instincts were in direct conflict with each other and could be overridden by experience.

Drive-Reduction Theory

A **drive** is a state of unrest or irritation that energizes particular behaviors to alleviate that state. In other words, a drive is a psychological expression of an internal need. For example, when a person

19

becomes hungry, the need for food prompts a drive, which in turn activates a response—in this case, to get some food.

Drives are thought to originate within an individual without requiring any external factors to motivate behavior. Drives aid survival by creating states of discomfort that inherently motivate organisms to satisfy unmet needs (the only way to remove the discomfort). **Primary drives**, including the needs for food, water, and warmth, motivate us to keep our bodily processes in balance, or homeostasis. **Homeostasis** is a dynamic state of bodily equilibrium through which we maintain an optimal, relatively stable set of internal conditions. These internal conditions include blood pressure, blood glucose, and body temperature, among other factors.

Homeostasis is usually controlled by negative feedback loops. A common real-world example of a negative feedback loop is a thermostat. A thermostat is set to a desired temperature, and sensors monitor the air temperature in relation to that set point. If the air temperature drops below the set point, the thermostat turns the heat on; if the temperature warms up above the set point, the thermostat turns the heat off. That simple principle is enough to keep your home at a comfortable temperature. Negative feedback loops in the body operate the same way. When your body is too low on nutrients or energy, feedback systems release hormones that turn on the hunger drive and motivate eating. After you consume enough food, feedback is sent to your brain to turn off the hunger drive, so you stop eating. In short, homeostasis is like your body's personal thermostat.

While primary drives stem from biological needs, other drives are learned through experience. These are called **secondary drives**, which are drives that motivate you to act as though you have unmet basic needs. For example, the desire for money is a secondary drive. Having too little money motivates many behaviors—such as getting a job, taking out a loan, and even stealing—to obtain more funds.

The **drive-reduction theory** of motivation maintains that, when you have a physiological need, your body creates an aroused state that motivates you to reduce the need. In other words, imbalances to the body's internal environment generate motivations, which cause you to act in ways that restore homeostasis. For example, if your internal temperature lowers below an optimal level, your body reacts: you feel "chilled" and are thereby motivated to seek warmth—perhaps by turning up your home thermostat!

Arousal Theory

Drive-reduction theory can account for a lot of motivated behaviors, but not all of them. For example, consider curiosity. Humans and other animals cannot resist checking out new and unusual parts of their environments. People travel, ride roller coasters, are fascinated with technology, and browse through shops, libraries, and other places. Such behaviors create an increase in **arousal**, which is the body's general level of activation. Arousal is reflected in heart rate, muscle tension, brain activity, blood pressure, and other bodily systems. Arousal can be lowered by going to sleep, meditating, relaxing, or taking certain drugs such as depressants. Arousal increases in response to hunger and thirst, stimulant drugs, and engaging in stimulating behaviors (e.g., riding a roller coaster). Because people often try to increase or decrease their levels of arousal, some psychologists believe that motivation is tied to the regulation of arousal.

19

Arousal theory states that people perform actions in order to maintain an optimal level of arousal: seeking to increase arousal when it falls below their optimal level, and to decrease arousal when it rises above their optimum level. Most people perform best, and may feel at their best, when arousal is moderate, but people differ in the exact level of arousal that is optimal. These differences in optimal arousal may explain why some people are bolder or shyer, for example.

The **Yerkes-Dodson Law** suggests that performance and arousal are directly related. An increase in arousal up to a certain level can help to boost performance. Once arousal exceeds the optimal level, performance starts to diminish. The optimal level of arousal may vary with different types of tasks.

The law was first proposed by psychologists Robert Yerkes and John Dillingham Dodson in 1908. In an experiment, they discovered that rats could be motivated to complete a maze with slight electrical shocks. But, when the shocks were of a higher degree, their performance level decreased and they just wildly ran about seeking for an escape. It was clear from the experiment that arousal levels helped to focus attention and motivation on the task at hand, but only up to a certain point.

The Yerkes-Dodson law can be graphed as a U-shaped function between the level of arousal and performance, as shown in the following figure.

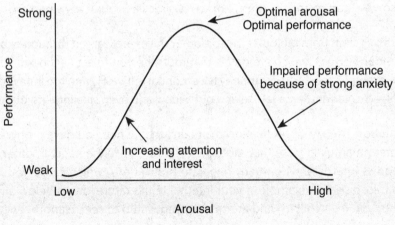

Yerkes-Dodson Law

Incentive Theory

Instinct, drive-reduction, and arousal theories of motivation all focus on internal processes that cause people to behave in certain ways. **Incentive theory** maintains that behavior is motivated not by need or arousal, but by the desire to pursue rewards and to avoid punishments. People are drawn toward behaviors that offer positive incentives and are pushed away from behaviors associated with negative incentives. According to incentive theory, if you expect that some behavior (such as taking the AP Psychology exam) will lead to a valued outcome (earning college credit), you will be motivated to engage in that behavior.

19

Maslow's Hierarchy of Needs

Needs are also motivators that influence human behavior. A **need** is an internal deficiency that may energize behavior. Motivation can be described as how we allocate our energy and resources to best satisfy these needs. Motivation thus determines which behaviors are most important to undertake, how much effort will be expended, and for how long the effort will be maintained.

Humanistic psychologist Abraham Maslow observed that certain needs yield a greater influence on our motivation when unsatisfied and established what is referred to as **Maslow's hierarchy of needs**. Maslow classified needs into five groups and assigned different levels of priority to each group.

The hierarchy is typically displayed as a pyramid, as shown in the following figure, in which the most basic, essential, and important needs are at the base. These are called *physiological needs*, and include food, water, oxygen, and so on. The second level contains *safety needs*, which include personal safety and security for one's family, job, property, and so forth. The third level is made up of *needs for love and belonging*. People need both to love and to be loved, as well as to belong and to be accepted by family and community. The fourth level includes *esteem needs*, like self-esteem, achievement, respect, and recognition from others. At the highest level are *self-actualization needs*. **Self-actualization** means reaching your fullest potential, developing yourself and pursuing a life course that you find meaningful and satisfying.

Maslow's Hierarchy of Needs

According to Maslow, every person feels a need to self-actualize, although many are limited in their capacity to pursue this need because of unsatisfied needs at lower levels. Maslow theorized that a person's highest motivational priority would be to fulfill the lowest level of unmet need. For example, a person who is both hungry (a physiological need) and lonely (a love and belonging need) would be more motivated to obtain food than to make friends.

A common criticism of Maslow's theory challenges his assumption that people must satisfy lower-level needs before they can achieve self-actualization and other higher-level needs. Many people around the world live in conditions of material deprivation in which physiological and safety needs cannot always be satisfied, and yet such people are often motivated to build relationships and communities or to pursue projects they find personally fulfilling. Critics of Maslow contend that people can be motivated to satisfy needs on various levels at the same time, or even to pursue higher-level needs before lower-level ones. Such critics grant that there are different types of needs that motivate people to act, but deny that these needs are hierarchical.

Eating and Hunger

Biological Bases for Hunger

What causes hunger? The most important signals about the body's need for food are sent from the blood to the brain. Researchers discovered these blood-generated triggers by giving starving rats injections of blood taken from well-fed rats. After the injection, the starving rats were offered food but did not eat it.

The nervous and endocrine systems regulate hunger to prevent nutrient deficiencies and maintain stable body weight. When blood glucose (sugar) levels drop, the brain automatically triggers a hunger feeling. When glucose levels rise, the pancreas releases insulin, a hormone that helps cells metabolize glucose. Insulin provides a signal that the body is full. As mentioned in Chapter 14, the brain's hypothalamus plays the primary role in monitoring blood signals about the need to eat. The hypothalamus detects levels of insulin and other hunger-related hormones and responds with signals that either increase hunger and reduce energy usage or reduce hunger and increase energy usage. This explains why you sometimes start to feel tired when you are hungry—your body is conserving energy.

The Psychology of Hunger

There is more to hunger than the feelings prompted by an empty stomach. For example, eating is powerfully affected by the appearance, aroma, and flavor of food. This explains why many people still want dessert despite declaring themselves "full" after a meal.

Eating is also affected by social and cultural factors. For example, you may be tempted to eat with your friends, even if you are not hungry. What you eat is often influenced by your culture. In some parts of the world, eating insects or alligators is considered perfectly normal. In places such as India, eating beef is viewed as abnormal and offensive. In short, eating serves more than a mere physiological function.

19

For some people, the biological or psychological processes that regulate hunger and eating may not function properly—resulting in the medical condition of obesity or in an eating disorder such as anorexia nervosa.

> ✔ **AP Expert Note**
>
> **Feeding and Eating Disorders**
>
> The DSM-5 categorizes anorexia nervosa, bulimia nervosa, binge eating disorder, and other similar disorders under the heading of feeding and eating disorders. See Chapter 20 on Clinical Psychology to learn more about these disorders.

Obesity

Obesity is a medical condition in which a person is severely overweight. More specifically, a person is considered obese when he or she has a *body mass index* of more than 30. The U.S. Centers for Disease Control and Prevention (the CDC) estimates that more than 65 percent of Americans are overweight. Approximately 35 percent of American adults and 17 percent of American children are further classified as obese. Obesity is associated with a number of health problems, such as increased risk for heart attack, diabetes, high blood pressure, and even dementia.

So how do people become obese? Body weight is determined by a combination of food intake and energy output. When one eats too much, the excess energy from the food is stored as fat. Those who are obese tend to consume too many food calories and have lower activity levels. But contrary to popular opinion, there are several important underlying factors that can contribute to development and maintenance of an obese state. Some people may have a genetic predisposition to obesity. Others may not have learned proper eating habits from their parents. And other people may have trouble managing stress, prompting them to overeat. Indeed, studies have verified that stress can trigger a person's impulse to eat.

Solutions to obesity come in the form of dieting, exercise, counseling, and medical treatment. Some medical treatments include drugs that help regulate eating and hunger or surgery to restructure the stomach or intestines to reduce the physical space for food. The most effective weight-loss programs are typically designed to reduce food intake, to change habits and attitudes about food and eating, and to increase physical activity. On the other hand, rapid weight-loss programs, such as extreme calorie reduction and certain diet pills, have largely proved ineffectual in the long run. Rapid weight loss that is not managed by a medical doctor can also increase the risks for other health problems.

Sexual Behavior and Motivation

While an individual can survive without sex, it is essential for reproduction and the continuation of the human species. Given the evolutionary importance of reproduction, it is no surprise that nearly everyone possesses a sex drive. The term **sex drive** refers to the strength of one's motivation to engage in sexual behavior.

Sexual motivation and behavior are strongly influenced by a person's sexual orientation. **Sexual orientation** describes, for example, a person's level of romantic and erotic attraction to members of the same sex (homosexual), opposite sex (heterosexual), both sexes (bisexual), or neither sex (asexual). Research suggests that a person's sexual orientation is influenced by a combination of biological, psychological, social, and culture-specific factors.

The Study of Sexual Behavior

As a scientific topic, sexual behavior can be challenging to study because many are hesitant to answer questions about their sexual practices. But such information is vital for researchers who study topics like differences in sexuality, gender differences in sexual motivation and behavior, sexual orientation, sexual dysfunctions, and sexually transmitted diseases. Despite the challenge, sexual motivation has been widely studied. Two of the most famous sets of studies are those by Kinsey and by Masters and Johnson.

In 1948, Alfred Kinsey reported his findings on sexual behavior based on interviews with people from a broad range of sociocultural backgrounds. Kinsey hoped to identify what sexual behaviors people were participating in, how often, with whom, and at what age they began. Kinsey and his colleagues surveyed thousands of individuals and, based on the data collected, developed a novel approach to defining human sexuality. They created a graded scale, called the Kinsey Scale, to define a person's sexuality. Prior to Kinsey, people were generally considered to be either heterosexual or homosexual. Instead of this rigid approach, Kinsey saw sexual behavior on a continuum that rarely described individuals as either strictly homosexual or heterosexual.

William Masters and Virginia Johnson published another important study of sexual motivation. Their study involved physiological measurement of sexual arousal. The results led Masters and Johnson to propose a four-stage human *sexual response cycle:* excitement, plateau, orgasm, and resolution. One of the most significant conclusions of the study was that men and women experience similar physical responses to sex.

Biology of Sex

Physiologically, humans are motivated to engage in sexual behavior based on the secretion of hormones, including estrogens, progesterone, and androgens. There is a strong association between hormone concentration and sexual desire. Another biological factor for sexual motivation is smell; certain odors have been shown to increase sexual desire and activity. Cognition is also important, as shown by one study that measured physiological arousal in people watching sexually explicit videos. The results showed that both men and women experienced the same levels of arousal while watching, but women more often reported being unaroused or having feelings of disgust based on subjective interviews. Finally, culture and society influence what is deemed appropriate sexual behavior, the age at which it is deemed appropriate, and with whom.

19

Sexual Dysfunctions

Sexual dysfunctions are more common than many people believe. People who have such dysfunctions can receive psychological counseling, medical treatment, or both. Disorders come in a variety of forms, with two of the most widespread being desire disorders, in which patients have little to no sexual motivation despite an expressed desire to be motivated in such a way, and arousal disorders, in which patients desire sexual activity but cannot become sexually aroused. Other disorders include the inability to have orgasms and pain-related disorders that make sexual activity uncomfortable.

STRESS

LEARNING OBJECTIVE

- Explain stress theories and stress's effect on well being

Stress is the emotional and physiological process that occurs as individuals confront challenging environmental circumstances. These environmental circumstances are called **stressors**. A stressor disrupts or threatens to disrupt people's daily routines and often causes them to adjust their behavior. Common stressors include:

- Environmental factors: uncomfortable temperatures, loud sounds, bad weather
- Daily mishaps: running late, losing items, unexpected setbacks
- Workplace or academic demands: taking exams, completing difficult projects
- Social expectations: demands placed on individuals by society, family, and friends
- Chemical and biological stressors: diet, alcohol, drugs, pathogens, allergies, medications, medical conditions

Stressors are classified as either negative or positive. A negative stressor creates **distress**, whereas a positive stressor creates **eustress**. Positive stressors can include life events such as graduating from high school, choosing a college, and going to prom.

Reacting to Stress

Adjustments made due to stressors are referred to as **stress reactions**. Stress reactions are psychological, behavioral, and physiological responses such as tiredness, anxiety, and even nausea. Several factors influence the frequency and severity of stress reactions in people. First, if you can predict and control your stressors, you are better able to handle the stress. Second, how you interpret a stressor impacts the stress reaction. Third, if you have adequate social support, you tend to manage stress better. Finally, learning and practicing stress coping skills, such as meditation and exercise, can help you to minimize your stress reactions.

Your interpretation of stress is referred to as cognitive appraisal. **Cognitive appraisal** is the subjective evaluation of a situation that induces stress. When you encounter a stressor, you perform an initial evaluation of the environment and the associated threat. The appraisal begins with the identification of eustress or distress. Next, you evaluate whether you can cope with the stress. This evaluation includes assessments of: *harm*, or damage caused by the stressor; *threat*, or the potential for future damage caused by the stressor; and *challenge*, or the potential to overcome and possibly benefit from the stressor. Individuals who perceive themselves as having the ability to cope with the stressor experience less stress than those who don't. In general, appraisal and stress level are personal, as individuals have different skills, abilities, and coping mechanisms. Some situations require ongoing monitoring through constant reappraisal, such as when you feel like you are being followed.

Measuring Stress

In 1967, psychiatrists Thomas Holmes and Richard Rahe decided to study whether stress contributes to illness. They surveyed more than 5,000 patients and asked them to say whether they had experienced any of a series of 43 life events in the previous two years. Each event, called a *life change unit* (LCU), had a different "weight" for stress. The more events the patient had experienced and the larger the weight of each event, the higher his or her score. The higher the score, the more likely the patient was to develop a mental disorder or physical illness. Their questionnaire is called the *Social Readjustment Rating Scale* (SRRS).

General Adaptation Syndrome

Hans Selye (pronounced "SELL-yay") was the first researcher to identify stress as a medical issue and to study the side effects of stress on people. After studying animals' reactions to various stressors (such as trauma and electric shock) and observing how subjects tended to respond in the same way to particular stressors, he developed a theory on stress called **general adaptation syndrome (GAS)**.

Selye saw GAS as having three distinct phases. In the first phase, you experience an *alarm* reaction due to the stressor, as your brain activates your sympathetic nervous system. Heart rate, blood sugar, and blood pressure increase, preparing your body to deal with the stress challenge. The second phase is referred to as the *resistance* phase, in which the continuous release of hormones allows your sympathetic nervous system to remain engaged to fight the stressor. In the last phase, you experience *exhaustion* when your body can no longer maintain an elevated response with sympathetic nervous system activity. When exhausted, you become more susceptible to illnesses and medical conditions (such as ulcers and high blood pressure), organ systems can begin to deteriorate (including heart disease), and in extreme cases death can result.

Coping with Stress

Strategies for coping with stress fall into two groups. *Problem-focused strategies* involve working to overcome a stressor, such as reaching out to family and friends for social support, confronting the issue head-on, and creating and following a plan of problem-solving actions.

19

Emotionally focused strategies center on changing your feelings about a stressor. They include taking responsibility for the issue, engaging in self-control, distancing yourself from the issue, wishful thinking, and using positive reappraisal to focus on positive outcomes instead of the stressor. Additionally, coping strategies may be positively adaptive (such as reaching out to loved ones for support) or negatively adaptive (like turning to drugs and alcohol).

Individuals can also engage in stress management to reduce their stress levels. Exercise is a powerful stress management tool that not only improves health, but also enhances mood. Exercise releases endorphins and other chemicals that promote positive feelings. Relaxation techniques, including meditation, deep breathing, and progressive muscle relaxation have also been found to reduce stress. Additionally, studies have shown that engaging in a spiritual practice helps to manage stress.

EMOTION

High-Yield

LEARNING OBJECTIVES

- Distinguish among major theories of emotion
- Identify the influences of culture on emotional expression

An **emotion** is a psychological and physiological response characterized by pleasure, pain, and/or other feelings. Like the word motivation, the word emotion is derived from the Latin *movere*, meaning "to move," and indeed our emotions often move us to act in distinctive ways. Virtually everyone agrees that love, hate, fear, joy, sorrow, and anger are emotions. But what makes an emotion different from an impulse or a thought? Psychological research has shed some light on this and related questions:

- An emotion is usually temporary, lasting perhaps only a few minutes.
- An emotion can be positive (pleasurable), negative (painful), or a mixture of both. Some feelings, for example, can be bittersweet, such as leaving your friends and family to go on an exciting trip.
- Emotions can vary in intensity. For instance, getting a top grade on your English exam may make you somewhat pleased, a little happy, or ecstatic, depending on the circumstances.
- Emotions alter your thought process. For example, anxiety about an upcoming event may narrow your attention to focus more on that event.
- Emotions tend to cause us to act. If you are really upset about a problem at your school, you may be motivated to seek a solution.

Three Elements of Emotion

There are three distinct but related aspects of emotions: the physiological response, the behavioral response, and the cognitive response.

A *physiological response* consists of a change in levels of arousal through activation of the sympathetic or parasympathetic nervous systems. The physiological component of emotion includes changes in heart rate, breathing rate, skin temperature, and blood pressure.

A *behavioral response* includes facial expressions and body language. For example, a smile, a friendly hand gesture, or even a subtle head tilt toward someone are commonly recognized as warm and happy signals. On the other hand, a frown, slumping of the shoulders, and looking downwards are recognized as sad signals.

A *cognitive response* concerns the subjective interpretation of the feeling being experienced. Determination of one's emotion is partly based on one's memories of past experiences and perceptions about the cause of the emotion.

Theories of Emotion

As just explained, emotions are a combination of physiological arousal, behavior, and thought. For decades, psychologists have been theorizing about how these components fit together. Different theories disagree, for example, about whether the physiological arousal or the conscious experience of the emotion comes first.

Another disagreement concerns the interaction between thinking and feeling: does cognition always precede emotion? Early psychologists believed that the cognitive component of emotion led to the physiological component, which then produced the behavioral component. For example, the feeling of joy would start with the perception and recognition of a positive stimulus, which would cause physiological changes like increased heart rate, which would then result in joyful behavior like smiling and laughing. This explanation assumes that feeling and interpretation come before arousal, which comes before action. Four prominent psychological theories on the emotions offer alternative explanations: the James-Lange theory, the Cannon-Bard theory, the two-factor theory, and the appraisal theory.

James-Lange Theory

William James, the founder of functionalism, believed that emotions begin with physiological responses. In other words, physiological changes come first and feelings come second. Around the same time, a physician named Carl Lange developed a similar theory, so the explanation shared by the two is referred to as the James-Lange theory of emotion. According to the **James-Lange theory**, a stimulus results in physiological arousal that in turn leads to a secondary response, which is the feeling of emotion. For example, bumping into someone in a dark room is a stimulus for elevated heart rate and blood pressure. These physiological responses result in the cognitive labeling of the event as fearful: "I must be afraid because my heart is racing and my blood pressure is high."

James believed that when peripheral organs receive information and respond, that response is then assigned an emotion by the brain. A consequence of this view is that someone with severe spinal cord injuries (whose brain does not communicate with the peripheral nervous system) would be expected to experience decreased levels of emotion. Research, however, has shown this to be false; spinal cord injury patients show the same level of emotion after their injuries as before.

Cannon-Bard Theory

American physiologist Walter Cannon believed that the James-Lange theory was implausible, that the body's responses were not different enough to produce different emotions. Do elevated blood pressure and a racing heart indicate love, anger, surprise, or fear? Cannon and another researcher named Philip Bard theorized that physiological arousal and emotional experience occur at the same time. According to this view, the thalamus simultaneously routes information to the brain's cortex (prompting the awareness of emotion) and to the sympathetic nervous system (causing the body's arousal). So if you saw a snake, the **Cannon-Bard theory** of emotion maintains that the cognitive and physiological components of your fear would occur simultaneously, and would then prompt the behavioral component: "I am afraid because I see a snake and my heart is racing ... Let me out of here!"

Two-Factor Theory and Appraisal Theory

Another theory on emotion is called the **two-factor theory**, or the Schachter-Singer theory (named after its creators). It states that your physiology and your cognition (perceptions, interpretations, and memories) combine to create emotion. In other words, both arousal and the labeling of arousal must occur in order for an emotion to be experienced. According to the two-factor theory, someone seeing a snake might conclude: "I am afraid of this snake because my heart is racing and because I believe snakes to be scary."

Richard Lazarus also believed that cognition was important to the generation of emotion. His **appraisal theory of emotion** maintains that cognition happens first, sometimes unconsciously. The nature of the emotion experienced as a result of a stimulus is determined by two factors: a primary appraisal, which looks at the meaning of the event, and a secondary appraisal, which assesses how well equipped the individual is to cope with the stimulus. These factors should sound familiar: Lazarus applied these types of appraisal to stress as well as emotion, as discussed in the previous section.

Each of these models is similar to one of the previously discussed theories. The Schachter-Singer theory is similar to the James-Lange theory in that both believe that arousal precedes emotion. Appraisal theory is similar to the Cannon-Bard theory in that both believe that the emotional response and the physiological response occur simultaneously.

Cultural Impact on Emotion

Some emotions seem to be universal, appearing in all human beings irrespective of culture. American psychologist Paul Ekman claims there are seven basic emotions recognized by everyone: happiness, sadness, contempt, surprise, fear, disgust, and anger. Across cultures, adults and children tend to cry when upset and smile when happy.

Although cultures share basic emotions, they can vary significantly in how much emotion they show. Cultures that encourage individuality, as in the United States and Europe, tend to display a lot of visible emotions. In Chinese and many other Asian cultures with a more collectivist orientation, personal emotions are less visible.

Culture can also differ in recognizing emotions. In one study, for example, a group of Americans and a group of Japanese were shown a series of facial expressions. Both groups agreed on which faces exhibited happiness and sadness, but often disagreed about which faces showed anger, disgust, and fear. There are also differences in recognizing the emotional significance of tone of voice. One study suggested that Westerners were best at recognizing happy tones of voice while East Asians were best at recognizing sad tones of voice.

Finally, some emotions seem to be specific to particular cultures or subcultures, to be found only in particular times and places. For example, you may be familiar with FOMO, the so-called "fear of missing out," which seems to be unique to a generation that's grown up in an age of social media. Thus, while emotion is a biological and cognitive phenomenon, it is undeniably also a sociocultural phenomenon.

PERSONALITY THEORIES

LEARNING OBJECTIVE

- Distinguish among major personality theories

The study of personality is an effort to describe and classify the factors that make every human being into a unique person. More concretely, **personality** is the set of thoughts, feelings, traits, and behaviors that are characteristic of a person and that are consistent over time and in different situations. There are many different theories of personality, and the AP Psychology exam expects you to be able to compare and contrast them.

Type and Trait Theories

If you have ever taken an online quiz that tells you which television show character you most resemble or which jungle animal you would be, you are familiar with type and trait theories of personality. These perspectives are limited to descriptions or classifications, grouping people by their characteristics without really caring about how or why people gained those characteristics in the first place. Specifically, **type theories** say that people's personalities can be classified into one group or another as a whole, while **trait theories** say that all people possess classifiable traits (consistent tendencies in behavior) that they express to different degrees and that add together in different combinations to make a unique personality—but the two are similar enough that we will consider them together.

Grouping people by types and traits is a practice that existed well before modern psychology. Some ancient Greek and Roman thinkers believed that everyone's health was a result of the balance of four bodily fluids called humors and that individual differences in the balance of humors led to distinct personality types. Medical treatments to restore the balance of these humors (in order to cure personality disorders) were popular in European medicine as recently as the nineteenth century. In the early twentieth century, William Sheldon proposed a system of classification by

19

body shape called somatotypes. Sheldon presumed that all short, stocky people were jolly, all tall people were high-strung and aloof, and people in between were strong and well-adjusted. Like humorism, somatotypes are interesting as a historical type theory, but they are no longer taken seriously by psychologists.

One more modern and widely known type theory classifies people into type-A and type-B personalities. People with **type-A** personalities are said to be outgoing and ambitious but can be compulsive, impatient, and prone to anxiety, while people with **type-B** personalities are generally laid-back and relaxed. There has been some research to suggest that people with type-A personalities are more prone to heart attacks and other cardiovascular problems, but these results are controversial, and many studies have demonstrated a limited or nonexistent correlation.

> ✔ **AP Expert Note**
>
> The Myers-Briggs Type Inventory is an example of a personality assessment that is based on the type perspective. It, and other such assessments, will be discussed in the next section.

While type perspectives classify whole people into different groups, trait perspectives label clusters of similar behaviors that are typically found together. For example, people who are more reserved and less outspoken in groups tend to enjoy alone time and avoid overstimulation. Trait theorists maintain that each individual is made up of different combinations of these traits.

Hans and Sybil Eysenck pioneered the **PEN model** of personality traits. PEN is an acronym that designates the three traits that the Eysencks focused on. People who score highly in **psychoticism** tend to be aggressive, stubborn non-conformists. Those with high **extraversion** are outgoing and thrive on the external stimulation of being around others. Finally, those with high **neuroticism** are prone to anxiety and will experience a fight-or-flight reaction in response to even minor stressors. Low scores on these three dimensions are known as socialization, introversion, and stability, respectively.

More recently, Paul Costa and Robert McCrae expanded the PEN model to what is known as the **Big Five**, which reorganizes and adds to the original three factors. As the name would suggest, this model uses five factors that can be remembered using the acronym OCEAN: **openness to experience** (curious vs. cautious), **conscientiousness** (organized vs. careless), *extraversion* (extraverted vs. introverted), **agreeableness** (friendly vs. detached), and *neuroticism* (neurotic vs. stable).

Some traits may be more important to a person than others. Gordon Allport identified three kinds of traits that carry different weights in making up an individual's personality. *Cardinal traits* are traits that are most important to an individual and that guide most of the person's actions. Ebenezer Scrooge, for example, has greed as his cardinal trait, whereas King Arthur's cardinal trait might be nobility. Allport believed that not everyone develops a cardinal trait, but that everyone has central and secondary traits. A *central trait* is a major part of someone's personality and is always present. A *secondary trait* is a part of someone's personality that might only manifest in certain situations.

19

Behaviorist and Biopsychological Approaches

While type and trait theories merely attempt to classify existing aspects of personality, the behaviorist and biopsychological approaches are both interested in how personality develops. In some ways, these two approaches could not be more different, since they find themselves on opposite sides of the nature versus nurture debate. On the other hand, they have in common a belief that the origins of personality can be completely explained: to a behaviorist, personality is developed primarily through experience, while a biopsychologist believes that your genes most greatly influence who you are to become.

The **biopsychological approach** to personality is relatively straightforward. Genes determine the structure of the nervous system, which in turn determines neurotransmitter activity and therefore how much influence each nervous structure has in the way you act and react to your environment. For example, people with a mutation in the DRD2 and DRD4 genes, both of which code for dopamine receptors, have fewer such receptors in their brains to transmit feelings of pleasure and satisfaction. These people must overindulge in pleasurable stimuli to obtain the same reward as those without the mutation, and thus are prone to addictive and thrill-seeking behaviors.

In contrast, the **behaviorist approach** presumes that people start as a blank slate, and that their personality is determined entirely by experience. As behaviorist John B. Watson famously quipped, "Give me a dozen healthy infants, well-formed, and my own specified world to bring them up in and I'll guarantee to take any one at random and train him to become any type of specialist I might select—doctor, lawyer, artist, merchant-chief and, yes, even beggar-man and thief, regardless of his talents, penchants, tendencies, abilities, vocations, and race of his ancestors." Often, major life changes impact personality, as when people become parents for the first time: people who are carefree or even reckless can find themselves acting with much more caution throughout all aspects of their lives when they are responsible for a newborn.

The Social Cognitive Perspective

As discussed, behaviorism presumes that people are shaped by their environments. Adherents to the **social cognitive perspective** believe that while this is true, it is also a two-way street: people shape their environments to match their personalities. This idea, proposed by Albert Bandura, is called **reciprocal determinism**: people's thoughts, feelings, beliefs, and environment all interact to determine their actions in a given situation. For example, a person who is extraverted might be more likely to network in college by joining clubs, which could lead to more employment opportunities after graduation. The extravert might take a job in a large city, an environment that would encourage different behaviors than life in a small suburban town. According to this perspective, personality, environment, and behavior are all linked to each other, and changing any one of them has effects on the others.

The Psychoanalytic Perspective

Like the biopsychological, behaviorist, and social cognitive approaches, the psychoanalytic perspective seeks to explain personality rather than simply describe or classify it (as the type and

19

trait perspectives do). But while these other approaches look to external (non-mental) factors to explain personality, the men and women who developed the **psychoanalytic** or **psychodynamic perspective** look deep inside the unconscious mind to find the roots of human behavior.

Freud

It is impossible to talk about psychoanalysis without talking about Sigmund Freud. As discussed in Chapter 18, Freud believed that personality develops as the result of unconscious desires and conflicts. Freud's best-known contribution to the study of personality is the **structural model**, which organizes the conscious and unconscious mind into three structures: the id, the ego, and the superego.

The **id** consists of all of the basic, primal urges and instincts to survive and reproduce. It operates according to the **pleasure principle**, the drive for instant gratification and the relief of pent-up tension, or *catharsis*. When you are born, the id is completely dominant. Babies cry when they have an instinctive need that is not being met and stop crying once the need is fulfilled. **Primary process** thinking, the style of thought generated by the id, is therefore simple, primal, and aimed at seeking pleasure and avoiding pain, much like the kind of thought you would associate with babies. Adults engage in primary process thinking as well, manifested as daydreaming or fantasy. When these fantasies are used to imagine satisfying an urge that would be unacceptable to act out, the adult is said to be engaged in **wish fulfillment**.

Where the id desires satisfaction of basic needs, the **superego** is focused on creating the ideal self. Think of the superego as the personality's perfectionist, always judging your actions. The superego can be divided into two subsystems: the **conscience**, which responds by causing feelings of guilt when you succumb to the urges of the id, and the **ego-ideal**, which responds with feelings of pride when you overcome those urges.

If these were the only two aspects of your personality, you'd never be happy. Suppressing your base instincts would cause the id to be dissatisfied, but giving into them would cause guilt brought about by the superego. The third entity in the structural model, the **ego**, works as a referee for the id and superego. You can't always act on every desire you have, nor will you ever be as perfect as the superego would want, so the ego suppresses the needs of the other two entities according to the **reality principle**, allowing you to put off instant gratification or fulfill your desires in socially acceptable ways. This mode of thought—seeking to relieve the tension caused by delaying gratification—is called **secondary process**.

When the anxiety caused by the clash between the id and the superego becomes too great, the ego uses **defense mechanisms** to relieve the tension. There are many different defense mechanisms, but they all have two things in common: they are all unconscious (except suppression), and they all deny, distort, or falsify reality in some way. The following table summarizes the most important defense mechanisms that you should know for the exam.

19

Defense Mechanisms		
Mechanism	**Definition**	**Example**
Repression	The ego pushing an unwanted or socially unacceptable feeling out of conscious awareness	Forgetting a traumatic childhood experience that is too painful to think about
Suppression	Consciously setting aside thoughts or feelings that would be unhelpful in the current situation	Counting to ten when feeling angry to prevent speaking or acting negatively in response to that feeling
Regression	Reverting to an earlier stage of emotional or mental development in response to stress	An adult becoming overwhelmed with stress and whining or throwing temper tantrums, rather than dealing with her emotions in a more mature manner
Reaction formation	Turning an unwanted thought or feeling into its opposite	Developing an infatuation with an unattainable person, but unconsciously turning those feelings of love into hate and lashing out against the person
Projection	Attributing your own unwanted feelings to others	A teenager's thoughts of *I hate my parents* becoming *My parents hate me*
Rationalization	Justifying unacceptable behaviors to make them more acceptable to yourself or others and to hide your true motivations	Someone procrastinating on a big project because he is nervous that he could fail coming up with excuses, such as not being able to get started until his office is clean
Displacement	Redirecting an unwanted feeling from one target to another	A young child who is sent to his room for misbehavior punching his pillow rather than directing his anger at his parents
Sublimation	Transforming an undesirable feeling or drive into a socially acceptable one	A person who has uncontrollable aggressive urges channeling that energy into playing a contact sport, such as boxing or rugby, or even into something unrelated, such as business success or artistic creativity

Jung

While Freud pioneered psychoanalysis, others thinkers built on his foundations. Carl Jung is perhaps the most well known of Freud's associates. Where Freud believed that the source of your urges and emotions was the libido and was largely sexual in nature, Jung felt that sexuality was only one part of personal development. Jung also had a different view of the structural model. He maintained that the ego represented the entirety of the conscious mind, and that the unconscious could be divided into two parts: the **personal unconscious**, which is any part of the personality or memory that is not currently conscious because it has been forgotten or repressed (which is essentially Freud's conception of the unconscious), and the **collective unconscious**, which represents the idea that all people, because of our common ancestry, share the same instincts and emotionally-charged symbols. These emotional symbols are known as **archetypes**.

There are four commonly cited Jungian archetypes. The **persona** is the part of your personality that you present to the outside world. It represents the way you'd like others to see you, emphasizing your positive qualities and burying your negative ones. The **shadow** archetype is the part of your personality that you generally dislike and try to hide. The other two archetypes, the **anima** and the **animus**, represent feminine qualities in men and masculine qualities in women, respectively. For example, in Jung's theory, the anima is the part of a man's personality that is emotional, while the animus is the part of a woman's personality that is ambitious and power-seeking. Jung believed that the self was the sum of all of the conscious and unconscious aspects of your personality.

Adler

Like Jung, Alfred Adler emphasized social motivations for behavior over sexual ones. Adler is the originator of the concept of the **inferiority complex**, which is a person's feelings of incompleteness or imperfection. Striving for superiority, according to Adler, drives behavior.

Horney

Along with Adler and Jung, Karen Horney (pronounced HORN-eye) disagreed with Freud's focus on sexuality and sought to distance the study of personality from Freud's more controversial, male-focused concepts such as the notion of penis envy. Her most important contributions to psychoanalysis involve the ways in which parenting styles affect a child's personality and behaviors later in life. Inadequate parenting can cause insecurity and helplessness, which Horney called **basic anxiety**, while neglect and rejection cause anger known as **basic hostility**. To overcome basic anxiety or hostility, children use three strategies to govern their relationships with others: **moving toward** people to obtain their goodwill, **moving against** people to gain the upper hand, and **moving away**, or withdrawing, from people. Healthy children are able to use any or all of these strategies depending on the situation, but maladjusted children fixate on one, and this fixation is carried into adulthood.

The Humanistic Perspective

The **humanistic perspective** is similar to psychoanalysis in that it considers internal influences on personality rather than only external factors. However, while psychoanalysis focuses on undesirable and troubling urges, the humanistic perspective focuses on the positive aspects of personality and the ways in which healthy people strive toward self-realization.

Abraham Maslow, whose hierarchy of needs was discussed earlier in this chapter, was a humanist who studied famous people such as Ludwig van Beethoven, Albert Einstein, and Eleanor Roosevelt, who he felt had lived healthy and productive lives. He identified several traits that these exceptional people had in common, such as a non-hostile sense of humor, originality, creativity, and the ability to act spontaneously. He also noted that these people were more likely to have what he called **peak experiences**, deeply moving events in a person's life that have important and long-lasting effects on the individual.

19

✔ **AP Expert Note**

Client-centered therapy, pioneered by Carl Rogers, is based in the humanist approach of treating the patient as a whole and focusing on the positive aspects of his or her personality. See Chapter 20 on Clinical Psychology for more on this topic.

PERSONALITY RESEARCH AND ASSESSMENTS

LEARNING OBJECTIVES

- Contrast personality psychology research methods
- List, and evaluate for reliability and validity, common personality assessments

Personality Research Methods

Psychologists who wish to learn more about personality have two major approaches that they can employ: case studies and surveys. Each has advantages and disadvantages in terms of what can be learned and how reliable they are.

Case studies look closely at a small subset of a population. Psychologists can conduct a case study of a community, a small group, an event, or an individual. In conducting a case study, psychologists often use direct observation of the subject to obtain qualitative and quantitative data of the subject's actions. The researchers may also have the subject complete personal diaries, questionnaires, inventories, or unstructured interviews. Case studies allow researchers to study a subject in a great deal of depth and can provide insight into the lives of people whose circumstances are rare or would be unethical to replicate, such as those with a brain injury or genetic disorder. On the other hand, case studies require a large investment of time and often cannot be generalized to the overall population.

Surveys take the form of questionnaires and inventories. These can have closed-ended questions, for which subjects pick from a number of preconstructed responses, or open-ended questions, for which subjects can express their thoughts and feelings in their own words. Closed-ended question surveys are faster to administer and easier to score than open-ended question surveys, but provide less opportunity for detail and nuance.

✔ **AP Expert Note**

For more on case studies, surveys, and other research methods, see Chapter 13.

Personality Assessments

Earlier in the chapter, we examined the perspectives through which personality can be viewed. The assessments that psychologists use to study personality each fit into one of these perspectives. In general, personality assessments can be grouped into one of two types: objective or projective.

Objective tests use self-report questionnaires and tend to focus on types or traits. For example, the **Myers-Briggs Type Indicator** (**MBTI**) seeks to sort people into personality types based on psychological functions proposed by Carl Jung. The test presumes that everyone's personality can be described on a continuum of each of four ways of interacting with the world: Extraversion (E) versus Introversion (I), Sensing (S) versus Intuition (N), Thinking (T) versus Feeling (F), and Judging (J) versus Perceiving (P). The test determines which half of each function is dominant and groups people by type (for example, "INTJ"). The **Keirsey Temperament Sorter** works similarly but provides names and descriptions for each of the personality types, such as "the Architect" or "the Provider." These tests are widely used in business settings but are criticized for poor internal and external validity. Additionally, critics feel that these tests use vague terminology such that the results might apply to any personality type, a phenomenon known as the Forer effect.

✔ AP Expert Note

The Forer Effect

A well-known series of studies demonstrated the Forer effect (also known as the Barnum effect) by giving participants a horoscope and asking them how well it described them personally. Most participants believed that the horoscope described them well, even though everyone had received the exact same horoscope!

The **Minnesota Multiphasic Personality Inventory** (**MMPI-2**) is another objective test widely used to assess both personality traits and the presence of psychological disorders. It is a true-false test that presents participants with statements such as "My daily life is full of things that keep me interested." The test places participants on scales of, for example, femininity/masculinity, depression, mania, introversion, and so on. The results also include assessments of how likely it is that the participant is answering dishonestly. Other examples of objective tests include the Beck Depressive Inventory and the Occupational Personality Questionnaire, which is based on the Big Five personality factor model.

Projective tests are based on the psychoanalytic concept of projection, discussed in the previous section. They presume that, when presented with ambiguous stimuli, people will interpret them in ways that reflect their own unconscious thoughts and feelings. The **Rorschach inkblot test** asks participants to describe what they see on cards with abstract designs, while the **Thematic Apperception Test** presents participants with a series of images and asks them to tell a story about what is happening. Other common projective tests include the draw-a-person task, as well as sentence completion and word association tasks.

Critics of projective tests express concern over their internal validity; these tests might reveal more about a participant's most recent experiences or conscious thoughts at the time of testing than they do about unconscious feelings. Further, psychologists who do not subscribe to the psychoanalytic structural model may not consider the Freudian conception of the unconscious valid in the first place.

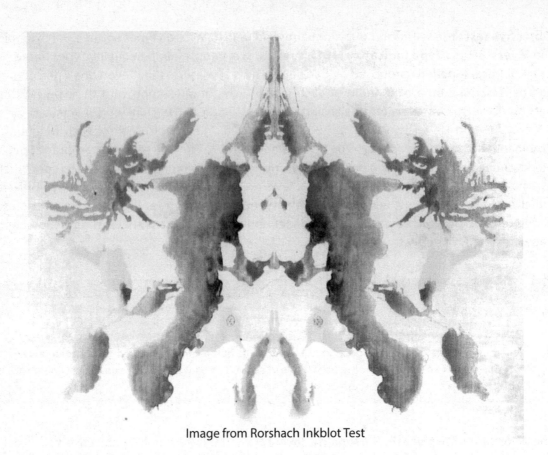

Image from Rorshach Inkblot Test

PERSONALITY AND CULTURE

LEARNING OBJECTIVE

- Explain the possible influence of cultural context on self-concept and other aspects of personality development

19

Childhood socialization, as it occurs within a particular culture, shapes people's thoughts, feelings, and behaviors and provides values and norms that children need to master to fit into adult society. Margaret Mead, for example, conducted an extended survey of Samoan culture and found, among other things, that children are generally ignored by adults until they reach marriageable age. As a result, Samoan children tend to develop more competitive or aggressive temperaments to garner attention from others.

While the AP Psychology exam won't ask you to know much about specific cultures, one general trend that you will be asked about is the difference between collectivist and individualistic cultures. North American and European societies tend to be more **individualistic**. Such cultures place an emphasis on individual goals and personal achievement. In contrast, Asian, African, and South American countries tend to be **collectivist**. People in these cultures are seen primarily as members of a family or larger social group, and the achievements of the individual reflect directly on the family group. Individualistic cultures focus on individual rights, while norms and rules in collectivist countries promote unity and selflessness. As a result, each type of culture defines certain personality traits as being desirable. For collectivist cultures, honesty and generosity are valued traits, while in individualistic cultures, assertiveness and independence are emphasized.

IMPORTANT CONTRIBUTORS

LEARNING OBJECTIVE

- Recognize important contributors to the psychology of motivation, emotion, and personality

See the list of important contributors to the study of motivation, emotion, stress, and personality in the Rapid Review section of Chapter 10.

 # NEXT STEP: PRACTICE

Go to Rapid Review and Practice Chapter 10 or to your online quizzes at kaptest.com for exam-like practice on this topic.

Haven't registered your book yet? Go to kaptest.com/moreonline to begin.

CHAPTER 20

Clinical Psychology

While many psychologists study how the mind *functions*, a significant number of psychologists, particularly in the field of clinical psychology, focus on how the mind *malfunctions*. These psychologists investigate **abnormal behavior**, broadly defined as any maladaptive action or cognitive process that defies social norms or is otherwise atypical, as well as the psychological disorders believed to cause such behavior. In this chapter, we will consider a variety of theories about the causes of abnormal behavior, discuss the classification of psychological disorders, and examine the various frameworks for treatment.

WHAT ARE PSYCHOLOGICAL DISORDERS?

LEARNING OBJECTIVES

- Summarize past and present conceptions of psychological disorders
- Assess the strengths and weaknesses of various theoretical perspectives on psychological disorders

Historical Conceptions

Every community has had its share of people who so regularly transgress social expectations that other members of the community cannot help but think that there is something wrong with them. Explanations for why some people behave so abnormally have varied throughout history (and prehistory), but they broadly fall into two categories. On the one hand is the perspective that some external force causes people to act irregularly; on the other hand is the view that some internal problem is responsible.

The external force view is based on the notion that when people behave in highly unusual ways, they are literally not themselves: something else is acting through them. Advocates of this view often believe in *possession*, the idea that "evil spirits" or other supernatural forces can take control of an individual's body, forcing him or her to behave abnormally. Societies throughout history have used techniques such as trephination (drilling small holes into a person's skull) or exorcism (using ritual prayers and ceremonies to draw evil spirits from a person) in an attempt to cure possession. Of course, misguided practices like these would usually do nothing to end the abnormal behavior, and communities would adopt more extreme measures to deal with "possessed" people, such as ostracism, exile, torture, or even execution.

In contrast to this perspective, which arguably caused more suffering than it alleviated, is the view that abnormal behavior is the result of some internal dysfunction. For example, ancient Greek and Roman civilizations treated abnormal behavior more like a health problem, and even classified a number of distinct mental disorders, such as melancholia, mania, dementia, and hysteria. Some ancient thinkers even attempted to explain these disorders medically. The Greek physician Hippocrates, after whom the Hippocratic Oath is named, believed mental disorders were caused by an imbalance in four bodily fluids, known as the *humors*. The humors include blood, phlegm, yellow bile, and black bile. According to the humorist view, an excess or deficiency in any of these fluids could cause mental illness.

While the medical explanations for abnormal behavior would eventually predominate over the moral explanations, there was very little physicians could do for those with mental disorders. Beginning in the Middle Ages, institutions were created in parts of the Islamic world and Europe to house those who were deemed "mad" or "insane." These asylums for the mentally ill could vary widely in their conditions; some were set up as humane places for treatment, but many others were designed only to isolate the mentally ill, often in horrifying and inhumane conditions.

Fortunately, as a more medical perspective of mental illness became prominent, there were greater calls for humanitarian treatment of the mentally ill. In the nineteenth century in particular, a large-scale movement emerged to reform asylums and to treat the mentally ill with dignity, respect, and compassion. Dorothea Dix was one noteworthy figure who helped to found a number of state-run asylums in the United States and Europe that were committed to humane treatment.

The nineteenth century is also noteworthy for transforming the debate on the causes of abnormal behavior. With the possession view no longer credible, a dispute grew between two perspectives that agreed that abnormal behavior had internal causes but disagreed about the nature of those causes: the *somatogenic*, which proposed physiological causes, and the *psychogenic*, which proposed psychological causes. The somatogenic perspective was an updated version of Hippocrates' view, treating mental illness like any other bodily disease. In contrast, individuals like Sigmund Freud, who adopted a psychogenic perspective, believed disorders to be the result of childhood trauma and unconscious conflicts and employed non-physiological treatments like hypnosis and talk therapy to alleviate symptoms.

During the twentieth century, this debate between the psychogenic and the somatogenic views continued. Beginning in the 1950s, the somatogenic view gained the upper hand with the discovery of psychotropic drugs that could effectively treat a variety of symptoms, including depression, anxiety, and psychosis. These more effective treatments, along with social factors, eventually led to a policy of **deinstitutionalization**, in which patients in asylums and psychiatric hospitals were released back into their communities in great numbers. In the United States, for example, the institutionalized population declined from nearly 600,000 in the middle of the twentieth century to less than 100,000 by century's end. While reintegration into the community often proved beneficial for patients, many patients who were economically disadvantaged simply found themselves homeless and neglected.

Contemporary Models

The Medical Model

The **medical model** of psychological disorders has a long history, as can be seen from the previous section. This view dates back to at least Hippocrates, but it has been considerably refined as modern scientific medicine has revolutionized healthcare. The basic idea behind the medical model is that abnormal behaviors are symptoms of an underlying disease. As such, this model typically advocates the use of psychopharmaceuticals and other proven medical technologies as treatments. This view is so pervasive that we regularly use phrases like "mental health" and "mental illness," often without realizing that they assume a medical orientation.

Strengths of the medical model include the fact that medical treatments are highly effective for a wide range of disorders. The medical model has proven to be successful in treating a variety of physiological symptoms, so it only makes sense that it would enjoy similar success with psychological ones. The medical model is also strongly supported by numerous experiments and other quantitative research.

Among the medical model's limitations is the way that medicalization can creep into everyday phenomena that civilizations have regarded as a normal part of human existence for centuries. There is a danger, for instance, that the medical perspective will pathologize unpleasant emotions like fear and sadness, so that even sensible expressions of these feelings will be viewed as symptoms, rather than natural responses to the human condition. Moreover, like the biological model, the medical model can be reductive, reducing all disorders to a matter of biology and eliminating the role of responsibility and choice. Finally, the medical model has the potential of focusing excessively on the symptoms, which are relatively easy to treat, while ignoring underlying causes (which require greater research to discover).

The Psychoanalytic Model

The **psychoanalytic model**, sometimes called the psychodynamic model, is the psychogenic perspective originally formulated by Freud. According to this view, unconscious parts of the mind (such as the id, ego, and superego, discussed in Chapter 19) and the conflicts between these parts are the underlying causes of psychological (and some physiological) symptoms. These unconscious processes are purportedly shaped by childhood trauma and other experiences, which have often been lost to conscious memory due to repression and other mechanisms. According to this model, psychological disorders are best treated by uncovering the unconscious causes and bringing to consciousness the repressed traumas and conflicts that produce symptoms.

One strength of the psychoanalytic model is that practitioners claim some success in treating patients. For example, Freud was able to restore functioning to a number of women diagnosed with hysteria. In addition, this model respects meaningful aspects of life like childhood experiences, which may be ignored by reductive approaches like the medical and biological. The psychoanalytic model was also one of the first to be applied in psychotherapy, so it has undoubtedly shaped the way that other psychotherapies have developed.

20

Downsides of the model include the fact that many of its concepts are neither well-defined nor easily operationalized in experiments. Indeed, evidence in favor of the model tends to depend highly on case studies (such as the many that Freud himself wrote about), with very limited quantitative research in its support. Some critics go so far as to contend that the psychoanalytic model is inherently unverifiable, meaning that it could never be adequately tested in experiments. Moreover, psychoanalysis seeks to reduce most symptoms to a limited set of unconscious causes, meaning effective treatment cannot be provided for a wide variety of illnesses.

The Humanistic Model

The **humanistic model** of psychological disorders adopts the optimistic perspective of humanistic psychology, which maintains that human beings possess the freedom and the capacity to grow and flourish. The goal of humanistic psychology is self-actualization, the full realization of an individual's unique potential. As conceptualized in Maslow's hierarchy of needs, human beings must achieve fulfillment on a variety of levels before reaching self-actualization. Thus, the humanistic model characterizes psychological disorders as temporary stumbling blocks on the path to a fuller, richer life. The proper treatment for such problems, according to this model, would be something like Rogerian client-centered therapy (discussed later in this chapter), in which the therapist constantly affirms the value of the client and his or her life choices.

Perhaps the greatest strength of the humanistic model is its positive outlook. For individuals who suffer from disorders like depression that lower self-esteem, the optimism of humanism can provide a healthy counterbalance. Indeed, viewing a disorder as a temporary obstacle on the road to self-actualization is far more heartening than viewing it as an illness that requires medical intervention. Humanism also takes the ideas of freedom and responsibility more seriously than other models, which have the danger of explaining the causes of abnormal behavior without leaving room for human agency.

Disadvantages include a lack of empirical support; as was true of the psychoanalytic model, some humanistic concepts are ill-defined and hard to quantify. In addition, the humanistic model may have difficulty explaining the origins of conditions like schizophrenia and other psychotic disorders, and the use of techniques like unconditional positive regard could prove counterproductive for disorders in which an individual's self-worth is pathologically inflated, such as narcissistic personality disorder.

The Cognitive Model

According to the **cognitive model** of psychological disorders, abnormal behaviors are the results of faulty beliefs and maladaptive emotional responses. For example, individuals with depression have distorted views about themselves and the world around them, highlighting bad features and minimizing good ones, while underestimating their abilities to bring about positive changes. The cognitive model stresses the insight that many things in life are good or bad only because they are perceived to be that way; simply adopting a more optimistic outlook can actually make a person's world better. Advocates of this model propose the use of cognitive therapy, such as the approach developed by Aaron Beck, to alleviate symptoms. Cognitive therapeutic strategies are discussed in more detail later in this chapter.

One strength of the model is that it helps to explain and treat particular psychological disorders, such as depression and anxiety, quite well. Like other psychogenic perspectives, the cognitive model doesn't attempt to reduce psychological disorders to biological illnesses, but instead emphasizes distinctly human elements like thoughts and feelings that give existence meaning.

Weaknesses of the cognitive model include its limited ability to explain the causes of psychological disorders. Some disorders include symptoms that cannot be so easily traced to distorted beliefs and feelings, an issue that similarly plagues the psychoanalytic model. Consequently, cognitive therapy doesn't provide effective treatment for a number of mental health problems.

The Biological Model

The **biological model** of mental health maintains that psychological disorders ultimately have biological causes. Even more so than the medical model, this model seeks to understand the brain chemistry and physiology that underlie abnormal behavior. Advocates of this model also often take an interest in genetic and evolutionary explanations, seeking to understand the extent to which psychological disorders are inherited and the reasons that such disorders continue to persist even when they seem maladaptive. The most common treatment approach under the biological model is the use of psychotropic drugs that help to restore chemical balances.

One strength of the biological model is how it can explain psychological disorders in terms of specific biochemistry. When a condition can be linked to a particular chemical, it can be precisely targeted with drugs like agonists, antagonists, and reuptake inhibitors (described in Chapter 14 on the Biological Bases of Behavior). In addition, like the closely related medical model, the biological model possesses a wealth of empirical support. Moreover, the emphasis on genetics and evolution helps to give a broader perspective on the causes of mental illness, including not only how psychological disorders happen but also why they persist in the human species.

Weaknesses of the biological model include its limited focus on physiological causes, with no place for mental and social phenomena that human beings find meaningful and valuable. The biological model allows no real place for human freedom or responsibility, instead reducing complex phenomena to relatively simple cause-and-effect processes. In addition, there are gaps in the research supporting this model; many conclusions are based on studies of nonhuman animals, so they may not adequately generalize to human beings. Finally, the treatments advocated by this model may often be effective, but many come with substantial side effects that result from manipulating neurotransmitter or hormone levels.

The Sociocultural Model

The **sociocultural model** of psychological disorders incorporates insight from social psychology, sociology, and anthropology to explain abnormal behavior. In this perspective, behaviors are recognized as abnormal only within a particular cultural and historical context. Unlike other models that view abnormal behavior as symptomatic of an individual patient's underlying disorder, the sociocultural model sees the existence of mental health patients as symptoms of larger, underlying social problems like poverty, oppression, and injustice. Consequently, a sociocultural approach is more likely to look beyond the treatment of individual patients and instead to advocate wide-scale interventions through mechanisms such as public policy, which can address social problems directly.

One advantage of this model is its recognition of cultural differences in ideas of abnormal behavior and psychological disorders. Unlike other views that can privilege one cultural perspective over others, the sociocultural model affirms human diversity. In addition, the increased cultural awareness promoted by this view has helped therapists to work with a broader range of patients and to deal with these patients in more culturally sensitive ways.

The sociocultural model is limited insofar as it's difficult to investigate experimentally. Broad social problems cannot be adequately reproduced in the lab. In addition, recognition of a wide array of social influences makes it harder to isolate specific variables. Finally, the sociocultural model has little to say about what causes specific individuals to develop disorders. It may, for instance, be able to explain why a particular minority group has a higher incidence of depression, but it cannot say why some members of that group develop depression, while others do not.

The Behavioral Model

Unlike most of the other models discussed, the **behavioral model** of abnormal behavior does not concern itself with underlying psychological disorders. Instead, it views abnormal behavior like any other kind of behavior, as the product of conditioning and other learning from the environment. Behavioral psychologists use the principles of classical conditioning, operant conditioning, and observational learning (discussed in Chapter 16 on Learning) to explain why abnormal behaviors arise. To reduce the frequency of abnormal behaviors, this model advocates the application of learning principles in techniques such as behavioral therapy.

The greatest strength of the behavioral model is that it relies solely on observable, quantifiable phenomena (the frequency of specific behaviors), so it is relatively easy to test experimentally. Moreover, behavioral therapy has proven effective at treating disorders such as obsessive-compulsive disorder and specific phobias.

This model also carries a number of limitations, most notably in its refusal to consider underlying causes beyond learning. Some critics allege that the view is overly simplistic, ignoring the broad array of biological, psychological, and social factors that influence abnormal behavior. There is also evidence that some behavioral treatments can be relatively short-lived in their effectiveness; without ongoing reinforcement, newly learned adaptive behaviors may soon be extinguished.

DIAGNOSTIC CATEGORIES

High-Yield

LEARNING OBJECTIVES

- Recognize the American Psychiatric Association's *Diagnostic and Statistical Manual of Mental Disorders* (DSM) as the main basis of diagnostic judgments

- Identify the major diagnostic categories of psychological disorders and their corresponding symptoms

The ***Diagnostic and Statistical Manual of Mental Disorders*** (**DSM**) is a diagnostic tool published by the American Psychiatric Association and used by clinicians to categorize and diagnose psychological disorders. Now in its fifth edition, the manual organizes disorders into 20 categories, several of which are discussed below. It is important to note that the DSM-5 does not classify disorders by their origin, but rather by the symptoms by which each disorder is characterized. The use of the DSM-5 has enabled more consistent diagnosis and treatment of mental health problems.

Below are twelve major diagnostic categories, based on descriptions provided by the DSM-5. Some of these categories contain just a few disorders, while others contain more than a dozen. Here, we highlight the material most likely to be featured on the AP psychology exam: the characteristics that define each category and the most common disorders under each heading.

Anxiety Disorders

Anxiety disorders include more than a dozen subtypes characterized by **fear** (an emotional response to a perceived or real threat, resulting in autonomic arousal) and **anxiety** (expectation of a threat, resulting in hypervigilance, evasive behaviors, and bodily tension). The subtypes of anxiety disorders are differentiated by what induces the anxiety and by what kind of behavior results from the anxiety. Anxiety disorders are the most common psychological disorder affecting adults and are more prevalent in women than in men. These disorders differ from normal worry or stress because they impair the patient's ability to function.

Generalized anxiety disorder is defined as excessive worry about numerous aspects of life on more days than not over a period of at least six months. To qualify for this diagnosis, the patient must present at least three of the following symptoms during that period: restlessness or feeling on edge, irritability, muscle tension, fatigue, disturbed sleep, and difficulty concentrating.

Specific phobias are characterized by an irrational fear of an individual object or situation that compels the patient to avoid that stimulus at all costs, with symptoms lasting six months or more. Phobias differ from fear in that the degree of anxiety resulting from the condition exceeds the actual danger posed by the stimulus. The DSM-5 recognizes numerous stimuli that may act as a phobic stimulus, including animals, natural phenomena like storms, and social situations. Arguably,

20

any stimulus can be the focus of a specific phobia. Below are a few of the most common specific phobias:

- Acrophobia: the irrational fear of heights
- Claustrophobia: the irrational fear of enclosed spaces
- Arachnophobia: the irrational fear of spiders
- Agoraphobia: the irrational fear of public or open spaces

Panic disorder is an anxiety disorder characterized by repeat, unexpected panic attacks. **Panic attacks** involve the acute onset of intense anxiety and are accompanied by at least four of the following symptoms: fear, hyperventilation, heart palpitations, sweating, shaking, and a sense of unreality. Panic attacks can be extremely serious, and for the attacks to warrant a diagnosis of "panic disorder," they must be unexpected, meaning there is no reasonably stressful stimulus that might otherwise induce the attack.

Social anxiety disorder is anxiety resulting from social or performance situations that the patient perceives to be overwhelmingly stressful with potential to cause them embarrassment.

Dissociative Disorders

Dissociative disorders allow an individual to evade stress by adopting a different identity. The patient retains a realistic sense of the world beyond his or her self, but the patient believes that he or she actually is a different person.

Depersonalization/derealization disorder causes a feeling of being detached from one's mind and body or from the surrounding environment. Depersonalization may result in failure to recognize one's own reflection or photograph, whereas derealization is characterized by a feeling of dreamlike existence. Depersonalization and derealization may be experienced at the same time or individually, and the disorder often impairs normal daily functioning. Memory is not affected.

Dissociative amnesia is diagnosed when a patient is unable to recall past experiences beyond normal gaps in memory. This type of forgetfulness is considered "dissociative" because the amnesia does not correlate with brain trauma, such as a concussion, or with a neurological disorder; instead, the onset is correlated with emotional trauma. Patients with dissociative amnesia may experience a subtype of the disorder known as **dissociative fugue**, in which he or she expresses confusion over identity. In cases of fugue, individuals may flee to new locations, construct entire histories for new identities, and forget their actual identities, potentially for years.

Dissociative identity disorder (**DID**) was previously known as multiple personality disorder and is considered a form of mental escape from trauma or stress. This disorder is a source of controversy in diagnostics, with some evidence supporting the contention that DID is therapist-induced. DID may be diagnosed when two or more distinct personalities alternatively direct a patient's behavior. The various personalities often have opposing elements that the individual struggles to express cohesively and which therefore surface as distinct personalities. Individuals with this disorder exhibit gaps in memory when switching between personalities and often struggle to function socially and occupationally.

Feeding and Eating Disorders

Feeding and eating disorders are characterized by obsessive eating habits and an unhealthy relationship with food. Overwhelming concern about one's physical appearance also generally accompanies these disorders. They have historically been considered more prevalent in women than in men and usually arise during adolescence.

Anorexia nervosa is characterized by the fear of gaining weight, a very strong inclination to lose weight, a low body mass index (BMI), and habitually restrictive eating. Patients suffering from anorexia commonly deny the problem, hide their behavior, and feel shame over the weight they perceive they need to lose.

Bulimia nervosa is characterized by episodes of excessive food consumption, otherwise known as binge eating, followed by intentional vomiting or the use of laxatives after meals. Bulimic patients usually have a normal BMI. An obsession with weight loss usually accompanies the eating and purging habits.

Binge eating disorder is characterized by a lack of control during a binging episode, or by restrictive eating habits such as consuming excessive amounts of food in a limited time period. Patients with binge eating disorder often eat alone, eat when they are not hungry, or eat until they are uncomfortable. Binge eating is significantly more severe than typical overeating.

Somatic Symptom and Related Disorders

Somatic symptom and related disorders are characterized by a pattern of physical symptoms that result in stress and impair normal daily functioning. Patients with somatoform disorders often falsely attribute their symptoms to an underlying medical condition, although their symptoms are better explained by psychological factors.

Somatic symptom disorder may be diagnosed when a patient experiences at least one somatic symptom, regardless of whether or not it is linked to an underlying medical condition, and is overwhelmingly concerned with the problem. The patient must devote an unreasonable amount of time or attention to the issue or experience anxiety due to their preoccupation to qualify for a diagnosis.

Conversion disorder is characterized by unexplained inhibition of voluntary functions. Examples of inhibited sensory or motor functions include paralysis and blindness. These symptoms appear in the absence of a traumatic brain injury or other neuroanatomical change, but normally follow a traumatic event. It is theorized that the brain converts stress into physical symptoms in cases of conversion disorder.

20

Illness anxiety disorder, known as hypochondriasis in earlier versions of the DSM, is a disorder characterized by constant, invasive thoughts about having or developing a severe medical condition. Patients with illness anxiety disorder are overly concerned with their health and may fear diagnosis of a condition so immensely that they entirely avoid doctor's appointments. Alternatively, their fears may prompt them to visit a physician frequently. Individuals with this disorder may frequently and incorrectly attribute normal bodily changes to an underlying problem.

Obsessive-Compulsive and Related Disorders

Obsessive-compulsive and related disorders are characterized by unwanted obsessions that cause fear, anxiety, or negative thoughts, followed by compelling urges to perform a behavior, otherwise known as a compulsion, that reduces the distress. To meet criteria for a diagnosis in this category, the obsessions and compulsions must be time-consuming and cause significant stress as a direct result of the disorder. This category includes hoarding, trichotillomania (hair-pulling disorder), excoriation (skin-picking disorder), and most commonly, obsessive-compulsive disorder and body dysmorphic disorder.

Obsessive-compulsive disorder (OCD) is characterized by the presence of **obsessions** (intrusive, recurring impulses) and **compulsions** (repetitive actions). The obsessions result in the patient experiencing stress and the compulsions relieve that stress. This cycle commonly inhibits the patient's normal functioning.

Body dysmorphic disorder involves a skewed perception of one's physical appearance, often with a negative focus on one specific body part. The patient is preoccupied with an inaccurate view of a normal body part to the point that day-to-day life is affected by the dysmorphia. Patients with this disorder may seek extreme solutions to correct their perceived flaws.

Depressive Disorders

Sadness is a normal emotion, especially when experienced as a result of distressing events. When sadness reaches a certain level of severity and duration, however, an individual may be suffering from depression, especially when these intense emotions interfere with normal daily functioning. **Depressive disorders** are unipolar in that low feelings are not paralleled by the occasional manic episode, as is the case with bipolar disorders.

Major depressive disorder consists of depressive episodes that last at least two weeks or longer. The patient may experience a persistent depressed mood, anhedonia (lack of interest in formerly enjoyable activities), weight loss or gain, disturbed sleep or appetite, feelings of guilt, difficulty concentrating, and potentially thoughts of suicide. Depression is twice as likely to occur in women as in men.

Dysthymia is otherwise known as persistent depressive disorder. Patients with dysthymia exhibit similar symptoms to those seen in a major depressive individual, but to a lesser degree of severity. This chronic condition usually persists for at least two years.

Seasonal affective disorder (**SAD**) is a form of depression that follows a seasonal pattern. SAD is not a stand-alone diagnosis in the DSM-5, but is essentially major depressive disorder brought on by seasonal changes (usually in the winter). **Bright light therapy**, in which the patient is exposed to a bright, artificial light for a period each day during the triggering season, is sometimes an effective treatment.

Bipolar and Related Disorders

Bipolar and related disorders are characterized by oscillation between extremes of depressive and manic episodes. **Depressive episodes** are characterized by inactivity, inhibition, and feelings of helplessness. **Manic episodes** are characterized by constant activity, an elevated mood, inflated self-esteem, decreased need for sleep, and distractibility. Manic episodes generally persist for shorter periods than depressive episodes.

Bipolar I disorder involves manic episodes with or without the presence of depressive episodes. A patient with bipolar I will be prone to severe mania that impairs his or her normal functioning, as well as psychotic episodes.

Bipolar II disorder involves hypomanic episodes—periods of mania not sufficient in duration or severity to be considered manic episodes—as well as at least one major depressive episode.

Cyclothymic disorder is a bipolar-related disorder in which the patient experiences hypomanic episodes and dysthymic episodes that are not severe enough to qualify as major depressive.

Personality Disorders

Personality disorders are characterized by rigid, maladjusted behavior that impairs cognitive, emotional, or interpersonal functioning. This category of disorders is distinct from the other diagnostic categories in that patients suffering from personality disorders believe that their behavior is normal, whereas patients suffering from other types of psychological conditions are able to recognize their behavior as problematic. The ten major personality disorders are grouped into three clusters: A, B, and C.

Cluster A

Cluster A includes conditions generally considered to be odd or eccentric by unaffected people and contains the following three disorders:

- **Paranoid personality disorder** is characterized by mistrust of others due to suspicion of their motives.

- **Schizotypal personality disorder** is characterized by strange patterns of thinking, sometimes including extreme superstition and belief in clairvoyance.

- **Schizoid personality disorder** is diagnosed in cases of detachment from emotions and social interactions. These patients exhibit poor social skills.

20

Cluster B

Cluster B includes behavior generally considered to be dramatic, emotional, or erratic by unaffected individuals. This category contains the following four disorders:

- **Antisocial personality disorder** is marked by total disregard for others. Patients with this condition are three times more likely to be male. Patients are often characterized by others as aggressive, deceitful, and without remorse.

- **Borderline personality disorder** is characterized by an unstable mood and self-image; intense interpersonal interactions; disturbed identity, goals, and values; and an overwhelming fear of abandonment. This disorder is twice as likely to occur in women as in men.

- **Histrionic personality disorder** is characterized by overwhelming attention-seeking behavior, sometimes masked as extreme extraversion.

- **Narcissistic personality disorder** is characterized by feelings of entitlement, a delusional perspective of the patient's importance and successes, a need for admiration, and vulnerable self-esteem. These individuals are usually perceived as caring little, if at all, for the well being of others.

Cluster C

Cluster C encompasses behavior considered to be anxious or fearful by unaffected people. The following three disorders fall into this cluster:

- **Avoidant personality disorder** is characterized by extreme shyness accompanied by an intense fear of rejection and criticism. These patients are usually isolated socially, even though they have a strong wish to be accepted and to experience affection.

- **Dependent personality disorder** is marked by dependence on one other individual to make decisions for the patient, as well as by the patient's intense need to be constantly reassured about his or her choices.

- **Obsessive-compulsive personality disorder** (**OCPD**) is characterized by stubbornness and perfectionist tendencies. These individuals embrace rules and order, dislike change, and stick to rigid routines. OCPD differs from obsessive-compulsive disorder (OCD) primarily in that individuals with OCD view their obsessive-compulsive behaviors as a problem, while individuals with OCPD don't.

Schizophrenia Spectrum and Other Psychotic Disorders

The category of **psychotic disorders** in the DSM-5 possesses two distinctive types of symptoms: positive and negative. **Positive symptoms** are in addition to normal behavior, and include delusions, hallucinations, disorganized thoughts, and catatonic behavior. **Negative symptoms** are those that detract from normal behavior, and include avolition (decreased motivation) and disturbance of affect (unusual or decreased emotional expression).

Schizophrenia is the archetypal psychotic disorder. Schizophrenia is a disorder of general psychosis, otherwise known as a break between reality and the perception of reality. To be diagnosed with schizophrenia, the patient must exhibit at least two of the following symptoms, one of which must be one of the first three symptoms: delusions (strange and false beliefs), hallucinations, disorganized speech, catatonic behavior (a pattern of extreme psycho-motor functions), and negative symptoms. Furthermore, the patient must exhibit these symptoms for a period longer than six months to qualify for a diagnosis.

In previous versions of the DSM, schizophrenia was divided into distinguishable subtypes, such as Type I and Type II schizophrenia, but the DSM-5 no longer recognizes these distinctions, instead considering this psychotic disorder to be a spectrum. Subtypes for the disorder were eliminated because individuals with schizophrenia do not normally exhibit stable symptoms, with variation in both positive and negative symptoms common.

Neurodevelopmental Disorders

Neurodevelopmental disorders normally become evident during early development, with most cases emerging before grade school. Developmental challenges with social, academic, or occupational functioning may be evident across any of these disorders. This category includes several dozen conditions, some of which highlight very specific impairments, while others include a wide array of challenges. Oftentimes, a patient will exhibit more than one of these conditions, with certain combinations (such as autism and intellectual disabilities) occurring more commonly than others.

Attention deficit hyperactivity disorder (**ADHD**) is characterized by inattention, disorganization, and impulsivity beyond the degree expected for peers developing normally. Patients with ADHD have a hard time waiting, tend to fidget, may be defiant, and struggle to stay on task. This condition often leads to impaired social, academic, or occupational functioning when left untreated.

Autism spectrum disorder is characterized by a tendency towards sameness; restricted behaviors, interests, and activities; communication deficits; and difficulty with social interactions and nonverbal elements of communication. Occasionally, autistic patients also exhibit heightened abilities beyond the norm in specific tasks.

Specific learning disorder is a condition diagnosed when a patient's deficit is specific to one developmental field of perception or processing. The disorder first becomes evident when an individual struggles to learn the foundational principles underlying an academic subject, resulting in lower than average performance relative to peers. Examples of specific learning disorders are *dyslexia* (challenges with word recognition and spelling) and *dyscalculia* (challenges with numerical processing and arithmetic).

Intellectual disability, also known as **intellectual developmental disorder**, is characterized by general deficiencies in reasoning, judgment, abstract thinking, problem solving, and other mental tasks. This disorder normally inhibits patients' ability to adapt to change and to learn from their environment due to delayed conceptual, practical, and social development. Intellectual disabilities are diagnosed when individuals fail to meet developmental benchmarks that are

20

anticipated for their peers, normally before the age at which standardized testing could similarly indicate the disorder.

Trauma- and Stressor-Related Disorders

Trauma- and stressor-related disorders include disorders that result when a patient experiences a particularly traumatic or stressful event and are characterized by variable stress reactions, including but not limited to dissociation, anhedonia, fear, anxiety, anger, and dysphoria. The most common of these disorders is posttraumatic stress disorder, but reactive adjustment disorder, acute stress disorder, adjustment disorders, and several other rare trauma- and stressor-related disorders exist.

Posttraumatic stress disorder (**PTSD**) is characterized by disturbing memories, flashbacks, or nightmares that cause the patient to relive the event that induced the disorder. Individuals with PTSD routinely avoid stimuli associated with the traumatic event itself and generally experience negative changes in mood or thought when exposed to such stimuli, which may partially or severely affect day-to-day functioning. To be diagnosed with PTSD, the patient must experience symptoms for longer than one month.

Neurocognitive Disorders

Neurocognitive disorders are characterized by a decline in various mental abilities, which results in the patient's gradual loss of independence, thus interfering with daily living. The DSM-5 classifies neurocognitive disorders as being either minor or major depending on the degree to which the disorder limits the patient. The two most common major disorders are discussed below, but there are several others, such as Huntington's disease and prion diseases such as Creutzfeldt-Jakob disease, that similarly result in general cognitive decline.

Alzheimer's disease is a degenerative brain disorder marked by progressive memory loss, disorientation, changes in behavior, atrophy of the brain (especially acetylcholinergic neurons), and a tendency to misplace things. To be diagnosed with this disease, the patient must exhibit several of these symptoms.

Parkinson's disease is characterized by tremors, slurred and softened speech, instability, and trouble with standing upright and moving freely. Parkinson's is caused by atrophy of dopaminergic neurons and is progressive. A patient with Parkinson's may exhibit mild decline of select mental functions, or they may experience what is referred to as "global dementia," meaning all critical mental abilities are affected by the disease.

DIAGNOSTIC LABELS

LEARNING OBJECTIVE

- List the pros and cons of assigning diagnostic labels

In the preceding section, you saw many of the **diagnostic labels** featured in the DSM-5, but the manual includes many others as well. In fact, any patient who seeks help from a clinician—whether a counselor, licensed social worker, psychologist, or psychiatrist—will generally be diagnosed with a disorder listed in the DSM-5 prior to receiving any treatment. These labels are now so common that nearly half of U.S. citizens will receive at least one DSM diagnosis at some point in their lives. But what are the advantages and disadvantages of using diagnostic labels?

One significant advantage is the consistency that diagnostic labels and their specified criteria allows. This consistency can be found both in clinical practice, insofar as diagnoses of and treatments for specific disorders are more regular even between different practitioners, as well as in research, with well-established disorders being easier to recognize and measure in experiments and other studies. Diagnostic labels can also be useful tools for patients. Many patients feel empowered by being able to put a name to the problems they are experiencing, seeing it as the first step in alleviating their distress. Diagnostic labels may also reduce some of the stigma historically associated with psychological disorders by giving them a more clinical veneer; people are generally more likely to judge others for their moral failings than for their medical problems.

Drawbacks of diagnostic labels include the fact that they are imperfect tools that may reflect the biases of particular cultures. Moreover, they can be misapplied by practitioners with their own personal biases. Another disadvantage is that some people may be suffering from symptoms that don't fit the criteria for any single category; indeed, it is not uncommon for patients to partially fulfill the criteria for many disorders without perfectly fitting any one diagnosis. A further downside is the tendency of these labels to be applied to an increasing array of conditions, many of which may be of only questionable clinical significance. Even though some patients are empowered by these labels, many are disempowered. A patient may treat a label as a kind of self-fulfilling prophecy, allowing his or her diagnosis to excuse maladaptive behavior associated with the disorder. Furthermore, other people may latch onto these labels and discriminate against those diagnosed with them. Others may view all of a patient's behavior through the prism of the diagnosis.

This last disadvantage of diagnostic labels was corroborated in a famous study conducted by David Rosenhan in 1973. The **Rosenhan experiment** sought to investigate how psychiatric labels affected the perceptions of clinical practitioners. Toward that end, Rosenhan and seven other psychologically well-adjusted individuals played the role of psychiatric "pseudopatients." These pseudopatients presented themselves at a number of psychiatric hospitals and offered a similar, simple complaint, claiming to hear voices that said words like "empty," "hollow," and "thud." Most of the pseudopatients received a diagnosis of schizophrenia and a prescription for antipsychotics. However, despite feigning no other symptoms after being admitted, the pseudopatients stayed an average of 19 days before being released, and none of the staff at any of the hospitals recognized the sanity of any pseudopatient. Indeed, even when released, the pseudopatients generally had to agree to stay on the antipsychotic medications.

While the Rosenhan experiment has detractors who object to it for its use of deception or for other reasons, it does support the criticism that diagnostic labels change the ways that people are treated. People who are regarded as mental health patients may find it harder to form relationships, to find gainful employment, or simply to be taken seriously by others. Indeed, the pseudopatients in Rosenhan's study reported feeling powerless, bored, tired, and seemingly invisible to nurses and other staff. Because of these potential stigmas, psychiatric labels are generally regarded as confidential information, just like any other medical diagnosis.

PSYCHOLOGY AND THE LAW

LEARNING OBJECTIVE

- Describe the interaction of psychology and the judicial system

The judicial system interacts with clinical psychology in a number of ways, two of which are particularly important to know for the AP Psychology exam. The first concerns confidentiality and its limits, while the second concerns the legal notion of insanity.

Personal health information is protected in the United States by HIPAA (Health Insurance Portability and Accountability Act of 1996) regulations, which mandate **confidentiality**. Unless a patient specifically agrees to disclose health information to specific others, the information cannot legally be disseminated. This includes psychiatric diagnoses, prescriptions or other treatment regimens, and any information discussed during psychotherapy. There are exceptions to these restrictions, particularly when a therapist has reason to believe that a client poses a danger to him- or herself or to other people. In such cases, therapists have a responsibility to report these dangers to appropriate authorities or to take other measures to avoid the possibility of harm, such as the involuntary commitment of the patient to a psychiatric institution.

Insanity is a legal category, not a psychiatric one. An individual deemed to be insane is incapable of telling the difference between right and wrong, which means he or she cannot be held fully responsible for his or her actions. Psychologists and psychiatrists often serve as expert witnesses when defendants attempt to plead insanity. During their testimony, these expert witnesses are permitted to disclose personal health information that would otherwise be considered confidential (another exception to HIPAA regulations). Defendants found not guilty by reason of insanity are typically committed for long stays in psychiatric hospitals and are often released only on condition of abiding by certain rules, such as continued administration of a psychiatric medication.

WHAT IS PSYCHOLOGICAL TREATMENT?

LEARNING OBJECTIVE

- Summarize psychological treatment's primary characteristics

Psychological treatment helps people with and without psychological disorders live happier, healthier, and more productive lives. Psychological treatment is provided by **mental health professionals**, including psychologists, medical doctors and nurses, social workers, and licensed counselors. Regardless of the person providing the treatment, the two most common forms of treatment are psychotherapy (i.e., talk therapy) and pharmacological treatment (i.e., drug therapy).

Psychotherapy is typically an ongoing interaction between a patient and a mental health professional, often referred to as a therapist, in which the two discuss the patient's experiences and symptoms. (Sometimes psychotherapy involves more than one patient, as in family and group therapy, discussed later in this chapter.) The goal of psychotherapy is to alleviate psychological distress and increase psychological well being. Sigmund Freud first introduced the idea of a "talking cure" to remedy psychological distress in the early twentieth century. During psychotherapy, mental health professionals will frequently collect a patient's psychosocial history, including information about the patient's symptoms, functioning, family, and goals for treatment. The content of psychotherapy varies depending on the treatment orientation of the mental health professional. Psychotherapy may include *psychoeducation* (education about relevant psychological concepts), worksheets, roleplaying, and other activities. Often, psychotherapy is focused on promoting a change in the patient's thoughts, feelings, self-concept, or behavior.

With **pharmacological treatment**, a mental health professional prescribes a drug to alleviate psychological distress. According to recent estimates, drug therapy is very common, with nearly one in five adults taking medication for a psychological or behavioral disorder. In addition to a prescription, pharmacological treatment often includes a discussion of possible side effects and monitoring of the symptoms' response to the treatment. Not all mental health professionals have the ability to provide pharmacological treatment. In the United States, most psychotropic medications are prescribed by primary care physicians, although nurse practitioners and physician assistants may also prescribe medication. In some states, psychologists with a special license are also permitted to prescribe psychotropic medications.

Psychotherapy and pharmacological treatment may take place in different settings depending on the severity of the patient's distress. For example, people with incapacitating psychological symptoms may require inpatient treatment, during which they reside in a medical facility and receive psychological treatment daily. Modern inpatient care dates back to Dorothea Dix, who campaigned for the creation of state institutions to help care for people with psychological disorders. Although Dix intended state institutions to eliminate the abuse of mentally ill patients, the quality of life for people in institutions continued to be a concern for activists. Now, community outpatient treatment is far more common than state institutional care. It is very common for patients in outpatient treatment to receive both psychotherapy and pharmacological treatment from mental health professionals.

20

Moral Treatment

Psychological treatment was transformed by the activism of Dorothea Dix. Dix began advocating for reform after visiting a local prison and viewing the abusive "treatments," which included shackles, isolation, and physical punishment. The state institutions she founded focused on *moral treatment* as an alternative to these barbaric treatments. Arising from European models, moral treatment was characterized by regular walks, healthy diets, and environments with natural light. Until deinstitutionalization (see earlier in this chapter), institutions were the dominant treatment setting for mental illness.

The next section describes specific approaches to psychological treatment. Although these approaches are diverse, they do share a number of common features. Psychological treatment is collaborative, meaning that the individual receiving treatment and the person providing the treatment communicate about the best treatment plan. All psychological treatment is also confidential, meaning that a mental health professional will maintain the patient's privacy. Many mental health professionals risk losing their licenses if they violate confidentiality. However, there are exceptions (see earlier in this chapter for more details about the laws surrounding confidentiality). Finally, in recent years, psychological treatment has prioritized empirically based treatments—those supported by scientific evidence. To that end, recent research has focused on identifying effective treatments by investigating how well particular approaches alleviate distress or reduce specific symptoms.

TREATMENT ORIENTATIONS AND FORMATS

LEARNING OBJECTIVE

- Identify major treatment orientations and formats and their influence on treatment

Treatment Orientations

The type of treatment that a therapist chooses to use depends on how the therapist approaches psychological disorders and therapy. **Theoretical orientation** refers to a therapist's belief system about the cause and nature of psychological distress and the appropriate treatment. Theoretical orientation influences the therapist's choice of intervention, techniques, and even the goal of treatment. There are hundreds of different theories about psychological treatment, but the most common include: psychodynamic, humanistic, behavioral, cognitive, biomedical, and integrated approaches. These approaches to treatment stem from the dominant models of abnormal behavior described earlier in this chapter.

Psychodynamic Therapies

Sigmund Freud is considered the founder of psychoanalytic therapy, which over time evolved into modern psychodynamic therapy. Therapists with a psychodynamic orientation generally view psychological disorders to be the results of unconscious conflicts (see earlier in this chapter) between the id, ego, and superego (see Chapter 19). The goal of psychodynamic therapy is to bring repressed emotions into consciousness and reduce the conflict.

Psychodynamic therapists employ a number of specific techniques to access the unconscious. **Dream interpretation** is a technique which analyzes the meaning of symbols from dreams. For example, dreaming about falling is often associated with a fear of losing control. **Free association** is a technique in which the patient is instructed to "think out loud" and say everything that comes to mind. Psychodynamic therapies often discuss the relationship between the patient and the therapist, especially the phenomenon of transference. **Transference** occurs when feelings directed at one person become redirected to another person, often the therapist. For example, a patient who is angry at her mother may begin to feel angry at her therapist because both people try to care for the patient.

Humanistic Therapies

Humanistic therapy arose from the philosophies of humanistic psychologists like Abraham Maslow, who believed that psychological distress is caused by environments that limit people's ability to develop and flourish. The goal of humanistic therapy is **self-actualization**, or the individual's ability to live up to his or her full human potential. There are three main manifestations of humanistic therapy: client-centered, Gestalt, and existential.

Client-centered therapy, pioneered by Carl Rogers in the 1950s, is the most popular humanistic approach. Client-centered therapy views patients as "clients" who are equal partners with the therapist, and encourages these clients to be authentic and build a healthy self concept. An essential component of client-centered therapy is **unconditional positive regard**, in which the therapist communicates positive feelings and acceptance regardless of what the client says or does. **Active listening** is another client-centered technique in which the therapist verbally and non-verbally communicates interest in what the patient is saying in order to encourage openness. In client-centered therapy, an open, empathetic, genuine, and authentic therapist is essential.

The other humanistic approaches also believe in the importance of self-actualization. **Gestalt therapy**, developed by Fritz Perls, maintains that psychological distress occurs when patients focus on what might be, could be, or should be, rather than focusing on the present moment. Gestalt therapists encourage patients to become fully immersed in their emotions and experiences during therapy sessions. **Existential therapy**, which was popularized by Irving Yalom, is based on the hypothesis that people are distressed when their lives lack meaning. Existential therapists help patients find meaning in their lives even during times of immense suffering.

Behavioral Therapies

Behavioral therapy is a direct consequence of the behaviorist movement, which shifted focus from the "black box" of the mind towards observable phenomena, specifically behaviors. Behaviorists like B.F. Skinner believed that the basic principles of classical conditioning, operant conditioning,

20

and other types of learning could help patients improve their functioning. Behavioral therapists explain common psychological symptoms (e.g., those associated with depression and anxiety) as natural, learned responses to environmental conditions. For example, a number of the symptoms of depression are very similar to the **learned helplessness** observed in dogs who were repeatedly shocked with no way to escape (see Chapter 16).

The goal of behavioral therapy is to increase or decrease the frequency of certain behaviors. The targeted behavior might be a bad habit like smoking or a routine activity like teeth brushing. Modern day behavioral therapists use **applied behavioral analysis** (**ABA**) to help identify factors in the environment that may be reinforcing or punishing behaviors. After this initial analysis, a plan is made to modify environmental conditions to be consistent with the desired behavior change. **Token economies**, in which patients earn tokens (symbolic rewards, such as plastic coins or points) for good behavior, is one method of reinforcement used to change environmental conditions. The tokens can be exchanged for "real world" rewards, like stickers or an enjoyable activity.

Mary Cover-Jones, inspired by her mentor John Watson, was one of the first people to apply classical conditioning techniques to treatment. She documented her successful efforts to cure a child's rabbit phobia by pairing rabbits with a positive stimulus. Cover-Jones' efforts contributed to the development of one the most popular modern techniques in behavioral therapy, **systematic desensitization**, which is primarily used to treat phobias by creating new associations between fearful and relaxing stimuli. **Aversion therapy**, or aversive conditioning, is another behavioral technique derived from classical conditioning, in which a habitual or addictive behavior is paired with an aversive stimulus. See Chapter 16 for more on classical conditioning, systematic desensitization, and aversion therapy.

Cognitive Therapies

Cognitive therapy became popular during the cognitive revolution in psychology in the 1960s, and arose as a challenge to traditional psychodynamic approaches. Albert Ellis, an early pioneer of cognitive therapy, called his approach **rational-emotive behavior therapy**. He believed that therapy should focus on rational analysis of thought, rather than on uncovering unconscious motivations.

Cognitive therapists believe that psychological distress results from **cognitive distortions**, which are automatic and irrational perceptions of the world that contribute to feelings of anxiety or depression. Often, these distortions stem from a **core belief**, which is a deeply held belief that guides an individual's thoughts. Overgeneralization, when broad conclusions are drawn from very little evidence, is a common cognitive distortion that leads to negative feelings. For example, a patient who was called lazy one time might overgeneralize this feedback and think she was a lazy person despite being very successful in her work.

Patients in cognitive therapy are often asked to keep a **thought log**, where they write down their automatic thoughts throughout the day. During therapy, cognitive therapists use **Socratic questioning** to help patients identify cognitive distortions and core beliefs. Cognitive therapists encourage their patients to be more flexible and adaptive in their thinking using a process called

cognitive restructuring, in which patients challenge irrational beliefs and replace them with more realistic ones.

Since its origin, cognitive therapy has evolved into several specific treatment approaches. The most popular modern approach is **cognitive behavioral therapy (CBT)**, which was introduced by Aaron Beck. CBT combines both cognitive and behavioral techniques to identify solutions to patients' concerns. Recently, **third wave cognitive therapies**, including dialectical behavior therapy (DBT) and acceptance and commitment therapy (ACT), have also become popular. Compared to other cognitive therapies, third wave therapies focus more on values and techniques like **mindfulness** (cultivating a state of conscious awareness) to manage psychological distress.

Biomedical Therapies

Biomedical therapies are treatments that are consistent with the medical model of psychological disorders. According to the medical model, psychological distress is the result of structural problems or chemical imbalances in the patient's brain. There are three main types of biomedical therapy: psychopharmacology, electroconvulsive therapy (ECT), and psychosurgery.

Psychopharmacology is the most common biomedical treatment for mental disorders. Psychotropic medications, which are drugs that influence an individual's thoughts, emotions, and behavior, emerged as treatments in the 1950s. Most psychotropic medications change levels of certain neurotransmitters in the brain (see Chapter 14). Frequently, psychotropic medications that were originally used to treat a specific disorder are eventually expanded to treat a variety of disorders (e.g., SSRIs). See the table below for a list of drugs worth knowing for the exam.

Drug Type	Date of Introduction	Targeted Disorder(s)
Tricyclic antidepressants (TCAs)	1960s	depressive disorders
Selective serotonin reuptake inhibitors (SSRIs; e.g., Prozac)	1990s	depressive and anxiety disorders
Benzodiazepines (e.g., Valium)	1960s	anxiety disorders
Lithium carbonate	1950s	bipolar disorders
Atypical anti-psychotics (e.g., Clozapine)	1990s	schizophrenia

Electroconvulsive therapy (ECT) is a medical procedure that is conducted under anesthesia and delivers small electric currents to the brain to deliberately cause a seizure. Inducing a seizure can help treat severe depression and catatonia by changing levels of neurotransmitters in the brain. Modern ECT is very safe, but earlier versions of the procedure sometimes caused serious brain damage. This dark history may explain the stigma that is attached to "shock therapy." In recent years, deep brain stimulation, which historically has been used to treat Parkinson's, has been used to treat OCD. **Deep brain stimulation** is more invasive than ECT, since it requires implanting an electrode in the brain to deliver electric currents directly.

20

Psychosurgery is a medical technique in which part of the brain is removed or deliberately damaged. The most famous, and controversial, type of psychosurgery is frontal lobe lobotomy, which was popular in the 1940s and '50s. Although frontal lobe lobotomies often left patients with serious mental deficits, modern psychosurgery is more precise but nevertheless remains controversial. Modern psychosurgery is reserved for severe cases of depression and OCD, and typically targets the limbic system, which is implicated in emotion regulation.

Integrated Therapies

Most therapists do not rigidly adhere to one approach when treating a patient. **Eclectic therapy**, in which a therapist intentionally draws from a variety of treatment approaches, is one of the most common types of therapy. Some eclectic therapists apply the **transtheoretical model**, an integrative approach to behavior change that can be adapted to any psychotherapy treatment. According to the transtheoretical model, people vary in their "stage of change," or their readiness to make changes in their lives. Therapists who work from this perspective customize their interventions based on whether patients are in the precontemplation (not ready for change), contemplation (getting ready), preparation (ready), or action (making the change) stage.

Treatment Formats

In addition to the variety of theoretical orientations, psychotherapy can also be classified into four formats: individual, group, couple, and family psychotherapy. **Individual psychotherapy** is a format in which a patient and mental health professional meet one-on-one. In contrast, **group psychotherapy** is a format in which multiple patients meet with one or two mental health professionals at the same time. Although the mental health professional(s) will lead the group discussion, all of the patients are expected to participate. Some treatment approaches (e.g., dialectical behavior therapy) are frequently implemented using both formats, while most approaches can be implemented in either format.

While both individual and group therapy employ similar techniques, treat a similar range of mental disorders, and have similar levels of efficacy, there are some key differences between the formats. First, individual therapy focuses on the specific problems and goals of the person seeking treatment, while group therapy focuses on a common problem or goal shared by all members, such as addiction to a substance. Unlike individual therapy, group therapy allows participants to learn from the experience of other members, to receive support from peers, and to practice interpersonal skills. Finally, in individual therapy, the process depends on the rapport established between the therapist and patient, while group therapy also draws upon the relationships between group members as a part of the therapeutic process.

In addition to individual and group therapy, two other therapy formats in which more than one person seeks treatment for a shared distress are worth noting. **Couples psychotherapy** is when a therapist provides psychological treatment to romantic partners. Similarly, **family psychotherapy** is when a therapist provides psychological treatment to a family unit. Due to the unique circumstances of these formats, they often employ different treatment approaches than individual and group psychotherapy. A common approach to couples and family therapy is called **systemic therapy**, which focuses on how people are influenced by complex family systems.

HOW EFFECTIVE IS TREATMENT?

LEARNING OBJECTIVE

- Assess particular treatments' effects on particular psychological disorders

Hundreds of studies have found that, overall, psychotherapy helps people make positive changes in their lives. Reviews of these studies show that the average person who engages in psychotherapy is better off by the end of treatment than 80 percent of those who don't receive treatment at all. **Meta-analysis studies**, which analyze the results of many studies at once, have demonstrated that psychotherapy reduces disability, morbidity, and mortality; improves work functioning; and decreases psychiatric hospitalization. In recent years, psychology has emphasized the importance of **evidence-based practice** (**EBP**). EBP is defined as the effective integration of three components in psychotherapy: the best research evidence available; the patient's specific context, including culture, preferences, and characteristics; and the therapist's clinical expertise.

Evidence-Based Treatment

The first component of evidence-based practice is the use of **evidence-based treatments** (**EBTs**). When research demonstrates that a treatment is effective at reducing psychological distress, it is considered an EBT. The gold standard in determining whether a treatment is evidence-based is a **randomized controlled trial**. In a randomized controlled trial, patients are randomly assigned to one of two conditions. In the experimental condition, a patient receives the treatment being evaluated. In the control condition, the patient receives another treatment, called the placebo treatment (for a review of experimental methods, see Chapter 13). At the end of the study, the researchers compare the symptoms of the patients in the two conditions. If the experimental treatment improves symptoms significantly more than the placebo, it is considered an EBT.

Randomized controlled trials have compared the effectiveness of psychotherapy to pharmacological treatments. The results suggest that the effects on symptoms are comparable, and a combination of both treatments produces the best results for depression and anxiety. However, there is some evidence that the results of psychotherapy are more long-lasting, and psychotherapy does not come with the same risk of side effects. Despite this evidence, the use of psychotherapy has decreased over the last decade alongside the rapid increase in pharmacological treatments.

Since 1995, the American Psychological Association (APA) has regularly updated a list of EBTs for specific disorders based on the available research. Treatments are considered "well established" if they demonstrate results that are either superior to a placebo or similar to those for another established treatment. The majority of established EBTs identified by the APA are derived from cognitive therapy, most notably cognitive behavioral therapy. Specifically, CBT is consistently identified as an evidence-based treatment for depression and related disorders. Exposure-based behavior therapies that include systematic desensitization are the most well-established approaches for anxiety disorders. The dominance of cognitive and behavioral approaches is unsurprising, considering that these approaches value an empirical and rational approach to treatment. Other approaches, including humanistic and psychodynamic approaches, have historically been less successful (and invested) in providing research evidence for their effectiveness.

Common Factors

Common factors theory challenges the assumption that a specific psychotherapy approach is superior to another. Many randomized controlled trials that compared the effectiveness of different therapeutic approaches in treating certain disorders have found that the two approaches were equivalent in effectiveness. Instead of trying to find the best treatment, common factors advocates argue that research should work on identifying the components that are effective in *all* therapeutic approaches. Specifically, prominent common factors theorists propose that the bond between the client and therapist, the client's expectations for therapy, the structure of therapy, and the placebo effect account for most of the effectiveness in therapy.

THERAPY AND CULTURE

LEARNING OBJECTIVE

- Explain the impact of cultural and ethnic context on the selection and outcome of treatment

Cultural Context

Culture is defined as a collection of experiences, language, values, attitudes, and beliefs that are shared by a group in a specific place and time. Culture plays a big role in shaping our **worldview**, or how we interpret and understand the world around us. Culture can include belonging to a racial or ethnic group, a religious identity, a geographic location, or a specific gender and sexual orientation. Culture may also apply to a specific workplace, church, or family. Cultural differences should not be assumed rigid, since not all people within a certain culture are exactly the same.

When considering the role of culture in treatment, there are trade-offs between using a universal approach and using a culturally sensitive one. A universal approach maintains that human behavior (including abnormal behavior) shares common characteristics that will respond similarly to specific treatment techniques. Under this "one size fits all" perspective, culture is largely unimportant. In contrast, a culturally sensitive approach maintains that culture impacts the way an individual thinks, behaves, and feels—and, consequently, that culture impacts the experience and expression of psychological distress. In fact, some disorders described in the DSM-5 are **culture-bound syndromes**, which occur exclusively within a particular cultural context. For example, latah, a common phenomenon in Indonesia, describes uncontrollable singing, dancing, and laughing after experiencing an emotional shock.

According to the culturally sensitive view, culture influences a variety of factors important to treatment, including:

- Expectations about physical touch (e.g., handshakes, hugs)

- Level of comfort with eye contact

- Openness to self-disclosure

- Mental illness stigma

- Beliefs about the origins of mental illness

- Trust in healthcare systems and providers

- Values surrounding family, work, health, etc.

- Communication style (e.g., direct, passive)

Increasingly, mental health professionals agree that a culturally sensitive approach to therapy is important, especially considering that members of some racial and ethnic groups are often short-changed by traditional psychotherapy approaches.

Differential Outcomes

Members of different racial and ethnic groups tend to experience different therapeutic outcomes in the United States. For one, whites are considerably more likely than other groups to seek psychological treatment when experiencing psychological distress. This is believed to occur because of decreased access to psychological treatment for some racial and ethnic groups, due to lack of healthcare insurance, low socioeconomic status, or geographic location. Furthermore, such individuals are more likely to terminate psychological treatment early. In addition to decreased access, racism and the cultural context of traditional psychotherapy approaches are also contributing factors.

Racism

Some prospective patients are mistrustful of psychological treatment due to concerns about institutionalized racism. Indeed, misdiagnosis is often higher for members of some racial and ethnic groups due to a lack of cultural sensitivity. In one study, therapists were presented with two case studies that were identical except for the race of the patient. Therapists who read about a black patient tended to perceive the patient as more impaired, more untrustworthy, and more dangerous compared to therapists who read about a white patient. Furthermore, racist experiments like the Tuskegee Syphilis Experiment (see Chapter 13) allowed black men to suffer without treatment for decades. Experiences of racism and fears of racism likely contribute to the high attrition rates for non-white patients.

20

Eurocentrism

Historically, psychotherapy has focused on the treatment of white patients. Therefore, virtually all of the dominant treatment approaches are **Eurocentric**, meaning they are derived from a white European worldview and value system. Members of racial and ethnic groups who do not share a Eurocentric worldview are sometimes uncomfortable with traditional psychotherapy approaches and conceptualizations of illness. For example, in some Asian cultures, it is common for psychological complaints to be experienced as physiological symptoms, such as a stomachache. In collectivist cultures, the family and community are valued over the individual, so traditional psychotherapy's focus on an individual's thoughts and feelings may seem inappropriate. Finally, the self-disclosure required by traditional psychotherapy approaches is discouraged in many cultures. When an individual with a non-Eurocentric worldview is treated with a Eurocentric therapy approach, it is unsurprising that dropout rates are higher.

Solutions

Studies have identified factors that reduce the early termination rate for non-white patients. Non-white patients who are matched with a non-white therapist are less likely to terminate treatment compared to patients matched with a white therapist. However, this is a limited solution considering the discrepancies in racial representation among mental health professionals. Research has also found that multiculturally sensitive treatments (described below) are effective at reducing early termination rates for non-white patients.

Multicultural Competence

In response to the research on differential outcomes, mental health professionals have attempted to incorporate multiculturalism into traditional psychotherapy approaches. **Multiculturalism** is the integration, acceptance, and embrace of cultural differences. **Multicultural competence** is a related idea that refers to mental health professionals' ability to work with patients who are different than themselves in terms of race, gender, ethnicity, sexual orientation, and/or socioeconomic status. According to psychologist Derald W. Sue, a multiculturally competent therapist is defined as having three characteristics: self-awareness of his or her own cultural context and worldview, knowledge of the cultural contexts of other groups, and adoption of appropriate multicultural treatments.

Multicultural Treatments

Traditional psychotherapy approaches can be modified to be more culturally sensitive. For example, a psychodynamic therapist would typically not accept gifts from a patient, but a multiculturally competent therapist might accept a gift from a patient whose culture values gift-giving in relationships. A multiculturally sensitive, or multiculturally informed, intervention is a treatment approach that tries specially to address a particular cultural context. For example, a treatment may be developed to address the concerns of gay black men struggling with depression. A meta-analysis revealed that multiculturally sensitive interventions are superior at reducing psychological distress compared to traditional therapeutic approaches. Social justice therapy and Afrocentric therapy are two specific examples of multiculturally sensitive treatment approaches.

Social Justice Therapy

Social justice therapy recognizes that many patients face structural and institutional issues that influence their psychological well being. Patients from marginalized groups (including some racial and ethnic groups, women, disabled people, gender and sexual minorities, and immigrants) often experience discrimination, prejudice, and even violence that impacts their mental health. Marginalized groups often do not have equal access to societal resources, including housing and employment. Thus, a social justice therapist will often advocate for patients outside of the conventional role as therapist. For example, a social justice therapist might aid a patient in bringing a discrimination lawsuit against the patient's employer or in communicating with the patient's landlord to prevent eviction.

Afrocentric Therapy

First introduced by Frederick Phillips, **Afrocentric therapy** is rooted in African values, rather than Eurocentric values. Afrocentric therapy was founded as a spiritually based psychotherapy that is complementary to African American culture and community, rather than opposed to it. The five principles of Afrocentric therapy are harmony, balance, interconnectedness, cultural awareness, and authenticity. The goal of Afrocentric therapy is to help the patient find harmony in the natural order of the world.

PREVENTION STRATEGIES

LEARNING OBJECTIVE

- List tactics designed to promote resilience and competence

In a way, **prevention** is the most effective psychological treatment. Prevention of mental illness has a number of benefits, including improvements in individuals' well being and positive economic and social changes. Prevention efforts are often cost effective, since they usually cost less than psychological treatment. Similar to other psychological interventions, prevention should be evidence-based. Specifically, evidence-based prevention programs are rigorously evaluated based on outcomes, ideally compared to a control group.

Risk factors for mental illness include both genetic and environmental influences. Prevention programs might address mitigating environmental risk factors, such as child abuse, poverty, and violence in neighborhoods. Prevention efforts may also target specific populations with a higher risk of developing mental illness, including individuals with a family history of mental illness or with certain temperaments (e.g., pessimism). In addition to addressing risk, strength promotion is essential to effective prevention. Often, prevention programs will target social and emotional skills, including self-esteem, communication, and problem solving.

Types of Prevention

Prevention can take place in schools, neighborhoods, the workplace, or even on highway billboards. Prevention efforts can be universal, meaning that they are directed at all people. For example, anti-tobacco prevention campaigns attempt to reach people of all ages through commercials, advertisements, and billboards. Prevention can also be targeted, meaning that it attempts to prevent a specific problem for a specific community, like prevention of postpartum depression in mothers of newborns.

Health Promotion

Health promotion efforts aim to equip people with life skills related to their psychological or physical health. Health prevention programs often target **competence**, the ability to navigate the appropriate social, emotional, cognitive, and behavioral tasks at different developmental stages. For example, a school might teach elementary students emotion regulation skills in an effort to increase their emotional and social competence. There is evidence that the development of emotion regulation skills is associated with lessened risk of mood and conduct-related disorders.

Building Resilience

Resilience-building prevention programs prevent mental health problems by proactively strengthening families and children. **Resilience** is the ability to thrive, develop, and succeed despite adverse circumstances, such as exposure to trauma. Resilience is the ability to turn a high-risk situation into a positive outcome. Specifically, self-esteem, self-reliance, self-reflection, problem-solving abilities, and social skills are considered characteristics of resilience. There is evidence that increasing resilience is effective at lowering rates of depression, teen pregnancy, and suicide.

Levels of Prevention

In addition to being universal or targeted, prevention falls into three levels: primary, secondary, and tertiary. *Primary prevention* aims to avoid the occurrence of a disorder altogether. Most primary interventions target individuals and groups who have a high risk of developing a mental illness. Primary prevention programs might include incorporating mindfulness in schools, increasing social support for at-risk youth, and providing resources for victims of violence.

Secondary prevention includes methods to diagnose and treat a disorder in its early stages before it causes significant distress. Often, this decreases the overall prevalence of a disorder. An example of a secondary prevention program is using mental health screeners in primary care doctor offices. If an individual is experiencing depression symptoms, they can be referred for therapy, which may prevent them from developing a more severe or persistent mood disorder.

Tertiary prevention efforts prevent the negative impact of existing disorders. One example of tertiary prevention is Alcoholics Anonymous (AA), which prevents relapse of substance abuse disorders. Tertiary prevention addresses the after-effects of mental illness, including providing services to a community following a suicide.

IMPORTANT CONTRIBUTORS

LEARNING OBJECTIVE

- Recognize important contributors to clinical psychology

See the list of important contributors to clinical psychology in the Rapid Review section of Chapter 11.

 ## NEXT STEP: PRACTICE

Go to Rapid Review and Practice Chapter 11 or to your online quizzes at kaptest.com for exam-like practice on this topic.

Haven't registered your book yet? Go to kaptest.com/moreonline to begin.

CHAPTER 21

Social Psychology

Social psychology is the field of psychology that studies interaction between people and its effects on individual and group behavior. Essentially, social psychology aims to understand behavior and other psychological phenomena within a social context. In this chapter, we'll look at social behavior from three distinct perspectives: social behavior within individuals, group behavior, and behavior within diverse societies.

INTRAPERSONAL SOCIAL PHENOMENA

LEARNING OBJECTIVES

- Describe attitude formation and change
- Explain motives through the use of attribution theory
- Discuss factors contributing to attraction, altruism, and aggression

The topics discussed in this first section encompass a range of diverse phenomena. The common thread is that they involve the cognition, emotion, or behavior of a single individual in response to the social world. Because these topics largely concern how individuals think and feel about other people, we'll just refer to them broadly as intrapersonal social phenomena.

Attitudes

Attitudes are beliefs and feelings that predispose us to respond in specific ways to particular people, objects, or situations. Learning and other environmental factors have the greatest influence on initial attitude formation, particularly the attitudes expressed by parents early in development and, later, by peers. However, attitudes are one of the more flexible aspects of human psychology, so they are subject to change throughout life. Psychologists have identified two broad ways in which individuals tend to be persuaded to change their beliefs or feelings about something.

The **central route to persuasion** is based upon the content of the message. For example, suppose you're looking to buy a new phone because you've broken your old one (again). You see an ad for a new type of smart phone with a guaranteed unbreakable screen and an extended warranty that covers replacement for any other damages. If these reasons convince you to buy the phone, you've been persuaded through the central route.

The second approach, the **peripheral route to persuasion**, is based upon anything other than the message's content. If you decide to buy that new phone because you find the model in the ad attractive or because your best friend told you to buy it, you've been persuaded through the peripheral route.

Persuasive Techniques

In addition to the two broad routes of persuasion, the AP Psychology exam sometimes tests a few specific persuasive techniques. The **mere-exposure effect** (also covered in Chapter 14) is the tendency to develop a positive attitude towards something simply by virtue of encountering it frequently. Even universally recognized companies will spend a lot on advertising in order to increase exposure of their brands to the public, causing more people to adopt favorable attitudes about them.

The **foot-in-the-door technique** involves the use of an initial small request to encourage compliance prior to a second larger request. It's named after the tactic used by door-to-door salesmen back in the day, when they would literally put their feet in potential customers' open doorways to continue the conversation and increase the chance of a sale. For example, say your friend asked to borrow five dollars yesterday and you readily agreed, but today she comes back and asks to borrow twenty more. The fact that you helped her the first time makes it a bit harder to say no the second time, even though the request is more extreme.

In contrast, the **door-in-the-face technique** involves making an outrageous request at first (the kind that would get a door shut on a salesman's face), before making a smaller request that seems more reasonable by comparison. For example, if your friend first asked to borrow a hundred bucks and you laughed in her face, you might be more inclined to agree when she comes back and asks for "only" twenty-five. While opposite in their approaches, note that both the foot-in-the-door and the door-in-the-face techniques could achieve the same result—getting your friend the $25 she wanted in the first place.

> ✔ **AP Expert Note**
>
> **Cognitive Dissonance**
>
> While not exactly a type of persuasion, cognitive dissonance is another phenomenon that can lead to changes in people's attitudes. **Cognitive dissonance** is an uncomfortable state of mind that arises when individuals recognize inconsistencies in themselves, often conflicts between behaviors and beliefs. Psychologist Leon Festinger discovered in his research that individuals experiencing cognitive dissonance are more likely to change their attitudes than their actions. For example, a habitual smoker is more likely to call his beliefs about the dangers of cigarettes into question than to quit smoking.

Attribution Theory

Attribution theory aims to explain how people assign causes to actions taken by themselves or other people, and events that occur to themselves or other people. These attributions vary along two axes: dispositional vs. situational and stable vs. unstable.

A **dispositional attribution**, also known as a personal or internal attribution, assigns responsibility for a behavior or outcome to the person involved. In contrast, a **situational attribution**, or external attribution, assigns responsibility to the circumstances surrounding the action or event. A **stable attribution** maintains that a cause is ongoing and relatively constant, while an **unstable attribution** credits a one-time source. For example, if your friend earned an A on his most recent biology test, you would be making a dispositional-stable attribution if you credited his intelligence, but a situational-unstable attribution if you believed his teacher just happened to make one easy test.

According to social psychologist Harold Kelley, people make attributions on the basis of three types of cues: consistency, distinctiveness, and consensus. *Consistency* cues concern how an individual behaves in the same situation over time. *Distinctiveness* cues concern how an individual acts in distinct but similar situations. *Consensus* cues concern how other people act in the same situation. For example, if your friend tends to do well on a broad range of biology assignments (distinctiveness cues) and his classmates tended to earn Cs and Ds on the test (consensus cues), you would be more inclined to make a dispositional attribution for his A grade. If you knew he earned an A on every biology test he's taken this semester (consistency cues), you would be more likely to make a stable attribution.

Attribution Biases

Even though people respond to cues, most of us don't make attributions based on a rational, objective assessment of circumstances. Instead we often fall prey to a number of biases and errors that incline us to make particular types of faulty attributions. The most important of these are the fundamental attribution error, self-serving bias, and the just-world hypothesis.

The **fundamental attribution error** is the tendency to make dispositional attributions, rather than situational attributions, about other people's behavior. For example, you'd be committing the fundamental attribution error if you assumed that the quiet girl you met at the party last night was shy, rather than considering the possibility that she might simply have been exhausted after a long day. A related phenomenon is that people often view the same behavior under different lenses depending on whether they are acting or observing; *actor-observer bias* is the tendency to make dispositional attributions for other people and situational attributions for oneself with respect to similar behaviors.

Self-serving bias is the tendency to make favorable attributions about oneself. We tend to make dispositional attributions about the good actions we do and the good outcomes we experience, but situational attributions about the bad. For instance, if you believe you earned an A on your history test because you are a smart and diligent student, but got that C on your trigonometry test because your math teacher doesn't make fair exams, you may be guilty of self-serving bias.

According to the **just-world hypothesis**, good things happen to good people and bad things happen to bad people. Like the fundamental attribution error, this hypothesis tends to lead people to make dispositional attributions about others. If someone is successful or experiences other positive outcomes, according to the just-world hypothesis, it is because he or she has a good disposition. This bias tends to be most pernicious, however, when applied to people who suffer misfortunes: it can lead to an attitude of blaming victims for adverse consequences beyond their control.

Attraction, Altruism, and Aggression

Attraction

Attraction concerns the ways in which people take interest in and feel positively towards others. While usually used in a romantic or sexual sense, attraction can also be platonic when it describes the characteristics we find appealing in friends. Research has revealed that romantic attraction is influenced by a number of factors, the most noteworthy of which are physical attractiveness, proximity, similarity, and reciprocal liking.

Perhaps the most intuitive determinant of romantic attraction is **physical attractiveness**, the possession of outward physiological characteristics deemed to be appealing. While physical attractiveness is certainly influenced by cultural standards, research has revealed that some characteristics are relatively universal across times and places. Most notable is symmetry, particularly facial symmetry. Individuals across cultures consistently prefer more symmetrical faces over less symmetrical ones. There are also characteristics of attractiveness that seem consistent within particular genders and sexual orientations. For example, while heterosexual men can vary widely in their preferences about body weight based on cultural and individual factors, almost all heterosexual men seem to prefer an "hourglass" figure in women, consisting of a waist-to-hip ratio of approximately 0.7. Evolutionary psychologists believe that this ratio is a reflection of reproductive fitness, since wider hips ease the birthing process.

> ✔ **AP Expert Note**
>
> **The Matching Hypothesis**
>
> Rather than pursuing the most attractive partner possible, many people are drawn to individuals who are roughly equal in attractiveness to themselves. This tendency is referred to as the **matching hypothesis** and is believed to be evolutionarily adaptive, allowing a broader range of people to find mates and reproduce.

Proximity refers to the relative closeness of a person geographically. You are more likely to be attracted to people who live near you, particularly those you see on a regular basis. Part of the explanation for this may be the mere-exposure effect, described earlier.

Similarity refers to characteristics that people have in common. We tend to be more attracted to people when they share with us characteristics like socioeconomic class, religion, education level, personality, and interests. While traits that seem exotic to us can sometimes be appealing in the short term, research suggests that it is more generally the case that "birds of a feather flock together" than that "opposites attract" when seeking long-term partners.

21

Finally, **reciprocal liking** refers to the tendency to like people who like us. Even though there are plenty of exceptions, you are generally more likely to be attracted to a person if you believe that he or she is attracted to you.

Altruism

Altruism refers to prosocial behavior, typically behavior that imposes a cost on the actor while conferring a benefit on one or more other individuals. Altruistic behavior doesn't seem to make sense from an evolutionary perspective because it appears to decrease the fitness of an organism with altruistic tendencies while increasing the fitness of potential competitors—and yet we see examples of such behavior every day. Even if prosocial behavior is primarily learned from experience, the frequency of this type of behavior in human beings (and occasionally other animals) suggests it must have some biological basis. Evolutionary psychologists and other researchers have proposed several explanations for the existence of altruism.

One evolutionary explanation for altruism is known as **kin selection**. This account acknowledges that you tend to be more altruistic towards people who are related to you; you are more willing to sacrifice for individuals who share more of your genes. For example, while sacrificing yourself to save your children would end your life, your genes (which may have predisposed you to act that way) remain in the gene pool as long as your children survive.

Kin selection, however, cannot account for the tendency to help unrelated people, such as friends. **Reciprocity**, or reciprocal altruism, however, helps to explain such prosocial behavior. According to this account, you are more likely to help someone when you believe that he or she will help you back. When you have established relationships with friends, colleagues, and acquaintances, you almost automatically keep track of the give and take in your interactions. Indeed, human beings are naturally adept at detecting cheaters, individuals who have a tendency to take from others without giving back. A wide variety of social mechanisms and institutions have been established to punish cheaters, ensuring that they are less likely to benefit from the largess of their more benevolent peers.

Nevertheless, neither kin selection nor reciprocal altruism explains why many people act kindly toward strangers, including people they'll never meet again. One possible explanation for this is based on the process of **sexual selection**, the tendency for genes that increase reproductive fitness to perpetuate. In cross-cultural surveys, both men and women tend to rate kindness as one of the most desirable characteristics in a mate, often ranking it even more highly than physical attractiveness. According to the sexual selection hypothesis, people engage in altruistic behaviors because it makes them more appealing to potential mates and indicates their high levels of fitness (they can afford to make sacrifices without endangering their survival).

But even sexual selection doesn't explain the phenomena of anonymous donors and other discreet acts of kindness. Indeed, none of these explanations account for the actual motives of most prosocial actors, who are not behaving kindly in order to pass on their genes, but who tend to act out of genuine feelings of empathy, responsibility, and benevolence.

21

Aggression

Aggression is any type of behavior, physical or verbal, that is intended to harm or destroy. Twin studies and brain imaging studies (both discussed in Chapter 14) have shown that aggressive tendencies have a significant genetic and neurological basis, with aggressive individuals more likely to have abnormalities in the amygdala or frontal lobe and to possess higher testosterone levels. However, much aggressive behavior is thought to be learned, as demonstrated, for instance, in Albert Bandura's Bobo doll experiment (introduced in Chapter 16). Bandura's results seemed to suggest that observational learning plays a key role in the development of aggression.

Aggression is often divided into two types. **Instrumental aggression**, also known as "cold" aggression, refers to behaviors that harm in order to attain a specific goal. For instance, a playground bully looking for some extra cash might intimidate or threaten other students in order to obtain their lunch money. In contrast, **hostile aggression**, or "hot" aggression, refers to behaviors performed simply for the sake of inflicting pain. For example, a student subjected to incessant taunting finally snaps and strikes one of his tormentors in a fit of rage.

> ✔ **AP Expert Note**
>
> The **frustration-aggression model** maintains that aggressive behavior results from unsatisfied desires. When an individual's needs are unmet, he or she is more likely to lash out at others in frustration.

GROUP PSYCHOLOGY High-Yield

LEARNING OBJECTIVES

- Anticipate the effect of others' presence on individuals' behavior
- Describe individuals' responses to others' expectations
- Predict ways in which behavior can affect a self-fulfilling prophecy
- Summarize specific types of group behavior in terms of structure and function

When individuals gather together in groups, their behavior begins to change. In social psychology, a **group** is defined as two or more people who interact in some way. Members of groups may share a common worldview, purpose, or identity, or they might just happen to be in the same location. In a broad sense, society as a whole counts as a group, but social psychologists are typically interested in considerably smaller groups.

Groups tend to possess a number of characteristics, regardless of size. **Norms** are expectations about how group members behave. **Roles** refer to specific positions within the group governed by particular norms, such as special privileges or responsibilities. Norms and roles are often implicit, but more formally structured groups occasionally make them explicit. Specific patterns of interactions between members are known as **relations**. Groups often overlap, and most people are members of many different groups of a variety of types. For example, you are likely a member of a family, one or more groups of friends, a school, an athletic team or other extracurricular organization, and a nation, among other groups. In each of the groups you belong to, you follow different norms, adopt different roles, and share different relations with other members.

The Presence of Others

Even the most impersonal type of group, a crowd of people in the same location, exerts influence on the behavior of its members. Indeed, the mere presence of one or more other individuals can have an impact on how people behave, influencing whether they intervene in a crisis or how well they perform in a competition. Indeed, other people can bring out both the best and the worst in you.

Other people can bring out your best when their presence encourages you to perform at a higher level. **Social facilitation** refers to the tendency for people to perform simple tasks and tasks they've extensively practiced better in front of an audience. For instance, runners tend to go faster when participating in a marathon than when practicing on the treadmill. This feeling of social pressure that drives people to do better is not just confined to athletics, but extends to a wide range of phenomena from cheering louder in a crowd to reeling in a fishing line faster when being watched. (However, for difficult or novel tasks, having an audience can actually decrease performance.)

On the other hand, sometimes the presence of others can bring out your worst. The infamous case of **Kitty Genovese** is often cited as an example. Ms. Genovese was a young woman who was brutally murdered outside of her New York City apartment in 1964. According to the original reporting of the incident (which was later discovered to be inaccurate), despite Kitty's repeated screaming as she was stabbed to death over the course of half an hour, none of the dozens of neighbors who witnessed the crime made any effort to help. The tendency not to intervene while in a crowd is referred to as the **bystander effect**. Psychologists believe that this results from the **diffusion of responsibility** (the tendency to assume less responsibility for taking action when more people are present) experienced by members of a crowd. With so many other people around, it's easy to assume that someone else will step up and do what needs to be done.

> **✔ AP Expert Note**
>
> **Social Loafing**
>
> Another phenomenon believed to result from the diffusion of responsibility is social loafing. **Social loafing** refers to the tendency for some members of a group with a common goal to avoid doing their fair share of work to accomplish the goal. Social loafers tend to assume that other members of the group will pick up their slack, but if a group contains too many loafers, it will likely fail at its goal. Social loafing is more likely to occur in larger groups.

Social Expectations

Groups that are more structured than crowds tend to contain more norms and other expectations that more significantly influence how individuals in the group behave. The most important phenomena relating to social expectations include groupthink, conformity, obedience to authority, and self-fulfilling prophecies.

21

Groupthink

Groupthink, a term coined by Irving Janis, refers to the tendency of particular groups to make poor decisions as a result of members' desire to maintain harmony. The classic example of group-think that Janis relied upon is the Bay of Pigs invasion, when the John F. Kennedy administration launched an ill-fated Cuban invasion in 1961 after uncritically accepting a flawed CIA plan. Janis contrasted this with the JFK administration's more successful handling of the Cuban Missile Crisis a year later, in which greater critical thinking and better decision making prevented a nuclear war. Groups are more likely to be susceptible to groupthink when they are highly cohesive (members are well-acquainted and try to promote friendly interactions and reduce conflict), insulated from outside opinions, and lacking in clear rules for decision making.

Conformity

Conformity is the tendency for people to follow social norms; it often involves mimicking the attitudes or behaviors of a group's majority. The **Asch conformity experiment** is one of the most famous studies of this phenomenon. Solomon Asch enlisted a number of confederates, actors who pretended to be part of the experiment, to sometimes give obviously wrong information in a simple task involving matching the lengths of lines, using cards like the ones in the figure below. Asch put these confederates and an unwitting participant in a room and asked them to say out loud which lines matched in length. Participants would generally go along with the group, often even when confederates gave an obviously wrong answer. For example, if all the confederates claimed that line A matched the line on the first card, the participant would be more likely to say A as well, even though C was clearly correct.

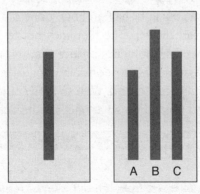

Cards from the Asch Conformity Experiment

Asch conducted additional experiments and discovered three factors that influence whether individuals give into peer pressure:

- Unanimity: The participant was more likely to conform when the group's opinion was unanimous.

- Lack of dissent: If just one confederate disagreed with the majority, the participant was more likely to dissent as well.

- Size of discrepancy: The bigger the difference between the majority opinion and the correct answer, the less likely the participant would conform.

Asch also discovered, contrary to his hypothesis, that group sizes larger than three confederates did *not* significantly influence the conformity of the participant.

Obedience

While conformity involves following implicit norms (no one told the participants in the Asch experiment to go along with the majority), **obedience** requires following the explicit directives of an authority figure. Obedience is sometimes also distinguished from **compliance**, in which individuals satisfy explicit requests from peers (as in the foot-in-the-door and door-in-the-face techniques discussed earlier in this chapter). What distinguishes obedience is that instructions come from an **authority**, an individual in a position of social power.

The most important research on obedience was the **Milgram experiment**, conducted by Stanley Milgram. Participants believed they were involved in a learning experiment, acting as "teachers" who would give shocks of increasing voltage to "learners" in another room. Unknown to the participants, the learners were confederates only pretending to be shocked, with scripted responses like screams, requests to stop the experiment, complaints of having a heart condition, and eventually silence (meant to suggest unconsciousness or death). Whenever a participant was unwilling to administer a shock, a researcher in a white lab coat would urge him or her to go on, using increasingly demanding language. A surprising number of participants continued administering shocks up to the maximum voltage, even though it seemed likely that the learner was being harmed or killed.

Milgram conducted variations on his initial experiment and discovered a number of factors affecting the likelihood of obedience. Participants were less likely to obey if they had more interaction with the learner, such as when they were placed in the same room together. Obedience also decreased when the original researcher left the room and was replaced by another in the middle of the experiment. Finally, obedience plummeted when participants shared the room with supposed peers (confederates portraying future participants).

Self-Fulfilling Prophecies

A **self-fulfilling prophecy** is a set of expectations about a social situation that causes that situation to come into being. For example, if a teacher believes that a student is destined to fail out of school, the way she treats that student could discourage him and be a decisive factor in his decision to drop out. Her belief that he was a failure was a self-fulfilling prophecy, because he would not have failed had she believed otherwise.

Research has shown this to be a more powerful effect than you might suspect. In one revealing study, Robert Rosenthal found evidence for the **Pygmalion effect**, the tendency for higher expectations to lead to improved educational performance. In the study, a group of students selected at random saw greater increases in IQ than their peers simply because their teachers were told that this group possessed exceptional abilities. With other factors controlled, it was clear that the expectation alone was enough to bring about the reality.

21

Group Behavior

Members of groups sometimes adopt extreme or destructive patterns of behavior not typically seen in solitary individuals. Three of these phenomena that are commonly tested on the AP Psychology exam are deindividuation, group polarization, and social traps.

Deindividuation

Deindividuation refers to loss of self-identity within a group, often accompanied by uncharacteristic behavior. Individuals in such a state can behave in ways they never would ordinarily. A deindividuated person is more likely to act impulsively and antisocially, perhaps even lashing out violently at a common target of the group. Deindividuation is more likely to occur in situations characterized by high arousal and high anonymity.

One of the most well-known studies on this phenomenon was the **Stanford prison experiment**, conducted by Philip Zimbardo. Students from Stanford University were assigned roles as prisoners or guards in a simulated prison environment. Despite plans to continue the experiment for two weeks, it was ended after only six days because of the levels of physical and psychological abuse that the "guards" were inflicting on the "prisoners." It was claimed by Zimbardo that none of the students involved showed evidence of prior sadistic tendencies; it seems that "guards" simply lost themselves in the role they were playing. The results supported the hypothesis that actual guards in American prisons sometimes behave cruelly towards prisoners due to deindividuation rather than sadism. However, later critiques found that there was profound selection bias in Zimbardo's initial design for selecting volunteers, that participants may not have been randomly assigned to groups, and that Zimbardo himself frequently interfered with the students and encouraged maladaptive behavior, suggesting the results of the study may not necessarily apply to the general population.

Group Polarization

Group polarization is the tendency for groups to adopt more extreme positions and to make more extreme decisions than the members of the group would individually. For example, members of political groups often find their opinions shifting in the direction of the group's tendencies as they gradually adopt more and more radical positions. Psychologists believe that members' opinions shift due to discussions in which more extreme views become normalized, coming to seem less shocking than they would when encountered in other contexts. Group polarization may help to explain the behavior of extremist groups like terrorist organizations, as well as the tendency for social media to enhance political polarization.

Social Traps

A **social trap** is a situation in which individuals within a group act in their own short-term self-interest to the overall long-term detriment of the group. This idea is closely linked to a phenomenon in ecology called the "tragedy of the commons," which describes situations in which a group resource, called a commons, is overused and eventually depleted. For example, an individual fishing

21

company is incentivized to catch as many fish as possible in order to compete against other fishing companies and maximize profits. When many fishing companies do the same thing, however, the result is overfishing, which leads to the depletion of fish stocks and guarantees that the companies will have a harder time earning a profit later.

Perhaps you've been a part of a group project that requires a task which is difficult or time consuming. If no one in the group is willing to complete this part of the project, each might gain some short-term reward such as free time or reduced stress, but the quality of the project will suffer overall. Social traps and the tragedy of the commons could be avoided through individual restraint or concerted efforts at cooperation, but often some kind of external regulation is required to ensure that the long-term best interests of everyone are promoted.

SOCIETY AND DIVERSITY

LEARNING OBJECTIVES

- Describe the influence of gender, race, and ethnicity on self-concept and interpersonal relations
- List factors tending to create stereotypes, prejudice, and discrimination among members of groups

Social and Cultural Categories

Social and cultural categories such as gender, race, and ethnicity play important psychological roles, both for individuals and groups. For individuals, these categories can affect your **self-concept**, the collection of ways you define yourself. Individuals typically adopt both a **gender identity**—based on whether they see themselves as masculine, feminine, androgynous, gender-fluid, or undifferentiated—and a **sexual orientation**, such as heterosexual, homosexual, bisexual, or asexual, which describes the type of people to whom they are romantically or sexually attracted. In addition, self-concept can also be influenced by **ethnic identity**, belonging to one or more ethnic groups in which members share a common ancestry, cultural heritage, and language.

Social and cultural categories also have interpersonal effects, insofar as members of one group may treat members of other groups differently. Some of the effects most commonly tested on the AP Psychology exam are stereotypes, prejudice, and discrimination.

Stereotypes, Prejudice, and Discrimination

Human beings often distinguish between in-groups and out-groups. An **in-group** is simply a group you belong to, while an **out-group** is one you don't belong to. Typically, stereotypes, prejudice, and discrimination favor members of in-groups and disfavor members of out-groups. While inter-related, each of these concepts is distinct. **Stereotypes** are cognitive: they are beliefs about the characteristics that define a group, typically based on limited and superficial information. **Prejudice** is affective: it is an irrational attitude and a negative emotional response toward a particular group, often formed prior to extensive contact with the group. **Discrimination** is behavioral: it refers to differential treatment of members of different groups.

For example, suppose you were born in Pittsburgh and are a devoted fan of its local football team, but you have recently moved to Baltimore, home of your team's dreaded rival. If you believed that all fans of the Baltimore team are obnoxious, you would possess a stereotype. If you consequently felt annoyed whenever dealing with Baltimore fans, you would exhibit prejudice. Finally, if you refused to sit next to a Baltimore fan at a restaurant or bar, you'd be engaged in discrimination.

When applied to specific groups, these phenomena are given distinctive names. **Racism** refers to stereotyping, prejudice, or discrimination directed against members of marginalized racial or ethnic groups, while **sexism** is based on sex or gender and is typically directed against women. **Ethnocentrism** is a similar phenomenon in which people presume to judge other cultures, including cultures that they have no experience of, on the basis of the values of their own culture.

The important thing to stress about all of these phenomena is that they are irrational, unsupported by evidence, and harmful. Even stereotypes, which might seem innocuous when compared to outright prejudice and discrimination, have been shown to produce negative consequences. For example, stereotypes can shape self-fulfilling prophecies, discussed earlier in the section on group psychology. In addition, there is **stereotype threat**, in which concern about confirming a negative stereotype can lead a member of a stereotyped group to perform worse. Research has shown, for instance, that women tend to perform worse on math tests as compared to a control group when reminded of the unjustified stereotype that men are better than women at math.

Of course, because discrimination involves behavior, it is likely to cause the most harm, especially when it is embedded in social institutions. While **individual discrimination** occurs when one person discriminates against a group, **institutional discrimination** refers to discriminatory treatment by social, cultural, or governmental organizations. Those familiar with American history will recognize that it includes long stretches of institutional discrimination against African Americans and other marginalized groups, from slavery to Jim Crow to continuing disparities in policing and rates of incarceration.

Counteracting Stereotypes, Prejudice, and Discrimination

Many researchers believe that stereotypes, prejudice, and discriminatory behavior are learned. That means it is possible to unlearn them and perhaps to prevent future generations of people from falling into these unfortunate tendencies. One technique for counteracting them is the creation of **superordinate goals**, shared objectives that require cooperation between groups to accomplish.

The famous **Robbers Cave experiment** conducted by Muzafer Sherif demonstrated both how prejudices can be learned and how superordinate goals can counteract them. Sherif and his colleagues separated 11-year-old boys at a summer camp into two groups and helped to cultivate a group identity for each, including feelings of animosity toward the rival group. Before long, members of the two groups began to develop stereotypes and prejudices against the other group, with physical aggression sometimes resulting when the groups met. The researchers then shifted their focus and created situations in which the two groups had to work together to accomplish goals that neither group could accomplish on its own. As the children cooperated to accomplish these superordinate goals, relations between the two groups improved.

IMPORTANT CONTRIBUTORS

LEARNING OBJECTIVE

- Recognize important contributors to social psychology

See the list of important contributors to social psychology in the Rapid Review section of Chapter 12.

 ## NEXT STEP: PRACTICE

Go to Rapid Review and Practice Chapter 12 or to your online quizzes at kaptest.com for exam-like practice on this topic.

Haven't registered your book yet? Go to kaptest.com/moreonline to begin.

PART 4

Practice Exams

HOW TO TAKE THE PRACTICE EXAMS

The final section of this book consists of six full-length practice exams. Taking a practice AP Psychology exam gives you an idea of what it's like to answer AP questions under conditions that approximate those of the real exam. You'll find out which areas you're strong in and where additional review may be required. Any mistakes you make now are ones you won't make on the actual exam, as long as you take the time to learn where you went wrong.

The six full-length practice exams in this book each include 100 multiple-choice questions and two free-response questions, just like the real exam. You should allow yourself 70 minutes for the multiple-choice questions in Section I and 50 minutes for both free-response questions in Section II. Before taking a practice exam, find a quiet place where you can work uninterrupted, and bring blank lined paper for the free-response questions. (The proctor will provide lined paper when you take the official exam.) Time yourself according to the time limit given at the beginning of each section. It's okay to take a short break between sections, but for the most accurate results, you should approximate real test conditions as much as possible.

As you take the practice exams, remember to pace yourself and to use the multiple-choice and free-response strategies reviewed in Chapters 2 and 3. Above all, approach the exam with a confident attitude. Just think to yourself that you're going to get a great score because you've reviewed the material and learned the strategies in this book.

After taking each practice exam, complete the following steps:

1. Self-score your multiple-choice section by using the Answer Key following the exam. You can also use the breakdown tables that follow the Answer Key to assess your performance on each topic.

2. Review the Answers and Explanations for the exam you completed. These detailed explanations are located immediately after the Answer Key and breakdown tables for each exam and can be helpful even when you answer questions correctly by reviewing additional testable information.

3. Self-score your free-response questions using the scoring guidelines and sample essays in the Answers and Explanations. Comparing your writing to these exam-like samples will help you to assess how AP readers would likely score your essay.

4. Enter your raw results into the online scoring tool (found in your online book companion at kaptest.com) for the exam you completed to see what your overall score out of 5 would be with a similar performance on the official exam. (If you haven't registered your book yet, go to kaptest.com/moreonline to begin.)

Good luck!

Practice Exam 1
Answer Grid

1. Ⓐ Ⓑ Ⓒ Ⓓ Ⓔ   26. Ⓐ Ⓑ Ⓒ Ⓓ Ⓔ   51. Ⓐ Ⓑ Ⓒ Ⓓ Ⓔ   76. Ⓐ Ⓑ Ⓒ Ⓓ Ⓔ
2. Ⓐ Ⓑ Ⓒ Ⓓ Ⓔ   27. Ⓐ Ⓑ Ⓒ Ⓓ Ⓔ   52. Ⓐ Ⓑ Ⓒ Ⓓ Ⓔ   77. Ⓐ Ⓑ Ⓒ Ⓓ Ⓔ
3. Ⓐ Ⓑ Ⓒ Ⓓ Ⓔ   28. Ⓐ Ⓑ Ⓒ Ⓓ Ⓔ   53. Ⓐ Ⓑ Ⓒ Ⓓ Ⓔ   78. Ⓐ Ⓑ Ⓒ Ⓓ Ⓔ
4. Ⓐ Ⓑ Ⓒ Ⓓ Ⓔ   29. Ⓐ Ⓑ Ⓒ Ⓓ Ⓔ   54. Ⓐ Ⓑ Ⓒ Ⓓ Ⓔ   79. Ⓐ Ⓑ Ⓒ Ⓓ Ⓔ
5. Ⓐ Ⓑ Ⓒ Ⓓ Ⓔ   30. Ⓐ Ⓑ Ⓒ Ⓓ Ⓔ   55. Ⓐ Ⓑ Ⓒ Ⓓ Ⓔ   80. Ⓐ Ⓑ Ⓒ Ⓓ Ⓔ
6. Ⓐ Ⓑ Ⓒ Ⓓ Ⓔ   31. Ⓐ Ⓑ Ⓒ Ⓓ Ⓔ   56. Ⓐ Ⓑ Ⓒ Ⓓ Ⓔ   81. Ⓐ Ⓑ Ⓒ Ⓓ Ⓔ
7. Ⓐ Ⓑ Ⓒ Ⓓ Ⓔ   32. Ⓐ Ⓑ Ⓒ Ⓓ Ⓔ   57. Ⓐ Ⓑ Ⓒ Ⓓ Ⓔ   82. Ⓐ Ⓑ Ⓒ Ⓓ Ⓔ
8. Ⓐ Ⓑ Ⓒ Ⓓ Ⓔ   33. Ⓐ Ⓑ Ⓒ Ⓓ Ⓔ   58. Ⓐ Ⓑ Ⓒ Ⓓ Ⓔ   83. Ⓐ Ⓑ Ⓒ Ⓓ Ⓔ
9. Ⓐ Ⓑ Ⓒ Ⓓ Ⓔ   34. Ⓐ Ⓑ Ⓒ Ⓓ Ⓔ   59. Ⓐ Ⓑ Ⓒ Ⓓ Ⓔ   84. Ⓐ Ⓑ Ⓒ Ⓓ Ⓔ
10. Ⓐ Ⓑ Ⓒ Ⓓ Ⓔ   35. Ⓐ Ⓑ Ⓒ Ⓓ Ⓔ   60. Ⓐ Ⓑ Ⓒ Ⓓ Ⓔ   85. Ⓐ Ⓑ Ⓒ Ⓓ Ⓔ
11. Ⓐ Ⓑ Ⓒ Ⓓ Ⓔ   36. Ⓐ Ⓑ Ⓒ Ⓓ Ⓔ   61. Ⓐ Ⓑ Ⓒ Ⓓ Ⓔ   86. Ⓐ Ⓑ Ⓒ Ⓓ Ⓔ
12. Ⓐ Ⓑ Ⓒ Ⓓ Ⓔ   37. Ⓐ Ⓑ Ⓒ Ⓓ Ⓔ   62. Ⓐ Ⓑ Ⓒ Ⓓ Ⓔ   87. Ⓐ Ⓑ Ⓒ Ⓓ Ⓔ
13. Ⓐ Ⓑ Ⓒ Ⓓ Ⓔ   38. Ⓐ Ⓑ Ⓒ Ⓓ Ⓔ   63. Ⓐ Ⓑ Ⓒ Ⓓ Ⓔ   88. Ⓐ Ⓑ Ⓒ Ⓓ Ⓔ
14. Ⓐ Ⓑ Ⓒ Ⓓ Ⓔ   39. Ⓐ Ⓑ Ⓒ Ⓓ Ⓔ   64. Ⓐ Ⓑ Ⓒ Ⓓ Ⓔ   89. Ⓐ Ⓑ Ⓒ Ⓓ Ⓔ
15. Ⓐ Ⓑ Ⓒ Ⓓ Ⓔ   40. Ⓐ Ⓑ Ⓒ Ⓓ Ⓔ   65. Ⓐ Ⓑ Ⓒ Ⓓ Ⓔ   90. Ⓐ Ⓑ Ⓒ Ⓓ Ⓔ
16. Ⓐ Ⓑ Ⓒ Ⓓ Ⓔ   41. Ⓐ Ⓑ Ⓒ Ⓓ Ⓔ   66. Ⓐ Ⓑ Ⓒ Ⓓ Ⓔ   91. Ⓐ Ⓑ Ⓒ Ⓓ Ⓔ
17. Ⓐ Ⓑ Ⓒ Ⓓ Ⓔ   42. Ⓐ Ⓑ Ⓒ Ⓓ Ⓔ   67. Ⓐ Ⓑ Ⓒ Ⓓ Ⓔ   92. Ⓐ Ⓑ Ⓒ Ⓓ Ⓔ
18. Ⓐ Ⓑ Ⓒ Ⓓ Ⓔ   43. Ⓐ Ⓑ Ⓒ Ⓓ Ⓔ   68. Ⓐ Ⓑ Ⓒ Ⓓ Ⓔ   93. Ⓐ Ⓑ Ⓒ Ⓓ Ⓔ
19. Ⓐ Ⓑ Ⓒ Ⓓ Ⓔ   44. Ⓐ Ⓑ Ⓒ Ⓓ Ⓔ   69. Ⓐ Ⓑ Ⓒ Ⓓ Ⓔ   94. Ⓐ Ⓑ Ⓒ Ⓓ Ⓔ
20. Ⓐ Ⓑ Ⓒ Ⓓ Ⓔ   45. Ⓐ Ⓑ Ⓒ Ⓓ Ⓔ   70. Ⓐ Ⓑ Ⓒ Ⓓ Ⓔ   95. Ⓐ Ⓑ Ⓒ Ⓓ Ⓔ
21. Ⓐ Ⓑ Ⓒ Ⓓ Ⓔ   46. Ⓐ Ⓑ Ⓒ Ⓓ Ⓔ   71. Ⓐ Ⓑ Ⓒ Ⓓ Ⓔ   96. Ⓐ Ⓑ Ⓒ Ⓓ Ⓔ
22. Ⓐ Ⓑ Ⓒ Ⓓ Ⓔ   47. Ⓐ Ⓑ Ⓒ Ⓓ Ⓔ   72. Ⓐ Ⓑ Ⓒ Ⓓ Ⓔ   97. Ⓐ Ⓑ Ⓒ Ⓓ Ⓔ
23. Ⓐ Ⓑ Ⓒ Ⓓ Ⓔ   48. Ⓐ Ⓑ Ⓒ Ⓓ Ⓔ   73. Ⓐ Ⓑ Ⓒ Ⓓ Ⓔ   98. Ⓐ Ⓑ Ⓒ Ⓓ Ⓔ
24. Ⓐ Ⓑ Ⓒ Ⓓ Ⓔ   49. Ⓐ Ⓑ Ⓒ Ⓓ Ⓔ   74. Ⓐ Ⓑ Ⓒ Ⓓ Ⓔ   99. Ⓐ Ⓑ Ⓒ Ⓓ Ⓔ
25. Ⓐ Ⓑ Ⓒ Ⓓ Ⓔ   50. Ⓐ Ⓑ Ⓒ Ⓓ Ⓔ   75. Ⓐ Ⓑ Ⓒ Ⓓ Ⓔ   100. Ⓐ Ⓑ Ⓒ Ⓓ Ⓔ

SECTION I

70 Minutes—100 Questions

Percent of total grade: 66⅔

Directions Answer the following 100 question in 70 minutes. Select the best answer for each and fill in the corresponding letter on your answer grid or a sheet of scratch paper.

1. If a psychologist investigates the effects of a high-fat diet on weight loss, the type of diet would be the

   (A) placebo

   (B) operational definition

   (C) dependent variable

   (D) independent variable

   (E) control condition

2. For six weeks, or ever since he failed his law school exam, Miles has been unable to go to work and class, and he prefers to stay at home by himself. Also, he feels tired throughout the day and does not believe he will graduate from law school. Miles is likely experiencing

   (A) panic attacks

   (B) bipolar I disorder

   (C) depression

   (D) conversion disorder

   (E) antisocial personality disorder

3. The study of emotions has been of interest to psychologists for many years, leading to the development of different theories. Which of the following controversies is most associated with these theories?

   (A) Whether people really have emotions

   (B) Whether emotions are felt during dreaming

   (C) Whether emotions happen before or after physiological response

   (D) Whether people "make up" their own emotions

   (E) Whether people are unaware of their own emotions

4. If a person's score on the WAIS is the mean, his IQ score would be about what percentile?

   (A) 2

   (B) 10

   (C) 16

   (D) 50

   (E) 84

5. When people see a circle that is partially completed with only broken lines around the perimeter, their minds fill in the spaces and they perceive an intact circle. Gestalt psychologists refer to this principle as

   (A) continuity

   (B) figure-ground

   (C) similarity

   (D) proximity

   (E) closure

GO ON TO THE NEXT PAGE

6. Jean Piaget's major contribution to theories of child development stems from his studies on

    (A) social development

    (B) cognitive development

    (C) recessive gene inheritance

    (D) physical development

    (E) IQ scores and heredity

7. In his pioneering work on early development, Harry Harlow examined how food was delivered to infant monkeys. His work with monkeys and surrogate mothers suggests that

    (A) bottle-fed infants are less attached to their mothers than breast-fed infants

    (B) infants prefer to be around their mothers

    (C) contact comfort is more important than provision of food

    (D) infant monkeys generally refuse all milk except that of their own mothers

    (E) infants will cling to any object that provides food

8. A professor wants to investigate the behavior of shoppers in a mall clothing store, so with permission he sets up a hidden video camera to record the behavior of the shoppers. This is an example of what type of research?

    (A) Experiment

    (B) Longitudinal study

    (C) Survey

    (D) Case study

    (E) Naturalistic observation

9. In an experiment, over a series of trials, food is paired with a loud noise. Later, the loud noise continues to occur but is no longer paired with food. This experiment is probably studying

    (A) extinction

    (B) learned helplessness

    (C) taste aversion

    (D) reinforcement

    (E) encoding specificity

10. People typically believe that flying in an airplane is more dangerous than driving a car. However, research has shown that more people die in car crashes every year than in airplane disasters. Which of the following could best explain this misconception?

    (A) Actor-observer bias

    (B) The availability heuristic

    (C) Groupthink

    (D) The representativeness heuristic

    (E) Social loafing

11. Most likely to criticize Skinner's theory on language acquisition would be

    (A) Raymond Cattell

    (B) Noam Chomsky

    (C) Lev Vygotsky

    (D) Walter Mischel

    (E) Jean Piaget

12. Which of the following disorders supposedly involves a patient having multiple personalities?

    (A) Bipolar I disorder

    (B) Antisocial personality disorder

    (C) Borderline personality disorder

    (D) Schizophrenia

    (E) Dissociative identity disorder

GO ON TO THE NEXT PAGE

13. An Olympic speed skater had never been able to beat a time of 4:50 in a race. During the Olympics, however, he ended up beating his best time. This exemplifies the concept of

    (A) compliance

    (B) self-fulfilling prophecy

    (C) social facilitation

    (D) foot-in-the-door

    (E) groupthink

14. Which of the following characterizes a child in the preoperational stage of cognitive development, as described by Jean Piaget?

    (A) The child can solve high-level logical problems.

    (B) Given long division, the child can solve a problem using a variety of strategies.

    (C) The child cannot speak yet.

    (D) The child can understand and produce language but can solve only simple logical problems.

    (E) The child can perform conservation tasks.

15. Which of the following provides the best example of a correlational study?

    (A) A psychologist gives one group of rats a drug and another group a placebo to see the effect of the drug on learning.

    (B) A psychologist examines a client's background to help provide therapy.

    (C) A psychologist analyzes case studies to determine how traits vary among people.

    (D) A psychologist attempts to determine the relationship between income and IQ by examining participants' tax returns and WAIS scores.

    (E) A psychologist gives students exams before and after taking a course to determine if the course improved learning.

16. Which of the following systems is responsible for the "fight or flight" response?

    (A) Somatic nervous system

    (B) Parasympathetic nervous system

    (C) Sympathetic nervous system

    (D) Limbic system

    (E) Central nervous system

17. Dr. Fredrick notices that the subjects who take his test of mechanical reasoning several times over a one-year period have virtually identical scores. This suggests that this test has

    (A) high content validity

    (B) high reliability

    (C) high predictive validity

    (D) a large standard deviation

    (E) been standardized

18. In a normal distribution, approximately what percentage of cases will fall within one standard deviation of the mean?

    (A) 34%

    (B) 50%

    (C) 68%

    (D) 95%

    (E) 100%

19. Each time a puff of air is administered to the eye of a rabbit, the rabbit blinks its eye. Before the puff of air, the experimenter rings a bell. Eventually, the bell elicits the blink. The bell would be labeled the

    (A) unconditioned response

    (B) conditioned response

    (C) unconditioned stimulus

    (D) conditioned stimulus

    (E) learned stimulus

GO ON TO THE NEXT PAGE

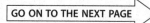

20. One example of a mood disorder is

    (A) schizophrenia

    (B) posttraumatic stress disorder

    (C) bipolar I disorder

    (D) obsessive-compulsive disorder

    (E) conversion disorder

21. After a head injury, a patient has experienced a range of problems including difficulty with muscle coordination and walking. Which of the following areas was most likely damaged?

    (A) Thalamus

    (B) Parietal lobe

    (C) Amygdala

    (D) Cerebellum

    (E) Hypothalamus

22. If a diagnostic test for depression is given to people who have been diagnosed with depression and people who have no signs of depression, and both groups receive very similar scores, then this suggests that the test

    (A) has not been standardized

    (B) has not been factor-analyzed

    (C) is not reliable

    (D) is not valid

    (E) does not produce scores that form a normal distribution

23. Which psychologist developed the first modern test of intelligence?

    (A) Henry Murray

    (B) Alfred Binet

    (C) David Wechsler

    (D) Sigmund Freud

    (E) B.F. Skinner

24. A teacher notices that one of her students is having extreme difficulty listening to directions, staying on task, and focusing. This child is potentially exhibiting symptoms of

    (A) schizophrenia

    (B) depression

    (C) attention deficit hyperactivity disorder

    (D) autism

    (E) bipolar II disorder

25. What is the primary excitatory neurotransmitter in the nervous system?

    (A) Dopamine

    (B) GABA

    (C) Serotonin

    (D) Glutamate

    (E) Norepinephrine

GO ON TO THE NEXT PAGE

Questions 26–29 are based on the following.

Researchers wanted to determine whether an advanced learning program (ALP) implemented during elementary school had long-term impacts on students' academic performance. They examined the academic records of all high school seniors who participated in the same ALP from fourth through eighth grade and compared their grade point averages (GPAs) to those of seniors who had not participated in the program. The results appear in the graph below.

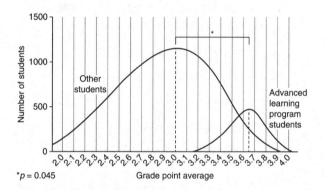

*$p = 0.045$

26. Which of the following would be the most reasonable null hypothesis for this research?

(A) Students in the advanced learning program will perform better than other students.

(B) The advanced learning program helps students perform better when they reach high school.

(C) Students who experienced the ALP will perform the same in high school as non-ALP students.

(D) Students currently in the ALP perform the same as students not currently in the ALP.

(E) Students cannot be influenced by early childhood learning programs.

27. The researchers ran a *t*-test and found the *p*-value to be 0.045. This means that

(A) the difference between the two groups is not statistically significant

(B) 4.5% of ALP students perform at the same level as non-ALP students

(C) there is a 4.5% chance that the conclusion of this study is valid

(D) it is highly probable that the difference between the two groups is not due to chance

(E) the means of the two groups are too close together to draw a meaningful conclusion

28. Suppose that only children with high IQ scores were admitted to the ALP in fourth grade. What would this imply about the validity of the researchers' likely conclusion?

(A) It would strengthen the conclusion that the ALP was responsible for improved academic performance.

(B) It would strengthen the conclusion that the ALP had no significant impact on academic performance.

(C) It would be irrelevant to the researchers' likely conclusion.

(D) It would weaken the conclusion that the ALP was responsible for improved academic performance.

(E) It would weaken the conclusion that the ALP had no significant impact on academic performance.

GO ON TO THE NEXT PAGE

29. Many other studies of this ALP were unable to replicate the results of the original study. What does this suggest about the original study?

    (A) The original study resulted in a type I error.

    (B) The original study resulted in a type II error.

    (C) Participants in the original study were influenced by the placebo effect.

    (D) The original study had faulty coding.

    (E) Participants in the original study were vulnerable to the Hawthorne effect.

30. According to Maslow's hierarchy of needs, creativity belongs to which of the following levels?

    (A) Esteem

    (B) Physiological

    (C) Intrinsic

    (D) Love and belonging

    (E) Self-actualization

31. In children with severe epilepsy, hemispherectomy, or removal of half of the brain, is considered as a possible therapy. What is the most likely outcome of this treatment?

    (A) Due to decreased neuroplasticity, the brain would never recover.

    (B) Due to increased neuroplasticity, the brain would eventually recover almost completely.

    (C) Due to increased speeds of neurotransmission, the brain would never recover.

    (D) Due to increased speeds of neurotransmission, the brain would recover most major functions.

    (E) Because the missing hemisphere controlled no important brain functions, there would be no adverse consequences.

32. The brain structure implicated in hunger, thirst, and other basic motivations is the

    (A) thalamus

    (B) medulla

    (C) hypothalamus

    (D) frontal lobe

    (E) temporal lobe

33. The process of repeating a previously published scientific experiment by using different participants but following the original experiment's specifications is called

    (A) random sampling

    (B) correlational research

    (C) replication

    (D) naturalistic observation

    (E) the double-blind procedure

34. Phil sees that Tony flunks a test in math. Because of this, Phil thinks that Tony is not very bright. Later, Phil flunks a math test. Phil believes that this is because the teacher hates him and graded him unfairly. This is an example of

    (A) the halo effect

    (B) the recency effect

    (C) social loafing

    (D) groupthink

    (E) actor-observer bias

GO ON TO THE NEXT PAGE

35. Which of the following is NOT a potential drawback of using diagnostic labels to categorize persons with psychological disorders?

    (A) Stigmatizing the disorders that have been labeled

    (B) Underemphasizing important differences among individuals

    (C) Overemphasizing the labels when referring to the individuals

    (D) Facilitating the development of a treatment program

    (E) Creating biased perceptions of those with disorders

36. When Ms. Ettson asks her students to solve a problem by generating as many answers as possible, she is asking them to show their

    (A) neural plasticity

    (B) factor analysis

    (C) divergent thinking

    (D) predictive validity

    (E) convergent thinking

37. Salespeople paid on commission who maintain high levels of perseverance despite infrequent sales display the effect of

    (A) a fixed ratio schedule

    (B) negative reinforcement

    (C) a fixed interval schedule

    (D) positive reinforcement

    (E) a variable ratio schedule

38. Which test do psychologists use most frequently to assess students' developmental delays?

    (A) Stanford-Binet Intelligence Test

    (B) MMPI-2

    (C) The Wechsler scales

    (D) Thematic Apperception Test

    (E) IRT

39. A person hears a horrifying scream, runs away, and feels afraid. This sequence is predicted by which of the following theories of emotion?

    (A) Social construction theory

    (B) Cannon-Bard theory

    (C) Schachter-Singer theory

    (D) Dual processing theory

    (E) James-Lange theory

40. Who is most well known for studying the influence of misleading information on eyewitness testimony?

    (A) Frederic Bartlett

    (B) Elizabeth Loftus

    (C) Ernst Weber

    (D) B.F. Skinner

    (E) John Watson

41. Which of the following is the Freudian stage during which a boy suffers from the Oedipus complex?

    (A) Oral

    (B) Latency

    (C) Genital

    (D) Phallic

    (E) Anal

GO ON TO THE NEXT PAGE

42. A man has a stroke. Following the stroke, he suffers from impaired speech comprehension. This would most probably be diagnosed as

    (A) Broca's aphasia

    (B) dyslexia

    (C) aphagia

    (D) Wernicke's aphasia

    (E) dyspraxia

43. Zimbardo's prison experiment suggested that both cruel and meek behavior could be elicited from ordinary people because of the power of

    (A) inherited traits

    (B) genetic predispositions

    (C) learned helplessness

    (D) deindividuation

    (E) groupthink

44. To solve a problem in an experiment, participants must use a book to adjust the height of a chair. The book must be used creatively. This experiment is most directly concerned with

    (A) demand characteristics

    (B) intelligence

    (C) functional fixedness

    (D) semantic priming

    (E) learned helplessness

45. Trait theory is often criticized because it

    (A) places too great an emphasis on early childhood experiences

    (B) focuses too heavily on the role of reinforcement and punishment

    (C) overestimates the consistency of behavior in different situations

    (D) underestimates the influence of heredity in personality development

    (E) overemphasizes positive traits

46. Client-centered therapy differs from psychoanalysis most substantially in that the client-centered therapist

    (A) is more controlling

    (B) tries to use free association to uncover hidden urges

    (C) encourages expression of feelings without judgment from the therapist

    (D) forces regression to earlier ages

    (E) believes that clients are often mistaken about the reasons they behave the way they do

47. Visual illusions can be informative because they demonstrate ways that the human visual system can be fooled. The reason people typically see illusions is that

    (A) the size of the retinal image remains constant

    (B) motion parallax tends to make objects appear larger

    (C) afterimages distort the true image

    (D) people use prior knowledge to interpret sensory information

    (E) the size of the retinal image is increasing

48. An example of a biological therapy is

    (A) token economies

    (B) operant conditioning

    (C) electroconvulsive therapy

    (D) classical conditioning

    (E) insight therapy

GO ON TO THE NEXT PAGE

49. Albert Bandura investigated aggression in several of his studies. In his most famous study, he found that

    (A) frustration is necessary for aggressive behavior

    (B) observation of aggression increases aggressive behavior in children

    (C) girls have a stronger innate tendency toward aggression than boys

    (D) direct expression of hostile feelings is not common in children

    (E) adult models have no impact on aggression in children

50. Wendy believes that her mother treats everyone badly because she does not like people. But, in reality, Wendy is the one who does not like people. The tendency to attribute one's own feelings and thoughts to an external object is known as

    (A) projection

    (B) compensation

    (C) denial

    (D) displacement

    (E) sublimation

51. Which of the following correctly links a psychologist with a concept or theory that he developed?

    (A) Jung: collective unconscious

    (B) Skinner: structuralism

    (C) Wundt: operant conditioning

    (D) Freud: classical conditioning

    (E) Piaget: clinical psychology

52. "Motivation comes largely from an attempt to achieve a state of balance or equilibrium among competing drives." Which of the following terms is associated with this theory?

    (A) Homeopathy

    (B) Homeostasis

    (C) Entropy

    (D) Complacency

    (E) Cognitive dissonance

53. A patient goes to a therapist and complains that he does not feel it is safe to leave his house. In fact, he has organized his entire existence in such a way that he almost never has to leave. This person is likely to be suffering from

    (A) a personality disorder

    (B) schizophrenia

    (C) obsessive-compulsive disorder

    (D) a somatic symptom disorder

    (E) agoraphobia

54. A child calls her mother "Mommy." One day, when she sees another woman at the park, she calls out "Mommy!" After a short time, the child learns that other adult women go by different names, and she begins to use the word "lady." This is an example of

    (A) accommodation

    (B) adaptation

    (C) organization

    (D) equilibration

    (E) assimilation

GO ON TO THE NEXT PAGE

55. Which of the following parenting styles tends to produce the most well-adjusted children?

    (A) Indulgent

    (B) Permissive

    (C) Strict

    (D) Authoritarian

    (E) Authoritative

56. The goal of attribution theory is to

    (A) explain how individuals attempt to understand the behavior of others

    (B) teach people that they are rarely accurate in their perceptions of others

    (C) understand breakthroughs in attitude measurement

    (D) develop good procedures for studying obedience

    (E) construct a clear understanding of psychopathologies

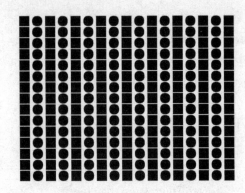

57. When Judy looks at the picture above, she describes it as columns of circles and squares, while her friend Tom describes it as one big rectangle when he looks at it. Which of the following statements most accurately describes this scenario?

    (A) Judy's perspective can be explained using the law of closure.

    (B) Tom's perception is influenced by the law of proximity.

    (C) Judy is using kinesthesis when perceiving the image.

    (D) Tom is being mislead by the Müller-Lyer illusion.

    (E) Neither Tom nor Judy are influenced by Gestalt principles.

GO ON TO THE NEXT PAGE

58. If someone takes antipsychotic medication for too long, he or she may suffer from symptoms that mimic which of the following medical conditions?

    (A) Parkinson's disease

    (B) Nicotine addiction

    (C) Blindness

    (D) Alzheimer's disease

    (E) Dysphasia

59. Barry does poorly on a quiz and says to his friend that it was the teacher's fault for not teaching him well enough. Which of the following most likely represents the maladaptive cognitive process at work here?

    (A) Internal locus of control

    (B) Top-down processing

    (C) Bottom-up processing

    (D) External locus of control

    (E) Heuristics

60. One common method for treating addictions is

    (A) aversion therapy

    (B) electroconvulsive therapy

    (C) psychoanalysis

    (D) transactional analysis

    (E) client-centered psychotherapy

61. If a researcher wants to study which areas of a person's brain are most active when he or she solves complicated math problems, the researcher should use a(n)

    (A) X-ray

    (B) brain lesion

    (C) MRI

    (D) PET scan

    (E) EEG

62. Research on social facilitation has demonstrated that if an individual is with other people, performance of

    (A) all tasks improves

    (B) all tasks deteriorates

    (C) simple and well-practiced tasks improves

    (D) simple and well-practiced tasks deteriorates

    (E) difficult and unfamiliar tasks improves

63. Which of the following theories provides a different perspective on color vision than the first major psychological theory on the subject?

    (A) Frequency theory

    (B) Localization theory

    (C) Opponent-process theory

    (D) Volley theory

    (E) Trichromatic theory

64. While reciting the alphabet, Freddie says the first 10 letters correctly but then slips up and recites the remaining letters in incorrect order. This is specifically an example of

    (A) selective attention

    (B) the recency effect

    (C) the short-term memory effect

    (D) the serial position effect

    (E) the primacy effect

65. Lithium is most commonly prescribed for

    (A) bipolar disorders

    (B) schizophrenia

    (C) major depressive disorder

    (D) personality disorders

    (E) somatic symptom disorders

GO ON TO THE NEXT PAGE

66. Hans Selye argued that we often overreact to stressful situations when we are already stressed. The term he and others use to describe this process is

    (A) global assessment of functioning

    (B) general adaptation syndrome

    (C) opponent-process theory

    (D) the Hawthorne effect

    (E) systematic desensitization

67. According to Piaget, a child who knows that clay does not change in size when it changes shape is probably

    (A) in the sensorimotor stage of cognitive development

    (B) between one and two years old

    (C) too young to learn a complex logical skill

    (D) able to understand conservation of mass

    (E) in the preoperational stage of cognitive development

Questions 68–70 are based on the following.

Mr. Ramirez sponsors a high school quiz bowl team. Team members must maintain a certain grade point average and attend practice two afternoons per week. At the end of each school year, Mr. Ramirez hosts a party for the team members to reward their performance. The following criteria apply:

- If the team has won its district tournament, Mr. Ramirez serves hot dogs, cake, and ice cream, and each team member receives a certificate.

- If the team has won the state tournament, he serves hot dogs, cake, and ice cream, and each team member receives a trophy.

- If the team has not won any tournaments, he serves hot dogs only.

68. The reward structure Mr. Ramirez has implemented for the quiz bowl team is an example of what type of motivation?

    (A) Introverted

    (B) Extraverted

    (C) Intrinsic

    (D) Extrinsic

    (E) Instinctive

69. One of the members of the quiz bowl team, Sasha, throws a tantrum and threatens to drop out of school when she is told that her grade point average is a bit too low to continue being on the team next semester. Which Freudian defense mechanism best accounts for this type of age-inappropriate behavior?

    (A) Sublimation

    (B) Regression

    (C) Displacement

    (D) Reaction formation

    (E) Rationalization

70. Suppose that, as a fun activity for the party, Mr. Ramirez gives the team a projective personality assessment. Of the following, he would most likely administer the

    (A) Myers-Briggs Type Indicator

    (B) MMPI-2

    (C) Beck Depression Inventory

    (D) Thematic Apperception Test

    (E) Kiersey Temperament Sorter

GO ON TO THE NEXT PAGE

71. Baumrind identified several styles of parenting. They included

    (A) autocratic, democratic, and laissez-faire

    (B) securely attached, insecurely attached, and loosely attached

    (C) authoritarian, authoritative, and permissive

    (D) moving against, moving toward, and moving away from

    (E) protective, semi-protective, and overbearing

72. The DSM is important for clinical psychology primarily because it

    (A) focuses on the etiology of mental disorders

    (B) offers a biological system of assessment

    (C) provides psychologists with consistent criteria for diagnosis

    (D) endorses a completely behavioral perspective

    (E) helps psychologists understand personality

73. During a group project, a few members of the team do not carry their weight and leave most of the work to the others. This is an example of

    (A) social loafing

    (B) groupthink

    (C) self-fulfilling prophecy

    (D) the Hawthorne effect

    (E) deindividuation

74. "Paradoxical sleep" is so called because

    (A) its EEG pattern is much less active than would be expected in sleep

    (B) it is so easy to wake someone in paradoxical sleep

    (C) its EEG pattern resembles that of the waking state more than that of slow-wave sleep

    (D) it is apparently unnecessary, since organisms deprived of paradoxical sleep do not compensate for the loss when allowed to resume sleeping

    (E) investigators are unsure what transpires during this sleep stage

75. To test whether a new drug to reduce hyperactivity is effective, a researcher would give a pill with the drug to one group and a pill that appears identical but does not contain the drug to a second group. Which of the following best describes the second group?

    (A) Control group

    (B) Random sample

    (C) Case study

    (D) Experimental group

    (E) Independent variable

76. Which of the following accurately matches a psychologist with his most well-known theory?

    (A) Wundt: attribution theory

    (B) Bandura: social learning theory

    (C) James: cognitive dissonance theory

    (D) Watson: instinctual drift

    (E) Skinner: depth perception

GO ON TO THE NEXT PAGE

77. A patient has a fear of crossing bridges. To help this person, the therapist designs a treatment involving slow introduction into bridge crossing. This is paired with relaxation techniques. This therapeutic technique is called

    (A) flooding

    (B) systematic desensitization

    (C) implosion

    (D) psychoanalysis

    (E) time out

78. Which of the following theoretical approaches is John Watson most well known for?

    (A) Biological

    (B) Social

    (C) Behavioral

    (D) Humanistic

    (E) Cognitive

79. "Children can perform at a higher level with support than they can without." The theory that posits this is

    (A) Jean Piaget's theory of conservation

    (B) Sigmund Freud's theory of psychosexual development

    (C) B.F. Skinner's theory of operant conditioning

    (D) Lev Vygotsky's theory of the zone of proximal development

    (E) Wilhelm Wundt's theory of consciousness

80. Human physiology undergoes slight changes that recur in cycles lasting approximately 24 hours. Blood pressure, body temperature, and hormone secretion are all susceptible to this kind of regular variation, with levels peaking and dipping at particular times during the day or night. These cycles are known as

    (A) narcoleptic patterns

    (B) circadian rhythms

    (C) sleep-wake cycles

    (D) sleep spindles

    (E) cataplexy

81. Which of the following statements is most likely to produce cognitive dissonance?

    (A) "I plan to spend my life doing this job, even though I hate it."

    (B) "I love to exercise because it makes me feel better."

    (C) "I often read because I am stimulated by the material."

    (D) "I find myself speeding, but I love the fear of getting caught."

    (E) "I will stop working when I feel that I have done all I can."

82. Which of the following is true of the structures of the eye?

    (A) Object discrimination is worst in the fovea.

    (B) Object discrimination is best in the fovea.

    (C) Color discrimination is best in the fovea.

    (D) Color discrimination is best at the periphery of the retina.

    (E) Visual sensitivity is the same across the retina.

GO ON TO THE NEXT PAGE

83. Operant conditioning was first described by

    (A) John Watson

    (B) B.F. Skinner

    (C) Wilhelm Wundt

    (D) Jean Piaget

    (E) Ivan Pavlov

84. Drugs such as morphine are classified as narcotics. Which neurochemicals are these like?

    (A) Endogenous endorphins

    (B) Epinephrine

    (C) Norepinephrine

    (D) Serotonin

    (E) L-dopa

85. In Milgram's experiments on obedience,

    (A) most participants refused to administer the shocks

    (B) most participants did obey the command to give the shocks

    (C) about half the participants gave the shocks

    (D) participants with poor moral reasoning skills gave the shocks

    (E) female participants shocked more than male participants

86. A large number of people observe a hit-and-run accident, yet no one reports it to the police. This is an example of

    (A) groupthink

    (B) diffusion of responsibility

    (C) altruism

    (D) stereotyping

    (E) reinforcement

87. One mnemonic technique involves associating a list of items to remember with a mental map of specific places. This technique is called

    (A) state-dependent learning

    (B) the method of loci

    (C) natural language mnemonics

    (D) chunking

    (E) the peg-word method

88. Paul experienced a traumatic injury to his ear which resulted in damage to a small, specific region of the cochlea. Despite this damage, Paul is able to hear all pitches that he was able to hear prior to his injury. What theory of pitch perception is most *weakened* by this evidence?

    (A) Temporal theory

    (B) Volley theory

    (C) Place theory

    (D) Opponent-process theory

    (E) Perceptual constancy

89. A psychologist believes that her client's aggressive behavior can be attributed to the client's history of being rewarded for showing aggression. This psychologist probably belongs to the same school of psychological thought as

    (A) Carl Jung

    (B) Sigmund Freud

    (C) Carl Rogers

    (D) B.F. Skinner

    (E) Charles Darwin

GO ON TO THE NEXT PAGE

90. When participants have problems learning new information because old information is causing them confusion, psychologists call this

    (A) proactive interference

    (B) anterograde inhibition

    (C) retroactive interference

    (D) interference theory

    (E) state-dependent learning

Questions 91–92 are based on the following.

A researcher set up an experiment in which a rat is placed in a cage with a green button that releases a food pellet. However, when the green button is pressed, the food pellet is released only after one minute has elapsed following the first button press. The researcher measured how many times the rat presses the green button while waiting for the food pellet. The results of the experiment are presented in the graph below.

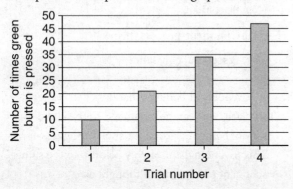

91. Based on the experiment described above, what effect would most likely be observed when decreasing the 1-minute wait period to 30 seconds?

    (A) The food pellet will become a weaker reinforcer due to the size principle.

    (B) The green button will become a stronger positive reinforcer.

    (C) The food pellet will become a stronger negative reinforcer.

    (D) The food pellet will become a stronger reinforcer due to the immediacy principle.

    (E) The food pellet will become a weaker reinforcer due to the satiation principle.

92. Which of the following provides the most plausible explanation for the results shown in the graph?

    (A) The increase in number of button presses is a coping mechanism for the rat in order to increase its stress.

    (B) The subject is pressing the button as an avoidance mechanism.

    (C) The food pellet is becoming a more effective reinforcement due to expectancy.

    (D) The increase in button pressing is due to escape conditioning.

    (E) The rat's button-pressing behavior increases in frequency due to classical conditioning.

93. According to Carl Jung, which archetype represents the feminine side of men?

    (A) Persona

    (B) Anima

    (C) Animus

    (D) Shadow

    (E) Self

94. Laetitia is grounded, but her father will allow her to go to a concert with her friends this weekend if she completes all of her chores this week. This is best considered an example of

    (A) positive reinforcement

    (B) negative reinforcement

    (C) punishment

    (D) classical conditioning

    (E) an unconditioned response

GO ON TO THE NEXT PAGE

95. Bipolar I disorder is

    (A) a severe form of clinical depression

    (B) characterized by manic episodes

    (C) a form of schizophrenia

    (D) extremely common in the United States

    (E) treated best by using psychoanalysis

96. When a person is in a room and the lights are dimmed significantly, her vision changes. Which of the following statements best describes this change?

    (A) Vision improves for color but diminishes for black and white

    (B) Vision improves immediately

    (C) Vision improves for black and white but diminishes for color

    (D) Vision does not improve in any way

    (E) Vision goes away completely

97. What part of the brain is most closely associated with visual processing?

    (A) Cerebellum

    (B) Frontal lobe

    (C) Parietal lobe

    (D) Temporal lobe

    (E) Occipital lobe

98. Which of the following cues is important in helping people to perceive depth?

    (A) Binocular convergence

    (B) Binocular disparity

    (C) Convergence

    (D) Visual acuity

    (E) Space location

99. What is the name of the method, developed by psychologists Wilhelm Wundt and Edward Titchener, in which subjects were asked to monitor and report their sensory experiences of differently colored objects?

    (A) Structuralism

    (B) Spaced practice

    (C) Introspection

    (D) Rehearsal

    (E) Psychoanalysis

100. Which of the following studies is likely to be completed by someone who is interested in developmental psychology?

    (A) A study of memory

    (B) An investigation into age-related changes in social relations

    (C) The study of reinforcement in infant rats

    (D) The impact of dopamine and other neuro-chemicals on memory

    (E) The causes of obedience

END OF SECTION I

SECTION II

50 Minutes—2 Questions

Percent of total grade: 33⅓

Directions Answer both of the following questions in 50 minutes. Lists of facts are insufficient to earn points; you must write essays that answer the questions thoughtfully with sound arguments that employ the proper terms from psychology. Use scratch paper to write out your responses.

1. Alana recently attended her first fencing match and enjoyed it so much that she began taking fencing lessons. After the first week, she threatened to quit because she was so frustrated, and even yelled at her parents a few times when they picked her up from her lessons. In an attempt to placate Alana after her lessons, her parents eventually start taking her for ice cream after every fencing lesson.

    Part A

    Explain how each of these terms or concepts relate to this scenario.

    - Procedural memory
    - Displacement
    - Operant conditioning

    Part B

    Explain how each of the following terms would help Alana and those around her cope with her frustration at her current level of fencing.

    - Metacognition
    - Scaffolding
    - Intrinsic motivation
    - Social learning

2. Dr. Smith is interested in determining the relationship between intelligence and success in life. He begins designing an observational study of 1000 people to assess how intelligence affects success in life.

    Part A

    - Identify a plausible operational definition of the dependent variable in Dr. Smith's study.
    - Identify the most likely operational definition of the independent variable in Dr. Smith's study.
    - Explain why Dr. Smith might be worried about the validity of his study.

Part B

Explain how each of the following might have relevance to Dr. Smith's study.

- Stereotype threat
- Sampling
- Confounding variables

Part C

Below is a histogram of the IQs of people in Dr. Smith's study. Is this a representative sample of the general population? Explain why or why not.

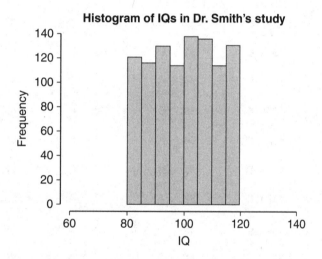

END OF SECTION II

STOP

END OF EXAM

ANSWER KEY

Section I

1. D	16. C	31. B	46. C	61. D	76. B	91. D
2. C	17. B	32. C	47. D	62. C	77. B	92. C
3. C	18. C	33. C	48. C	63. C	78. C	93. B
4. D	19. D	34. E	49. B	64. E	79. D	94. B
5. E	20. C	35. D	50. A	65. A	80. B	95. B
6. B	21. D	36. C	51. A	66. B	81. A	96. C
7. C	22. D	37. E	52. B	67. D	82. C	97. E
8. E	23. B	38. C	53. E	68. D	83. B	98. B
9. A	24. C	39. E	54. A	69. B	84. A	99. C
10. B	25. D	40. B	55. E	70. D	85. B	100. B
11. B	26. C	41. D	56. A	71. C	86. B	
12. E	27. D	42. D	57. B	72. C	87. B	
13. C	28. D	43. D	58. A	73. A	88. C	
14. D	29. A	44. C	59. D	74. C	89. D	
15. D	30. E	45. C	60. A	75. A	90. A	

Section II

1. See Answers and Explanations

2. See Answers and Explanations

PRACTICE EXAM 1 BREAKDOWN: ASSESS YOUR STRENGTHS

Use the following tables to determine which topics you are already strong in and which topics you need to review most.

Topic	Questions
Scientific Foundations of Psychology	1, 8, 15, 26, 27, 28, 29, 33, 51, 75, 76, 78, 89, 99
Biological Bases of Behavior	16, 21, 25, 31, 42, 61, 74, 80, 84, 97
Sensation and Perception	5, 47, 57, 63, 82, 88, 96, 98
Learning	9, 19, 37, 49, 83, 91, 92, 94
Cognitive Psychology	4, 10, 11, 17, 18, 22, 23, 36, 38, 40, 44, 59, 64, 87, 90
Developmental Psychology	6, 7, 14, 54, 55, 67, 71, 79, 100
Motivation, Emotion, and Personality	3, 30, 32, 39, 41, 45, 50, 52, 66, 68, 69, 70, 93
Clinical Psychology	2, 12, 20, 24, 35, 46, 48, 53, 58, 60, 65, 72, 77, 95
Social Psychology	13, 34, 43, 56, 62, 73, 81, 85, 86

Topic	Chapters	Questions on Exam	Number You Got Correct
Scientific Foundations of Psychology	4, 13	14	
Biological Bases of Behavior	5, 14	10	
Sensation and Perception	6, 15	8	
Learning	7, 16	8	
Cognitive Psychology	8, 17	15	
Developmental Psychology	9, 18	9	
Motivation, Emotion, and Personality	10, 19	13	
Clinical Psychology	11, 20	14	
Social Psychology	12, 21	9	

PRACTICE EXAM 1 ANSWERS AND EXPLANATIONS

SECTION I

1. D

Topic: Scientific Foundations of Psychology

In an experiment, the dependent variable depends upon the independent variable. In other words, changes to the independent variable (manipulated by the researcher) are expected to cause corresponding changes to the dependent variable (measured by the researcher). Because the psychologist is investigating how a high-fat diet affects weight loss, the type of diet is the independent variable, **(D)**. (A) is incorrect because there is no indication that a placebo, a substance or treatment with no therapeutic effect that is often administered as a control in experiments, is used in the psychologist's study. (B) is incorrect because an operational definition indicates how a particular construct will be measured in an experiment. (C) is incorrect because weight loss is the dependent variable in this case. (E) is incorrect because a control condition (such as a diet with a standard amount of fat) is not specified in the question stem.

2. C

Topic: Clinical Psychology

Given that Miles has been unable to engage in basic activities such as going to work and school for several weeks, and is bleak about his prospects of graduating law school, he is showing signs of depression. **(C)** is correct. Panic attacks are marked by rapid, acute episodes of anxiety. This does not accurately describe Miles, making (A) incorrect. A person suffering from bipolar I disorder fluctuates between periods of extreme hyperactivity and periods of deep depression. There is no indication that Miles has periods of extreme hyperactivity, so (B) is incorrect. A conversion disorder is a type of somatic symptom disorder in which a person suffers due to a heightened level of stress about an upcoming event. (D) is incorrect. Those with antisocial personality disorder often violate the rights of other people, making (E) incorrect.

3. C

Topic: Motivation, Emotion, and Personality

Most of the research on emotion, especially the early research, focused on whether emotions happened before or after physiological response. For instance, in the James-Lange theory, a physiological response comes before the experience of emotion, while in the Cannon-Bard theory, emotion precedes physiological response. **(C)** is thus correct. (A) is incorrect because psychologists of emotion do not generally dispute the existence of emotions. (B) is incorrect because the primary controversy concerns the timing between emotion and physiology, not whether we experience emotions in dreams. (D) is incorrect because psychologists of emotion generally accept that individuals actually experience the emotions they claim to feel. (E) is incorrect because psychologists of emotion generally believe that individuals have some consciousness of their own emotions.

4. D

Topic: Cognitive Psychology

The Weschsler Adult Intelligence Scale functions the same as any other measurement scale. If a score is at the mean on any scale, half (50%) of the scores on the scale are lower and half are higher. This translates to the 50th percentile, **(D)**.

5. E

Topic: Sensation and Perception

According to the Gestalt principle of closure, a person mentally fills in the gaps and perceives an object as a whole. **(E)** is correct. According to the principle of continuity, (A), an individual sees contiguous parts as belonging to a larger whole. The principle of figure-ground, (B), allows someone to see an object in an image as being in either the foreground or background. Similarity, (C), means that one sees similar things as belonging together. Proximity, (D), means that an individual sees things that are closer together as connected.

6. B

Topic: Developmental Psychology

Piaget spent most of his career trying to understand how children develop the skills to engage in higher-level cognitive functions. **(B)** is thus correct. The other choices present issues that may be of interest to many developmental psychologists, but Piaget focused almost exclusively on cognitive development.

7. C

Topic: Developmental Psychology

In Harlow's research, there were two food sources the monkey could feed from: a wire "mother" or a cloth-covered "mother." The infants were much more likely to feed from the cloth mother than the wire mother, suggesting that warmth and support are even more important to young monkeys than food. **(C)** is thus correct. The other choices present conclusions not supported by Harlow's research.

8. E

Topic: Scientific Foundations of Psychology

In naturalistic observation, the researcher wants to view the participants (in this case, shoppers) in their most natural habitat (in this case, a clothing store). Remember that the cardinal rule of naturalistic observation is not to disturb the group being watched, so the professor is careful to use the hidden camera. **(E)** is correct. This kind of research allows for the observation of behavior but does not allow for controls, such as in an experiment, (A). Surveys, (C), and case studies, (D), do not involve this kind of direct observation, and a longitudinal study, (B), is normally carried out over several years.

9. A

Topic: Learning

Extinction is the process of breaking a connection between a conditioned stimulus and a conditioned response. If the connection is not made for several trials, the stimulus will no longer lead to the response. In the scenario described in the question stem, the food serves as an unconditioned stimulus, while the loud noise is the conditioned stimulus. An unconditioned response, such as salivation, would eventually become a conditioned response to the loud noise after several pairings.

Removing the food in subsequent trials, however, would weaken this connection between the loud noise and salivation, likely causing extinction. **(A)** is thus correct. (B), (C), and (D) are incorrect because learned helplessness, taste aversion, and reinforcement pertain to operant conditioning, not classical conditioning. Encoding specificity refers to a concept in cognitive psychology, so (E) is also incorrect.

10. B

Topic: Cognitive Psychology

The availability heuristic refers to the tendency of people to rely on information that is readily available to make judgments about the probability of an event occurring, rather than on the true probability of it actually happening. Because plane crashes tend to be more widely publicized than car crashes, it is not surprising that many people regard flying as more dangerous. **(B)** is correct. This type of heuristic differs from the representativeness heuristic, (D), in that the latter judges the likelihood of an event based on the known outcome of a similar event. (A) is the tendency for a person to believe that his or her behavior is due to external causes while other people's behavior is internally motivated. (C) occurs when the members of a group make decisions based on a desire for group harmony; this can lead to poor decisions. (E) is the phenomenon that occurs when a person works less hard while working within a group.

11. B

Topic: Cognitive Psychology

Of the psychologists listed, Noam Chomsky would be most likely to criticize Skinner's theory on language acquisition. In fact, one of the biggest debates in language acquisition concerns the difference between these two psychologists' views. Skinner, a behaviorist, stated that children learn language by imitating adults and through reinforcement. According to Chomsky, language acquisition comes not through learning principles alone. Instead, he argues that the ability to speak is inborn, and that the environment helps shape our language skills. Chomsky argues that Skinner's theory does not adequately account for language learning because language acquisition occurs too rapidly. **(B)** is correct. Cattell, (A), is known for his analysis of personality and intelligence. Vygotsky, (C), did important work analyzing how social and cultural factors impact child development. Mischel, (D), is known for his work on cognitive and emotional self-control. Piaget, (E), is well known for his work on cognitive development, which describes how children are able to deal with logical problems at different ages.

12. E

Topic: Clinical Psychology

Dissociative identity disorder was formerly called multiple personality disorder. It is a rare and controversial disorder in which individuals supposedly alternate between two or more distinct identities. **(E)** is thus correct. (A) is incorrect because bipolar I disorder is a mood disorder characterized by alternation between periods of depression and mania. (B) is incorrect because antisocial personality disorder is a personality disorder characterized by regular disregard or violation of the rights of other people. (C) is incorrect because borderline personality disorder is a personality disorder characterized by instability in interpersonal relationships, sense of self, and emotional states. (D) is incorrect because schizophrenia is a mental disorder in which individuals lose touch with reality and engage in abnormal social behaviors.

13. C

Topic: Social Psychology

Social facilitation is the phenomenon in which a person performs better at some activities while in the presence of others than he or she would if acting alone. The question stem describes exactly this kind of scenario, making **(C)** correct. (A) is incorrect because compliance occurs when behavior changes due to a request. (B) is a belief that comes true because one is acting as if it is already true. According to the foot-in-the-door technique, (D), a person is more likely to comply with a larger request when he or she has already complied with a smaller request. (E) refers to a situation in which a group makes decisions based on a desire for group harmony rather than on accurate analysis.

14. D

Topic: Developmental Psychology

A child in the preoperational stage has acquired some basic logical skills and language abilities, but a child in this stage cannot understand conservation (the idea that quantity remains the same even if shape changes), solve

complex logical problems, or do long division. A child is typically in this stage between ages 2 and 6. **(D)** is thus correct. (A) occurs during the formal operational stage, in which a child—usually around 12 years old—can conduct complex logical thought; this is the fourth and highest level of cognitive development, according to Piaget. (B) and (E) happen during the concrete operational stage (the third stage), usually occurring between the ages of 7 and 11. (C) occurs during the first stage, referred to as the sensorimotor stage.

15. D

Topic: Scientific Foundations of Psychology

In a correlational study, a psychologist will attempt to determine if there is a relationship between two variables that already exist in the world. Thus, an investigation of the relationship between income and IQ, as in **(D)**, presents one example of a correlational study. (A) is incorrect because it provides an example of a controlled experiment. (B) is incorrect because it is more like a case study. (C) is incorrect because it is an analysis of multiple case studies. (E) is incorrect because it describes another experiment.

16. C

Topic: Biological Bases of Behavior

The sympathetic nervous system, which is part of the peripheral nervous system, helps organisms prepare for a response when a situation calls for one. For example, if someone is scared, the sympathetic nervous system prepares the person to respond appropriately. While the sympathetic division of the nervous system uses energy to arouse a person, the parasympathetic division works to calm the person down and save energy. **(C)** is thus correct, and (B) is incorrect. (A) is the part of the peripheral nervous system that controls skeletal muscles. (D) is the part of the nervous system that is associated with emotions and motives for basic needs. The central nervous system, (E), consists of the brain and spinal column, and is distinct from the peripheral nervous system.

17. B

Topic: Cognitive Psychology

A test that yields consistent results when taken multiple times is one that has high reliability, specifically test-retest reliability. **(B)** is thus correct. None of the other choices reflect the information provided. (A) is incorrect because a test with high content validity will actually measure the phenomenon it is supposed to. (C) is incorrect because a test with high predictive validity will allow accurate predictions of behavior based on test results. (D) is incorrect because a test with a large standard deviation will show a wide spread in results between multiple test-takers. (E) is incorrect because a standardized test is one that is always taken and scored in the same manner.

18. C

Topic: Cognitive Psychology

In a normal distribution, 34 percent of the scores fall between the mean and one standard deviation above the mean. However, another 34 percent of scores fall between the mean and one standard deviation *below* it. Thus, all scores within one standard deviation of the mean will comprise 68 percent of the total number of scores in a normal distribution. **(C)** is correct.

19. D

Topic: Learning

In this example, the bell serves as a conditioned stimulus, **(D)**, because it eventually comes to have the same effect as the unconditioned stimulus after conditioning. (A) and (B) are incorrect because the blink is both the unconditioned response and the conditioned response. (C) is incorrect because the unconditioned stimulus is the puff of air. (E) is incorrect because "learned stimulus" is not a term used in classical conditioning.

20. C

Topic: Clinical Psychology

Bipolar I disorder is classified as a mood disorder because most sufferers cycle between episodes of mania (elevated mood) and depression (diminished mood). **(C)** is thus correct. (A) is incorrect because schizophrenia is not characterized as a mood disorder, but belongs to a separate category. (B) and (D) are incorrect because PTSD and OCD belong to distinct classes of disorders. (E) is incorrect because conversion disorder is a type of somatic symptom disorder.

21. D

Topic: Biological Bases of Behavior

The cerebellum is the region in which voluntary motor movements and balance are coordinated, so damage there would likely cause the symptoms described in the question stem. **(D)** is correct. Damage to the thalamus and parietal lobe, (A) and (B), would each result in diminished sensory perception; damage to the amygdala, (C), would affect the experience of fear; and damage to the hypothalamus, (E), would alter the body's ability to regulate hormonal production and maintain homeostasis.

22. D

Topic: Cognitive Psychology

A test that is supposed to be an indicator of depression should result in markedly different scores for groups of depressed people and non-depressed people. That the scores of both groups are similar suggests that the test does not measure what it is supposed to. In other words, the test is not valid, **(D)**. (A) and (B) are incorrect because no information is provided concerning whether the test has been standardized (administered and scored consistently) or factor-analyzed (subjected to specific statistical techniques). (C) is incorrect because there is no indication of whether individuals score consistently when taking the test multiple times. (E) is incorrect because no information is provided about the distribution of scores.

23. B

Topic: Cognitive Psychology

Alfred Binet was hired by the French government to develop a test to determine how well students would likely perform in school. Binet's test diverged from other measures at the time and forged a new way of thinking about intelligence. Eventually, other tests of intelligence were developed along the same lines as Binet's. **(B)** is correct. (A) is incorrect because Murray studied personality, not intelligence. (C) is incorrect because Wechsler developed two later intelligence tests, the WAIS and WISC. (D) is incorrect because Freud was a clinician who developed the therapeutic method of psychoanalysis. (E) is incorrect because Skinner's work was in behavioral psychology.

24. C

Topic: Clinical Psychology

Attention deficit hyperactivity disorder (ADHD) is a common diagnosis among children today. A child with ADHD will tend to have extreme difficulty sitting still, paying attention, and following directions, and will become easily distracted. **(C)** is thus correct. (A) is characterized by disorganized and delusional thought patterns, disturbed perceptions, and inappropriate behavior. (B) is characterized by persistent negative mood and lack of interest in activities. Autism, (D), is a disorder that appears in childhood and is characterized by a deficient ability to communicate, socialize, and interact with others. A person with bipolar II disorder, (E), alternates between periods of hypomania and depression.

25. D

Topic: Biological Bases of Behavior

Glutamate is the primary excitatory neurotransmitter in the nervous system; it has the effect of making a post-synaptic neuron more likely to fire an action potential. **(D)** is thus correct. The other choices are incorrect because they list either inhibitory neurotransmitters, ones that make a postsynaptic neuron *less* likely to fire, or mixed neurotransmitters, whose effects are determined by the receptor type on the postsynaptic neuron.

26. C

Topic: Scientific Foundations of Psychology

The null hypothesis is the assertion that no relationship exists between the variables of interest in the study. In this case, the null hypothesis would be that there is no relationship between past attendance of the ALP and high school GPA. In other words, past ALP students and non-ALP students will perform similarly, as suggested correctly in **(C)**. (A) and (B) are incorrect because they are expressions of the alternative hypothesis, what the researchers expected to find. (D) is incorrect because the study examined former ALP students, not current ones. (E) is incorrect because it is too broad; the study only examined a single program.

27. D

Topic: Scientific Foundations of Psychology

The p-value is a measure that indicates the probability that the null hypothesis is true based on the results of the study. More specifically, it describes the probability that the results of the experiment occurred due to random chance. The lower the p-value, the more confident one can be that the results of the experiment are statistically significant. A p-value of 0.045 means that there is only a 4.5% chance that the results are due to chance and a 95.5% chance that they are not, so **(D)** is correct. (A) and (E) are incorrect because they directly contradict the results of the t-test. (B) and (C) are incorrect because they misinterpret the meaning of p-value.

28. D

Topic: Scientific Foundations of Psychology

If only high-achieving students are admitted into the ALP, the claim that the program itself was the cause of students' improved high-school performance would be weakened. There would be no way to distinguish whether the program helps its students to perform better or whether its students were already high-performing to begin with. The results of the study would likely lead the researchers to conclude that the ALP helps academic performance, but the hypothetical in the question stem would weaken that conclusion, making **(D)** correct. (A) is incorrect because it suggests the opposite. (B) and (E) are incorrect because they misstate the likely conclusion of the study. (C) is incorrect because the hypothetical situation is indeed relevant to the study's conclusion.

29. A

Topic: Scientific Foundations of Psychology

If the original study's claims are unable to be reproduced by multiple other studies, it is likely that this study's results were due to chance, meaning that the null hypothesis (that there were no high-school performance differences between ALP and non-ALP students) was wrongly rejected. This is known as a false positive, or type I error, as stated correctly in **(A)**. (B) is incorrect because type II error is a false negative, the improper rejection of a relationship between the variables in the study. (C) is incorrect because there were no placebos administered in the study. (D) is incorrect because coding was not necessary to operationalize the variables in the study. (E) is incorrect because there is no suggestion that the participants in the original study were even aware that they were being studied: the original researchers only needed to look at existing academic records to gather data.

30. E

Topic: Motivation, Emotion, and Personality

Maslow arranges human needs in a hierarchy of five levels. According to Maslow, it is very difficult, if not impossible, to address higher-level needs before more basic needs are met. Creativity, along with self-fulfillment and personal growth, is a higher-order need found at the top level of the hierarchy, self-actualization; **(E)** is correct. Esteem needs are directly below self-actualization and include achievement, social status, and responsibility; (A) is incorrect. Physiological needs, including food, water, sex, and sleep, are the most basic needs at the bottom of the hierarchy, so (B) is incorrect. Intrinsic is not represented in Maslow's hierarchy of needs but instead refers to behavior that is motivated by internal satisfaction; (C) is incorrect. Love and belonging needs such as family and relationships are psychological, occurring after safety and before esteem. (D) is incorrect.

31. B

Topic: Biological Bases of Behavior

Neuroplasticity is the ability of the brain to make lasting changes over time and is responsible for recovery after traumatic injury. Neuroplasticity tends to peak earlier in life, during infancy and childhood. While a hemispherectomy would likely permanently disable an adult, whose brain would be unable to adapt to losing such a large quantity of developed brain tissue, a child's brain would be much more likely to adapt to the change, modifying itself to take over functions ordinarily performed by the missing half. **(B)** is thus correct. (A) is incorrect because neuroplasticity tends to be higher in children, not lower. (C) and (D) refer to speed of neurotransmission, which is most impacted by presence of myelination and by aging. Speed of neurotransmission is not directly related to recovery from trauma, though there are some declines in processing and neurotransmission speeds seen with advanced age. So, while

children and young adults may have relatively fast neurotransmission of some signals compared to adults, this wouldn't be expected to have a major impact on recovery from traumatic brain injury or surgery. (E) is incorrect because important functions are performed by both hemispheres of the brain.

32. C

Topic: Motivation, Emotion, and Personality

Basic motivations like hunger and thirst are controlled by the hypothalamus. **(C)** is thus correct. (A) is incorrect because the thalamus relays sensory information. (B) is incorrect because the medulla controls autonomic behavior, such as breathing and heart rate. (D) is incorrect because the frontal lobe regulates higher-order processes. (E) is incorrect because the temporal lobe is involved with language and hearing.

33. C

Topic: Scientific Foundations of Psychology

For results of scientific research to be considered significant and robust, the results must hold true for more than one set of subjects. It is vital that researchers repeat the work of others to determine if results apply to a larger population than the relatively small sample in the original study. This process is known as replication, **(C)**. Random sampling, (A), and the double-blind procedure, (E), are important to experimental design, but neither one requires repeating a study. Correlational research, (B), and naturalistic observation, (D), are two other types of research, distinct from experimentation.

34. E

Topic: Social Psychology

In actor-observer bias, people tend to attribute their own failures to external factors, while they attribute others' failures to internal processes. This describes precisely the scenario in the question stem, making **(E)** correct. The halo effect, (A), is the tendency to see someone in a positive light no matter what. The recency effect, (B), is a cognitive term concerning short-term memory. Social loafing, (C), is the idea that one works less hard when working with others. (D) refers to a situation in which a group makes decisions based on a desire for group harmony rather than on accurate analysis.

35. D

Topic: Clinical Psychology

One of the benefits of diagnostic labeling is that labels can help healthcare professionals accurately outline treatment programs. **(D)** is correct since this choice represents something that is NOT a drawback. Drawbacks of labeling include the possible stigmatization of particular disorders and the individuals suffering from them, as well as the creation of biased perceptions. (A), (C), and (E) are incorrect. Also, when a person is labeled as having a disorder, the person's individual differences are often clouded by the overuse of the condition's label. (B) is incorrect.

36. C

Topic: Cognitive Psychology

Divergent thinking refers to the capacity to explore multiple avenues of thought when investigating a problem. This describes precisely the skill specified in the question stem. **(C)** is correct. Neural plasticity, (A), refers to the brain's internal ability to change over time, a process that would not happen during a class period. Factor analysis, (B), and predictive validity, (D), are both terms related to designing psychometric tests. Convergent thinking, (E), looks for one possible correct solution to a problem, making it the opposite of divergent thinking.

37. E

Topic: Learning

Salespeople paid on commission are unable to predict when reinforcement is going to occur. Thus, the behavior is on a variable ratio schedule of reinforcement, in which sporadic but unpredictable reinforcement leads to maintenance of behavior even if the reinforcement comes very infrequently. **(E)** is correct. (A) and (C) are incorrect because the schedule of reinforcement is not fixed, either with respect to ratio or interval. (B) is incorrect because negative reinforcement is the removal of an adverse stimulus in order to increase the frequency of a behavior. (D) is incorrect because positive reinforcement is the presentation of a pleasant stimulus in order to increase the frequency of a behavior. While a commission is a type of positive reinforcement for making a sale, the question stem emphasizes the infrequent nature of these reinforcements, which makes **(E)** the better answer.

38. C

Topic: Cognitive Psychology

The other exams are useful, but the Wechsler scales (which include the Wechsler Preschool and Primary Scale of Intelligence, or WPPSI, and the Wechsler Intelligence Scale for Children, or WISC) are the measures of choice among school psychologists for assessing developmental delays. **(C)** is thus correct. (A) is a commonly used test to measure IQ (intelligence quotient), but it does not provide as much useful data to school psychologists as do the Wechsler scales. The MMPI-2 (Minnesota Multiphasic Personality Inventory) is the most widely used personality test, but it is not often used to measure students' developmental delays. (B) is incorrect. The Thematic Apperception Test (TAT) is a test in which people express their feelings and interests through stories. (D) is incorrect. IRT, which stands for "item response theory," is a component of test design, but not an actual test to measure development, making (E) incorrect.

39. E

Topic: Motivation, Emotion, and Personality

The James-Lange theory maintains that a physiological response takes place before an emotion is experienced. **(E)** is thus correct. (A) is concerned with how one thinks about and uses categories to structure his or her social life and experiences. According to the Cannon-Bard theory, (B), emotion precedes physiological response. In this scenario, the Cannon-Bard theory would likely say that the person hears the scream, feels afraid, and therefore runs away. (C) suggests that one's emotional response is determined by his or her cognitive interpretation and physiological response to a situation. (D) is the principle that information is processed both consciously and unconsciously at the same time.

40. B

Topic: Cognitive Psychology

Elizabeth Loftus conducted groundbreaking work on the unreliability of memory, including the creation of false memories and what is known as the misinformation effect, in which eyewitnesses seem to change their recollection of an event based on leading questions or the presentation of other types of misinformation. **(B)** is thus correct. (A) is incorrect because Bartlett studied memory distortions, but not with eyewitnesses. (C) is incorrect because Weber studied sensory processes, and (D) and (E) are incorrect because Skinner and Watson were behavioral psychologists, so they focused more on behavior than on memory.

41. D

Topic: Motivation, Emotion, and Personality

According to Freud and Jung, during the phallic stage, a child might suffer from an uncomfortable attraction to the parent of the opposite sex (the Oedipus and Electra complexes). This is purportedly an unconscious attraction but one that causes a great deal of anxiety. **(D)** is thus correct. (A) is the first stage of development, during which a child tends to discover the nature of an object by tasting it. Occurring after the phallic stage, the latency stage, (B), is when a child focuses on learning, play, and social skill development. (C) is the final stage, which starts during adolescence and is characterized by the development of sexual impulses on a conscious level. The anal stage, (E), generally occurs when a child is two years old. The child starts learning socially acceptable behavior, including toilet training.

42. D

Topic: Biological Bases of Behavior

Damage to Wernicke's area would result in what has been called receptive aphasia, in which an individual has difficulty comprehending speech. **(D)** is correct. Damage to Broca's area would result in speech production difficulties, making (A) incorrect. (B) is incorrect because dyslexia is a reading disorder, (C) is incorrect because aphagia is a swallowing disorder, and (E) is incorrect because dyspraxia is another kind of language production disorder.

43. D

Topic: Social Psychology

Zimbardo's experiment lasted only six days, but it turned regular college students into sadistic guards and compliant prisoners, supposedly due to the deindividuation that arose after assigning those social roles to the students. **(D)** is thus correct. The experiment suggested that the power of the situation can have enormous effects on human behavior and mental processes, irrespective of inborn inclinations from traits, (A), or genetics, (B). Learned

helplessness, (C), only refers to passive and helpless behavior when an individual gives up after continuous adversity, which may apply to the meekness of the "prisoners," but not to the cruelty of the "guards." Groupthink, (E), involves conformity to a group, which is not applicable in this case.

44. C

Topic: Cognitive Psychology

In such a problem, a person needs to think creatively and not be bound by the normal uses of an object. Functional fixedness is the tendency to think of objects as having only a single, conventional use; the described experiment would measure participants' capacity to go beyond functional fixedness and think creatively. Thus, **(C)** is correct. A demand characteristic, (A), is a cue picked up on by a participant of an experiment that causes the participant to act differently, perhaps in a way that the participant thinks the researcher wants. (B) is incorrect because the problem requires creative thinking in particular, not intelligence in general. (D) relates to how someone processes the meaning of a word; for example, a person may comprehend the meaning of an unfamiliar word if it is associated or linked to a more common word. (E) is a phenomenon that occurs when a person or animal gives up trying to do something due to a lack of hope for success.

45. C

Topic: Motivation, Emotion, and Personality

Trait theorists believe that human personalities are a collection of fixed characteristics (like introversion or curiosity) that may vary slightly but in general remain constant over time. **(C)** correctly reflects the primary criticism leveled against trait theory, which is that people will often act differently depending on the situations they find themselves in. (E) is incorrect because trait theory includes traits that can be viewed as positive or negative, while (A) is a criticism of psychoanalytic theory, (B) of behavioral theory, and (D) of social-cognitive theories of personality.

46. C

Topic: Clinical Psychology

Client-centered therapy focuses on the client, creating a safe space for him or her to express what he or she feels and thinks without judgment. This is substantially different from psychoanalysis, in which the expression of feelings is subject to more scrutiny by the therapist, who may believe that there are deeper, unconscious issues at stake. **(C)** is thus correct. The other answer choices present characteristics that are commonly associated with psychoanalysis.

47. D

Topic: Sensation and Perception

Many of our perceptual abilities are rooted in the fact that we use prior knowledge to interpret our experiences in the world. Visual illusions occur because our typically reliable visual system is fooled by some cue that is normally reliable with respect to a particular perceptual experience. **(D)** is thus correct. The other choices are incorrect because they list standard visual cues.

48. C

Topic: Clinical Psychology

Electroconvulsive therapy is a procedure in which an electric shock is passed through a patient's brain to help alleviate depression. The procedure is rarely used, but it is effective in some cases because it directly affects the biological functioning of the brain. **(C)** is thus correct. A token economy, (A), is a system for reinforcing desirable behaviors with points or tokens (similar to coins) that can be traded in for a reward. (B) is a process in which responses, or behaviors, are learned based on positive or negative consequences. (D) is a learning process in which a neutral stimulus is paired with a stimulus that triggers a reflexive response until the neutral stimulus by itself starts to trigger a similar response. Insight therapy, (E), is a clinical technique in which a therapist helps patients understand how their thoughts, feelings, actions, and events from the past are influencing their current mental well-being.

49. B

Topic: Learning

Bandura discovered in the famous Bobo doll experiment that if a child witnesses an adult acting in an aggressive manner toward a doll, the child is more likely to act that way toward the doll too. **(B)** is thus correct. One of the remarkable conclusions of Bandura's experiment was that a child did not have to be frustrated before committing

an aggressive act, which makes (A) incorrect. (C) is incorrect because Bandura's results suggested that boys were more aggressive than girls. (D) and (E) are incorrect because Bandura's results indicated that, given an aggressive adult model, a child could act in a hostile manner.

50. A

Topic: Motivation, Emotion, and Personality

Projection is a defense mechanism in which an individual believes that other people possess undesirable characteristics that the individual him- or herself possesses. **(A)** is thus correct. The other choices present different defense mechanisms not described in the question stem. (B) occurs when one strives to make up for unconscious fears or beliefs, such as feelings of inferiority. (C) occurs when someone strongly rejects, or denies, the existence of a negative impulse. (D) occurs when someone deflects an impulse from its true source to a less threatening source. (E) occurs when someone replaces an unacceptable impulse with a more socially acceptable behavior or action; for example, if someone is angry, instead of engaging in a violent act, the person might engage in athletics.

51. A

Topic: Scientific Foundations of Psychology

In contrast to Freud, Jung maintained that aspects of the unconscious belonged not merely to individuals, but were collectively shared by all human beings. **(A)** is thus correct. (B) is incorrect because Skinner developed the theory of operant conditioning, while (C) is incorrect because Wundt developed structuralism. (D) is incorrect because Freud developed psychoanalysis (classical conditioning, in contrast, was first demonstrated in experiments by Pavlov). (E) is incorrect because Piaget was a developmental psychologist, not a clinical psychologist.

52. B

Topic: Motivation, Emotion, and Personality

The concept of homeostasis suggests that human beings need to maintain a proper physiological and psychological balance to ensure mental and physical health. **(B)** is thus correct. (A) is a term that describes an alternative, naturalistic system of medicine. Entropy, (C), is a term related to the amount of disorder within a system. (D) is a term that describes a feeling of satisfaction with one's current level of achievement. Cognitive dissonance, (E), is the idea that attitude change is motivated by a desire to reduce tension caused by inconsistencies between thoughts and behaviors.

53. E

Topic: Clinical Psychology

Agoraphobia is a type of anxiety disorder in which a person is afraid to leave his or her home. This describes precisely the patient in the question stem, making **(E)** correct. (A) is incorrect because a personality disorder is typically not recognized as an impairment by the one suffering from it, but the patient in the question complains about having an issue to his therapist. (B) is incorrect because schizophrenia is characterized by delusions, hallucinations, and other symptoms that the patient does not suffer from. (C) is incorrect because OCD is a disorder involving obsessive thoughts and compulsive, anxiety-reducing behavior. (D) is incorrect because somatic symptom disorders occur when psychological symptoms are manifested as physiological ailments or disabilities.

54. A

Topic: Developmental Psychology

Accommodation occurs when a child develops a new schema to account for differences in experience. In this case, the child accommodates by differentiating the category of women into "Mommy" and other ladies. **(A)** is thus correct. (B) is incorrect because adaptation is the general process of attempting to understand and fit into one's environment. (C) and (D) are incorrect because organization and equilibration are both processes of "fixing" existing schemata. (E) is incorrect because assimilation refers to the process of fitting a new experience into an existing schema.

55. E

Topic: Developmental Psychology

Authoritative parents demand a lot of their children but also offer them a lot of emotional support, which tends to produce children who have high self-esteem and good social skills. **(E)** is thus correct. (A) and (B) are incorrect because indulgent or permissive parenting is responsive but not demanding, often leading to impulsive and ego-centric children. (C) and (D) are incorrect because strict

or authoritarian parenting is demanding but not responsive, often diminishing the self-esteem and social skills of children.

56. A

Topic: Social Psychology

To create an understanding of the world, psychologists are interested in why people behave the way they do. The role of attribution theory is to understand how people interpret the motivations for behavior. **(A)** is correct. While attribution theory may conclude that people sometimes have misconceptions about others, (B) distorts the goal of this theory. (C), (D), and (E) are related to attribution theory, but none of these accurately characterizes the theory's main goal.

57. B

Topic: Sensation and Perception

The law of closure is the tendency to fill in gaps in recognizable patterns, perceiving discontinuous figures as wholes, thus eliminating (A). The law of proximity is perceiving objects that are close to each other as forming a group, which fits Tom's perspective in the question stem, making **(B)** correct. Kinesthesis is a somatic sense of the movement of your body in space, which makes (C) incorrect. (D) can be eliminated because the Müller-Lyer illusion consists of two line segments, one with arrows pointing inward and one with arrows pointing outward. (E) is incorrect because both Tom and Judy are influenced by Gestalt principles, with Tom using the law of proximity and Judy using the law of similarity.

58. A

Topic: Clinical Psychology

Early antipsychotic drugs—chlorpromazine in particular—had very strong effects on the muscles. The drug led to twitching and the development of tics reminiscent of Parkinson's disease. **(A)** is correct. (B) is incorrect because antipsychotics do not mimic nicotine addiction. Antipsychotic medicine has not been shown to cause blindness, making (C) incorrect. (D) is incorrect because Alzheimer's is a distinct neurocognitive disorder not associated with the effects of antipsychotics. (E) is a language disorder marked by difficulty speaking, which is not a problem associated with antipsychotic mediation.

59. D

Topic: Cognitive Psychology

Because Barry is citing an outside factor to explain the consequences of his behavior, he is suggesting an external locus of control. **(D)** is thus correct. If Barry had an internal locus of control, he would offer reasons based on his own behaviors or qualities, such as a failure to spend enough time studying; thus, (A) is incorrect. (B) is incorrect because top-down processing is when people begin with the big picture before focusing on details. (C) is incorrect because bottom-up processing is when people begin with the small details before focusing on the big picture. (E) is incorrect because heuristics are fast decision-making tools that are based on limited information, which is not what is described in the question stem.

60. A

Topic: Clinical Psychology

For addictions, aversion therapy, in which addictive behaviors are paired with unpleasant stimuli, is one common treatment. This type of classical conditioning can reduce the desire to repeat the addictive behavior. **(A)** is thus correct. The remaining choices are not often used for treating addictions. (B) is sometimes used to treat severe depression and mania. (C) is a technique designed to help clients work through their unconscious thoughts and emotions. (D) is a method that helps clients examine their relationships and interactions in hopes of gaining insight. (E) is a type of therapy that offers a supportive and nurturing environment, giving the client unconditional positive regard and allowing any thoughts and feelings to be expressed.

61. D

Topic: Biological Bases of Behavior

Of the options presented, only a PET (positron emission tomography) scan shows the activity occurring in specific brain areas. **(D)** is thus correct. (A) and (C) are incorrect because X-rays and MRIs can only show the structure of the brain. (B) is incorrect because a brain lesion is a type of damage to a particular part of the brain, not an imaging technique. (E) is incorrect because an EEG can only show the brain's overall electrical activity, not the activity in specific regions.

62. C

Topic: Social Psychology

According to the research on social facilitation, when you're in the presence of an audience, your performance improves on tasks that are simple or that you've practiced extensively, making **(C)** correct and (B) and (D) incorrect. Your performance on difficult and unfamiliar tasks actually tends to get worse in the presence of an audience, so (A) and (E) are incorrect.

63. C

Topic: Sensation and Perception

The first major psychological theory of color vision was the trichromatic theory, which maintained that the retina only codes for three colors. The later opponent-process theory allowed for a more complete understanding of color vision by explaining how human beings use a variety of oppositions to perceive color. **(C)** is thus correct. (A), (B), and (D) are incorrect because the frequency, localization, and volley theories are all related to hearing, not sight. (E) is incorrect because, as noted, the trichromatic theory was the original theory of vision.

64. E

Topic: Cognitive Psychology

The primacy effect is the tendency of people to remember the first several items in a long list better than items that occupy other positions in the list. **(E)** is thus correct. (A) is incorrect because selective attention (the tendency of people to pay attention to some parts of their experience more than others) is typically associated with perception, not memory. (B) is incorrect because the recency effect is the tendency to better remember the last items in a list, the ones that were presented most recently. (C) is incorrect because short-term memory is the capacity to retain a small amount of information for a short period of time, but this tends to be limited to fewer than 10 items; in addition, there is no psychological phenomenon called "the short-term memory effect." (D) is incorrect because the serial position effect refers to the combination of the primacy and recency effects (that is, the tendency for people to remember the first and last items better than the middle items), but the question stem only specifies that Freddy remembers the first 10 letters, making **(E)** the better answer.

65. A

Topic: Clinical Psychology

Lithium salts, though originally developed in the 1950s, are still a common treatment for individuals suffering from bipolar disorders. **(A)** is correct. The other disorders listed tend to be treated with drugs developed in the last 30 years or so, such as SSRIs (selective serotonin reuptake inhibitors) like Prozac (fluoxetine), used for major depressive disorder.

66. B

Topic: Motivation, Emotion, and Personality

The general adaptation syndrome occurs when the body prepares itself to deal with stress. Individuals become hypersensitive to stressful situations and struggle with even small annoyances. **(B)** is thus correct. (A) refers to a scale that measures how serious a mental illness may be. (C) is a theory of color vision. The Hawthorne effect, (D), describes how subjects of a study alter their behavior due to their awareness of being observed. Systematic desensitization, (E), is a type of exposure therapy used to treat phobias.

67. D

Topic: Developmental Psychology

According to Piaget, the ability to recognize conservation of quantities like mass is a key cognitive skill. A child who can tell that the amount of clay does not change even as its shape is molded recognizes the conservation of mass. **(D)** is thus correct. (A) and (E) are incorrect because the conservation of mass is typically recognized in Piaget's concrete operational stage, not the sensorimotor or preoperational stages. (B) is incorrect because children up through age two are typically in the sensorimotor stage, not the concrete operational stage. (C) is incorrect because children in the concrete operational stage are typically capable of learning some complex logical skills.

68. D

Topic: Motivation, Emotion, and Personality

Mr. Ramirez offers food in exchange for participation on the team, and the number of options increases with the team's performance. Because this provides an extrinsic, rather than intrinsic, source of motivation, **(D)** is correct

and (C) is incorrect. (A) and (B) are eliminated because introverted and extraverted refer to personality traits and not a type of motivation. Instinctive refers to inborn, fixed patterns of behavior that present in response to certain stimuli and are often species-specific; (E) is incorrect.

69. B

Topic: Motivation, Emotion, and Personality

Regression is the act of reverting to an earlier stage of emotional development in response to stress. A high school student throwing a tantrum would be an example of regression, making **(B)** correct. Sublimation is a defense mechanism marked by transforming an undesirable feeling or drive into a socially acceptable one, eliminating (A). (C) and (D) are incorrect because displacement is the defense mechanism marked by redirecting an unwanted feeling from one target to another, while reaction formation is marked by turning an unwanted thought or feeling into its opposite. Lastly, (E) is eliminated because rationalization is a defense mechanism marked by justifying unacceptable behaviors to make them more acceptable to yourself or others and to hide your true motivations.

70. D

Topic: Motivation, Emotion, and Personality

A projective type personality test is based on the idea that people will interpret ambiguous stimuli in ways that reflect their unconscious thoughts and feelings. The only projective test on the list is the Thematic Apperception Test, making **(D)** correct. The Myers-Briggs Type Indicator, MMPI-2, Beck Depression Inventory, and Keirsey Temperament Sorter are all objective (not projective) personality tests, eliminating (A), (B), (C), and (E).

71. C

Topic: Developmental Psychology

According to Baumrind, parents have different styles of raising their children. The authoritarian parent exerts a great deal of control, while the permissive parent permits just about anything. The authoritative parent has control, yet is willing to allow the child to explore the world and make choices. **(C)** is correct. Baumrind's three styles are still widely accepted in psychology today, but the other choices do not describe generally accepted parenting styles.

72. C

Topic: Clinical Psychology

The DSM (*Diagnostic and Statistical Manual of Mental Disorders*) is important to clinical psychologists and psychiatrists mainly because they use the book to apply a consistent system of diagnosing disorders. Generally speaking, the symptoms are clearly set out in the book to allow two independent professionals to see a patient and come to the same diagnosis from the symptoms presented. **(C)** is thus correct. (A) is incorrect because the DSM focuses on the diagnosis of mental disorders rather than their etiology (that is, the study of their causes). (B) is incorrect because the system of assessment in the DSM is not primarily biological, but relies on many symptoms that manifest psychologically. (D) is incorrect because the DSM does not endorse the behavioral perspective over other theoretical approaches. (E) is incorrect because the DSM concerns psychological disorders in particular, not personality in general.

73. A

Topic: Social Psychology

Social loafing occurs when an individual uses membership in a group to avoid taking personal responsibility, with the expectation that others in the group will be able to pick up the slack. **(A)** is thus correct. Groupthink, (B), refers to a situation in which a group makes decisions based on a desire for group harmony rather than on accurate analysis. A self-fulfilling prophecy, (C), is a belief that comes true because someone is acting as if it is already true. The Hawthorne effect, (D), describes how subjects of a study alter their behavior due to their awareness of being observed. Deindividuation, (E), is a mental state in which a member of a group becomes submerged in the group and loses his or her individual identity. The person may then engage in behavior that he or she would not normally do.

74. C

Topic: Biological Bases of Behavior

Paradoxical sleep occurs during REM (rapid eye movement) sleep, when brain waves are very similar to a waking state. A person in paradoxical sleep is probably dreaming and is typically easily awoken. Human beings seem to need to enter this stage of sleep because, if denied paradoxical sleep, people will enter REM more quickly and remain in it longer than normal the next time they fall sleep. The term "paradoxical" applies because it would appear that humans need sleep to rest, yet the brain seems more active than at rest during this stage. **(C)** is thus correct. (A) is incorrect because the EEG pattern suggests greater-than-expected activity, not lesser. (B) is incorrect because REM sleep is not called "paradoxical" simply because it is easier to wake people in that stage, but rather because it looks more like waking brain activity, as already noted. (D) is incorrect because it is factually inaccurate; as noted, paradoxical sleep seems to be necessary. (E) is incorrect because psychologists know that dreaming occurs during this stage.

75. A

Topic: Scientific Foundations of Psychology

In a simple experiment such as the one described in the question stem, the experimental group and the control group will be placed in almost identical circumstances, with the only difference being that the experimental group receives a treatment while the control group does not. To better achieve this effect, control groups often receive a placebo, like the ineffective pill given to the second group described in the question stem. **(A)** is thus correct. (B) is incorrect because a random sample is a group selected at random to be representative of a larger population. Typically, only after a random sample is selected would it then be divided into experimental and control groups. (C) is incorrect because a case study is an in-depth investigation of one particular subject, often just a single patient. (D) is incorrect because the first group is the experimental group. (E) is incorrect because the independent variable is the quantity or quality that is manipulated in the experiment; in this case, it would be the presence (or absence) of the drug.

76. B

Topic: Scientific Foundations of Psychology

Bandura is famous for his work on social learning theory (what is now called social cognitive theory), which includes the concept of vicarious reinforcement. This theory maintains that individuals can learn not simply by being directly punished or reinforced, but also by watching others receive punishment or reinforcement. **(B)** is thus correct. The other choices are incorrect because Wundt, (A), is primarily known for structuralism; James, (C), for functionalism, the stream of consciousness, and the James-Lange theory of emotions; Watson, (D), for behaviorism and classical conditioning; and Skinner, (E), for behaviorism and operant conditioning.

77. B

Topic: Clinical Psychology

Systematic desensitization is the process of treating a phobia (such as the one described in the question stem) by gradually increasing the intensity of exposure to sources of fear, so that the patient can eventually avoid succumbing to excessive anxiety when presented with objects of fear in the future. **(B)** is correct. (A) is a technique that puts a patient in a fearful but harmless situation to expose the person to a fear for an extended period in order to diminish the fear. (C) describes a technique in which the patient imagines his or her most intense fear for long periods of time with the goal of reducing the fear. The goal of psychoanalysis, (D), is to help the patient uncover the unconscious conflicts that give rise to anxiety. (E) describes a technique that might be used on children to reduce misbehavior.

78. C

Topic: Scientific Foundations of Psychology

Watson's work focused almost exclusively on the role of the environment on behavior. Watson argued that psychologists should reject the notions of consciousness and mental events and instead examine how a person's environment has an impact on his or her subsequent behavior. **(C)** is thus correct. A biological approach, (A), focuses on how genetics and physiology affect behavior and mental processes. A social approach, (B), focuses on how people influence and are influenced by other people. The humanistic approach, (D), focuses on a person's inner capacities for growth and self-fulfillment. Cognitive psychologists, (E), seek to understand how people process information, including perception, thoughts, language, memory, and attention.

79. D

Topic: Developmental Psychology

According to Vygotsky, a child's zone of proximal development (ZPD) is the area in which a child can solve problems or perform tasks with guidance that he or she would otherwise be unable to complete. **(D)** is thus correct. Piaget's theory of conservation, (A), states that children in the concrete operational stage start to realize that when a material changes shape or direction, the material does not fundamentally change. (B) concerns the development of personality as a child passes through distinct psychosexual stages. (C) is incorrect because Skinner's theory of operant conditioning concerns the use of reinforcement and punishment to alter the frequency of behaviors. Wundt's theory of consciousness, (E), involved using introspection to better understand the structural elements of the mind.

80. B

Topic: Biological Bases of Behavior

A circadian rhythm is a physiological cycle that people develop if they are on consistent schedules. In such cycles, body temperature, heart rate, and so on will increase or decrease at roughly the same times each day as a way of preparing the body for resting or waking. **(B)** is correct. Narcolepsy is a sleep disorder resulting in an abnormal sleep pattern, making (A) incorrect. (C) refers to a person's regular sleep and wake patterns; normally a person is awake for approximately 16 hours a day and asleep for about 8 hours. Circadian rhythms are related to, but distinct from, sleep-wake cycles. (D) is a term that describes spikes of brain activity that occur during stage 2 of sleep. Cataplexy, (E), is a sudden and uncontrollable muscle weakness that is often triggered by a strong emotion, such as or laughter or excitement.

81. A

Topic: Social Psychology

Cognitive dissonance is a discomfort caused by having beliefs or habits that conflict. When a person is working at a job even though he or she hates it, this will cause a great deal of dissonance. To resolve this, the person might quit or adjust her perspective to emphasize the more enjoyable parts of the job. **(A)** is correct. The remaining choices present more consistent attitudes, and thus do not represent any kind of cognitive dissonance.

82. C

Topic: Sensation and Perception

The fovea is the part of the eye with the greatest degree of visual acuity. Any information that is directed onto the fovea is going to be the information that is most clearly and easily recognized, including color discrimination. **(C)** is correct. Object discrimination occurs in the temporal lobe of the brain, making (A) and (B) incorrect. (D) is incorrect because the fovea is at the center of the retina, not at the periphery. Visual sensitivity, (E), is not uniform across the retina; the retinal cells called the rods and cones differ in how they process incoming stimuli.

83. B

Topic: Learning

Skinner became interested in behaviorism after reading books by Pavlov, Watson, and Thorndike. However, he believed that the emphasis on classical conditioning was missing many of the behaviors that humans and other animals produce. Thus, he coined the term *operant conditioning* to try to describe how operant, or voluntary, behaviors are learned. **(B)** is correct. Watson, (A), is known for his early work on behaviorism, but not for operant conditioning, which came later. Wilhelm Wundt, (C), did some of the earliest work in psychology and is credited with opening the first psychology lab. Piaget, (D), worked on cognitive development, in particular focusing on how children develop. Pavlov, (E), was a physiologist who is famous for his pioneering work on classical conditioning.

84. A

Topic: Biological Bases of Behavior

Endogenous means "naturally occurring," and endorphins are the body's natural response to alleviating pain. Thus, the narcotics that serve to dull pain are similar to these naturally occurring chemicals (albeit more effective). **(A)** is correct. (B) and (C) are stress hormones that prepare the body for fight or flight. (D) is a neurotransmitter that affects mood, sleep, and appetite, and (E) is a precursor

to the neurotransmitter dopamine; neither are considered narcotics.

85. B

Topic: Social Psychology

The point of the Milgram study was to demonstrate that participants were willing to give shocks if they were told to do so by an authority figure. Thus, even in situations in which participants might report they wouldn't do so, Milgram demonstrated that under the right conditions, most participants are willing to do things if they are told to. **(B)** is correct, and (A) and (C) incorrect. People of different levels of moral reasoning were willing to give the shocks, making (D) incorrect. While the original Milgram experiment only tested males, subsequent studies did not show significant differences between males and females, making (E) incorrect.

86. B

Topic: Social Psychology

Diffusion of responsibility occurs when a group of people all believe someone else is going to deal with the situation. If everyone in the group assumes that someone else will report the hit and run, then no one may end up reporting it. **(B)** is correct. Groupthink, (A), occurs when people act in a way to maintain good relations within their group, often resulting in poor decision-making. Altruism, (C), refers to behavior which helps other people more than oneself. Stereotyping, (D), involves adopting beliefs about an individual based on generalized beliefs about a group of which that person is a member. (E) refers to any consequence that leads to an increase in the probability of a behavior occurring again.

87. B

Topic: Cognitive Psychology

The method of loci is a mnemonic technique, or a memory aid, that involves associating whatever needs to be remembered with familiar places or known visual images. A mental map of specific places is an example of the method of loci, making **(B)** correct. (A) is incorrect because state-dependent learning refers to the capacity to remember things when in the same state of consciousness as when they were first learned. Natural language mnemonics, (C), use language to create the mnemonic (such as using HOMES to remember the Great Lakes: Huron, Ontario, Michigan, Erie, and Superior). Chunking, (D), involves grouping information into meaningful units so that they can be better stored. The peg-word method, (E), is a memory aid that involves linking words with numbers.

88. C

Topic: Sensation and Perception

There are multiple theories about how information on pitch is sensed and transmitted at the ear. In Paul's case, damage has occurred to one specific region of the cochlea. According to place theory, different tones are detected by unique locations in the cochlea. If this theory were accurate, you would expect Paul's ear damage to result in decreased detection of a tone or group of tones. **(C)** is thus correct. Temporal theory, (A), holds that pitch is encoded by firing rate of stereocilia, which would not necessarily be affected by damage to only one cochlear region. Likewise, volley theory, (B), holds that the phasic firing of different neurons is required for perception of sound, again meaning that damage to a specific cochlear region may not necessarily result in loss of perception of a specific pitch. Opponent-process theory, (D), and perceptual constancy, (E), both describe vision, not hearing.

89. D

Topic: Scientific Foundations of Psychology

The psychologist here is focused on the client's behavior rather than his or her mental processes. Additionally, she believes that the client's behavior results from environmental influences—in this case, a history of rewards. Since behaviorism is the study of observable behavior and focuses on the influence of environment on behavior, this psychologist is most likely a behaviorist. B.F. Skinner is the only behaviorist among the psychologists listed in the choices, so **(D)** is correct. In contrast, Carl Jung, (A), and Sigmund Freud, (B), were part of the psychodynamic approach; Carl Rogers, (C), was a humanistic psychologist; and Charles Darwin, (E), is known for his influence on evolutionary psychology.

90. A

Topic: Cognitive Psychology

Proactive interference occurs when old information intrudes on one's ability to recall newly learned information. **(A)** is correct. Retroactive interference, (C), occurs when one is trying to remember old information, but new information gets in the way. Both proactive and retroactive interference are components of interference theory, (D). (B) and (E) are unrelated to this specific scenario.

91. D

Topic: Learning

From the experiment description, it is evident that the food pellet serves as a positive reinforcement, since the graph demonstrates that the frequency of the behavior is increasing, and the food pellet is being added and not removed (as in negative reinforcement) following the press. This eliminates (B) and (C), neither of which identifies the food pellet as a positive reinforcer. Immediacy refers to the principle in which the more quickly the reinforcement is delivered, the more likely behavior will occur, which certainly applies to the described scenario, making **(D)** correct. (A) and (E) are incorrect because decreasing the time delay will actually make the pellet a stronger reinforcer. The size principle refers to the the idea that a bigger reinforcement is more likely to produce the desired behavior, so it does not apply here. The satiation principle refers to an increase in the effectiveness of a reinforcer due to a longer time of deprivation, which also does not apply.

92. C

Topic: Learning

The graph illustrates that the rat is increasing the number of button presses with each trial, even though the conditions and time frame for pellet release remain the same. As such, the answer should include an explanation that reflects this trend. (A) is incorrect because coping consists of the behavioral and cognitive strategies used to manage stress, not increase it. (B) and (D) can be eliminated because avoidance refers to preventing potential negative effects in the future, and escape means eliminating a negative effect that has already occurred. Expectancy refers to the anticipation of future events or relationships based on past experiences. In the setting of the experiment, because the rat has associated pressing a button with the release of a food pellet, the expectancy principle is increasing this behavior; **(C)** is correct. (E) is incorrect because the experiment described in the stimulus is an example of operant, not classical, conditioning.

93. B

Topic: Motivation, Emotion, and Personality

According to Jung, we have several archetypes in our collective unconscious. These are patterns of behavior or images that have an impact on our behavior. Jung referred to the feminine side of men as the anima, making **(B)** correct. A person's persona, (A), is the image that he or she wishes to project to others. The animus, (C), is what Jung referred to as the masculine side of women. The shadow archetype, (D), represents a person's negative aspects that he or she does not want to share with others. Self, (E), for Jung signified the unification of consciousness and unconsciousness in a person, thus representing the psyche as a whole.

94. B

Topic: Learning

Negative reinforcement is the removal of adverse stimuli for the sake of increasing the frequency of a behavior. Laetitia's father is offering to remove the adverse situation of her being grounded in order for her to do her chores, a clear case of negative reinforcement, **(B)**. (A) is incorrect because positive reinforcement consists of supplying a desirable stimulus in order to increase behavior. (C) is incorrect because punishment results in a decrease in behavior. (D) and (E) are incorrect because the example in the question stem involves operant conditioning, not classical conditioning.

95. B

Topic: Clinical Psychology

Bipolar I disorder is characterized by manic episodes, which sometimes alternate with depressive episodes. **(B)** is thus correct. (A) is incorrect because bipolar I

disorder is not a severe form of depression. (C) is incorrect because schizophrenia is a completely different disorder. (D) is incorrect because bipolar I disorder affects only about one to three percent of Americans. (E) is incorrect because psychoanalysis has not been shown to be particularly effective at treating bipolar I disorder.

96. C

Topic: Sensation and Perception

In the visual system, two kinds of cells on the retina capture photons of light: rods and cones. Cones (located mostly in the fovea) are primarily responsible for color, and rods (located mostly in the periphery) are responsible for black and white. Cones require more light to activate than rods, so in a dark room black-and-white vision will improve, while color vision diminishes. That means (A) is incorrect and **(C)** is correct. (B) is incorrect because it takes some time for the eye to become adjusted to darkness; improvement in black-and-white vision will not occur immediately. (D) is incorrect because black-and-white vision eventually improves in darker conditions. (E) is incorrect because a small amount of ambient light in a dark room will still allow for limited black-and-white vision.

97. E

Topic: Biological Bases of Behavior

The occipital lobe contains the visual cortex, where visual information is processed. **(E)** is correct. (A) is incorrect because the cerebellum is associated with motor control and balance. (B) is incorrect because the frontal lobe is associated with executive control functions. (C) is incorrect because the parietal lobe is associated with sensory processing and integration. (D) is incorrect because the temporal lobe is associated with hearing and language comprehension.

98. B

Topic: Sensation and Perception

The concept of binocular disparity suggests that because a person has two eyes, each with slightly different views of the world, he or she is able to see depth. A person fuses together the information from the two images to create an image with depth. **(B)** is correct. (A) is the phenomenon in which your eyes rotate inwards to focus on an object based on how far away the object is. For the same reason, (C) is incorrect. (D) refers to how *sharp* a person's vision is, and (E) relates to a person's range of vision.

99. C

Topic: Scientific Foundations of Psychology

While it was first developed by Wundt, Titchener expanded the method known as introspection. Long before the advent of brain imaging technology, Titchener wanted to know how brains worked, and to do that he asked subjects to report their moment-by-moment sensations. With this data, Titchener went on to develop the theory of structuralism, which suggested how the mind is structured from its most basic elements. **(C)** is therefore correct. While Wundt and Titchener developed structuralism, (A) is too broad to be correct. Spaced practice, (B), is a learning strategy in which something is learned over several short sessions rather than all at once. (D) is also a learning strategy involving repetition and analysis. (E) is a method of psychotherapy developed by Freud that seeks to help clients gain insight into and work through unconscious thoughts and emotions presumed to cause mental problems.

100. B

Topic: Developmental Psychology

Developmental psychologists specialize in trying to understand the development of mental processes and behavior over a lifetime. **(B)** is correct. (A) would be carried out by a cognitive psychologist, (C) by a behaviorist, (D) by a biological psychologist or neuroscientist, and (E) by a social psychologist.

SECTION II

1. This question is worth 7 points, 3 for Part A, which connects the concepts to the situation, and 4 for Part B, which requires explaining how the terms might help Alana cope with her frustration. The following is a sample student response that would receive full credit, with indications of where points would be awarded in parentheses:

   Procedural memory (also known as implicit or non-declarative memory) is used when a person is actively doing something he or she knows how to do. Alana has not yet learned how to perform fencing movements, and so she has not developed the procedural memory that she has with other motor movements like walking and catching a ball, but this will likely improve over time with practice. **(1 POINT)**

   Displacement is a defense mechanism, identified by Sigmund Freud, in which people direct their emotions, such as anger, at someone or something other than the source of that emotion. Alana is displacing her anger (resulting from the difficulty she is having with her fencing lessons) onto her parents, who serve as a convenient target even though they are not responsible for her frustration. **(1 POINT)**

   Operant conditioning happens when an association is formed between a behavior and a consequence. A pleasant consequence is a reinforcement, which increases the behavior's frequency, while an unpleasant consequence is a punishment, which decreases the behavior's frequency. In this case, Alana's parents are using operant conditioning by rewarding Alana's behavior of attending fencing practice with ice cream, a positive reinforcement. **(1 POINT)**

   Metacognition involves thinking about one's own thinking or being aware of one's own awareness. It is a higher-order thinking skill and involves self-awareness about one's own skills and development. If Alana was engaging in metacognition about her skills, she would realize that becoming an expert at fencing takes more than just a short time practicing, and that she should adjust her expectations about improving to avoid more frustration in the future. **(1 POINT)**

   Scaffolding is a term applicable to Vygotsky's zone of proximal development, the area in which students are capable of learning with the assistance of a teacher. In scaffolding, a teacher provides some of the structure necessary to solve a problem or perform a task, requiring the student to fill in the remaining gaps to complete it, eventually enabling the student to perform entirely on her own. Alana should ask her fencing instructor for additional scaffolding in guiding her through the new techniques, since she is just starting out, with the understanding that this assistance will gradually be reduced as Alana becomes more proficient. **(1 POINT)**

   Intrinsic motivation refers to an internal desire to accomplish something, without the need for external rewards like money or trophies. Alana will need to develop internal motivation to keep fencing or she might remain unhappy and continue to act out, even if her parents are taking her out for ice cream. In fact, by providing an external motivator, the ice cream, Alana's parents might be reducing her intrinsic motivation to fence. **(1 POINT)**

   Social learning is our ability to change our behavior based on experiences that we see happen to others. Alana could take time to watch not only her instructor but also the other students, and she may learn to model their behavior in order to improve her own performance. **(1 POINT)**

2. This question is worth 7 points, 3 for Part A, 3 for Part B, and 1 for Part C. The following is a sample student response that would receive full credit, with indications of where points would be awarded in parentheses:

Dr. Smith would most likely define the independent variable of intelligence as a score on an IQ test, and could define the dependent variable of success in life as income over a five-year span. **(2 POINTS)**

Dr. Smith is likely concerned about the validity of the results because he wants to make claims about the relationship between intelligence and success. To do so, he needs to recognize that some studies have questioned whether IQ is a valid measure of intelligence, and that there may be other measures that could be used to measure intelligence in this study. **(1 POINT)**

Stereotype threat happens when performance is decreased due to a negative stereotype based on an individual's identity. For example, there is some evidence that members of particular groups do worse on IQ tests when reminded of negative stereotypes about their group. If Dr. Smith administers new IQ tests to his participants, he should be careful to avoid calling attention to these stereotypes, or he'll risk adversely affecting his results. **(1 POINT)** Sampling refers to selecting participants who represent the population being studied, allowing conclusions to be generalized from sample to population. If Dr. Smith does not select a representative sample for this study, it cannot be generalized to populations outside his study sample, so he will likely want to use some kind of random sampling. **(1 POINT)** Dr. Smith needs to be aware, and control for, confounding variables that might influence his study. For instance, success in life might be tied to parental success, which would confound this study unless parental income was controlled for. **(1 POINT)**

Because Dr. Smith is studying intelligence, he should be aware that IQ scores fall on a normal distribution, with a mean of 100 and a standard deviation of 15. The graph that shows the IQs of the participants in the study does not appear to have a normal distribution. There should be a bell-shaped curve with decreasing numbers of individuals with IQs below 80 and above 120, and there should be more individuals clustered at 100 than at 80 or 120. Since there are absolutely no individuals with IQs below 80 or above 120, it appears as though the data has been truncated or cherry-picked in some way. Therefore, Dr. Smith's results might not be generalizable since his population is not representative of the population as a whole. **(1 POINT)**

Practice Exam 2
Answer Grid

1. Ⓐ Ⓑ Ⓒ Ⓓ Ⓔ	26. Ⓐ Ⓑ Ⓒ Ⓓ Ⓔ	51. Ⓐ Ⓑ Ⓒ Ⓓ Ⓔ	76. Ⓐ Ⓑ Ⓒ Ⓓ Ⓔ
2. Ⓐ Ⓑ Ⓒ Ⓓ Ⓔ	27. Ⓐ Ⓑ Ⓒ Ⓓ Ⓔ	52. Ⓐ Ⓑ Ⓒ Ⓓ Ⓔ	77. Ⓐ Ⓑ Ⓒ Ⓓ Ⓔ
3. Ⓐ Ⓑ Ⓒ Ⓓ Ⓔ	28. Ⓐ Ⓑ Ⓒ Ⓓ Ⓔ	53. Ⓐ Ⓑ Ⓒ Ⓓ Ⓔ	78. Ⓐ Ⓑ Ⓒ Ⓓ Ⓔ
4. Ⓐ Ⓑ Ⓒ Ⓓ Ⓔ	29. Ⓐ Ⓑ Ⓒ Ⓓ Ⓔ	54. Ⓐ Ⓑ Ⓒ Ⓓ Ⓔ	79. Ⓐ Ⓑ Ⓒ Ⓓ Ⓔ
5. Ⓐ Ⓑ Ⓒ Ⓓ Ⓔ	30. Ⓐ Ⓑ Ⓒ Ⓓ Ⓔ	55. Ⓐ Ⓑ Ⓒ Ⓓ Ⓔ	80. Ⓐ Ⓑ Ⓒ Ⓓ Ⓔ
6. Ⓐ Ⓑ Ⓒ Ⓓ Ⓔ	31. Ⓐ Ⓑ Ⓒ Ⓓ Ⓔ	56. Ⓐ Ⓑ Ⓒ Ⓓ Ⓔ	81. Ⓐ Ⓑ Ⓒ Ⓓ Ⓔ
7. Ⓐ Ⓑ Ⓒ Ⓓ Ⓔ	32. Ⓐ Ⓑ Ⓒ Ⓓ Ⓔ	57. Ⓐ Ⓑ Ⓒ Ⓓ Ⓔ	82. Ⓐ Ⓑ Ⓒ Ⓓ Ⓔ
8. Ⓐ Ⓑ Ⓒ Ⓓ Ⓔ	33. Ⓐ Ⓑ Ⓒ Ⓓ Ⓔ	58. Ⓐ Ⓑ Ⓒ Ⓓ Ⓔ	83. Ⓐ Ⓑ Ⓒ Ⓓ Ⓔ
9. Ⓐ Ⓑ Ⓒ Ⓓ Ⓔ	34. Ⓐ Ⓑ Ⓒ Ⓓ Ⓔ	59. Ⓐ Ⓑ Ⓒ Ⓓ Ⓔ	84. Ⓐ Ⓑ Ⓒ Ⓓ Ⓔ
10. Ⓐ Ⓑ Ⓒ Ⓓ Ⓔ	35. Ⓐ Ⓑ Ⓒ Ⓓ Ⓔ	60. Ⓐ Ⓑ Ⓒ Ⓓ Ⓔ	85. Ⓐ Ⓑ Ⓒ Ⓓ Ⓔ
11. Ⓐ Ⓑ Ⓒ Ⓓ Ⓔ	36. Ⓐ Ⓑ Ⓒ Ⓓ Ⓔ	61. Ⓐ Ⓑ Ⓒ Ⓓ Ⓔ	86. Ⓐ Ⓑ Ⓒ Ⓓ Ⓔ
12. Ⓐ Ⓑ Ⓒ Ⓓ Ⓔ	37. Ⓐ Ⓑ Ⓒ Ⓓ Ⓔ	62. Ⓐ Ⓑ Ⓒ Ⓓ Ⓔ	87. Ⓐ Ⓑ Ⓒ Ⓓ Ⓔ
13. Ⓐ Ⓑ Ⓒ Ⓓ Ⓔ	38. Ⓐ Ⓑ Ⓒ Ⓓ Ⓔ	63. Ⓐ Ⓑ Ⓒ Ⓓ Ⓔ	88. Ⓐ Ⓑ Ⓒ Ⓓ Ⓔ
14. Ⓐ Ⓑ Ⓒ Ⓓ Ⓔ	39. Ⓐ Ⓑ Ⓒ Ⓓ Ⓔ	64. Ⓐ Ⓑ Ⓒ Ⓓ Ⓔ	89. Ⓐ Ⓑ Ⓒ Ⓓ Ⓔ
15. Ⓐ Ⓑ Ⓒ Ⓓ Ⓔ	40. Ⓐ Ⓑ Ⓒ Ⓓ Ⓔ	65. Ⓐ Ⓑ Ⓒ Ⓓ Ⓔ	90. Ⓐ Ⓑ Ⓒ Ⓓ Ⓔ
16. Ⓐ Ⓑ Ⓒ Ⓓ Ⓔ	41. Ⓐ Ⓑ Ⓒ Ⓓ Ⓔ	66. Ⓐ Ⓑ Ⓒ Ⓓ Ⓔ	91. Ⓐ Ⓑ Ⓒ Ⓓ Ⓔ
17. Ⓐ Ⓑ Ⓒ Ⓓ Ⓔ	42. Ⓐ Ⓑ Ⓒ Ⓓ Ⓔ	67. Ⓐ Ⓑ Ⓒ Ⓓ Ⓔ	92. Ⓐ Ⓑ Ⓒ Ⓓ Ⓔ
18. Ⓐ Ⓑ Ⓒ Ⓓ Ⓔ	43. Ⓐ Ⓑ Ⓒ Ⓓ Ⓔ	68. Ⓐ Ⓑ Ⓒ Ⓓ Ⓔ	93. Ⓐ Ⓑ Ⓒ Ⓓ Ⓔ
19. Ⓐ Ⓑ Ⓒ Ⓓ Ⓔ	44. Ⓐ Ⓑ Ⓒ Ⓓ Ⓔ	69. Ⓐ Ⓑ Ⓒ Ⓓ Ⓔ	94. Ⓐ Ⓑ Ⓒ Ⓓ Ⓔ
20. Ⓐ Ⓑ Ⓒ Ⓓ Ⓔ	45. Ⓐ Ⓑ Ⓒ Ⓓ Ⓔ	70. Ⓐ Ⓑ Ⓒ Ⓓ Ⓔ	95. Ⓐ Ⓑ Ⓒ Ⓓ Ⓔ
21. Ⓐ Ⓑ Ⓒ Ⓓ Ⓔ	46. Ⓐ Ⓑ Ⓒ Ⓓ Ⓔ	71. Ⓐ Ⓑ Ⓒ Ⓓ Ⓔ	96. Ⓐ Ⓑ Ⓒ Ⓓ Ⓔ
22. Ⓐ Ⓑ Ⓒ Ⓓ Ⓔ	47. Ⓐ Ⓑ Ⓒ Ⓓ Ⓔ	72. Ⓐ Ⓑ Ⓒ Ⓓ Ⓔ	97. Ⓐ Ⓑ Ⓒ Ⓓ Ⓔ
23. Ⓐ Ⓑ Ⓒ Ⓓ Ⓔ	48. Ⓐ Ⓑ Ⓒ Ⓓ Ⓔ	73. Ⓐ Ⓑ Ⓒ Ⓓ Ⓔ	98. Ⓐ Ⓑ Ⓒ Ⓓ Ⓔ
24. Ⓐ Ⓑ Ⓒ Ⓓ Ⓔ	49. Ⓐ Ⓑ Ⓒ Ⓓ Ⓔ	74. Ⓐ Ⓑ Ⓒ Ⓓ Ⓔ	99. Ⓐ Ⓑ Ⓒ Ⓓ Ⓔ
25. Ⓐ Ⓑ Ⓒ Ⓓ Ⓔ	50. Ⓐ Ⓑ Ⓒ Ⓓ Ⓔ	75. Ⓐ Ⓑ Ⓒ Ⓓ Ⓔ	100. Ⓐ Ⓑ Ⓒ Ⓓ Ⓔ

SECTION I

70 Minutes—100 Questions

Percent of total grade: 66⅔

Directions Answer the following 100 question in 70 minutes. Select the best answer for each and fill in the corresponding letter on your answer grid or a sheet of scratch paper.

1. Dave has trouble sleeping because he stops breathing and wakes up several times a night. Dave most likely suffers from

   (A) narcolepsy

   (B) cataplexy

   (C) sleep apnea

   (D) insomnia

   (E) somnambulism

2. If a researcher found that rich people rate themselves as less happy than poor people do, then she could say that wealth and happiness are

   (A) positively correlated

   (B) negatively correlated

   (C) independent variables

   (D) dependent variables

   (E) causally related

3. Heuristics could be considered more useful than algorithms because they

   (A) consider all potential solutions to a problem

   (B) involve a random trial-and-error approach

   (C) are faster than algorithms

   (D) are examples of formal operational thought

   (E) incorporate mental sets

4. "People are primarily motivated to alleviate internal tension caused by basic biological needs like hunger and thirst in order to maintain homeostasis." This statement is supported by which theory of motivation?

   (A) Humanistic

   (B) Arousal

   (C) Drive-reduction

   (D) Instinct

   (E) Incentive

5. Lawrence Kohlberg is well known for his theory of moral development, but Carol Gilligan strongly criticized his theory. Gilligan's primary criticism concerned

   (A) sex differences in orientations toward morality

   (B) vagueness about the ages that children reach certain levels

   (C) an inability to generalize to other cultures

   (D) the way that Kohlberg defined justice

   (E) a lack of coherence with other theories of development

GO ON TO THE NEXT PAGE

6. Fred did not get a high score on his IQ test. He says that it is because IQ tests are inherently biased—that they do not accurately reflect his true abilities. According to Fred, his high intelligence is confirmed by the number of advanced classes he is taking in school. Which of the following best describes the attributions that Fred makes?

(A) Dispositional attributions

(B) The fundamental attribution error

(C) Self-serving bias

(D) Situational attributions

(E) Actor-observer bias

7. The disorder that is characterized by a flagrant disregard for the rights of others and a lack of remorse for one's actions is called

(A) paranoid personality disorder

(B) histrionic personality disorder

(C) bipolar I disorder

(D) borderline personality disorder

(E) antisocial personality disorder

8. Which of the following researchers made the argument that intelligence is composed of many more qualities than just traditional math and verbal skills?

(A) Alfred Binet

(B) Lewis Terman

(C) Howard Gardner

(D) David Wechsler

(E) John Piaget

9. Which of the following is NOT used by cognitive psychologists to measure cognitive processes?

(A) Eye movements

(B) Gaze duration

(C) Latency

(D) Semantic recognition

(E) Free association

10. If you look at a specially modified version of the American flag that uses green, black, and yellow in place of the regular colors and then look at a white screen, you will briefly see the American flag with its proper colors. This is best explained by

(A) opponent-process theory

(B) tri-color theory

(C) place theory

(D) frequency theory

(E) gate-control theory

11. According to Piaget, at what stage does a child typically develop understanding of the concept of conservation?

(A) Preoperational

(B) Presensorimotor

(C) Formal operational

(D) Concrete operational

(E) Sensorimotor

12. Maslow's theory of motivation involves

(A) the hierarchy of needs

(B) the just-world hypothesis

(C) locus of control

(D) the collective unconscious

(E) the need for achievement

GO ON TO THE NEXT PAGE

13. Tammy wanted to remember a list of items she needed to buy at the mall, without writing that list down. While at the mall, she was able to remember the last few items on the list but not the rest. She was demonstrating the effect of

    (A) chunking

    (B) mnemonics

    (C) recency

    (D) primacy

    (E) iconic memory

14. Of the following treatments, which would most likely be used with patients who suffer from developmental delays?

    (A) Token economy

    (B) Psychoanalysis

    (C) Cognitive therapy

    (D) Systematic desensitization

    (E) Client-centered therapy

Questions 15–16 are based on the following.

While most people would perceive the image below as a star, those with a brain injury might perceive it as a series of dashed lines.

15. For someone with a brain injury, which Gestalt principle is being disrupted when they perceive the image as a series of dashed lines and not as the shape of a star?

    (A) Continuity

    (B) Bottom-up processing

    (C) Closure

    (D) Similarity

    (E) Proximity

16. What process occurs as the light from the dashed lines hits the cornea of the eye and is turned into action potentials that the brain can interpret and process?

    (A) Subliminal processing

    (B) Transduction

    (C) Sensory adaptation

    (D) Sensorineural loss

    (E) Good continuation

17. Which personality disorder is characterized by a tendency to use binary judgments like "good" and "bad" and difficulty identifying "shades of gray" in daily life?

    (A) Schizoid

    (B) Narcissistic

    (C) Bipolar

    (D) Borderline

    (E) Antisocial

18. Who was the psychologist who developed the first stage-based theory of cognitive development?

    (A) Sigmund Freud

    (B) Jean Piaget

    (C) Erik Erikson

    (D) Harry Harlow

    (E) Carol Gilligan

GO ON TO THE NEXT PAGE

19. Wilhelm Wundt is known for

    (A) developing the concept of Gestalt psychology

    (B) working at Harvard University

    (C) developing the first lab in experimental psychology

    (D) developing behaviorism

    (E) studying sleep disorders

20. If you were in a car accident and damaged your hippocampus, you would probably experience problems with

    (A) memory

    (B) sensory processing

    (C) motor control

    (D) language

    (E) vision

21. In the majority of people, the left hemisphere is dominant for

    (A) vision

    (B) thought

    (C) language

    (D) memory

    (E) attention

22. The typical IQ test has a mean of 100 and a standard deviation of 15. If you scored 115, approximately what percentage of others who have taken the test scored lower than you?

    (A) 34

    (B) 48

    (C) 68

    (D) 84

    (E) 98

23. Depth perception is obtained by a variety of cues in the environment. Which of the following cues is based on the different images a person gets from her eyes because of their distinct positions in her head?

    (A) Interposition

    (B) Linear perspective

    (C) Context

    (D) Localization

    (E) Binocular disparity

24. Not helping a person in need because you are only one person among many in a group is explained by which of the following concepts from social psychology?

    (A) Diffusion of responsibility

    (B) Groupthink

    (C) Stereotyping

    (D) Just-world hypothesis

    (E) Fundamental attribution error

25. While hiking in the woods, Joey sees a bear and his body secretes hormones from his adrenal glands. Which of the following is the most likely physical response?

    (A) Increased heart rate

    (B) Decreased pupil size

    (C) Decreased heart rate

    (D) Increased gut motility

    (E) Decreased breathing rate

GO ON TO THE NEXT PAGE

26. I see a lion, my heart starts racing, I start trembling, and I remember that my parents were killed by lions. From these inputs, I realize I feel both afraid and angry. This understanding of emotion is most consistent with the

    (A) two-factor theory

    (B) Cannon-Bard theory

    (C) opponent-process theory

    (D) encoding specificity principle

    (E) availability heuristic

27. Which of the following is NOT a Jungian archetype?

    (A) Persona

    (B) Shadow

    (C) Anima

    (D) Animus

    (E) Superego

28. A central tenet of the Gestalt school is that

    (A) studying consciousness is essential to understanding psychology

    (B) our minds fail to organize sensory information

    (C) a perception must be studied in its whole or molar form

    (D) only things that can be independently observed are important for psychology

    (E) biology is the most important element in understanding behavior

29. A normal distribution is in the shape of a

    (A) bell curve

    (B) chi square

    (C) scatterplot

    (D) bimodal distribution

    (E) skewed distribution

30. Victor has been hugging and tickling his younger brother incessantly. His psychoanalyst believes, due to interviews with Victor, that he has been frequently fantasizing about punching, kicking, and biting his brother. Based on this information, the psychoanalyst most likely believes that Victor is experiencing

    (A) sublimation

    (B) projection

    (C) displacement

    (D) reaction formation

    (E) repression

31. Albert Bandura argues that reinforcement does not need to be directly experienced for it to have an impact on behavior. This phenomenon is called

    (A) social loafing

    (B) vicarious reinforcement

    (C) operant conditioning

    (D) classical conditioning

    (E) attribution theory

GO ON TO THE NEXT PAGE

32. Psychological research suggests that you are more likely to prefer something if you have seen it before. Individuals prefer stimuli they have previously encountered, even in experiments in which the stimuli are only presented subliminally, below the threshold of participants' conscious awareness. This is called

    (A) groupthink

    (B) the halo effect

    (C) the mere-exposure effect

    (D) the levels-of-processing effect

    (E) spreading activation

33. Which of the following is commonly used to treat anxiety disorder?

    (A) Morphine

    (B) Benzodiazepines

    (C) Chlorpromazine

    (D) Risperidone

    (E) Lithium salts

34. Stanley Milgram's classic experiment in social psychology is most closely associated with

    (A) persuasion

    (B) authority

    (C) leadership

    (D) altruism

    (E) attraction

35. The concepts of introversion and extraversion were measured in a tool created by

    (A) Carl Rogers

    (B) Hans Eysenck

    (C) George Kelly

    (D) Joseph Wolpe

    (E) Wilhelm Wundt

36. "Give me a group of infants, and if I could control the world in which they are raised, I could predict which will become doctors and which will become sculptors." This statement is similar to one made by

    (A) John Watson

    (B) Sigmund Freud

    (C) Wilhelm Wundt

    (D) Carl Rogers

    (E) Edward Titchener

37. Two pins are placed so close to each other on a subject's finger that they are perceived as a single point. This is because the pins have not reached the

    (A) absolute threshold

    (B) just-noticeable difference

    (C) threshold

    (D) signal detection

    (E) action potential

38. A department store offers salespeople a bonus if they sell a certain number of items during a month. The bonus serves as a(n)

    (A) intrinsic motivation

    (B) cognitive dissonance

    (C) extrinsic motivation

    (D) conditioned stimulus

    (E) punishment

39. Which of the following did Kohlberg use when assessing someone's moral development?

    (A) The prisoner's dilemma

    (B) The Heinz dilemma

    (C) The riddle of the sphinx

    (D) The twin paradox

    (E) Zeno's paradox

GO ON TO THE NEXT PAGE

40. Francine raged at her therapist when she failed to get a perfect score on her history exam. Her therapist remarked in a very relaxed manner how absurd her logic was, because she was still earning an A in the class. The way her therapist responded was most typical of what kind of therapy?

    (A) Client-centered

    (B) Psychoanalytic

    (C) Behavioral

    (D) Cognitive

    (E) Biomedical

41. Of the following statistics, which is the most commonly used measure of spread among scores?

    (A) Mean

    (B) Kurtosis

    (C) Mode

    (D) Skewness

    (E) Standard deviation

Questions 42–43 are based on the following.

A therapist interviews Brian to determine what concerns he has and what kind of treatment might be helpful. During the interview, Brian reports that for the past several weeks, he has consistently felt "blue" and "down" and has lost interest in previously enjoyable activities. He denies having any current medical concerns or issues with misusing substances.

42. Brian's therapist suspects that Brian suffers from some type of depressive disorder. Which of the following actions would help the therapist to rule out an alternate diagnosis for Brian?

    (A) Assess whether Brian experiences persistent feelings of worthlessness

    (B) Ask whether Brian has problems with functioning in daily activities

    (C) Observe how Brian responds to an antidepressant medication

    (D) Ask whether Brian experiences any feelings of hopelessness

    (E) Determine whether Brian has a history of manic symptoms

43. Several days after the initial interview, Brian goes to see his primary care physician and receives a diagnosis of major depressive disorder. The diagnosis is then relayed with Brian's permission to his therapist. In keeping with evidence-based treatment principles, the therapist would probably recommend which of the following to Brian?

    (A) Psychodynamic therapy

    (B) Cognitive behavioral therapy

    (C) Existential therapy

    (D) Group therapy

    (E) Social justice therapy

GO ON TO THE NEXT PAGE

44. On the way to the beach, Juan's car stops running and overheats. He has no water, but he does have several drinks. Eventually, he comes to the realization that he could pour some sugar-free iced tea into his radiator as a temporary measure to allow him to reach his destination. Which of the following obstacles has Juan overcome?

    (A) A schema

    (B) A script

    (C) An algorithm

    (D) Metacognition

    (E) Functional fixedness

45. In most people, the occipital lobe is responsible for

    (A) vision

    (B) muscle movement

    (C) language

    (D) memory

    (E) attention

46. A social psychologist finds that he can get students to remember math answers on an easy test more quickly when they have to compete with each other to give the answer. This is an example of

    (A) the James-Lange theory

    (B) social comparison theory

    (C) the Cannon-Bard theory

    (D) levels of processing

    (E) social facilitation

47. The research by Harry Harlow that used wire and cloth surrogate mothers demonstrated the importance of

    (A) contact comfort

    (B) family resemblance

    (C) instinctual drift

    (D) cognitive economy

    (E) display characteristics

48. Broca's area is responsible for

    (A) visual acuity

    (B) speech production

    (C) color vision

    (D) memory

    (E) auditory processing

49. A type I error occurs whenever

    (A) a true null hypothesis is accepted

    (B) a false null hypothesis is not rejected

    (C) a false null hypothesis is rejected

    (D) a true null hypothesis is rejected

    (E) a statistically insignificant result is obtained

50. Carl Rogers would say which of the following is important in the development of personality?

    (A) Reciprocal determinism

    (B) Self-efficacy

    (C) Collective unconscious

    (D) Temperament

    (E) Self-concept

GO ON TO THE NEXT PAGE

51. A researcher describes a particular concept as "a score between 5 and 5.2 on the scale." This is called a(n)

    (A) empirical verification
    (B) controlled observation
    (C) operational definition
    (D) statistical study
    (E) hypothesis test

52. After hearing about them often in the news, Paula believes that shark attacks are so common that she refuses to vacation at the beach. This is most likely an example of

    (A) divergent thinking
    (B) the availability heuristic
    (C) confirmation bias
    (D) belief perseverance
    (E) insight

53. The WAIS and WISC are types of

    (A) personality tests based on trait theories
    (B) intelligence tests
    (C) normal distributions
    (D) measures of central tendency
    (E) reliability measures for academic tests

54. The receptive field in the eye with the greatest amount of visual acuity is the

    (A) fovea
    (B) retina
    (C) sclera
    (D) lens
    (E) cornea

55. John has problems interacting with people. His communication skills are poor, and he often falsely believes that he is the leader of a country and that political opponents are out to get him. John would probably be diagnosed with

    (A) dissociative identity disorder
    (B) dissociative fugue
    (C) bipolar I disorder
    (D) obsessive-compulsive disorder
    (E) schizophrenia

56. Being awakened is most disruptive to typical sleep patterns if it occurs during which stage of sleep?

    (A) Stage 1
    (B) Stage 2
    (C) REM sleep
    (D) Stage 3
    (E) Stage 4

57. The reinforcement schedule that causes behavior to be most difficult to extinguish is a

    (A) fixed ratio schedule
    (B) variable ratio schedule
    (C) fixed interval schedule
    (D) variable interval schedule
    (E) continuous schedule

58. In obsessive-compulsive disorder, an obsession and a compulsion are, respectively,

    (A) controllable and uncontrollable
    (B) an uncontrollable thought and an uncontrollable behavior
    (C) neurotic and psychotic
    (D) the result of trauma and self-generated
    (E) associated with personality disorders and not associated with personality disorders

GO ON TO THE NEXT PAGE

59. Of the following individuals, who is most responsible for developing the concept of classical conditioning?

    (A) B.F. Skinner

    (B) E.L. Thorndike

    (C) Jean Piaget

    (D) Ivan Pavlov

    (E) John B. Watson

60. The method of loci is an example of

    (A) the primacy effect

    (B) the recency effect

    (C) a mnemonic

    (D) a heuristic

    (E) an algorithm

61. Facial expressions that are associated with particular emotions, such as surprise or fear, are

    (A) very similar throughout the world

    (B) learned in early childhood

    (C) different in individualist and collectivist cultures

    (D) more similar in women than in men

    (E) more similar in adults than in children or adolescents

62. Dr. Rosen is conducting a medical study on the causes of a particular psychological disorder. Charles, one of her patients who suffers from this disorder, has undergone brain imaging and is participating in her medical study. Before Dr. Rosen can release her work to others, she must

    (A) ask at least one other doctor to verify Charles' diagnosis

    (B) clearly indicate the features of the brain that show up on the images

    (C) compare Charles' images to at least one other person's images

    (D) show Charles the images before releasing the results of her study

    (E) obtain Charles' written consent to release his medical information

63. In an experiment, participants were asked to remember a lengthy list of words. Several hours later, when asked to recall as many words as they could, many participants wrote down words that were similar in meaning to the actual words. This is an example of

    (A) memory decay

    (B) visual encoding

    (C) source amnesia

    (D) acoustic encoding

    (E) semantic encoding

64. When Nancy was in high school, she ate lunch at 10:15 a.m. every day. As an adult, she now tends to get hungry around 10:15 a.m. most days. The time of day is a(n)

    (A) unconditioned stimulus

    (B) conditioned stimulus

    (C) unconditioned response

    (D) conditioned response

    (E) neutral stimulus

GO ON TO THE NEXT PAGE

65. If a child is now able to solve complex problems, she is probably in which stage of cognitive development, according to Piaget?

    (A) Sensorimotor

    (B) Presensorimotor

    (C) Preoperational

    (D) Concrete operational

    (E) Formal operational

66. The concept in social psychology that suggests that people will do things simply because others are doing them is

    (A) conformity

    (B) attribution

    (C) compliance

    (D) groupthink

    (E) altruism

67. In his longitudinal study of gifted children, Lewis Terman found that the children

    (A) were more emotional and less healthy than a control group

    (B) were healthy, well-adjusted, and performed well academically

    (C) were often bullied and marginalized by their peers

    (D) felt they had been scarred by being labeled and thus refused to participate

    (E) cared more deeply about saving the planet than a control group

68. Philip Zimbardo is most associated with which of the following famous studies?

    (A) Obedience study

    (B) Robbers Cave experiment

    (C) Stanford prison study

    (D) Bystander intervention study

    (E) Nonsense syllable study

69. One main criticism of personality tests is that they

    (A) deal with inherent traits versus learned behaviors

    (B) focus on specific personality traits

    (C) focus too heavily on positive personality traits

    (D) focus too heavily on negative personality traits

    (E) use self-reporting survey methods

70. With regards to intelligence tests, reliability and validity, respectively, refer to

    (A) the ability to measure individuals and the ability to measure groups

    (B) the consistency of the measurements of a test and the extent to which a test measures what it intends to measure

    (C) consistency from test to test and consistency within a given test

    (D) the extent to which a test measures what it intends to measure and the measurements of a test

    (E) the ability of the test administrator and the success of the test

71. The psychologist who trained with Wundt and traveled to the United States to set up one of the first psychology labs at Cornell University was

    (A) William James

    (B) Edward Titchener

    (C) B.F. Skinner

    (D) Stanley Milgram

    (E) John Watson

72. Willie spent a year of his life stranded on a desert island. Though he was rescued, he still suffers from anxiety and impaired ability to function normally. Willie would most likely be diagnosed with

    (A) seasonal-affective disorder

    (B) insomnia

    (C) borderline personality disorder

    (D) learned helplessness

    (E) posttraumatic stress disorder

73. Assume you are interested in helping your dog develop the ability to urinate in the same location every time. To do this, you start by providing many rewards to go outside, and gradually you reward the behavior only as it begins to get closer to the desired location. This is a process called

    (A) modeling

    (B) method of loci

    (C) observational learning

    (D) shaping

    (E) extinction

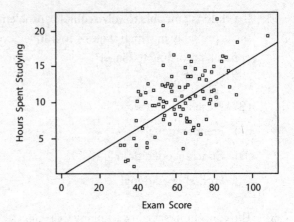

74. The graph above presents the results of a study that examined the relationship between time spent studying and exam scores. What can be inferred from the results of this study?

    (A) Both time spent studying and exam scores have increased in recent years.

    (B) More time spent studying causes students to receive higher exam scores.

    (C) Students with higher exam scores are more likely to enjoy studying.

    (D) The amount of time spent studying positively correlates with exam score.

    (E) The amount of time spent studying negatively correlates with exam score.

75. If two individuals have the same phenotype, they must

    (A) have the same genes

    (B) have the same expressed traits for a particular gene

    (C) possess the same number of chromosomes

    (D) be the same gender

    (E) be identical twins

GO ON TO THE NEXT PAGE

76. Delusions and hallucinations are most likely to be reported by those who have which of the following disorders?

(A) Dissociative identity disorder

(B) Schizophrenia

(C) Borderline personality disorder

(D) Major depressive disorder

(E) Generalized anxiety disorder

77. Which of the following practices best characterizes the psychological perspective of William James?

(A) Observing human behavior to determine the function of that behavior in the human environment

(B) Using animal models to examine how and why stimuli produce certain behaviors in those animals

(C) Understanding the structure of the mind through introspection of sensations, feelings, and thoughts

(D) Advocating that there is inherent good in humans that can be accessed by client-centered therapy

(E) Interviewing patients to reveal their unconscious motivations through dream analysis and word associations

78. Myelin serves to provide

(A) faster nerve conduction times

(B) slower nerve conduction times

(C) rerouting of nerve impulses

(D) axon replication

(E) closer connection of neurons

79. The stage during which people typically dream is characterized by

(A) alpha waves

(B) beta waves

(C) delta waves

(D) rapid eye movements

(E) theta waves

80. Of the following individuals, who is most closely associated with the concept of imprinting?

(A) Abraham Maslow

(B) John Bowlby

(C) Jean Piaget

(D) Sigmund Freud

(E) Konrad Lorenz

81. Which of the following is the most important level of language, according to Chomsky?

(A) Semantic

(B) Syntactic

(C) Pragmatic

(D) Morphemic

(E) Phonemic

82. Which of the following is based on the principles of classical conditioning?

(A) Token economies

(B) Differential reinforcement

(C) Aversion therapy

(D) Contingency

(E) Unconditional positive regard

GO ON TO THE NEXT PAGE

Questions 83–84 are based on the following.

Tom is an avid fan of martial arts star Michael Howard, and decides to determine if certain factors provide a stronger motivation for his star to win a competition compared to others. To achieve this, Tom records factors that he thinks may be motivating Michael Howard to win across various martial arts events: the size of the crowd at the event and the monetary award for first place. The results can be seen in the table below:

	Competition 1	Competition 2	Competition 3
Crowd size (number of people)	1,211	10,321	8,756
Monetary reward for 1st place	$50,000	$100,000	$150,000
Outcome for Michael Howard	Loss	Win	Win

83. If Tom looks exclusively at the monetary reward, could he reasonably conclude that it is an effective factor in motivating Michael Howard?

    (A) Yes, because the monetary award is an instinctive motivation factor.

    (B) No, because Michael Howard is motivated only by intrinsic factors.

    (C) Yes, because the monetary award can be a strong secondary drive.

    (D) No, because the monetary amount does not correlate with the outcome of the event.

    (E) Yes, because the monetary award is part of self-actualization.

84. Suppose a fourth competition is added to the table, which was attended by 20,000 people and was nationally televised, and which resulted in a loss. Assuming that these four competition results are representative of Michael Howard's typical performance and looking only at the crowd size, this set of outcomes would best be explained by

    (A) instinct theory

    (B) drive-reduction theory

    (C) arousal theory

    (D) James-Lange theory

    (E) Cannon-Bard theory

85. Some psychological tests are designed by comparing a population of individuals who exhibit a disorder with "normals." Which of the following tests would be an example of such a measure?

    (A) Myers-Briggs

    (B) Rorschach

    (C) Thematic Apperception Test (TAT)

    (D) MMPI-2

    (E) Remote Associates Test

86. People with Parkinson's disease can be treated with L-DOPA, a drug that is chemically very similar to dopamine, and that is designed to mimic the effects of dopamine on neurons once it has entered the brain. What type of drug is L-DOPA?

    (A) Dopamine receptor antagonist

    (B) Dopamine reuptake inhibitor

    (C) Dopamine receptor agonist

    (D) Dopamine inhibitor

    (E) Selective dopamine reuptake inhibitor

GO ON TO THE NEXT PAGE

87. Which of the following does NOT lead to an increase in behavior?

    (A) Punishment

    (B) Positive reinforcement

    (C) Negative reinforcement

    (D) Shaping

    (E) Vicarious reinforcement

88. "I believe that I am a good person who does the right thing whenever I can. However, when my friend asked me to lend him money when he was short on his rent last month, I refused, even though I had some extra savings. But, no, that was the right thing to do after all, because lending him money would have just made him dependent on me, which would weaken his character." This line of thinking is most consistent with

    (A) social comparison theory

    (B) cognitive dissonance theory

    (C) the just-world hypothesis

    (D) the foot-in-the-door technique

    (E) a naive perspective

89. A one-year-old infant says his first word, "dada." This child

    (A) appears delayed linguistically

    (B) requires further testing to determine if he is developmentally delayed

    (C) is displaying appropriate behavior for his age

    (D) may be delayed, depending on what language he is learning

    (E) is definitely ahead of most normal children

90. Which of the following terms is NOT associated with Rogerian, client-centered therapy?

    (A) Empathy

    (B) Unconditional positive regard

    (C) Repression of anxiety

    (D) Positive trusting environment

    (E) Nondirective

91. Of the following correlation coefficients, which shows the strongest relationship between two variables?

    (A) −0.79

    (B) 0

    (C) 0.2

    (D) 0.68

    (E) 1.1

92. The concept of learned helplessness was developed by

    (A) B.F. Skinner

    (B) Albert Bandura

    (C) Martin Seligman

    (D) Joseph Wolpe

    (E) John B. Watson

93. The scientist who would reject the teachings of the early psychologists and be LEAST likely to study mental processes would be

    (A) Jean Piaget

    (B) William James

    (C) Edward Titchener

    (D) John Watson

    (E) Wilhelm Wundt

GO ON TO THE NEXT PAGE

94. Your friend says he saw a stranger running from the police, claiming that "she must have been a really evil person." You ask him about last week when he ran from the police and he says, "Yeah, but that's because I was just in the wrong place at the wrong time." This is an example of

(A) the fundamental attribution error

(B) the just-world hypothesis

(C) the availability heuristic

(D) cognitive dissonance

(E) groupthink

95. When Ms. Jennings analyzed the grades on her students' last psychology test, she found that the scores had a very small standard deviation. This would suggest that

(A) only a few students took the test, and most were absent

(B) the scores tended to be very different from one another

(C) students were confused about the content and left several answers blank

(D) the scores tended to be very similar to one another

(E) very few students were absent, and most students took the test

96. The "blind spot" refers to

(A) the area of the retina that only contains rods

(B) the area of the retina where cones cluster

(C) the area where the optic nerve exits the retina

(D) the place in the optic chiasm where the optic nerves cross

(E) the area on the cornea where an astigmatism occurs

97. In an experimental study on how sleep deprivation could affect a person's mental alertness, mental alertness is the

(A) dependent variable

(B) independent variable

(C) experimental condition

(D) control condition

(E) double-blind procedure

98. To diagnose mental disorders, a majority of psychologists follow a prescribed diagnostic approach based on

(A) established criteria set forth by the DSM

(B) the views of a particular school of psychology

(C) case studies compiled by well-known psychologists

(D) historical data that has been collected for many years

(E) the findings of the latest mental health studies

GO ON TO THE NEXT PAGE

99. Which one of the following does NOT accurately match the intelligence type to the scenario in which it is being used?

   (A) Crystallized intelligence: recalling the dates of a famous battle in the Civil War

   (B) Fluid intelligence: navigating around a road closure caused by construction

   (C) Fluid intelligence: winning a 1990s sitcom trivia game for a monetary prize

   (D) Fluid intelligence: creating a strategy to beat an opponent at a board game

   (E) Crystallized intelligence: reciting a soliloquy from *Hamlet* in front of an audience

100. During development, a fertilized egg can split. If it does, it results in

   (A) a developmental delay

   (B) a learning disability

   (C) identical twins

   (D) fetal alcohol syndrome

   (E) Down syndrome

END OF SECTION I

SECTION II
50 Minutes—2 Questions
Percent of total grade: 33⅓

Directions Answer both of the following questions in 50 minutes. Lists of facts are insufficient to earn points; you must write essays that answer the questions thoughtfully with sound arguments that employ the proper terms from psychology. Use scratch paper to write out your responses.

1. Elias is about to begin a training program for new math teachers at a nearby high school, where many of the students are struggling with math. For each of the following concepts, explain how they are relevant in Elias's preparation for teaching these struggling students.

   - Self-fulfilling prophecy

   - Formal operational thinking

   - Selective attention

   - Just-world hypothesis

   - Learned helplessness

   - Mnemonic devices

   - Maslow's hierarchy of needs

2. Dr. Maxwell wants to investigate the effects of caffeine consumption on mathematical ability in middle school girls. She selects a local middle school and has a computer select 50 of the 250 girls at random to be part of the experiment. The computer then randomly divides the girls into two groups. Each group takes a similar-looking pill, but it contains caffeine for only one of the groups; then the girls are given a standardized math test containing a series of challenging problems and each girl is assigned a score. At the end of the experiment, Dr. Maxwell concludes that, on average, caffeine does boost mathematical performance.

   Part A

   Identify each of the following for this experiment.

   - Independent variable

   - Dependent variable

   - Random assignment

   - Confounding variables

Part B

Construct a bar graph of the outcome that Dr. Maxwell found using the axes below. Provide labels for the axes and be sure to demonstrate the major trend in the data.

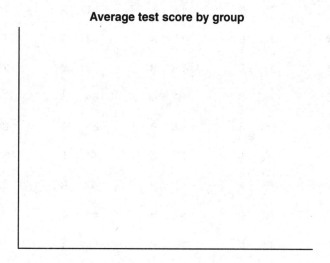

Average test score by group

Part C

Explain how the graph reflects Dr. Maxwell's conclusions.

END OF SECTION II

STOP

END OF EXAM

ANSWER KEY

Section I

1.	C	16.	B	31.	B	46.	E	61.	A	76.	B
2.	B	17.	D	32.	C	47.	A	62.	E	77.	A
3.	C	18.	B	33.	B	48.	B	63.	E	78.	A
4.	C	19.	C	34.	B	49.	D	64.	B	79.	D
5.	A	20.	A	35.	B	50.	E	65.	E	80.	E
6.	C	21.	C	36.	A	51.	C	66.	A	81.	B
7.	E	22.	D	37.	B	52.	B	67.	B	82.	C
8.	C	23.	E	38.	C	53.	B	68.	C	83.	C
9.	E	24.	A	39.	B	54.	A	69.	E	84.	C
10.	A	25.	A	40.	D	55.	E	70.	B	85.	D
11.	D	26.	A	41.	E	56.	C	71.	B	86.	C
12.	A	27.	E	42.	E	57.	B	72.	E	87.	A
13.	C	28.	C	43.	B	58.	B	73.	D	88.	B
14.	A	29.	A	44.	E	59.	D	74.	D	89.	C
15.	C	30.	A	45.	A	60.	C	75.	B	90.	C

91.	A
92.	C
93.	D
94.	A
95.	D
96.	C
97.	A
98.	A
99.	C
100.	C

Section II

1. See Answers and Explanations

2. See Answers and Explanations

PRACTICE EXAM 2 BREAKDOWN: ASSESS YOUR STRENGTHS

Use the following tables to determine which topics you are already strong in and which topics you need to review most.

Topic	Questions
Scientific Foundations of Psychology	2, 19, 41, 49, 51, 71, 74, 77, 91, 93, 95, 97
Biological Bases of Behavior	1, 20, 21, 45, 48, 56, 75, 78, 79, 86
Sensation and Perception	10, 15, 16, 23, 28, 37, 54, 96
Learning	31, 36, 57, 59, 64, 73, 82, 87, 92
Cognitive Psychology	3, 8, 9, 13, 22, 29, 44, 52, 53, 60, 63, 67, 70, 81, 99
Developmental Psychology	5, 11, 18, 39, 47, 65, 80, 89, 100
Motivation, Emotion, and Personality	4, 12, 25, 26, 27, 30, 35, 38, 50, 61, 69, 83, 84, 85
Clinical Psychology	7, 14, 17, 33, 40, 42, 43, 55, 58, 62, 72, 76, 90, 98
Social Psychology	6, 24, 32, 34, 46, 66, 68, 88, 94

Topic	Chapters	Questions on Exam	Number You Got Correct
Scientific Foundations of Psychology	4, 13	12	
Biological Bases of Behavior	5, 14	10	
Sensation and Perception	6, 15	8	
Learning	7, 16	9	
Cognitive Psychology	8, 17	15	
Developmental Psychology	9, 18	9	
Motivation, Emotion, and Personality	10, 19	14	
Clinical Psychology	11, 20	14	
Social Psychology	12, 21	9	

PRACTICE EXAM 2 ANSWERS AND EXPLANATIONS

SECTION I

1. C

Topic: Biological Bases of Behavior

Sleep apnea is a condition in which a person periodically stops breathing while sleeping, causing him or her to wake up to start breathing again. Often, sufferers do not remember waking up, but the episodes can cause serious drowsiness. This describes what Dave is suffering from, making **(C)** correct. Narcolepsy occurs when one falls asleep at unpredictable times; eliminate (A). Cataplexy can cause a person to lose muscle control, especially due to emotional triggers such as laughing or crying; eliminate (B). (D) is incorrect because insomnia is a sleep disorder in which a person has trouble falling or staying asleep, and (E) is incorrect because somnambulism is a sleep disorder associated with sleepwalking.

2. B

Topic: Scientific Foundations of Psychology

Correlation measures the extent to which two variables, or factors, are associated. Correlation, however, does not prove causation. If one factor increases as another factor decreases, the correlation is said to be negative. Here, as people have more monetary wealth, they rate themselves as less happy. As one factor increases, another factor decreases, so this is a negative correlation, making **(B)** correct. (A) is incorrect because a positive correlation occurs when two factors either both increase or both decrease. (C), (D), and (E) are all incorrect because these terms relate to experiments. In an experiment, an independent variable is manipulated by the researcher, and the dependent variable is what is measured. Through experimentation, a researcher can seek to determine if two variables are causally related.

3. C

Topic: Cognitive Psychology

A heuristic is a mental shortcut to a solution while an algorithm is a step-by-step process to find the correct solution. In problem solving, an algorithm usually takes more time than a heuristic. **(C)** is correct. Since a heuristic is a mental shortcut, it would not involve considering all potential solutions or engaging in a random trial-and-error approach, so eliminate (A) and (B). Formal operational thought involves thinking logically about abstract concepts, so eliminate (D). A mental set refers to a person's tendency to approach a problem with a mindset that has worked previously; this can often impede a person's ability to find a fresh perspective, making (E) incorrect.

4. C

Topic: Motivation, Emotion, and Personality

According to drive-reduction theory, developed by Clark L. Hull in 1943, motivation stems from the desire to resolve internal tension caused by basic biological needs like hunger, thirst, and sex. Therefore, **(C)** is correct. The humanistic theory of motivation, best exemplified by Maslow's hierarchy of needs, states that after satisfying basic biological needs, people seek to fulfill emotional, spiritual, and self-actualizing needs; (A) is incorrect. (B) is incorrect because arousal theory states that people pursue activities in order to reach an optimal level of arousal or excitement, choosing exciting activities (e.g., rock climbing, watching a scary movie) to increase arousal and relaxing activities (e.g., meditating, napping) to decrease arousal. While instinct theory touches upon biological needs, it claims that people's motivation is solely rooted in evolved biological instincts and does not address internal tension; thus, (D) is incorrect. Incentive theory (behaviorist theory) states that people are motivated by reinforcement and punishment (incentives), so (E) is incorrect.

5. A

Topic: Developmental Psychology

The biggest issue in the debate between Gilligan and Kohlberg concerned gender differences in morality. Gilligan claimed that Kohlberg's theory is limited in that it only incorporates a masculine perspective. **(A)** is correct. Gilligan did not challenge Kohlberg on the ages of development, cultural matters, the definition of justice, or coherence with other theories, making (B), (C), (D), and (E) incorrect.

6. C
Topic: Social Psychology

Self-serving bias is the tendency for individuals to make internal (or dispositional) attributions about their successes but external (or situational) attributions about their failures. Fred is attributing his placement in advanced classes to an internal cause—his high intelligence—but is also attributing his failure to get a high IQ score to an external cause—the supposed bias of the test. **(C)** is thus correct. (A) and (D) are incorrect because Fred is making both dispositional and situational attributions, not just one or the other. The fundamental attribution error refers to the tendency to attribute another person's behavior to internal causes, so (B) is incorrect. Actor-observer bias is the tendency to attribute other people's actions to dispositional factors while attributing one's own actions to situational factors. Fred makes both internal and external attributions about himself and does not make any attributions about others, so (E) is incorrect.

7. E
Topic: Clinical Psychology

The hallmark of antisocial personality disorder is the lack of regard for the rights and feelings of others. Such a person would not feel remorse for his or her actions. **(E)** is correct. (A) is incorrect because there is no indication of paranoia in this description. Histrionic personality disorder, (B), results in very dramatic, relationship-impairing behavior. Most patients with bipolar I disorder alternate between periods of mania and periods of depression; eliminate (C). Someone with borderline personality disorder, (D), is emotionally unstable and tends to see situations or people as either all good or all bad.

8. C
Topic: Cognitive Psychology

Howard Gardner argues that traditional intelligence tests do not measure intelligence well. Rather, according to Gardner, each person possesses eight distinct intelligences, each to a varying degree. **(C)** is correct. Binet, Terman, and Wechsler all worked on more traditional forms of intelligence tests, making (A), (B), and (D) incorrect. Piaget, (E), is best known for his work on the cognitive development of children.

9. E
Topic: Cognitive Psychology

Free association is a technique used by practitioners of psychoanalysis to attempt to extract information from the unconscious. It is a therapeutic technique, rather than a way to measure cognitive processes, making **(E)** correct. The other measures—eye movements, gaze duration, latency, and semantic recognition—are typically used to study internal mental processes by cognitive psychologists, making (A), (B), (C), and (D) incorrect.

10. A
Topic: Sensation and Perception

The retina contains color receptors, and as visual information leaves the receptors, according to opponent-process theory, the information is analyzed in terms of three sets of opponent colors: red-green, yellow-blue, and white-black. This theory explains the afterimage effect described in the question stem; after tiring your neural response to black, green, and yellow, you should see their opponent colors. **(A)** is correct. The tri-color theory states that the retina contains three distinct color receptors—one sensitive to red, one to green, and one to blue. When stimulated in combination, these receptors can produce the perception of color. This does not explain the afterimage effect described in the question, so eliminate (B). Place and frequency theories have to do with hearing, making (C) and (D) incorrect. Gate-control theory has to do with pain signals; eliminate (E).

11. D
Topic: Developmental Psychology

Conservation is the principle that things stay the same (in amount or quantity) regardless of whether their forms change. Piaget believed that during the concrete operational stage (stage 3), children gain the mental capacity to understand the concept of conservation. **(D)** is correct. Prior to the concrete operational stage, children do not have the ability to understand that things can change shape and still maintain quantity. During stages 1 (sensorimotor) and 2 (preoperational), children lack the mental capacity to comprehend concrete logic, so eliminate (A) and (E). Presensorimotor is not a stage defined by Piaget, so eliminate (B). Formal operational stage is the last stage of development, according to Piaget's theory, so eliminate (C).

12. A

Topic: Motivation, Emotion, and Personality

Maslow's most notable contribution to psychology is the hierarchy of needs, a theory in which he argues that humans have needs on a variety of levels, with lower-level needs (such as for food and shelter) requiring satisfaction before higher-level needs (such as for security, love, and self-esteem). According to Maslow, after a person has met needs at all the lower levels, he or she can then pursue self-actualization, the full realization of his or her potential as an individual. **(A)** is correct. (B) is incorrect because the just-world hypothesis is a concept from social psychology. (C) is incorrect because locus of control provides the framework for Julian Rotter's theory of personality. (D) is incorrect because the collective unconscious is part of Carl Jung's theory of personality. (E) is incorrect because the need for achievement was a personality concept investigated by Henry Murray and David McClelland.

13. C

Topic: Cognitive Psychology

The recency effect suggests that when people try to remember a list, they tend to remember the last few items on the list more easily because they encountered those items more recently. **(C)** is correct. Chunking refers to grouping information to organize it better, and mnemonics are memory aids, making (A) and (B) incorrect. The primacy effect, (D), suggests that people remember information at the beginning of a list better because they have more time to rehearse the information and transfer it to long-term memory. Iconic memory, (E), relates to a very short-lived picture-image memory.

14. A

Topic: Clinical Psychology

People with developmental delays often have difficulty with basic, everyday activities. A token economy is a conditioning procedure in which a person receives a token for exhibiting proper behavior. The person can then trade the tokens for an actual reward or treat. The person develops an association between the token and the reward, resulting in a behavior modification. **(A)** is correct. The other systems—psychoanalysis, cognitive therapy, systematic desensitization, and client-centered therapy—are not commonly used for people with developmental delays, making (B), (C), (D), and (E) incorrect.

15. C

Topic: Sensation and Perception

The perception of whole shapes as opposed to a series of dashed lines comes from the Gestalt principle of closure. This principle states that humans organize things they perceive into whole objects as opposed to collections of parts. Since the person with a brain injury is not seeing the image as a star, the principle of closure is being disrupted and **(C)** is correct. Continuity is the principle of grouping objects together because they follow a pattern, such as forming a line or shape; (A) is incorrect. Bottom-up processing is not being disrupted because the person with a brain injury is still perceiving the lines; (B) is incorrect. Similarity is how objects are perceived as grouped when they have similar characteristics; (D) is incorrect. Proximity is how objects are perceived as grouped because they are close together when viewed; (E) is incorrect.

16. B

Topic: Sensation and Perception

Human perception involves sensation, the stimulation of a sensory receptor by something in the environment, turning into action potentials that the brain can interpret through the process of transduction. This means that **(B)** is correct. Subliminal processing is the processing of signals below the threshold for perception; (A) is incorrect. Sensory adaptation is when constant stimulation of a sense can lead to lack of perception by that sense, such as not perceiving a smell when it has been present for a long time; (C) is incorrect. Sensorineural loss is when a sense no longer works because the neurons and the sensory cells undergo some kind of disconnect, like in some types of hearing loss; (D) is incorrect. Good continuation refers to when human brains perceive continuous lines (as opposed to a series of smaller lines) in complete shapes; (E) is incorrect.

17. D

Topic: Clinical Psychology

A person with borderline personality disorder sometimes has trouble understanding the differences between someone making a mistake and someone actually being a bad person. He or she may judge things as either good or bad, recognizing no intermediates. **(D)** is thus correct. A schizoid personality involves a lack of engagement and emotion, making (A) incorrect. Those with narcissistic, (B), and antisocial, (E), personality disorders have difficulty dealing with the fact that their behavior has consequences. Bipolar disorders, (C), are not personality disorders, but are characterized by fluctuations between periods of mania and periods of depression.

18. B

Topic: Developmental Psychology

Jean Piaget is credited with developing the first stage-based theory of cognitive development. Piaget developed a theory that described how people are able to deal with logical problems differently at different points in their lives. **(B)** is correct. Freud, Erikson, Harlow, and Gilligan all contributed to developmental psychology, but their theories did not concern cognitive development specifically; eliminate (A), (C), (D), and (E).

19. C

Topic: Scientific Foundations of Psychology

Wilhelm Wundt is credited with starting the first lab in experimental psychology. He began the lab at the University of Leipzig in 1879. **(C)** is correct. Max Wertheimer, Kurt Koffka, and Wolfgang Köhler developed Gestalt psychology, eliminating (A). William James was the early experimental psychologist who worked at Harvard, not Wundt, so (B) is incorrect. James B. Watson and, later, B.F. Skinner made the most important contributions to behaviorism, making (D) incorrect. Lastly, Wundt was not known for any major work on sleep disorders, (E).

20. A

Topic: Biological Bases of Behavior

The hippocampus is the part of the brain that processes memories. Damage to this region results in the inability to form new memories, making **(A)** correct. The other skills are associated with different parts of the brain: sensory processing in the parietal lobe, motor control in the frontal lobe, language in the temporal lobe, and vision in the occipital lobe, making (B), (C), (D), and (E) incorrect.

21. C

Topic: Biological Bases of Behavior

Language is localized for a significant majority of people in the left hemisphere. Damage to this region results in a language and speech problems. **(C)** is correct. Both the left and right sides are responsible for vision, thinking, memory, and attention, making the remaining choices incorrect.

22. D

Topic: Cognitive Psychology

A typical set of IQ scores fits a normal distribution. According to the rules for normal distributions, about 68 percent of test-takers will score within one standard deviation above or below the mean. Since the mean is 100, half the test-takers score less than 100. Then, from 100 to one standard deviation above 100, there are about 34 percent (half of 68 percent) of scorers. Given that each standard deviation is 15 points, a score of 115 is one standard deviation above the mean. So, scoring 115 means you would outscore $50 + 34 = 84$ percent of test-takers. **(D)** is correct. (A) represents the percentage of scorers between the mean and 115. (B) reverses the order of the digits of the correct answer. (C) represents the percentage of scorers who fall between 85 and 115 (in other words, between one standard deviation below and one standard deviation above the mean). (E) represents the percentage that score below 130 (two standard deviations above the mean).

23. E

Topic: Sensation and Perception

The concept of binocular disparity suggests that because humans have two eyes, each with slightly different views of the world, they are able to see depth. A person fuses together the information from the two images to create an image with depth. **(E)** is correct. Interposition, linear perspective, and context are all cues for depth, but they do not require both eyes; (A), (B), and (C) incorrect. (D) is incorrect because localization is not a term associated with depth perception.

24. A

Topic: Social Psychology

If an individual is in a group, he or she often assumes that someone else in that group will help a person in distress. This is called diffusion of responsibility. **(A)** is correct. (B) is incorrect because groupthink is way of thinking that occurs when you want to maintain harmony within a decision-making group, even when you may privately disagree. (C) is incorrect because a stereotype is a generalized belief about a group of people. The just-world hypothesis, (D), is the belief that the world is basically just, and that people get what they deserve. The fundamental attribution error, (E), occurs when you overemphasize the internal characteristics of a person and ignore external circumstances when judging a person's behavior.

25. A

Topic: Motivation, Emotion, and Personality

In this situation, Joey is most likely experiencing fear, which will cause a "fight-or-flight" or sympathetic response. Adrenal glands produce the hormones responsible for the fight-or-flight response, which includes increased heart rate, increased pupil size, and decreased gut motility. **(A)** is thus correct. (B) is incorrect because Joey's pupils would increase in size to let more light in so he could see the bear (and any possible escape routes) more clearly. (C) is incorrect because Joey's heart rate would increase, as already noted. (D) is incorrect because Joey's gut motility would actually decrease; increased focus on digestion is part of the parasympathetic "rest and digest" response. (E) is incorrect because breathing rate would increase to allow increased blood flow, in case Joey needed to defend himself or get away quickly.

26. A

Topic: Motivation, Emotion, and Personality

This example is most consistent with the two-factor or Schachter-Singer theory, which holds that physiological arousal and cognitive label work together to dictate emotional interpretation. The feelings of fear and anger are dependent upon both physiological response and identification of the lion as a viable threat. **(A)** is correct. (B) is incorrect because the Cannon-Bard theory states that emotional and physiological reactions occur simultaneously. The opponent-process theory, (C), relates to vision and how people see color, and the encoding specificity

principle, (D), relates to memory. The availability heuristic, (E), involves making judgments about the frequency of events based on limited or inaccurate information.

27. E

Topic: Motivation, Emotion, and Personality

The superego is a psychoanalytic concept that Freud identified as the part of personality that acts as a person's conscience. The superego is the moral principle, wanting to do what is right at all times. **(E)** is correct. The other choices are all part of Carl Jung's theory of archetypes. A person's persona, (A), is the image that he or she wishes to project to others. The shadow archetype, (B), represents a person's negative aspects that he or she does not want to share with others. The anima, (C), relates to the notion of femininity for a male, while the animus, (D), relates to the notion of masculinity for a female.

28. C

Topic: Sensation and Perception

A main idea for Gestalt psychologists is that we cannot understand complex phenomena by looking at individual pieces, but rather, we need to look at the entire whole. Our minds work to organize separate sensory inputs into organized wholes. Thus, **(C)** is correct, and (B) is incorrect. While Gestalt psychologists may study conscious thoughts, (A) does not describe a central tenet of the Gestalt school. (D) and (E) are claims that run counter to Gestalt psychology.

29. A

Topic: Cognitive Psychology

A normal distribution of data forms a symmetrical bell-shaped curve in which the mean, median, and mode are equal and located in the center of the distribution and the percentages of scores falling between standard deviations are fixed by a formula. **(A)** is correct. The remaining choices all represent data displays that do not have the appearance of a bell-shaped normal distribution. A chi-square distribution, (B), is skewed to the right. A scatterplot, (C), is a set of ordered pairs graphed in the coordinate plane. A bimodal distribution, (D), will have two distinct peaks in its curve that represent the two modes of the data set, and a skewed distribution, (E), will have a lot of data values that fall either to the left or to the right of the mean.

30. A

Topic: Motivation, Emotion, and Personality

Sublimation occurs when a desire that is socially unacceptable is replaced by a more socially acceptable behavior or desire. For example, rather than screaming at people, you might take to writing them angry letters that are never sent. **(A)** is correct. (B) is incorrect because projection occurs when you see the issues that bother you in someone else, rather than yourself. Displacement, (C), occurs when you take out your anxiety on someone other than the person who caused it. (D) is incorrect because reaction formation occurs when you engage in the opposite of an anxiety-producing behavior. Repression, (E), occurs when you push the cause of a strong anxiety deep into your unconscious.

31. B

Topic: Learning

Bandura's work was groundbreaking in that it suggested that reinforcement does not need to be given directly to the individual for it to be effective. Rather, vicarious reinforcement, a type of social learning, can lead to an increase in behavior. **(B)** is correct. Social loafing, (A), occurs when a member of a group does not contribute much effort because he or she believes the other members will complete the group's task. Operant conditioning suggests that behavior is controlled by the consequences of that behavior, while classical conditioning suggests that some behavior is controlled by learned associations; (C) and (D) are incorrect. Attribution theory, (E), maintains that people often infer the reasons that someone might engage in a behavior by observing that person.

32. C

Topic: Social Psychology

The mere-exposure effect suggests that if you see something, even if you do not prefer it at that point, and then you see it again in a different context, you may then prefer it simply because of the prior exposure. **(C)** is correct. Groupthink, (A), is way of thinking that occurs when you want to maintain harmony within a decision-making group. The halo effect, (B), is the notion that you perceive someone with one good quality as having many other good qualities as well. The levels-of-processing effect concerns the relationship between memory and the depth of mental processing, while spreading activation concerns how memories are organized; eliminate (D) and (E).

33. B

Topic: Clinical Psychology

Anxiety disorders are commonly treated with benzodiazepines, which work to depress central nervous system activity. **(B)** is correct. Morphine is used to treat severe pain, making (A) incorrect. Chlorpromazine and risperidone are both antipsychotic drugs that are mainly used tc treat schizophrenia, making (C) and (D) incorrect. (E) is incorrect because lithium is used to treat bipolar disorders.

34. B

Topic: Social Psychology

In Milgram's research, he found that participants were willing to administer an electric shock to a person if they were told to do so, even if it was against their better judgment. One conclusion of the experiment was the suggestion that participants will do whatever they are told, if they believe the person telling them to do it is an authority figure. **(B)** is correct. Persuasion and leadership were only indirectly associated with the experiment; eliminate (A) and (C). Altruism, (D), and attraction, (E), were not factors in the experiment.

35. B

Topic: Motivation, Emotion, and Personality

The Eysenck Personality Inventory is a forced-choice tool that yields a score that allows the researcher to determine a person's level of introversion/extraversion; **(B)** is correct. Carl Rogers (notable for humanistic psychology), George Kelly (a personality psychologist), Joseph Wolpe (a behavioral therapist), and Wilhelm Wundt (a founder of modern psychology) did not develop any known techniques for measuring introversion or extraversion. (A), (C), (D), and (E) are incorrect.

36. A

Topic: Learning

In Watson's famous paper in 1913, he claimed that if he had control over a person's environment, he could create whatever characteristics he desired in that person. He wrote, " . . . give me a dozen healthy young infants. . . . I will take any one and create . . . a doctor, a lawyer, and yes, even a beggar-man and thief. . . ." **(A)** is correct. Freud, Wundt, Rogers, and Titchener did not make any such similar claim, making the remaining options incorrect.

37. B

Topic: Sensation and Perception

The just-noticeable difference is the amount of difference in similar stimuli required to perceive a difference between the two stimuli. **(B)** is correct. The absolute threshold, (A), is the intensity required to detect the existence of a stimulus. A threshold is a general term referring to a minimal necessary value, making (C) incorrect. (D) is incorrect because signal detection is the ability to discern the difference between a pattern and random noise. (E) is incorrect because an action potential is the signal transmitted by neurons.

38. C

Topic: Motivation, Emotion, and Personality

Extrinsic motivation is motivation derived from rewards coming from an outside source. A bonus given to a salesperson is an excellent example of extrinsic motivation; **(C)** is correct. (A) is incorrect because intrinsic motivation refers to motivation that comes from internal sources—this is self-motivation. Cognitive dissonance, (B), refers to the discomfort that people feel when having conflicting thoughts. Conditioned stimulus refers to a phenomenon in classical conditioning, while punishment is a phenomenon in operant conditioning; eliminate (D) and (E).

39. B

Topic: Developmental Psychology

The Heinz dilemma is a famous moral dilemma in which a participant is asked to choose between stealing a medicine and saving a loved one's life or following the law but allowing the loved one to die. Kohlberg assessed a participant's moral development not on the answer that he or she gave, but on the reasoning he or she provided. **(B)** is correct. The remaining answer choices are not moral dilemmas, making them incorrect.

40. D

Topic: Clinical Psychology

Since the therapist is telling Francine that her logic is absurd, the therapist is responding in the manner of a cognitive therapist. A cognitive therapist challenges the irrational thinking of patients so that they begin to change the way they think. **(D)** is correct. A client-centered therapist, (A), would offer unconditional regard and support, and would not challenge her irrational thinking. A therapist using a psychoanalytic, behavioral, or biomedical approach would be more likely to use other therapeutic techniques. (B), (C), and (E) are incorrect.

41. E

Topic: Scientific Foundations of Psychology

The standard deviation reveals how much, on average, each score differs from the mean. **(E)** is correct. The mean is the average value of the data set, the mode is the most frequently occurring score in the distribution, and skewness and kurtosis reveal information about the shape of the distribution, making (A), (B), (C), and (D) incorrect.

42. E

Topic: Clinical Psychology

To rule out non-depressive diagnoses, Brian's therapist would need to determine whether Brian experiences symptoms of other categories of mood disorders (e.g., bipolar disorders) or of other kinds of disorders. If the therapist determines that Brian does not have a history of symptoms of hypomania or mania, for example, the therapist is in a better position to rule out bipolar diagnoses. Thus, **(E)** is correct. For the record: the actions in (A) and (D) could help the therapist to corroborate a depressive diagnosis—but not to rule out a non-depressive diagnosis. (B) could pertain to practically any mental disorder and thus does not help to rule out a non-depressive diagnosis. (C) is incorrect because Brian's response to a medication would not be sufficient information to rule out alternate diagnoses.

43. B

Topic: Clinical Psychology

Brian's diagnosis is major depressive disorder. Of all psychological therapies for depression, cognitive behavioral therapy has the most empirical evidence in favor of its effectiveness. So, **(B)** is correct. The other choices may occasionally be effective treatments for depression, but there is no extensive evidence that any of them is particularly effective at treating depressive disorders.

44. E

Topic: Cognitive Psychology

Functional fixedness refers to the process of not being able to "think outside the box." In this example, Juan is able to deduce a solution by thinking about the problem in a unique way. **(E)** is correct. Schemata, scripts, and algorithms would generally not be considered obstacles, so (A), (B), and (C) are incorrect. Metacognition refers to your ability to describe your thoughts, making (D) incorrect.

45. A

Topic: Biological Bases of Behavior

The occipital lobe is the part of the cerebral cortex in the back of the brain. This is the area that processes information received from the visual field. **(A)** is correct. Muscle movement, memory, and attention are associated more with the frontal lobe, making (B), (D), and (E) incorrect. Language, (C), is controlled by the left hemisphere in more than 90 percent of the population and is not associated with the occipital lobe.

46. E

Topic: Social Psychology

Social facilitation theory argues that if you are in the presence of other people, you will perform better at some activities than you would attempting them alone. **(E)** is correct. (A), (B), and (C) refer to theories of emotions, and (D) is associated with cognitive psychology.

47. A

Topic: Developmental Psychology

In Harlow's research, infant monkeys preferred a terry-cloth surrogate mother over a wire-frame mother, even when the wire-frame mother was the only one that provided a source of food. These results suggested that contact comfort was even more important than food provision for the infants. **(A)** is thus correct. The remaining choices have nothing to do with Harlow's research.

48. B

Topic: Biological Bases of Behavior

Broca's area is located at the junction between the temporal and frontal lobes. Damage to this area results in a decreased ability to produce speech clearly. **(B)** is correct. Damage to the occipital lobe would result in decreased ability to see clearly or see color, and damage to the frontal lobe would produce problems with memory. Eliminate (A), (C), and (D). Auditory processing, (E), occurs in the temporal lobe.

49. D

Topic: Scientific Foundations of Psychology

In an experiment, a type I error occurs when a true null hypothesis is rejected as false. **(D)** is correct. Eliminate (B) because when a false null hypothesis is not rejected, it is called a type II error. (A), (C), and (E) are not considered errors.

50. E

Topic: Motivation, Emotion, and Personality

Carl Rogers was a humanistic psychologist. His views on personality development centered around people's thoughts and feelings about themselves, which he termed their self-concept, which means that **(E)** is correct. The remaining choices were important to other psychologists. (A) and (B) are associated with Albert Bandura. (C) is associated with Carl Jung. (D) is associated with Hans and Sybil Eysenck and their work on personality development.

51. C

Topic: Scientific Foundations of Psychology

Operational definitions are quantifiable, measurable descriptions of particular concepts, used to conduct research on those concepts. **(C)** is correct. Empirical verification, (A), would involve checking the accuracy of the data, and controlled observation, (B), would be involved in an experimental study. Hypothesis testing is a type of statistical study, not merely a description of a measuring scale, making (D) and (E) incorrect.

52. B

Topic: Cognitive Psychology

The availability heuristic is used when you make judgments about the frequency of events based on limited or inaccurate information. Paula believes shark attacks are common only because information about them is so readily available in her mind, due to the many news stories she has heard about them. **(B)** is correct. (A) is incorrect because divergent thinking refers to the generation of a variety of possibilities when considering a problem. (C) is incorrect because confirmation bias occurs when you seek information to back up what you already think is true. Belief perseverance, (D), relates to how beliefs remain in your memories. (E) is incorrect because an insight is a sudden flash of understanding.

53. B

Topic: Cognitive Psychology

The WAIS and WISC were developed by psychologist David Wechsler to measure several different kinds of intelligence, including block design, basic math, and vocabulary. WAIS stands for Wechsler Adult Intelligence Scale and WISC is the Wechsler Intelligence Scale for Children. **(B)** is correct. These tests are not based on trait theories, (A), are not types of distributions, (C), and are not measures of central tendency, (D), or reliability, (E).

54. A

Topic: Sensation and Perception

The fovea is a pit in the middle area of the retina in which cones are very concentrated, making it the part of the eye with the greatest degree of visual acuity. When you look at something, the image falls on the fovea. **(A)** is correct.

The retina is the entire structure that contains the receptor cells; eliminate (B). The sclera, (C), is the white part of the eye that provides structure. The lens, (D), and cornea, (E), work together to help focus the image on the retina.

55. E

Topic: Clinical Psychology

John's inability to interact with other people coupled with his delusions of being someone else and of being threatened indicate that he is suffering from schizophrenia. **(E)** is correct. Dissociative identity disorder, formerly known as multiple personality disorder, is a rare condition in which a person alternates between two or more distinct personalities. This does not accurately characterize John, making (A) incorrect. Someone with dissociative fugue would forget his or her past and essentially recreate a new personal history. Eliminate (B). A person with bipolar I disorder typically fluctuates between periods of extreme hyperactivity and periods of depression, making (C) incorrect. There is no indication that John has obsessive-compulsive tendencies; eliminate (D).

56. C

Topic: Biological Bases of Behavior

During stage 1 sleep, you are barely asleep; in stage 2, you are in a light sleep; and in stages 3 and 4, you are in a deeper sleep. Sometimes referred to as a fifth stage, REM sleep is when you dream, with your brain in a state of heightened activity compared to other stages. If you are awakened during REM sleep, the next time you go to sleep, you will slip into REM sleep more quickly and spend more time in that stage. This is called the rebound effect. Systematically disrupting REM sleep can lead to both physiological and psychological disturbances. **(C)** is correct.

57. B

Topic: Learning

With a variable ratio schedule, the subject is rewarded after so many behaviors—but the number of behaviors needed to get the reward varies. As such, if an animal works faster, it can get the reward sooner. Experiments have shown that with this type of schedule, the behavior is slowest to disappear once the reward stops. **(B)** is correct. With variable interval (D), the reward comes on a varying time schedule—not based on the behavior of the animal or person. Since the reward does not depend on the behavior frequency, the behavior goes away more quickly once the rewards stop, making (D) incorrect. Studies have shown that with fixed schedules, the behavior will cease more quickly than with variable schedules, making (A) and (C) incorrect. Likewise, (E) is incorrect because, with continuous reinforcement, the behavior tends to stop shortly after the reward disappears.

58. B

Topic: Clinical Psychology

With obsessive-compulsive disorder (OCD), both the obsession and the compulsion are uncontrollable. The obsession is a thought that causes anxiety, and the compulsion is considered an impulse. The impulse is what drives the person to try to help stop the anxiety. An OCD patient, for example, might have obsessive thoughts about leaving the stove on. To alleviate that thought, the patient will check the stove repeatedly throughout the night to help calm the anxiety. **(B)** is correct. Since the obsession is not controllable, eliminate (A). The terms neurotic and psychotic, (C), do not describe this condition. OCD is not the result of trauma, so (D) is incorrect. It is not considered a personality disorder, so (E) is incorrect.

59. D

Topic: Learning

Ivan Pavlov, a Russian physiologist, developed the concept of classical conditioning, but he did it quite by chance. He was examining digestion in dogs and, by happenstance, found that if he paired sound with the delivery of food, the animal would salivate. Further, he found that the salivation could be controlled by this stimulus. **(D)** is correct. Skinner, (A), and Thorndike, (B), were later behaviorists, and Piaget, (C), worked in child development. Watson did work with classical conditioning, but he did not develop the concept and borrowed heavily from the work of Pavlov, so (E) is incorrect.

60. C

Topic: Cognitive Psychology

The method of loci is a mnemonic, or a memory aid, that involves associating whatever needs to be remembered

with familiar places or known visual images. **(C)** is correct. The primacy effect, (A), is the tendency to remember the first few items on a list better than other items, while the recency effect, (B), is the tendency to remember the last few items on a list better than other items. A heuristic is a mental shortcut and an algorithm is a step-by-step problem solving strategy; eliminate (D) and (E).

61. A

Topic: Motivation, Emotion, and Personality

While Charles Darwin was one of the first to observe the similarities in facial expressions between humans and animals, it was psychologist Paul Ekman who discovered the similarity in human facial expressions throughout the world. Until Ekman's work in the 1960s, emotions and their accompanying facial expressions were thought to be culturally determined. **(A)** is correct. This contradicted any notion that such expressions are learned, or dependent on culture, gender, or age; eliminate (B), (C), (D), and (E).

62. E

Topic: Clinical Psychology

Healthcare professionals are legally bound by confidentiality laws to protect the privacy of their patients' medical information. Without Charles' written consent, Dr. Rosen would be unable to disclose, or share, Charles' brain images or any other medical information, making **(E)** correct. While the other options may be useful for Dr. Rosen to consider, she would not be legally obligated to carry out any of them, making (A), (B), (C), and (D) incorrect.

63. E

Topic: Cognitive Psychology

Encoding refers to the way that information enters through the senses and then gets sent to the brain for further processing. In this experiment, remembering the words that were similar in meaning is an example of semantic (that is, meaning-based) encoding. **(E)** is correct. Memory decay, (A), and source amnesia, (C), would make it more likely that the participants could not recall the words and would not explain the participants' ability to remember similar words. Acoustic encoding, (D), refers to information that one hears, and visual encoding, (B), to what one sees.

64. B

Topic: Learning

A conditioned stimulus is one that causes a response after training or repetition. After eating lunch so many times at 10:15 a.m., Nancy has learned to associate that time with hunger. Thus, the reflex of hunger begins to occur around 10:15 a.m., regardless of whether Nancy is actually hungry. **(B)** is correct. Given the conditioning, eliminate (A), (C), and (E). The hunger is the conditioned response, so eliminate (D).

65. E

Topic: Developmental Psychology

Complex logical problem-solving skills are markers that a person has entered the final stage of cognitive development in Piaget's theory: formal operations (stage 4). **(E)** is correct. During stages 1 (sensorimotor) and 2 (preoperational), children lack the mental capacity to comprehend logic, so eliminate (A) and (C). Presensorimotor, (B), is not a stage defined by Piaget. In stage 3 (concrete operational), children learn to solve simple problems, but are not yet capable of abstract and complex logic, making (D) incorrect.

66. A

Topic: Social Psychology

In conformity situations, participants often change their behavior (and opinions) when faced with others who make a different choice. **(A)** is correct. Attribution theory, (B), refers to our interpretations of others' actions. Compliance, (C), occurs when people change their behavior due to a request. Groupthink, (D), occurs when people act in order to maintain good relations within their group, often resulting in poor decision-making. Altruism, (E), refers to behavior that helps other people more than it helps oneself.

67. B

Topic: Cognitive Psychology

One of the most prominent studies of gifted individuals was Lewis Terman's longitudinal study of gifted students whom he called "Terman's Termites." Individuals from the study scored higher than average in terms of family income, physical and mental health, and reported happiness. Terman's research disproved a popular misconception that gifted individuals were not well adjusted or socially successful. **(B)** is correct. Since the gifted students proved to be healthy and well-adjusted, eliminate (A), (C), and (D). (E) does not represent an outcome of Terman's study.

68. C

Topic: Social Psychology

The Stanford prison study was completed in 1971 by Philip Zimbardo and his associates. In this study, 24 students were chosen, with half playing the role of guards and half playing the role of prisoners. The study was set to run two weeks, but Zimbardo had to stop the experiment after only six days because prisoners and guards alike had completely adopted the roles that they had been given and were treating each other badly. The study revealed that situational circumstances strongly influence behavior; **(C)** is correct. Stanley Milgram is notable for doing an obedience study in which participants were tested to see if they would give an electric shock to another person, making (A) incorrect. The Robbers Cave experiment, (B), was performed by Muzafer Sherif to study intergroup behavior. Zimbardo never studied bystander intervention, (D), nor did he use nonsense syllables, (E), in his research.

69. E

Topic: Motivation, Emotion, and Personality

Much of the criticism of personality measures is that they rely heavily on self-reporting survey methods, which are not always the most accurate measures of behavior. The research on surveys suggests that people will sometimes tell the researcher what they think the researcher wants to hear. Similarly, participants often lie on surveys for a variety of reasons. **(E)** is correct. Not all personality tests measure traits, so (A) and (B) are incorrect. (C) and (D) are criticisms that may apply to particular surveys, but not to personality tests in general.

70. B

Topic: Cognitive Psychology

The concepts of reliability and validity are essential in psychological testing. Reliability refers to the extent to which a test measures a construct consistently, while validity refers to the extent to which the test measures what it is supposed to measure. A test can be reliable and not be valid. That is, a test may yield the same score again and again, but it may not be an accurate measure of what it is intended to measure. **(B)** is correct. The other choices all relate to aspects of testing, but none of these options accurately describes the concepts of reliability and validity.

71. B
Topic: Scientific Foundations of Psychology

Edward Titchener was one of Wilhelm Wundt's most famous students, and he was enormously influential in developing a lab at Cornell. **(B)** is correct. James, Skinner, Milgram, and Watson did not train with Wundt, making the other choices incorrect.

72. E
Topic: Clinical Psychology

Sometimes, after a highly stressful event, a person may suffer from posttraumatic stress disorder, in which he or she may re-experience the anxiety-inducing event and the emotions that went along with it for many years after the actual event occurred. **(E)** is correct. Seasonal-affective disorder, (A), is a condition in which people who have otherwise normal mental health exhibit depressive symptoms during the part of the year when there is less daylight, normally during the winter. Insomnia, (B), is a sleep disorder. Someone with borderline personality disorder, (C), tends to view most people and things as either good or bad. Learned helplessness results when a person believes that nothing he or she can do will produce positive outcomes; eliminate (D).

73. D
Topic: Learning

The process of shaping by successive approximations is often used to train an animal, such as the dog in this case, to engage in a complex behavior. **(D)** is correct. Modeling, (A), is a form of observational learning, (C), in which a person or animal learns by observing and imitating the behavior of another. The method of loci, (B), is a mnemonic technique that involves associating whatever needs to be remembered with familiar places or known visual images. (E) is incorrect because extinction is the process of breaking a connection between a conditioned stimulus and a conditioned response.

74. D
Topic: Scientific Foundations of Psychology

The graph shown is a scatterplot, which provides a visual representation of a correlation. This means that the study described in the question is a correlational study, a study that examines the relationship between two different variables. Since the line in the scatterplot slants upward, the correlation is positive. In other words, as time spent studying increases, so too does exam score. This makes **(D)** correct. (A) is incorrect because the study was examining the relationship between two variables, rather than a change over time. (B) is incorrect because correlation does not imply causation. Although it is true that students who spend more time studying receive higher exam scores, without random assignment, there is not sufficient information to infer that more study time causes a higher exam score. The causal relationship might go the other way, or there could be some third factor which causes both. (C) is incorrect because the graph does not present any information about how much students enjoy studying. (E) is incorrect because the scatterplot shows a positive, rather than negative, correlation.

75. B
Topic: Biological Bases of Behavior

A phenotype refers to the physiological expression of an organism's genetic code. So if two individuals have the same phenotype, or physical characteristic, then they must have the same expressed trait for a gene, making **(B)** correct. They would not have to have all of the same genes, so eliminate (A). Individuals would not necessarily need to possess the same number of chromosomes to share a phenotype, so (C) is incorrect. (D) is incorrect because individuals of different genders can still share phenotypes. To share a common physical trait, the two individuals would not have to be identical twins, so eliminate (E).

76. B
Topic: Clinical Psychology

Delusions and hallucinations are common occurrences for most individuals with schizophrenia. Delusions are false beliefs, such as thinking that you are someone else—the queen of England, for example—while hallucinations are false sensory experiences that can be visual (seeing things that are not present) or auditory (troubling noises or voices). **(B)** is correct. While it is possible that those with other disorders could experience delusions or hallucinations, it is not nearly as common, making the remaining choices incorrect.

77. A

Topic: Scientific Foundations of Psychology

William James was an early functionalist psychologist. Functionalists hope to explain how behavior helps organisms operate in their world and focuses on the functions those behaviors serve, which means **(A)** is correct. (B) is incorrect because it is associated with behaviorists like Pavlov, Watson, and Skinner. (C) is incorrect because it is associated with structuralists like Wilhelm Wundt. (D) is incorrect because it is associated with humanists like Maslow and Rogers. (E) is incorrect because it is associated with psychoanalysts like Sigmund Freud.

78. A

Topic: Biological Bases of Behavior

Myelin is a fatty substance that wraps itself around axons to produce faster action potentials. Myelin is most common in the cortex, where fast-acting neural transmission is essential for the higher-level cognitive functioning that occurs in that region of the brain. It is also essential for fast-twitch muscle control. **(A)** is correct, and (B) is incorrect. The myelin does not reroute nerve impulses, replicate axons, or provide closer neuron connections—eliminate (C), (D), and (E).

79. D

Topic: Biological Bases of Behavior

Dreaming typically occurs during REM (rapid eye movement) sleep, when the brain is more active than during other stages of the sleep cycle. **(D)** is thus correct. (A), (B), (C), and (E) are types of brain waves that can be detected in a variety of states of consciousness. None of them are particularly associated with dreaming.

80. E

Topic: Developmental Psychology

Konrad Lorenz did a great deal of work looking at inborn behaviors. He found that ducklings will imprint or bond with the first organism that they see after birth. **(E)** is correct. Maslow is known for his hierarchy of needs, Bowlby for his work on attachment theory, Piaget for cognitive

development, and Freud for psychoanalysis, making (A), (B), (C), and (D) incorrect.

81. B

Topic: Cognitive Psychology

According to Chomsky, syntax is what provides language with a great deal of its meaning. That is, the placement of a word in a sentence helps us determine the part of speech and, eventually, the meaning of the word. **(B)** is correct. Semantics, (A), refers to the rules we use to derive meaning from words, and pragmatics, (C), refers to how language is used. A morpheme, (D), refers to the smallest unit of language that has meaning, and a phoneme, (E), is the smallest distinct unit of sound.

82. C

Topic: Learning

Aversion therapy is a process that relies on pairing a previously pleasurable stimulus with a stressful or unpleasant situation. Eventually, instead of inducing pleasure, the stimulus will be avoided. **(C)** is correct. (A), (B), and (D) rely on operant conditioning principles. Unconditional positive regard, (E), is a concept in humanistic psychology.

83. C

Topic: Motivation, Emotion, and Personality

According to the table provided, the two higher monetary rewards did coincide with Michael Howard winning the competition. Thus it could reasonably be considered an effective motivation factor, eliminating (B) and (D). Among the remaining answers, **(C)** is correct because monetary award would fall into the category of secondary drives according to drive-reduction theory. (A) and (E) are incorrect because instinctive refers to inborn, fixed patterns of behavior that present in response to certain stimuli and are often species-specific, while self-actualization is a stage in Maslow's hierarchy of needs that is not related to the monetary rewards.

84. C

Topic: Motivation, Emotion, and Personality

Examining data from the table, it is evident that as the crowd size increased, Michael Howard started to win competitions. However, with the addition of a fourth competition where crowd size has increased dramatically, the performance dropped and resulted in a loss of the event. As such, it can be assumed that there is an optimal range in terms of size of the crowd that results in optimal performance, which best fits arousal theory and the Yerkes-Dodson law, making **(C)** correct. None of the theories provided in the other choices adequately explains this result. (A) is eliminated because instinct theory is based on the work of Darwin, stating that people perform certain behaviors due to instincts developed through generations of evolution. (B) is incorrect due to drive-reduction theory stating that imbalances to your body's internal environment generate drives that cause you to act in ways that restore homeostasis. Lastly, (D) and (E) are eliminated because both of them are theories of emotion and are not relevant to the scenario above.

85. D

Topic: Motivation, Emotion, and Personality

The MMPI-2 (Minnesota Multiphasic Personality Inventory) was developed by comparing the results of "normal" individuals, people who had not been diagnosed with any psychological disorder, with individuals who were committed for a variety of disorders. **(D)** is thus correct. (A) is incorrect because Myers-Briggs is a personality test that divides individuals into one of sixteen types based on four dimensions of characteristics, so it does not involve comparisons between psychologically healthy individuals and those suffering from disorders. The TAT and Rorschach tests involve individuals offering interpretations of ambiguous pictures, which does not allow for easy comparisons between groups; (B) and (C) are incorrect. The Remote Associates Test, (E), is a test of creativity that would also not allow for easy comparisons.

86. C

Topic: Biological Bases of Behavior

L-DOPA is described as a drug that acts like dopamine once in the brain, making it a dopamine receptor agonist. **(C)** is correct. Receptor antagonists make it harder to activate a receptor for the given compound, so (A) is incorrect. (C) and (E) describe reuptake inhibitors, which do not mimic the target neurotransmitter, but instead increase its concentration by decreasing uptake of the neurotransmitter at the synapse. Finally, dopamine inhibitor, (D), is not language used to describe drug action, and even if it were, L-DOPA does not inhibit dopamine.

87. A

Topic: Learning

Punishment is designed to decrease the probability of a behavior occurring. According to B.F. Skinner, punishment should not be used unless there is no other choice, because it carries possible side effects. Also, Skinner argued that unless punishment is consistent and severe enough, it will not be effective. **(A)** is correct. A positive reinforcement is a reward given to an individual that results in an increase in behavior, making (B) incorrect. A negative reinforcement has the same effect, but works through the removal of an adverse stimulus; (C) is incorrect. (D) is incorrect because shaping is a technique of selective reinforcement used to condition a specific behavior. (E) is incorrect because vicarious reinforcement occurs when an individual sees another person rewarded for a behavior; this act of observation also increases the frequency of behavior in the observer.

88. B

Topic: Social Psychology

According to cognitive dissonance theory, when your thoughts and behaviors do not coincide, you experience tension, or dissonance. In the example provided in the question stem, the speaker believes herself to be a good person, but then takes an action which does not seem so good. To prevent her from rejecting her belief in her own goodness, she then comes up with an after-the-fact rationalization, which allows her to think that she did do the right thing by not helping her friend. This is a classic case of cognitive dissonance and its resolution, making **(B)** correct. According to social comparison theory, (A), we estimate our worth based on how we compare with others, but no such comparison is offered in the example. According to the belief in a just world, (C), we live in a fair, just world, where actions have predictable, appropriate consequences; the example, however, does not include observations about how fair the world is. (D) is incorrect because the foot-in-the-door phenomenon involves an effort to get someone to complete a demanding task by having them first agree to complete a less demanding task, which is clearly not relevant here. (E) is incorrect because the example does not necessarily suggest a naive worldview.

89. C

Topic: Developmental Psychology

Typically, a child will speak his or her first word—or something that sounds like a word—at about one year old. **(C)** is thus correct. Since this is a normal, expected occurrence, eliminate (A), (B), and (D), because the child would not be considered developmentally delayed (regardless of the language being learned). On the other hand, the child would not be considered ahead of most children based solely on his first word; eliminate (E).

90. C

Topic: Clinical Psychology

Repression of anxiety is a concept most commonly associated with Freudian psychoanalysis, making **(C)** correct. According to Roger's client-centered therapy, a successful approach relies on the therapist developing an empathetic understanding, delivering unconditional positive regard, and maintaining a trusting, nondirective relationship with the client. (A), (B), (D), and (E) are incorrect.

91. A

Topic: Scientific Foundations of Psychology

A correlation coefficient reveals two things: (1) the absolute value of the number indicates the strength of the relationship, and (2) the sign indicates the direction of the relationship. The closer the value is to 1 or −1, the stronger the relationship between the two variables. A positive sign indicates that the relationship is direct (as one variable changes, the other changes in the same direction), while a negative sign indicates that the relationship is inverse (as one variable changes, the other changes in the opposite direction). Because the question asks only for the strength of the relationship, and not the direction, **(A)** is correct. (B) is incorrect because a correlation coefficient of 0 suggests no relationship between the variables at all. (C) and (D) are incorrect because they have lower absolute values than −0.79, so both suggest weaker relationships. (E) is incorrect because correlation coefficients cannot be less than −1 or greater than 1.

92. C

Topic: Learning

Learned helplessness occurs when an organism has been placed in an adverse situation from which it cannot escape. After several attempts that are unsuccessful, the animal will stop trying to escape. Later, even if the situation changes and it becomes clear that the animal could escape, it will not try because it has learned that it cannot. Martin Seligman studied this phenomenon and coined the term "learned helplessness" to describe it. **(C)** is correct. B.F. Skinner, (A), is known for his work on operant conditioning. Albert Bandura, (B), is notable for his work on social learning. Wolpe is associated with systematic desensitization, and Watson is associated with behaviorism, making (D) and (E) incorrect.

93. D

Topic: Scientific Foundations of Psychology

John Watson established the psychological school of behaviorism and promoted the belief that the only subject matter that scientific psychologists can study is observable behavior. **(D)** is correct. All of the other choices are psychologists who were very much interested in how the mind is structured (Titchener and Wundt), how the mind functions (James), and how the mind changes over time as people grow (Piaget), making the remaining options incorrect.

94. A

Topic: Social Psychology

The fundamental attribution error suggests that we tend to make dispositional (internal to the individual) attributions about the causes of other people's behavior, rather than situational or external, as compared to a propensity to make more balanced attributions about our own behavior. In other words, we often believe that someone else does something because of who he or she is—rather than due to the situation that the person is in. **(A)** is thus correct. According to the just-world hypothesis, (B), we live in a just world where people face consequences that they deserve, but the quoted statement describes the actions of a supposedly bad person, not the consequences that the person faces. (C) is incorrect because the availability heuristic happens when we make judgments about the frequency of events based on limited or inaccurate information. According to cognitive dissonance theory, (D), when our thoughts and behaviors do not coincide, we experience tension, or dissonance. Groupthink, (E), occurs when people act in a way to maintain good relations within their group, often resulting in poor decision-making.

95. D

Topic: Scientific Foundations of Psychology

Standard deviation is a measure of how dispersed data values are. A set of data in which the values are widely spread out has a large standard deviation. The smaller the standard deviation is, the closer the data is to the mean and the more similar the scores are to each other. Since the grades have a very small standard deviation, the scores are very close together, making **(D)** correct. (A) and (E) are incorrect because the number of students does not make the standard deviation smaller. (B) is incorrect because if the scores were very different, or spread out a lot, then the standard deviation would be large. (C) is incorrect because no information is provided about the actual test grades; the small deviation could have been due to all of the students scoring very well.

96. C

Topic: Sensation and Perception

The blind spot is on the back of the retina where the optic nerve exits the eye. At that point, there are no receptor cells, and thus, no visual information is received there. The brain compensates for this by "filling in the blank" during normal visual processes. **(C)** is correct. (A) is incorrect because the area of the retina where rods are located would pick up visual information; rods are necessary for peripheral vision. (B) is incorrect because the area where cones cluster is the fovea, where visual acuity is greatest. The optic chiasm, (D), is located in the brain. Since the blind spot is on the retina, not the cornea, eliminate (E).

97. A

Topic: Scientific Foundations of Psychology

In an experiment, the phenomenon that is being studied and measured is the dependent variable. The variable that the researcher controls and manipulates (in order to see its effect on the dependent variable) is called the independent variable. In the example provided, the independent variable is the amount of sleep deprivation and the dependent variable is mental alertness. **(A)** is thus correct and (B) incorrect. Experimental conditions, (C), and control conditions, (D), as well as the double-blind procedure, (E), are components of experimental design distinct from the dependent and independent variables.

98. A

Topic: Clinical Psychology

A vast majority of psychologists and health care professionals diagnose psychological disorders based on the American Psychiatric Association's DSM, that is, the *Diagnostic and Statistical Manual of Mental Disorders*. **(A)** is correct. Psychologists may be influenced by a particular school of psychology, certain case studies, historical data, and the findings of recent studies. However, none of these options accurately describes the prescribed diagnostic approach taken by a majority of psychologists, making (B), (C), (D), and (E) incorrect.

99. C

Topic: Cognitive Psychology

Fluid intelligence is the type of intelligence that encompasses problem solving and reacting to novel situations. On the other hand, crystallized intelligence has to do with acquiring and retrieving knowledge. To answer this question, you must find the choice that improperly matches the type of intelligence with the scenario. (A) is incorrect because it properly matches crystallized intelligence with recalling a specific fact. (B) is incorrect because it properly matches fluid intelligence with solving a novel problem. **(C)** is correct because it improperly matches fluid intelligence and an activity that requires previously gained knowledge, specifically knowledge of 1990s sitcoms. (D) is incorrect because it properly matches fluid intelligence with responding to novel situations. (E) is incorrect because it properly matches crystallized intelligence with memorization of knowledge.

100. C

Topic: Developmental Psychology

When a fertilized egg splits into two embryos, the result is identical twins, who have the same genetic information. **(C)** is correct. A developmental delay or learning disability is unlikely to result simply due to the splitting of an egg, so (A) and (B) are incorrect. Fetal alcohol syndrome, (D), is a birth defect caused by excessive alcohol consumption during pregnancy. Down syndrome, (E), is caused by the possession of an extra 21st chromosome, which would not result merely from the splitting of an egg.

SECTION II

1. This question is worth 7 points, 1 point each for accurately providing an appropriate example of each concept. (NOTE: You do not need to define each term explicitly, but it must be clear from your answer that you know what it means.) The following is a sample student response that would receive full credit, with indications of where points would be awarded in parentheses:

Elias must be aware of the dangers of a self-fulfilling prophecy to be sure that he does not come into the school thinking that these children are failures at math. If students perceive that he thinks they are not smart or not good at math, then they may act that way, thus reinforcing his belief and making it come true. (**1 POINT**)

Piaget's theory of cognitive development maintains that formal operational thinking, the capacity to deal with abstract concepts such as those found in math, is typically not developed until early adolescence or later. Elias should be prepared for the possibility that some of his students have not yet reached the formal operational stage, so they may not yet have mastered the ability to deal with many mathematical concepts. (**1 POINT**)

Humans have only a finite amount of attention, and must be selective about what they pay attention to. A student who is busy texting or playing with smart phone apps in class is not paying full attention to the teacher, which will negatively impact his or her learning. Elias might counter this by regularly shifting activities to keep students engaged or by restricting the use of distracting technologies in class. (**1 POINT**)

According to the just-world hypothesis, people get the outcomes in their lives that they deserve. If Elias's students believe this, they might think that they do poorly in math because they are bad people. This would likely affect their motivation and cause stress for low-performing students, and so Elias should be prepared to dispel this type of thinking. (**1 POINT**)

If students repeatedly experience failure in a math classroom, they may give up, refusing to participate in class, do homework, study, or make an effort when taking tests. Elias should know that even when he gives students new tools and strategies for solving problems, some may shut down and say, "This will never work"—just like the dogs in Seligman's learned helplessness experiments who could have escaped electric shocks but had given up trying. To avoid this, Elias should start struggling students off with simple problems within their abilities, so they have some evidence that they are capable of succeeding at math. (**1 POINT**)

A great way to teach students to learn anything is by teaching them mnemonics, and perhaps even helping them to create their own. If Elias can help students to learn or invent catchy sayings or memorable acronyms, such as PEMDAS (parentheses, exponents, multiplication, division, addition, subtraction) for the order of operations, they may more easily be able to remember the formulas and procedures required in his class. (**1 POINT**)

Elias's students not performing well in class could have a variety of explanations. One such explanation is that they are not having their basic needs met, which in turn makes it difficult for them to be motivated to participate in school work. Elias should be aware that this might be the case and look for resources to help ensure the lower levels of Maslow's hierarchy are being met for his students, so that they can be motivated to succeed in their school work. (**1 POINT**)

2. This question is worth 7 points, 4 points for Part A, 2 points for Part B, and 1 point for Part C. The following is a sample student response that would receive full credit, with indications of where points would be awarded in parentheses:

In this example, the independent variable would be the consumption of caffeine. (**1 POINT**) The dependent variable would be the girls' mathematical ability, as quantified by their scores on the standardized math test. (**1 POINT**)

Since a computer was used to randomly place participants in each group, Dr. Maxwell's study uses random assignment, which can help to limit bias that could occur if the groups were divided another way. (**1 POINT**)

In this example, there are many potential confounding variables. If one group was given the puzzles early in the day and the other group got them in the afternoon, then time of day would be confounding. Similarly, if there were a systematic difference between the members of the control and experimental groups, for instance if members of the experimental group were more likely to belong to the school's math club, then this would present another confounding variable. Random assignment helps to reduce the likelihood of confounding variables, but may not eliminate them completely. (**1 POINT**)

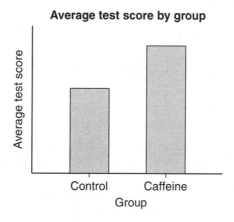

[Your bar graph should have the labels "group" (or "experimental group") on the *x*-axis and "average test score" (or something similar) on the *y*-axis. (**1 POINT**) The data should show that the group that was given caffeine has a higher bar than the group that was not given caffeine. (**1 POINT**)]

Because the group that was given caffeine has a higher average math score than the group that was given a placebo, as indicated in the completed graph, Dr. Maxwell finds support for her conclusion that caffeine enhances mathematical performance. (**1 POINT**)

Practice Exam 3
Answer Grid

1. (A)(B)(C)(D)(E)	26. (A)(B)(C)(D)(E)	51. (A)(B)(C)(D)(E)	76. (A)(B)(C)(D)(E)
2. (A)(B)(C)(D)(E)	27. (A)(B)(C)(D)(E)	52. (A)(B)(C)(D)(E)	77. (A)(B)(C)(D)(E)
3. (A)(B)(C)(D)(E)	28. (A)(B)(C)(D)(E)	53. (A)(B)(C)(D)(E)	78. (A)(B)(C)(D)(E)
4. (A)(B)(C)(D)(E)	29. (A)(B)(C)(D)(E)	54. (A)(B)(C)(D)(E)	79. (A)(B)(C)(D)(E)
5. (A)(B)(C)(D)(E)	30. (A)(B)(C)(D)(E)	55. (A)(B)(C)(D)(E)	80. (A)(B)(C)(D)(E)
6. (A)(B)(C)(D)(E)	31. (A)(B)(C)(D)(E)	56. (A)(B)(C)(D)(E)	81. (A)(B)(C)(D)(E)
7. (A)(B)(C)(D)(E)	32. (A)(B)(C)(D)(E)	57. (A)(B)(C)(D)(E)	82. (A)(B)(C)(D)(E)
8. (A)(B)(C)(D)(E)	33. (A)(B)(C)(D)(E)	58. (A)(B)(C)(D)(E)	83. (A)(B)(C)(D)(E)
9. (A)(B)(C)(D)(E)	34. (A)(B)(C)(D)(E)	59. (A)(B)(C)(D)(E)	84. (A)(B)(C)(D)(E)
10. (A)(B)(C)(D)(E)	35. (A)(B)(C)(D)(E)	60. (A)(B)(C)(D)(E)	85. (A)(B)(C)(D)(E)
11. (A)(B)(C)(D)(E)	36. (A)(B)(C)(D)(E)	61. (A)(B)(C)(D)(E)	86. (A)(B)(C)(D)(E)
12. (A)(B)(C)(D)(E)	37. (A)(B)(C)(D)(E)	62. (A)(B)(C)(D)(E)	87. (A)(B)(C)(D)(E)
13. (A)(B)(C)(D)(E)	38. (A)(B)(C)(D)(E)	63. (A)(B)(C)(D)(E)	88. (A)(B)(C)(D)(E)
14. (A)(B)(C)(D)(E)	39. (A)(B)(C)(D)(E)	64. (A)(B)(C)(D)(E)	89. (A)(B)(C)(D)(E)
15. (A)(B)(C)(D)(E)	40. (A)(B)(C)(D)(E)	65. (A)(B)(C)(D)(E)	90. (A)(B)(C)(D)(E)
16. (A)(B)(C)(D)(E)	41. (A)(B)(C)(D)(E)	66. (A)(B)(C)(D)(E)	91. (A)(B)(C)(D)(E)
17. (A)(B)(C)(D)(E)	42. (A)(B)(C)(D)(E)	67. (A)(B)(C)(D)(E)	92. (A)(B)(C)(D)(E)
18. (A)(B)(C)(D)(E)	43. (A)(B)(C)(D)(E)	68. (A)(B)(C)(D)(E)	93. (A)(B)(C)(D)(E)
19. (A)(B)(C)(D)(E)	44. (A)(B)(C)(D)(E)	69. (A)(B)(C)(D)(E)	94. (A)(B)(C)(D)(E)
20. (A)(B)(C)(D)(E)	45. (A)(B)(C)(D)(E)	70. (A)(B)(C)(D)(E)	95. (A)(B)(C)(D)(E)
21. (A)(B)(C)(D)(E)	46. (A)(B)(C)(D)(E)	71. (A)(B)(C)(D)(E)	96. (A)(B)(C)(D)(E)
22. (A)(B)(C)(D)(E)	47. (A)(B)(C)(D)(E)	72. (A)(B)(C)(D)(E)	97. (A)(B)(C)(D)(E)
23. (A)(B)(C)(D)(E)	48. (A)(B)(C)(D)(E)	73. (A)(B)(C)(D)(E)	98. (A)(B)(C)(D)(E)
24. (A)(B)(C)(D)(E)	49. (A)(B)(C)(D)(E)	74. (A)(B)(C)(D)(E)	99. (A)(B)(C)(D)(E)
25. (A)(B)(C)(D)(E)	50. (A)(B)(C)(D)(E)	75. (A)(B)(C)(D)(E)	100. (A)(B)(C)(D)(E)

SECTION I
70 Minutes—100 Questions
Percent of total grade: 66⅔

Directions Answer the following 100 question in 70 minutes. Select the best answer for each and fill in the corresponding letter on your answer grid or a sheet of scratch paper.

1. Which of the following is an example of the Flynn effect?

    (A) A female student scores lower on a test than she otherwise would have after being reminded of a negative stereotype about women.

    (B) Due to alcohol exposure in utero, an individual experiences cognitive deficits and has an IQ score below 70.

    (C) The mean score on an IQ test administered to teenagers in 1960 was 100. The mean score on the same test administered in 2010 was 130.

    (D) An intellectually gifted child fails to develop proper social skills. Later in life, he is not well-adjusted or successful socially.

    (E) An individual performs poorly on an intelligence test despite being very creative because the test does not consider creativity as a type of intelligence.

2. In addition to the four stages, Piaget's theory of cognitive development also included all of the following concepts EXCEPT

    (A) assimilation

    (B) adaptation

    (C) schemata

    (D) the reality principle

    (E) accommodation

3. Cassidy designs an experiment to determine the minimum difference between two weights required for her friends to accurately differentiate between the two. Cassidy's goal is to develop a predictive rule that will estimate how much weight must be added to a starting weight to produce a noticeable difference. Cassidy's experiment is looking for the principle known as

    (A) the all-or-none phenomenon

    (B) the law of similarity

    (C) the disconfirmation principle

    (D) the Yerkes-Dodson law

    (E) Weber's law

4. While running, Zara trips and twists her ankle. She can either limp the remaining half-mile home or call her unfriendly neighbor to ask for help. Kurt Lewin would describe this as an

    (A) approach-avoidance conflict

    (B) approach-approach conflict

    (C) avoidance-avoidance conflict

    (D) intrapersonal conflict

    (E) interpersonal conflict

GO ON TO THE NEXT PAGE

499 | K

5. For the past few months, Sara has been refusing to practice for class presentations because it makes her anxious. A cognitive psychologist would want to

   (A) know about Sara's dreams over the past few months

   (B) understand Sara's experience as a whole, rather than focusing on each incident separately

   (C) observe Sara's behavior as she practiced for a presentation

   (D) study Sara's neural activity as she practiced for a presentation

   (E) determine whether memories of past events are affecting Sara's behavior

6. Which of the following researchers studied how children were attached to their caregivers and their responses to encountering strangers?

   (A) Diana Baumrind

   (B) Jean Piaget

   (C) Carol Gilligan

   (D) Konrad Lorenz

   (E) Mary Ainsworth

7. Suppose that Leonard makes the decision not to speed because he does not want to have to pay a fine for speeding. Based on Kohlberg's theory, which stage of moral development would this type of behavior fall under?

   (A) Post-conventional

   (B) Pre-conventional

   (C) Universal ethical principles

   (D) Interpersonal accord and conformity

   (E) Conventional

8. Patients with schizophrenia are known to experience all of the following symptoms EXCEPT

   (A) delusions of grandeur

   (B) disordered thinking

   (C) inappropriate affect

   (D) dissociative fugue

   (E) catatonic episodes

9. Which of the following represents a humanistic approach to the treatment of abnormal behavior?

   (A) Using free association and dream interpretation to gain insight into the unconscious origins of the behavior

   (B) Using active listening to encourage patients to get in touch with their conscious feelings

   (C) Using aversive conditioning to train the patient to associate an unpleasant state with an unwanted behavior

   (D) Identifying errors in the patient's style of thinking and teaching new, more constructive ways to process information

   (E) Administering drugs that are specifically indicated to target the patient's abnormal behavior

10. Amanda and Andrew have recently started dating each other. They met through a guild in a massively multiplayer online roleplaying game and video chat regularly. Amanda lives in London, and Andrew lives in Honolulu. Which of the following factors is least likely to have contributed to their attraction to one another?

   (A) Similarity

   (B) Reciprocal liking

   (C) Physical attractiveness

   (D) The matching hypothesis

   (E) Proximity

GO ON TO THE NEXT PAGE

11. What is the process of moving memories from short-term memory to long-term memory?

    (A) Memory consolidation

    (B) Memory encoding

    (C) Memory recall

    (D) Memory rehearsal

    (E) Memory relearning

12. The expansion of which neuroanatomical structure suggests that humans are a species capable of advanced executive functions?

    (A) Medulla

    (B) Prefrontal cortex

    (C) Spinal cord

    (D) Olfactory bulb

    (E) Cerebellum

13. Grace's parents have noticed that she has rapid, frequent mood swings and difficulty forming and maintaining relationships with her peers. Grace is likely to be suffering from

    (A) borderline personality disorder

    (B) bipolar I disorder

    (C) antisocial personality disorder

    (D) social phobia

    (E) avoidant personality disorder

14. Michael is a museum curator attending the opening night event for a new museum. Michael moves through the noisy crowd of hundreds of people while looking for his colleague, and quickly turns around when he hears someone say his name. What concept best explains why Michael responded?

    (A) Dishabituation

    (B) Controlled processing

    (C) Divided attention

    (D) The cocktail-party phenomenon

    (E) Alternating attention

15. Pain is typically most intense in the moments immediately following an injury but, over a short period of time, begins to dull. If the same neurological signals are being sent to the brain but a person is not experiencing as much pain, this is an example of

    (A) sensory adaptation

    (B) top-down processing

    (C) inattentional blindness

    (D) trichromatic theory

    (E) opponent-process theory

16. Which of the following is an example of observational learning?

    (A) A puppy learns how to climb stairs by mimicking the actions of the family cat.

    (B) A baby starts to cry when he sees his mother enter the room to let her know he is hungry.

    (C) A toddler stops touching the stove after she burns her hand.

    (D) A child bikes to school on the same route his dad usually drives him on.

    (E) A teenager meets his friend's parents and understands some of his friend's mannerisms.

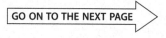

GO ON TO THE NEXT PAGE

17. Which field in psychology is focused on designing tests that measure constructs such as intelligence?

    (A) Cognitive neuroscience

    (B) Psychometrics

    (C) Human factors

    (D) School psychology

    (E) Developmental psychology

18. Physical symptoms that cannot be explained by a medical condition are most likely to be reported by those who have which of the following disorders?

    (A) Dysthymic disorder

    (B) Conversion disorder

    (C) Obsessive-compulsive disorder

    (D) Histrionic personality disorder

    (E) Dissociative amnesia

19. An individual is most likely to conform to a group if he or she

    (A) is joining a group of at least three people

    (B) is confident and secure in his or her ability

    (C) is interacting with others who hold diverse opinions

    (D) is part of a highly individualistic culture

    (E) is committed to a specific idea or worldview

20. Which of the following is an example of the door-in-the-face technique?

    (A) After agreeing to buy a necklace from a salesperson, you agree to buy a shirt.

    (B) After declining to purchase a product for $100, you agree to buy a product for $50.

    (C) After purchasing an expensive watch, you regret your purchase and decide to return it.

    (D) After noticing that an item is buy one get one free, you buy two despite only needing one.

    (E) After deciding not to make any new purchases, you change your mind after noticing a sale.

21. A twin study finds that genetic relatedness closely correlates with shyness, regardless of environment. What approach to personality theory does this data support?

    (A) Behaviorist

    (B) Biopsychological

    (C) Social cognitive

    (D) Psychoanalytic

    (E) Humanistic

22. A psychologist who believes that people feel sad solely because they cry and happy solely because they smile most likely subscribes to the

    (A) two-factor theory of emotion

    (B) Cannon-Bard theory of emotion

    (C) Schachter-Singer theory of emotion

    (D) James-Lange theory of emotion

    (E) evolutionary theory of emotion

GO ON TO THE NEXT PAGE

23. Which of the following is NOT true in the process of forming a new memory?

(A) Preserved memories remain out of consciousness until needed.

(B) Information is stored in memory.

(C) Sensory memory is the last stage in the process.

(D) Stored memory is recalled consciously when needed.

(E) Information is encoded into a utilizable form.

24. To gain insight into the experiences of only children, a psychologist conducts in-depth interviews with children who do not have siblings. This is an example of

(A) quantitative research

(B) qualitative research

(C) observational research

(D) experimental research

(E) correlational research

25. The brain's plasticity allows neuronal connections to develop and adapt to new environments. The anatomical change to neural networks that occurs in response to learning is called

(A) shaping

(B) conditioning

(C) neurotransmitter modification

(D) pruning

(E) mapping

26. Shortly before beginning a test, an examinee is reminded of a negative stereotype about a group that he belongs to. As a result, he receives a lower test score than he otherwise would have received. This is an example of

(A) stereotype threat

(B) groupthink

(C) culture-fairness

(D) poor reliability

(E) learned helplessness

27. In Vygotsky's cognitive development theory, a more knowledgeable other (MKO) most likely would NOT be a

(A) grandchild

(B) computer

(C) hamster

(D) parent

(E) teenager

28. A teenager feels hungry whenever he sees his mother's car pulling into the driveway. This is most likely an example of

(A) latent learning

(B) classical conditioning

(C) operant conditioning

(D) secondary reinforcement

(E) observational learning

GO ON TO THE NEXT PAGE

29. A researcher finds that the correlation coefficient between two variables is –0.81. The relationship between these two variables can best be classified as

    (A) weak and direct

    (B) weak and inverse

    (C) strong and direct

    (D) strong and inverse

    (E) no correlation

30. Which of the following is NOT a manifestation of antisocial personality disorder?

    (A) Disregarding social norms and laws

    (B) Lacking remorse

    (C) Lying continuously

    (D) Withdrawing from others

    (E) Risking the well being of others for one's own benefit

31. Electroconvulsive therapy (ECT)

    (A) is sometimes used to treat catatonia

    (B) results in fewer side effects than traditional forms of treatment

    (C) is used more frequently than psychopharmacology

    (D) has no effect on brain chemistry

    (E) has no known side effects

32. When viewing the above figure, most people are able to distinguish a triangle due to the brain's perception of subjective contours. This is an example of

    (A) top-down processing

    (B) the law of good continuation

    (C) the law of closure

    (D) bottom-up processing

    (E) data-driven processing

33. Which of the following psychologists distinguished between primary process and secondary process thinking?

    (A) Lev Vygotsky

    (B) Carl Wernicke

    (C) Noam Chomsky

    (D) Sigmund Freud

    (E) Paul Broca

GO ON TO THE NEXT PAGE

Questions 34–37 are based on the following.

Disorders of perceptions can have grave effects on those suffering from them. For instance, patients suffering from vertigo can feel nauseous or dizzy at any time. Patients suffering from pain disorders like chronic pain syndrome can have debilitating pain that makes even simple tasks difficult to manage. Treatments can be as varied as the causes of these disorders. Vertigo can be treated by anti-inflammatory drugs while chronic pain syndrome can often be managed by therapy in combination with medication.

34. In those suffering from vertigo, which of the following senses is being affected?

    (A) Thermoception

    (B) Nociception

    (C) Olfaction

    (D) Proprioception

    (E) Depth perception

35. Those with vertigo caused by inflammation can also have inflammation in their cochlea. Which of the following would be another sense that could be affected by this inflammation?

    (A) Vision

    (B) Hearing

    (C) Nociception

    (D) Thermoception

    (E) Gustation

36. Which of the following medications would an individual suffering from chronic pain syndrome most likely use for treatment?

    (A) Depressants

    (B) Stimulants

    (C) Hallucinogens

    (D) Statins

    (E) Narcotics

37. Patients suffering from chronic pain syndrome often have strong negative and sometimes catastrophic thoughts that correlate with their intensity of pain. What type of therapy would most likely be used to help such patients challenge these thoughts and establish more optimistic beliefs?

    (A) Psychoanalysis

    (B) Cognitive therapy

    (C) Client-centered therapy

    (D) Aversion therapy

    (E) Systemic therapy

38. A researcher is conducting an experiment to determine whether listening to music while completing a memory task improves performance on that task. The only difference between the experimental group and control group should be

    (A) whether the participants listen to music while completing the task

    (B) whether the participants receive a debriefing at the conclusion of the study

    (C) whether the participants enjoy listening to music on a regular basis

    (D) which genre of music the participants prefer listening to

    (E) which type of memory task the participants receive

39. According to Diana Baumrind, an authoritarian parent is

    (A) demanding but not responsive

    (B) demanding and responsive

    (C) not demanding but responsive

    (D) not demanding and not responsive

    (E) also called authoritative

GO ON TO THE NEXT PAGE

40. The Yerkes-Dodson law is a component of which theory of motivation?

    (A) Drive-reduction theory

    (B) Opponent-process theory

    (C) Incentive theory

    (D) Management theory

    (E) Arousal theory

41. At a company meeting, employees refrain from voicing any disagreement with the group's decisions because they want to maintain harmony in the group. As a result, the group makes a decision that later causes the company to lose money. This is an example of

    (A) anchoring

    (B) standardization

    (C) discrimination

    (D) groupthink

    (E) social learning

42. Where in the neuron are excitatory and inhibitory electrical potentials summated prior to an action potential?

    (A) Axon hillock

    (B) Soma

    (C) Dendritic spines

    (D) Nodes of Ranvier

    (E) Axon

43. All of the following are characteristic of REM sleep EXCEPT

    (A) muscle paralysis

    (B) dreaming

    (C) hypnagogic hallucinations

    (D) similar physiology to a wakeful state

    (E) increase in intensity toward the end of the night

44. Which psychological perspective stresses the importance of free will?

    (A) The psychoanalytic perspective

    (B) The behavioral perspective

    (C) The humanist perspective

    (D) The biopsychosocial perspective

    (E) The cognitive perspective

45. Split-brain is a condition in which the left and right hemispheres function independently of one another and is normally the result of a corpus callosotomy, in which the corpus callosum is surgically severed. Dr. William P. Van Wagenen developed this procedure to treat what condition?

    (A) Schizophrenia

    (B) Autism

    (C) Down syndrome

    (D) Depression

    (E) Epilepsy

46. A test that assumes that personality is mostly unconscious but can be revealed by responses to ambiguous stimuli is

    (A) projective

    (B) objective

    (C) the inner experience method

    (D) the descriptive experience sampling (DES) method

    (E) the articulated thoughts in simulated situations (ATSS) method

GO ON TO THE NEXT PAGE

47. A test that aims to measure overall academic ability includes reading comprehension questions, but not math questions. Since this test does not measure all facets of academic ability, it has poor

   (A) test-retest reliability

   (B) split-half reliability

   (C) predictive validity

   (D) inter-rater reliability

   (E) content validity

48. Which of the following treatments would be supported by Mary Cover-Jones?

   (A) Presenting a toddler who is scared of loud noises with a piece of chocolate every time he hears a loud noise

   (B) Training a patient to control his thoughts in order to then control his behaviors and emotions

   (C) Encouraging a patient to actively develop self-awareness and self-acceptance

   (D) Presenting a teenager with a token every time a desired behavior is exhibited and later allowing the teenager to exchange the token for a reward

   (E) Bringing together a family in order to focus on changing disruptive patterns of communication

49. Acquisition occurs when

   (A) practice results in a permanent change in behavior

   (B) an individual responds only to one stimulus, inhibiting responses to all other stimuli

   (C) repeat exposure to a stimulus results in a diminished emotional response

   (D) the stimulus evokes the conditioned response

   (E) an extinguished response reappears spontaneously after time has passed

50. A speaker gives a presentation that argues in favor of a new city policy. You decide that, because the speaker spoke clearly and confidently, you now agree with the new policy as well. Which term describes how you formed this new attitude?

   (A) Foot-in-the-door technique

   (B) Situational attribution

   (C) Normative social influence

   (D) Central route to persuasion

   (E) Peripheral route to persuasion

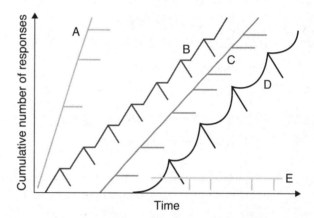

51. Assuming each dash in the above figure represents the addition of a reinforcer, which learning curve represents a variable ratio reinforcement schedule?

   (A) A

   (B) B

   (C) C

   (D) D

   (E) E

GO ON TO THE NEXT PAGE

52. A parrot is trained to speak whenever its owner whistles. However, a few weeks later, the parrot speaks anytime it hears whistling or singing. This is an example of

    (A) extinction

    (B) acquisition

    (C) spontaneous recovery

    (D) higher order conditioning

    (E) generalization

53. Which of the following can be used to prevent a placebo effect in research?

    (A) Descriptive statistics

    (B) Inferential statistics

    (C) Informed consent

    (D) A correlational study

    (E) A double-blind procedure

54. Which of the following is not one of the Big Five personality traits characterized by Costa and McCrae?

    (A) Conscientiousness

    (B) Openness to experience

    (C) Neuroticism

    (D) Extraversion

    (E) Psychoticism

55. One of the three main factors that make mnemonics useful for improving memory is

    (A) covariation

    (B) focused attention

    (C) sustained attention

    (D) imagination

    (E) selective attention

56. After hearing about a serious car accident that resulted in injuries to both drivers, a man concludes that the drivers must have been speeding and therefore brought the injuries on themselves. This is an example of

    (A) situational attribution

    (B) scapegoat theory

    (C) the just-world hypothesis

    (D) ingroup bias

    (E) prejudice

57. Jenny does not really enjoy interacting with others, so she mostly does activities on her own. She finds a job that involves little interaction with others, and ultimately winds up working from home most days. This interdependence of environment and personality is addressed by the theory of

    (A) the pleasure principle

    (B) basic hostility

    (C) reciprocal determinism

    (D) peak experience

    (E) shaping

58. Danny has been struggling to perfect his recipe for crab cakes. He has spent the last year varying the salt levels in his recipe, but has not solved the problem. Danny is engaging in

    (A) overconfidence

    (B) expertise

    (C) divergent thinking

    (D) convergent thinking

    (E) confirmation bias

GO ON TO THE NEXT PAGE

59. Robert Rescorla is best known for

(A) experimentally demonstrating the establishment of a conditioned reflex

(B) demonstrating the involvement of cognitive processes in classical conditioning

(C) discovering the process of imprinting in baby ducks

(D) establishing the concept of learned helplessness

(E) recognizing the importance of touch in normal development

60. The Rosenhan study demonstrated

(A) that psychological labels could have effects on the way that patients were treated

(B) that humans and animals can display learned helplessness if they believe an adverse situation is unavoidable

(C) that people will act against their own judgment in order to obey people in positions of authority

(D) that increasing someone's expectations of another person will result in the other person performing at a higher level

(E) that memories can be easily manipulated by using techniques like leading questions

61. John's psychiatrist prescribes him Prozac for his major depressive disorder. What treatment approach is John's doctor using?

(A) Cognitive

(B) Behavioral

(C) Humanistic

(D) Biomedical

(E) Psychoanalytic

62. Which of the following terms is correctly matched with its definition?

(A) Positive skew: a distribution with a mean greater than the median and a right lean

(B) Standard deviation: the difference between the top and bottom data value

(C) Positive correlation: when two variables in a study change in the same direction

(D) Mean: the middle value of a dataset arranged from least to greatest

(E) Confounding variable: a variable that is manipulated in an experiment

63. Which of the following is NOT involved in a reflex arc?

(A) Afferent nerve fibers

(B) Effector muscle or organ

(C) Sensory nerve endings

(D) Motor cortex

(E) Spinal cord

64. A hiring manager creates a test to measure job applicants' potential for future success. This is an example of a(n)

(A) aptitude test

(B) achievement test

(C) projective test

(D) standardized test

(E) intelligence test

65. Which type of study can be used to determine whether a causal relationship exists?

(A) Case study

(B) Survey

(C) Controlled experiment

(D) Naturalistic observation

(E) Structured observation

GO ON TO THE NEXT PAGE

66. Metacognition is defined as the

    (A) ability to think rationally, analyze situations, and solve problems

    (B) awareness of the elements of the environment through physical sensation

    (C) listing of options without critiquing them, analyzing those options, and then choosing one

    (D) awareness and understanding of one's own thought processes

    (E) reliance on oneself alone for any sense of purpose or meaning

67. A study finds that children learned to solve complex mathematical problems best by first watching their teachers go through them, then working through similar problems as a team, and finally trying them alone. Which of the following ideas best explains these findings?

    (A) Gestalt principles

    (B) Information processing theory

    (C) Zone of proximal development

    (D) Trial-and-error

    (E) Mental set

68. Which of the following is an example of a secondary reinforcer?

    (A) Praise

    (B) Food

    (C) Water

    (D) Sleep

    (E) Shelter

69. Which of the following is an example of standardization?

    (A) An intern purchases a new wardrobe to better match co-workers' style of dress.

    (B) A researcher ensures that all subjects participate in her study at the same time of day.

    (C) Two young children enter each stage of language acquisition in the same order.

    (D) A test developer specifies the conditions under which the test should be administered.

    (E) An institutional review board reviews a research proposal to determine whether it meets ethical standards.

Questions 70–71 are based on the following.

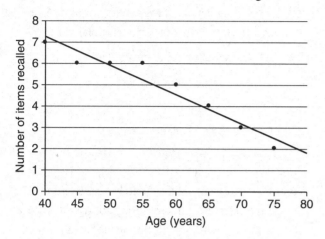

In an experiment, investigators read a series of words to adults aged 40-80. Subjects were then asked to recall as many words as possible. The results are summarized in the graph above.

70. The researchers have finished their study and are hoping to publish their results in a developmental psychology journal. Based on the data presented in the graph, which of the following would be an appropriate title for their paper?

    (A) Comparing physiological differences in younger versus older adults

    (B) Cohort study on socioemotional selectivity theory

    (C) Effect of self-reference on item recall

    (D) Case study analyzing the relationship between divided attention and memory

    (E) Analysis of the cognitive effects of aging in adults

71. In order to complete this task, a participant in the study would be activating his or her

    (A) semantic memory

    (B) episodic memory

    (C) working memory

    (D) declarative memory

    (E) procedural memory

72. Before participating in a research study, participants are entitled to

    (A) debriefing

    (B) informed consent

    (C) incentives

    (D) anonymity

    (E) confidentiality

73. Although nonverbal expressions of emotion differ across cultures, people in different cultures are able to identify the same seven basic emotions. Which psychologist is known for the original research that revealed this?

    (A) Paul Ekman

    (B) Albert Bandura

    (C) Hans Selye

    (D) Alfred Kinsey

    (E) Robert Rosenthal

74. For which of the following is it true that acute activation results in increased immune function, while chronic activation results in decreased immune function?

    (A) Prefrontal cortex

    (B) Mammillary bodies

    (C) Hypothalamic-pituitary-adrenal axis

    (D) Reticular formation

    (E) Hippocampus

GO ON TO THE NEXT PAGE

75. After the death of his mother two weeks ago, James tells his doctor that he has been feeling listless and lonely, and he is unsure how to work through his feelings. Of the following, the first response that James' doctor would be likely to suggest given this context is

    (A) antidepressants

    (B) electroconvulsive therapy

    (C) group therapy

    (D) counterconditioning

    (E) free association

76. Which of the following is NOT true of the *Diagnostic and Statistical Manual of Mental Disorders*?

    (A) It is constantly being revised and updated.

    (B) It catalogs the etiology of recognized psychological disorders.

    (C) It serves as the primary reference for psychologists making diagnoses.

    (D) All cultural disorders are not included in the DSM.

    (E) Critics argue that it makes the diagnostic process seem more objective than it actually is.

77. The role of an institutional review board (IRB) is to

    (A) guarantee that all research being conducted by an institution is methodologically sound

    (B) determine if research results are statistically significant

    (C) procure grants to fund research at an institution

    (D) evaluate studies within an institution and select the best ones to publish

    (E) ensure that all studies conducted within an institution uphold ethical standards

78. Revisiting the scene of a crime often aids victims in recalling details of the event to assist police investigations. This scenario is explained by

    (A) the serial position effect

    (B) state-dependent memory

    (C) context effects

    (D) the recency effect

    (E) the spacing effect

79. A sixteen-year-old boy switches back and forth between many different groups of friends before settling in with one group. According to Erikson's stages of personality development, which stage is the boy currently at?

    (A) Industry vs. inferiority

    (B) Intimacy vs. isolation

    (C) Initiative vs. guilt

    (D) Identity vs. role confusion

    (E) Autonomy vs. shame

80. Dahlia broke the rules and ate several cookies before dinner, so her mom took away her computer. This is an example of

    (A) positive reinforcement

    (B) negative reinforcement

    (C) positive punishment

    (D) negative punishment

    (E) shaping

GO ON TO THE NEXT PAGE

81. Which of the following is an example of a situational attribution?

    (A) A teacher attributes a student's poor test performance to a lack of motivation.

    (B) A parent attributes a child's tantrum to the child not having slept the night before.

    (C) A supervisor attributes an employee's recent success to his own good management.

    (D) A runner attributes her recent win in a race to her own natural running skill.

    (E) A volunteer attributes a donor's willingness to give to his generous nature.

82. Which of the following ideas was most central to individual psychology, Alfred Adler's distinctive psychodynamic approach?

    (A) Extinction

    (B) The inferiority complex

    (C) Sublimation

    (D) Post-conventional morality

    (E) Means-ends analysis

83. Which of the following studies would use random assignment?

    (A) A study examining the effect of caffeine on athletic performance immediately following intake

    (B) A study determining the prevalence of generalized anxiety disorder within a specified region

    (C) A study comparing males and females on digit span memorization

    (D) A study investigating the correlation between income and spatial reasoning skills

    (E) A study observing how adolescents interact with one another at school dances

84. Which language theorist is known for the concept of the language acquisition device?

    (A) B.F. Skinner

    (B) Noam Chomsky

    (C) Lev Vygotsky

    (D) Jean Piaget

    (E) George A. Miller

85. The terminal button is associated with

    (A) releasing neurotransmitters into the synapse

    (B) receiving signals from other neurons

    (C) transmitting an action potential down a neuron

    (D) enhancing action potential transmission

    (E) containing the nucleus and cellular structures

86. Which of the following statements about cognition and world cultures is LEAST accurate?

    (A) People across cultures search for cause-and-effect relationships to understand the world better.

    (B) North Americans do not often have self-serving biases.

    (C) Family and conformity are of primary importance to people in Latin America, Asia, and Africa.

    (D) Individuals from Africa more often have self-effacing biases.

    (E) Individual values and goals are most important to peoples in North America and Western Europe.

GO ON TO THE NEXT PAGE

87. Which of the following is NOT true regarding an individual experiencing prolonged stress?

   (A) The stress can make the individual more vulnerable to disease.

   (B) The individual's sympathetic nervous system is activated.

   (C) The individual's body can become depleted of resources.

   (D) The condition often results from a perceived sense of control over events.

   (E) Hormones are released to maintain the body's resistance.

88. Which of the following is NOT a Gestalt principle?

   (A) Closure

   (B) Continuity

   (C) Proximity

   (D) Similarity

   (E) Transduction

89. The desire to cultivate respect from others would be categorized by Maslow as a(n)

   (A) physiological need

   (B) safety need

   (C) esteem need

   (D) love and belonging need

   (E) self-actualization need

90. A researcher studying the biological basis of obesity is able to induce obesity in a rat by repeatedly stimulating a specific region in its brain. This region is the

   (A) amygdala

   (B) hippocampus

   (C) thalamus

   (D) reticular formation

   (E) lateral hypothalamus

91. A man spends a lot of his time volunteering at several charities, even though he receives no compensation for doing so. This is an example of

   (A) altruism

   (B) obedience

   (C) commitment

   (D) reinforcement

   (E) attachment

92. Which of the following statements about intelligence would be consistent with Robert Sternberg's theory of intelligence?

   (A) Intelligence is made up of three parts: practical, creative and analytical.

   (B) Intelligence has a facet called emotional intelligence that encompasses intra- and interpersonal relationships.

   (C) There are at least eight types of intelligence, including linguistic, musical, and logical-mathematical.

   (D) Intelligence consists of one single factor that can be measured with IQ tests.

   (E) There are two factors to intelligence, crystallized intelligence and fluid intelligence.

GO ON TO THE NEXT PAGE

Questions 93–95 are based on the following.

A psychologist uses a standard mood inventory to track Martha's reported mood for each of 14 consecutive one-week periods, and the results are shown in the graph below. A score of 0 represents a clinically normal or stable mood. Greater than 0 indicates an elevated mood, while less than 0 indicates a depressed mood. Scores between −100 and −50 or between 50 and 100 are considered severe.

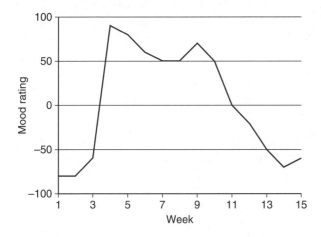

93. Assuming that the results in the graph provide an accurate reflection of Martha's changes in mood over time, Martha most likely suffers from which of the following?

(A) Major depressive disorder

(B) Seasonal affective disorder

(C) Cyclothymic disorder

(D) Bipolar I disorder

(E) Bipolar II disorder

94. Which of the following symptoms would Martha be most likely to display during week 9?

(A) Phobia

(B) Anhedonia

(C) Delusions

(D) Avolition

(E) Catatonia

95. Martha's prescribing psychologist would most likely advise Martha to take which of the following types of medication to manage her full range of symptoms?

(A) A lithium salt

(B) A tricyclic antidepressant

(C) A selective serotonin reuptake inhibitor

(D) An atypical antipsychotic

(E) A benzodiazepine

96. Results of a study are statistically significant if

(A) there is a large effect size

(B) there is no type I error

(C) the null hypothesis is rejected

(D) the correlation between variables is positive

(E) the p-value obtained is greater than 0.05

97. A child cries every time he is exposed to snakes. Which of the following is NOT a suitable mechanism for extinguishing this behavior?

(A) Stress inoculation training

(B) Exposure therapy

(C) Aversive conditioning

(D) Cognitive behavior therapy

(E) Systematic desensitization

98. Mary Whiton Calkins is known for

(A) leading the movement to treat the insane as mentally ill

(B) being the first woman president of the American Psychological Association

(C) improving conditions in jails and poor-houses throughout the United States

(D) being the first woman to receive a Ph.D. in psychology

(E) studying how the cerebral hemispheres of the brain communicate with each other

GO ON TO THE NEXT PAGE

99. A pregnant mother of two young children gets sick with rubella, usually a mild childhood rash and fever. For whom is this illness most likely to result in the most severe outcomes?

    (A) The two children

    (B) The mother

    (C) The fetus

    (D) Other exposed family members

    (E) People with limited immune systems in the community

100. Suppose that a twin study found that skill at playing billiards has a strong genetic component. Which group would be expected to be the most similar with respect to this skill?

    (A) Random strangers

    (B) Fraternal twins raised together

    (C) Fraternal twins raised apart

    (D) Identical twins raised together

    (E) Identical twins raised apart

END OF SECTION I

SECTION II BEGINS ON THE NEXT PAGE

SECTION II
50 Minutes—2 Questions
Percent of total grade: 33⅓

Directions Answer both of the following questions in 50 minutes. Lists of facts are insufficient to earn points; you must write essays that answer the questions thoughtfully with sound arguments that employ the proper terms from psychology. Use scratch paper to write out your responses.

1. For most of his life, Jack has experienced debilitating anxiety when he finds himself needing to go higher than the third or fourth story of a building. When he is high up in a building, his heart starts racing and he begins sweating, along with feeling a great fear of falling. He has recently been offered a new job that would really help his career, but he would have to work near the top of a skyscraper. Jack is certain he cannot work productively at such a height, so he seeks out a behavioral therapist to help him overcome his fear.

   Define the following terms and explain how each concept relates to Jack's situation.

   - Phobia

   - Sympathetic nervous system

   - Amygdala

   - Counterconditioning

   - Exposure therapy

   - Positive reinforcement

   - Richard Lazarus's appraisal theory of emotion

2. A researcher designs a day care room containing a curtain that divides the room in half. This researcher is studying how children of different ages react to their mother disappearing behind this curtain. While the mother sits in the room, the children crawl/walk around and happily explore the curtain while ignoring the other children, often leaving the mother's side. At some point the mother then steps behind the curtain so her child cannot see her. When this happens, many children have a negative reaction and start to cry. The mother reappears on the other side of the curtain and researchers then measure the surprised reactions of the children. The results of the study are shown on the following graph.

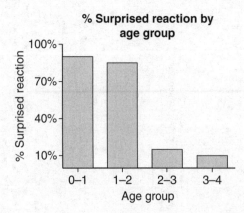

% Surprised reaction by age group

Part A

Define the following terms and explain how each concept is exhibited in this study.

- Object permanence
- Secure attachment

Part B

Identify each of the following for this study.

- Dependent variable
- Independent variable

Part C

Identify the major findings of this study with respect to object permanence, and explain how the graph supports these findings.

END OF SECTION II

STOP

END OF EXAM

ANSWER KEY

Section I

1.	C	16.	A	31.	A	46.	A	61.	D	76.	B	91.	A
2.	D	17.	B	32.	A	47.	E	62.	C	77.	E	92.	A
3.	E	18.	B	33.	D	48.	A	63.	D	78.	C	93.	D
4.	C	19.	A	34.	D	49.	D	64.	A	79.	D	94.	C
5.	E	20.	B	35.	B	50.	E	65.	C	80.	D	95.	A
6.	E	21.	B	36.	E	51.	A	66.	D	81.	B	96.	C
7.	B	22.	D	37.	B	52.	E	67.	C	82.	B	97.	C
8.	D	23.	C	38.	A	53.	E	68.	A	83.	A	98.	B
9.	B	24.	B	39.	A	54.	E	69.	D	84.	B	99.	C
10.	E	25.	D	40.	E	55.	D	70.	E	85.	A	100.	D
11.	A	26.	A	41.	D	56.	C	71.	C	86.	B		
12.	B	27.	C	42.	A	57.	C	72.	B	87.	D		
13.	A	28.	B	43.	C	58.	D	73.	A	88.	E		
14.	D	29.	D	44.	C	59.	B	74.	C	89.	C		
15.	A	30.	D	45.	E	60.	A	75.	C	90.	E		

Section II

1. See Answers and Explanations

2. See Answers and Explanations

PRACTICE EXAM 3 BREAKDOWN: ASSESS YOUR STRENGTHS

Use the following tables to determine which topics you are already strong in and which topics you need to review most.

Topic	Questions
Scientific Foundations of Psychology	17, 24, 29, 38, 44, 53, 62, 65, 72, 77, 83, 96, 98
Biological Bases of Behavior	12, 25, 36, 42, 43, 45, 63, 74, 85, 100
Sensation and Perception	3, 14, 15, 32, 34, 35, 88
Learning	16, 28, 49, 51, 52, 59, 68, 80, 97
Cognitive Psychology	1, 5, 11, 23, 47, 55, 58, 64, 66, 69, 71, 78, 84, 86, 92
Developmental Psychology	2, 6, 7, 27, 39, 67, 70, 99
Motivation, Emotion, and Personality	4, 21, 22, 33, 40, 46, 54, 57, 73, 79, 82, 87, 89, 90
Clinical Psychology	8, 9, 13, 18, 30, 31, 37, 48, 60, 61, 75, 76, 93, 94, 95
Social Psychology	10, 19, 20, 26, 41, 50, 56, 81, 91

Topic	Chapters	Questions on Exam	Number You Got Correct
Scientific Foundations of Psychology	4, 13	13	
Biological Bases of Behavior	5, 14	10	
Sensation and Perception	6, 15	7	
Learning	7, 16	9	
Cognitive Psychology	8, 17	15	
Developmental Psychology	9, 18	8	
Motivation, Emotion, and Personality	10, 19	14	
Clinical Psychology	11, 20	15	
Social Psychology	12, 21	9	

PRACTICE EXAM 3 ANSWERS AND EXPLANATIONS

SECTION I

1. C

Topic: Cognitive Psychology

The Flynn effect is an unexplained phenomenon wherein intelligence test scores have been steadily increasing over generations. Thus, **(C)** is correct because it illustrates an increase in IQ scores over time. (A) is an example of stereotype threat; (B) illustrates Fetal Alcohol Syndrome; (D) summarizes a theory that was disproven by Terman's study of gifted individuals; and (E) demonstrates a criticism of intelligence tests that do not measure intelligence on multiple dimensions.

2. D

Topic: Developmental Psychology

The reality principle is a concept in Freud's model of personality, not Piaget's theory of cognitive development; **(D)** is therefore correct. (C) is incorrect because schemata are included in Piaget's theory and are defined as the basic building blocks of knowledge. (B) is incorrect because Piaget believed that adaptation was the result of intellectual growth. Two processes resulted in this adaptation: assimilation and accommodation. In the former, a schema that already exists is utilized in a new sensory stimulus; the latter requires changing an existing schema to include new information. Consequently, (A) and (E) are also incorrect.

3. E

Topic: Sensation and Perception

Weber's law states that there is a constant ratio between (1) the change in stimulus magnitude needed to produce a just-noticeable difference and (2) the magnitude of the original stimulus. Cassidy asks her friends to tell her when they are first able to notice a change in weight, indicating that her experiment is investigating this constant ratio, making **(E)** correct. The all-or-none phenomenon, (A), is the observation that once the threshold potential of a neuron is reached, the neuron will fire an action potential regardless of the strength of the stimulus. If that threshold potential is not reached, no response is observed.

The law of similarity, (B), is a Gestalt principle that holds that objects that appear similar to one another will be grouped together by the individual perceiving the stimuli. The disconfirmation principle, (C), is the idea that if an experiment is performed in which the evidence fails to support the hypothesis, the hypothesis must be reconsidered. The Yerkes-Dodson law, (D), maintains that performance at a given task is optimal under conditions of moderate arousal.

4. C

Topic: Motivation, Emotion, and Personality

An avoidance-avoidance conflict is one in which an individual has to choose between two equally unattractive options. Since limping home in pain and calling an unfriendly neighbor are both undesirable options, **(C)** is correct. An approach-avoidance conflict occurs when an individual must decide whether to pursue or avoid something that has both positive and negative aspects, eliminating (A). An approach-approach conflict occurs when an individual must choose between two equally attractive options. Since this is the opposite of what is described in the question stem, (B) is incorrect. An intrapersonal conflict is an internal conflict that can develop from one's thoughts, ideas, values, or predispositions, eliminating (D). An interpersonal conflict is a conflict between multiple individuals. Though Zara has an interpersonal conflict with her neighbor, this type of conflict does not represent the choice she is being forced to make, eliminating (E).

5. E

Topic: Cognitive Psychology

Cognitive psychologists study how mental processes such as perception, thinking, learning, and memory impact behavior. They believe that the rules people use to interpret the world are an important part of understanding why people think and act the way they do. Since a cognitive psychologist would be interested in how Sara's acquisition and processing of information in her past would affect her thoughts and behaviors now, **(E)** is correct. (A) is more characteristic of a psychoanalytic approach. (B) is more characteristic of Gestalt psychology.

(C) is more characteristic of a behavioristic approach. (D) is more characteristic of a biopsychology or neuroscience approach.

6. E
Topic: Developmental Psychology

Mary Ainsworth is responsible for the development of attachment theory, which identifies four different types of attachment children can form with their caregivers. These attachment types influence the way that children respond when encountering new people. **(E)** is therefore correct. Baumrind, (A), is best known for her work on parenting styles. Piaget, (B), is best known for his stages of childhood development. Gilligan, (C), was primarily interested in moral development and is known for her criticisms of Lawrence Kohlberg's theory. Lorenz, (D), is best known for his work on imprinting.

7. B
Topic: Developmental Psychology

According to Kohlberg's stages of moral development, making a decision simply to avoid personal punishment would be considered to be pre-conventional morality, specifically the obedience and punishment orientation. This makes **(B)** the correct answer. (D) and (E) are incorrect because conventional morality, including the interpersonal accord and conformity substage, is about making moral decisions based on social expectations or law and order. (A) and (C) are incorrect because post-conventional morality, including the universal ethical principles substage, involves an individual making moral decisions based on the good of all or a universal ethical code for humankind.

8. D
Topic: Clinical Psychology

Dissociative fugue is a dissociative disorder in which people lose some or all memories of their past. It is not a symptom of schizophrenia, but a distinct condition. Thus, **(D)** is correct. Symptoms of schizophrenia include delusions of persecution or grandeur, disordered thinking, hallucinations, the creation of neologisms, nonsensical word associations, inappropriate affect, flat affect, and catatonic episodes, so (A), (B), (C), and (E) are incorrect.

9. B
Topic: Clinical Psychology

The goal of humanistic therapy is to help patients develop a healthier sense of self. Since encouraging patients to get in touch with their own emotions is an important first step in achieving self-actualization, **(B)** is correct. (A) is more indicative of the psychoanalytic approach, which uses free association and dream analysis to better understand the unconscious mind. (C) is an example of a behavioral therapy, using stimuli to affect observable behaviors. (D) is more indicative of the cognitive approach to therapy, which investigates how dysfunctional styles of thought lead to abnormal behaviors. (E) is an example of biomedical therapy, which attempts to directly alter biological functioning through medication, electric shock, or surgery.

10. E
Topic: Social Psychology

Proximity refers to the relative closeness of individuals geographically. Closer proximity is associated with increased attraction. Because Amanda and Andrew live on virtually opposite sides of the globe, they do not share proximity, making **(E)** correct. (A), (B), (C), and (D) all refer to other aspects of attraction that are not necessarily affected by the distance between Amanda and Andrew, especially since they are aware of each others' appearances and do interact regularly.

11. A
Topic: Cognitive Psychology

When memories are moved from short-term memory to long-term memory, this process is called memory consolidation, which means that **(A)** is correct. Encoding is the process by which information gets into the brain, so (B) is incorrect. Recall and relearning are both ways for memories to go from long-term memory to short-term memory; (C) and (E) are incorrect. Rehearsal maintains memories in the short-term memory but is not involved in moving memories from short-term to long-term, so (D) is incorrect.

12. B

Topic: Biological Bases of Behavior

The prefrontal cortex is responsible for higher-level thought processes such as problem-solving, emotional expression, and judgment, making **(B)** correct. This structure is highly developed in humans, while more primitive organisms feature less complex prefrontal cortices as well as fewer higher-level functions. The medulla, (A), is responsible for autonomic functions and is not more developed in organisms capable of advanced thought—the medulla of a mouse accomplishes roughly the same functions as the human medulla. The length of the spinal cord, (C), correlates with the organism's size, not with its evolutionary complexity. While the olfactory bulb, (D), grew as organisms developed a better sense of smell, several organisms feature much larger olfactory bulbs than humans, such as bears and sharks. The cerebellum, (E), is primarily involved in coordinating movement, although it may also play a role in some higher-level processes such as language and attention, but not to the extent achieved by the prefrontal cortex.

13. A

Topic: Clinical Psychology

Borderline personality disorder is characterized by lack of stability in interpersonal relationships, self-image, and emotion. Individuals tend to experience rapid mood swings, impulsivity, angry outbursts, and an intense fear of abandonment. Thus, **(A)** is correct. Bipolar I disorder is a mood disorder in which an individual typically alternates between periods of depression and mania. Though Grace does experience mood swings, the fact that they are rapid and that a description of these moods as depressed or euphoric is not provided in the question stem makes (B) incorrect. Individuals with antisocial personality disorder exhibit a lack of remorse for wrongdoing. They frequently ignore rules and laws and are often aggressive and ruthless, making (C) incorrect. Social phobia is characterized by an intense fear of social situations. Though Grace has trouble maintaining friendships, since the question stem does not state that this is because she is purposely avoiding social situations, (D) can be eliminated. (E) is incorrect because avoidant personality disorder is characterized by inhibition in social situations, feelings of inadequacy, and an oversensitivity to criticism.

14. D

Topic: Sensation and Perception

Michael is exhibiting a type of selective attention known as the cocktail-party phenomenon, **(D)**. Michael is able to move through the crowd while ignoring the many conversations he passes by but is still able to respond when he senses a meaningful stimulus, his name. Dishabituation is the recovery of a response to a stimulus after habituation has occurred. The question stem does not indicate that Michael has been habituated to his name, in which case he would generally ignore his name when he hears it, so (A) is incorrect. Controlled processing occurs when an individual gives undivided attention to a task in order to accomplish it. Controlled processing is primarily used in new or complex tasks, which would not apply to searching for a friend, so (B) is incorrect. Divided attention uses automatic processing to accomplish multiple tasks at once. In this scenario, Michael is actively looking for his colleague and passively filtering out all of the other conversations, and thus he is not actively performing multiple tasks at once, making (C) incorrect. Alternating attention is the ability to shift one's attention back and forth between multiple attention-demanding tasks. In this scenario, Michael is only focused on finding his colleague and is not giving attention to the background noise, making (E) incorrect.

15. A

Topic: Sensation and Perception

When a stimulus is persistent, the brain can adapt to no longer perceive the stimulus, even though it is still being sensed. This disconnect between stimulus and perception is called sensory adaptation, and so **(A)** is correct. Top-down processing occurs when your sensations are influenced by your previous experience, so (B) is incorrect. (C) is incorrect because inattentional blindness occurs when your focus is intent on one stimulus and you miss other cues in your visual field. Trichromatic theory and opponent-process theory are accounts of how humans process color, so (D) and (E) are incorrect.

16. A

Topic: Learning

Observational learning is defined as learning behaviors by watching others. Since the puppy learns how to climb by watching the cat, **(A)** is correct. (B) is incorrect because crying to indicate hunger is an instinctual behavior. (C) is incorrect because the toddler did not learn to stop touching the stove by observing someone else. (D) is an example of latent learning. While (E) involves an individual learning something from an observation he makes, this example does not fit the definition of observational learning.

17. B
Topic: Scientific Foundations of Psychology

Psychometrics is a subfield of psychology that focuses on the design, validation, and evaluation of tests, including intelligence tests. This makes **(B)** correct. (D) may be tempting because school psychologists often make use of intelligence tests; however, the field of school psychology is not centered on the development of tests. Cognitive neuroscience, (A), involves the study of the biological phenomena underpinning cognition; human factors, (C), is a subfield of industrial and organizational psychology; and developmental psychology, (E), investigates psychological development across the lifespan.

18. B
Topic: Clinical Psychology

Conversion disorder is a somatoform disorder in which an individual displays a physical symptom that cannot be explained by a medical or chemical cause. Thus, **(B)** is correct. Dysthymic disorder, (A), is a mood disorder consisting of mild depression lasting for at least two years. Obsessive-compulsive disorder, (C), is a disorder characterized by uncontrollable, recurring thoughts (obsessions) and behaviors (compulsions) that an individual feels must be repeated over and over again. Histrionic personality disorder, (D), is characterized by excessive attention-seeking emotions and behavior. Dissociative amnesia, (E), is characterized by a sudden inability to recall important personal information.

19. A
Topic: Social Psychology

One factor that has been found to increase likelihood of conformity is larger group size, specifically a group size of three or more people. This makes **(A)** correct. (B), (C),

(D), and (E) all illustrate situations that decrease, rather than increase, likelihood of conformity.

20. B
Topic: Social Psychology

According to the door-in-the-face phenomenon, you will comply with a reasonable request after first being presented with a more extreme request. Thus, **(B)** is correct because it shows first declining a larger request and then complying with a more reasonable request. (A) may be tempting because it illustrates the foot-in-the-door phenomenon (complying with a larger request after first complying with a smaller request), but this is distinct from door-in-the-face. The other answer choices demonstrate neither of these phenomena.

21. B
Topic: Motivation, Emotion, and Personality

The biopsychological approach to personality holds that genetics determine neurological traits, which in turn determine behavior. A twin study that finds strong genetic effects for personality traits supports this theory, making **(B)** correct. The behaviorist approach, (A), would predict the opposite results: that environment, not genetics, would dictate behavior. (C), (D), and (E) are all theoretical approaches that consider variables beyond genetics and environment, making them incorrect.

22. D
Topic: Motivation, Emotion, and Personality

The James-Lange theory states that after a stimulus causes a physiological response, the body interprets this response to produce an emotion. Thus, feeling an emotion (sadness) in response to the body's physiological response (crying) fits the James-Lange theory of emotion, making **(D)** correct. The Schachter-Singer theory of emotion, also known as the two-factor theory of emotion, focuses on the interaction between physiological arousal and the cognitive interpretation of that arousal. It involves taking an extra step to process whether the physiological response of crying is due to happiness or sadness, before assigning an emotion. Thus, (A) and (C) are incorrect. The Cannon-Bard theory states that an emotion-arousing stimulus simultaneously triggers a physiological response and an emotional response, making (B) incorrect. The evolutionary theory of emotion states that emotions are innate responses to stimuli, eliminating (E).

23. C
Topic: Cognitive Psychology

The first stage of memory formation is the collection of sensory data from one's surroundings exactly as seen or heard. **(C)** is correct because sensory memory is the first—not the last—stage in the process. When a new memory is formed, information is encoded, stored in memory unconsciously, and retrieved consciously when needed. Consequently, (A), (B), (D), and (E) are incorrect.

24. B
Topic: Scientific Foundations of Psychology

Since the researcher here is using interviews to collect data, the data will be in the form of words rather than numbers. Since qualitative research is the term for research that deals with non-numerical data, **(B)** is the correct answer. Quantitative research, (A), is the opposite of qualitative research because it involves numerical, or quantifiable, data. (C) is incorrect because observational research would involve the researcher observing the children and describing their behaviors rather than interviewing them directly. (D) and (E) are incorrect because they are both types of quantitative, rather than qualitative, research.

25. D
Topic: Biological Bases of Behavior

Synaptic pruning is the process by which neural networks adjust to improve execution of repeated behaviors and actions. As an individual learns, synapses form and disappear to strengthen certain networks and eliminate others via pruning. **(D)** is correct. (A) and (B) are behavioral methods by which learning can be achieved, not anatomical changes, and are thus incorrect. Neurotransmitters are not modified; only axons and dendrites change in response to learning, so (C) is incorrect. Topographical maps of some senses exist in the brain (such as touch at the sensory cortex), but alterations in neuronal connections are called pruning, not mapping, (E).

26. A
Topic: Social Psychology

Stereotype threat occurs when people show lower test performance due to being reminded of a negative stereotype about a group they belong to prior to taking the test. Thus, **(A)** is correct. (B) is incorrect because groupthink refers to a process that occurs within a group rather than within an individual. (C) is incorrect because culture-fairness can help to prevent the phenomenon being described. (D) is incorrect because poor reliability indicates a flaw in the design of a test, whereas the question describes circumstances surrounding the administration of a test. (E) is a phenomenon in social psychology in which an individual is conditioned to believe that he or she has no control over a situation. This choice may be tempting, but keep in mind that the question stem does not state that the examinee feels that the exam is beyond his control.

27. C
Topic: Developmental Psychology

Vygotsky's more knowledgeable other (MKO) is any person or thing with a higher level of understanding than the learning individual. Because hamsters are nonhuman animals with a diminished understanding of the world compared to human beings, they are extremely unlikely to serve as MKOs. **(C)** is thus correct. (A), (B), (D), and (E) are incorrect because all could be MKOs. If a grandchild were teaching his or her grandparent how to use a television remote control or some other technological gadget, the grandchild would be serving as an MKO. Because some computer programs are educational, a computer could be an MKO for an adult or child. A parent, teacher, or coach would be obvious MKOs for children. Finally, a teenager could be an MKO for an adult if the teen were teaching the adult some cultural skill popular among the young, such as freestyle rapping.

28. B
Topic: Learning

Classical conditioning is a process in which a neutral stimulus is paired with a stimulus that evokes a specific response until the previously neutral stimulus comes to evoke a similar response. In this example, the mother pulling into the driveway began as the neutral stimulus but has now become a conditioned stimulus causing a conditioned response: the teenager's feelings of hunger. Thus, **(B)** is correct. (A) is incorrect because latent learning is a type of learning that becomes obvious only when a reinforcement is given for demonstrating it. (C) is incorrect because operant conditioning is a type of learning in which a behavior is strengthened or diminished if followed by a reinforcer or punisher, respectively. (D) is incorrect because secondary reinforcement occurs when a stimulus reinforces a behavior after it has been associated with a primary reinforcer. Examples of secondary reinforcement include money and praise. (E) is incorrect because observational learning is defined as learning behaviors by watching other individuals receive rewards or punishments.

29. D

Topic: Scientific Foundations of Psychology

Correlation coefficients reveal two characteristics of a relationship between variables: direction and strength. The sign indicates the direction (positive indicates a direct relationship and negative indicates an inverse relationship). The magnitude, on the other hand, indicates the strength of the relationship. Values closer to 1 or −1 indicate stronger relationships, whereas values closer to 0 indicate weaker relationships. If the correlation is 0, then there is no relationship. Since −0.81 is a non-zero number, (E) is incorrect. Furthermore, the sign is negative, which means that the correlation must be inverse. This eliminates (A) and (C). Finally, since −0.81 is close to −1, the correlation is strong. This makes **(D)** correct and (B) incorrect.

30. D

Topic: Clinical Psychology

The *Diagnostic and Statistical Manual of Mental Disorders* (DSM-5) describes 10 types of personality disorders that are grouped into 3 discrete clusters—A, B, and C—based on the similarities of the disorders. Behavior that is erratic and histrionic describes Cluster B, to which antisocial personality disorder belongs. (A), (B), (C), and (E) can be eliminated because disregarding social norms and laws, lacking remorse, lying continuously, and risking the well being of others for one's own benefit all describe symptoms of antisocial personality disorder. That means **(D)** is correct. Withdrawing from others is a symptom of schizoid personality disorder, which is a

Cluster A personality disorder that is characterized by eccentric and odd behavior.

31. A

Topic: Clinical Psychology

Electroconvulsive therapy is sometimes used for patients suffering from catatonia, a symptom involving physical immobility associated with schizophrenia and other disorders, making **(A)** correct. ECT is known for having worse side effects than psychopharmacology, such as memory loss, brief seizures, or loss of consciousness, eliminating (B) and (E). As a result, it is used less frequently than psychopharmacology, eliminating (C). ECT is an example of a biomedical therapy, which attempts to directly alter biological functioning. The quick stimulations that are administered during ECT treatments cause changes in brain chemistry, making (D) incorrect.

32. A

Topic: Sensation and Perception

Bottom-up processing, (D), and data-driven processing, (E), are alternative names for the same concept, wherein the brain takes in individual sensory stimuli and combines them together to create a cohesive image before determining what the object is. Gestalt principles use the opposite form of processing, known as top-down processing, or conceptually driven processing, wherein the brain recognizes the whole object first and then recognizes the components based on these expectations. **(A)** is correct. The question stem describes the Gestalt principle, "subjective contours," which the brain employs when forming a closed triangle. (B) and (C) are Gestalt principles that describe other processing phenomena. The law of good continuation, (B), says that elements that appear to follow in the same pathway tend to be grouped together. The law of closure, (C), says that when a space is enclosed by a contour, it tends to be perceived as a complete figure.

33. D

Topic: Motivation, Emotion, and Personality

In his structural model of personality, Freud distinguished between primary process thinking, generated by the id, which aims at immediate gratification, and secondary process thinking, generated by the ego, which seeks to relieve the tension caused by delaying gratification. **(D)** is correct. The remaining choices name psychologists known for other ideas. (A) is incorrect because Vygotsky was a developmental psychologist who adopted a sociocultural approach and was known for ideas such as the zone of proximal development (ZPD). (B) and (E) are incorrect because Wernicke and Broca were scientists who studied speech disorders; they are the namesakes of Wernicke's area and Broca's area, regions in the brain responsible for speech comprehension and speech production, respectively. (C) is incorrect because Chomsky developed the idea of a universal grammar.

34. D

Topic: Sensation and Perception

Those suffering from vertigo have issues with their vestibular sense. This sense comes from specialized structures in the inner ear that allow humans to sense their position in space, or proprioception. Since proprioception is affected in those suffering from vertigo, **(D)** is correct. Thermoception is the perception of temperature, so (A) is incorrect. Nociception is the perception of pain; (B) is incorrect. Olfaction is the perception of scent, making (C) incorrect. Depth perception has to do with determining the distance of objects and is not affected by vertigo; (E) is incorrect.

35. B

Topic: Sensation and Perception

Inflammatory vertigo is caused by inflammation in the inner ear. The structures associated with vestibular sense (the semicircular canals) are very close to the cochlea. The cochlea is the structure associated with turning vibrations in the air into nerve impulses, or the perception of sound. Therefore, if vertigo is caused by inflammation, hearing might also be affected, and **(B)** is correct. None of the other senses are associated with the inner ear and therefore (A), (C), (D), and (E) are incorrect.

36. E

Topic: Biological Bases of Behavior

Narcotics, also referred to as opioids, act globally to decrease pain and reduce sensation. In fact, despite being addictive, they are commonly prescribed for chronic pain

due to their efficacy. **(E)** is correct. While the other drug classes listed in (A), (B), (C), and (D) may have some secondary effects that could reduce pain, relief of severe pain is not their primary function.

37. B

Topic: Clinical Psychology

Some types of cognitive therapy use a process called cognitive restructuring, which challenges irrational or unhelpful beliefs and replaces them with more realistic and productive ones. Thus, a cognitive approach could be especially helpful for treating the described aspect of chronic pain syndrome, so **(B)** is correct. The remaining choices present types of therapy that do not primarily focus on challenging beliefs and establishing new ones. (A) is incorrect because psychoanalysis is a type of therapy that focuses primarily on the unconscious, while the chronic pain sufferer's issues are with conscious sensations and beliefs. (C) is incorrect because client-centered therapy is a humanistic approach that focuses on authenticity and self-esteem. (D) is incorrect because aversion therapy is a behavioral technique primarily used to treat addictions and bad habits. (E) is incorrect because systemic therapy is typically only used for couples or families.

38. A

Topic: Scientific Foundations of Psychology

In an experiment, the only difference between the experimental group and the control group should involve the independent variable. In the experiment described, the independent variable is music. More specifically, it is listening to music while completing a task. Thus, the experimental group would listen to music while completing the task while the control group would not, making **(A)** correct. (B) is incorrect because all participants should receive a similar debriefing after a study ends. (C) and (D) may be tempting because they both mention music. However, they are incorrect because they are inconsistent with what the experimenter is measuring. Here, the experimenter is interested in the effect of listening to music, rather than enjoyment of music or of a specific music genre. (E) is incorrect because the memory task should be constant between the two groups.

39. A

Topic: Developmental Psychology

Diana Baumrind's theory of parenting typologies classifies authoritarian parents as highly demanding but unresponsive. **(A)** is correct. (B) and (E) are incorrect because an authoritative parent is both demanding and responsive. (C) is incorrect because an indulgent parent is not demanding but responsive. Neglectful parents are considered to be not demanding and not responsive, making (D) incorrect.

40. E

Topic: Motivation, Emotion, and Personality

Arousal theory states that humans and animals are motivated by activities that help them achieve their optimum level of excitement or arousal. The Yerkes-Dodson law, which is a component of this theory, states that while an increase in arousal can boost performance, once the arousal surpasses the optimal level, the individual's performance will diminish. Thus, **(E)** is correct. Drive-reduction theory maintains that a physiological need creates an aroused tension state, also known as a drive, that motivates an organism to satisfy or reduce the need, eliminating (A). (B) is incorrect because opponent process theory is an explanation of color vision. (C) is incorrect because incentive theory maintains that behavior is directed toward attaining desirable stimuli and avoiding unwanted stimuli. Theory X of management theory states that managers believe employees will work when offered rewards or threatened with punishments while theory Y of management theory states that managers believe employees are internally motivated to do good work. Thus, (D) can be eliminated.

41. D

Topic: Social Psychology

Groupthink occurs when a desire for harmony in a decision-making group outweighs consideration of realistic alternatives. As a result, the group will end up making a riskier decision than an individual within the group would have made. In this example, the group makes a decision that proves detrimental to the company because group members do not voice their concern with the decision being made. **(D)** is correct.

(A) refers to a tendency to rely too heavily on the first piece of information received on a topic, and it typically happens at the individual level rather than the group level. (B) is a term used in psychometrics that refers to using consistent content and procedures when administering a test. (C) refers to unjustifiable negative behavior toward members of an outgroup. (E) refers to a theory of learning that maintains that people learn social behavior by observing others being rewarded and punished.

42. A

Topic: Biological Bases of Behavior

The axon hillock is the summation point of all electrical potentials that have been received by the dendrites of the neuron. At the axon hillock, if the absolute threshold is reached, the neuron will propagate an action potential down the axon. If not, there will be no action potential. **(A)** is correct. The soma, (B), and the dendritic spines, (C), only conduct potentials and are not involved in summation. The nodes of Ranvier, (D), and the axon, (E), only propagate action potentials and are not involved in summation.

43. C

Topic: Biological Bases of Behavior

Hypnagogic hallucinations are characteristic of the first stage of non-REM sleep, which is a transitional state between wakefulness and dreaming. Hypnagogic hallucinations can be auditory or visual in nature, and are often reminiscent of an activity the subject was engaged in prior to entering the sleep cycle. Because it is not characteristic of REM sleep, **(C)** is correct. Dreaming, (B), is perhaps the most well-known aspect of REM sleep, but muscle paralysis, (A), goes hand-in-hand with dreaming: the body effectively becomes paralyzed during dreaming to prevent the sleeping individual from acting out his or her dreams, which could potentially be dangerous. One of the distinguishing characteristics of REM sleep is that it shares similar physiology with the wakeful state, so (D) is incorrect. Because the mind is active while the body is paralyzed, REM sleep is sometimes called paradoxical sleep. Finally, (E) is incorrect because REM sleep increases in intensity toward the end of the night.

44. C

Topic: Scientific Foundations of Psychology

The humanist perspective stresses the importance of individual choice and free will, making **(C)** correct. The psychoanalytic perspective, (A), stresses the importance of exploring and understanding the unconscious mind. The behavioral perspective, (B), explores how stimuli affect observable behaviors. The biopsychosocial perspective, (D), maintains that biological, psychological, and social factors all play a role in human behavior and the development of psychological disorders. The cognitive perspective, (E), examines human thought and behavior in terms of how information is interpreted, processed, and remembered.

45. E

Topic: Biological Bases of Behavior

The intensity of seizures manifesting near the corpus callosum may be reduced through a corpus callosotomy, which inhibits the propagation of a seizure between hemispheres of the brain. Seizures are the primary symptom in epileptic persons; indeed, the corpus callosotomy was designed to treat epilepsy. **(E)** is therefore correct. While split-brain people face some drawbacks, such as their cerebral hemispheres working in opposition to one another due to lack of communication, the condition is often considered preferable to the intense seizures caused by epilepsy. The conditions in (A), (B), (C), and (D) are not normally treated with invasive surgery but are instead treated with pharmacological approaches.

46. A

Topic: Motivation, Emotion, and Personality

Projective tests such as the Rorschach test, which utilizes cards with ambiguous inkblots, and the Thematic Apperception Test (TAT), which involves storytelling about vague scenes, theoretically allow unconscious thoughts or motives to be exposed through an individual's responses. **(A)** is therefore correct. Self-reporting on objective tests assumes that personality is conscious, so (B) can be eliminated. (C), (D), and (E) are incorrect for a similar reason, presupposing that personality is a matter of conscious, rather than unconscious, factors. The inner experience, DES, and ATSS methods are all based on a type of introspection, in which subjects attempt to articulate aspects of their conscious experience.

47. E

Topic: Cognitive Psychology

Remember that, in testing, reliability refers to consistency and validity refers to accuracy. Since this question refers to a problem with test accuracy, (A) and (B) can be eliminated. Content validity, **(E)**, is the degree to which a test measures the total construct that it is meant to measure. Since the test described in the question stem is not measuring the full construct of academic ability because it fails to measure math skills, this test has poor content validity. Thus, **(E)** is correct. (C) refers to whether test results relate to another measure of the same construct and (D) refers to whether the results of different individuals judging a task are similar.

48. A

Topic: Clinical Psychology

Mary Cover-Jones was a developmental psychologist who used classical conditioning to counter-condition a four-year-old's fear of rabbits. She began by placing the rabbit a distance away from the child and slowly moving it closer. As the rabbit came closer, the child was given candy. Eventually, the child was able to touch the rabbit without crying. Thus, since **(A)** describes provision of a new desirable stimulus in order to eradicate an unwanted behavior, it is correct. (B) is an example of cognitive-behavioral therapy. (C) is an example of a humanistic treatment. (D) is an example of token economy, which is based on the principles of operant conditioning. (E) is an example of a type of group therapy in which a family can come together to evaluate their behavior, set goals, and practice coping strategies.

49. D

Topic: Learning

Acquisition is the initial stage in classical conditioning. It is the phase in which the neutral stimulus is paired with the unconditioned stimulus and comes to evoke a conditioned response. Thus, **(D)** is correct. (A) is incorrect because it describes learning, defined as the process by which experience or practice leads to a relatively permanent change in behavior. (B) is incorrect because it describes discrimination, a process in which an individual learns to respond to only one stimulus and to inhibit the response to all other stimuli. (C) is incorrect because it describes habituation, which occurs when repeat exposure to a single stimulus results in a diminished response to that stimulus. (E) is incorrect because it describes the process of spontaneous recovery, in which the conditioned response reappears after having disappeared for a while.

50. E

Topic: Social Psychology

In this example, you are forming your opinion based on incidental cues (like the speaker's manner of speaking) rather than the content of the argument presented. The tendency of being influenced by these incidental cues is known as the peripheral route to persuasion, making **(E)** correct. (A) refers to the technique of getting someone to comply with a large request by first having them comply with a smaller request. (B) refers to an assumption that a person's behavior can be attributed to the situation at hand rather than his or her disposition. (C) refers to the influence that results from a person's desire to gain approval from others. (D) is incorrect because the central route to persuasion involves focusing on the content of an argument rather than the context.

51. A

Topic: Learning

Ratio reinforcement schedules are characterized by their rapid response rates, and variable ratio schedules occur when the response is reinforced after a random number of responses. For example, in a lab setting, a rat may receive a food pellet after pressing a bar once, then four times, then three times, then once again. Since **(A)** shows the delivery of a reinforcer after a random number of rapid responses, it is correct. (B) indicates a fixed ratio schedule, in which a response is consistently reinforced after a specific number of responses have been performed. Like the variable ratio schedule, the response rate is high. However, during this schedule, there are pauses after reinforcement, indicated by the horizontal components. (C) indicates a variable interval schedule, in which a response is rewarded after a random amount of time has elapsed. This schedule is characterized by low and steady response rates. (D) indicates a fixed interval schedule, in which the response is rewarded only after a specific amount of time has passed. It can be easily

identified by the lack of responses directly after the reinforcer is administered (the flatter regions), and the subsequent increase in responses near the end (the steeper regions) of the interval. (E) represents a scenario where the behavior is already being performed and the addition of a reinforcer has no effect on the response rate.

52. E

Topic: Learning

Generalization is the tendency to respond to stimuli that are similar to the conditioned stimuli. The classic example of generalization occurred during John Watson's Little Albert experiment in which Albert, who was initially only afraid of white rats, came to be afraid of all animals with white fur. Thus, **(E)** is correct. (A) is incorrect because extinction occurs when the conditioned stimulus, after being unpaired with the unconditioned stimulus, no longer evokes the conditioned response. (B) is incorrect because acquisition is the initial stage of classical conditioning in which the neutral stimulus is paired with the unconditioned stimulus and comes to evoke a conditioned response. (C) is incorrect because spontaneous recovery is the reappearance of the conditioned response after a period of extinction. (D) is incorrect because higher order conditioning is a process in which a neutral stimulus becomes a conditioned stimulus after being paired with a previously conditioned stimulus.

53. E

Topic: Scientific Foundations of Psychology

The placebo effect occurs when participants in an experiment show a change due to knowledge that they are receiving treatment rather than due to the treatment itself. Thus, to prevent a placebo effect from confounding the results of a study, participants should not know whether they are receiving a placebo. A double-blind procedure is employed when neither the experimenters nor the participants know which participants are in the experimental group versus the control group. This prevents participants in the experimental group from knowing that they are receiving the "true" treatment. Thus, **(E)** is correct. (A) is incorrect because descriptive statistics are used to describe the characteristics of data gathered in a study. (B) is incorrect because inferential statistics are used to make inferences from collected data. (C) is incorrect because informed consent is an ethical obligation of research in which subjects voluntarily decide to participate in research only after receiving sufficient knowledge about it. (D) is incorrect because a correlational study looks for relationships between variables.

54. E

Topic: Motivation, Emotion, and Personality

The Big Five personality traits include conscientiousness, openness to experience, agreeableness, extraversion, and neuroticism. (A), (B), (C), and (D) are incorrect. Psychoticism, **(E)**, was a trait included in the original PEN model that was not included in the Big Five, and is thus correct.

55. D

Topic: Cognitive Psychology

Imagination, association, and location are the three main parameters used in mnemonics to improve memory. Imagination is used to design and strengthen the association needed to build an effective mnemonic. The more vividly one visualizes something in the imagination, the easier it will be to recall. **(D)** is thus correct. Covariation is an attribution principle developed by Harold Kelley, so (A) is incorrect. (B), (C), and (E) are incorrect because they are types of attention, which is a distinct cognitive process.

56. C

Topic: Social Psychology

The just-world hypothesis is the tendency to believe that the world is just and, therefore, that people generally deserve what they get and get what they deserve. In this example, the man assumes that the injuries the drivers received were the result of their own poor driving, despite having no information to back up this idea, so **(C)** is correct. (A) is incorrect because a situational attribution assigns blame for an outcome to the circumstances, but the man is blaming characteristics of the drivers themselves. (B) is incorrect because scapegoat theory typically applies when someone is blamed for things going wrong in the world rather than for things going wrong in his or her own life. (D) is incorrect because ingroup bias refers to a favoring of one's own group, and the question does not mention group membership of either the man or the drivers. (E) is incorrect because prejudice is a cognitive bias against members of a certain group, and, again, the question does not mention group membership.

57. C

Topic: Motivation, Emotion, and Personality

Reciprocal determinism is part of the social cognitive perspective of personality, and holds that people's thoughts and environment interact to determine their actions. **(C)** is correct. (A), (B), and (D) all describe theories of personality that are not related to the interplay between innate traits and environment. (E), shaping, refers to behavioral training.

58. D

Topic: Cognitive Psychology

Danny is repeating the same step over and over in hopes of finding a new solution, indicating that he is using convergent thinking. **(D)** is correct. There is insufficient information in the question stem to determine whether overconfidence, (A), or confirmation bias, (E), is affecting Danny's problem solving process. Expertise, (B), or divergent thinking, (C), would likely help Danny find the right answer to his crab cake dilemma.

59. B

Topic: Learning

Robert Rescorla was an American psychologist who devised experiments to demonstrate the involvement of cognitive processes in classical conditioning. More specifically, he discovered that subjects were able to predict the likelihood that an unconditioned stimulus would occur. Thus, **(B)** is correct. Ivan Pavlov developed the process of classical conditioning, demonstrating how a neutral stimulus could come to evoke a conditioned response or reflex, eliminating (A). Konrad Lorenz studied how baby ducks imprinted on the first thing they saw move after birth, eliminating (C). Martin Seligman and Steven Maier used dogs to establish the concept of learned helplessness, a psychological condition in which a human or animal has learned to believe that nothing can be done to escape pain or discomfort, eliminating (D). Harry Harlow studied baby monkeys and their attachment to surrogate wireframe mothers. He discovered that the monkeys preferred the surrogate mother covered by soft terrycloth over the surrogate mother that was uncovered, even when the uncovered mother was the only one to provide food. Thus, (E) can be eliminated.

60. A

Topic: Clinical Psychology

The Rosenhan study identified the consequences of diagnostic labels. David Rosenhan sent individuals to various hospitals and instructed them to claim they heard voices in order to be admitted and diagnosed with schizophrenia. Following their diagnoses, the individuals halted any abnormal behaviors. However, their actions continued to be interpreted in terms of their diagnosed mental illness. Thus, **(A)** is correct. Martin Seligman and Steven Maier used dogs to establish the concept of learned helplessness, a psychological condition in which a human or animal has learned to believe an adverse situation is inescapable, eliminating (B). Through his obedience studies, Stanley Milgram demonstrated that people will obey orders they are uncomfortable with if they come from a voice of authority, eliminating (C). Robert Rosenthal demonstrated the Pygmalion effect by showing how a person's high expectations for another individual result in high performance by that individual, eliminating (D). Elizabeth Loftus demonstrated how leading questions could be used to create false memories, eliminating (E).

61. D

Topic: Clinical Psychology

Biomedical therapy attempts to alter biological functioning directly through medication, electric shock, or surgery. Thus, prescribing a drug is a type of biomedical therapy, making **(D)** correct. The cognitive approach, (A), investigates how dysfunctional styles of thought lead to abnormal behaviors. Thus, a cognitive approach would involve exploring the patient's thought processes to better understand the disorder. Behavioral therapy, (B), uses manipulatable stimuli to affect observable behaviors. The goal of humanistic therapy, (C), is to help patients develop a healthier sense of self through active listening and talk therapy. The psychoanalytic approach, (E), uses free association and dream analysis to better understand the unconscious mind.

62. C

Topic: Scientific Foundations of Psychology

Positive skew happens when the mean is less than the median and the curve has a left lean, so (A) is incorrect.

Standard deviation is a measurement of the variation of a data set, while the range is the difference between the top and bottom value; (B) is incorrect. Positive correlation happens when two variables change in the same direction in a scientific study, which means **(C)** is correct. The mean is the sum of all values divided by the number of values, while the median is the middle value in a dataset arrange from least to greatest; (D) is incorrect. Confounding variables are variables that are not measured that could affect the outcome of a study, whereas the independent variable is the variable that is manipulated in an experiment, so (E) is incorrect.

63. D

Topic: Biological Bases of Behavior

A reflex arc is a neural pathway that does not involve complex neural structures such as those found in the brain above the brain stem, including but not limited to the motor cortex, **(D)**. Instead, sensory nerve endings, (C), send impulses to afferent nerve fibers, (A), which synapse with an interneuron in the spinal cord, (E). The interneuron then synapses with efferent nerve fibers, which stimulate an effector muscle, (B), resulting in a reflex. This type of neural action is much faster than neural impulses, which route through the brain. Sensory analysis and perception of the reflex event do involve the brain after the reflex occurs.

64. A

Topic: Cognitive Psychology

Since the test designed by the hiring manager is measuring potential rather than acquired knowledge, it is an aptitude test. This makes **(A)** correct. An achievement test measures already acquired knowledge, which makes (B) incorrect. (C) is a type of personality test that is based on ambiguous stimuli. Since this test is not a personality test, (C) must be incorrect. Although it is possible that the hiring manager's test could be standardized, the question stem does not specify whether this is the case, making (D) incorrect. Regarding (E), the question stem does not specify whether the test is measuring intelligence, since it is possible that the test is measuring applicants' potential for success in other domains, such as physical strength. This makes (E) incorrect.

65. C

Topic: Scientific Foundations of Psychology

To conclude that there is a causal relationship between two variables, a researcher must conduct a study in which everything is held constant except for the conditions of the independent variable. A controlled experiment, **(C)**, is the only type of study that uses this type of procedure. (A) refers to an in-depth study that examines a single subject. (B) refers to a study that collects self-reported data from participants. (D) refers to a technique whereby participants are observed in their natural environment, and (E) refers to a similar technique whereby participants are observed in a more structured environment. What differentiates experiments from these other types of studies is that experiments involve manipulating one or more independent variables and randomly assigning participants to experimental or control conditions.

66. D

Topic: Cognitive Psychology

The knowledge of one's own cognitive processes and the ability to control these processes by organizing, monitoring, and modifying them as a function of learning is metacognition. **(D)** is correct. (A) is incorrect because it is a definition of intelligence. (B) is incorrect because it defines perception. (C) is incorrect because it describes decision-making. (E) is incorrect because it describes a kind of self-reliance.

67. C

Topic: Developmental Psychology

These findings are best described by the zone of proximal development, **(C)**, an idea developed by Lev Vygotsky that suggests that children learn best if guided by a teacher or more experienced peer, particularly if given some structural aids. (A) is incorrect because Gestalt principles describe ways that perceptual wholes are organized. The information processing theory, (B), is a way of looking at human cognition like a computer, but this situation does not describe the initial processing or encoding. Trial-and-error, (D), is incorrect because the situation does not describe the children practicing the same problem over and over to correct their mistakes. A mental set, (E), is the tendency to repeat the same actions or steps that have resulted in positive outcomes in the past.

68. A

Topic: Learning

A secondary reinforcer has no inherent value. It can only be used as a reinforcer when it is linked to a primary reinforcer. For example, praise is linked to affection, while money can be linked to food or shelter. Thus, **(A)** is correct. (B), (C), (D), and (E) all indicate primary reinforcers, which are innate reinforcers that satisfy physiological needs.

69. D

Topic: Cognitive Psychology

Standardization is a term used in psychometrics. It involves both the utilization of test scores from a large sample to determine individual performance compared to other test takers, as well as ensuring that a test is always administered under the same conditions. A test developer who is working to ensure similar conditions across test administrations is an example of standardization; thus, **(D)** is correct. The other choices do not deal with testing, so they could not be examples of standardization.

70. E

Topic: Developmental Psychology

Due to deterioration in the prefrontal cortex, older adults experience significant impairments in their working memory, episodic memory, and semantic memory. **(E)** correctly describes the effect shown and would be an appropriate name for a paper based on the results of the graph. All of the other choices do not describe the inverse relationship between recall ability and older age as presented in the graph, and would thus be inappropriate titles for a paper based on those results.

71. C

Topic: Cognitive Psychology

In order to repeat a list of words immediately after reciting it, subjects would need to use short-term memory. Specifically, the subjects would activate working memory, which enables people to temporarily hold new information that is not (yet) stored in long-term memory. **(C)** is thus correct. The other choices are incorrect because they refer to types of long-term memory.

72. B

Topic: Scientific Foundations of Psychology

Prior to participating in a research study, participants must be made aware of the risks of participation and agree to participate without coercion. This process is known as informed consent, **(B)**. Although participants are also entitled to debriefing, (A), anonymity, (D), and confidentiality, (E), these considerations become relevant after the participant has already participated. Although many researchers may offer incentives, (C), participants are not inherently entitled to incentives in all cases.

73. A

Topic: Motivation, Emotion, and Personality

Paul Ekman studied facial expressions and their ties to emotion. He claimed that the seven basic emotions of anger, disgust, fear, happiness, sadness, contempt, and surprise were universal emotions that were expressed the same way in all cultures, making **(A)** correct. Albert Bandura, (B), is known for his Bobo doll experiment, which investigated whether social behaviors like aggression could be acquired through observation and imitation. Hans Selye, (C), is known for developing the general adaptation syndrome model of the body's stress response. Alfred Kinsey, (D), is known for his controversial research on human sexuality. Robert Rosenthal, (E), is known for studying the effects of non-verbal communication and self-fulfilling prophecies. He also demonstrated the Pygmalion effect by showing how students who were liked by their teachers performed better in school.

74. C

Topic: Biological Bases of Behavior

The hypothalamic-pituitary-adrenal axis regulates the body's production of cortisol and, in turn, the stress response. Acute stress can heighten the body's immune preparedness, whereas chronic stress can cause abnormal or suppressed immune responses. **(C)** is correct. The prefrontal cortex, (A), is involved in higher level processing. The mammillary bodies, (B), are involved in spatial memory and recall. The reticular formation, (D), is primarily responsible for regulating the sleep-wake cycle as well as some autonomic functions. The hippocampus, (E), is associated with long-term memory and learning.

75. C

Topic: Clinical Psychology

In group therapy, a therapist meets with several people at once. Groups are beneficial because they allow people to feel less alone in dealing with their problems. Group members discuss their experiences and offer different ways of coping. They also provide each other with acceptance and support. Since James is feeling depressed and alone, having him undergo therapy with a group of individuals with similar experiences is likely to provide him with the support and coping strategies he needs. Thus, **(C)** is correct. Since James has a reasonable explanation for his sadness, it is unlikely that a doctor would automatically prescribe antidepressants without attempting some form of talk therapy, eliminating (A). Electroconvulsive therapy is used in extreme cases of depression when other forms of treatment have been ineffective, eliminating (B). Counterconditioning is used to replace an unpleasant conditioned response with a pleasant one. Since that does not apply to James' situation, (D) can be eliminated. Free association is an integral part of the psychoanalytic approach to treatment that stresses the importance of exploring and understanding the unconscious mind. Since the cause of James' feelings is already known, this will likely not be a useful approach for alleviating his feelings of loneliness and providing him with useful coping strategies. Thus, (E) is incorrect.

76. B

Topic: Clinical Psychology

The *Diagnostic and Statistical Manual of Mental Disorders* (DSM) is used by psychologists and psychiatrists to diagnose psychological disorders, eliminating (C). **(B)** is correct because the DSM focuses on the diagnoses of mental disorders, rather than their etiology, or causes. The first version of the DSM was published in 1952, and it has been revised several times since then, eliminating (A). Some critics state that having a diagnostic tool like the DSM makes the process of diagnosing psychological disorders seem objective when it is, in fact, very subjective since, for example, a rambunctious child who displays hyperactive behavior could be diagnosed with attention deficit hyperactivity disorder by one psychologist but stated to be normal by another. Thus, (E) is incorrect. Though the DSM recognizes the existence of culture-specific disorders, only a few are actually listed in the DSM, eliminating (D).

77. E

Topic: Scientific Foundations of Psychology

An institutional review board is an entity within an institution that reviews all human-subjects research studies to ensure that the researchers are upholding ethical standards, such as obtaining informed consent and debriefing participants. Thus, **(E)** is correct. Important to note is that the IRB is only involved with upholding ethical standards, rather than experimental design quality or results interpretation, which is why the other choices are incorrect.

78. C

Topic: Cognitive Psychology

Context effects refer to circumstances in which memory recall is aided by being in the same physical location where encoding took place, such as when a victim revisits the scene of a crime. **(C)** is thus correct. The serial position effect, (A), is the tendency for list items to be more easily recalled if they are the first few or last few items on the list. The recency effect, (D), is related to the serial position effect and explains the tendency to remember latter items from a list due to short-term memory. The recency effect diminishes when an individual is asked to recall the first items on the list. The concept of state-dependent memory, (B), holds that a person's mental state can affect recall; for example, it is easier to remember events when you are in the same mood as you were when you experienced them. The spacing effect, (E), suggests that the longer the amount of time between sessions of relearning, the greater the retention of the information later on.

79. D

Topic: Motivation, Emotion, and Personality

According to Erikson's stages of personality development, the stage that occurs during the teenage and early adult years, between twelve and twenty, is called identity vs. role confusion. In this stage, people either become steadfast about who they are or have personalities that shift from day to day. Based on the boy's age and the description of his behavior, **(D)** is correct. The other stages occur at different ages and involve different issues than the ones that the boy faces.

80. D

Topic: Learning

The removal of something in order to decrease incidence of a behavior is a negative punishment. **(D)** is correct. Addition of something in order to increase incidence of a behavior is a positive reinforcement, (A). Negative reinforcement, (B), is removal of something to increase incidence of a behavior. Positive punishment, (C), is addition of something to decrease incidence of a behavior. (E), shaping, is a method of slowly training a simple behavior to eventually elicit a desired, complex behavior.

81. B

Topic: Social Psychology

A situational attribution occurs when someone attributes another's behavior to the surrounding situation rather than to inherent personality traits. In contrast, a dispositional attribution occurs when someone attributes another's behavior to his or her personality. Thus, **(B)** is correct because it is the only choice in which someone (the parent) is attributing another's behavior (the child's tantrum) to the surrounding situation. (A), (D), and (E) are all dispositional attributions, while (C) attributes someone else's success to the individual making the attribution.

82. B

Topic: Motivation, Emotion, and Personality

According to Adler, human beings naturally develop feelings of inferiority in childhood, as they face a world in which they are relatively helpless and dependent on parents or other adults for survival. Some individuals, in large part due to setting excessively high standards for themselves, are trapped in an inferiority complex, in which they believe that nothing they do is good enough. Adler suggested that these feelings of inferiority are often unconscious, but they manifest themselves in neurotic personalities and behavior. Because the concept of the inferiority complex is central to Adler's theory, **(B)** is correct. (A) can be eliminated because extinction is a term in operant conditioning. Sublimation, a Freudian term, is the conversion of socially unacceptable desires into socially acceptable ones, so (C) is incorrect. Post-conventional morality is a level in Lawrence Kohlberg's stages of moral development, so (D) can be eliminated. Means-ends analysis is one method of problem solving, so (E) is also incorrect.

83. A

Topic: Scientific Foundations of Psychology

Random assignment is taking research participants and randomly dividing them into experimental groups and control groups. By having assignment to the experimental condition be random, rather than systematic, the researcher can ensure that there are no differences between the two groups, on average, other than the experimental condition. As such, random assignment would be used in an experimental study. The only true experiment listed among the choices is **(A)**.

84. B

Topic: Cognitive Psychology

The language acquisition device is a theoretical pathway in the brain that allows infants to process and absorb language rules, and was theorized by Noam Chomsky. **(B)** is correct. While Skinner, (A), Vygotsky, (C), Piaget, (D), and Miller, (E), all have theories related to learning and/or cognition, they are not responsible for this particular theory.

85. A

Topic: Biological Bases of Behavior

The terminal button releases neurotransmitters into the synapse, making **(A)** correct. (B) describes dendrites, (C) describes the axon, (D) describes myelination, and (E) describes the cell body, or soma.

86. B

Topic: Cognitive Psychology

Self-serving bias occurs when one's personal successes are attributed to internal characteristics like skill and one's personal failures are attributed to external characteristics like bad luck. In contrast, self-effacing bias occurs when personal successes are attributed externally and personal failures are attributed internally. While many cultures in

Africa do indeed promote self-effacing biases, which makes (D) incorrect, cultures in North America, particularly in the U.S. and Canada, tend to promote self-serving biases. **(B)** is thus correct because it presents the least accurate statement. (A) is incorrect because the search for causal explanations is indeed universal. (C) and (E) are incorrect because cultures in Latin America, Asia, and Africa tend to be more collectivist, while cultures in North America and Western Europe tend to be more individualistic.

87. D

Topic: Motivation, Emotion, and Personality

(D) is correct because a perceived sense of control over events can actually help decrease stress. Hans Selye's general adaptation syndrome model maintains that the body responds to stress in three states: alarm, resistance, and exhaustion. During the alarm reaction, the sympathetic nervous system is activated to provide the energy needed to cope with stressors, eliminating (B). During the resistance stage, hormones are released to maintain the body's state of high alert, eliminating (E). If resistance lasts too long, the body can significantly deplete its resources, eliminating (C). As a result of this resource depletion, the body can be more vulnerable to diseases, eliminating (A).

88. E

Topic: Sensation and Perception

Transduction refers to the conversion of one form of energy into another, such as when sensory stimuli are converted into neural signals. It is not a Gestalt principle, so **(E)** is correct. The remaining choices are incorrect because they are Gestalt principles. (A) refers to the tendency to fill in gaps in discontinuous figures. (B) refers to the tendency to group objects that follow a continuous pattern. (C) refers to the tendency to group objects that are close together. (D) refers to the tendency to group objects with the same color, shape, or size.

89. C

Topic: Motivation, Emotion, and Personality

Maslow's hierarchy of needs consists of physiological needs, like air, food, and water; safety needs, like shelter and stability; love and belonging needs, like friendship and family; esteem needs, like confidence, achievement, and respect; and self-actualization needs, like the need to live up to one's full potential. Because the need for respect is an esteem need, **(C)** is correct.

90. E

Topic: Motivation, Emotion, and Personality

The lateral hypothalamus is the feeding center of the brain. Stimulation of this region produces hunger. Thus, overstimulation of this region can lead to obesity, making **(E)** correct. (A) is incorrect because the amygdala is involved in emotion and memory formation. (B) is incorrect because the hippocampus is integral in the establishment of long term memories. (C) is incorrect because the thalamus serves as the relay station of the brain, ensuring that information gets to the right location. (D) is incorrect because the reticular formation is responsible for arousing the cortex to ensure that the brain is alert and attentive to new stimuli.

91. A

Topic: Social Psychology

Altruism refers to partaking in prosocial behavior without self-interested motives. Since the man in this example is volunteering and does not stand to gain anything from doing so, **(A)** is correct. (B) refers to compliance with orders or requests from an authority figure. Obedience is not relevant to this example because the man was not told to do charity work. (C) is a component of romantic love that is present in mature relationships. (D) is a method of increasing a certain behavior by introducing rewards or taking away unpleasant stimuli. Since the man is not receiving any compensation for his volunteer work, he would not be receiving any sort of reinforcement. (E) refers to an emotional bond with another person. Since the question does not mention the man having an emotional bond with another person, this choice is incorrect.

92. A

Topic: Cognitive Psychology

Robert Sternberg's theory of intelligence is called the triarchic theory of intelligence. He argues that there are three parts to intelligence: practical, creative, and analytical intelligence, which means that **(A)** is correct. The remaining choices are incorrect because they are associated with other theories of intelligence. (B) represents the views of Daniel Goleman. (C) represents Howard Gardner's multiple intelligence theory. (D) represents Charles Spearman's view about the g factor, or generalized intelligence. (E) represents Raymond Cattell's theory of intelligence.

93. D

Topic: Clinical Psychology

Most of the disorders among the answer choices could account for the appearance of depressive episodes in the first three weeks and last three weeks of the graph. However, the presence of Martha's severely elevated mood, a likely indication of a manic episode, during weeks 4–6— and again during weeks 8–10—is sufficient to rule out less severe bipolar disorders such as (C) and (E) and non-bipolar depressive disorders such as (A) and (B). **(D)** is correct because bipolar I disorder would best account for both the severely elevated and the severely depressed moods shown in the graph.

94. C

Topic: Clinical Psychology

Since Martha's mood was extremely elevated during week 9, she was most likely suffering from a manic episode. Whereas (A), (B), (D), and (E) are not characteristic of a manic episode, **(C)** can occur during such an episode and is thus correct.

95. A

Topic: Clinical Psychology

Martha's nondepressive symptoms relate to mania, or severely elevated mood. Since lithium salts like lithium carbonate are often used to treat bipolar disorders, **(A)** is correct. For the record: (B) and (C) treat depressive symptoms but not manic ones. (D) and (E), respectively, treat psychotic and anxious symptoms, neither of which is indicated as a concern of Martha or her therapist.

96. C

Topic: Scientific Foundations of Psychology

The null hypothesis in an experiment maintains that there is no difference between experimental and control groups beyond what would be expected by chance alone. Thus, rejecting the null hypothesis means that there is a difference between groups that is not due to chance alone. This is another way of saying that results are statistically significant, which makes **(C)** correct. (A) is incorrect because statistical significance has no bearing on effect size. (B) is incorrect because type I error occurs when a null hypothesis is rejected that should have been affirmed; the lack of type I error does not guarantee statistical significance because, for example, there is no type I error when results are correctly found not to be statistically significant and a null hypothesis is correctly affirmed. (D) is incorrect because the direction of a correlation has no bearing on statistical significance. (E) may be tempting, but keep in mind that for results to be statistically significant, the p-value should be less than 0.05 (and sometimes less than 0.01).

97. C

Topic: Learning

In aversive conditioning, also known as aversion therapy, an unpleasant stimulus is associated with an unwanted behavior in order to create an aversion to the behavior. It is commonly used to treat conditions like alcoholism in adults or bedwetting in children. In this case, since the child is already crying in response to an unpleasant stimulus, pairing his crying with another unpleasant stimulus is unlikely to have any therapeutic effect. Thus, **(C)** is correct. Cognitive behavior therapy is a form of therapy that combines behavioral techniques with cognitive techniques. Stress inoculation training is a type of cognitive behavior therapy in which individuals are taught to restructure how they think about stressful situations. Because encouraging the child to think about why he cries in response to the animal is an important step in extinguishing the behavior, (A) and (D) can be eliminated. Exposure therapy treats anxieties (like the fear of snakes) via behavioral techniques such as systematic desensitization, which associates a pleasant, relaxed state with gradually increasing anxiety-triggering stimuli, eliminating (B) and (E).

98. B

Topic: Scientific Foundations of Psychology

Mary Whiton Calkins was an American psychologist who conducted research on memory, personality, and dreams. Though she was denied her doctorate from Harvard after completing all the necessary requirements, she later went on to become the first woman president of the American Psychological Association, making **(B)** correct. Dorothea Dix was a reformer and pioneer in the movement to treat the insane as mentally ill, rather than as delinquent, in the 1820s. She was also responsible for improving conditions in jails, poorhouses, and insane asylums throughout the U.S. and Canada. Thus, (A) and (C) are incorrect because they describe Dorothea Dix rather than Mary Whiton Calkins. Margaret Floy Washburn was the first woman to receive a Ph.D. in psychology, eliminating (D). Roger Sperry and Michael Gazzaniga made important advancements in understanding how the cerebral hemispheres communicate with each other, eliminating (E).

99. C

Topic: Developmental Psychology

Illness during pregnancy is most dangerous to the fetus, making **(C)** correct. The other choices are incorrect because rubella is often mild in children, adults, and even those with limited immune systems, but can put a fetus at increased risk of birth defects like congenital deafness and cardiac problems.

100. D

Topic: Biological Bases of Behavior

Identical twins share all of their genes, so they are very likely to be similar with respect to traits that have a strong genetic component. Being raised in the same environment is likely to make them even more similar. Thus, **(D)** is correct. (A) is incorrect because random strangers are unlikely to share many genes in common. (B) and (C) are incorrect because fraternal twins only share about half of their genes, just like siblings born at different times. (E) is incorrect because identical twins raised apart are brought up in different environments, which may affect the development of particular traits, even those with strong genetic components.

SECTION II

1. This question is worth 7 points, 1 point for each definition and correct application to the situation. The following is a sample student response that would receive full credit, with indications of where points would be awarded in parentheses:

    A phobia is the irrational fear of a thing or situation; the presence of a phobia inhibits an individual from engaging in normal activities and often results in anxiety. Jack experiences an irrational fear of heights that inhibits him from accepting an otherwise great job, which makes his condition a phobia rather than a simple fear. (**1 POINT**)

    The sympathetic nervous system controls the body's "fight-or-flight" response. When placed in stressful situations, the sympathetic nervous system will elevate the heart rate and blood pressure, dilate the pupils, open the airways, and decrease digestive rates in order to prepare the body for handling the stressful stimulus. Because Jack perceives height as a stressful stimulus, his body's sympathetic nervous system is activated, thereby causing the physiological changes associated with his anxiety. (**1 POINT**)

    The amygdala is the primary neuroanatomical structure for handling fear reactions. As part of the limbic system, the amygdala plays a role in implicit emotional memory, specifically fear and aggression. When Jack finds himself at higher elevations, activity in the amygdala is responsible for producing the emotion of fear. The amygdala directs the autonomic responses associated with his fear of heights, such as physiological arousal. (**1 POINT**)

    Counterconditioning is used in behavioral therapy to help individuals change their responses to stimuli that cause them to react negatively. In this case, the response that Jack is trying to modify is his debilitating anxiety and the stimulus that causes this is being high up in a building. His behavioral therapist can work with Jack to change this response using something like exposure therapy. (**1 POINT**) Exposure therapy involves incremental exposures to whatever an individual fears in order to accustom that person to the feared object or situation over time. The goal of exposure therapy is to extinguish the fear altogether. Jack's therapist may use exposure therapy to gradually decrease Jack's fear of heights. By bringing Jack to the fourth, then fifth, then sixth floor of the skyscraper only once he is comfortable at a given level, Jack may eventually feel comfortable at the floor on which he is expected to work. (**1 POINT**)

    Positive reinforcement increases the frequency of a given behavior by offering a favorable reward in return for the performance of the desired behavior. As Jack complies with each step of the therapeutic program his psychologist works him through, his psychologist might offer an immediate positive reinforcement, such as praise, in order to further encourage the behavior. Ultimately, the psychologist would want Jack to be able to work in a tall building, with the final reward being his ability to successfully perform his new job without interference from his fear of heights. (**1 POINT**)

    Richard Lazarus's appraisal theory of emotion states that the emotions that are elicited by a specific situation are appraised by the brain first and that appraisal leads to emotional and physiological responses. In Jack's case, his brain is appraising height as a danger to himself, which leads to his emotion of fear as well as his physiological symptoms of a fast heart-rate and sweating. (**1 POINT**)

2. This question is worth 7 points, 4 points for Part A (with each term offering 1 point for identification and 1 point for application), 2 points for Part B, and 1 point for Part C. The following is a sample student response that would receive full credit, with indications of where points would be awarded in parentheses:

Object permanence is the recognition that objects do not disappear when they are not immediately in view. (**1 POINT**) The children in the younger age groups have not yet developed object permanence. The younger children are more surprised when their mothers reemerge from behind the curtain, as if they had magically disappeared when they went behind the curtain, then again magically re-appeared on the other side. A child that has developed an understanding of object permanence would not likely demonstrate surprise at his or her mother reappearing on the opposite side of the curtain, as we see in the older age group. (**1 POINT**)

Secure attachment is an attachment style in which a child has a stable caregiver that acts as a base to which the child can return, therefore allowing the child to go out and explore without anxiety. (**1 POINT**) The children demonstrate secure attachment to their mothers because they are willing to leave their mothers' sides to explore the new environment. Additionally, the children begin to feel upset when their mothers first move out of their sight while in the new environment. When the mothers reappear, the children again show that they are happy because they are comforted by their mothers' presence. (**1 POINT**)

In this study, the independent variable is the age group of the children. (**1 POINT**) The dependent variable shown in the graph is the percentage of children who had a surprised reaction to their mothers reappearing. (**1 POINT**)

This study shows that object permanence develops some time around 2 years of age. This is the case because the children in the study are surprised that their mother has reappeared at a much lower rate in the 2-3 years age range, while the surprise rate is high for the 0-1 and 1-2 years age ranges. (**1 POINT**)

Practice Exam 4
Answer Grid

1. Ⓐ Ⓑ Ⓒ Ⓓ Ⓔ	26. Ⓐ Ⓑ Ⓒ Ⓓ Ⓔ	51. Ⓐ Ⓑ Ⓒ Ⓓ Ⓔ	76. Ⓐ Ⓑ Ⓒ Ⓓ Ⓔ
2. Ⓐ Ⓑ Ⓒ Ⓓ Ⓔ	27. Ⓐ Ⓑ Ⓒ Ⓓ Ⓔ	52. Ⓐ Ⓑ Ⓒ Ⓓ Ⓔ	77. Ⓐ Ⓑ Ⓒ Ⓓ Ⓔ
3. Ⓐ Ⓑ Ⓒ Ⓓ Ⓔ	28. Ⓐ Ⓑ Ⓒ Ⓓ Ⓔ	53. Ⓐ Ⓑ Ⓒ Ⓓ Ⓔ	78. Ⓐ Ⓑ Ⓒ Ⓓ Ⓔ
4. Ⓐ Ⓑ Ⓒ Ⓓ Ⓔ	29. Ⓐ Ⓑ Ⓒ Ⓓ Ⓔ	54. Ⓐ Ⓑ Ⓒ Ⓓ Ⓔ	79. Ⓐ Ⓑ Ⓒ Ⓓ Ⓔ
5. Ⓐ Ⓑ Ⓒ Ⓓ Ⓔ	30. Ⓐ Ⓑ Ⓒ Ⓓ Ⓔ	55. Ⓐ Ⓑ Ⓒ Ⓓ Ⓔ	80. Ⓐ Ⓑ Ⓒ Ⓓ Ⓔ
6. Ⓐ Ⓑ Ⓒ Ⓓ Ⓔ	31. Ⓐ Ⓑ Ⓒ Ⓓ Ⓔ	56. Ⓐ Ⓑ Ⓒ Ⓓ Ⓔ	81. Ⓐ Ⓑ Ⓒ Ⓓ Ⓔ
7. Ⓐ Ⓑ Ⓒ Ⓓ Ⓔ	32. Ⓐ Ⓑ Ⓒ Ⓓ Ⓔ	57. Ⓐ Ⓑ Ⓒ Ⓓ Ⓔ	82. Ⓐ Ⓑ Ⓒ Ⓓ Ⓔ
8. Ⓐ Ⓑ Ⓒ Ⓓ Ⓔ	33. Ⓐ Ⓑ Ⓒ Ⓓ Ⓔ	58. Ⓐ Ⓑ Ⓒ Ⓓ Ⓔ	83. Ⓐ Ⓑ Ⓒ Ⓓ Ⓔ
9. Ⓐ Ⓑ Ⓒ Ⓓ Ⓔ	34. Ⓐ Ⓑ Ⓒ Ⓓ Ⓔ	59. Ⓐ Ⓑ Ⓒ Ⓓ Ⓔ	84. Ⓐ Ⓑ Ⓒ Ⓓ Ⓔ
10. Ⓐ Ⓑ Ⓒ Ⓓ Ⓔ	35. Ⓐ Ⓑ Ⓒ Ⓓ Ⓔ	60. Ⓐ Ⓑ Ⓒ Ⓓ Ⓔ	85. Ⓐ Ⓑ Ⓒ Ⓓ Ⓔ
11. Ⓐ Ⓑ Ⓒ Ⓓ Ⓔ	36. Ⓐ Ⓑ Ⓒ Ⓓ Ⓔ	61. Ⓐ Ⓑ Ⓒ Ⓓ Ⓔ	86. Ⓐ Ⓑ Ⓒ Ⓓ Ⓔ
12. Ⓐ Ⓑ Ⓒ Ⓓ Ⓔ	37. Ⓐ Ⓑ Ⓒ Ⓓ Ⓔ	62. Ⓐ Ⓑ Ⓒ Ⓓ Ⓔ	87. Ⓐ Ⓑ Ⓒ Ⓓ Ⓔ
13. Ⓐ Ⓑ Ⓒ Ⓓ Ⓔ	38. Ⓐ Ⓑ Ⓒ Ⓓ Ⓔ	63. Ⓐ Ⓑ Ⓒ Ⓓ Ⓔ	88. Ⓐ Ⓑ Ⓒ Ⓓ Ⓔ
14. Ⓐ Ⓑ Ⓒ Ⓓ Ⓔ	39. Ⓐ Ⓑ Ⓒ Ⓓ Ⓔ	64. Ⓐ Ⓑ Ⓒ Ⓓ Ⓔ	89. Ⓐ Ⓑ Ⓒ Ⓓ Ⓔ
15. Ⓐ Ⓑ Ⓒ Ⓓ Ⓔ	40. Ⓐ Ⓑ Ⓒ Ⓓ Ⓔ	65. Ⓐ Ⓑ Ⓒ Ⓓ Ⓔ	90. Ⓐ Ⓑ Ⓒ Ⓓ Ⓔ
16. Ⓐ Ⓑ Ⓒ Ⓓ Ⓔ	41. Ⓐ Ⓑ Ⓒ Ⓓ Ⓔ	66. Ⓐ Ⓑ Ⓒ Ⓓ Ⓔ	91. Ⓐ Ⓑ Ⓒ Ⓓ Ⓔ
17. Ⓐ Ⓑ Ⓒ Ⓓ Ⓔ	42. Ⓐ Ⓑ Ⓒ Ⓓ Ⓔ	67. Ⓐ Ⓑ Ⓒ Ⓓ Ⓔ	92. Ⓐ Ⓑ Ⓒ Ⓓ Ⓔ
18. Ⓐ Ⓑ Ⓒ Ⓓ Ⓔ	43. Ⓐ Ⓑ Ⓒ Ⓓ Ⓔ	68. Ⓐ Ⓑ Ⓒ Ⓓ Ⓔ	93. Ⓐ Ⓑ Ⓒ Ⓓ Ⓔ
19. Ⓐ Ⓑ Ⓒ Ⓓ Ⓔ	44. Ⓐ Ⓑ Ⓒ Ⓓ Ⓔ	69. Ⓐ Ⓑ Ⓒ Ⓓ Ⓔ	94. Ⓐ Ⓑ Ⓒ Ⓓ Ⓔ
20. Ⓐ Ⓑ Ⓒ Ⓓ Ⓔ	45. Ⓐ Ⓑ Ⓒ Ⓓ Ⓔ	70. Ⓐ Ⓑ Ⓒ Ⓓ Ⓔ	95. Ⓐ Ⓑ Ⓒ Ⓓ Ⓔ
21. Ⓐ Ⓑ Ⓒ Ⓓ Ⓔ	46. Ⓐ Ⓑ Ⓒ Ⓓ Ⓔ	71. Ⓐ Ⓑ Ⓒ Ⓓ Ⓔ	96. Ⓐ Ⓑ Ⓒ Ⓓ Ⓔ
22. Ⓐ Ⓑ Ⓒ Ⓓ Ⓔ	47. Ⓐ Ⓑ Ⓒ Ⓓ Ⓔ	72. Ⓐ Ⓑ Ⓒ Ⓓ Ⓔ	97. Ⓐ Ⓑ Ⓒ Ⓓ Ⓔ
23. Ⓐ Ⓑ Ⓒ Ⓓ Ⓔ	48. Ⓐ Ⓑ Ⓒ Ⓓ Ⓔ	73. Ⓐ Ⓑ Ⓒ Ⓓ Ⓔ	98. Ⓐ Ⓑ Ⓒ Ⓓ Ⓔ
24. Ⓐ Ⓑ Ⓒ Ⓓ Ⓔ	49. Ⓐ Ⓑ Ⓒ Ⓓ Ⓔ	74. Ⓐ Ⓑ Ⓒ Ⓓ Ⓔ	99. Ⓐ Ⓑ Ⓒ Ⓓ Ⓔ
25. Ⓐ Ⓑ Ⓒ Ⓓ Ⓔ	50. Ⓐ Ⓑ Ⓒ Ⓓ Ⓔ	75. Ⓐ Ⓑ Ⓒ Ⓓ Ⓔ	100. Ⓐ Ⓑ Ⓒ Ⓓ Ⓔ

SECTION I

70 Minutes—100 Questions

Percent of total grade: 66⅔

Directions Answer the following 100 questions in 70 minutes. Select the best answer for each and fill in the corresponding letter on your answer grid or a sheet of scratch paper.

1. Josh is an adult who tends to rush into romantic relationships. He often feels insecure about his partner's feelings and constantly questions whether she loves him to the same extent that he loves her. Josh would best be described as having

   (A) a secure attachment style

   (B) an anxious-preoccupied attachment style

   (C) a dismissive-avoidant attachment style

   (D) a fearful-avoidant attachment style

   (E) an ambivalent attachment style

2. Alice believes her anxiety disorder results from persistent thoughts she has about being a failure. Which of the following models of abnormal behavior is most consistent with her belief?

   (A) Psychodynamic model

   (B) Humanistic model

   (C) Biological model

   (D) Sociocultural model

   (E) Cognitive model

3. The Bay of Pigs invasion, in which a group of people accepted a flawed plan without criticism, is a classic example of

   (A) the diffusion of responsibility

   (B) the bystander effect

   (C) norms

   (D) roles

   (E) groupthink

4. A student arrives at a classroom five minutes before class is supposed to start, but finds that the door is closed and many other students are standing in the hallway by the door. The student presumes that the door is locked and stands in the hallway with her peers without attempting to open the door. What kind of learning has this student demonstrated?

   (A) Observational

   (B) Insight

   (C) Emotional

   (D) Latent

   (E) Cognitive mapping

5. Laurel, who has been saving up for a new car, is ecstatic when she is offered an extra shift at the restaurant she works at. However, the shift coincides with a concert that she was excited to attend. Kurt Lewin would describe this as an

   (A) approach-avoidance conflict

   (B) approach-approach conflict

   (C) avoidance-avoidance conflict

   (D) intrapersonal conflict

   (E) interpersonal conflict

GO ON TO THE NEXT PAGE

6. A parent with a permissive parenting style would be considered

    (A) both demanding and responsive

    (B) not demanding but responsive

    (C) demanding but not responsive

    (D) neither demanding nor responsive

    (E) to have the most effective parenting style

7. Elizabeth buys groceries for her sister when she is running low on money but refuses to do the same for her friend. With which explanation for the origin of altruism is this behavior most consistent?

    (A) The matching hypothesis

    (B) The anonymous donor effect

    (C) Sexual selection

    (D) Reciprocity

    (E) Kin selection

8. Which lobe of the cerebral cortex manages hearing and language comprehension?

    (A) Parietal

    (B) Temporal

    (C) Frontal

    (D) Occipital

    (E) All of the above

9. When Leah first moves into her new apartment, she notices a distinct, foul smell. By the end of the day, she no longer notices it. However, when she leaves for work and returns the next day, she notices again. Leah has experienced

    (A) the cocktail party effect

    (B) adaptation

    (C) sensitization

    (D) dishabituation

    (E) selective attention

10. Which of the following is NOT a typical effect of psychedelic drugs?

    (A) Altered mood

    (B) Increased heart rate

    (C) Diminished sensation

    (D) Hallucinations

    (E) Distorted perception

11. Which of the following best characterizes a recognized difference between cognitive psychology and behavioral psychology?

    (A) Cognitive psychology focuses on the ego, while behavioral psychology focuses on the id.

    (B) Behavioral psychology focuses on the superego, while cognitive psychology focuses on the ego.

    (C) Behavioral psychology focuses on learning, while cognitive psychology focuses on information processing.

    (D) Cognitive psychology focuses on observable behavior, while behavioral psychology focuses on internal processes.

    (E) Both focus on observable behavior; there is no significant difference.

GO ON TO THE NEXT PAGE

12. Which of the following statements about schedules of reinforcement is true?

    (A) A continuous schedule of reinforcement is a specific kind of interval reinforcement schedule.

    (B) Variable interval schedules provide a reward every time a behavior is performed over a random period of time.

    (C) Variable schedules generally lead to a larger increase in behavior than fixed schedules.

    (D) Ratio schedules generally lead to a larger increase in behavior than interval schedules.

    (E) Fixed schedules generally lead to a larger increase in behavior than ratio schedules.

13. The person who revised the first IQ test to include the use of an IQ formula was

    (A) Francis Galton

    (B) Alfred Binet

    (C) Theodore Simon

    (D) Charles Spearman

    (E) Lewis Terman

14. Lilly is having trouble staying awake during the day. Several times a day, she is overcome with excessive sleepiness—so much so that it is almost impossible for her not to fall asleep. Lilly probably suffers from

    (A) enuresis

    (B) cataplexy

    (C) night terrors

    (D) somnambulism

    (E) narcolepsy

15. A student memorizes a list of ten items. According to empirical findings about memory, if asked to recall the items a day later, the student is LEAST likely to be able to recall the

    (A) first item

    (B) third item

    (C) fifth item

    (D) ninth item

    (E) tenth item

16. Which thinker is known for the concept of the *tabula rasa*, or the blank slate?

    (A) Plato

    (B) Aristotle

    (C) Descartes

    (D) Locke

    (E) Darwin

17. In the word "grasping," the "-ing" at the end of the word is an example of

    (A) a phoneme

    (B) a morpheme

    (C) syntax

    (D) semantics

    (E) pragmatics

18. Suppose a study finds only a weak correlation between IQ and the ability to solve word problems in math, with higher-IQ individuals tending to solve such problems more capably. Of the following, the correlation coefficient in this study would most likely be

    (A) −0.98

    (B) −0.56

    (C) 0.00

    (D) +0.17

    (E) +0.99

GO ON TO THE NEXT PAGE

19. Suppose a psychologist believed that people can be grouped based on the color of shirt they like to wear and claimed that people who wear red shirts are passionate and impulsive, whereas people who wear blue shirts are controlled and cerebral. This proposal would be classified as a

    (A) type theory

    (B) trait theory

    (C) humanist theory

    (D) behavioral theory

    (E) psychoanalytic theory

20. Andrew finds Shannon attractive because she is so generous to other people, even strangers. With respect to explanations for the existence of altruism, this is most consistent with

    (A) the matching hypothesis

    (B) reciprocal liking

    (C) sexual selection

    (D) reciprocity

    (E) kin selection

21. According to Carl Jung, which of the following archetypes represents the part of your personality that you present to the world?

    (A) Self

    (B) Persona

    (C) Shadow

    (D) Animus

    (E) Anima

22. Karen is so afraid of heights that it impedes her ability to function. This frustrates her, but nothing she does seems to alleviate her fears. Karen is probably suffering from

    (A) a specific phobia

    (B) generalized anxiety disorder

    (C) obsessive-compulsive disorder

    (D) a personality disorder

    (E) post-traumatic stress disorder

23. With every generation, mean intelligence scores increase, requiring IQ norms to be recalculated. This increase in intelligence scores over time is known as

    (A) the triarchic theory of intelligence

    (B) savant syndrome

    (C) general intelligence factor

    (D) the Flynn effect

    (E) fluid intelligence

24. A confounding variable

    (A) makes the mean greater than anticipated

    (B) makes the mean less than anticipated

    (C) influences the dependent variable

    (D) causes participants to feel deceived

    (E) is controlled by the researcher

25. Suppose that a mother and father are frequently fighting with their teenage son and decide to seek family psychotherapy. Which of the following approaches would their therapist most likely use?

    (A) Humanistic therapy

    (B) Cognitive therapy

    (C) Systemic therapy

    (D) Psychodynamic therapy

    (E) Eclectic therapy

GO ON TO THE NEXT PAGE

26. Generally speaking, if a person has a particular genetic disease, there is a 50 percent chance that his or her sibling will also have the disease. If an afflicted person has a fraternal twin, what is the chance that the fraternal twin has the same genetic disease?

    (A) 0%

    (B) 25%

    (C) 50%

    (D) 75%

    (E) 100%

27. The concept most associated with behavioral therapy is

    (A) dream analysis

    (B) unconditional positive regard

    (C) reinforcement

    (D) cognitive restructuring

    (E) transference

28. A teenager who is usually quiet and shy finds himself screaming at a soccer referee when he is among a group of rowdy soccer fans at a game. This is best seen as an example of

    (A) deindividuation

    (B) social loafing

    (C) social facilitation

    (D) group polarization

    (E) conformity

29. Robert believes that opposites attract, or in other words, that people are drawn to others who are radically different from themselves. Which common attribute of attractiveness has been shown by research to suggest the contrary?

    (A) Similarity

    (B) Physical attractiveness

    (C) Proximity

    (D) Sexual selection

    (E) Reciprocal liking

30. One day in February, a 25-year-old female is questioned by the police, who believe her to be a witness to a robbery committed earlier that day. Her face matches the picture found in a wallet recovered from the suspected robber, but she has no memory of the robbery and she shows no signs of brain damage. Assuming she was actually there, which of the following diagnoses best matches her symptoms?

    (A) Agoraphobia

    (B) Major depressive disorder

    (C) Seasonal affective disorder

    (D) Dissociative amnesia

    (E) Generalized anxiety disorder

31. A client believes he is beginning to develop feelings for his therapist. He previously had the same feelings for someone else. According to Freudian theory, this is a process called

    (A) active listening

    (B) thought log

    (C) cognitive restructuring

    (D) transference

    (E) Socratic questioning

GO ON TO THE NEXT PAGE

32. A researcher finds that students who were paid to perform certain activities were less likely to continue those activities when the payment stopped than students who were not paid, even though both groups had the same initial level of interest in the activity. This suggests that

    (A) the extrinsic motivator was more powerful than the intrinsic motivator

    (B) the extrinsic motivator interfered with the intrinsic motivator

    (C) the reinforcement schedule of the extrinsic motivator was insufficient

    (D) the extrinsic motivator was not satisfying a drive

    (E) the extrinsic motivator was not causing dopamine release

33. When his teacher is watching him in class, Seth is a model student. However, as soon as his teacher leaves the room, he begins to distract other students. This situation is most analogous to

    (A) hindsight bias

    (B) imprinting

    (C) ingroup bias

    (D) groupthink

    (E) the Hawthorne effect

Questions 34–37 are based on the following.

Pamela wants her husband Paul to do more chores around the house instead of playing the computer games that he loves. Toward this end, she decides that for every hour of chores that Paul completes, she will offer him his favorite snack, chocolate. In an effort to improve her husband's overall health, Pamela offers him a plate of steamed vegetables, which Paul neither likes nor dislikes, whenever he plays video games. After a while, she notices that Paul can eat steamed vegetables with enjoyment without playing computer games at the same time.

34. In the scenario above, Paul receiving chocolate for every hour of completed chores would be an example of a

    (A) continuous schedule

    (B) fixed ratio schedule

    (C) variable ratio schedule

    (D) fixed interval schedule

    (E) variable interval schedule

35. If, at first, Pamela had to guide Paul to complete a full hour of chores in incremental steps by providing chocolate each time he completed part of the task, this would most closely resemble

    (A) shaping

    (B) latent learning

    (C) secondary reinforcement

    (D) token reinforcement

    (E) satiation

36. In the situation described above, the plate of steamed vegetables, when first introduced to Paul, is

    (A) a conditioned stimulus

    (B) an unconditioned stimulus

    (C) a neutral stimulus

    (D) an unconditioned response

    (E) a conditioned response

37. Which psychologist is most responsible for providing the theoretical foundation that explains Paul's changed behavior in response to the chocolate?

    (A) Ivan Pavlov

    (B) B.F. Skinner

    (C) John Garcia

    (D) Albert Bandura

    (E) Robert Rescorla

GO ON TO THE NEXT PAGE

38. Many people find that if they get a new phone number, they have trouble remembering it and may at first accidentally give out their old phone number. This is an example of

    (A) retroactive interference

    (B) proactive interference

    (C) anterograde amnesia

    (D) retrograde amnesia

    (E) source amnesia

39. Charles Spearman referred to the ability of individuals to solve complex problems as

    (A) performance scales

    (B) creative intelligence

    (C) practical intelligence

    (D) the g factor

    (E) savant syndrome

40. Which of the following provides an example of how a social role influences behavior?

    (A) When a child enters the first grade, she enjoys playing on the playground.

    (B) At the end of the school year, a teacher feels disappointed.

    (C) When a colleague is promoted to manager, she begins to boss people around in the office.

    (D) A man is happy to become a parent after the birth of his first child.

    (E) A boy laughs ecstatically when he dresses up as an astronaut for Halloween.

41. Which of the following describes the controversial and discredited theory that cranial shape and size correlate with intelligence and character?

    (A) Psychophysics

    (B) Phrenology

    (C) Eugenics

    (D) Parapsychology

    (E) Psychoanalysis

42. Suppose José wanted to conduct a study that investigated two existing groups to determine how members of these groups differed with respect to a number of psychological traits. Which of the following statistics would be most useful for formulating conclusions in his study?

    (A) Mean

    (B) Standard deviation

    (C) Median

    (D) Mode

    (E) Correlation coefficient

43. Which of the following represents the main disagreement between the nativist and behavioral perspectives on language acquisition?

    (A) The timing of the development of linguistic abilities

    (B) Whether there are language differences between boys and girls

    (C) The order in which young children learn grammatical concepts

    (D) Whether the ability to acquire language is learned or innate

    (E) None of the above

GO ON TO THE NEXT PAGE

44. Which of the following is specifically an example of prejudice?

    (A) Daniel feels angry with all women because of his ex-girlfriend.

    (B) Anthony believes women are bad at math.

    (C) Brad refuses to hire women at his mechanic shop.

    (D) Ronald disallows women from competing in his poker competition.

    (E) Patrick is convinced that all women possess strong maternal instincts.

Questions 45–47 are based on the following.

Adam just started preschool and recently has been trying to assert his independence. Every day, Adam insists on getting dressed, tying his shoes, and using the potty by himself. One day before school, Adam tries to put his schoolbooks into his backpack, but they are too heavy. When Adam's older brother, Jack, tries to help, Adam gets upset and claims that he can do it all by himself.

45. According to Erik Erikson, Adam is experiencing which developmental conflict?

    (A) Identity vs. role confusion

    (B) Trust vs. mistrust

    (C) Autonomy vs. shame and doubt

    (D) Initiative vs. guilt

    (E) Generativity vs. stagnation

46. Adam is in the preoperational stage. Which of the following behaviors would Adam be expected to develop and exhibit during this stage?

    (A) Object permanence

    (B) Egocentrism

    (C) Conservation

    (D) Abstract reasoning

    (E) Conformity

47. Jack is currently in the pre-conventional stage of moral development. According to Kohlberg, Jack would most likely attempt to help Adam because Jack

    (A) wants to make life easier for Adam

    (B) feels guilty that Adam is struggling

    (C) would want Adam to help Jack if the roles were reversed

    (D) wants their mother to give Jack candy

    (E) wants the reputation of being a good brother

48. A woman associates a song with a happy experience and finds that listening to the song always cheers her up. For several days in a row, she plays the song while driving to work, and soon discovers that driving to work puts her in a good mood, even after she stops playing the song. This is an example of

    (A) response extinction

    (B) spontaneous recovery

    (C) stimulus generalization

    (D) stimulus discrimination

    (E) higher order conditioning

49. Which of the following therapeutic approaches encourages patients to reassess their established patterns of thinking and develop more realistic and empowering beliefs about their circumstances and capabilities?

    (A) Cognitive

    (B) Psychoanalytic

    (C) Humanistic

    (D) Behavioral

    (E) Biological

GO ON TO THE NEXT PAGE

50. When the above picture is shown to a person, even though half of it is obscured, the image of a cat is still discernible. This is an example of

    (A) the law of proximity

    (B) the law of similarity

    (C) the law of continuity

    (D) the law of closure

    (E) Weber's law

51. Which of the following was characteristic of the moral treatment advocated by Dorothea Dix and other nineteenth-century reformers?

    (A) Regular diet and exercise

    (B) Bible study

    (C) Group psychotherapy

    (D) Biomedical treatment

    (E) Cognitive restructuring

52. Studies on split-brain patients by Roger Sperry revealed that

    (A) the brain has a contralateral organization

    (B) the dominant cerebral hemisphere is always the left

    (C) split-brain patients have two consciousnesses

    (D) language abilities are usually managed by the left hemisphere

    (E) spatial abilities are usually managed by the left hemisphere

53. "Colorless green ideas sleep furiously" is an example used by linguist Noam Chomsky to argue that sentences can be proper but still not make sense. At what level is this sentence ambiguous?

    (A) Semantic

    (B) Lexical

    (C) Syntactic

    (D) Phonemic

    (E) Morphemic

54. The basal ganglia are a network of well-connected nuclei responsible for many processes, including habit formation, emotion, voluntary movement, and procedural learning. Which of the following statements about the basal ganglia is true?

    (A) They are involved in lower cognitive functions and are located in the hindbrain.

    (B) They are involved in higher cognitive functions and are located in the midbrain.

    (C) They are involved in lower cognitive functions and are located in the forebrain.

    (D) They are involved in lower cognitive functions and are located in the midbrain.

    (E) They are involved in higher cognitive functions and are located in the forebrain.

GO ON TO THE NEXT PAGE

55. During which of Piaget's developmental stages would a child begin to understand that quantities remain constant even when their outward appearances change?

    (A) Sensorimotor

    (B) Preoperational

    (C) Concrete operational

    (D) Formal operational

    (E) Oral

56. Anna loves to play imagination games with her friends. She feels confident in her ability to be a leader among her peers and often initiates new friendships. According to Erikson, Anna is flourishing in which of the following psychosocial stages?

    (A) Trust vs. mistrust

    (B) Autonomy vs. shame and doubt

    (C) Initiative vs. guilt

    (D) Industry vs. inferiority

    (E) Intimacy vs. isolation

57. Konrad Lorenz noticed that young goslings form an instinctive attachment to the first moving object they see within a critical period after hatching. While this instinctual tendency has not been observed in humans, it has been seen in other animals. This phenomenon is known as

    (A) attachment

    (B) temperament

    (C) imprinting

    (D) habituation

    (E) gestation

58. During an experiment, Demarius is shown a handwritten letter "B" that is easy to identify. However, when that same letter is later shown to him while surrounded by the numbers "7" and "9" on each side, Demarius identifies it instead as the number "8." This change in perception can best be explained by

    (A) bottom-up processing

    (B) the proximity principle

    (C) Weber's Law

    (D) top-down processing

    (E) the cocktail party effect

59. Ellen pushed another child out of the way to get to a toy. What type of aggression did Ellen demonstrate?

    (A) Hostile

    (B) Instrumental

    (C) Beneficial

    (D) Hot

    (E) Adaptive

60. Which of the following is NOT taken into account in the social cognitive perspective of personality?

    (A) Rewards or punishments for behaviors

    (B) Unconscious desires of the id

    (C) Observations of others

    (D) Physical location

    (E) Thoughts, feelings, and beliefs

61. Which of the following drugs is most likely to be prescribed for patients with schizophrenia?

    (A) Benzodiazepines

    (B) Tricyclic antidepressants

    (C) Selective serotonin reuptake inhibitors

    (D) Atypical anti-psychotics

    (E) Lithium salts

GO ON TO THE NEXT PAGE ⇨

62. Psychologists are creating an assessment tool to determine if individuals would be well suited to a career in air traffic control. They first administer the exam to a representative sample to serve as a source for comparison, making certain that all individuals take the test under the same testing conditions. The psychologists are focused on establishing

    (A) standardization

    (B) content validity

    (C) construct validity

    (D) test-retest reliability

    (E) split-half reliability

63. Which psychologist was responsible for finding a general intelligence factor that accounted for up to 50 percent of variability in intelligence scores?

    (A) L.L. Thurstone

    (B) Howard Gardner

    (C) Robert Sternberg

    (D) Charles Spearman

    (E) Daniel Goleman

64. The condition popularly known as multiple personality disorder is classified by the DSM-5 as

    (A) a psychotic disorder

    (B) a dissociative disorder

    (C) an anxiety disorder

    (D) a trauma- and stressor-related disorder

    (E) a personality disorder

65. According to the psychoanalytic perspective, which of the following is responsible for primary process thinking?

    (A) The id

    (B) The ego

    (C) The shadow

    (D) The persona

    (E) The superego

66. A correlation of +0.90 between variables a and b indicates

    (A) a weak inverse relationship between a and b

    (B) that variable a caused variable b to occur

    (C) that variable b caused variable a to occur

    (D) a strong direct relationship between a and b

    (E) no relationship between a and b

67. A mathematician is looking for a step-by-step method that can be applied to a certain type of problem and will always produce a correct answer. This mathematician is trying to create

    (A) a heuristic

    (B) an algorithm

    (C) a mnemonic

    (D) an insight

    (E) a mental set

68. The statistical process that reveals common aspects among large groups of variables is known as

    (A) the Flynn effect

    (B) factor analysis

    (C) test-retest reliability

    (D) construct validity

    (E) content validity

GO ON TO THE NEXT PAGE

69. Which model of psychological disorders maintains that abnormal behaviors arise from unconscious mental processes?

    (A) Psychoanalytic

    (B) Cognitive

    (C) Sociocultural

    (D) Medical

    (E) Humanistic

70. An individual who is prone to anxiety and becomes easily frustrated is likely to score highly on which of the following Big Five traits?

    (A) Openness to experience

    (B) Conscientiousness

    (C) Extraversion

    (D) Agreeableness

    (E) Neuroticism

71. Which of the following disorders does NOT necessarily require the existence of depressive or dysthymic episodes?

    (A) Major depressive disorder

    (B) Dysthymia

    (C) Seasonal affective disorder

    (D) Bipolar I disorder

    (E) Bipolar II disorder

72. Researchers studying the perception of brightness find that 50 percent of their 500 participants are able to discriminate between two lights with brightnesses of 100 lumens and 107 lumens. Which of the following would most reasonably be expected when the same 500 participants are asked to discriminate between two lights with brightnesses of 200 and 207 lumens?

    (A) None of the participants will be able to distinguish between the two stimuli.

    (B) Fewer than 50 percent of the participants will be able to distinguish between the two stimuli.

    (C) Exactly 50 percent of the participants will be able to distinguish between the two stimuli.

    (D) More than 50 percent of the participants will be able to distinguish between the two stimuli.

    (E) Nothing can be predicted about the number of participants who will be able to distinguish between the two stimuli.

73. Which of the following is the stage of sleep characterized by the slowest brain waves?

    (A) NREM stage 1

    (B) NREM stage 2

    (C) NREM stage 3

    (D) NREM stage 4

    (E) REM

GO ON TO THE NEXT PAGE

Questions 74–75 are based on the following.

Researchers asked participants to assess the relative probabilities of various events by responding to a series of prompts. The results for one of the prompts appears in the graph below. Note that the correct response to that prompt was actually "less likely." The results for the other prompts largely followed the same trend.

Prompt: "A deadly shark attack is _____ than/as death from a vending machine."

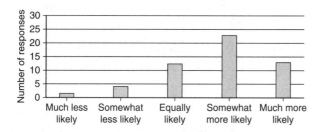

74. The data obtained above best serve as a demonstration of which of the following phenomena?

   (A) The availability heuristic

   (B) Priming

   (C) The Flynn effect

   (D) Insight

   (E) Divergent thinking

75. If some of the participants demonstrated belief perseverance, which of the following would most likely be true of those participants?

   (A) They will quickly come to regret not making the right choice initially.

   (B) When presented with evidence that their original responses are incorrect, their confidence in those responses will decrease.

   (C) When asked about the same situation in the future, their new responses will not correlate with their original responses.

   (D) When presented with evidence that their original responses are incorrect, their confidence in them will remain about the same.

   (E) Those with lower intelligence will be more susceptible to belief perseverance than those with higher intelligence.

76. Which of the following best describes a principle of signal detection theory?

   (A) An individual's response to a stimulus does not depend upon environment or mental state.

   (B) There is a difference between the images seen by each eye, which can be used to gauge distance.

   (C) There is a cognitive component to sensation, which explains why a stimulus might be sensed in one situation but not in another.

   (D) The retina has three types of color receptors: red-sensitive receptors, green-sensitive receptors, and blue-sensitive receptors.

   (E) Individuals possess a somatic sense of the movement of their bodies in space.

GO ON TO THE NEXT PAGE

77. Learning to reduce negative emotional responses to particular stimuli through careful, repeat exposure is a technique most commonly used to treat

    (A) depression

    (B) a phobia

    (C) an addiction

    (D) chronic pain

    (E) relationship problems

78. Suppose that a researcher wished to train a pigeon to jump through a hoop on command. Which of the following is an example of the use of shaping in training for the desired behavior?

    (A) First reward the pigeon for perching on the hoop, then only reward the pigeon for perching on the hoop and jumping off to the opposite side, then only for jumping through without perching.

    (B) Reward the pigeon for jumping through the hoop once, then reward it only for jumping through twice, then three times, steadily increasing the number of times the behavior must be performed.

    (C) Steadily decrease the size of the reward for performing the behavior until the pigeon jumps through the hoop out of habit rather than in anticipation of a reward.

    (D) Provide a large hoop at first so that the pigeon is more likely to accidentally jump through it, then change the shape of the hoop over time to make it more challenging.

    (E) Reward the pigeon both for jumping through the hoop and for pecking at a button in the cage so that the pigeon learns to associate the reward with both an instinctive behavior and a learned one.

79. Which of the following would provide the most support for the Schachter-Singer theory of emotion?

    (A) An individual who is given a tranquilizer feels angry when the people around him act angry.

    (B) A person who is given a dose of epinephrine feels angry when the people around him act angry.

    (C) A patient with a spinal cord injury exhibits a diminished level of emotion after her injuries compared to before.

    (D) A hiker simultaneously starts sweating and feeling scared when she encounters a bear in the woods.

    (E) A young man senses his heartbeat speeding up and concludes that he must be excited.

80. Which of the following correctly identifies the names of the three ossicles inside the ear?

    (A) Stapes, pinna, and cochlea

    (B) Incus, stapes, and pinna

    (C) Malleus, incus, and cochlea

    (D) Malleus, stapes, and cochlea

    (E) Malleus, incus, and stapes

81. The chemical messengers that enable communication between neurons are

    (A) hormones

    (B) synapses

    (C) neurotransmitters

    (D) dendrites

    (E) axons

GO ON TO THE NEXT PAGE

82. Which of the following statements about facial expressions is true?

    (A) All cultures recognize and display the same emotions.

    (B) In all cultures, children learn to recognize and display emotions by watching their parents.

    (C) All cultures recognize and display the same facial expressions for anger.

    (D) Cultures are unable to recognize or display emotions from other cultures.

    (E) All cultures recognize the same emotions but display them in different ways.

83. The existence of which of the following paranormal phenomena has been robustly supported by scientific research?

    (A) Clairvoyance

    (B) Psychokinesis

    (C) Telepathy

    (D) Precognition

    (E) None of the above

84. What was an unintended consequence of deinstitutionalization?

    (A) Fewer patients in asylums

    (B) More homelessness

    (C) Fewer people diagnosed with mental illnesses

    (D) More patients integrated into communities

    (E) More people seeking treatment

85. After conducting an experiment on the effects of rap music on test performance in fifth graders, Dr. Sanchez tells a colleague that her study showed that exposure to any music and test performance are positively correlated. Her colleague would likely be most concerned about there being an issue with the study's

    (A) internal validity

    (B) face validity

    (C) construct validity

    (D) external validity

    (E) concurrent validity

86. Psychologists often talk about the body's ability to deal with pain. Which of the following has been described as a natural painkiller?

    (A) GABA

    (B) Dopamine

    (C) Serotonin

    (D) Endorphins

    (E) Ibuprofen

87. A positive correlation indicates that two variables are

    (A) inversely related

    (B) unrelated

    (C) weakly related

    (D) directly related

    (E) strongly related

GO ON TO THE NEXT PAGE

88. Selective serotonin reuptake inhibitors (SSRIs) operate by

    (A) limiting the reabsorption of serotonin by the synapses

    (B) creating the serotonin that is released into the synapses

    (C) increasing sensitivity to serotonin

    (D) mimicking the effects of serotonin

    (E) creating new connections between synapses

89. Which of the following did both Watson and Skinner believe was the biggest determinant of future behavior?

    (A) Inborn tendencies

    (B) Temperament

    (C) Environment

    (D) Thoughts

    (E) Memories

90. Which of the following is NOT typically used to ensure that participants in psychological studies are treated ethically?

    (A) Informed consent

    (B) Approval by the APA

    (C) Debriefing

    (D) Confidentiality

    (E) Approval by an IRB

91. Suppose that a certain sound causes neurons in a person's cochlea to fire at a particular rate, while a different sound of a higher pitch causes those same neurons to fire at a higher rate. This observation would most support

    (A) gate-control theory

    (B) temporal theory

    (C) opponent-process theory

    (D) place theory

    (E) volley theory

92. Which of the following best expresses the biological perspective of personality?

    (A) Animals of the same species should all have the same basic personality traits.

    (B) Personality is determined by body type, of which there are three: endomorph, ectomorph, and mesomorph.

    (C) Personality is most influenced by things learned from one's closest biological relatives.

    (D) Genes control the development of the nervous system and so have an effect on personality.

    (E) Personality is determined by the balance or imbalance of the four bodily fluids called humors.

93. Which of the following best describes a type II error?

    (A) Affirming a false null hypothesis

    (B) Affirming a true null hypothesis

    (C) Rejecting a true null hypothesis

    (D) Rejecting a false null hypothesis

    (E) Affirming a false alternative hypothesis

94. According to Abraham Maslow, which of the following needs can only be pursued after all the others have been satisfied?

    (A) Hunger

    (B) Thirst

    (C) Self-esteem

    (D) Self-actualization

    (E) Belonging

GO ON TO THE NEXT PAGE

95. Human infants are born with a number of reflexes that enable their growth and development. Which of the following is NOT one of these reflexes?

   (A) Grasping

   (B) Moro

   (C) Rooting

   (D) Standing

   (E) Babinski

96. Homeostasis is defined as

   (A) a state of irritation that results in a behavior intended to alleviate it

   (B) the tendency of organisms to maintain a balanced internal state

   (C) inborn, fixed patterns of behavior that present in response to certain stimuli

   (D) an internal desire or deficiency that can motivate behavior

   (E) the physiological and psychological state of being active and alert

97. Mnemonics aid in remembering because they always provide

   (A) a catchy tune

   (B) instant, photographic memorization

   (C) organization for recall

   (D) context

   (E) a bigger short-term memory

98. When Darien's friend trips on the stairs, Darien calls him clumsy. But when Darien trips on the stairs, he blames the faulty design of the stairs. This can best be characterized as an example of

   (A) the diffusion of responsibility

   (B) the bystander effect

   (C) group polarization

   (D) the fundamental attribution error

   (E) social facilitation

99. When talking to a friend, Chrystal states, "I love being a teacher. Everyday, I feel fulfilled because I know I am doing my best to help my students learn." Chrystal is most likely experiencing

   (A) intrinsic motivation

   (B) punishment

   (C) groupthink

   (D) extrinsic motivation

   (E) negative reinforcement

100. Which of the following is a recognized potential weakness of the medical model of abnormal behavior?

   (A) The medical model pathologizes healthy human emotions.

   (B) The medical model does not provide effective treatments.

   (C) The medical model is not supported by research.

   (D) The medical model is a brand new approach to treatment.

   (E) The medical model focuses on causes, not symptoms.

END OF SECTION I

SECTION II
50 Minutes—2 Questions
Percent of total grade: 33⅓

Directions Answer both of the following questions in 50 minutes. Lists of facts are insufficient to earn points; you must write essays that answer the questions thoughtfully with sound arguments that employ the proper terms from psychology. Use scratch paper to write out your responses.

1. Jordan is a senior in high school studying for a psychology test at the end of the semester. Normally, Jordan does very well in school, and she wants to do very well on this test. However, Jordan is struggling to remember much from her psychology class this semester and has been unmotivated to read the material. Fortunately, her teacher has made audio recordings of every lecture available to the students. Following the suggestion of someone who took the class last year, Jordan plans on listening to these recordings for the two days before the test in order to catch up and learn the material from the class. The teacher has also provided presentation slides that Jordan plans to review separately.

   Explain the following terms and relate them to Jordan's study plan for this test.

   - Herman Ebbinghaus' spacing effect

   - Encoding

   - The cochlea and hair cells in the human ear

   - The hippocampus

   - Achievement motivation

   - Visual cortex

   - Social norms

2. In the fifth version of the *Diagnostic and Statistical Manual of Mental Disorders* (DSM-5), posttraumatic stress disorder (PTSD) is now part of a group called trauma- and stressor-related disorders. Dr. Kerry is studying how various treatment regimens can help patients suffering from PTSD get better and judging their efficacy by age category. To do this, she gathers a sample of 300 people and treats 100 of them with psychotherapy only (PO), 100 with psychotherapy and medication (P+M), and 100 of them with medication only (MO). Within each group, the treatment efficacy is assessed for four age categories: 18–28, 29–39, 40–50, and 51+. Dr. Kerry hypothesizes that patients receiving psychotherapy and medication will have the largest reduction in symptoms. The resulting decrease in PTSD symptoms is shown in the following table. Assume all differences are statistically significant.

Age Category	Treatment	Reduction in Symptoms
18-28	PO	13%
29-39	PO	11%
40-50	PO	10%
51+	PO	14%
18-28	P+M	18%
29-39	P+M	16%
40-50	P+M	15%
51+	P+M	11%
18-28	MO	10%
29-39	MO	13%
40-50	MO	14%
51+	MO	15%

Part A

Identify each of the following in this study:

- The two independent variables
- The dependent variable

Part B

- Explain the causes of posttraumatic stress disorder according to the DSM-5.
- Calculate the mean reduction in symptoms for each treatment group.
- Explain whether or not Dr. Kerry's hypothesis is supported in general.
- Explain why it was important for Dr. Kerry to group participants by age in this study.

END OF SECTION II

STOP

END OF EXAM

ANSWER KEY

Section I

1. B	16. D	31. D	46. B	61. D	76. C	91. B
2. E	17. B	32. B	47. D	62. A	77. B	92. D
3. E	18. D	33. E	48. E	63. D	78. A	93. A
4. A	19. A	34. D	49. A	64. B	79. B	94. D
5. B	20. C	35. A	50. D	65. A	80. E	95. D
6. B	21. B	36. C	51. A	66. D	81. C	96. B
7. E	22. A	37. B	52. D	67. B	82. C	97. C
8. B	23. D	38. B	53. A	68. B	83. E	98. D
9. D	24. C	39. D	54. E	69. A	84. B	99. A
10. C	25. C	40. C	55. C	70. E	85. D	100. A
11. C	26. C	41. B	56. C	71. D	86. D	
12. D	27. C	42. E	57. C	72. B	87. D	
13. E	28. A	43. D	58. D	73. D	88. A	
14. E	29. A	44. A	59. B	74. A	89. C	
15. C	30. D	45. C	60. B	75. D	90. B	

Section II

1. See Answers and Explanations

2. See Answers and Explanations

PRACTICE EXAM 4 BREAKDOWN: ASSESS YOUR STRENGTHS

Use the following tables to determine which topics you are already strong in and which topics you need to review most.

Topic	Questions
Scientific Foundations of Psychology	11, 16, 18, 24, 33, 41, 42, 66, 85, 87, 89, 90, 93
Biological Bases of Behavior	8, 10, 14, 26, 52, 54, 73, 81, 86, 88
Sensation and Perception	9, 50, 58, 72, 76, 80, 83, 91
Learning	4, 12, 34, 35, 36, 37, 48, 77, 78
Cognitive Psychology	13, 15, 17, 23, 38, 39, 43, 53, 62, 63, 67, 68, 74, 75, 97
Developmental Psychology	1, 6, 45, 46, 47, 55, 56, 57, 95
Motivation, Emotion, and Personality	5, 19, 21, 32, 60, 65, 70, 79, 82, 92, 94, 96, 99
Clinical Psychology	2, 22, 25, 27, 30, 31, 49, 51, 61, 64, 69, 71, 84, 100
Social Psychology	3, 7, 20, 28, 29, 40, 44, 59, 98

Topic	Chapters	Questions on Exam	Number You Got Correct
Scientific Foundations of Psychology	4, 13	13	
Biological Bases of Behavior	5, 14	10	
Sensation and Perception	6, 15	8	
Learning	7, 16	9	
Cognitive Psychology	8, 17	15	
Developmental Psychology	9, 18	9	
Motivation, Emotion, and Personality	10, 19	13	
Clinical Psychology	11, 20	14	
Social Psychology	12, 21	9	

PRACTICE EXAM 4 ANSWERS AND EXPLANATIONS

SECTION I

1. B

Topic: Developmental Psychology

An individual who tends to seek high levels of intimacy quickly and to feel insecure about his partner's love would best be described as having an anxious-preoccupied attachment style. **(B)** is correct. An individual with a secure attachment style, (A), would be able to form intimate relationships and would feel secure about her partner's love. Individuals with a dismissive-avoidant attachment style, (C), tend to avoid intimacy altogether. Individuals with a fearful-avoidant attachment style, (D), wish to form intimate relationships, but also fear getting too close to others. An ambivalent attachment style, (E), refers to an attachment style between infants and primary caregivers in which the infant feels separation anxiety when its caregiver leaves that is not resolved when its caregiver returns.

2. E

Topic: Clinical Psychology

(E) is correct because the cognitive model identifies faulty belief as the primary origin of abnormal behavior. (A) would attribute the anxiety to repression or unconscious conflicts, (B) to a lack of self-actualization, (C) to an imbalance in neurotransmitters, and (D) to factors in the broader social environment.

3. E

Topic: Social Psychology

Groupthink, a term coined by Irving Janis, refers to the tendency of particular groups to make poor decisions as a result of their members' desire to maintain harmony, with the Bay of Pigs invasion being Janis' classic example; **(E)** is correct. (A) and (B) are incorrect because they describe the behavior of individuals in crowds or large groups. (C) and (D) are incorrect because norms are social expectations, while roles are positions within a group.

4. A

Topic: Learning

Because this student is changing her behavior based on her observations of those around her, this is an example of observational learning, and so **(A)** is correct. Insight learning is a sudden realization of the solution to a problem, but this student is not solving a problem in the example, so (B) can be eliminated. Emotional learning is the notion that emotions can affect our ability to learn; a lack of emotional content in this example means (C) can be eliminated. Latent learning is learning that occurs without a reward and is only manifested later when a reward is present. Since this student is changing her behavior immediately, (D) cannot be correct. Finally, cognitive mapping, (E), is not a part of the story, since the student is not attempting to learn anything about the geography or location of the hallway.

5. B

Topic: Motivation, Emotion, and Personality

An approach-approach conflict occurs when an individual must choose between two equally attractive options. Since making more money and attending a fun concert are both good options, **(B)** is correct. An approach-avoidance conflict occurs when an individual must decide whether to pursue or avoid something that has both positive and negative aspects, eliminating (A). An avoidance-avoidance conflict is one in which an individual must choose between two equally unattractive options. Since this is the opposite of what is described in the question stem, (C) is incorrect. An intrapersonal conflict is an internal conflict that can develop from one's thoughts, ideas, values, or predispositions, eliminating (D). An interpersonal conflict, (E), is a conflict between multiple individuals.

6. B

Topic: Developmental Psychology

Permissive parenting, also known as indulgent parenting, is a style of parenting in which parents are responsive but not demanding; they tend to establish inconsistent rules and avoid confrontation. **(B)** is correct. (A) characterizes authoritative parenting, (C) characterizes authoritarian or strict parenting, and (D) characterizes neglectful parenting. (E) is incorrect because authoritative parenting tends to produce better outcomes for children than permissive parenting.

7. E

Topic: Social Psychology

(E) is correct because kin selection theory proposes that individuals are more likely to be altruistic toward family members who share their genes as an indirect way of ensuring that (some of) their genes stay in the gene pool. (A) is incorrect because it is a hypothesis about attraction, not altruism. (B) is incorrect because the tendency for people to donate money anonymously is difficult to explain with existing theories on altruism. (C) is incorrect because it explains why people are altruistic toward others (sometimes even strangers) in public ways that can make them seem more attractive to potential mates. (D) is incorrect because it explains why people are altruistic toward people who help them back.

8. B

Topic: Biological Bases of Behavior

The temporal lobe controls hearing and the comprehension of language, so **(B)** is correct. (A) is incorrect because the parietal lobe regulates sensory perception and integration. (C) is incorrect because the frontal lobe is involved with voluntary motion and higher cognitive functions. (D) is incorrect because the occipital lobe controls vision. (E) is incorrect because hearing and language comprehension are localized to the temporal lobe, not regulated by all four lobes.

9. D

Topic: Sensation and Perception

Habituation occurs when an individual stops paying attention to repetitive stimuli, as when Leah stopped noticing the smell. Dishabituation then occurs if new stimuli cause the individual to notice the original repetitive stimulus again, as Leah did when she came home (after hours of being exposed to other smells). Thus, **(D)** is correct. Adaptation, (B), is the process by which people adapt to different levels of stimulation. Sensitization, (C), is characterized by increased responsiveness to a stimulus. Selective attention, (E), is the process by which individuals are able to focus on specific stimuli while ignoring all other stimuli. The cocktail party effect, (A), is an example of selective attention in which individuals are able to focus on one voice in a room full of others.

10. C

Topic: Biological Bases of Behavior

Psychedelic drugs, or hallucinogens, tend to alter mood, increase heart rate, induce hallucinations, and distort perception; (A), (B), (D), and (E) are incorrect. Hallucinogens tend to enhance, rather than diminish, sensation, so **(C)** is correct.

11. C

Topic: Scientific Foundations of Psychology

Behavioral psychology primarily deals with conditioning and other types of learning, while cognitive psychology is more concerned with internal processes such as information processing. **(C)** is thus correct. (A) and (B) are incorrect because the id, ego, and superego are actually psychoanalytic concepts developed by Sigmund Freud, who was neither a behaviorist nor a cognitive psychologist. (D) is incorrect because it reverses the two approaches. (E) is incorrect because cognitive psychology does not primarily concern observable behavior.

12. D

Topic: Learning

In general, fixed ratio and variable ratio schedules lead to greater increases in behavior than fixed or variable interval schedules, so **(D)** is correct. (A) can be eliminated because continuous schedules are a kind of fixed ratio schedule in which the reward is given every time the behavior is performed. (B) is close to providing a correct definition of variable interval, except that the reward is given once at the end of the random interval rather than every time the behavior is performed (which would make it a continuous fixed ratio schedule). (C) gets the order of effectiveness wrong, since fixed ratio schedules are generally stronger than variable interval schedules. Finally, (E) provides two categories of schedule that cannot be directly compared, since fixed ratio is one of the four kinds of schedules, and it cannot be stronger or weaker than itself.

13. E

Topic: Cognitive Psychology

Terman developed the first IQ test that utilized the IQ formula and allowed for testing on adults (the Stanford-Binet). **(E)** is correct. Galton, (A), founded psychometrics and the concept of nature versus nurture. Binet, (B), created the first method for measuring intelligence and the concept of mental age, but his test did not use the IQ formula or norms. Simon, (C), collaborated with Binet to create the Simon-Binet test. Spearman, (D), developed a theory of intelligence based on the g factor.

14. E

Topic: Biological Bases of Behavior

Lilly likely has narcolepsy, a disorder that results in an inability to stay awake during the day; **(E)** is correct. Enuresis is the medical term for involuntary urination, often associated with bed-wetting at night; (A) is incorrect. Cataplexy, the sudden onset of muscle weakness or paralysis, is a condition often associated with narcolepsy, so (B) is incorrect. (C) is also incorrect; night terrors are characterized by waking from non-rapid eye movement (NREM) sleep with feelings of terror or dread. Somnambulism is a sleep disorder marked by walking or performing other behaviors during sleep; (D) is incorrect.

15. C

Topic: Cognitive Psychology

Because of the serial position effect, you are more likely to be able to recall list items presented both very early, like (A) and (B), and very late, like (D) and (E). Items in the middle are forgotten more easily, so **(C)** is correct.

16. D

Topic: Scientific Foundations of Psychology

John Locke was an empiricist philosopher who maintained that the human mind was a *tabula rasa*, a blank slate upon which experience would write, shaping

individuals to become whatever their experiences would make them. **(D)** is correct. (A) and (B) are incorrect because Plato and Aristotle were ancient philosophers who concerned themselves with other issues, such as the development of virtue and the location where thoughts originated in the body. (C) is incorrect because René Descartes was the modern philosopher known primarily for his theory of mind-body dualism. (E) is incorrect because Charles Darwin was a biologist known for his theory of evolution through natural selection.

17. B

Topic: Cognitive Psychology

A morpheme is the smallest unit of language that has meaning. The "-ing" at the end of the word "grasping" indicates an ongoing action, making it a morpheme. **(B)** is correct. (A) is incorrect because a phoneme is the smallest unit of sound in a language, but "-ing" is composed of multiple distinct sounds, which are represented by the letters that make it up. (C), (D), and (E) are incorrect because they are concepts that pertain to combinations of words, whereas the example in this question refers to a single part of a single word. Syntax refers to how words are combined to form sentences, semantics refers to the rules that govern how we derive meaning from phrases or sentences, and pragmatics refers to the dependence of language on context and other preexisting knowledge.

18. D

Topic: Scientific Foundations of Psychology

Correlation coefficients range in value from −1 to +1, with the sign determining the direction of the relationship and the absolute value determining the relative strength. The question stem describes a weak, positive (because when IQ is high, problem solving ability is also high) correlation, which would only describe **(D)**. (A) and (B) are negative correlations, (C) is no correlation, and (E) is a strongly positive correlation.

19. A

Topic: Motivation, Emotion, and Personality

This theory separates people into groups and describes the qualities that each group shares. This is thus a type theory, so **(A)** is correct. Trait theories start from the opposite direction, listing individual traits that form various combinations to make each person a little different from everyone else. Since this psychologist is saying that all people who wear a certain color shirt share the same traits, (B) is incorrect. Humanist, behavioral, and psychoanalytic theories all seek to describe where behaviors and traits come from rather than focusing on the traits and types themselves, so (C), (D), and (E) can be eliminated as well.

20. C
Topic: Social Psychology

(C) is correct because sexual selection theory proposes that individuals act altruistically in order to attract mates. (A) and (B) are incorrect because they pertain to attraction, not altruism. (D) is incorrect because it explains why people help others who help them, while (E) is incorrect because it refers to the tendency for individuals to behave selflessly toward family members as an indirect way of perpetuating their genes.

21. B
Topic: Motivation, Emotion, and Personality

The persona, **(B)**, is Jung's psychodynamic archetype that represents the part of the personality that an individual presents to the world. The shadow, (C), is the undesirable part that an individual hides. The animus, (D), encompasses a woman's masculine traits, and the anima, (E), encompasses a man's feminine traits. The self, (A), is not an archetype for Jung, but is rather the sum of all of the conscious and unconscious parts of the personality.

22. A
Topic: Clinical Psychology

An irrational and maladaptive fear of heights is known as acrophobia, one of the specific phobias. **(A)** is correct. (B) involves excessive worry about numerous aspects of life, not about one specific trigger. (C) is characterized by recurring urges and repetitive behaviors. Personality disorders are not recognized as problems by the people who suffer from them, but Karen sees her fear of heights as frustrating; (D) is incorrect. (E) involves disturbing memories of a particular traumatic incident, which is not suggested in the description of Karen's disorder.

23. D
Topic: Cognitive Psychology

Psychologist James Flynn was the first to document the increase in mean intelligence scores over time within the population; **(D)** is thus correct. (A) is incorrect because the triarchic theory of intelligence, proposed by Robert Sternberg, maintains that three distinct capacities make up intelligence. Savant syndrome, (B), is a condition characterized by limited general mental ability but exceptional ability in a single skill. General intelligence factor, (C), is the factor identified by Charles Spearman that has been found to account for 40 to 50 percent of variation in intelligence scores. Fluid intelligence, (E), refers to the ability to solve novel problems.

24. C
Topic: Scientific Foundations of Psychology

Confounding variables are variables other than independent variables that influence the results of an experiment by affecting the dependent variable. **(C)** is thus correct. (A) and (B) are incorrect because confounding variables can have different effects on the data. (D) is incorrect because confounding variables have no general connection to deception. (E) is incorrect because confounding variables are uncontrolled; if the researcher controlled them, then they could not influence the dependent variable.

25. C
Topic: Clinical Psychology

Systemic therapy, **(C)**, is correct because this approach is often used in couple and family therapy due to its focus on how people are influenced by complex family systems. The other choices are incorrect because they are common approaches for individual psychotherapy.

26. C
Topic: Biological Bases of Behavior

Unlike identical twins, who originate from a single fertilized egg and thus have identical genetics, fraternal twins are born when two separate eggs are fertilized at the same time. They are twins only insofar as they gestate at the same time, but otherwise they are exactly like any pair of siblings born at different times, sharing only about half of their genes in common (they may even be different sexes). Thus, the chance of a person having the same genetic disease that his or her fraternal twin has is 50 percent, **(C)**. (E) may be tempting because identical twins have identical genes, so they would share the same genetic disorders—but this question asked about fraternal twins.

27. C

Topic: Clinical Psychology

In behavioral therapy, the goal is to apply learning principles, such as reinforcement and punishment, to change patients' behaviors. **(C)** is thus correct. (A) and (E) are associated with psychoanalysis, (B) is associated with client-centered therapy, and (D) is associated with cognitive therapy.

28. A

Topic: Social Psychology

Deindividuation occurs in situations characterized by high arousal and anonymity when an individual experiences loss of self-awareness and self-restraint. In this example, the teenager is relatively anonymous because he is in a large group of other soccer fans, and he is highly aroused because he is at a rowdy game. Thus, he has lost self-restraint and uncharacteristically begun yelling at a referee. **(A)** is correct. (B) refers to the tendency for people in a group to put forth less effort when completing a task. The question does not say that the teenager is putting forth less effort due to the presence of other fans, so this choice is incorrect. (C) refers to a magnifying effect of the presence of others on one's ability to perform some tasks. (D) refers to an increase in a group's initial tendencies over the course of discussion within that group. (E) may be tempting because it may seem as though the teenager is conforming to the expectations of the other soccer fans. However, the question does not state that he is partaking in the same behaviors as the other fans; rather, he is influenced by the general rowdy atmosphere.

29. A

Topic: Social Psychology

(A) is correct; similarity refers to the tendency to be attracted to people with characteristics like yours, the contrary of what Robert believes. (B) refers to the

tendency to be attracted to outward beauty, (C) refers to the tendency to pick partners who are nearby, (D) refers to the evolutionary process in which genes that increase reproductive fitness perpetuate, and (E) refers to the tendency to like people who like you.

30. D

Topic: Clinical Psychology

Individuals with dissociative amnesia experience a sudden inability to recall important personal information. This memory loss is often induced by a stressful event, such as the robbery mentioned in the question stem. Thus, **(D)** is correct. None of the other conditions listed matches the described symptoms. Individuals with agoraphobia, (A), are afraid to leave familiar spaces. Individuals with major depressive disorder, (B), experience two or more weeks of depressed moods, feelings of worthlessness, and diminished interest in most activities. Individuals with seasonal affective disorder, (C), experience episodes of depression that usually occur during the fall and winter months. These individuals often experience an improvement in mood during the spring and summer months. Individuals with generalized anxiety disorder, (E), are constantly plagued by excessive worries.

31. D

Topic: Clinical Psychology

Transference is the tendency to redirect feelings originally felt about one person to another person, often a therapist. **(D)** is thus correct. (A) is a technique used in client-centered therapy, while (B), (C), and (E) are all techniques used in cognitive therapy.

32. B

Topic: Motivation, Emotion, and Personality

Extrinsic motivation refers to behaviors that are driven by external rewards like money or praise. Conversely, intrinsic motivation refers to behaviors that are driven by internal rewards. Since both groups in the question stem are interested in the activity, even without a reward, both groups have intrinsic motivation to complete the activity. When payment, an extrinsic motivator, is added to one group and then removed, that group becomes less likely to complete the activity. Thus, the extrinsic motivator interfered negatively with the intrinsic motivator, making

(B) correct. Since the question stem does not state that the paid group performed the activity better or more frequently than the unpaid group, there is no way to claim that the extrinsic motivator was more powerful, eliminating (A). Since the group that was paid continued performing the behavior as long as the extrinsic motivator was present, it is likely that the reinforcement schedule was sufficient, and that the motivator was satisfying a drive and causing dopamine release, which is involved in reward-motivated behavior. Thus, (C), (D), and (E) can be eliminated.

33. E
Topic: Scientific Foundations of Psychology

The Hawthorne effect refers to changes that occur in people's behavior when they know they are being observed. When they are aware of being observed by a researcher, people tend to act in ways that make them look good—something they are less likely to do when they believe no one is watching. While the Hawthorne effect is usually used in research contexts, Seth's behavior reflects a similar effect, so **(E)** is correct. Hindsight bias is the inclination to believe that an event was predictable after the outcome is known. Since neither Seth nor the teacher made any predictions, (A) is incorrect. (B) is incorrect because imprinting is the process by which some nonhuman animals form attachments early on in their lives. Ingroup bias is the tendency to favor one's own group. Since Seth treats his classmates better when an outsider (his teacher) is present, (C) is incorrect. (D) is incorrect because groupthink occurs when groups make poor decisions because of individuals' desires to maintain harmony in the group.

34. D
Topic: Learning

The original scenario provided in the stimulus describes a situation in which the reward is given per fixed unit of time, which is an example of fixed interval reward schedule. This makes **(D)** correct. (A) is incorrect because a continuous schedule rewards every single instance of a desired behavior. (B) and (C) are incorrect because ratio-based schedules depend upon the number of times a behavior is done, not the interval of time passed. (E) is incorrect because the interval is fixed at one hour.

35. A
Topic: Learning

Sometimes a considerable amount of time is needed before a subject masters a new behavior. Instead of just waiting around for a prolonged period of time, the teacher can coax or nudge learners in the right direction by giving them rewards. This process, known as shaping, is analogous to the situation described in the question stem, thus making **(A)** correct. (B) is incorrect because latent learning is learning that occurs without any obvious reinforcement and remains unexpressed until reinforcement is provided. A secondary reinforcer is a learned reinforcer, one that has come to be associated with a primary reinforcer. Examples would include praise, approval, or money. Token reinforcement is a special type of secondary reinforcement; thus, both (C) and (D) are incorrect. (E) can be eliminated because satiation refers to the tendency to desire a particular reinforcer more after being deprived of it.

36. C
Topic: Learning

The stimulus states that Paul neither likes nor dislikes the steamed vegetables to begin with. As such, the plate of steamed vegetables evokes no response, either conditioned or unconditioned, making it a neutral stimulus. **(C)** is correct and (A) and (B) are incorrect. (D) and (E) are incorrect because the plate of vegetables is a stimulus, not a response.

37. B
Topic: Learning

When a subject receives a reward as a reinforcement for a given task, such as when Paul receives chocolate for doing chores, this is an example of operant conditioning. Among the names listed, B.F. Skinner is most closely associated with this type of learning, making **(B)** correct. The remaining choices are incorrect because they name thinkers who were known for other ideas. Ivan Pavlov conditioned dogs to salivate at the sound of a bell after repeated pairings with food, thereby discovering classical conditioning; (A) is incorrect. John Garcia discovered taste aversion when looking at the impact of radiation on rats, while Albert Bandura conducted the Bobo doll experiment, making (C) and (D) incorrect. Lastly, Robert Rescorla studied cognitive processes in classical conditioning; (E) is incorrect.

38. B
Topic: Cognitive Psychology

Since this situation involves one source of information making another source of information more difficult to remember, the correct answer involves interference, not amnesia (general memory loss), so (C), (D), and (E) can be eliminated. Here, old information is interfering with the memory of new information in a process known as proactive interference, so **(B)** is correct. (A) is incorrect because retroactive interference occurs when new information interferes with the memory of old information, which is the opposite of what is described.

39. D
Topic: Cognitive Psychology

The description in the question is of Spearman's construct known as the g factor; **(D)** is correct. Performance scales, (A), are intelligence tests that evaluate without the use of verbal measures. Creative intelligence, (B), and practical intelligence, (C), are both parts of Sternberg's triarchic theory. Savant syndrome, (E), is a condition in which someone has limited general mental ability but exceptional ability in a single skill.

40. C
Topic: Social Psychology

(C) is correct because it describes an individual who adopts a new social role (manager) and begins behaving differently (bossing people around). The remaining choices are incorrect because they describe emotional reactions to particular circumstances, not behaviors that are directly influenced by social roles.

41. B
Topic: Scientific Foundations of Psychology

Phrenology is the thoroughly debunked theory proposed by Gall and Spurzheim that psychological traits could be deduced from characteristics of the skull, such as its size and shape; **(B)** is correct. Psychophysics, (A), investigates the relationship between physical stimuli and the sensations they cause. Eugenics, (C), is also a controversial and

discredited idea, but it concerns misguided efforts to "perfect" the human race through controlled breeding and other interventions. Parapsychology, (D), also largely debunked, refers to the pseudoscientific investigation of extrasensory perception and other "paranormal" psychological phenomena. Psychoanalysis, (E), is the clinical and theoretical approach developed by Sigmund Freud that focuses on the unconscious.

42. E
Topic: Scientific Foundations of Psychology

Because José is simply interested in establishing relationships between variables (i.e., membership in a particular group and measures of specific psychological traits), he would find the use of correlation coefficients most helpful for formulating conclusions in his study. **(E)** is correct. While José might draw on the other statistics in the course of his analysis, the remaining choices are incorrect because his conclusions are specifically statements of correlation that describe how membership in a particular group relates to possession of particular characteristics.

43. D
Topic: Cognitive Psychology

The main difference between the cognitive and behavioral perspectives boils down to the source of language—behavioral psychologists argue that language is very similar to other behaviors and is learned through operant conditioning and observational learning, whereas cognitive psychologists argue that language capacity is "hardwired" and that we apply the rules we have learned to the input we receive during a critical period. **(D)** is correct and (E) is incorrect. The remaining choices are not subjects of particular disputes between nativists and behaviorists.

44. A
Topic: Social Psychology

(A) is correct because prejudice is an irrational and negative emotional response (in Daniel's case, anger) to a particular group of people (in this case, women). (B) and (E) are examples of stereotypes, overgeneralized beliefs about characteristics associated with a group or category of people. (C) and (D) are examples of discrimination, differential treatment of different groups of people.

45. C
Topic: Developmental Psychology

Adam is struggling to establish a sense of freedom and self-reliance by taking a more active role in his daily routine. Erikson called the conflict at this stage of development autonomy vs. shame and doubt; **(C)** is correct. Identity vs. role confusion, (A), describes children questioning what roles they want to play in society before deciding which identities best suit them. Trust vs. mistrust, (B), describes infants relying on caregivers to fulfill their basic needs and subsequently developing trust when those needs are met. When infants have caregivers who are neglectful or do not provide for them, a sense of suspicion and mistrust can develop, affecting the ability to form lasting relationships later in life. During the initiative vs. guilt conflict, (D), young children play with others their age and become secure in their ability to take initiative and make decisions. If children are given too much criticism when trying to self-express, they may develop a sense of guilt and conclude that they are a nuisance to others. Although (D) is a tempting choice, it is incorrect because this stage involves developing a sense of security and control over social interactions, whereas autonomy vs. shame and doubt involves developing a sense of control over physical skills, which better describes Adam's behavior. (E) is incorrect because generativity vs. stagnation describes the stage in which adults seek a sense of purpose through family and/or career development. Failure to establish such purpose can lead to a questioning of self-worth, as individuals doubt their capacity to contribute to society.

46. B
Topic: Developmental Psychology

Children in the preoperational stage are most likely to develop egocentrism, or self-centeredness, as a result of their inability to comprehend that others have different worldviews; **(B)** is correct. Children do not obtain conservation until the concrete operational stage, making (C) incorrect. Children develop object permanence, (A), during the sensorimotor stage. Abstract reasoning, (D), develops during the formal operational stage. Conformity, (E), is a sub-stage of Kohlberg's conventional stage of moral development.

47. D
Topic: Developmental Psychology

According to Kohlberg, children in the pre-conventional stage act in largely self-interested ways by trying to avoid punishment or gain rewards. **(D)** is correct because it presents an example of a reward that might plausibly motivate Jack. (A), (B), and (C) are incorrect because they suggest a greater level of empathy than is typically found in pre-conventional children. (E) is incorrect because it describes a motivation more likely to be found in the conventional stage.

48. E
Topic: Learning

In the described scenario, the happy experience is an unconditioned stimulus, and the song is a conditioned stimulus that causes the same feelings of happiness. This conditioned stimulus is then paired with driving to work, which becomes a new conditioned stimulus. In classical conditioning, when a conditioned stimulus is used to condition a response to *another* neutral stimulus, this is called higher order conditioning. **(E)** is correct. Since the woman is gaining rather than losing a conditioned response, this is not an example of (A), extinction. Because spontaneous recovery only happens after extinction, (B) is out as well. (C), generalization, would only be applicable if the two stimuli were similar, such as if many different songs evoked the feeling of happiness, rather than just the original song. (D), as the opposite of generalization, cannot be correct either, since discrimination involves experiencing a conditioned response as a result of a specific stimulus but not other, similar stimuli.

49. A
Topic: Clinical Psychology

The goal of cognitive therapy is to help patients understand the limitations of how they think about the world and establish more realistic patterns of thinking that can empower them to make positive changes in their lives. **(A)** is thus correct. The remaining choices are incorrect because the other approaches do not focus primarily on thoughts. (B) focuses on the unconscious, (C) encourages self-acceptance and self-actualization, (D) aims to change behavior, and (E) relies upon medical treatments, usually drugs.

50. D

Topic: Sensation and Perception

The tendency to fill in gaps in recognizable patterns, perceiving discontinuous figures as wholes, is an example of the law of closure, making **(D)** correct. (A), (B), and (C) can be eliminated because they name different Gestalt principles. The law of proximity is the tendency to perceive objects that are close to each other as forming a group. The law of similarity is the tendency to group objects that are similar in some way, such as color, shape, or size. The law of continuity is the tendency to group objects if they follow a continuous pattern, such as a line or shape. (E) is incorrect because Weber's law states that the size of the just noticeable difference (JND) varies in a constant ratio with the strength of the original stimulus, which is not relevant to the question.

51. A

Topic: Clinical Psychology

In the nineteenth century, moral treatment was characterized by regular walks, healthy diets, and environments with natural light, so **(A)** is correct. (B) is incorrect because the study of religious texts such as the Bible was not part of moral treatment. (C), (D), and (E) are modern psychological treatments.

52. D

Topic: Biological Bases of Behavior

Among Sperry's findings was that language abilities are typically managed by the left hemisphere of the cerebrum; **(D)** is correct. (A) is incorrect because the fact that the left cerebral hemisphere controls the right side of the body and vice versa was already known to Sperry and was used in the design of his research. (B) is incorrect because the dominant hemisphere is usually the left, but not always. (C) is incorrect because there is no evidence that split-brain patients have more than one consciousness. (E) is incorrect because spatial abilities are usually controlled by the right hemisphere, not the left.

53. A

Topic: Cognitive Psychology

The sentence is lexically correct (the words mean something), syntactically correct (the words are in the right order), phonemically correct (the sounds are appropriate), and morphemically correct (the words are put together correctly). This rules out (B), (C), (D), and (E), respectively. The sentence, however, is meaningless, because this combination of words contains logical contradictions and is therefore semantically ambiguous. **(A)** is correct.

54. E

Topic: Biological Bases of Behavior

The forebrain gives rise to the most evolutionarily advanced structures in the brain, which are generally responsible for more complex cognitive processes such as emotion and adaptive learning, making **(E)** correct. The midbrain and hindbrain give rise to less advanced structures such as the superior and inferior colliculi, responsible for sensorimotor reflexes; and the medulla, reticular formation, and cerebellum, responsible for vital functions, arousal, and movement, respectively. Due to the complex nature of the characteristics controlled and influenced by the basal ganglia, options (A), (B), (C), and (D) are all incorrect.

55. C

Topic: Developmental Psychology

Piaget found that children reach the cognitive milestone of conservation, the ability to determine that quantities remain constant even when their outward appearances change, during the concrete operational stage. **(C)** is correct. (A) and (B) are incorrect because children in these Piagetian stages are not yet able to understand conservation. (D) is incorrect because children in the formal operational stage have already mastered conservation. (E) is incorrect because the oral stage is one of the stages in Freud's theory, not Piaget's.

56. C

Topic: Developmental Psychology

In Erikson's third stage of psychosocial development, initiative vs. guilt, children begin to assert control through play and interactions with peers. Children who are successful in this stage will develop leadership skills and personal initiative. **(C)** is correct. Trust vs. mistrust, (A), is Erikson's first stage of psychosocial development and is marked by infants' explorations of their environment. Autonomy vs. shame and doubt, (B), is Erikson's second stage, when children start to make more choices for themselves. Industry vs. inferiority, (D), is Erikson's fourth stage, when children begin to gain competence in skills their peers value. Intimacy vs. isolation, (E), is Erikson's sixth stage and is marked by the conflict between forming intimate relationships with others and living in isolation.

57. C
Topic: Developmental Psychology

The phenomenon described in the question stem is called imprinting; **(C)** is correct. Attachment, (A), refers to the emotional bond between an infant and its primary caregiver. Temperament, (B), refers to an individual's characteristic pattern of emotional reactivity. Habituation, (D), refers to a decrease in response to a stimulus after repeated exposure to the stimulus in classical conditioning. Gestation, (E), is the period of development between conception and birth.

58. D
Topic: Sensation and Perception

(A) is incorrect because bottom-up processing is the perceptual process of integrating basic sensory data into a more complex whole. Top-down processing, on the other hand, is the perceptual process in which memories, expectations, and other factors give organization to the whole of perception, which describes what happened in the question stem, making **(D)** correct. (B) is eliminated because proximity is the tendency to perceive objects that are close to each other as forming a group. Weber's law states that the size of the just noticeable difference (JND) varies in a constant ratio with the strength of the original stimulus, making (C) incorrect. Lastly, (E) is eliminated because the cocktail party effect describes an individual's ability to focus on only one voice even with extensive and varied background noise.

59. B
Topic: Social Psychology

(B) is correct because instrumental aggression refers to behaviors that cause harm in order to attain a goal, in this case to get the toy. (A) and (D) are incorrect because these terms refer to aggression that stems from a desire to harm. (C) and (E) are not established terms in social psychology.

60. B
Topic: Motivation, Emotion, and Personality

The social cognitive perspective, and reciprocal determinism in particular, maintains that personality, behavior, and environment all interact and have an effect on each other. **(B)** is correct because the social cognitive perspective doesn't incorporate the psychoanalytic idea of the unconscious. The remaining choices represent characteristics taken into account by the social cognitive perspective.

61. D
Topic: Clinical Psychology

Antipsychotics, including atypical antipsychotics, are commonly prescribed to treat schizophrenia. **(D)** is correct. (A) is used to treat anxiety, (B) and (C) are used to treat anxiety and mood disorders, and (E) is most commonly used to treat bipolar disorders.

62. A
Topic: Cognitive Psychology

Standardization, **(A)**, involves creating a comparison group for the establishment of norms and maintaining consistent testing conditions for all participants, just as described in the stem. **(A)** is correct. Validity, as in (B) and (C), refers to a test's ability to measure what it is actually supposed to, which is not yet a consideration of the psychologists. Reliability, as in (D) and (E), refers to the consistency in test results, also not yet a consideration for the psychologists.

63. D
Topic: Cognitive Psychology

Charles Spearman, **(D)**, identified the g factor, which accounts for about half of variability in IQ scores and has been shown to correlate with social, educational, and economic success later in life. L.L. Thurstone, (A), disagreed with the theory of general intelligence, proposing instead seven independent intelligences. Howard Gardner, (B), also proposed a theory of multiple intelligences, challenging the commonly accepted definition of intelligence. Robert Sternberg, (C), proposed the triarchic theory of intelligence, in which analytical, creative, and practical abilities combine to form intelligence. Daniel Goleman, (E), is an advocate of the theory of emotional intelligence.

64. B

Topic: Clinical Psychology

Dissociative identity disorder (DID), popularly known as multiple personality disorder, is a dissociative disorder because it involves a disconnection from one's identity; patients suffering from DID have developed two or more distinct identities who often conflict and alternate in their control of behavior. **(B)** is correct. The remaining choices are incorrect because no other diagnostic category involves the development of multiple distinct identities.

65. A

Topic: Motivation, Emotion, and Personality

Primary process thinking is a concept in Freud's structural perspective. It is primal, instinctive, and based on seeking pleasure and avoiding pain; it is therefore a product of the id, **(A)**. The ego is responsible for secondary process thinking, so (B) is incorrect. (C) and (D) are incorrect because these are Jungian archetypes, not Freudian structures of the unconscious. (E) is incorrect because the superego is not associated with a particular type of thinking process.

66. D

Topic: Scientific Foundations of Psychology

A +0.90 correlation (on a scale of –1 to 1) is a very strong positive correlation, demonstrating that two variables are directly related; **(D)** is correct. (A) is incorrect because +0.90 is neither weak nor inverse (which would be a negative correlation). Correlations on their own can never indicate causation, so (B) and (C) are incorrect. No relationship between variables would be indicated by a correlation coefficient of zero, so (E) is incorrect.

67. B

Topic: Cognitive Psychology

Because the mathematician wants to be able to apply her method to all problems of a certain type and guarantee a result, she is looking to create an algorithm, **(B)**. A heuristic, (A), is a shortcut that is efficient but might not always work. Since she is not trying to memorize anything, a mnemonic, (C), would be inappropriate. (D) is incorrect because an insight is a sudden realization that solves a problem, rather than a rigorous method. A

mental set, (E), is a tendency to use old methods to solve new problems; this mathematician is seeking a completely new way of solving a problem, making (E) incorrect.

68. B

Topic: Cognitive Psychology

Factor analysis reduces a large number of potential variables by combining like items, making **(B)** correct. The Flynn effect, (A), refers to the increase in average IQ scores with each successive generation. Test-retest reliability, (C), is a test's ability to produce the same score when taken twice. Construct validity, (D), refers to a test's ability to measure an abstract idea. Content validity, (E), refers to how well a test measures the complete meaning of a concept.

69. A

Topic: Clinical Psychology

The psychoanalytic model holds that abnormal behavior results from repressed memories of childhood trauma, conflicts between the id, ego, and superego, and other unconscious mental processes. **(A)** is correct. All of the other choices postulate other causes (social, biological, etc.) for psychological disorders.

70. E

Topic: Motivation, Emotion, and Personality

Neuroticism is the Big Five trait associated with anxiety, worry, fear, and the fight-or-flight response, making **(E)** correct. The remaining choices are the other traits of the Big Five model.

71. D

Topic: Clinical Psychology

Bipolar I disorder is characterized by manic episodes and occasional psychotic episodes. While some patients with this disorder suffer from depressive episodes as well, not all do. **(D)** is therefore correct. (A), (B), and (C) are incorrect because these are all depressive disorders. (E) is incorrect because bipolar II disorder is characterized by hypomanic episodes and at least one major depressive episode.

72. B

Topic: Sensation and Perception

The result of the first experiment described in the question stem, in which half of the participants are able to discriminate between two stimuli, is the definition of the just-noticeable difference (JND) for that stimulus. Brightness follows Weber's law, which means that a larger stimulus requires a proportionately larger JND. According to that law, if the first intensity is doubled (from 100 to 200 lumens), the new JND would also roughly double, from 7 lumens to 14 lumens. However, the question asks about discriminating between intensities of 200 and 207 lumens, which is a difference of only half the JND for 200 lumens. While it is unreasonable to expect that absolutely none of the 500 participants would be able to tell the difference, eliminating (A), it is almost certain that fewer than half of them will be able to discriminate. **(B)** is thus correct. (C) and (D) directly contradict this expectation. (E) is incorrect because Weber's law allows psychologists to make predictions about the JND at particular intensities.

73. D

Topic: Biological Bases of Behavior

Stage 4 of NREM is the stage of sleep characterized by the slowest brain waves; **(D)** is correct. (A), (B), and (C) are incorrect because these shallower stages of NREM sleep involve relatively faster brain waves. During REM sleep, brain activity is more like the waking state, so brain waves in REM are considerably faster than they are in the other sleep stages; (E) is incorrect.

74. A

Topic: Cognitive Psychology

The availability heuristic is a mental bias that can occur when judgments are based on the information that is most easily brought to mind, rather than a more objective assessment. This study is asking participants to estimate the probability of dying due to particular causes, but most participants answer based only on what *seems* more obviously fatal (e.g., the shark attack). **(A)** is thus correct. The remaining choices describe phenomena that don't apply to the described scenario. Priming, (B), is the unconscious activation of particular associations that help with memory retrieval. The Flynn effect, (C), refers to the ongoing increase in average IQ scores over time, which requires IQ tests to

be renormalized periodically. Insight, (D), is a sudden and often completely new realization of the solution to a problem. Divergent thinking, (E), is cognition that produces many alternatives and promotes open-ended thought.

75. D

Topic: Cognitive Psychology

Belief perseverance is the tendency to maintain a belief even after the evidence used to form the belief is proven wrong. If some participants demonstrate belief perseverance, the confidence they have in their initial beliefs will remain the same, even after contrary evidence has been presented. This exactly describes the situation in **(D)**. (A) is incorrect because individuals with belief perseverance are unlikely to acknowledge that they are wrong, let alone to regret being wrong. (B) directly contradicts the phenomenon of belief perseverance. (C) is incorrect because people with belief perseverance are unlikely to change their answers. Belief perseverance is not correlated positively or negatively with intellectual abilities, so (E) is incorrect.

76. C

Topic: Sensation and Perception

Signal detection theory maintains that the same stimulus can elicit a different response in different situations, depending on an individual's surroundings and mental state. This makes **(C)** correct and eliminates (A). (B) is incorrect because it describes the concept of retinal disparity. (D) and (E) are incorrect because they describe trichromatic theory and kinesthesis, respectively.

77. B

Topic: Learning

Systematic desensitization, which involves carefully planned, repeat exposure to fear-inducing stimuli, is commonly used to treat phobias, so **(B)** is correct. (A) is incorrect because depression is usually treated with a combination of medication and cognitive behavioral therapy. (C) is incorrect because addictions are often treated using aversion therapy, which involves creating a negative emotional response to the object of addiction, not reducing an existing negative response. (D) is incorrect because chronic pain is typically treated with medication, and (E) is incorrect because relationship problems are not commonly treated with systematic desensitization.

78. A

Topic: Learning

Shaping is the process by which successively more complicated behaviors are rewarded, so the step-by-step approach in **(A)** is a way that this might reasonably be done. Shaping does not require a change in the schedule of reinforcement, as in (B), or the size of the reward, as in (C), so these can both be eliminated. (D) does mention shapes, but shaping is about rewarding successive steps in a behavior rather than increasing the difficulty of the task over time. Finally, (E) discusses associating multiple tasks with the same reward. While it is easier to train animals to perform behaviors that resemble instinctual behaviors, shaping would use an instinctive behavior as a step in a chain of successive behaviors rather than as a separate task.

79. B

Topic: Motivation, Emotion, and Personality

The Schachter-Singer theory states that emotional experience requires both the awareness and interpretation of physiological arousal. Thus, **(B)** must be correct because the individual is experiencing an emotion that is consistent with both his physiological reaction to the dose of adrenaline and his interpretation of his environment. (A) is incorrect because a tranquilizer would cause a physiological reaction associated with calmness, not anger. (C) and (E) are incorrect because they support the James-Lange theory of emotion, which states that emotional responses occur as a result of physiological arousal. (D) is incorrect because it supports the Cannon-Bard theory of emotion, which states that physiological arousal and emotional experience in response to a stimulus occur simultaneously.

80. E

Topic: Sensation and Perception

The three ossicles found inside the ear are the malleus, incus, and stapes; **(E)** is correct. The pinna is the external part of the ear, while the cochlea is a snail-shell-shaped, fluid-filled structure that contains auditory receptors. That eliminates (A), (B), (C), and (D).

81. C

Topic: Biological Bases of Behavior

Neurotransmitters carry messages from sending neurons across synapses to receptor sites on receiving neurons. **(C)** is correct. (A) is incorrect because hormones are endocrine signaling molecules that travel through the bloodstream. A synapse is a tiny gap between neurons, not a chemical messenger, making (B) incorrect. Dendrites, (D), and axons, (E), are structures of neurons, not chemical messengers.

82. C

Topic: Motivation, Emotion, and Personality

Paul Ekman's cross-cultural studies found that there are seven universal emotions—happiness, surprise, sadness, fear, disgust, contempt, and anger—which are each associated with a distinct facial expression and expressed the same way in all cultures, eliminating (D). Given that anger is one of these universal emotions, **(C)** must be correct. Other emotions, such as love or jealousy, are expressed differently in different cultures, and some emotions may not even be recognized in particular cultures, eliminating (A) and (E). (B) is incorrect because children who are blind have been observed to exhibit the facial expressions associated with the seven universal emotions, implying that there is an innate component to the expression of emotion.

83. E

Topic: Sensation and Perception

The pseudoscientific field of parapsychology purports to study "paranormal" phenomena, such as psychokinesis (moving objects with the mind) and extrasensory perception, which includes clairvoyance (perceiving events in other locations), telepathy (perceiving thoughts in other minds), and precognition (perceiving the future). None of these purported abilities have been empirically verified by research, making **(E)** correct and the other choices incorrect.

84. B

Topic: Clinical Psychology

(A) and (D) were the *intended* consequences of deinstitutionalization, which called for patients to be treated in their communities rather than in asylums. However, fewer patients in asylums contributed to increased homelessness, which was not intended, so **(B)** is correct. Deinstitutionalization primarily affected asylum patients and not the larger population; thus, (C) and (E) are incorrect.

85. D

Topic: Scientific Foundations of Psychology

External validity is the extent to which a study can be generalized beyond the sample. Since Dr. Sanchez specifically studied rap music but is claiming that exposure to any music increases test performance, the external validity of her experiment is called into question. Thus, **(D)** is correct. Internal validity, (A), is the degree to which the causal relationship between the independent and dependent variables can be established. A study with low internal validity has confounding variables that could be the cause of the effect on the dependent variable. Face validity, (B), is the degree to which a study or test appears to measure what it is supposed to. Construct validity, (C), is the extent to which a test measures what it claims to be measuring. Concurrent validity, (E), is the degree to which the score on one measuring scale correlates with the score from another measuring scale.

86. D

Topic: Biological Bases of Behavior

Endorphins are neurochemicals produced in the brain's hypothalamus and pituitary gland, and they work as natural painkillers. **(D)** is correct. (A), (B), and (C) are incorrect because GABA, dopamine, and serotonin are all neurotransmitters. (E) is incorrect because ibuprofen is a synthetic painkiller.

87. D

Topic: Scientific Foundations of Psychology

If two variables share a positive correlation, then as one increases, the other also increases. This is also known as a direct relationship, making **(D)** correct. (A) is incorrect because an inverse relationship yields a negative correlation. (B) is incorrect because a correlation of zero suggests that two variables are unrelated. (C) and (E) are incorrect because the relative strength of a correlation is determined by its absolute value, not by its positive or negative sign.

88. A

Topic: Biological Bases of Behavior

SSRIs are drugs that block the reuptake of serotonin, resulting in an increase in the amount of serotonin in the synapses at any given time. This increases the effect of the neurotransmitter, enhancing a person's mood. These drugs, such as Prozac, are often used as a treatment for depression, suggesting that serotonin may be an important neurotransmitter in the regulation of mood. **(A)** is correct. SSRIs do not actually create serotonin, increase sensitivity to serotonin, or mimic any type of effect; eliminate (B), (C), and (D). Also, SSRIs do not function by creating new connections between synapses, making (E) incorrect.

89. C

Topic: Scientific Foundations of Psychology

B.F. Skinner and John B. Watson were both behavioral psychologists who maintained that organisms are conditioned by their external environments to behave in particular ways; **(C)** is correct. (A) and (B) are incorrect because the behaviorists did not believe that innate characteristics such as inborn tendencies or temperament had much influence on behavior. (D) and (E) are incorrect because the behaviorists concerned themselves only with observable behaviors, not with internal mental phenomena such as thoughts and memories.

90. B

Topic: Scientific Foundations of Psychology

To ensure the ethical treatment of participants, researchers must first receive approval for their research proposal from an institutional review board (IRB), eliminating (E). After receiving such approval, researchers should provide participants with informed consent prior to beginning the study, eliminating (A), maintain the confidentiality of all participants as they conduct the study, eliminating (D), and debrief participants afterwards, eliminating (C). Only **(B)**, approval by the APA, is not ethically required.

While the American Psychological Association does provide guidelines on ethical research, it does not review or approve individual research proposals.

91. B

Topic: Sensation and Perception

The situation described in the question is most consistent with temporal or frequency theory, which states that pitch is perceived through the frequency at which neurons in the cochlea fire. This makes **(B)** correct. Gate-control theory maintains that the spinal cord acts like a neurological gate that can open or close to manage whether pain signals travel to the brain; (A) is incorrect. Opponent-process theory suggests that the retina has receptors for three opposing pairs of colors, eliminating (C). (D) is eliminated because it describes a competing theory that maintains that pitch is perceived through the activation of neurons at different locations on the cochlea. Volley theory might be tempting because it helps supplement temporal theory. However, volley theory states that higher frequencies (ones that exceed the rate at which action potentials can fire) are encoded through the firing of multiple neurons out of phase, which combine to produce a higher rate of firing than a single neuron alone. Because the question stem states that the same set of neurons is firing for both sounds, with no new neurons being recruited for the higher-pitched sound, (E) is incorrect.

92. D

Topic: Motivation, Emotion, and Personality

The biological perspective states that the nervous system develops at least in part as a result of genetic expression, so some aspects of personality can be traced back to genes. This matches **(D)**. (A) is not a part of the biological perspective, since biological theorists do not believe, for example, that all humans have the same personality. (B) and (E) are both historical type theories that are no longer believed to be true. The notion that personality is learned, regardless of whom it is learned from, is a position of the behavioral perspective, so (C) can be eliminated as well.

93. A

Topic: Scientific Foundations of Psychology

A type II error is also known as a false negative, the inaccurate endorsement of a null hypothesis that is actually false. **(A)** is thus correct. A type I error, or false positive, is affirming a false alternative hypothesis or rejecting a true null hypothesis; (C) and (E) are incorrect. (B) and (D) are incorrect because affirming a true null hypothesis and rejecting a false null hypothesis are not errors.

94. D

Topic: Motivation, Emotion, and Personality

Maslow claimed that individuals cannot attend to a need in the hierarchy of needs until they have fulfilled all other lower-priority needs. Thus, individuals will only be able to reach self-actualization after meeting their physiological needs, such as those of thirst and hunger, and their psychological needs, such as those of self-esteem and belonging, making **(D)** correct and the other choices incorrect.

95. D

Topic: Developmental Psychology

Infants, when supported upright, will successively march their feet, engaging in a kind of instinctive walking, though they do not have a reflex to attempt to stand up or to stay standing still. Standing is thus a learned behavior, making **(D)** correct. The remaining choices are all reflexes found in newborns. Grasping, (A), is the tendency for an infant to close his or her fingers into a fist when an object brushes the palm of his or her hand. Moro, (B), is the startle reflex. Rooting, (C), is the tendency for an infant to turn his or her head to the side when an object brushes either cheek in search of a nipple for feeding. The Babinski reflex, (E), is the tendency for the toes to fan out when an object brushes the sole of the foot.

96. B

Topic: Motivation, Emotion, and Personality

Homeostasis is the tendency for organisms to maintain a stable internal state by constantly making tiny adjustments in response to external and internal changes. Thus,

(B) is correct. (A) matches the definition of a drive, (C) matches the definition of an instinct, (D) matches the definition of a need, and (E) matches the definition of arousal.

97. C
Topic: Cognitive Psychology

Mnemonics are memory aids that organize information in ways that make it easier to recall, making **(C)** correct. While some mnemonics may use catchy tunes, not all do, so (A) is incorrect. Mnemonics do not provide people with photographic memories, so (B) is incorrect. Many mnemonics bear no meaningful connection to the information they help a person memorize, so mnemonics do not necessarily provide context, as in (D). Mnemonics do not affect the size of short-term memory, so (E) is incorrect.

98. D
Topic: Social Psychology

The fundamental attribution error is the tendency to make dispositional attributions (e.g., he is clumsy), rather than situational attributions (e.g., the stairs are tricky), about other people's behavior. **(D)** is correct. None of the other choices are relevant to attributions. (A) and (B) are incorrect because they refer to the behavior of individuals in larger groups. (C) refers to the tendency of members of a group to adopt more extreme positions over time, while (E) refers to the tendency to perform some tasks better in front of an audience.

99. A
Topic: Motivation, Emotion, and Personality

Intrinsic motivation refers to behaviors that are driven by internal rewards such as enjoyment and satisfaction. Since Chrystal enjoys her job and feels satisfied by it, **(A)** is correct. Chrystal is not being punished, so (B) is incorrect. Since the question stem does not indicate that a group is making a decision, (C) is incorrect. Extrinsic motivation refers to behaviors that are driven by the desire to receive a reward or avoid punishment. Because Chrystal does not mention things like money or social status as reasons for why she loves her job, (D) is incorrect. (E) is incorrect because negative reinforcement is the removal of an aversive stimulus, which does not apply to Chrystal's situation.

100. A
Topic: Clinical Psychology

One unfortunate tendency of the medical model is to classify an increasingly broad range of human behavior (sometimes even healthy emotional responses) as symptomatic of mental illness—that is, to pathologize such behavior. **(A)** is thus correct. The remaining choices are incorrect: the medical model encourages effective medical treatments, is supported by research, is a time-tested approach, and focuses on symptoms, not causes.

SECTION II

1. This question is worth 7 points, 1 point for each explanation and correct application to the situation. The following is a sample student response that would receive full credit, with indications of where points would be awarded in parentheses:

    Herman Ebbinghaus' spacing effect describes how learning is greater when practice with material is spaced out over time, rather than occurring all at once. In this case, Jordan is not spacing out her learning and is trying to cram it all into the two days before her test, so her memorization might not be as good as it would be if she spaced out her studying over a longer period of time. (**1 POINT**)

    Encoding is how information gets into our brains. In this case, Jordan has acoustic encoding from listening to the lectures and visual encoding from viewing the teacher's presentations. To enhance memory, Jordan might want to also participate in semantic encoding, thinking about the meaning of the concepts presented, to help better remember the material she is trying to learn. (**1 POINT**)

    The cochlea is where vibrations caused by sound are turned into neural impulses by hair cells. The hair cells turn those vibrations into action potentials that eventually make it to the brain for processing through the auditory nerve. Jordan's cochlea and hair cells will be active as she listens to the recorded lectures. (**1 POINT**)

    The hippocampus is essential in turning new learning into long-term memories, a process known as consolidation. In Jordan's case, her hippocampus is essential for turning the things she hears and remembers from her studying into long-term memories that she can use to answer questions on her exam. (**1 POINT**)

    Since Jordan is normally a high achiever, her motivation for doing well on this test might be because of her need to gain honors or success, which is achievement motivation. This motivation would explain why Jordan would like to do well on this psychology test, regardless of her interest in psychology. (**1 POINT**)

    The visual cortex is the part of the brain where the visual information that Jordan studies, i.e. the presentation slides, will be processed. The visual cortex is located in the occipital lobe of the brain. (**1 POINT**)

    Social norms come from a culture and represent the expected behavior and roles of people within that society. Since Jordan is a high-achieving student, she might be expected to do well on this psychology test because of that status. Also, since it was suggested to her that listening to the lecture recordings was a good way to study, she might feel as though the social norms for getting a good grade in this class involve listening to the lecture recordings and learning in that manner. (**1 POINT**)

2. This question is worth 7 points: 3 for Part A and 4 for Part B. The following is a sample student response that would receive full credit, with indications of where points would be awarded in parentheses:

    For this experiment, one independent variable is the treatment regimen, since it is being varied for different groups in the experiment. (**1 POINT**) The other independent variable in this study is age category, since it changes treatment efficacy. (**1 POINT**) The dependent variable is the reduction in PTSD symptoms, since it is hypothesized that it is being directly affected by the treatment regimen and age category. (**1 POINT**)

Posttraumatic stress disorder is one of the few disorders that has an explicit cause in the DSM-5. It is caused by exposure to a traumatic experience that involves sexual or physical violence or actual or threatened death. (**1 POINT**)

To calculate the mean reduction in symptoms, add together each of the reductions for each treatment category and then divide by 4, since there are 4 measurements per category. For PO, this should be (13+11+10+14)/4 = 48/4 = 12% reduction. For P+M, this should be (18+16+15+11)/4 = 60/4 = 15% reduction. for MO, this should be (10+13+14+15)/4 = 52/4 = 13% reduction. (**1 POINT**) Because the reduction for P+M is higher than either PO or MO, Dr. Kerry's hypothesis is supported and P+M seems to be the most effective treatment. (**1 POINT**)

While the mean reduction in symptoms is greatest for P+M, this trend does not hold for each age group. Specifically, the 51+ age group has higher reduction in symptoms for both PO and MO treatment regimens. This might imply that the treatment recommendations that Dr. Kerry makes from this study will only be applicable to those 50 years old and under. (**1 POINT**)

Practice Exam 5
Answer Grid

1. Ⓐ Ⓑ Ⓒ Ⓓ Ⓔ
2. Ⓐ Ⓑ Ⓒ Ⓓ Ⓔ
3. Ⓐ Ⓑ Ⓒ Ⓓ Ⓔ
4. Ⓐ Ⓑ Ⓒ Ⓓ Ⓔ
5. Ⓐ Ⓑ Ⓒ Ⓓ Ⓔ
6. Ⓐ Ⓑ Ⓒ Ⓓ Ⓔ
7. Ⓐ Ⓑ Ⓒ Ⓓ Ⓔ
8. Ⓐ Ⓑ Ⓒ Ⓓ Ⓔ
9. Ⓐ Ⓑ Ⓒ Ⓓ Ⓔ
10. Ⓐ Ⓑ Ⓒ Ⓓ Ⓔ
11. Ⓐ Ⓑ Ⓒ Ⓓ Ⓔ
12. Ⓐ Ⓑ Ⓒ Ⓓ Ⓔ
13. Ⓐ Ⓑ Ⓒ Ⓓ Ⓔ
14. Ⓐ Ⓑ Ⓒ Ⓓ Ⓔ
15. Ⓐ Ⓑ Ⓒ Ⓓ Ⓔ
16. Ⓐ Ⓑ Ⓒ Ⓓ Ⓔ
17. Ⓐ Ⓑ Ⓒ Ⓓ Ⓔ
18. Ⓐ Ⓑ Ⓒ Ⓓ Ⓔ
19. Ⓐ Ⓑ Ⓒ Ⓓ Ⓔ
20. Ⓐ Ⓑ Ⓒ Ⓓ Ⓔ
21. Ⓐ Ⓑ Ⓒ Ⓓ Ⓔ
22. Ⓐ Ⓑ Ⓒ Ⓓ Ⓔ
23. Ⓐ Ⓑ Ⓒ Ⓓ Ⓔ
24. Ⓐ Ⓑ Ⓒ Ⓓ Ⓔ
25. Ⓐ Ⓑ Ⓒ Ⓓ Ⓔ

26. Ⓐ Ⓑ Ⓒ Ⓓ Ⓔ
27. Ⓐ Ⓑ Ⓒ Ⓓ Ⓔ
28. Ⓐ Ⓑ Ⓒ Ⓓ Ⓔ
29. Ⓐ Ⓑ Ⓒ Ⓓ Ⓔ
30. Ⓐ Ⓑ Ⓒ Ⓓ Ⓔ
31. Ⓐ Ⓑ Ⓒ Ⓓ Ⓔ
32. Ⓐ Ⓑ Ⓒ Ⓓ Ⓔ
33. Ⓐ Ⓑ Ⓒ Ⓓ Ⓔ
34. Ⓐ Ⓑ Ⓒ Ⓓ Ⓔ
35. Ⓐ Ⓑ Ⓒ Ⓓ Ⓔ
36. Ⓐ Ⓑ Ⓒ Ⓓ Ⓔ
37. Ⓐ Ⓑ Ⓒ Ⓓ Ⓔ
38. Ⓐ Ⓑ Ⓒ Ⓓ Ⓔ
39. Ⓐ Ⓑ Ⓒ Ⓓ Ⓔ
40. Ⓐ Ⓑ Ⓒ Ⓓ Ⓔ
41. Ⓐ Ⓑ Ⓒ Ⓓ Ⓔ
42. Ⓐ Ⓑ Ⓒ Ⓓ Ⓔ
43. Ⓐ Ⓑ Ⓒ Ⓓ Ⓔ
44. Ⓐ Ⓑ Ⓒ Ⓓ Ⓔ
45. Ⓐ Ⓑ Ⓒ Ⓓ Ⓔ
46. Ⓐ Ⓑ Ⓒ Ⓓ Ⓔ
47. Ⓐ Ⓑ Ⓒ Ⓓ Ⓔ
48. Ⓐ Ⓑ Ⓒ Ⓓ Ⓔ
49. Ⓐ Ⓑ Ⓒ Ⓓ Ⓔ
50. Ⓐ Ⓑ Ⓒ Ⓓ Ⓔ

51. Ⓐ Ⓑ Ⓒ Ⓓ Ⓔ
52. Ⓐ Ⓑ Ⓒ Ⓓ Ⓔ
53. Ⓐ Ⓑ Ⓒ Ⓓ Ⓔ
54. Ⓐ Ⓑ Ⓒ Ⓓ Ⓔ
55. Ⓐ Ⓑ Ⓒ Ⓓ Ⓔ
56. Ⓐ Ⓑ Ⓒ Ⓓ Ⓔ
57. Ⓐ Ⓑ Ⓒ Ⓓ Ⓔ
58. Ⓐ Ⓑ Ⓒ Ⓓ Ⓔ
59. Ⓐ Ⓑ Ⓒ Ⓓ Ⓔ
60. Ⓐ Ⓑ Ⓒ Ⓓ Ⓔ
61. Ⓐ Ⓑ Ⓒ Ⓓ Ⓔ
62. Ⓐ Ⓑ Ⓒ Ⓓ Ⓔ
63. Ⓐ Ⓑ Ⓒ Ⓓ Ⓔ
64. Ⓐ Ⓑ Ⓒ Ⓓ Ⓔ
65. Ⓐ Ⓑ Ⓒ Ⓓ Ⓔ
66. Ⓐ Ⓑ Ⓒ Ⓓ Ⓔ
67. Ⓐ Ⓑ Ⓒ Ⓓ Ⓔ
68. Ⓐ Ⓑ Ⓒ Ⓓ Ⓔ
69. Ⓐ Ⓑ Ⓒ Ⓓ Ⓔ
70. Ⓐ Ⓑ Ⓒ Ⓓ Ⓔ
71. Ⓐ Ⓑ Ⓒ Ⓓ Ⓔ
72. Ⓐ Ⓑ Ⓒ Ⓓ Ⓔ
73. Ⓐ Ⓑ Ⓒ Ⓓ Ⓔ
74. Ⓐ Ⓑ Ⓒ Ⓓ Ⓔ
75. Ⓐ Ⓑ Ⓒ Ⓓ Ⓔ

76. Ⓐ Ⓑ Ⓒ Ⓓ Ⓔ
77. Ⓐ Ⓑ Ⓒ Ⓓ Ⓔ
78. Ⓐ Ⓑ Ⓒ Ⓓ Ⓔ
79. Ⓐ Ⓑ Ⓒ Ⓓ Ⓔ
80. Ⓐ Ⓑ Ⓒ Ⓓ Ⓔ
81. Ⓐ Ⓑ Ⓒ Ⓓ Ⓔ
82. Ⓐ Ⓑ Ⓒ Ⓓ Ⓔ
83. Ⓐ Ⓑ Ⓒ Ⓓ Ⓔ
84. Ⓐ Ⓑ Ⓒ Ⓓ Ⓔ
85. Ⓐ Ⓑ Ⓒ Ⓓ Ⓔ
86. Ⓐ Ⓑ Ⓒ Ⓓ Ⓔ
87. Ⓐ Ⓑ Ⓒ Ⓓ Ⓔ
88. Ⓐ Ⓑ Ⓒ Ⓓ Ⓔ
89. Ⓐ Ⓑ Ⓒ Ⓓ Ⓔ
90. Ⓐ Ⓑ Ⓒ Ⓓ Ⓔ
91. Ⓐ Ⓑ Ⓒ Ⓓ Ⓔ
92. Ⓐ Ⓑ Ⓒ Ⓓ Ⓔ
93. Ⓐ Ⓑ Ⓒ Ⓓ Ⓔ
94. Ⓐ Ⓑ Ⓒ Ⓓ Ⓔ
95. Ⓐ Ⓑ Ⓒ Ⓓ Ⓔ
96. Ⓐ Ⓑ Ⓒ Ⓓ Ⓔ
97. Ⓐ Ⓑ Ⓒ Ⓓ Ⓔ
98. Ⓐ Ⓑ Ⓒ Ⓓ Ⓔ
99. Ⓐ Ⓑ Ⓒ Ⓓ Ⓔ
100. Ⓐ Ⓑ Ⓒ Ⓓ Ⓔ

SECTION I

70 Minutes—100 Questions

Percent of total grade: 66⅔

Directions Answer the following 100 questions in 70 minutes. Select the best answer for each and fill in the corresponding letter on your answer grid or a sheet of scratch paper.

1. Mitch is a college student who finds students from other countries intolerable. Every time he hears classmates speaking another language in public, he gets frustrated and thinks to himself that they should just learn English. He imagines that most of them are lazy rich kids who take spots that should be reserved for harder-working local students. Of the following, Mitch is most clearly exhibiting

   (A) prejudice

   (B) individual discrimination

   (C) racism

   (D) stereotype threat

   (E) institutional discrimination

2. Which of the following is a kinesthetic binocular cue for depth perception?

   (A) Stereopsis

   (B) Convergence

   (C) Parallax

   (D) Interposition

   (E) Texture gradient

3. Which of the following perspectives explains personality by emphasizing the potential for personal growth and self-empowerment?

   (A) Humanistic theory

   (B) Psychoanalytic theory

   (C) Type theory

   (D) Biopsychological theory

   (E) Trait theory

4. A paper entitled "The Role of Imagery in Memory Processes" would most likely be written by a

   (A) biological psychologist

   (B) cognitive psychologist

   (C) sociocultural psychologist

   (D) psychodynamic psychologist

   (E) behavioral psychologist

5. Which of the following did Wolfgang Köhler provide evidence of when one of his chimps fastened two sticks together to reach a bunch of bananas?

   (A) Operant conditioning

   (B) Vicarious reinforcement

   (C) Classical conditioning

   (D) Heuristics

   (E) Insight

GO ON TO THE NEXT PAGE

6. Which of the following graphs best displays the
   relationship between a person's level of arousal
   and his or her performance on a challenging
   task?

(A)

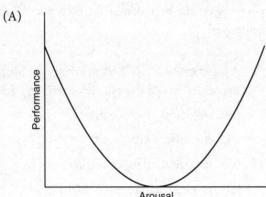

(B)

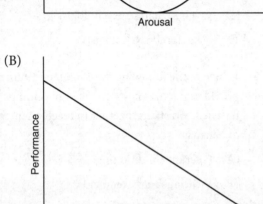

(C)

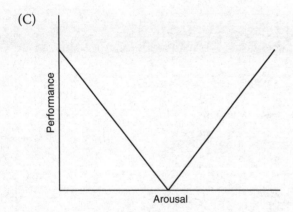

(D)

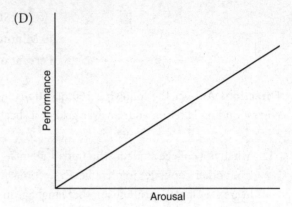

(E)

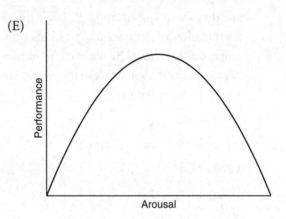

GO ON TO THE NEXT PAGE

7. If a researcher wants to study the changes in a patient's neural activity as the patient draws a picture, the researcher should use which of the following?

(A) EEG

(B) MRI

(C) CT

(D) fMRI

(E) X-ray

8. Research shows that people with a family history of alcohol dependence are four times more likely to develop the condition themselves. It is also known that peer and parental influence can increase or decrease this risk. This scenario is best seen as an example of the interaction between

(A) internal locus of control and external locus of control

(B) attitudes and behaviors

(C) id and superego

(D) nature and nurture

(E) primary and secondary groups

9. Fatima begins seeing a therapist, who encourages her to express her feelings openly. During the sessions, the therapist often echoes the ideas that Fatima expresses and always responds with acceptance and affirmation. Which of the following best characterizes this type of therapy?

(A) Client-centered therapy

(B) Group therapy

(C) Behavior modification

(D) Psychoanalysis

(E) Systematic desensitization

10. What is unique about personality disorders compared to other diagnostic categories?

(A) Personality disorders impair cognitive functioning.

(B) A symptom of personality disorders is interpersonal problems.

(C) Personality disorder patients believe their behavior is normal.

(D) Personality disorders include maladaptive behavior.

(E) Personality disorders are characterized by flexible behavior.

11. Dr. Baldwin is a psychologist who conducts personality testing but does not subscribe to the structural model. Thus, she would be least likely to make use of which of the following in her work?

(A) Myers-Briggs Type Indicator

(B) Thematic Apperception Test

(C) Keirsey Temperament Sorter

(D) Minnesota Multiphasic Personality Inventory-2

(E) She is equally likely to use any of the above.

12. In experiments with rats, destroying the ventromedial hypothalamus leads to which of the following?

(A) An increased sensation of thirst

(B) Increased sweating to compensate for higher internal temperatures

(C) A total lack of interest in sexual activity

(D) Decreased food consumption, to the point of near starvation

(E) Increased food consumption, to the point of dangerous obesity

GO ON TO THE NEXT PAGE

13. A slot machine, a gambling device that dispenses cash rewards after a random number of pulls, is an example of what type of reinforcement schedule?

    (A) Fixed ratio

    (B) Variable ratio

    (C) Fixed interval

    (D) Variable interval

    (E) Continuous

14. Which of the following processes will lead to a longer-lasting memory?

    (A) Deep processing

    (B) Shallow processing

    (C) Automatic processing

    (D) Information processing

    (E) Executive processing

Questions 15–16 are based on the following.

A team of policy analysts sought to determine whether a particular housing proposition (Proposition 12) was popular in the local community. Surveys were submitted electronically to all the residents in the neighborhood, which includes around 18,000 adults. After two weeks, 117 responses were returned. Below are the questions the analysts asked:

Q1. Do you support Proposition 12?

Q2. How happy are you with the current housing situation in the city?

Q3. Are you concerned about the fiscal deficit that Proposition 12 will bring to the city?

Q4. Are you troubled by the new residents who will flood into the city if Proposition 12 passes?

15. The survey results showed that respondents were overwhelmingly against Proposition 12. The researchers concluded that Proposition 12 is unpopular in the community. Which of the following is a reason to doubt that the researchers' conclusion is valid?

    (A) Extreme results are not possible on surveys.

    (B) Surveys are usually a poor tool to assess general opinions.

    (C) Surveys need to have at least twenty questions to be informative.

    (D) The researchers failed to include opinions of former residents.

    (E) The low number of returns likely produced a nonresponse bias.

16. This survey likely exhibits surveyor bias because

    (A) there were only four total questions on the survey

    (B) Q3 and Q4 contain potentially controversial assumptions

    (C) the survey was not administered to randomly assigned groups

    (D) the researchers surveyed both homeowners and renters

    (E) electronic surveys are unlikely to reflect people's real opinions

GO ON TO THE NEXT PAGE

17. An experiment with a high degree of internal validity

    (A) indicates no relationship between independent and dependent variables

    (B) successfully controls potential confounding variables

    (C) is generalizable to populations outside of the one sampled

    (D) can be generalized only to the sampled population

    (E) cannot be used to support conclusions about causal relationships

18. Which of the following would a psychologist use if she wanted to be sure that the participants in her experiments were representative of the larger population?

    (A) Random assignment

    (B) Replication

    (C) Correlation

    (D) Naturalistic observation

    (E) Random sampling

19. Assuming that each of the pairs of groups mentioned below initially holds strong negative feelings for each other, which of the following scenarios best reflects the findings of Muzafer Sherif's Robbers Cave experiment?

    (A) A camp counselor shows two opposing boy scout troops the value of cooperation by having the two groups eat lunch together and share activity space every day.

    (B) A daycare teacher gets two groups of children to stop fighting by assigning them to various individual chores around the center like arranging books and cleaning the eating area.

    (C) A politician unites members from two opposing political parties by delivering uplifting speeches full of appeals to abstract human values and universal ethical principles.

    (D) The mayor of a city ends a labor dispute between a union and a major corporation by encouraging the corporation to raise hourly wages in exchange for a local tax break.

    (E) A high school football coach brings upperclassmen and underclassmen players together by setting them the common task of beating a rival high school team in an upcoming game.

GO ON TO THE NEXT PAGE

20. Motion sickness is said to be caused by discrepancies among sensory systems. For example, when Cynthia reads in a moving vehicle, the image she sees remains stationary while her body perceives motion and acceleration, which causes her to experience nausea and dizziness. Cynthia's motion sickness results from a conflict between the visual sense and which of the following?

    (A) The thalamus

    (B) Proprioception

    (C) Nociception

    (D) The limbic system

    (E) The vestibular sense

21. Which of the following is a measure of central tendency?

    (A) Correlation coefficient

    (B) Range

    (C) Mean

    (D) Standard deviation

    (E) Variance

22. After hitting his head in a car crash, a patient no longer experiences fear when confronted with the things he was once afraid of. Based on this information, which of the following areas was most likely damaged during the accident?

    (A) Hippocampus

    (B) Thalamus

    (C) Cerebellum

    (D) Amygdala

    (E) Broca's area

23. Which of the following approaches to psychology focuses on the concept of self-actualization?

    (A) Behavioral

    (B) Cognitive

    (C) Sociocultural

    (D) Humanistic

    (E) Biological

24. The most important difference between Kohlberg's and Gilligan's perspectives on moral development is that Gilligan

    (A) avoids dividing moral development into discrete stages

    (B) cares more about moral judgments than the reasoning behind them

    (C) focuses on the role of empathy and benevolence in moral reasoning

    (D) focuses on the role of social rules and cues in moral reasoning

    (E) believes there are types of moral reasoning not all people are capable of

25. A new test is being designed to predict scholastic performance. The test is split into different versions, which are administered months apart. If the scores are similar across these different administrations of the test, then this test has high

    (A) equivalent-form reliability

    (B) test-retest reliability

    (C) split-half reliability

    (D) face validity

    (E) content validity

GO ON TO THE NEXT PAGE

26. Each of the following brain regions plays a role in emotional processing except the

    (A) amygdala

    (B) hippocampus

    (C) hypothalamus

    (D) thalamus

    (E) cerebellum

27. Recent research has indicated that advertisements that focus on the appearance of the product are more effective than advertisements that focus on what the product actually does. Which of the following best characterizes the type of persuasion used in appearance-focused advertising?

    (A) Foot-in-the-door technique

    (B) Door-in-the-face technique

    (C) Peripheral route

    (D) Central route

    (E) Mere-exposure effect

28. Matthew has been depressed since his divorce. Which of the following explanations is most consistent with a humanistic explanation for his symptoms?

    (A) Matthew's depression stems from his negative thoughts about the divorce.

    (B) Matthew's depression stems from his unsatisfied need for love and belonging.

    (C) Matthew's depression stems from a change in his neurotransmitter levels.

    (D) Matthew's depression stems from repressed childhood memories of his parents' divorce.

    (E) Matthew's depression stems from his learned responses to environmental stimuli.

29. Sarah finds that the pain medication she was prescribed no longer offers the same pain relief as it did when she started taking it. As a result, she begins to take more and more of the medication to achieve the same relief. Her behavior best aligns with which of the following theories?

    (A) Drive-reduction theory

    (B) Arousal theory

    (C) Instinct theory

    (D) Incentive theory

    (E) Opponent-process theory

30. Dog trainers often use a clicker, a device that emits a distinctive clicking sound, in their training. When a dog performs a desired behavior, the trainer will simultaneously feed the dog a treat and use the clicker. With time, the trainer can use the clicker alone, without a treat, to train the dog. After being used in this way, the clicker can best be characterized as an example of

    (A) a primary reinforcer

    (B) a secondary reinforcer

    (C) a neutral stimulus

    (D) a conditioned response

    (E) an unconditioned response

31. A teratogen is a substance that can cause

    (A) birth defects

    (B) genetic mutations

    (C) cancer

    (D) changes in mood

    (E) a stress response

GO ON TO THE NEXT PAGE

32. Which of the following famous studies was conducted by Albert Bandura?

    (A) Taste aversion with rats and radiation

    (B) Learned helplessness with dogs and electric shocks

    (C) The Little Albert experiment

    (D) Classical conditioning with dogs and bells

    (E) The Bobo doll experiment

33. A severe intellectual disability is characterized by an ability to complete basic tasks, but with a need for considerable support in daily life. The IQ score range for a severe intellectual disability is

    (A) 0–25

    (B) 25–40

    (C) 55–70

    (D) 70–130

    (E) 130–145

34. Participants in a study are presented with a stimulus comprised of a field of randomly placed dots. In some trials, an additional group of ten dots, arranged in a circle, is placed somewhere within the stimulus. For each trial, participants are asked to indicate whether the circle of dots is present. Which of the following best describes the subject of this study?

    (A) The Gestalt principle of continuity

    (B) Weber's law

    (C) Top-down processing

    (D) Visual transduction

    (E) Signal detection

35. Peter studies for an hour each night leading up to an exam, whereas his brother Paul studies for several hours on the night before the exam. A month after the exam, Peter still remembers much of what he studied, but Paul does not. This is an example of the

    (A) self-reference effect

    (B) primacy effect

    (C) recency effect

    (D) misinformation effect

    (E) spacing effect

36. A study in which only the researchers know whether participants are in control or experimental groups is referred to as a

    (A) single-blind study

    (B) double-blind study

    (C) confounder

    (D) placebo

    (E) case study

37. In 1986, the explosion of the *Challenger* Space Shuttle triggered an investigation into the disaster. Investigators found that NASA senior personnel repeatedly ignored the concerns of their engineers and opted to bypass their own safety rules, considering those decisions acceptable risks. According to some commentators, these staff members were motivated by a desire to reduce internal conflict and promote consensus. The behavior of the NASA senior staff could best be characterized as an example of

    (A) ethnocentrism

    (B) the fundamental attribution error

    (C) discrimination

    (D) groupthink

    (E) group polarization

GO ON TO THE NEXT PAGE

38. The tendency to use old patterns to solve new problems is referred to as

   (A) belief perseverance

   (B) functional fixedness

   (C) a mental set

   (D) anchoring

   (E) confirmation bias

39. A test designed to predict current mastery of a subject would be considered what type of test?

   (A) Achievement

   (B) Aptitude

   (C) Power

   (D) Abstract

   (E) Speed

40. Stress hormones are primarily secreted by the

   (A) ovaries

   (B) testes

   (C) adrenals

   (D) thyroid

   (E) pituitary

41. According to Lev Vygotsky's concept of the zone of proximal development, complicated but achievable learning occurs best

   (A) algorithmically, through structured trial-and-error

   (B) heuristically, through insight and creative thinking

   (C) institutionally, in the presence of other children learning the same task

   (D) operantly, through the use of rewards and punishments

   (E) socially, in the presence of a more knowledgeable other

42. Which of the following maintains that dreams result from the brain's attempt to make sense of images, sensations, and other neural activities that occur during sleep?

   (A) The activation-synthesis hypothesis

   (B) Information-processing theory

   (C) Psychoanalytic theory

   (D) The manifest content

   (E) The latent content

43. The phenomenon in which people develop false memories based on inaccurate information they were provided after the fact is called

   (A) the misinformation effect

   (B) déjà vu

   (C) source amnesia

   (D) memory decay

   (E) interference

44. Which of the following is NOT a symptom of autism spectrum disorder?

   (A) Restricted interests

   (B) Communication deficits

   (C) Difficulty with social interactions

   (D) Mood swings

   (E) Tendency towards sameness

GO ON TO THE NEXT PAGE

45. Which of the following would be expected of a child in the concrete operational stage of development?

   (A) The ability to fully understand the concept of freedom but not the ability to explain why others might value that freedom

   (B) The ability to understand that an object does not disappear when out of sight but not the ability to understand that others might still be able to see the object

   (C) The ability to understand conservation of liquid in different containers but not the ability to understand that repeated lying might make others distrustful

   (D) The ability to plan a strategy for solving a problem but not the ability to persevere through trial-and-error solutions

   (E) The ability to create new schemata but not the ability to adjust those schemata in response to new experiences that conflict with them

46. The term *operationalization* is best described as

   (A) utilizing more than one independent variable

   (B) defining variables quantitatively

   (C) creating an experiment

   (D) measuring a correlation

   (E) choosing appropriate statistical procedures

47. Parents take their teenage son to a psychologist because they suspect he has a learning disability. The psychologist has the son take the Wechsler Intelligence Scale for Children (WISC) in order to assess

   (A) baseline symptoms of depression

   (B) how his feelings influence his interpretations of ambiguous images

   (C) his mental age in relation to other children at his age

   (D) his verbal and non-verbal intelligence

   (E) his creative intelligence

Questions 48–50 are based on the following.

In an experiment, researchers randomly assigned college students in an introductory calculus class into four groups. All groups were given the same set of questions in an exam, but the exam began with a brief introductory statement that differed for each group, establishing differing expectations for student performance, as follows:

Group A: The introduction stated that most students are expected to pass the exam.
Group B: The introduction stated that most students are expected to fail the exam.
Group C: The introduction included statistics that showed female students performing worse than male students on similar exams.
Group D: The introduction contained no information on expected performance.

The results of the experiment are given in the bar graph below:

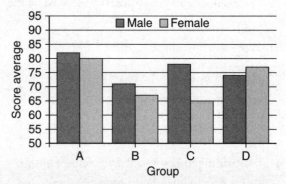

48. Which of the following best accounts for the disparity in average exam scores for Group C?

   (A) Groupthink

   (B) Situational attribution

   (C) Stereotype threat

   (D) The just-world hypothesis

   (E) Compliance

GO ON TO THE NEXT PAGE

49. What phenomenon best explains the performance differences between Groups A and B?

    (A) Social facilitation

    (B) Group polarization

    (C) Self-serving bias

    (D) Unstable attribution

    (E) The Pygmalion effect

50. Suppose Group D had not been included in the experiment, and the calculus students had instead been randomly assigned only to the first three groups. What effect would this have on the study?

    (A) The study's internal validity would be strengthened.

    (B) The study's internal validity would be weakened.

    (C) The study's external validity would be strengthened.

    (D) The study's external validity would be weakened.

    (E) There would be no effect on the study's internal or external validity.

51. Alfred Adler is most associated with which of the following ideas?

    (A) Basic anxiety

    (B) Peak experiences

    (C) The inferiority complex

    (D) The structural model

    (E) Personality archetypes

52. Which of the following is an inhibitory neurotransmitter that is stimulated by benzodiazepines to decrease activity in the central nervous system as a treatment for anxiety disorders?

    (A) Acetylcholine

    (B) Dopamine

    (C) GABA

    (D) Glutamate

    (E) Norepinephrine

53. During the 1970s in Peru, anchovy fishing was a lucrative and productive venture. Because so many individuals fished the anchovies, the population of anchovies crashed, leading to economic turmoil. This is an example of which psychological phenomenon?

    (A) Superordinate goals

    (B) The bystander effect

    (C) The prisoner's dilemma

    (D) A social trap

    (E) Social inhibition

54. Participants in a study are asked to stare at the center of a red circle on a yellow background on a screen for one minute, after which the screen displays a blank white stimulus. According to opponent-process theory, what afterimage should the participants report seeing?

    (A) A blue circle on a green background

    (B) A green circle on a blue background

    (C) A red circle on a yellow background

    (D) A yellow circle on a red background

    (E) No afterimage; just the blank white stimulus

GO ON TO THE NEXT PAGE

55. A therapist is helping Marcus learn to overcome his fear of public spaces by exposing him to public areas in small increments: standing in an empty public space, walking in a quiet public library, sitting in a crowded cafe, and so on. What type of strategy is she using?

    (A) Partial reinforcement

    (B) Aversion therapy

    (C) Systematic desensitization

    (D) Latent learning

    (E) Coping

56. Which of the following is an area of psychology that is often criticized for offering theories that cannot be empirically tested?

    (A) Cognitive

    (B) Behavioral

    (C) Biological

    (D) Sociocultural

    (E) Humanistic

57. Although Jerry cannot immediately remember one of the terms for his biology exam when given its definition, he can correctly identify it when given a word bank. Here, Jerry is demonstrating

    (A) recall

    (B) relearning

    (C) rehearsal

    (D) recognition

    (E) repetition

58. Suppose that you want to compare people aged 6, 26, 46, and 66 on how many "close friends" they think they have. You match these participants on where they live, their race, and their religion. Such a study would most likely be considered a

    (A) case study

    (B) cross-sectional study

    (C) longitudinal study

    (D) controlled experiment

    (E) naturalistic observation

59. Electroconvulsive therapy (ECT) is a treatment that has received a great deal of bad press. However, it can be an effective therapy for a small group of disorders, including

    (A) somatic symptom disorder

    (B) anxiety disorders

    (C) personality disorders

    (D) major depressive disorder

    (E) sleep apnea

GO ON TO THE NEXT PAGE

60. A gym wanted to improve its members' attendance rate through an incentive program. They tested three separate programs over the course of a year. First, they randomly assigned all their members into three groups. Members in Group 1 were informed that they would receive a small gift card after every 30 hours they spent at the gym. Members in Group 2 were only told that they would receive small gift cards for spending more time at the gym. They were not told precisely how long, and in fact their gift cards were awarded after a random number of hours at the gym. Instead of gift cards, members of Group 3 had their gym memberships for the entire year discounted at a small rate. The average number of hours spent at the gym before the incentive programs and after them are shown in the bar graph below.

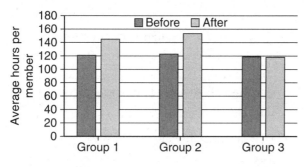

Which of the following best explains why members of Group 2 saw a larger average increase than members of Group 1?

(A) Behaviors learned from continuous schedules are more prone to extinction when the reinforcement stops.

(B) Behaviors learned from partial schedules are more prone to extinction when the reinforcement stops.

(C) Fixed reinforcement schedules tend to be more effective than variable reinforcement schedules.

(D) Variable reinforcement schedules tend to be more effective than fixed reinforcement schedules.

(E) There was a systematic bias in the compositions of the different groups.

61. Which of the following structures plays the greatest role in the maintenance of homeostasis?

(A) Thalamus

(B) Hippocampus

(C) Hypothalamus

(D) Pituitary

(E) Amygdala

GO ON TO THE NEXT PAGE

62. A man takes a personality test and learns only that he is classified as "ESFP." Which of the following personality tests did the man most likely take?

    (A) The Rorschach test

    (B) The Myers-Briggs Type Indicator

    (C) The Thematic Apperception Test

    (D) The Keirsey Temperament Sorter

    (E) The Minnesota Multiphasic Personality Inventory-2

63. Judy's dad takes away her beloved video game console because Judy failed to keep a promise to clean her room. This provides an example of

    (A) positive reinforcement

    (B) negative reinforcement

    (C) positive punishment

    (D) negative punishment

    (E) neutral punishment

64. Which of the following would be an example of a projective test?

    (A) A survey of yes/no questions that asks whether participants have had certain life experiences

    (B) A questionnaire that asks participants to agree or disagree with statements regarding their personality

    (C) An open-ended writing task in which participants are asked to describe the time they felt most afraid

    (D) A creative task in which participants are asked to listen to a piece of music and make up a story for it

    (E) A task in which participants are presented with several objects and asked to solve a physical puzzle with them

65. Which of the following correlation coefficients reflects the weakest degree of relationship between two variables?

    (A) −0.99

    (B) −0.45

    (C) −0.11

    (D) 0.34

    (E) 1.00

66. Which of the following is a technique used in Freudian therapy?

    (A) Free association

    (B) Free recall

    (C) Exposure therapy

    (D) Systematic desensitization

    (E) Biofeedback

67. An elderly man requires constant reminders that he has a doctor's appointment every other Thursday, but is able to remember that his children and grandchildren visit him on the same day. This is an example of

    (A) socioemotional selectivity

    (B) retrograde amnesia

    (C) anterograde amnesia

    (D) synaptic pruning

    (E) symptoms of Alzheimer's disease

68. Which of the following neurotransmitters plays an essential role in activating the "fight or flight" response?

    (A) Dopamine

    (B) Serotonin

    (C) Norepinephrine

    (D) Acetylcholine

    (E) GABA

GO ON TO THE NEXT PAGE

69. Psychoanalysis is a form of therapy most closely associated with the work of

    (A) Joseph Wolpe

    (B) Carl Rogers

    (C) Wilhelm Wundt

    (D) Noam Chomsky

    (E) Sigmund Freud

70. Flashbulb memories are typically

    (A) more accurate than other types of memories

    (B) less vivid than other types of memories

    (C) associated with emotional experiences

    (D) procedural memories

    (E) encoded before the age of 5

71. After tripping on stage in the school play, Zoey is so embarrassed that she is actively trying to forget the experience. Zoey is using a process called

    (A) repression

    (B) suppression

    (C) rehearsal

    (D) memory decay

    (E) interference

72. Which of the following statements about language would B.F. Skinner most likely agree with?

    (A) Humans have an internal language acquisition device.

    (B) Different languages share a universal grammar.

    (C) People who were not exposed to language during their critical period will not be able to speak.

    (D) Children learn to speak by imitating the speech of their parents.

    (E) Learning principles do not explain the rapid vocabulary development that occurs in childhood.

73. According to Abraham Maslow, which of the following needs must be satisfied before any of the others can be satisfied?

    (A) Health insurance

    (B) Access to drinkable water

    (C) Self-respect

    (D) Self-fulfillment

    (E) Membership on a sports team

74. Although Sally has not been actively watching a clock, she can tell that it is currently around noontime. This is an example of

    (A) automatic processing

    (B) effortful processing

    (C) focused attention

    (D) divided attention

    (E) selective attention

GO ON TO THE NEXT PAGE

75. All of the following types of cells are located in both the central and peripheral nervous systems except

    (A) interneurons

    (B) glial cells

    (C) afferent neurons

    (D) efferent neurons

    (E) sensory neurons

Questions 76–77 are based on the following.

An electroencephalogram (EEG) can be used to analyze how someone sleeps by measuring the electrical activity of the brain. The following waves are examples of EEG readings for the four stages of non-REM sleep I–IV.

I

II

III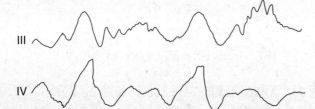

IV

76. What types of features are seen in the EEG labeled IV?

    (A) Alpha waves

    (B) Beta waves

    (C) Delta waves

    (D) Sleep spindles

    (E) Theta waves

77. During normal sleep, a person will start in stage I and go through stages II and III sequentially before entering deep sleep, stage IV. Eventually, the sleeper will enter into REM (rapid eye movement) sleep. Which of the following presents the correct sequence of EEG readings most likely to be detected during the three stages of NREM sleep immediately prior to REM sleep?

    (A) IV, II, III

    (B) I, II, III

    (C) IV, II, I

    (D) IV, III, II

    (E) I, III, IV

78. Which of the following is a parenting style characterized by strict rules and a lack of encouragement that can result in poor social skills and low self-esteem?

    (A) Ambivalent

    (B) Authoritarian

    (C) Authoritative

    (D) Neglectful

    (E) Permissive

79. A pediatrician is testing the maturation of cognitive abilities in a three-year-old by playing peek-a-boo. According to Piaget's theory of cognitive development, which stage is ended with the development of object permanence?

    (A) Sensorimotor

    (B) Preoperational

    (C) Concrete operational

    (D) Formal operational

    (E) Postoperational

GO ON TO THE NEXT PAGE

80. The Gestalt principle of closure dictates that we tend to fill in gaps to perceive discontinuous figures as coherent wholes. As such, this principle is an example of

    (A) top-down processing

    (B) bottom-up processing

    (C) perceptual constancy

    (D) extrasensory perception

    (E) an afterimage

81. Which of the following research topics would most likely be investigated by a biological psychologist?

    (A) How damage to the amygdala affects a rat's social interactions

    (B) Which reward systems work best for potty training children

    (C) The role of close and distant neighbors on childhood development

    (D) Whether office reward or demerit systems best prevent worker tardiness

    (E) Which relative most impacts a child's future profession

82. According to the Schachter-Singer two-factor theory of emotion, which of the following best describes what happens before a person feels fear from seeing a venomous snake right in front of her?

    (A) Nothing would happen before she feels fear; rather, she would experience a physiological response and fear simultaneously.

    (B) She would appraise the situation and decide to be afraid.

    (C) She would apply a situation-appropriate cognitive label to her physiological response.

    (D) She would have a physiological response, making her heart start to pound.

    (E) She would have the fearful emotion first, followed by a physiological response such as her heart pounding.

83. Which IQ test determined IQ by dividing the mental age by the chronological age and then multiplying the result by 100?

    (A) Wechsler Adult Intelligence Scale

    (B) Wechsler Intelligence Scale for Children

    (C) Stanford-Binet IQ Test

    (D) MMPI-2

    (E) Thematic Apperception Test

84. Which of the following is the most likely match for the continent of origin and type of culture of someone who values family relationships over personal achievement?

    (A) Africa: individualistic

    (B) Asia: collectivist

    (C) Europe: individualistic

    (D) North America: collectivist

    (E) South America: individualistic

85. A cognitive therapist would most likely argue that a patient suffering from a panic disorder

    (A) has unresolved, unconscious conflicts between his id, ego, and superego

    (B) has acquired this anxiety response as a result of classical and operant conditioning

    (C) has an imbalance of neurotransmitters

    (D) is suffering from severe, irreversible brain damage

    (E) is displaying a dysfunctional style of thought

GO ON TO THE NEXT PAGE

86. Hippocrates believed mental disorders were caused by an imbalance in four bodily fluids, known as the humors. Hippocrates' view is most consistent with the

    (A) psychogenic model

    (B) psychoanalytic model

    (C) humanistic model

    (D) somatogenic model

    (E) cognitive model

87. Which of the following is an example of inattentional blindness?

    (A) A driver waiting to cross a busy intersection is so focused on oncoming traffic that he fails to notice the person in a chicken costume advertising a restaurant on the opposite corner.

    (B) An astronomer looking through a telescope at the night sky fails to notice a star because the light from that star falls on the part of her retina where the optic nerve is attached.

    (C) A child looks at a stimulus made of tightly packed dots. Most of the dots are red, but there is a set of green dots in the center that form an image of the number "2." The child is unable to perceive the number.

    (D) A patient enters a hospital waiting room and notices the hum of the fluorescent lights above her. After sitting for a few minutes, she no longer notices the sound.

    (E) A pedestrian stops at an intersection and watches intently for the signal to switch from "don't walk" to "walk." After a few seconds he begins to think about his plan for the rest of the day and fails to notice the signal change despite looking directly at it.

88. Which of the following statements describes a strength of the biological model of abnormal behavior?

    (A) The biological model encourages the development of effective drugs to treat mental illness.

    (B) The biological model encourages the use of social and cultural variables to explain abnormal behavior.

    (C) The biological model posits that mental illness has purely psychological causes.

    (D) The biological model explains how mental illness is influenced by context.

    (E) The biological model accounts for human freedom and responsibility.

89. Rose has been feeling wonderful, describing herself as being "on top of the world," and has been frantically working on her art projects day and night. Her friends have noticed that she talks extremely rapidly, is easily distracted, and does not seem to be sleeping. Of the following, Rose is most likely experiencing

    (A) a manic episode

    (B) a panic attack

    (C) a depressive episode

    (D) dissociative fugue

    (E) amnesia

GO ON TO THE NEXT PAGE

90. Tonga wants to become a dentist, but to do so he must first pass the entry exam for dental school. However, due to his multiple work responsibilities, he is unable to find the proper time and resources to prepare for the exam, and thus fails it multiple times. Eventually, Tonga gives up on dental school, and he even decides to stay at a job he hates because he stops believing he can find a better one. Of the following, Tonga can best be characterized as exhibiting

    (A) accidental conditioning

    (B) social learning

    (C) observational learning

    (D) self-efficacy

    (E) learned helplessness

91. The Rosenhan study revealed that

    (A) trained mental health workers easily identify pseudopatients

    (B) mental health patients do not like the use of diagnostic labels

    (C) diagnostic labels change the way that people are treated

    (D) diagnostic labels allow for consistency in clinical practice

    (E) patients feel empowered when diagnostic labels name their problems

92. The structure in the ear that is caused to vibrate directly by the ossicles is the

    (A) cochlea

    (B) oval window

    (C) tympanic membrane

    (D) basilar membrane

    (E) malleus

93. Which of the following is a reflex that is NOT expected to be observed in a newborn?

    (A) Moro

    (B) Babinski

    (C) Rooting

    (D) Grasping

    (E) Plantar

94. All of the following can occur as a result of chronic stress EXCEPT

    (A) a weakened immune system

    (B) high cortisol levels

    (C) high blood pressure

    (D) tissue damage

    (E) sleep disturbances

95. A new test is being developed to predict golfing ability. The questions asked on this test appear to test golfing knowledge, but it is not yet known whether the test will accurately predict performance. Based on this information, it is most reasonable to conclude that this test possesses high

    (A) criterion-related validity

    (B) concurrent validity

    (C) predictive validity

    (D) content validity

    (E) face validity

96. A rat presses a bar, and a targeted electrical shock is delivered to a specific part of its brain by a wire. The result is an increase in bar-pressing behavior. In this situation, the shock is serving as

    (A) an unconditioned stimulus

    (B) an unconditioned response

    (C) a punishment

    (D) a negative reinforcement

    (E) a positive reinforcement

GO ON TO THE NEXT PAGE

97. The parietal lobe is most closely associated with

    (A) visual processing

    (B) memory formation

    (C) auditory processing

    (D) sensory processing

    (E) high-level reasoning

98. A student reads from a book in a bright room. After finishing a chapter, he looks up from his book and through his window at a tree outside. If it is also a bright day outside, which of the following changes can be expected to occur?

    (A) The muscles attached to the lens relax, causing it to become rounder.

    (B) The iris constricts, reducing the size of the pupil.

    (C) Rod cells are activated, while cone cells regenerate their photopigments.

    (D) A higher proportion of the light entering the eye becomes focused on the fovea.

    (E) Muscles constrict and elongate the sclera, changing the focal point of light entering the eye.

99. Researchers explored different strategies for charity fundraising in an experiment. They investigated three approaches using three groups of randomly selected and randomly assigned participants. The groups differed as follows:

    Group A: The 100 participants were told individually that they should donate $5.
    Group B: All 100 participants were told in an assembly that they should each individually donate $5.
    Group C: All 100 participants were told in an assembly that they need to donate $500 as a group.

    After donations were collected, the results were as follows:

Group	Average Individual Donation
A	$4.53
B	$4.20
C	$2.89

    Which of the following social psychological phenomena best explains the experimental results?

    (A) Groupthink

    (B) Social loafing

    (C) Social facilitation

    (D) Conformity

    (E) Self-serving bias

GO ON TO THE NEXT PAGE

100. Karina struggles to make friends because she is confident that she will humiliate herself if she hangs out with her classmates. However, despite being very shy, she truly wishes to be accepted by her peers. Which of the following personality disorders would be the most appropriate diagnosis for Karina?

(A) Borderline

(B) Antisocial

(C) Avoidant

(D) Paranoid

(E) Schizoid

END OF SECTION I

SECTION II
50 Minutes—2 Questions
Percent of total grade: 33⅓

Directions Answer both of the following questions in 50 minutes. Lists of facts are insufficient to earn points; you must write essays that answer the questions thoughtfully with sound arguments that employ the proper terms from psychology. Use scratch paper to write out your responses.

1. Manuel and Zahra are considering having children. Manuel's side of the family has a history of schizophrenia, though Manuel does not have schizophrenia himself. Manuel is experiencing a lot of anxiety and stress about having children because of this family history, and after many weeks of this, he is feeling exhausted. Zahra is not showing outward signs of anxiety, but Zahra refuses to talk about Manuel's family history of schizophrenia whenever he brings it up.

   Part A

   Explain each of the following and discuss how they relate to this family.

   - Range of reaction
   - Symptoms of schizophrenia
   - Hypothalamic-pituitary-adrenal axis
   - General adaptation theory
   - Cognitive dissonance

   Part B

   Manuel decides to seek treatment for his anxiety. Explain how the clinician would treat Manuel for each of the different modalities of treatment listed.

   - Cognitive therapy
   - Humanistic therapy

2. Dr. Schmidt is interested in testing new therapeutic methods for children with depressive disorders. She is specifically studying a new selective serotonin reuptake inhibitor (SSRI). To evaluate the effectiveness of this new drug, children with depressive disorders are recruited and randomly assigned to either the experimental group, which receives the new drug, or the control group, which does not. All children involved are also given cognitive-behavioral therapy and evaluated by their therapists for reduction in depressive symptoms. Dr. Schmidt hypothesizes that the new drug combined with cognitive behavioral therapy will reduce the depressive symptoms more than cognitive behavioral therapy alone.

Part A

Explain how Dr. Schmidt could adjust her experiment to account for the following.

- Placebo effect
- Observer-expectancy effect

Part B

Explain why each of the following components of Dr. Schmidt's experiment is important for valid conclusions.

- Random assignment
- Control group

Part C

The study finds that the experimental group has an average 42% reduction in depressive symptoms with a standard deviation of 7%. Meanwhile, the control group has an average 40% reduction in depressive symptoms with a standard deviation of 8%.

- Identify the operational definition of the dependent variable in this study.
- Explain how the data does or does not support Dr. Schmidt's hypothesis.
- Explain how SSRIs strengthen the effect of serotonin in the brain.

END OF SECTION II

STOP

END OF EXAM

ANSWER KEY

Section I

1.	A	16.	B	31.	A	46.	B	61.	C	76.	C	91.	C
2.	B	17.	B	32.	E	47.	D	62.	B	77.	D	92.	B
3.	A	18.	E	33.	B	48.	C	63.	D	78.	B	93.	E
4.	B	19.	E	34.	E	49.	E	64.	D	79.	A	94.	B
5.	E	20.	E	35.	E	50.	B	65.	C	80.	A	95.	E
6.	E	21.	C	36.	A	51.	C	66.	A	81.	A	96.	E
7.	D	22.	D	37.	D	52.	C	67.	A	82.	C	97.	D
8.	D	23.	D	38.	C	53.	D	68.	C	83.	C	98.	A
9.	A	24.	C	39.	A	54.	B	69.	E	84.	B	99.	B
10.	C	25.	A	40.	C	55.	C	70.	C	85.	E	100.	C
11.	B	26.	E	41.	E	56.	E	71.	B	86.	D		
12.	E	27.	C	42.	A	57.	D	72.	D	87.	A		
13.	B	28.	B	43.	A	58.	B	73.	B	88.	A		
14.	A	29.	E	44.	D	59.	D	74.	A	89.	A		
15.	E	30.	B	45.	C	60.	D	75.	A	90.	E		

Section II

1. See Answers and Explanations

2. See Answers and Explanations

PRACTICE EXAM 5 BREAKDOWN: ASSESS YOUR STRENGTHS

Use the following tables to determine which topics you are already strong in and which topics you need to review most.

Topic	Questions
Scientific Foundations of Psychology	4, 15, 16, 17, 18, 21, 23, 36, 46, 50, 56, 58, 65, 81
Biological Bases of Behavior	7, 22, 26, 40, 42, 68, 75, 76, 77, 97
Sensation and Perception	2, 20, 34, 54, 80, 87, 92, 98
Learning	5, 13, 30, 32, 55, 60, 63, 90, 96
Cognitive Psychology	14, 25, 33, 35, 38, 39, 43, 47, 57, 70, 71, 72, 74, 83, 95
Developmental Psychology	8, 24, 31, 41, 45, 67, 78, 79, 93
Motivation, Emotion, and Personality	3, 6, 11, 12, 29, 51, 61, 62, 64, 73, 82, 84, 94
Clinical Psychology	9, 10, 28, 44, 52, 59, 66, 69, 85, 86, 88, 89, 91, 100
Social Psychology	1, 19, 27, 37, 48, 49, 53, 99

Topic	Chapters	Questions on Exam	Number You Got Correct
Scientific Foundations of Psychology	4, 13	14	
Biological Bases of Behavior	5, 14	10	
Sensation and Perception	6, 15	8	
Learning	7, 16	9	
Cognitive Psychology	8, 17	15	
Developmental Psychology	9, 18	9	
Motivation, Emotion, and Personality	10, 19	13	
Clinical Psychology	11, 20	14	
Social Psychology	12, 21	8	

PRACTICE EXAM 5 ANSWERS AND EXPLANATIONS

Section I

1. A

Topic: Social Psychology

Stereotypes are biased beliefs against a group, prejudice is a biased emotional reaction to a group, and discrimination is biased action against a group. The question stem describes Mitch's biased beliefs and feelings, but provides no evidence that Mitch is actively discriminating against students from other countries. Because he's demonstrating prejudice against foreign students, **(A)** is correct. (B) and (E) are incorrect because, as noted, Mitch is not described as taking action against foreign students. (C) is incorrect because no information is given about the race or ethnicity of these foreign students; it's possible that Mitch is also being racist, but there's no doubt that he's exhibiting prejudice either way. (D) is incorrect because stereotype threat is a response exhibited by people who are stereotyped, but in this example Mitch is the one who is stereotyping others.

2. B

Topic: Sensation and Perception

The question is asking for a binocular cue that is based on the kinesthetic sense. In other words, the correct answer will be the depth cue that uses both eyes and is based on sensation of the position of the eyes. This is convergence, **(B)**, which is the sensation of how crossed or parallel the eyes are when focused on an object. Stereopsis, (A), is a binocular cue, but it is perceptual rather than kinesthetic; the brain perceives depth due to slight differences in the images reaching each eye. Parallax (closer objects move more quickly than distant objects in our visual field as we change the position of our eyes), interposition (closer objects appear in front of and block more distant objects), and texture gradient (closer objects appear more detailed than distant objects) are all monocular depth perception cues, and so (C), (D), and (E) can also be eliminated.

3. A

Topic: Motivation, Emotion, and Personality

Humanistic theory emphasizes growth and self-realization in the study of personality, so **(A)** is correct. (B) is incorrect

because psychoanalytic theory focuses on the role of unconscious desires and conflicts in shaping personality. (C) and (E) are incorrect because type and trait theories don't try to explain personality; they only try to describe it. (D) is incorrect because the biopsychological theory emphasizes the role of genes and other biological factors in influencing personality.

4. B

Topic: Scientific Foundations of Psychology

Cognitive psychology focuses on cognitive processes such as memory, language, and information processing. Thus, a paper on imagery and memory would most likely be written by a cognitive psychologist, **(B)**. The remaining choices are incorrect because they describe approaches to psychology with different emphases: biological psychologists emphasize the brain and genetics, sociocultural psychologists emphasize social and cultural context, psychodynamic psychologists emphasize the unconscious mind, and behavioral psychologists emphasize observable behaviors.

5. E

Topic: Learning

In Köhler's study, chimps were presented with a problem: food was outside their reach, but they could use the materials in their cages to obtain the food. In most cases, the chimps did not arrive at a solution immediately, but after some time they were able to develop a strategy to obtain the food using what was available to them. Köhler referred to this as "insight." **(E)** is correct. (A) is incorrect because operant conditioning refers to learning that occurs as a result of reinforcement and punishment. (B) is incorrect because vicarious reinforcement is the observation of another individual being reinforced for a behavior, which in turn reinforces the observer to act in that same way. (C) is incorrect because classical conditioning is learning that occurs by pairing neutral stimuli with stimuli that instinctively produce responses in organisms, such as when a dog learns to salivate when it hears a dinner bell. (D) is incorrect because heuristics are problem-solving shortcuts that individuals use to solve complex problems.

6. E

Topic: Motivation, Emotion, and Personality

The relationship between arousal and performance is given in the Yerkes-Dodson law, which graphs as an inverted *U*. This indicates that performance increases as arousal increases, but only up to a certain optimal level, after which performance declines. Thus, **(E)** is correct. The remaining choices are incorrect because they fail to exhibit the proper relationship. (D) might be tempting because it captures the initial increase in performance at lower levels of arousal, but it is incorrect because it does not demonstrate the whole relationship.

7. D

Topic: Biological Bases of Behavior

An fMRI, or functional MRI, can measure brain activity by detecting changes in blood flow. Brain regions activated during a task (such as drawing a picture) experience increased blood flow, which can be detected by the fMRI. Thus, **(D)** is correct. (A) is incorrect because an EEG can only show the brain's overall electrical activity. So, while it can be used to detect large-scale brain activity, an EEG cannot be used to visualize activity in specific regions. (B), (C), and (E) are incorrect because these technologies can only be used to visualize brain structure, not neural activity.

8. D

Topic: Developmental Psychology

This scenario demonstrates that genetic factors can contribute to the likelihood of developing a disorder or disease, but that environmental factors can influence the expression of those genes. It is therefore a demonstration of the interaction between nature and nurture, **(D)**. Internal locus of control and external locus of control have to do with how individuals feel about the causes of their own behavior. Since the factors discussed do not involve cognition or the mental state of those with alcohol dependence, (A) can be eliminated, as can (B) and (C). Primary groups include individuals with a close bond to a person, such as family and close friends, while secondary groups include individuals with more superficial ties. Primary and secondary groups may include parents and peers, but the interaction between these groups is not the focus of this scenario, so (E) is incorrect.

9. A

Topic: Clinical Psychology

Client-centered therapy, developed by Carl Rogers, is a humanistic approach that focuses on helping the client recognize that she is of value. The therapist will listen to the issues as explained by the client and will always respond with unconditional positive regard, an attitude of support and acceptance regardless of what the client says, to help the client see that she is a valuable person with many strengths. This therapy is called client-centered because the client sets the direction of the therapy. **(A)** is correct. In the other forms of therapy given in the remaining choices, the therapist leads the session and is not always positive with his or her responses.

10. C

Topic: Clinical Psychology

(C) is correct because, unlike other disorders, patients with a personality disorder are often unable to recognize that their behavior is problematic. (A), (B), and (D) are incorrect because they are not unique to personality disorders. (E) is incorrect because personality disorders are characterized by rigid, maladjusted behavior.

11. B

Topic: Motivation, Emotion, and Personality

Projective personality tests, such as the Rorschach test, presuppose that examinees rely upon the defense mechanism of projection to complete them. The question stem indicates, however, that Dr. Baldwin does not endorse Freud's psychoanalytic structural model of personality, which includes projection and other unconscious defense mechanisms. Thus, Dr. Baldwin would likely not make use of projective tests with her patients, so **(B)**—an example of a projective personality test—is correct and (E) is incorrect. (A), (C), and (D) are all objective personality tests that do not assume the existence of projection or other aspects of the structural model.

12. E

Topic: Motivation, Emotion, and Personality

While the hypothalamus had long been believed to be the center of hunger regulation, it was not until the 1960s that experiments revealed that destruction of the ventromedial hypothalamus would lead rats to gorge themselves on food, as in **(E)**. These experiments also revealed that destruction of a different part of the structure, the lateral hypothalamus, would lead to starvation, (D). There is no evidence that destroying the ventromedial hypothalamus would affect thirst, (A), temperature regulation, (B), or sexual behavior, (C).

13. B
Topic: Learning

A variable ratio schedule is one in which a reinforcement is provided after a particular behavior is performed a randomized number of times. This precisely describes how a slot machine works, so **(B)** is correct. (A) is incorrect because a fixed ratio reinforcement schedule rewards behavior after it is performed a set number of times, but the slot machine's reward is more random. (C) and (D) are incorrect because interval-based reinforcement schedules space out the timing of rewards, either at a fixed or a variable amount, which is not how the slot machine is described in the question stem. (E) is incorrect because a continuous reinforcement schedule rewards every single instance of a behavior: it would be like a slot machine that you always won.

14. A
Topic: Cognitive Psychology

Deep processing is processing information with respect to its meaning rather than its sensory qualities. This typically results in longer-lasting memories of the information compared to shallow processing. **(A)** is correct and (B) is incorrect. (C) refers to the unconscious processing of information that is either incidental or well learned. As such, it does not typically produce lasting memories. (D) is the umbrella term for the different types of processing listed in the other answer options. (E) is not actually a term used in cognitive psychology.

15. E
Topic: Scientific Foundations of Psychology

Nonresponse bias is a distortion of data that can occur in surveys with a low response rate. Of the 18,000 surveys sent out, only a fraction (0.65%) are returned. This may cause distortion in the data because the sample may not be representative of the population. **(E)** is thus correct. (A) is incorrect because surveys sometimes produce extreme

results. (B) is incorrect because surveys are one of the best tools for assessing the opinions of many people. (C) is incorrect because surveys do not need to have a minimum length to be informative for investigators. The researchers are only interested in current residents' opinions, so previous residents are irrelevant in this context, making (D) incorrect.

16. B
Topic: Scientific Foundations of Psychology

Surveyor bias occurs when survey questions are written in ways that distort responses as a result of misleading wording or other controversial assumptions built into the questions. Among the questions included in the survey, Q3 highlights a negative aspect of the proposition, the "fiscal deficit" that it will supposedly cause, while Q4 uses loaded language like "troubled" and "flood into the city" that also suggests an anti-proposition bias. **(B)** is thus correct. (A) is incorrect because the number of questions has no impact on surveyor bias. (C) is incorrect because random assignment is generally utilized in controlled experiments but not in survey research. (D) is incorrect because the researchers were interested in the opinions of residents, which should include both renters and homeowners. (E) is incorrect because simply using electronic surveys does not result in surveyor bias; the content of the questions matters more for surveyor bias than the format.

17. B
Topic: Scientific Foundations of Psychology

Internal validity refers to the extent to which an experiment actually measures the independent variable's causal influence on the dependent variable. Internal validity is high if potential confounders are controlled, thereby ensuring that differences measured in the dependent variable could only be caused by manipulations to the independent variable. **(B)** is thus correct. (A) is incorrect because a study with high internal validity may or may not discover a relationship between independent and dependent variables; it depends on whether the results for the control group differ significantly from those for the experimental group. (C) and (D) are incorrect because generalizability pertains to external validity, not internal validity. (E) is incorrect because experiments with high internal validity can be, and often are, used to support causal conclusions.

18. E

Topic: Scientific Foundations of Psychology

Random sampling is a procedure in which a small sub-group (the sample) is selected for a study from a larger population at random, with an equal chance of any member of the population being selected. The element of random selection helps to ensure that the sample is representative of the population and to reduce the possibility of selection bias, which makes the results of psychological studies less generalizable. **(E)** is thus correct. In contrast, random assignment takes members of an already-selected sample and places them randomly into control and experimental groups to reduce the possibility of the groups having differences other than those intended by the experimental design. (A) is thus incorrect. (B) is incorrect because it refers to the practice of repeating already completed experiments to increase confidence in their conclusions. (C) is incorrect because correlation refers to the degree of relatedness between two variables. (D) is incorrect because naturalistic observation is a type of study in which a phenomenon is viewed in its natural environment.

19. E

Topic: Social Psychology

In the Robbers Cave experiment, Sherif was able to bring two competing groups of boys together by getting them to cooperate on superordinate goals, objectives that the groups shared but which required inter-group cooperation to achieve. **(E)** is correct because it presents an example of a superordinate goal, beating a rival football team, that brings the upperclassmen and the under-classmen on the team together. (A) may be tempting because it is set in a camp like the original experiment, but the two groups are being brought together only by sharing common spaces for lunch and activities, not by working together to accomplish superordinate goals. (B) is incorrect because the teacher stops the fighting only by distracting the students with individual tasks that don't require cooperation. (C) is incorrect because it describes a more passive way of uniting two groups with uplifting speeches, making no mention of the parties coming together to tackle shared objectives. (D) is incorrect because the two parties come together only through obtaining aims they already want (higher wages for the labor union, a tax break for the corporation), not by cooperating on new superordinate goals.

20. E

Topic: Sensation and Perception

The question describes a situation in which there is a conflict between visual information and perception of the body's motion. This sensation of movement is known as the vestibular sense, making **(E)** correct. (A), the thalamus, is a structure in the brain that relays sensory information to the cerebral cortex, but it has no direct role in sensing movement. Proprioception is the sense of the position of parts of the body in space. While Cynthia is experiencing motion due to the acceleration of the vehicle, the individual parts of her body are not moving, so (B) can be eliminated. (C) is incorrect because nociception is the sense of pain, which doesn't apply here. Finally, the limbic system is a collection of structures in the brain that influence memory, motivation, emotion, and learning. These functions are unrelated to sensation of movement, so (D) is incorrect.

21. C

Topic: Scientific Foundations of Psychology

The mean (the sum of the data divided by the number of data points) is one of the three commonly used measures of central tendency, so **(C)** is correct. (A) is incorrect because a correlation coefficient quantifies the relationship between two variables. (B), (D), and (E) are incorrect because they are measures of dispersion, not central tendency.

22. D

Topic: Biological Bases of Behavior

The amygdala is one component of the limbic system, which makes up the emotional center of the brain. It plays a major role in the expression of anger and the processing of fear. Thus, **(D)** is correct. The hippocampus, (A), is associated with the processing and integration of memories, rather than fear specifically. The thalamus, (B), is the relay center of the brain, responsible for receiving and relaying information about stimuli such as touch, taste, and sound from and to different parts of the body. Both the hippocampus and the thalamus are also parts of the limbic system. The cerebellum, (C), is part of the hindbrain and controls posture, movement, and balance. Broca's area, (E), is the area of the brain responsible for speech production.

23. D

Topic: Scientific Foundations of Psychology

Self-actualization is a term coined by humanistic psychologist Abraham Maslow, who defined it as the realization of an individual's unique potential. Self-actualization is the ultimate goal of humanistic approaches to psychotherapy. **(D)** is correct. The remaining choices are incorrect because they name approaches that do not emphasize self-actualization.

24. C

Topic: Developmental Psychology

Carol Gilligan believes that Kohlberg's stages of moral reasoning focus too much on duty and societal rules, and suggests that while many people often make moral decisions in other ways, this does not mean that their decisions are inferior. Gilligan structured her stages around empathy and benevolence instead, making **(C)** correct. Both Kohlberg and Gilligan organize development into stages, and both believe that not all people reason at the highest level, so (A) and (E) are incorrect. Choice (B) is backwards, since both theorists place more emphasis on the reasoning behind moral decisions than the decisions themselves. Finally, (D) describes Kohlberg's basis for his stages, not Gilligan's.

25. A

Topic: Cognitive Psychology

When a test is split into multiple different versions that are administered at different times, the correlation between the scores is a measure of equivalent-form reliability; **(A)** is correct. (B) is incorrect because assessing test-retest reliability requires two administrations of the exact same test at different times. (C) is incorrect because split-half reliability involves splitting the items on a single test in half and scoring each half separately. (D) is incorrect because face validity is a superficial measure of a test's ability to assess the skills it claims to. (E) is incorrect because content validity measures the extent to which a test accurately assesses the entire range of abilities it is designed to measure.

26. E

Topic: Biological Bases of Behavior

The limbic system makes up the emotional center of the brain and consists of the thalamus, (D), hippocampus, (B), amygdala, (A), and hypothalamus, (C). The cerebellum is part of the hindbrain and controls posture, movement, and balance; it does not play a notable role in the processing of emotions, making **(E)** correct.

27. C

Topic: Social Psychology

The peripheral route to persuasion is a method of persuasion that depends on factors other than the content of the message. An ad relying on outward appearance, rather than a set of reasons for buying the product, would be an example of the peripheral route; **(C)** is correct. (A) and (B) are incorrect because these methods require multiple interactions to operate: the foot-in-the-door technique consists of a small request followed by a larger request, while the door-in-the-face technique consists of a large request followed by a smaller request. (D) is incorrect because the central route depends on the content of the message. (E) is incorrect because the mere-exposure effect depends simply upon presenting the same idea repeatedly.

28. B

Topic: Clinical Psychology

(B) is correct because the humanistic model maintains that symptoms of mental illness come from a lack of meaning and fulfillment, such as when essential human needs (like those articulated in Maslow's hierarchy of needs, including love and belonging) go unfulfilled. The other choices present cognitive, (A), biological, (C), psychodynamic, (D), and behavioral, (E), explanations for the depression.

29. E

Topic: Motivation, Emotion, and Personality

The opponent-process theory of motivation states that people generally exist at a baseline with respect to their emotional state. However, when something moves them away from their baseline emotional state, they then experience the opposite emotion, which drives them back to baseline. This theory is commonly used to explain addictive behaviors because people first feel euphoria when consuming an addictive substance, followed by the negative feelings of coming down from a high. As tolerance to the drug increases, more and more of the drug is needed to produce the same euphoric feeling and combat the negative opponent process. Thus, **(E)** is correct. The remaining answer choices do not align as well with Sarah's described behavior. Drive-reduction theory, (A), states that imbalances to individuals' internal environments produce drives that cause them to perform behaviors that will lead to a restoration of homeostasis. Arousal theory, (B), states that individuals are motivated to perform behaviors in order to maintain an optimal arousal level. Instinct theory, (C), states that certain behaviors are driven by instincts that have been developed through generations of evolution. Incentive theory, (D), states that behaviors are motivated by the desire to attain rewards and avoid punishments.

30. B

Topic: Learning

A secondary reinforcer is a stimulus that an individual has been conditioned to desire through association with a primary reinforcer. In this scenario, the treat is the primary reinforcer, as the dog likely finds the treat to be intrinsically pleasant. By conditioning the dog to associate the clicks with the treat, the click then becomes a secondary reinforcer. **(B)** is correct. Prior to the training, the clicking sound was a neutral stimulus for the dog, but since the question specified the post-training period, (C) is incorrect. (D) and (E) are incorrect because the clicking is not a behavioral response, but a type of stimulus.

31. A

Topic: Developmental Psychology

A teratogen is defined as a substance that can cause birth defects, so **(A)** is correct. (B) and (C) are caused by mutagens and carcinogens, respectively. Changes in mood are typically caused by changes in neurotransmitters, and the stress response is caused by stress hormones, so (D) and (E) can be eliminated.

32. E

Topic: Learning

(E) is correct: Albert Bandura conducted the Bobo doll experiment, a powerful demonstration of observational learning in which children observing violent behaviors displayed similar aggression. The remaining studies were conducted by other psychologists. (A) describes John Garcia's experiment that showed rats developing an aversion for water due to association with the symptoms of radiation. (B) describes Martin Seligman's experiments that demonstrated learned helplessness in dogs. (C) was

John Watson's famous experiment in which a baby was conditioned to fear white rats and similar stimuli. (D) refers to Ivan Pavlov's efforts to condition dogs to salivate in response to the ringing of a dinner bell.

33. B

Topic: Cognitive Psychology

Individuals with IQs between 25 and 40 are classified as having severe intellectual disabilities; **(B)** is correct. (A) covers individuals with profound intellectual disabilities, while (C) covers individuals with mild intellectual disabilities. (D) is incorrect because it contains IQs within two standard deviations of the mean, which covers most (about 68%) of the population. (E) is incorrect because individuals with an IQ above 130 are considered intellectually gifted.

34. E

Topic: Sensation and Perception

Because the participants are asked whether they can detect a signal (the circle of ten dots) among random noise, the focus of this study is signal detection theory; **(E)** is correct. The Gestalt principle of continuity is relevant to the study; this principle says that objects are grouped when they follow a particular pattern, in this case a circle. However, the focus of the study is not whether participants see the signal stimulus *as a circle* or *as ten dots*, but only whether they see the pattern at all; thus, the principle of continuity is not the concept being investigated in the study, and (A) can be eliminated. Weber's law states that the just-noticeable difference between two stimuli is proportional to the intensity of the stimulus. This is not a feature of the study, so (B) is incorrect. Top-down processing, (C), is likewise incorrect; the study is not about using expectations to fill in details about the stimulus. Finally, (D) is incorrect because the study is about the perception of the stimulus rather than the sensation of it, so the process of transforming the light that enters the eye from the stimulus into electronic signals in the brain is not a focus of the study.

35. E

Topic: Cognitive Psychology

The spacing effect refers to the tendency for people to better remember material in the long term when they distribute their studying over a longer period of time. Since Peter, who distributed his study time, shows longer retention than Paul, who was cramming, this is an example of the spacing effect; **(E)** is correct. (A) refers to a tendency to better remember information when it is made relevant to oneself. In this example, neither brother used this strategy for studying. Both (B) and (C) are components of the serial position effect, which describes how the order of encoding affects recall. In this question, there is no mention of order; thus, both (B) and (C) are incorrect. (D) refers to a tendency for people to develop false memories after being given misinformation and is not relevant to this scenario.

36. A
Topic: Scientific Foundations of Psychology

In a single-blind study, researchers know the groups that participants belong to, but the participants themselves do not know; **(A)** is correct. This is in contrast to a double-blind study, (B), in which neither participants nor researchers know who is in which group. (C) is incorrect because a confounder, or confounding variable, is a variable other than an independent variable that influences the results of an experiment. (D) is incorrect because a placebo is not a type of study; placebos are used in some single-blind and double-blind studies to create control conditions. (E) is incorrect because a case study is a type of research in which only one or a few individuals are closely observed; case studies generally do not have experimental or control groups.

37. D
Topic: Social Psychology

Groupthink is a tendency in some groups to make poor decisions as a result of too much emphasis on maintaining harmony in the group. This describes the behavior of the NASA senior staff, who made disastrous decisions while trying to "reduce internal conflict and promote consensus." **(D)** is thus correct. (A) is incorrect because it refers to judging other cultures on the basis of the values of your own culture. The fundamental attribution error describes the tendency to attribute other people's behavior to dispositional rather than situational factors; it is not relevant to the described scenario, so (B) is incorrect. (C) is incorrect because discrimination is differential treatment of members of different groups. Group polarization is the tendency for groups to become more extreme in their beliefs and decisions over time; there's no evidence of increasing extremism in the senior staff, so (E) is incorrect.

38. C
Topic: Cognitive Psychology

A mental set is the tendency to use old patterns to solve new problems; **(C)** is correct. (A) is incorrect because belief perseverance is the tendency to make illogical conclusions in order to confirm your existing beliefs. (B) may be tempting, as it is also a form of fixation. However, (B) refers specifically to the tendency to think about familiar objects in familiar ways and does not necessarily apply to problem solving. Anchoring refers to a type of bias in which people rely too heavily on an initial piece of information they learned; (D) is incorrect. (E) is incorrect because confirmation bias is the tendency to disproportionately seek out pieces of information that support your preexisting viewpoints.

39. A
Topic: Cognitive Psychology

An achievement test is designed to assess current performance levels; **(A)** is correct. (B) is incorrect because an aptitude test is designed to predict future performance. Power tests, (C), present questions of increasing difficulty to determine the highest-level problem a person can solve. Abstract tests, (D), assess reasoning through the use of non-verbal questions, such as those containing shapes. Speed tests, (E), focus on assessing how many questions can be answered in a short amount of time.

40. C
Topic: Biological Bases of Behavior

The adrenal glands secrete hormones like cortisol and epinephrine (adrenaline), also known as stress hormones, which activate the sympathetic nervous system. **(C)** is correct. (A) and (B) are incorrect because the ovaries and testes secrete female and male sex hormones, respectively. (D) is incorrect because the thyroid secretes metabolic hormones. (E) is incorrect because the pituitary secretes hormones that regulate other endocrine glands.

41. E
Topic: Developmental Psychology

According to Vygotsky, skills that are just beyond the reach of what a child can learn on his or her own are best learned in the presence of someone who has already mastered that skill and can help the child to learn. This person is referred to as a "more knowledgeable other," so **(E)** is correct. The remaining choices reflect other perspectives on learning.

42. A

Topic: Biological Bases of Behavior

The activation-synthesis hypothesis states that dreams are the brain's interpretations of neural activity that occurs during REM sleep; **(A)** is correct. (B) is incorrect because information-processing theory maintains that dreams are a way for the brain to process stress. (C), (D), and (E) are incorrect because psychoanalytic theory views dreams as reflective of the unconscious mind, distinguishing between the manifest content you remember and the latent content that represents your unconscious thoughts and desires.

43. A

Topic: Cognitive Psychology

The misinformation effect refers to the tendency for people to develop false memories after being provided with information that distorts the details of an experience; **(A)** is correct. (B) refers to the feeling that a new experience is actually familiar, but this feeling is not necessarily brought on by misinformation. (C) is incorrect because source amnesia is a memory error in which a person may correctly remember the details of an experience but misremember the context. (D) is incorrect because memory decay is the natural process of slowly losing old memories over time. Interference, (E), may be tempting, as it refers to a memory retrieval error brought upon by the existence of other information. However, interference is a process that disrupts either the learning of new information or the recall of old information. By contrast, the misinformation effect refers to the alteration of already-formed memories.

44. D

Topic: Clinical Psychology

Mood swings are characteristic of bipolar disorders, but not autism spectrum disorder. **(D)** is thus correct. The remaining choices all present symptoms typically associated with autism spectrum disorder.

45. C

Topic: Developmental Psychology

The concrete operational stage is defined by the ability to reason concretely but not abstractly. As a result, **(C)** best describes this stage: conservation is a concrete idea, but the ability to reason about moral consequences is an abstract one. (A) is incorrect because freedom is likewise an abstract concept, so children would be able neither to understand nor to explain freedom before the formal operational stage. (B) is incorrect because both object permanence and theory of mind are features of the pre-operational stage and should be mastered before the concrete operational stage. (D) is the opposite of what would be expected; trial-and-error problem solving is expected in the concrete operational stage, but strategic planning doesn't develop until the formal operational stage. Finally, the ability to acquire and adjust schemata ("assimilation" and "accommodation," respectively) is present in the sensorimotor stage, so (E) can be eliminated.

46. B

Topic: Scientific Foundations of Psychology

Operationalization is the quantification of variables so that they can be more easily controlled or measured in research. **(B)** is correct. (A) is incorrect because researchers can operationalize variables in experiments with only one independent variable or with multiple variables. (C) is incorrect because operationalization is only one component of experimental design. (D) is incorrect because operationalization can be used in both experiments and correlational studies. (E) is incorrect because the choice of statistical procedures typically comes later in experimental design; variables must be quantified before measures of them can be statistically analyzed.

47. D

Topic: Cognitive Psychology

The Wechsler Intelligence Scale for Children (WISC) is a commonly used intelligence test specifically designed for children that measures intelligence using both verbal and non-verbal tasks. Thus, **(D)** is correct. (A) is incorrect because this would be assessed by a clinical test like the Beck Depression Inventory. (B) is incorrect because it describes projective personality tests, which assess unconscious thoughts and feelings based on the participant's interpretation of ambiguous stimuli. (C) refers to the original Stanford-Binet IQ test, which used Binet's concept of mental age to assess a person's intelligence in reference to others their same age. (E) is incorrect because the WISC measures verbal and non-verbal intelligence but does not specifically measure Sternberg's concept of creative intelligence, the ability to apply information to new situations.

48. C
Topic: Social Psychology

Stereotype threat is a phenomenon in which members of a stereotyped group perform worse on certain tasks when reminded of associated stereotypes. Female students in Group C were reminded of an unfounded stereotype about women performing worse than men in math, a clear instance of stereotype threat, which most likely explains why Group C is the only experimental group in which the female students performed significantly worse than the male students on average. **(C)** is correct. None of the other choices explain the gender disparity. (A) is incorrect because groupthink refers to the tendency of particular groups to make poor decisions as a result of members' desire to maintain harmony. (B) is incorrect because situational attribution refers to a type of attribution in which responsibility for an event or action is attributed to the circumstances of the situation rather than the character of the person(s) involved. (D) is incorrect because the just-world hypothesis is the belief that good things happen to good people and bad things happen to bad people. (E) is incorrect because compliance is when individuals follow explicit requests from peers.

49. E
Topic: Social Psychology

When told that most students are expected to pass this exam, Group A students performed better than the control (Group D); Group B students, who were told that most students are expected to fail, performed worse than the control. These are both examples of self-fulfilling prophecies, specifically the Pygmalion effect, the tendency for students to perform better when presented with more positive expectations. **(E)** is correct. (A) is incorrect because social facilitation is the tendency to perform practiced and simple tasks better in front of an audience, but there was no difference between Groups A and B in testing circumstances besides the differently worded

introduction. (B) is incorrect because group polarization describes a tendency for groups to move to extremes in beliefs and decisions, but it is not associated with differences between groups in average performance. (C) is incorrect because self-serving bias is the tendency to view personal successes as dispositional and personal failures as situational, which is not relevant to this experiment. (D) is incorrect because an unstable attribution is the belief that a result occurred due to a unique situation, which is again not relevant to the performance differences between Groups A and B.

50. B
Topic: Scientific Foundations of Psychology

The internal validity of a study is a measure of the extent to which it actually investigates what it is designed to. The experiment described sought to investigate how expectations influenced exam performance. However, the failure to include a proper control group like Group D (as suggested in the question stem) would make it more difficult to isolate the effect of the independent variable on the dependent variable, which would in turn decrease the internal validity of the study. Thus, **(B)** is correct and (A) and (E) are incorrect. External validity refers to the generalizability of a study to a larger population. Because random assignment is still being used on the same group of students irrespective of whether Group D is included, the external validity of the study would not be significantly affected; (C) and (D) are incorrect.

51. C
Topic: Motivation, Emotion, and Personality

Adler is most associated with **(C)**, the inferiority complex, which refers to a person's feelings of incompleteness or imperfection. Basic anxiety, (A), is an idea associated with Karen Horney, while peak experiences, (B), are from Abraham Maslow. The structural model, (D), and personality archetypes, (E), are attributed to Freud and Jung, respectively.

52. C
Topic: Clinical Psychology

Benzodiazepines reduce the activity of the central nervous system by increasing the activity of GABA, the main inhibitory neurotransmitter in the brain. They are commonly used for patients with anxiety disorders. Thus, **(C)** is correct. The other four choices are excitatory or mixed neurotransmitters.

53. D
Topic: Social Psychology

In this scenario, overfishing occurred because fishers saw the short-term gain they could obtain from harvesting as many anchovies as possible, but since the whole group behaved this way, there were major negative consequences for everyone. Seeking short-term individual gain to the long-term detriment of the group is known as a social trap, so **(D)** is correct. Superordinate goals are formed when people from competing sides come together to accomplish shared objectives, which often builds camaraderie between the sides; (A) is incorrect. The bystander effect occurs when people are less likely to intervene in a crisis due to the presence of many others on the scene; (B) is incorrect. The prisoner's dilemma is a thought experiment that demonstrates why cooperation may not occur between individuals, even when it is in their best interests to cooperate; (C) is incorrect. Social inhibition involves avoiding social situations because of anxieties associated with being thought of negatively in a group setting; (E) is incorrect.

54. B
Topic: Sensation and Perception

According to the opponent-process theory of vision, colors are detected by cone cells in pairs: red-green and blue-yellow. When looking at a stimulus made of one of the colors in a pair for a long time and then looking at a neutral stimulus, the brain perceives an afterimage of the other color in the pair. As a result, the red circle produces an afterimage of a green circle, and the yellow background produces an afterimage of a blue background. Therefore, **(B)** is correct. The remaining choices would not be predicted by opponent-process theory.

55. C
Topic: Learning

Systematic desensitization is a behavior modification technique that attempts to treat phobias through planned exposure to fearful stimuli, often in increasing increments.

This describes how the therapist is treating Marcus for his phobia, so **(C)** is correct. The remaining choices don't apply to the described scenario. Partial reinforcement, (A), refers to the use of reinforcement after a desired response only part of the time. Aversion therapy, (B), is a process of behavior modification that works by associating an undesirable habitual behavior with an aversive stimulus. Latent learning, (D), refers to learning that occurs without any obvious reinforcement and remains unexpressed until reinforcement is provided. Coping, (E), refers to the behavioral and cognitive strategies used to manage stress.

56. E
Topic: Scientific Foundations of Psychology

Because humanistic psychology is predominantly a clinical approach that focuses on individual freedom and self-actualization, humanistic psychologists often have difficulty formulating testable hypotheses and operationalizing variables. Consequently, humanistic psychology is often criticized for not being experimentally verifiable; **(E)** is correct. (A), (B), and (C) are incorrect because the theories of cognitive, behavioral, and biological psychology have often been tested in the lab. (D) is incorrect because sociocultural psychology, while difficult to test in laboratory settings since it tries to investigate larger social and cultural contexts, is still more suited to being empirically tested than humanistic psychology.

57. D
Topic: Cognitive Psychology

Recognition is the ability to correctly identify previously learned information from given stimuli. This is sometimes confused with recall, or the ability to reproduce memorized information without the use of retrieval cues. Since Jerry needs the retrieval cue of a word bank, he is demonstrating recognition rather than recall; **(D)** is correct and (A) is incorrect. (B) is incorrect because relearning is learning information that was previously memorized. Rehearsal refers to the repetition of a piece of information for the purpose of either keeping it in short-term memory or storing it in long-term memory; (C) is incorrect. (E) is incorrect because repetition is a method that Jerry may have used to memorize his terms, but it is not relevant to Jerry's current retrieval.

58. B

Topic: Scientific Foundations of Psychology

A cross-sectional study consists of observations conducted on a wide range of people at one particular point in time, providing a picture of a cross section of a population. The question stem describes exactly such a study, so **(B)** is correct. (A) is incorrect because a case study is an in-depth observation of one particular subject, which in psychology is often just a single individual. (C) is incorrect because a longitudinal study involves following a group of individuals (called a cohort) across a long span of time. (D) is incorrect because a psychological experiment involves more than just observation; it requires the manipulation of variables to create treatment and control conditions to which distinct individuals are assigned (typically randomly). This does not describe the study from the question stem. (E) is incorrect because a naturalistic observation involves examining subjects in their native environment, but the question stem does not suggest direct observation in a particular location; as described, it seems more likely that participants would simply fill out surveys about numbers of close friends.

59. D

Topic: Clinical Psychology

Although electroconvulsive therapy (ECT) is used very sparingly these days, it can still be an effective treatment for some forms of major depressive disorder and has been shown to reduce suicidal thoughts. **(D)** is correct. ECT would not be used to treat somatic symptom disorder, (A), anxiety disorders, (B), personality disorders, (C), or sleep apnea, (E).

60. D

Topic: Learning

According to research on operant conditioning, variable reinforcement schedules tend to produce larger changes in behavior than fixed reinforcement schedules. Because Group 2 received a reward after a variable number of hours, but Group 1 received a reward after a fixed number of hours, it makes sense that Group 2 would see a bigger positive change. **(D)** is correct and (C) is incorrect. (A) and (B) are incorrect because the reinforcements were not stopped at any point in the described study. While (A) does accurately describe the phenomenon known as

the partial reinforcement extinction effect, neither Group 1 nor Group 2 used a continuous schedule. (E) is incorrect because the groups were randomly assigned, so there should be no systematic biases in the compositions of their members.

61. C

Topic: Motivation, Emotion, and Personality

The hypothalamus secretes hormones that control the release of hormones by the pituitary gland, in addition to regulating sleep, blood pressure, hunger, and other basic drives. Thus, **(C)** is correct. The thalamus, (A), is considered the relay center of the brain, receiving sensory information from the body and ensuring it reaches the right part of the brain. The hippocampus, (B), is integral for memory formation. The pituitary, (D), a gland adjacent to the hypothalamus and regulated by it, produces hormones that affect functions throughout the body. The amygdala, (E), is responsible for regulating fear and aggression.

62. B

Topic: Motivation, Emotion, and Personality

The Myers-Briggs Type Indicator (MBTI) is the test that determines personality types along four different scales. Here, "ESFP" stands for "extraverted, sensing, feeling, perceiving," so **(B)** is correct. The Rorschach test and Thematic Apperception Test are projective tests, and so do not seek to label people by type; (A) and (C) are incorrect. (D) is incorrect because although it is similar to the MBTI, the Keirsey Temperament Sorter generates results that are descriptive labels, such as "the Champion" or "the Supervisor." Finally, (E) is incorrect because the Minnesota Multiphasic Personality Inventory-2 (MMPI-2) provides results across many different spectra, such as depression, mania, masculinity/femininity, and so on.

63. D

Topic: Learning

In operant conditioning, a punishment is a negative stimulus intended to reduce the frequency of a behavior. A positive punishment involves the presence of an aversive stimulus, while a negative punishment involves the absence of a pleasant stimulus. Because Judy loves her video games but is losing access to them for breaking her promise, she is receiving a negative punishment. **(D)** is correct and (C) is incorrect. (A) and (B) are incorrect because reinforcements reward desired behavior, but here Judy is being punished for undesired behavior. (E) is incorrect because neutral punishment is not a term recognized by behavioral psychologists.

64. D

Topic: Motivation, Emotion, and Personality

Projective tests present a participant with an ambiguous stimulus and ask the participant to interpret that stimulus, the idea being that the interpretation will present insight into the person's unconscious mind and personality. **(D)** is correct because it describes exactly such a scenario with the interpretation of a piece of music. None of the remaining choices present an ambiguous stimulus to interpret; therefore, they are not projective tests.

65. C

Topic: Scientific Foundations of Psychology

Correlation coefficients are mathematical expressions of the relationship between two variables. A coefficient with a negative sign indicates that as one variable increases, the other decreases, while a positive coefficient reflects that the variables move in the same direction. But the question here is about coefficient strength, and the strongest correlations are closest to 1 or −1, while the weakest are closest to 0. In this case, **(C)** is correct because it is closest to 0. The remaining choices reflect stronger correlations.

66. A

Topic: Clinical Psychology

Free association is a technique used by practitioners of Freudian psychoanalysis that analyzes the unconscious to help determine the cause of anxiety or stress. The belief is that by asking a person to say exactly what is on his or her mind when a certain word is said, the psychologist is able to determine what is happening in the unconscious. **(A)** is correct. Free recall, (B), is used in the study of memory. Exposure therapy, (C), involves exposing people to what they avoid or fear in order to help them overcome their anxieties; one type of exposure therapy is systematic desensitization, (D). Freud did not advocate for such techniques. Likewise, Freud did not use an approach involving biofeedback, (E).

67. A

Topic: Developmental Psychology

Socioemotional selectivity theory maintains that the elderly focus more on information that brings them emotional satisfaction and less on information that might be important to them in the future. The man described in the question stem is more readily able to recall such emotional information than information that might be relevant to his health, so **(A)** is correct. Retrograde amnesia and anterograde amnesia are the inability to recall old information or to make new memories, respectively. Since both of the events the man is trying to recall are happening at constant times in the future, neither of these would be responsible for the difference, so (B) and (C) can be eliminated. Synaptic pruning is the process through which synapses that are not frequently used are targeted for elimination. This process occurs mostly in adolescence, so it is unlikely to account for the difference in memory described here. Eliminate (D). Finally, needing reminders for a biweekly event is not a severe enough type of memory loss to be indicative of Alzheimer's disease, so (E) is incorrect.

68. C

Topic: Biological Bases of Behavior

When the body is exposed to stress, the sympathetic nervous system activates, causing the adrenal medulla to release epinephrine and norepinephrine, and the adrenal cortex to secrete cortisol. **(C)** is thus correct. The remaining choices are incorrect because they present neurotransmitters that are not involved in fight or flight.

69. E

Topic: Clinical Psychology

Psychoanalysis is a method of therapy developed by Freud that seeks to help clients gain insight into, and work through, unconscious thoughts and emotions presumed to cause mental problems. **(E)** is correct. Joseph Wolpe, (A), developed a technique of systematic desensitization to help people recover from fear and panic associated with phobias. Carl Rogers, (B), developed client-centered therapy. Wilhelm Wundt, (C), was one of the earliest researchers of consciousness. He used the method of introspection to help people better understand their mental processes. Much of Chomsky's work, (D), has centered on how humans learn language. While he has contributed work to many areas of psychology, he is not a clinical psychologist.

70. C

Topic: Cognitive Psychology

Flashbulb memories are memories of particularly emotional events, making **(C)** correct. Although flashbulb memories may contain more details than other types of memories, they are not necessarily more accurate; therefore, (A) is incorrect. (B) is incorrect because flashbulb memories are actually more vivid than other types of memories. (D) is incorrect because flashbulb memories are declarative, rather than procedural, memories. (E) is incorrect because people typically lose memories of events that occurred before the age of 5, a phenomenon known as infantile amnesia.

71. B

Topic: Cognitive Psychology

Suppression refers to the process of actively trying to put something out of one's mind. Since Zoey is indeed actively trying to put her tripping incident out of her mind, she is using suppression. **(B)** is correct. This is sometimes confused with repression, (A), which is a Freudian defense mechanism by which people unconsciously push away anxiety-inducing memories. (C) refers to the repetition of a piece of information in order to keep it in one's memory, which is the opposite of Zoey's goal. (D) refers to the natural, gradual loss of older memories over time. Since Zoey is actively trying not to remember her experience, she is not undergoing a natural or gradual process. (E) refers to a retrieval error caused by the existence of other information. Again, since Zoey is actively trying to forget her performance, she is not experiencing an accidental retrieval error.

72. D

Topic: Cognitive Psychology

B.F. Skinner proposed the behaviorist theory of language acquisition. A key tenet of this theory is that children learn language by imitating the speech of their parents and being rewarded for doing so; **(D)** is correct. (A), (B), (C), and (E) are incorrect because they represent the views

of language nativists like Noam Chomsky, which are in direct opposition to behaviorism on many points.

73. B

Topic: Motivation, Emotion, and Personality

Maslow's hierarchy of needs suggests that an individual cannot attend to a need at a particular level until they have fulfilled all other lower-priority needs. The five classifications of needs in order of priority are physiological needs, safety needs, needs for love and belonging, esteem needs, and self-actualization needs. Thus, before focusing on any other needs, an individual must first address his or her needs for food and water, making **(B)** correct. (A) is an example of a safety need, (C) is an example of an esteem need, (D) is an example of a self-actualization need, and (E) is an example of a love and belonging need.

74. A

Topic: Cognitive Psychology

Automatic processing refers to the processing of information that is either incidental or well-learned. It takes place at the unconscious level. Since Sally is not consciously processing the time throughout the day because she is not watching the clock, Sally's awareness that it is noontime is an example of automatic processing; **(A)** is correct. Effortful processing, (B), is the opposite of automatic processing because it takes place at the conscious level. (C), (D), and (E) are incorrect because they are all types of attention. Attention is the brain's ability to focus on stimuli or other information and thus would also take place at the conscious level.

75. A

Topic: Biological Bases of Behavior

Interneurons are found only in the brain and spinal cord, which make up the central nervous system, and not in the peripheral nervous system. Thus, **(A)** is correct. They serve to connect the sensory and motor segments of the nervous system. Glial cells, (B), are non-neuronal cells found in both the central and peripheral nervous systems. Glial cells include oligodendrocytes (in the CNS), astrocytes, microglia, and Schwann cells (in the PNS). Afferent neurons, (C), are sensory neurons, (E), that carry information to the spinal cord and the brain. Efferent neurons,

(D), are motor neurons that carry neural impulses away from the central nervous system toward the muscles.

76. C

Topic: Biological Bases of Behavior

The image labeled IV is the typical EEG of someone who is in non-REM (NREM) stage four sleep. During NREM stage four, the EEG will show almost exclusively delta waves. **(C)** is correct. (A) and (E) are associated with NREM sleep stages one and two (I and II). Delta waves, (B), are associated with both wakefulness and REM sleep. (D) is an EEG feature that occurs during NREM stage two sleep (II).

77. D

Topic: Biological Bases of Behavior

Before entering REM sleep, a person must typically first enter deep sleep, non-REM (NREM) stage IV, and then come back through NREM stages three and two before entering REM sleep. The figure shows the four different stages of NREM sleep, stages I–IV. Right before REM sleep, a person would be first in deep sleep, IV, then in NREM stage three sleep, III, and then in NREM stage two sleep, II, which means that **(D)** is correct.

78. B

Topic: Developmental Psychology

The question stem defines the authoritarian parenting style; **(B)** is correct. The authoritative parenting style, (C), is demanding but encouraging; the neglectful parenting style, (D), is cold and unresponsive; and the permissive parenting style, (E), is responsive but not demanding. Ambivalent, (A), is an attachment style, not a parenting style.

79. A

Topic: Developmental Psychology

Piaget's theory of cognitive development says that a child should develop object permanence during the end of the sensorimotor stage (when the child is about two), which makes **(A)** correct. (B), (C), and (D) are incorrect because object permanence is already well established in these stages. Postoperational, (E), is not a stage of Piaget's theory of cognitive development.

80. A

Topic: Sensation and Perception

Top-down processing is the style of processing in which we use expectations and prior experience to shape our perceptions of a stimulus. Most of the Gestalt principles are examples of this. Rather than seeing the individual pieces of such stimuli, we use our prior experience to fill in the gaps to perceive something that is more than the sum of its parts. Thus, **(A)** is correct. Bottom-up processing is the opposite, using the details to make determinations about an image. From the bottom up, we would see a stimulus like the one described in the question as its individual pieces, so (B) can be eliminated. Perceptual constancy is the ability to see objects as unchanging—constant in color, shape, size, and other properties—even when retinal images change due to distance or lighting, so (C) can be eliminated. Extrasensory perception is a parapsychological phenomenon in which people believe they can perceive things not directly presented to the senses, such as the future or the thoughts of others. While the principle described in the question is the perception of something beyond the explicit stimulus, it is not parapsychological, so (D) is incorrect. Finally, afterimages are perceived after seeing a stimulus for a long time and then looking at a neutral stimulus; the afterimage seems "burned" into your vision. Gestalt perceptions are not afterimages, so (E) is incorrect.

81. A

Topic: Scientific Foundations of Psychology

The biological approach to psychology emphasizes explanations based on brain anatomy and physiology. **(A)** presents a case that examines the role of a particular brain structure (the amygdala) on behavior, making it correct. (B) and (D) are incorrect because they are topics more likely to be studied by behavioral psychologists. (C) and (E) would more likely be studied by sociocultural and/or developmental psychologists.

82. C

Topic: Motivation, Emotion, and Personality

The Schachter-Singer two-factor theory of emotion states that two factors, cognitive and physiological, comprise emotions. A physiological reaction is given a label by a cognitive process that then leads to the emotion occurring. In this case, seeing the snake would cause the person's heart to race (a physiological response) and she would assign a cognitive label to this physiological response; only then would she feel the emotion of fear. This matches **(C)**, making it correct. (A) is incorrect because it characterizes the Cannon-Bard theory of emotion. (B) is incorrect because it characterizes Lazarus' appraisal theory of emotion. (D) is incorrect because it characterizes the James-Lange theory of emotion. (E) is incorrect because it is a reversal of the James-Lange theory.

83. C

Topic: Cognitive Psychology

The Stanford-Binet IQ Test was developed by Louis Terman as an attempt to provide an objective measure of intelligence. This early IQ test determined IQ by dividing mental age by chronological age and multiplying by 100. **(C)** is correct. (A) and (B) are incorrect because the Wechsler intelligence scales are modern tests of intelligence for adults and children; they never used the formula specified in the stem. The Minnesota Multiphasic Personality Inventory-2 (MMPI-2) is an objective personality test and not an intelligence test, so (D) is incorrect. (E) is incorrect because the Thematic Apperception Test (TAT) is a projective personality test, not an intelligence test.

84. B

Topic: Motivation, Emotion, and Personality

Cultures that value family over individuals are called "collectivist," so (A), (C), and (E) can be eliminated. Of the remaining choices, only **(B)** correctly matches the continent to its most common cultural type. (D) is incorrect because North American cultures tend to be individualistic.

85. E

Topic: Clinical Psychology

Cognitive psychologists study how mental processes such as perception, thinking, learning, and memory impact behavior. They believe that the rules people use to interpret the world are an important part of understanding why people think and act the way they do. Thus, a cognitive therapist would believe that an individual is suffering from a disorder due to an erroneous style of

thinking, making **(E)** correct. (A) is more characteristic of a psychoanalytic approach. (B) is more characteristic of a behavioral approach. (C) and (D) are more characteristic of a biological approach.

86. D

Topic: Clinical Psychology

(D) is correct because the somatogenic model proposes physiological causes (such as bodily humors) for mental illness. All the other choices are incorrect because they propose psychological causes for mental disorders.

87. A

Topic: Sensation and Perception

Inattentional blindness is a phenomenon in which a person's attention is so focused on one thing that he or she fails to recognize the presence of another stimulus. **(A)** is an example of this: the person is paying attention to the traffic and fails to see something rather obvious and ridiculous in his field of vision. The incorrect answers are examples of other kinds of blindness. (B) describes the blindspot, the part of the retina that contains no sensory cells. (C) is an example of color blindness. (D) describes habituation; in this case the stimulus is noticed but forgotten, whereas with inattentional blindness the stimulus is never noticed. Finally, (E) is an example of change blindness, in which an observer fails to notice when a stimulus in the perceptual field is altered.

88. A

Topic: Clinical Psychology

(A) is correct because the biological model attributes symptoms to differences in neurochemistry, which encourages research on effective drug treatments. All of the other choices are incorrect because they do not accurately describe the biological model. (B) and (C) are incorrect because the biological model relies upon physiological, genetic, and evolutionary explanations for mental illness, not cultural or psychological ones. (D) is incorrect because the biological model usually ignores the wider context, while (E) is incorrect because the biological model relies upon causal explanations, tending to ignore issues of freedom and responsibility.

89. A
Topic: Clinical Psychology

(A) is correct since manic episodes are characterized by frenetic activity, an elevated mood, inflated self-esteem, decreased desire for sleep, and distractibility. Rose's symptoms are not consistent with any of the other choices. Panic attacks, (B), are episodes of acute fear. Depressive episodes, (C), are periods of diminished mood and inactivity, the opposite of what Rose experiences. Dissociative fugue, (D), is a dissociative disorder in which patients construct new identities for themselves. Amnesia, (E), refers to memory loss.

90. E
Topic: Learning

Learned helplessness is a learned inability to overcome obstacles or avoid punishment. Tonga eventually gives up on his dreams and stops trying to overcome the obstacles in his life after experiencing repeat failures, so he is exhibiting learned helplessness. **(E)** is correct. The remaining choices don't apply to Tonga's situation. Accidental conditioning occurs when a behavior is, for coincidental reasons unconnected to the behavior, rewarded or punished. However, Tonga's inability to study is connected to his failure on the exam, so there's no coincidence there; (A) is incorrect. (B) and (C) are incorrect because they refer to the same phenomenon, in which behavior is learned by watching others, but no such observation is described in the question. (D) is incorrect because self-efficacy involves believing yourself capable of success, which is the opposite of what Tonga feels.

91. C
Topic: Clinical Psychology

In the Rosenhan study, confederates feigned symptoms of schizophrenia for the staff of several psychiatric hospitals. After gaining admittance to the facilities, the confederates ceased to feign symptoms, but were not identified as pseudopatients by any mental health worker within the facilities. Rosenhan concluded that the use of diagnostic labels, in this case schizophrenia, changed the way people were treated; **(C)** is correct. (A) is incorrect because the pseudopatients were not identified while admitted to the mental health hospitals. (B) and (E) are incorrect because the Rosenhan study did not survey

patients or ask for their beliefs on the use of diagnostic labels. Finally, (D) is incorrect because the Rosenhan study did not assess the consistency of clinical practice.

92. B
Topic: Sensation and Perception

Soundwaves entering the ear first vibrate the tympanic membrane, which in turn causes the ossicles, the small bones in the inner ear, to vibrate. These vibrations are then transferred to a membrane called the oval window before entering the cochlea, so **(B)** is correct. The cochlea, (A), is the fluid-filled structure that contains auditory receptors. It is not itself caused to vibrate; rather, vibration of the oval window causes the fluid inside the cochlea to carry vibrations to the hair cells. The tympanic membrane is the structure that causes the ossicles to vibrate rather than being vibrated by them, so (C) can be eliminated. The basilar membrane holds the hair cells and causes them to vibrate, and so (D) is incorrect. (E) can be eliminated because it is one of the ossicles.

93. E
Topic: Developmental Psychology

Of the reflexes mentioned, all but **(E)** are expected to be observed in newborns. The Moro (outstretching of arms in response to a loud noise), Babinski (fanning of toes in response to touching the bottom of the foot), rooting (turning the head towards anything touching the cheek), and grasping (holding tightly anything touching the palm) reflexes should all be present at birth and disappear over time. Between 12 months and 2 years, the Babinski reflex should be replaced by the plantar reflex, which is the curling of toes in response to touching the bottom of the foot. **(E)** is correct.

94. B
Topic: Motivation, Emotion, and Personality

Though acute stress is characterized by high cortisol levels (as per the first two stages of the general adaptation syndrome response), chronic stress occurs during the exhaustion stage and is characterized by low cortisol levels (since it becomes depleted and does not have a chance to be replenished). Thus, **(B)** is correct. Chronic stress is associated with immunosuppression, (A), hypertension, (C), tissue damage, (D), and sleep problems, (E).

95. E

Topic: Cognitive Psychology

Face validity is a superficial measure of a test's ability to measure performance. It is considered a weak form of validity because it does not measure whether a test actually predicts performance, only whether it appears to. Because the golfing test has only been assessed superficially, **(E)** is correct. The remaining choices would require a more extensive investigation to assess. Criterion-related validity, (A), describes a test's ability to predict performance correctly. Concurrent validity, (B), is a test's ability to assess current performance, while predictive validity, (C), is used to predict future performance. Content validity, (D), refers to the extent to which a test measures the entire range of an ability.

96. E

Topic: Learning

A positive reinforcement is a pleasant stimulus that is given to increase the frequency of a behavior. The shock given here increases behavior, so it must be serving as a positive reinforcement. **(E)** is correct. (A) and (B) are incorrect because the question stem describes a type of operant conditioning, not a type of classical conditioning. (C) is incorrect because a punishment is an adverse stimulus administered to decrease the frequency of a behavior. (D) is incorrect because a negative reinforcement involves removing an adverse stimulus to increase behavior, but in this case, the rat is given a stimulus, rather than having one taken away.

97. D

Topic: Biological Bases of Behavior

The parietal lobe, located in the middle of the brain, is associated with the processing of sensory information, such as taste, temperature, pressure, touch, and pain. Thus, **(D)** is correct. The occipital lobe, located at the back of the brain, is associated with the interpretation of visual information, eliminating (A). (B) is incorrect because memory formation is associated primarily with the hippocampus in the limbic system. The temporal lobe, located on each side of the brain, contains the primary auditory cortex, which is associated with the interpretation of auditory information, eliminating (C). (E) is incorrect because the frontal lobe, located at the front of the brain, is associated with higher-level cognition.

98. A

Topic: Sensation and Perception

The key to this question is to realize what is changing and what is not. The student is transitioning from focusing on a close object to focusing on a distant object. The part of the eye responsible for accommodating for distance is the lens: the shape of the lens changes as the muscles attached to it constrict and relax, and this changes the focal point of the light entering the eye, allowing us to focus on objects at different distances. **(A)** is the only choice that mentions this mechanism, and is therefore correct. Because both the room and the exterior environment are bright, we would not expect the iris to adjust the amount of light entering the eye, so (B) can be eliminated. (C) states that cone activity would be reduced and rod activity would be increased. If anything, the opposite would be true because cones are responsible for color vision. If the book is black and white, then rod cells would be most activated while reading, and cone cells would become activated when looking at the more colorful environment; if the book itself is colorful, then no change would be expected. Either way, this choice can be eliminated. There is no reason to expect that a change in focus would change the amount of light focused on the various parts of the retina, so (D) is incorrect. Finally, (E) can be eliminated because the shape of the sclera, the white part of the eye that gives it its overall structure, does not change when focusing at different distances.

99. B

Topic: Social Psychology

When individuals are made more aware of the fact that they are part of a group working toward the same goal, they will be less likely to work as hard individually. This phenomenon is known as social loafing, **(B)**, and it best explains the experimental results. The members of Group C donated substantially less than the other two groups because they were only informed of their group's collective responsibility, not the individual responsibility of each member. (A) is incorrect because groupthink requires collective decision making, but each participant decided how much to donate individually. (C) is incorrect because social facilitation is the tendency for people to perform well-rehearsed tasks better in front of an audience, which doesn't apply here. (D) is incorrect because the participants who were told in an assembly, where the pressure to conform would reasonably be larger, actually donated less than those told individually. (E) is incorrect because self-serving bias, which refers to the tendency to attribute personal successes to dispositional factors and personal failures to situational factors, doesn't apply here.

100. C

Topic: Clinical Psychology

Karina desires to be accepted by her peers, yet she is very shy and convinced that she will embarrass herself if she attempts to be social. These are symptoms of avoidant personality disorder, **(C)**, which is characterized by social isolation and fear of social rejection. (A) is incorrect because unlike patients with avoidant personality disorder, those with borderline personality disorder have an overwhelming fear of abandonment but generally do not fear social interaction. (B) is incorrect because those with antisocial personality disorder disregard and disrespect others, while those with avoidant personality disorder wish to be accepted socially but are afraid. Those suffering from paranoid personality disorder are suspicious and mistrustful of others. Karina is fearful of interacting socially with her classmates, but she is not suspicious of them, making (D) incorrect. Finally, although schizoid and avoidant personality disorders both involve social detachment, schizoid personality disorder patients are detached emotionally as well; (E) is incorrect.

Section II

1. This question is worth 7 points: 5 points for Part A and 2 points for Part B. The following is a sample student response that would receive full credit, with indications of where points would be awarded in parentheses:

Range of reaction is the idea that while genes set out the limits of what can happen in individuals, the environment also plays a crucial role in determining the phenotypes that individuals develop. In this case, though Manuel has a family history of schizophrenia, that does not mean that his future child will necessarily have schizophrenia. This knowledge might serve to assuage Manuel's stress about having a child with schizophrenia. (**1 POINT**)

Schizophrenia manifests in multiple ways, including hallucinations, delusions, disorganized thinking, abnormal motor behavior, and negative symptoms. These are the symptoms that Manuel and Zahra would need to be on the lookout for if they chose to have a child and were worried that he or she might develop the condition. (**1 POINT**)

The hypothalamic-pituitary-adrenal axis is a key biological part of stress responses. The hypothalamus stimulates the pituitary to release a hormone that in turn stimulates the adrenal glands to release cortisol, a stress hormone. This hormone is related to short-term effects like more energy and less pain sensitivity, but over time it can cause a weakened immune system and more illness. If Manuel remains stressed in the long term, he might experience detrimental effects on his health. (**1 POINT**)

General adaptation theory states that the body adapts to long-term stress through first being alarmed, then becoming resistant to the stress response, and eventually reaching the exhaustion stage where the stress starts to take a physical toll. Since Manuel is starting to feel physically exhausted by the stress of potentially having a schizophrenic child, it seems like he has entered into the exhaustion stage of general adaptation syndrome. (**1 POINT**)

Leon Festinger proposed cognitive dissonance as an explanation for why humans experience discomfort when there is conflict in their attitudes, behaviors, thoughts, beliefs, or opinions. One of the coping mechanisms for cognitive dissonance is denial, which could be relevant here. In this case, Zahra likely experiences cognitive dissonance between her desire to have children and her dread of the risks involved, so she is choosing to deny that those risks exist by not engaging with Manuel. (**1 POINT**)

If Manuel were to seek cognitive therapy, the therapist would help Manuel examine the thought processes that led him to have anxiety about the situation he is in. He would ask Manuel to examine how his thoughts lead him to his anxiety and help him challenge any beliefs he has that lead him to have an overly anxious reaction to the situation, such as the mistaken notion that genes are destiny, which may be leading Manuel to wrongly assume that any child he has will have schizophrenia. (**1 POINT**)

If Manuel were to seek humanistic therapy, the therapist would help Manuel examine his feelings by restating the things that Manuel tells him or her and offering clarifying remarks about those feelings. The therapist would also strive to help Manuel feel more accepting of himself by offering unconditional positive regard, which may help relieve some of his anxieties about the situation. Furthermore, the therapist would use a non-directive approach that does not give advice or interpret Manuel's feelings, but instead strives to help him understand those feelings. (**1 POINT**)

2. This question is worth 7 points: 2 points for Part A, 2 points for Part B, and 3 points for Part C. The following is a sample student response that would receive full credit, with indications of where points would be awarded in parentheses:

The placebo effect arises from people believing that taking medicine will help, so they respond positively when they receive anything that they believe is medicine, even if it's just a sugar pill. In this case, giving the control group a placebo pill that has no pharmacological effect would help determine whether or not the placebo effect was occurring for the new SSRI. (**1 POINT**) The observer-expectancy effect occurs when researchers influence the results of their experiments by treating or evaluating participants differently based on knowing the group they're in. Adding a placebo drug could help limit this effect by opening up the possibility of a double-blind experimental design. In the current design, it is harder to mask from the experimenters who is getting a pill and who isn't. However, in a design in which everyone receives a pill, it is easier to hide from the experimenters who gets the real drug and who gets the placebo. Such a double-blind design would allow for limits on the observer-expectancy effect, since no one would know who is in which group until the end of the study. (**1 POINT**)

Random assignment of the children into experimental and control groups helps limit bias arising from differences in group composition. By ensuring that each group is randomly assigned instead of picked by someone, the results become more internally valid and less susceptible to some confounding factor. (**1 POINT**) The control group here is important as a comparison. If there were no control group, the reduction in depressive symptoms would exist in a vacuum, and there would be no way to distinguish the effectiveness of the therapy from that of the drug. With the control group, Dr. Schmidt can compare the reduction in depressive symptoms between the two groups, enabling her to make conclusions about her hypothesis. (**1 POINT**)

The operational definition of the dependent variable is reduction in depressive symptoms. This is the variable that is being measured and that is affected by the type of treatment received (the independent variable). (**1 POINT**) The data does not support Dr. Schmidt's conclusion because the mean reductions in depressive symptoms are very close for the two groups, and the standard deviations are relatively large. This means there is likely no significant difference between the reduction in depressive symptoms for the two groups, so the new SSRI adds little of value for those receiving cognitive behavioral therapy. (**1 POINT**)

Selective serotonin reuptake inhibitors (SSRIs) prevent serotonin from being absorbed back into upstream neurons. This means that the serotonin stays in the synaptic cleft and can continue to stimulate the downstream neuron. This has the same effect as the upstream neuron releasing more serotonin and is thus how SSRIs can strengthen the effect of serotonin. (**1 POINT**)

Practice Exam 6
Answer Grid

1. Ⓐ Ⓑ Ⓒ Ⓓ Ⓔ
2. Ⓐ Ⓑ Ⓒ Ⓓ Ⓔ
3. Ⓐ Ⓑ Ⓒ Ⓓ Ⓔ
4. Ⓐ Ⓑ Ⓒ Ⓓ Ⓔ
5. Ⓐ Ⓑ Ⓒ Ⓓ Ⓔ
6. Ⓐ Ⓑ Ⓒ Ⓓ Ⓔ
7. Ⓐ Ⓑ Ⓒ Ⓓ Ⓔ
8. Ⓐ Ⓑ Ⓒ Ⓓ Ⓔ
9. Ⓐ Ⓑ Ⓒ Ⓓ Ⓔ
10. Ⓐ Ⓑ Ⓒ Ⓓ Ⓔ
11. Ⓐ Ⓑ Ⓒ Ⓓ Ⓔ
12. Ⓐ Ⓑ Ⓒ Ⓓ Ⓔ
13. Ⓐ Ⓑ Ⓒ Ⓓ Ⓔ
14. Ⓐ Ⓑ Ⓒ Ⓓ Ⓔ
15. Ⓐ Ⓑ Ⓒ Ⓓ Ⓔ
16. Ⓐ Ⓑ Ⓒ Ⓓ Ⓔ
17. Ⓐ Ⓑ Ⓒ Ⓓ Ⓔ
18. Ⓐ Ⓑ Ⓒ Ⓓ Ⓔ
19. Ⓐ Ⓑ Ⓒ Ⓓ Ⓔ
20. Ⓐ Ⓑ Ⓒ Ⓓ Ⓔ
21. Ⓐ Ⓑ Ⓒ Ⓓ Ⓔ
22. Ⓐ Ⓑ Ⓒ Ⓓ Ⓔ
23. Ⓐ Ⓑ Ⓒ Ⓓ Ⓔ
24. Ⓐ Ⓑ Ⓒ Ⓓ Ⓔ
25. Ⓐ Ⓑ Ⓒ Ⓓ Ⓔ

26. Ⓐ Ⓑ Ⓒ Ⓓ Ⓔ
27. Ⓐ Ⓑ Ⓒ Ⓓ Ⓔ
28. Ⓐ Ⓑ Ⓒ Ⓓ Ⓔ
29. Ⓐ Ⓑ Ⓒ Ⓓ Ⓔ
30. Ⓐ Ⓑ Ⓒ Ⓓ Ⓔ
31. Ⓐ Ⓑ Ⓒ Ⓓ Ⓔ
32. Ⓐ Ⓑ Ⓒ Ⓓ Ⓔ
33. Ⓐ Ⓑ Ⓒ Ⓓ Ⓔ
34. Ⓐ Ⓑ Ⓒ Ⓓ Ⓔ
35. Ⓐ Ⓑ Ⓒ Ⓓ Ⓔ
36. Ⓐ Ⓑ Ⓒ Ⓓ Ⓔ
37. Ⓐ Ⓑ Ⓒ Ⓓ Ⓔ
38. Ⓐ Ⓑ Ⓒ Ⓓ Ⓔ
39. Ⓐ Ⓑ Ⓒ Ⓓ Ⓔ
40. Ⓐ Ⓑ Ⓒ Ⓓ Ⓔ
41. Ⓐ Ⓑ Ⓒ Ⓓ Ⓔ
42. Ⓐ Ⓑ Ⓒ Ⓓ Ⓔ
43. Ⓐ Ⓑ Ⓒ Ⓓ Ⓔ
44. Ⓐ Ⓑ Ⓒ Ⓓ Ⓔ
45. Ⓐ Ⓑ Ⓒ Ⓓ Ⓔ
46. Ⓐ Ⓑ Ⓒ Ⓓ Ⓔ
47. Ⓐ Ⓑ Ⓒ Ⓓ Ⓔ
48. Ⓐ Ⓑ Ⓒ Ⓓ Ⓔ
49. Ⓐ Ⓑ Ⓒ Ⓓ Ⓔ
50. Ⓐ Ⓑ Ⓒ Ⓓ Ⓔ

51. Ⓐ Ⓑ Ⓒ Ⓓ Ⓔ
52. Ⓐ Ⓑ Ⓒ Ⓓ Ⓔ
53. Ⓐ Ⓑ Ⓒ Ⓓ Ⓔ
54. Ⓐ Ⓑ Ⓒ Ⓓ Ⓔ
55. Ⓐ Ⓑ Ⓒ Ⓓ Ⓔ
56. Ⓐ Ⓑ Ⓒ Ⓓ Ⓔ
57. Ⓐ Ⓑ Ⓒ Ⓓ Ⓔ
58. Ⓐ Ⓑ Ⓒ Ⓓ Ⓔ
59. Ⓐ Ⓑ Ⓒ Ⓓ Ⓔ
60. Ⓐ Ⓑ Ⓒ Ⓓ Ⓔ
61. Ⓐ Ⓑ Ⓒ Ⓓ Ⓔ
62. Ⓐ Ⓑ Ⓒ Ⓓ Ⓔ
63. Ⓐ Ⓑ Ⓒ Ⓓ Ⓔ
64. Ⓐ Ⓑ Ⓒ Ⓓ Ⓔ
65. Ⓐ Ⓑ Ⓒ Ⓓ Ⓔ
66. Ⓐ Ⓑ Ⓒ Ⓓ Ⓔ
67. Ⓐ Ⓑ Ⓒ Ⓓ Ⓔ
68. Ⓐ Ⓑ Ⓒ Ⓓ Ⓔ
69. Ⓐ Ⓑ Ⓒ Ⓓ Ⓔ
70. Ⓐ Ⓑ Ⓒ Ⓓ Ⓔ
71. Ⓐ Ⓑ Ⓒ Ⓓ Ⓔ
72. Ⓐ Ⓑ Ⓒ Ⓓ Ⓔ
73. Ⓐ Ⓑ Ⓒ Ⓓ Ⓔ
74. Ⓐ Ⓑ Ⓒ Ⓓ Ⓔ
75. Ⓐ Ⓑ Ⓒ Ⓓ Ⓔ

76. Ⓐ Ⓑ Ⓒ Ⓓ Ⓔ
77. Ⓐ Ⓑ Ⓒ Ⓓ Ⓔ
78. Ⓐ Ⓑ Ⓒ Ⓓ Ⓔ
79. Ⓐ Ⓑ Ⓒ Ⓓ Ⓔ
80. Ⓐ Ⓑ Ⓒ Ⓓ Ⓔ
81. Ⓐ Ⓑ Ⓒ Ⓓ Ⓔ
82. Ⓐ Ⓑ Ⓒ Ⓓ Ⓔ
83. Ⓐ Ⓑ Ⓒ Ⓓ Ⓔ
84. Ⓐ Ⓑ Ⓒ Ⓓ Ⓔ
85. Ⓐ Ⓑ Ⓒ Ⓓ Ⓔ
86. Ⓐ Ⓑ Ⓒ Ⓓ Ⓔ
87. Ⓐ Ⓑ Ⓒ Ⓓ Ⓔ
88. Ⓐ Ⓑ Ⓒ Ⓓ Ⓔ
89. Ⓐ Ⓑ Ⓒ Ⓓ Ⓔ
90. Ⓐ Ⓑ Ⓒ Ⓓ Ⓔ
91. Ⓐ Ⓑ Ⓒ Ⓓ Ⓔ
92. Ⓐ Ⓑ Ⓒ Ⓓ Ⓔ
93. Ⓐ Ⓑ Ⓒ Ⓓ Ⓔ
94. Ⓐ Ⓑ Ⓒ Ⓓ Ⓔ
95. Ⓐ Ⓑ Ⓒ Ⓓ Ⓔ
96. Ⓐ Ⓑ Ⓒ Ⓓ Ⓔ
97. Ⓐ Ⓑ Ⓒ Ⓓ Ⓔ
98. Ⓐ Ⓑ Ⓒ Ⓓ Ⓔ
99. Ⓐ Ⓑ Ⓒ Ⓓ Ⓔ
100. Ⓐ Ⓑ Ⓒ Ⓓ Ⓔ

SECTION I
70 Minutes—100 Questions
Percent of total grade: 66⅔

Directions Answer the following 100 questions in 70 minutes. Select the best answer for each and fill in the corresponding letter on your answer grid or a sheet of scratch paper.

1. Which of the following best describes the level of intellectual disability of an adult with an IQ of 50?

    (A) The individual is able to live independently.

    (B) The individual can only complete a handful of basic tasks alone.

    (C) The individual's academic performance is similar to that of an eight-year-old.

    (D) The individual is unable to communicate verbally.

    (E) The individual has an exceptional ability in one area despite limited intellectual capacity.

2. Which psychological perspectives on language do Noam Chomsky's and B.F. Skinner's ideas best represent, respectively?

    (A) Humanistic and behavioral

    (B) Sociocultural and biological

    (C) Biological and behavioral

    (D) Behavioral and biological

    (E) Biological and humanistic

3. Jack's score on his latest math test is one standard deviation above the mean. Jack's exam score would be closest to which of the following percentile values?

    (A) 20th

    (B) 33rd

    (C) 50th

    (D) 66th

    (E) 90th

4. A person approaches an elevator and presses the button to summon it. The elevator is slow to arrive, so the person continues to press the button a total of seven times before the elevator arrives. The next day, the same scenario is repeated, except that the elevator arrives after four button presses. If an operant conditioning researcher were to examine this scenario, he would probably argue that this is most analogous to a

    (A) fixed ratio schedule

    (B) fixed interval schedule

    (C) fixed frequency schedule

    (D) variable interval schedule

    (E) variable ratio schedule

5. Which of the following provides the best evidence for discontinuous development in children?

    (A) Children increase the complexity of their sentences gradually as they learn words.

    (B) Infants who previously lacked object permanence begin to recognize object permanence.

    (C) Children increase in height from infancy to adolescence.

    (D) Children learn independence by slowly gaining more responsibility around the house.

    (E) Toddlers increase their coordination until they can walk without support.

GO ON TO THE NEXT PAGE

6. Which of the following researchers conducted the Bobo doll experiment and demonstrated that aggression is learned by observing and modeling others?

    (A) John Garcia

    (B) Ivan Pavlov

    (C) Robert Rescorla

    (D) Albert Bandura

    (E) Edward Tolman

7. What are the two steps for modifying the schemata that children develop, according to Jean Piaget?

    (A) Denial and utilization

    (B) Assimilation and accommodation

    (C) Differentiation and disillusion

    (D) Bargaining and acceptance

    (E) Preoperation and conservation

8. Which of the following psychological disorders is more prevalent in men than in women?

    (A) Major depressive disorder

    (B) Panic disorder

    (C) Borderline personality disorder

    (D) Antisocial personality disorder

    (E) Posttraumatic stress disorder

9. A professor creates a new biology exam and wants to investigate it by using a test-retest reliability method. Which of the following scenarios would best achieve that goal?

    (A) The professor creates two different versions of the exam and administers them to two different groups of students at different times.

    (B) The professor creates two different versions of the exam and administers them to the same group of students.

    (C) The professor administers the same version of the exam to two different groups of students.

    (D) The professor administers the same version of the exam to the same group of students at two different times.

    (E) The professor creates two different versions of the exam and administers them to two different groups of students simultaneously.

10. A woman collapses suddenly on a subway platform. Based on social psychological research, which of the following would most likely transpire?

    (A) If there are relatively few people on the platform, then it is less likely that someone would approach the woman to help.

    (B) If there are no other women on the platform, then it is less likely that someone would approach the woman to help.

    (C) If there are lots of people on the platform, then it is less likely that someone would approach the woman to help.

    (D) If there are lots of people on the platform, then it is more likely that someone would approach the woman to help.

    (E) If the woman is from a foreign country, then she would likely only be helped by people from that same country.

GO ON TO THE NEXT PAGE

11. A researcher places a rat in a maze with no exit. After multiple attempts, the rat stops trying to escape the maze and simply sits in one place. The researcher then transfers the rat into a very simple maze with a clear exit, but the rat still makes no attempt to escape. This phenomenon can best be characterized as an example of

    (A) superstitious behavior

    (B) accidental conditioning

    (C) learned helplessness

    (D) emotional learning

    (E) systematic desensitization

12. Which theory of developmental psychology was proposed by Sigmund Freud?

    (A) Attachment theory

    (B) Social development theory

    (C) Psychosexual development theory

    (D) Cognitive development theory

    (E) Moral development theory

13. Susto, also called a "spirit attack," is a unique collection of physiological and psychological symptoms following an emotional event. It is commonly observed only in Latin American countries and is typically treated using folk remedies such as locally available herbs. Which of the following terms best describes this phenomenon?

    (A) Biomedical approach

    (B) Anxiety disorder

    (C) Posttraumatic stress disorder

    (D) Culture-bound syndrome

    (E) Biopsychosocial approach

14. After seeing a news report on skydiving, Mandy starts to believe that skydiving is dangerous. While on vacation, Mandy refuses to let her son go skydiving because she believes he will get injured; instead she takes him on a scenic drive around the island. Research has shown that motor vehicle accidents account for significantly more deaths each year than skydiving accidents. Which of the following would best explain Mandy's misconception?

    (A) Confirmation bias

    (B) Cognitive dissonance

    (C) The fundamental attribution error

    (D) The representativeness heuristic

    (E) The availability heuristic

GO ON TO THE NEXT PAGE

15. A study randomly assigned participants to one of two groups. Group 1 is asked to play a video game while completing the study, while Group 2 is asked to complete the study in silence. Both groups are read a set of words by the researcher and then asked to recall as many words as possible 30 seconds later. The results are listed in the table below.

Participant #	Group #	# Words Recalled
1	1	4
2	1	3
3	2	7
4	1	5
5	2	8
6	2	7
7	2	6
8	1	4
9	1	2
10	2	6

Which of the following concepts best accounts for the differences between the two groups?

(A) Shallow processing

(B) Inattentional blindness

(C) Selective attention

(D) Reticular formation

(E) Divided attention

16. Suppose a child psychologist conducts a study on the effects of exercise on IQ by randomly assigning children to groups that differ only in the hours of exercise they do each week. In this experiment, the number of hours of exercise would be the

(A) confounding variable

(B) population

(C) sample

(D) dependent variable

(E) independent variable

17. Which of the following concepts describes an individual's capacity to be influenced by information that is not consciously perceived?

(A) Hindsight bias

(B) Signal detection theory

(C) Just-noticeable difference

(D) Linear perspective

(E) Subliminal processing

GO ON TO THE NEXT PAGE

Questions 18–19 are based on the following.

An education company interviewed and hired a man named Karl for a position that recently opened up. One of the company interviewers reported the following after Karl's interview:

"Karl is well-dressed and well-groomed for the interview, which demonstrates a strong sense of professionalism and cleanliness in his words and actions. He also confidently cites his strong work ethic, perseverance, and creativity as reasons for his success in past employment."

A few months after being hired, Karl underwent a preliminary performance evaluation. One of his coworkers, a veteran of the company known for her reliability and forthrightness, reported the following during the evaluation process:

"Karl routinely shows up late for work, typically with no apology or excuse. He is often under-dressed, usually showing up to work in a t-shirt and sweatpants, and distracts other coworkers with inappropriate banter. The assignments he completes are frequently unpolished, but when you call his attention to this, he claims that he's being pulled in too many directions by competing priorities. Karl's desk area is so disorganized and slovenly that he recently caused an ant infestation at the office."

18. The interviewer made a dispositional attribution to explain Karl's professional appearance in the interview. Which of the following best explains why a situational attribution would be more appropriate for Karl's interview behavior?

(A) Karl's actual work habits diverged widely from his behavior during the interview.

(B) The coworker who evaluated Karl disliked him for arbitrary personal reasons.

(C) Karl got divorced shortly after starting the job and lost his passion for work.

(D) The quoted interviewer knew Karl from another job at which they both worked.

(E) Karl had no prior experience working in the education business.

19. Which of the following does Karl most clearly demonstrate in the explanations he gives for his own behavior, as reported by the interviewer and the coworker?

(A) The just-world hypothesis

(B) The fundamental attribution error

(C) The availability heuristic

(D) Nonresponse bias

(E) Self-serving bias

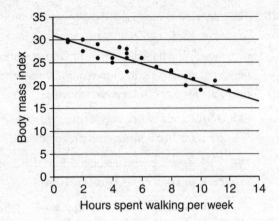

20. For a school project, Mia surveyed 25 of her classmates about their weekly activity level and their BMI. Some of her results are presented in the graph above. Which of the following could most reasonably be the correlation coefficient of the data presented in the above graph?

   (A) −1

   (B) −0.67

   (C) 0

   (D) 0.33

   (E) 1

21. Which of the following does NOT provide a reasonable explanation of altruism?

   (A) People behave altruistically toward people they know because they expect favors to be repaid later.

   (B) People behave altruistically toward family because there is an evolutionary benefit in helping kin.

   (C) People behave altruistically toward others because the benefits they experience are greater than the costs.

   (D) People behave altruistically toward others because displays of kindness are attractive to potential mates.

   (E) People behave altruistically toward others because they fear being called out as freeloaders.

22. Carl Wernicke found that damage to which area of the brain can disrupt an individual's ability to comprehend spoken words?

   (A) The right occipital lobe

   (B) The left frontal lobe

   (C) The thalamus

   (D) The left temporal lobe

   (E) The right parietal lobe

23. In 1848, Phineas Gage was working as a railroad foreman when an explosion drove an iron rod into his skull and through his frontal lobe. Miraculously, Gage survived, but he had several impairments following his accident. Which of the following resulted from the damage to Gage's frontal lobe?

   (A) Inability to hear high frequencies

   (B) Trouble with hand-eye coordination

   (C) Difficulty maintaining balance

   (D) Loss of appetite

   (E) Changes in personality

24. Tom regularly visits a psychodynamic therapist to address Tom's hostile disposition toward his father. After a few weeks, Tom begins to develop a hostile attitude towards the therapist, who he sees as acting silmilarly to his father. This situation is an example of

   (A) self-actualization

   (B) transference

   (C) free association

   (D) cognitive distortion

   (E) systematic desensitization

GO ON TO THE NEXT PAGE

25. Priscilla knowingly tries to deny her anxiety regarding heights while riding an airplane. Based on the structural model, which of the following is she most likely demonstrating?

   (A) Repression

   (B) Sublimation

   (C) Rationalization

   (D) Suppression

   (E) Regression

26. Which of the following situations most clearly illustrates the concept of intrinsic motivation?

   (A) Edgar, who dislikes being judged negatively by other people, did not attend a party.

   (B) Krystal, who is a restaurant server, worked overtime only to make more money.

   (C) Robert, who dislikes his aunt, nevertheless took her shopping out of a sense of obligation.

   (D) Isabel, who donated money to a charity group, wanted to be recognized for that action.

   (E) Julian, who enjoys gardening, spent the afternoon in his garden planting vegetables.

27. A psychologist is studying how seeing simple pictures affects patients' responses to a set of complex images. She presents different sets of simple images and then asks her patients what they see. Next, she presents the same set of complex images to each patient and asks what they see. She finds that patients who see the same set of simple images before viewing the complex images will often interpret the complex images similarly. This is an example of perceptions being influenced by

   (A) perceptual hypotheses

   (B) the principle of closure

   (C) similarity grouping

   (D) proximity grouping

   (E) figure-ground relationships

28. Which of the following properly characterizes the process by which action potentials are generated during gustation?

   (A) Fluid moves within the semicircular canals, which stimulates hair cells.

   (B) Pressure makes the cell membranes of nerve receptor cells more porous to ions.

   (C) Chemical compounds come into contact with receptor cells in the nose.

   (D) Chemical compounds come into contact with receptor cells on the tongue.

   (E) Hair cells in the cochlea react to vibrations within the cochlear fluid.

GO ON TO THE NEXT PAGE

29. Pàula was recently diagnosed with conversion disorder. Which of the following best describes the symptoms Pàula may be experiencing?

    (A) Impulsivity, difficulty concentrating, poor time management skills

    (B) Lack of empathy, low self-esteem, skewed perspective on her self-worth

    (C) Mood swings, preoccupation with physical appearance, extreme extroversion

    (D) Weight changes, anhedonia, excessive guilt

    (E) Unexplained inhibition of voluntary functions

30. When you are moderately excited, you are more likely to perform optimally. This is an example of

    (A) the Yerkes-Dodson law

    (B) the Hawthorne effect

    (C) instinct theory

    (D) actor-observer bias

    (E) incentive theory

31. A teacher recommends that her class use the spacing effect to remember the key terms on their upcoming psychology exam. Which of the following students successfully applies this technique?

    (A) Ahmad studies the vocabulary words for 30 minutes per night for the week leading up to the exam.

    (B) Anne places each vocabulary word in the context of her own life experience.

    (C) John visualizes the page on the textbook where the words appeared while taking the test.

    (D) Tomás recites the vocabulary words for an hour before the exam.

    (E) Sarah links the new vocabulary words to similar words she learned for the last test.

32. A woman has two sons, aged 9 and 11. If both children score a 110 on the Stanford-Binet IQ Test, then

    (A) only the 9-year-old's mental age is greater than his actual age

    (B) only the 11-year-old's mental age is greater than his actual age

    (C) only the 9-year-old's mental age is less than his actual age

    (D) only the 11-year-old's mental age is less than his actual age

    (E) both children have higher mental ages than actual ages

33. Valentina is a medical student who easily applies what she learned in the classroom to a patient setting. Valentina is showing a high level of

    (A) analytical intelligence

    (B) practical intelligence

    (C) fluid intelligence

    (D) intrapersonal intelligence

    (E) musical-rhythmic intelligence

34. The ultimate goal of humanistic therapy is

    (A) empowerment

    (B) cognitive restructuring

    (C) self-esteem

    (D) reducing repression

    (E) self-actualization

GO ON TO THE NEXT PAGE

35. In which of the following scenarios does a researcher most clearly violate ethical guidelines regarding research participation?

    (A) A researcher uses children in an experiment.

    (B) A researcher exposes patients to a drug that may have side effects.

    (C) A researcher tells his wife that one of his participants is in her yoga class.

    (D) A researcher does not let patients participate unless they sign a consent form.

    (E) A researcher tells participants which church he attends every Sunday.

36. Alvin is in a backpacking club, and the group is planning on a camping trip. Unfortunately for Alvin, the camping trip conflicts with his classes, and he decides not to go. Alvin's hiking partner in the club asks Alvin to skip class to come on the trip anyway. If Alvin goes on this trip, it would be an example of

    (A) groupthink

    (B) obedience

    (C) compliance

    (D) conformity

    (E) authority

37. In which of the following situations would a longitudinal study be the most appropriate research approach?

    (A) A researcher wants to study a patient who appears at his clinic with a rare disorder.

    (B) A researcher wants to study how adolescent behavior changes from middle to high school.

    (C) A researcher wants to investigate the side effects of a new blood pressure medication.

    (D) A researcher wants to establish a causal relationship between parenting style and childhood depression.

    (E) A researcher wants to publish her results in a scientific journal.

38. Presbycusis is the natural hearing loss observed in mammals as they age; it is usually high-pitched tones that are lost. Degeneration of what auditory structure normally causes this condition?

    (A) Pinna

    (B) Eustachian tube

    (C) Ossicles

    (D) Cochlea

    (E) Semicircular canals

39. Which of the following psychologists developed the idea of a universal grammar?

    (A) Noam Chomsky

    (B) Wolfgang Köhler

    (C) Sigmund Freud

    (D) Konrad Lorenz

    (E) Jean Piaget

GO ON TO THE NEXT PAGE

Questions 40–43 are based on the following.

Human nervous systems have many different subdivisions. The first major division is between the central nervous system and the peripheral nervous system. The brain, which is part of the central nervous system, is divided into three parts: forebrain, midbrain, and hindbrain. In the peripheral nervous system, sensory neurons are afferent neurons that take information towards the central nervous system. Motor neurons are efferent neurons that take information away from the central nervous system and towards their targets, such as muscles and glands.

40. Which of the following would NOT be found in the forebrain?

    (A) The auditory cortex

    (B) The limbic system

    (C) The medulla

    (D) The thalamus

    (E) Wernicke's area

41. Which of the following is NOT a part of the peripheral nervous system?

    (A) The autonomic nervous system

    (B) The optic nerve

    (C) The parasympathetic nervous system

    (D) The spinal cord

    (E) The sympathetic nervous system

42. Before a neurotransmitter is released by an efferent neuron, where does the neuron store those neurotransmitters?

    (A) In the synapse

    (B) In the cell body

    (C) Along the axon

    (D) In synaptic vesicles

    (E) In the myelin sheath

43. An afferent neuron is sending multiple signals that something is crawling on Jodie's arm. What must happen to the central nervous system neuron receiving signals from this afferent neuron before the sensation that something is on Jodie's arm will register in her brain?

    (A) The central nervous system neuron must become hyperpolarized.

    (B) The afferent neuron must become hyperpolarized.

    (C) The central nervous system neuron must reach the threshold potential.

    (D) The afferent neuron must reach resting potential.

    (E) The central nervous system neuron must reach resting potential.

44. A personality researcher asks 500 participants to each rate how much they identify with the statement, "I have experienced at least one unpleasant event in my life." All 500 participants responded that they strongly identified with that statement. This finding best illustrates which of the following?

    (A) Neuroticism

    (B) Reciprocal determinism

    (C) The Barnum effect

    (D) Reaction formation

    (E) Basic hostility

45. Which aspect of the structural model is responsible for causing feelings of pride when an individual overcomes the urges of the id?

    (A) Ego

    (B) Reality principle

    (C) Pleasure principle

    (D) Ego-ideal

    (E) Conscience

GO ON TO THE NEXT PAGE

46. Which of the following statements about emotions is best supported by psychological research?

    (A) They tend to disappear within a few hours.

    (B) They almost never motivate people to take actions.

    (C) They contain either positive or negative elements, but not both.

    (D) They rarely change the ways in which people think.

    (E) They tend to have little variation in intensity.

47. Which of the following would be classified as a depressive disorder in the DSM-5?

    (A) Body dysmorphic disorder

    (B) Depersonalization/derealization disorder

    (C) Anorexia nervosa

    (D) Dysthymia

    (E) Cyclothymic disorder

48. According to the Big Five model, the factor of neuroticism exists on a continuum from

    (A) detached to friendly

    (B) careless to organized

    (C) nonconforming to socialized

    (D) cautious to curious

    (E) anxious to stable

49. Which of the following theorists is best known for studying how parenting styles affect children's development?

    (A) Harry Harlow

    (B) Mary Ainsworth

    (C) Konrad Lorenz

    (D) Diana Baumrind

    (E) Albert Bandura

50. Attention deficit hyperactivity disorder is classified in the DSM-5 as a

    (A) neurodevelopmental disorder

    (B) personality disorder

    (C) trauma- and stressor-related disorder

    (D) anxiety disorder

    (E) dissociative disorder

51. According to Maslow's hierarchy of needs, ensuring the security of one's family generally must occur

    (A) before satisfying the need for emotional connection in one's family

    (B) after satisfying the need for a feeling of accomplishment

    (C) while satisfying the need for emotional connection in one's family

    (D) before satisfying the need for shelter

    (E) after satisfying the need for emotional connection in one's family

52. After the initial fight-or-flight response to a stressful event, the body begins to normalize. Which stage of general adaptation syndrome does this correspond to?

    (A) Exhaustion

    (B) Alarm

    (C) Recovery

    (D) Resistance

    (E) Homeostasis

GO ON TO THE NEXT PAGE

53. A gym teacher measured the amount of time six students took to run a mile and recorded the following results, in minutes: 5, 7, 7, 9, 10, 13. What was the median amount of time, in minutes, that these students took to run a mile?

    (A) 7

    (B) 7.5

    (C) 8

    (D) 8.5

    (E) 9

54. Which of the following best characterizes a difference between bipolar I and bipolar II?

    (A) Bipolar I is classified as a severe disorder, while bipolar II is a mild disorder.

    (B) Only patients with bipolar II must experience depressive episodes.

    (C) Patients with bipolar I experience dysthymic episodes, while those with bipolar II experience depressive episodes.

    (D) Only patients with bipolar I can have periods of mania.

    (E) Bipolar I must be treated in a psychiatric facility, while bipolar II patients can benefit from outpatient therapies.

55. Following a traumatic brain injury from an accident at work, Michael is told by his doctor that he is suffering from retrograde amnesia. Assuming this diagnosis is correct, one week after the accident, Michael would most likely not remember

    (A) how to ride a bike

    (B) where he put his car keys the night before

    (C) details of a family vacation he went on as a child

    (D) a list of words he is asked to repeat

    (E) his name and other autobiographical information

56. A researcher conditions a child to be afraid of white rats by pairing the display of a white rat with a loud noise. After a while, the child also becomes afraid of other animals with white fur. This is an example of

    (A) acquisition

    (B) stimulus discrimination

    (C) extinction

    (D) stimulus generalization

    (E) spontaneous recovery

57. Mr. Talikov notices that whenever he tries to teach mathematics in his class, the students are less likely to pay attention to the lesson; instead, the students talk amongst themselves. When Mr. Talikov promises to remove one of the quizzes from the course as a reward if the amount of talking between students is decreased, the class becomes much more attentive when learning mathematics. In this scenario, the act of removing one of the quizzes serves as

    (A) positive reinforcement

    (B) negative reinforcement

    (C) positive punishment

    (D) negative punishment

    (E) extinction

GO ON TO THE NEXT PAGE

58. After a molecule enters the nose, what is the pathway of the signal that produces olfaction in the brain?

    (A) Olfactory bulb > olfactory receptor > olfactory cortex

    (B) Olfactory cortex > olfactory bulb > olfactory receptor

    (C) Olfactory receptor > olfactory cortex > olfactory bulb

    (D) Olfactory bulb > olfactory cortex > olfactory receptor

    (E) Olfactory receptor > olfactory bulb > olfactory cortex

59. Tamara refuses to purchase health insurance because she believes that she will not become sick enough to require it. Later that year, however, she catches a particularly nasty form of flu and has to be hospitalized for several days. After this situation, Tamara would most likely be experiencing

    (A) hostile aggression toward family and friends

    (B) instrumental aggression toward the medical profession

    (C) cognitive dissonance

    (D) role conflict

    (E) the fundamental attribution error

60. Which of the following best characterizes the difference between internal and external validity?

    (A) Internal validity indicates whether a study measures what it is supposed to, while external validity determines how a particular variable will be measured.

    (B) Internal validity indicates whether an observational study or an experiment is used, while external validity indicates whether results are generalizable to the population.

    (C) Internal validity indicates whether results are generalizable to the population, while external validity indicates whether a study measures what it is supposed to.

    (D) Internal validity determines how a particular variable will be measured, while external validity determines how variables will be statistically analyzed.

    (E) Internal validity indicates whether a study measures what it is supposed to, while external validity indicates whether results are generalizable to the population.

61. In a quiet room, a person can detect a 1-decibel change in sound intensity, while in a large noisy theater, a larger difference in intensity is needed to detect a difference. This is best considered as an example of

    (A) an absolute threshold

    (B) a subliminal message

    (C) a difference threshold

    (D) sensory adaptation

    (E) transduction

GO ON TO THE NEXT PAGE

62. The type of study most capable of providing evidence of a causal relationship between variables is known as a

    (A) longitudinal study

    (B) cross-sectional study

    (C) controlled experiment

    (D) naturalistic observation

    (E) field experiment

63. A teacher administers a 100-question multiple-choice practice exam to her AP Psychology class. Since the practice test is long, the teacher divides the questions equally over two days. If scores were significantly better on the second day's portion of the exam, the test shows low levels of

    (A) split-half reliability

    (B) equivalent-form reliability

    (C) content validity

    (D) predictive validity

    (E) concurrent validity

64. A researcher replicates part of Mary Ainsworth's Strange Situation study: a mother brings her child into a room with toys, a stranger enters that room, the mother leaves the child in the room, and eventually the mother comes back to comfort the child. If the child did not change behavior when the mother was gone, and if the child was slow to show a positive reaction when the mother reentered the room to comfort the child, what type of attachment would there most likely be between mother and child?

    (A) Secure attachment

    (B) Avoidant attachment

    (C) Ambivalent attachment

    (D) Disorganized attachment

    (E) Permissive attachment

65. Which of the following is a behaviorist known for the law of effect, which served as the foundation for Skinner's operant conditioning theory?

    (A) Albert Bandura

    (B) Edward Tolman

    (C) Robert Rescorla

    (D) Edward Thorndike

    (E) John Watson

GO ON TO THE NEXT PAGE

Questions 66–69 refer to the following.

Participants in a research study were shown a short video clip of a convenience store robbery and instructed to remember as much as they could about the incident, especially the dialogue between the robber and the store clerk. Below is the transcript of the dialogue:

ROBBER: [shows gun] Get back and take out the money!
CLERK: Oh my...
ROBBER: Shut up if you don't want to get shot!
CLERK: Hey man, calm down, I'm...
ROBBER: Shut up and hurry up!
CLERK: Please don't shoot!
ROBBER: Hurry up. Fill this bag.
CLERK: Don't shoot, man! Don't shoot!
ROBBER: I told you to shut up if you don't want to die. Hurry it up!
CLERK: Okay! Okay! Don't shoot!
ROBBER: Put some drinks in the bag, and take off your watch.
CLERK: What?
ROBBER: I said take off your watch, are you deaf?
CLERK: Okay, okay! Just don't shoot, please don't shoot!
ROBBER: Come on, hurry up!

Two weeks later, participants were brought in for questioning about the event. The participants were separated into two groups, sorted randomly. The first group was asked, "When the robber was yelling at the clerk, what did the clerk keep repeating?" The second group was asked, "When the robber was talking to the clerk, what did the clerk keep repeating?"

66. Which of the following demonstrates the primacy effect?

(A) Participants have an easier time recalling the clothing of the robber versus the clothing of the clerk.

(B) Participants have an easier time recalling the first thing the robber said.

(C) Participants have an easier time recalling the last thing that transpired in the exchange.

(D) The clerk repeats "don't shoot" multiple times to reinforce this idea for the robber.

(E) Participants have an easier time recalling big features than small details of the event.

67. Which of the following could the researchers do to incorporate the concept of priming to facilitate participants' recall of the events in the short video clip?

(A) Ask participants to recall a separate memory from their youth first.

(B) Have participants do various mental games before recalling the video clip.

(C) Encourage participants to recall the events in reverse order.

(D) Induce a happy emotion in participants before having them recall the video clip.

(E) Take participants to the same convenience store shown in the video before recall.

GO ON TO THE NEXT PAGE

68. Researchers found that participants in the first group were more likely to recall the robber being more aggressive than he actually was, while participants in the second group were more likely to recall the robber being less aggressive than he actually was. Which of the following is most likely responsible for this difference?

    (A) Proactive interference

    (B) The misinformation effect

    (C) Retroactive interference

    (D) Source amnesia

    (E) Repression

69. Many of the participants in the study seemed to have formed false memories of the events. Which psychologist is known for the study of false memory formation?

    (A) David Dunning

    (B) George A. Miller

    (C) Howard Gardner

    (D) Elizabeth Loftus

    (E) Philip Zimbardo

70. Which of the following is another word for an evolved trait, according to Darwin's theory of evolution?

    (A) Fitness

    (B) Adaptation

    (C) Variation

    (D) Natural selection

    (E) Inheritance

71. Which theory of motivation focuses in part on avoiding punishments?

    (A) James-Lange theory

    (B) Incentive theory

    (C) Drive-reduction theory

    (D) Instinct theory

    (E) Arousal theory

72. A psychological researcher wants to determine whether people who are at least 70 years of age differ significantly from those who are under 70 years of age on the personality factor of openness to experience. The researcher would most likely use which of the following approaches?

    (A) Open-ended question survey

    (B) Unstructured interview

    (C) Personal diary

    (D) Case study

    (E) Close-ended question inventory

73. Based on Ekman's research, which of the following situations can best be characterized as the direct expression of a basic emotion?

    (A) Bret scrunches his nose in distaste when he smells spoiled food in his refrigerator.

    (B) Mia discusses her excitement with her friend about getting to go on a family vacation.

    (C) Wayne feels jealous that his coworker received a promotion at work.

    (D) Louisa feels tired after studying for a major academic exam.

    (E) Ernest is bored and stares blankly at his television screen for several hours.

GO ON TO THE NEXT PAGE

74. Obsessive-compulsive personality disorder (OCPD) is classified by the DSM-5 as

    (A) a Cluster A personality disorder

    (B) a Cluster B personality disorder

    (C) a Cluster C personality disorder

    (D) an obsessive-compulsive and related disorder

    (E) an anxiety disorder

75. Which of the following measures would be an example of a primary prevention strategy for adolescent nicotine use?

    (A) Offering smoking cessation programs in schools

    (B) Advertising the connection between smoking and lung cancer

    (C) Providing nicotine patches in schools

    (D) Regulating a decrease in the nicotine content of cigarettes

    (E) Educating parents to identify adolescent nicotine use

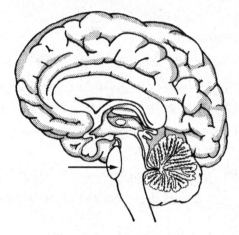

76. The arrow in the above illustration is pointing to which part of the brain?

    (A) Parietal lobe

    (B) Corpus callosum

    (C) Midbrain

    (D) Pons

    (E) Cerebral cortex

77. An agency discovers that black patients are more likely than white patients to quit therapy after the first session. Which of the following strategies would NOT be recommended to address this discrepancy?

    (A) Reduce potential barriers to accessing services

    (B) Encourage cognitive therapy techniques

    (C) Practice Afrocentric therapy techniques

    (D) Employ social justice therapy techniques

    (E) Provide racial sensitivity training to therapists

GO ON TO THE NEXT PAGE

78. A CT scan is most appropriate for which of the following?

    (A) To study metabolic activity in the brain

    (B) To observe changes in the brain while performing a task

    (C) To obtain a detailed, high–resolution image of neural soft tissue

    (D) To image a complex tumor

    (E) To record electrical activity in the brain

79. Which of the following would probably have the least influence on the height of an adolescent child?

    (A) Diet and nutrition

    (B) Medical conditions

    (C) Parenting style

    (D) Biological sex

    (E) Parental height

80. Which of the following best describes a famous experiment conducted by Philip Zimbardo?

    (A) Participants administered electric shocks of increasing voltage to an actor to gauge their obedience.

    (B) Student participants were assigned roles as prisoners or guards in a simulated jail environment.

    (C) Two opposing groups of boys at summer camp were brought together through cooperative projects.

    (D) Female students were reminded of a false and malicious stereotype prior to taking a math exam.

    (E) Participants judged the length of lines in the presence of confederates who deliberately judged wrongly.

81. John B. Watson's Little Albert study pioneered which psychological approach?

    (A) The sociocultural approach

    (B) Behaviorism

    (C) Functionalism

    (D) Structuralism

    (E) The psychodynamic approach

82. Which of the following correctly matches a structure of the eye with its function?

    (A) Fovea: a small indentation in the retina with a large number of cones

    (B) Iris: a small opening that allows light to enter the eye

    (C) Pupil: a transparent covering on the front of the eye

    (D) Lens: the colored portion of the eye that controls the size of its aperture

    (E) Cornea: a clear, curved structure in the eye that helps focus light on the retina

83. Which of the following could best be characterized as an example of ethnocentrism?

    (A) An American tourist is disgusted by a Peruvian dish, roasted whole guinea pig, because she believes that guinea pigs should only be kept as pets.

    (B) An ambassador from Italy insists that the olive oil made in Italy is much better tasting than olive oil made in California.

    (C) A political rally for a particular candidate is held in a partisan city that supports the candidate instead of a more neutral city.

    (D) A multinational corporation decides to exploit a recent fad in Asian media by launching several fad-themed promotions.

    (E) A religious group petitions outside of the capitol building, demanding equal treatment under the law for their group.

GO ON TO THE NEXT PAGE ⇒

84. A humanistic psychologist would most likely contend that, in the face of adversity,

    (A) parents play an important role in shaping their children's responses

    (B) people with high levels of serotonin will respond better than those with low levels

    (C) individuals are free to choose how to respond to the adverse situation

    (D) past experience will condition how a person responds to the new adverse event

    (E) unconscious conflicts influence whether a person develops anxiety

85. Suppose that your therapist focuses on childhood experiences, encourages cognitive restructuring, and employs unconditional positive regard. Which of the following would best describe your therapist's approach?

    (A) Eclectic

    (B) Cognitive

    (C) Psychodynamic

    (D) Humanistic

    (E) Mixed

86. A professor is interested in researching whether the ratio of time spent in REM sleep to time spent in NREM sleep influences the frequency of depressive symptoms in teenagers. Which psychological perspective best characterizes this research?

    (A) The biological approach

    (B) The cognitive approach

    (C) Behaviorism

    (D) Gestalt psychology

    (E) Psychoanalysis

87. Which of the following is a measure of the dispersion, or spread, of a dataset?

    (A) Correlation coefficient

    (B) Standard deviation

    (C) Mean

    (D) Median

    (E) Confidence interval

88. Which of the following properly describes binocular disparity?

    (A) Two parallel lines seem to converge in an image.

    (B) Color is coded in opponent pairs that can result in afterimages.

    (C) Sounds coming in one ear are louder, which means that an object is on that side.

    (D) Each eye sees a slightly different picture, which helps the human brain determine depth.

    (E) The pinnae of the ear direct sounds in a specific way that enables placement along a vertical axis.

89. What type of learning is considered a high-level process that involves thinking, anticipating, and other complex mental processes?

    (A) Latent learning

    (B) Cognitive learning

    (C) Insight learning

    (D) Emotional learning

    (E) Biofeedback learning

GO ON TO THE NEXT PAGE

90. A mother gets a call from the school psychologist saying that a school-wide IQ test revealed that her child is gifted. Which of the following is one possible value for the child's measured IQ?

    (A) 80

    (B) 103

    (C) 115

    (D) 127

    (E) 138

91. Which of the following best defines the behavioral term extinction?

    (A) It is conditioning with a negative reinforcer that reduces or removes the unpleasantness of something that already exists.

    (B) It is the tendency to respond to another stimulus that is similar but not identical to the original conditioned stimulus.

    (C) It is a loss of conditioned response after repeated presentation of an unconditioned stimulus without a conditioned stimulus.

    (D) It is the process of gradually molding behavior to a desired response by reinforcing successive approximations to it.

    (E) It is the cessation of responses after prolonged exposure to inescapable, continuous punishment.

92. Which of the following correctly characterizes how a sound reaches the brain?

    (A) Vibrations in the air vibrate the oval window, which vibrates the ossicles, causing them to vibrate the tympanic membrane. The tympanic membrane then passes these vibrations to the fluid in the cochlea, which in turn translates them into nerve impulses.

    (B) Vibrations in the air vibrate the tympanic membrane, which causes the hair cells in the cochlea to start vibrating. The ossicles of the ear then sense these vibrations and turn the vibrations into nerve impulses through the oval window.

    (C) Vibrations in the air cause the ossicles to shake the tympanic membrane. This membrane is located within the oval window, and thus these vibrations are passed to the fluid in the cochlea, which turns them into nerve impulses.

    (D) Vibrations in the air vibrate the tympanic membrane, which in turn vibrates the ossicles. They pass those vibrations to the oval window. These vibrations on the oval window permeate through the fluid in the cochlea, where they are turned into nerve impulses.

    (E) The cochlea is vibrated by the tympanic membrane directly. These vibrations then pass through the oval window to the ossicles, where the ossicles turn those vibrations into nerve impulses.

GO ON TO THE NEXT PAGE

93. A father cuts two equal pieces of cake for his two children, Santiago and Carlos, who are three years old and five years old, respectively. The father cuts Santiago's piece into smaller pieces to make it easier to eat but leaves Carlos' whole. Carlos gets mad at his father because he believes that Santiago is getting more cake than him. The lack of which principle of cognitive development would explain this reaction?

    (A) Egocentrism

    (B) Stranger anxiety

    (C) Abstract reasoning

    (D) Object permanence

    (E) Conservation

94. According to the socioemotional selectivity theory, which of the following behaviors would be expected in an aging adult?

    (A) Developing new friendships with strangers and cultivating those friendships into close friendships

    (B) Reducing the number of friendships but becoming closer with the friends that remain

    (C) Asking questions like "Who do I want to be?" in an attempt to figure out life

    (D) Slowly losing some cognitive abilities like memory and information processing

    (E) Finding meaning in life mainly through work and maintenance of family life

95. Mary is out for dinner with her friends and orders a regular-sized meal. After finishing the meal, she excuses herself to the bathroom and proceeds to purge herself. Despite doing this regularly, Mary has a normal BMI. Which of the following best classifies Mary's disorder?

    (A) Anorexia nervosa

    (B) Binge eating disorder

    (C) Bulimia nervosa

    (D) Somatic symptom disorder

    (E) Conversion disorder

96. Which of the following disorders is characterized by extreme superstitions and other strange patterns of thinking?

    (A) Schizoid personality disorder

    (B) Cyclothymic disorder

    (C) Histrionic personality disorder

    (D) Schizotypal personality disorder

    (E) Avoidant personality disorder

97. Which of the following is NOT an example of classical conditioning?

    (A) A child is conditioned to be afraid of an animal when presentation of the animal is paired with a loud noise.

    (B) Cats are conditioned to meow at the sound of a bell after repeated pairings of the bell with food.

    (C) A person who received shocks from pressing an elevator button is now afraid of pressing elevator buttons anywhere.

    (D) A person who happened to fall ill shortly after eating a particular fish now becomes nauseated at its smell or taste.

    (E) Children, after watching a video of a person being violent with a toy, show aggression when presented with that same toy.

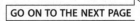

GO ON TO THE NEXT PAGE

98. Which perspective on personality assumes that people both respond to their environments and shape those environments to reflect their personalities?

    (A) Biopsychological

    (B) Psychodynamic

    (C) Behaviorist

    (D) Social cognitive

    (E) Psychoanalytic

99. As children mature into adolescence, they begin to prioritize peer relationships. Often, they will subsequently rebel against the views of their parents and adopt new views and styles. This is an example of which psychosocial developmental conflict described by Erik Erikson?

    (A) Identity vs. role confusion

    (B) Generativity vs. stagnation

    (C) Trust vs. mistrust

    (D) Initiative vs. guilt

    (E) Intimacy vs. isolation

100. Based on research about human attraction, which of the following scenarios is LEAST likely to occur?

    (A) Even with the rise of the internet, people are more likely to enter relationships with those who are geographically near.

    (B) Online dating sites, which often highlight members' photos, tend to garner more dates for their more attractive members.

    (C) Even when given access to more attractive potential partners, many people look for partners roughly equal in attractiveness.

    (D) Young people tend to be more attracted to individuals who continually show affection through texts and social media.

    (E) Romantic partners with fundamental personality differences are more likely to stay together than those who are similar.

END OF SECTION I

SECTION II BEGINS ON THE NEXT PAGE

SECTION II
50 Minutes—2 Questions
Percent of total grade: 33⅓

Directions Answer both of the following questions in 50 minutes. Lists of facts are insufficient to earn points; you must write essays that answer the questions thoughtfully with sound arguments that employ the proper terms from psychology. Use scratch paper to write out your responses.

1. Recently, Stefan has not been speaking with his sister Olivia because of a disagreement they had. Jakub, Stefan's 14-year-old son, recently asked Stefan about his aunt Olivia, but Stefan brushed him off and said Olivia was not a good person and they should not discuss her or speak with her. However, Jakub defied his father's wishes and called Olivia to chat about his recent score on a math test. Jakub did this because Olivia had earlier helped him with his homework by having him visualize the meanings of his math problems using shapes, a technique she often used while majoring in mathematics during college. Not long after all this, Jakub began ignoring his friend Samir because of a disagreement they had. One by one, Jakub's other friends also stopped speaking with Samir, even though they had nothing to do with Jakub and Samir's disagreement.

   Describe how each of the following concepts relates to this situation:

   • Conformity

   • Observational learning

   • Fundamental attribution error

   • Sigmund Freud's defense mechanisms

   • Lawrence Kohlberg's moral development theory

   • Erik Erikson's psychosocial development theory

   • Lev Vygotsky's more knowledgeable other

2. Parkinson's disease is a neurodegenerative disorder with increasing impairments as the disease progresses. It has also been linked to lower than expected amounts of dopamine produced in the brain. Since dancing has been linked to an increase in dopamine levels in people who enjoy it, a group of researchers wanted to determine if it can also have that effect on patients with Parkinson's disease. The goal of the study was to investigate the influence of tango dancing on the quality of life for people with early stage Parkinson's, as compared to swing dancing for the same cohort. From a cohort of 40 patients, two groups of 20 were formed. Those with last names beginning with the letters A through K were given 15 tango lessons, and those with last names beginning with the letters L through Z were provided with 15 swing lessons. The researchers administered a questionnaire to participants to assess symptoms after 5, 10, and 15 lessons and compared responses to the initial state prior to intervention. Neither group showed a significant decrease in the incidence of Parkinson's symptoms.

Part A

For the study described, identify each of the following:

- Independent variable
- Dependent variable

Part B

- Name two ways that the researchers could improve the internal validity of the study.

Part C

- Explain the role of dopamine in the human body and the effects of abnormal dopamine levels.
- Parkinson's disease is associated with resting tremors and loss of fine motor control. Which area of the brain is most likely affected?
- Dancing relies in part on having a good sense of balance. What physiological structures are necessary for maintaining balance?

END OF SECTION II

STOP

END OF EXAM

ANSWER KEY

Section I

1. C	16. E	31. A	46. A	61. C	76. D	91. C
2. C	17. E	32. E	47. D	62. C	77. B	92. D
3. D	18. A	33. B	48. E	63. B	78. D	93. E
4. E	19. E	34. E	49. D	64. B	79. C	94. B
5. B	20. B	35. C	50. A	65. D	80. B	95. C
6. D	21. C	36. C	51. A	66. B	81. B	96. D
7. B	22. D	37. B	52. D	67. E	82. A	97. E
8. D	23. E	38. D	53. C	68. B	83. A	98. D
9. D	24. B	39. A	54. B	69. D	84. C	99. A
10. C	25. D	40. C	55. C	70. B	85. A	100. E
11. C	26. E	41. D	56. D	71. B	86. A	
12. C	27. A	42. D	57. B	72. E	87. B	
13. D	28. D	43. C	58. E	73. A	88. D	
14. E	29. E	44. C	59. C	74. C	89. B	
15. E	30. A	45. D	60. E	75. B	90. E	

Section II

1. See Answers and Explanations

2. See Answers and Explanations

PRACTICE EXAM 6 BREAKDOWN: ASSESS YOUR STRENGTHS

Use the following tables to determine which topics you are already strong in and which topics you need to review most.

Topic	Questions
Scientific Foundations of Psychology	3, 16, 20, 35, 37, 39, 53, 60, 62, 81, 84, 86, 87
Biological Bases of Behavior	17, 22, 23, 40, 41, 42, 43, 70, 76, 78
Sensation and Perception	27, 28, 38, 58, 61, 82, 88, 92
Learning	4, 6, 11, 56, 57, 65, 89, 91, 97
Cognitive Psychology	1, 2, 9, 14, 15, 31, 32, 33, 55, 63, 66, 67, 68, 69, 90
Developmental Psychology	5, 7, 12, 49, 64, 79, 93, 94, 99
Motivation, Emotion, and Personality	25, 26, 30, 44, 45, 46, 48, 51, 52, 71, 72, 73, 98
Clinical Psychology	8, 13, 24, 29, 34, 47, 50, 54, 74, 75, 77, 85, 95, 96
Social Psychology	10, 18, 19, 21, 36, 59, 80, 83, 100

Topic	Chapters	Questions on Exam	Number You Got Correct
Scientific Foundations of Psychology	4, 13	13	
Biological Bases of Behavior	5, 14	10	
Sensation and Perception	6, 15	8	
Learning	7, 16	9	
Cognitive Psychology	8, 17	15	
Developmental Psychology	9, 18	9	
Motivation, Emotion, and Personality	10, 19	13	
Clinical Psychology	11, 20	14	
Social Psychology	12, 21	9	

PRACTICE EXAM 6 ANSWERS AND EXPLANATIONS

Section I

1. C

Topic: Cognitive Psychology

Individuals with an IQ between 40 and 55 are considered moderately disabled and generally attain a level of academic performance similar to a child in the second grade. Thus, **(C)** is correct. (A) is incorrect because independent living is more characteristic of individuals with only a mild intellectual disability (an IQ between 55 and 70). (B) is incorrect because it describes severely disabled individuals—those with an IQ between 25 and 40. Individuals who have trouble communicating, as in (D), are considered profoundly disabled and usually have an IQ of 25 or less. (E) describes savant syndrome, in which an individual with limited intellectual abilities excels at a single skill. Simply having an IQ of 50 does not guarantee that someone will be a savant, so (E) is incorrect.

2. C

Topic: Cognitive Psychology

The nativist, or biological, theory of language maintains that children do not just copy language that they hear, but are born with an innate understanding of grammar. This perspective is most commonly associated with linguist Noam Chomsky and his theory of universal grammar. That eliminates (A), (B), and (D). B.F. Skinner proposed that we learn language through our interactions with the environment, which best aligns with the behavioral perspective. Thus, **(C)** is correct and (E) is incorrect.

3. D

Topic: Scientific Foundations of Psychology

The 68–95–99.7 rule, also known as the empirical rule, says that 68% of the values lie within one standard deviation of the mean in a normal distribution. Hence, Jack's score is closest to the 66th percentile; **(D)** is correct. (A) and (B) are incorrect because they would represent scores below the mean, while (C) would represent a score exactly at the mean value. (E) is incorrect because it's closer to two standard deviations above the mean.

4. E

Topic: Learning

Since the number of button presses is different in each attempt to summon the elevator, this is most analogous to a variable ratio schedule, making **(E)** correct. (A) is incorrect because a fixed ratio schedule would involve the same number of button presses each time. (B) and (D) are incorrect because interval schedules depend upon the amount of time between reinforcements, rather than the number of behaviors (button presses). (C) is incorrect because fixed frequency is not an accepted term in operant conditioning.

5. B

Topic: Developmental Psychology

Discontinuous development presupposes that there are specific stages and ages when development occurs. In contrast, continuous development occurs when development relies on incremental changes that occur slowly and build upon earlier advances. Of the choices provided, the only one that describes a sudden (or discontinous) development event is **(B)**, making it correct. The remaining choices are examples of gradual change that would support continuous development, not discontinuous development.

6. D

Topic: Learning

The Bobo doll experiment was conducted by Albert Bandura, making **(D)** correct. John Garcia discovered taste aversion when looking at the impact of radiation on rats, eliminating (A). (B) and (C) are incorrect because both Pavlov and Rescorla studied classical conditioning. Edward Tolman was a behaviorist who developed the idea of latent learning by conducting experiments in which rats learned to run mazes even when reinforcement was withheld, eliminating (E).

7. B
Topic: Developmental Psychology

Jean Piaget proposed that schemata help children understand the world. These schemata allow children to interpret and organize information, which can then help them recognize things and learn. These schemata are not set in stone, and Piaget proposed a mechanism for how they are modified, known as assimilation and accommodation. First, children assimilate new knowledge by taking in information that is related to things that they already know. Then, they adjust their schemata to accommodate the new information they have learned. This means **(B)** is correct. The other choices do not present the terms that Piaget used to describe these processes.

8. D
Topic: Clinical Psychology

Patients with antisocial personality disorder lie, manipulate, and disregard others without remorse. **(D)** is correct because antisocial personality disorder is three times more common in men than in women. (A) and (B) are incorrect because the rates of anxiety disorders, such as panic disorder, and depressive disorders, such as major depressive disorder, are higher in women than in men. (C) and (E) are incorrect because research has shown that women are two times more likely than men to be diagnosed with borderline personality disorder or PTSD.

9. D
Topic: Cognitive Psychology

Test-retest reliability is a measure of reliability that compares scores on the same test by the same test-takers at two different times. This makes **(D)** correct. (A), (B), (C) and (E) describe other types of reliability testing.

10. C
Topic: Social Psychology

The bystander effect is an established psychological phenomenon in which people are less likely to help someone in need when they are part of a large crowd, due to the diffusion of responsibility among all the people present. **(C)** describes exactly this effect, making it correct. (A) and (D) are incorrect because they present the reverse. (B) is incorrect because there is no evidence that women would

be more likely to help a fellow woman than men would. (E) is incorrect because there is no evidence that nationality has such an influence on people's willingness to help.

11. C
Topic: Learning

The situation presented in the question stem is an example of the learned inability to overcome obstacles or avoid punishment, known as learned helplessness, making **(C)** correct. (A) and (B) are incorrect because superstitious behavior is learned through an accidental conditioning process, neither of which applies to the scenario described. (D) is eliminated because it describes how emotions and emotional state affect cognitive processes, including memory formation and retrieval. Lastly, systematic desensitization is a behavior modification technique that attempts to treat phobias through planned exposure to fearful stimuli, making (E) incorrect.

12. C
Topic: Developmental Psychology

Sigmund Freud's theory of development centered on children's pleasure-seeking behavior as focused on different parts of the body. He theorized that without proper parenting and nurturing, people could become stuck in one of the psychosexual stages, which could result in fixation on a particular body part. This became known as the psychosexual theory of development, which means **(C)** is correct. Attachment theory was developed by Harry Harlow, Mary Ainsworth, and Konrad Lorenz, among others, so (A) is incorrect. Social development theory was developed by Lev Vygotsky, making (B) incorrect. The cognitive theory of development was developed by Jean Piaget, making (D) incorrect. Moral development theory was developed by Lawrence Kohlberg, Carol Gilligan, and others; (E) is incorrect.

13. D
Topic: Clinical Psychology

Susto is a culture-bound syndrome, **(D)**, a psychological disorder that occurs exclusively within a particular cultural context. (A) and (E) are terms used to describe approaches to understanding psychological behavior. (B) and (C) are examples of psychological disorders in the DSM that are not localized to a specific culture.

14. E

Topic: Cognitive Psychology

The availability heuristic is a thinking strategy in which judgments are based on the information that first comes into a person's mind when evaluating a situation. The availability heuristic can lead to incorrect or biased judgments. If Mandy watched several reports on the news about skydiving incidents, she may think that skydiving accidents are a common occurrence, while in reality they are uncommon. Therefore, **(E)** correctly explains Mandy's misconception. (A) is incorrect because the question stem says that Mandy believed skydiving was dangerous only after watching the news. If she sought out these news reports because she thought skydiving was dangerous, then that would be an example of confirmation bias. (B) is incorrect because cognitive dissonance is a state of mind arising when people recognize inconsistencies in their beliefs. If Mandy went skydiving even though she believed it was extremely dangerous, that would be an example of cognitive dissonance. (C) is incorrect because the fundamental attribution error occurs when judgments of other people are based on perceived character traits and do not account for situational factors. (D) is incorrect because the representativeness heuristic is a thinking strategy in which one determines if something belongs within a group based on its similarity to other things within that group. If Mandy believed that air travel was dangerous, the representativeness heuristic might lead her to assume that airplanes, helicopters, and skydiving are equally dangerous because they all involve flying.

15. E

Topic: Cognitive Psychology

Participants in Group 1 were able to remember fewer words on average than those in Group 2. Group 1 may be experiencing the effects of divided attention because they were focusing on playing the video game in addition to remembering the words, which explains their reduced average recall compared to Group 2; **(E)** is correct. (A) is incorrect because shallow processing occurs when individuals use superficial aspects of information to remember it. Shallow processing causes less information to be remembered over the long term than deep processing, but since the participants were asked to immediately recall the words, shallow processing cannot explain the results in the table. (B) is incorrect because inattentional blindness refers to the failure to notice stimuli in plain sight; members of Group 1 were able to recall some of the words, which suggests that this concept does not apply. Selective attention, (C), does not explain the observed difference between groups, since Group 2 did not have more than one thing to focus on. Although the reticular formation is a collection of nuclei that contributes to attention by filtering incoming information, all participants would have this brain structure, and thus (D) is incorrect.

16. E

Topic: Scientific Foundations of Psychology

The independent variable in an experiment is the quantity that is manipulated to test its effects on one or more dependent variables. In this experiment, the number of hours spent exercising per week would be the independent variable; **(E)** is correct. (A) is incorrect because confounding variables are factors other than independent variables that influence the dependent variable, but time spent exercising is precisely what the psychologist seeks to investigate. (B) and (C) are incorrect because the population describes the larger group being investigated, while the sample is the subset of that group that participates in the study. (D) is incorrect because IQ score is the dependent variable.

17. E

Topic: Biological Bases of Behavior

In subliminal processing, the brain processes information beneath the level of conscious awareness, demonstrating that someone can be influenced by information even if he or she does not consciously perceive it. **(E)** is thus correct. Hindsight bias, (A), refers to the overconfidence that people have concerning their ability to predict an earlier event after being given full information. Signal detection theory, (B), relates to how participants are able to perceive information from the world. Just-noticeable difference refers to the ability to differentiate perceptions, and linear perspective relates to vision, making (C) and (D) incorrect.

18. A

Topic: Social Psychology

Unlike a dispositional attribution, which assigns responsibility for an action to characteristics of the actor, a situational attribution views the circumstances surrounding the action as more important. The interviewer assumed that Karl's professional appearance was a result of Karl's professionalism and cleanliness, but if that were true, Karl would behave that way in a wider variety of contexts, including daily work life. However, Karl's subsequent pattern of unprofessional work behavior suggests that he was only compelled to act professionally in the unique situation of the interview; **(A)** is correct. (B) is incorrect because it calls into question the objectivity of the coworker, which would make a situational attribution seem less appropriate rather than more appropriate. (C) is tempting because it provides a situational explanation of Karl's behavior on the job; however, the question asks specifically about why his interview behavior, not his work behavior, should receive a situational attribution. (D) is incorrect because the question stem does not mention whether Karl acted professionally in the previous job, so there is no way of knowing whether it would support a dispositional or situational attribution. (E) is incorrect because education-specific experience is not relevant to the issue of Karl's general professionalism and cleanliness (or lack thereof).

19. E

Topic: Social Psychology

Self-serving bias is the tendency to make dispositional attributions about your successes and situational attributions about your failures. Because Karl, according to the interviewer, explains his past successes using personal qualities such as a strong work ethic and perseverance, but, according to his coworker, explains his failures on assignments by situational factors such as competing priorities, Karl is clearly demonstrating self-serving bias. **(E)** is correct. (A) is incorrect because the just-world hypothesis is the view that people get what they deserve, but the concern in this question is only how Karl justifies his own behavior. (B) is incorrect because the fundamental attribution error is the tendency to make dispositional attributions for other people's behavior, but this question asks about attributions that Karl makes for his own behavior. (C) is incorrect because the availability heuristic is the tendency to make judgments based on the information most easily brought to mind, but the question concerns how Karl justifies his behavior, not how he makes judgments. (D) is incorrect because nonresponse bias refers to a distortion in results for surveys with low response rates, which isn't relevant to the described scenario.

20. B

Topic: Scientific Foundations of Psychology

A correlation coefficient describes how strong the association between two variables is. The graph depicts a strong, but not perfect, inverse relationship, which suggests a correlation coefficient with a value between −1 and 0. **(B)** is correct because it presents the only viable option. (A) is incorrect because several points in the graph are not on the trend line. If the correlation coefficient were −1, all points would fit the trend line perfectly. A coefficient of 0 would suggest no correlation between the variables, which clearly doesn't fit the data; (C) is incorrect. (D) and (E) are incorrect because they suggest a direct relationship, rather than an inverse one, between the two variables.

21. C

Topic: Social Psychology

Altruistic behavior is by definition behavior that imposes a net cost on the actor while providing a net benefit for one or more others. If the benefits to the actor were greater than the costs, it wouldn't be altruism. Thus, **(C)** cannot provide a reasonable explanation of altruism because it contradicts the meaning of the word. (A) is incorrect because it describes the reciprocity theory of altruism. (B) is incorrect because it describes the kin selection theory. (D) is incorrect because it describes the sexual selection theory of altruism. Finally, (E) is incorrect because it provides another evolutionary explanation of altruism, in which negative status as a freeloader decreases fitness.

22. D

Topic: Biological Bases of Behavior

Wernicke's area, which controls speech comprehension, is found in the temporal lobe of the dominant brain hemisphere, which is the left hemisphere in most people. Thus, **(D)** is correct. Remember that the temporal lobe is also the location of the primary auditory cortex, which is associated with the interpretation of auditory information. The occipital lobe, (A), is where visual information is processed. The left frontal lobe, (B), is the location of Broca's area, which is responsible for speech production. The thalamus, (C), is the relay center of the brain, responsible for receiving and relaying information about stimuli such as touch, taste, and sound from and to different parts of the body. It often sends information to the parietal lobe, (E), for further processing.

23. E

Topic: Biological Bases of Behavior

The frontal lobe controls voluntary movements, problem solving, and many aspects of personality, such as regulation of impulse control, social behavior, and sexual behavior. Damage to this area of the brain is expected to alter a patient's personality, and that's precisely what happened to Gage. **(E)** is correct. (A) is incorrect because hearing loss would more commonly result from damage to the temporal lobe, while (B) would more likely result from damage to the parietal lobe. (C) would most likely come from damage to the cerebellum, while (D) could result from damage to the hypothalamus.

24. B

Topic: Clinical Psychology

Transference is a term from psychodynamic therapy to describe when feelings directed at one person become redirected to another person, often the therapist. This makes **(B)** correct. Self-actualization is a term from humanistic therapy that refers to an individual's ability to live up to his or her full human potential, making (A) incorrect. Free association is a tempting answer because it is another psychodynamic term, but it refers to a technique in which the patient is instructed to "think out loud" to help access the unconscious, eliminating (C). Cognitive distortion is an automatic and irrational perception of the world that contributes to feelings of anxiety or depression, which does not fit the situation in the question, making (D) incorrect. (E) is also eliminated because systematic desensitization is a behavioral therapy used to treat phobias by gradually associating feared stimuli with relaxing stimuli.

25. D

Topic: Motivation, Emotion, and Personality

All defense mechanisms in Freud's structural model twist or outright deny reality, but only the defense mechanism of suppression is conscious. Since this question indicates that Priscilla knows that she is trying to deny her anxiety, she is using suppression; **(D)** is correct. All of the remaining choices are unconscious defense mechanisms.

26. E

Topic: Motivation, Emotion, and Personality

Intrinsic motivation is driven by internal factors such as personal enjoyment. This precisely describes the behavior of Julian, who gardens because he enjoys it; **(E)** is correct. The remaining choices are descriptions of extrinsic motivation, in which external rewards or punishments motivate behavior.

27. A

Topic: Sensation and Perception

All of human perception is based on educated guesses about reality. These educated guesses are influenced by a variety of factors including upbringing, personality, and other situational variables. The educated guesses made when interpreting complex sensory information are called perceptual hypotheses. In this case, the psychologist is influencing the perceptual hypotheses of her test subjects by showing them simple pictures, a procedure which then shapes how they perceive the more complex pictures; **(A)** is correct. Closure involves perceiving completed objects even when parts of them are missing, so (B) is incorrect. Similarity grouping refers to grouping things that are alike into a set, so (C) is incorrect. Proximity grouping refers to grouping things based on how close they are to one another, so (D) is incorrect. The figure-ground relationship refers to the distinction between an object of focus in a perceptual field and the surrounding background, which doesn't apply here; (E) is incorrect.

28. D

Topic: Sensation and Perception

Gustation is the sense of taste. When chemicals come into contact with receptors on the tongue, located in the papillae, they generate action potentials that are interpreted in the brain as tastes, which means that **(D)** is correct. (A) is incorrect because it describes the vestibular sense. (B) is incorrect because it describes how action potentials are produced in tactile sensations. (C) is incorrect because it describes how action potentials are generated in olfaction (smell). (E) is incorrect because it describes how action potentials are generated in hearing.

29. E

Topic: Clinical Psychology

Patients with conversion disorder have neurological symptoms, such as paralysis, seizures, or blindness, that cannot be explained by an underlying medical condition. **(E)** describes exactly such a symptom, making it correct. The remaining choices are incorrect because they describe the symptoms of other disorders. (A) describes symptoms of ADHD, (B) describes symptoms of narcissistic personality disorder, (C) describes symptoms of histrionic personality disorder, and (D) describes symptoms of major depressive disorder.

30. A

Topic: Motivation, Emotion, and Personality

According to the Yerkes-Dodson law, people do not perform tasks well at low levels of arousal or at very high levels of arousal. Rather, performance is best when people are at moderate levels of arousal. **(A)** is correct. (B) is incorrect because the Hawthorne effect suggests that people alter their behavior when being observed. Instinct theory, (C), focuses on genetically predisposed behavior, and incentive theory, (E), maintains that motivation comes from rewards and punishments. Actor-observer bias, (D), refers to a tendency to attribute other people's behaviors to internal causes, while attributing your own behavior to external causes.

31. A

Topic: Cognitive Psychology

The spacing effect refers to the finding that studying in multiple sessions over time leads to higher retention of information than studying for the same amount of time in a single session. By studying for 30 minutes a day over the course of a week, Ahmad is utilizing the spacing effect; **(A)** is correct. (B) is incorrect because Anne is using the self-reference effect. John is using visual encoding to remember the words as images of the textbook page they were on; (C) is incorrect. (D) is incorrect because Tomás is using repetition to keep the words in his short-term memory, which is called maintenance rehearsal. Finally, Sarah is using elaborative rehearsal in order to connect the new vocabulary words with existing knowledge of previously learned words. Hence, (E) is incorrect.

32. E

Topic: Cognitive Psychology

In the early 1900s, psychologist Alfred Binet developed the concept of a child's mental age to measure intelligence in comparison to the average child at that age. So, if both sons showed typical performance, the 9-year-old would have a mental age of 9 and the 11-year-old would have a mental age of 11. In the Stanford-Binet IQ Test, IQ is calculated by taking mental age divided by actual age and multiplying by 100. Children with an average mental age have an IQ of 100, since the mental age divided by the actual age would equal 1. In this case, both children have IQs above 100, so their mental ages must both be greater than their actual ages; **(E)** is correct. The use of the word "only" makes (A) and (B) incorrect because both children's mental ages are greater than their actual ages. (C) and (D) are incorrect because children with mental ages less than their actual ages would have IQs lower than 100.

33. B

Topic: Cognitive Psychology

Practical intelligence, part of Sternberg's triarchic theory, is the ability to apply knowledge to daily life. By easily applying classroom knowledge to real-word settings, Valentina is displaying a high level of practical intelligence; **(B)** is correct. (A) is incorrect because analytical intelligence refers to the intelligence associated with traditional academic performance. People display fluid intelligence when they are able to complete a task without any prior knowledge relating to the task. However, Valentina is applying prior knowledge, so (C) is incorrect. (D) is incorrect because intrapersonal intelligence concerns personal growth and self-reflection, which isn't immediately relevant to Valentina's situation as described. Finally, musical-rhythmic intelligence is the intelligence associated with appreciation of musical qualities; (E) is incorrect.

34. E

Topic: Clinical Psychology

Self-actualization is the ultimate goal of humanistic therapy because it represents the full realization of an individual's unique potential. **(E)** is correct. (A) and (C) might be goals of a variety of therapeutic approaches, including humanistic therapy, but neither is the *ultimate* goal of humanistic therapy. (B) is a goal of cognitive therapy. (D) is a goal of psychodynamic therapy.

35. C
Topic: Scientific Foundations of Psychology

Current ethical guidelines require that researchers maintain strict confidentiality, with only limited exceptions, and do not readily disclose information that could identify patients in their studies. Thus, a researcher telling his wife that one of his participants is in her yoga class would unambiguously be a breach of ethical guidelines; **(C)** is correct. Vulnerable populations, such as children, may be included in research as long as proper consent is obtained from the patient or a guardian; (A) is incorrect because it is not necessarily a violation of ethics, provided that parental permission has been given. (B) is incorrect because patients may be exposed to drugs with side effects as long as proper consent has been obtained. Under ethical guidelines, researchers must obtain informed consent from all research participants; (D) is consistent with this guideline, making it incorrect. Although it may not be appropriate in all instances, it is not unethical for a researcher to disclose information about his or her personal life; (E) is incorrect.

36. C
Topic: Social Psychology

Compliance occurs when an individual follows the requests of peers. Since Alvin's hiking partner is a peer, **(C)** is correct. (A) is incorrect because groupthink describes a process of poor decision making as a result of the desire to preserve harmony in a group. (B) is incorrect because obedience requires following an authority's orders, but Alvin's partner is a peer, not an authority figure. (D) is incorrect because conformity is the adherence to unstated social norms, but this scenario involves an explicit request. (E) is incorrect because authority refers to a position of social power, but Alvin and his partner are peers.

37. B
Topic: Scientific Foundations of Psychology

A longitudinal study is a type of observational study that follows a group of participants over time in order to measure how individuals change. A longitudinal study

that investigated a specific group of adolescents beginning in middle school and continuing through high school would be the best format for **(B)**, making it correct. (A) is incorrect because it would be more appropriate for a case study. (C) and (D) are incorrect because they would be better suited to controlled experiments. (E) is incorrect because journals publish a wide range of types of research, including longitudinal studies, controlled experiments, and others.

38. D
Topic: Sensation and Perception

The cochlea is the structure that houses the basilar membrane, which vibrates in response to pitch and is therefore the structure that degrades in cases of presbycusis. **(D)** is correct. The pinna, (A), is the cartilaginous outer ear and is not involved in detecting pitch; the pinna directs sounds into the auditory canal. The eustachian tube, (B), connects the middle ear to the nasal cavity in order to equalize pressure between the middle ear and the external environment. The ossicles, (C), consist of the stapes, incus, and malleus. The role of these three small bones is to transmit and amplify the vibrations from the tympanic membrane to the inner ear. (E) is incorrect because the semicircular canals of the inner ear are three perpendicular tubes lined with cilia that detect motion of a liquid called endolymph. Motion of the endolymph is transmitted to the brain to help orient the body and keep the head and body balanced.

39. A
Topic: Scientific Foundations of Psychology

Noam Chomsky argued that children do not simply repeat language that they hear, but are born with an innate understanding of grammar, a kind of universal grammar; **(A)** is correct. The remaining choices present psychologists known for other ideas. Wolfgang Köhler's research on problem-solving abilities in chimpanzees contributed to the creation of Gestalt psychology. Sigmund Freud is most notable for developing psychoanalysis and his theory that psychological disorders are the result of repressed memories and conflicts within the unconscious mind. Konrad Lorenz was a biological psychologist who discovered the innate form of attachment known as imprinting. Finally, Jean Piaget is best known for his theory of child cognitive development.

40. C

Topic: Biological Bases of Behavior

The forebrain includes the two hemispheres of the cerebral cortex and is the largest part of the brain. Since it encompasses the cerebral cortex, both the auditory cortex and Wernicke's area are found in the forebrain, so (A) and (E) are incorrect. It also encompasses the limbic system and subcortical structures such as the thalamus, which means (B) and (D) are incorrect. That leaves the medulla, which is found in the hindbrain; **(C)** is correct.

41. D

Topic: Biological Bases of Behavior

All parts of the nervous system that are not part of the central nervous system belong to the peripheral nervous system, which has two divisions, the autonomic nervous system and the somatic nervous system. The autonomic nervous system is further divided into the parasympathetic nervous system and the sympathetic nervous system, eliminating (A), (C), and (E). The central nervous system has two parts, the brain and the spinal cord, which means that **(D)** is not part of the peripheral nervous system and is correct. The optic nerve is an afferent neuron of the peripheral nervous system that takes signals towards the central nervous system, which means that (B) is incorrect.

42. D

Topic: Biological Bases of Behavior

Neurotransmitters are stored in the axon terminals that are located at the end of axons. Within these terminal buttons, there are small, membrane-bound sacs of neurotransmitters called synaptic vesicles that can bind to the cell membrane of the synaptic terminal and release the neurotransmitters into the synapse. Thus, **(D)** is correct. If the neurotransmitters were stored in the synapse, they would be able to bind to receptors and would possibly be degraded, so (A) is incorrect. (B) and (C) are too far away from the synapse to be able to be efficiently mobilized when neurotransmitters need to be released by axon terminals, so they are incorrect. Finally, the myelin sheath is not part of the neuron or any other cell but is a structure surrounding the neuron. It would not have a place to store neurotransmitters, so (E) is incorrect.

43. C

Topic: Biological Bases of Behavior

For a nerve to fire, it must first reach the threshold potential, which in turn causes an action potential. For Jodie's brain to realize that something is crawling on her arm, a nerve inside her brain must have an action potential. To do this, a nerve in her central nervous system must reach the threshold potential through depolarization; **(C)** is correct. If a nerve's membrane potential is hyperpolarized or at resting potential, no signal is happening, and so (A), (B), (D), and (E) are incorrect.

44. C

Topic: Motivation, Emotion, and Personality

If the fact that everyone strongly identified with the researcher's statement does not surprise you, it is because that statement identifies a normal human experience that practically everyone has at least once—and often more than once—during their lifespan. Thus, the generic language of that statement does not help to discriminate effectively between different personality types. This phenomenon is known as the Forer, or Barnum, effect, so **(C)** is correct. The remaining choices describe other phenomena. (A) is one of the factors in the Big Five model of personality traits. (B) is a concept of the social cognitive theory of personality. (D) is one of the defense mechanisms of Freud's structural model of personality. (E) is a concept from Horney's psychoanalytic theory of personality.

45. D

Topic: Motivation, Emotion, and Personality

According to Freud's structural model, the superego is divided into two aspects: the conscience, which makes you feel guilty when you follow the whims of your id, and the ego-ideal, which makes you feel proud when you deny those whims. Thus, **(D)** is correct and (E) is incorrect. (A) and (B) are incorrect because the ego is the referee between the id and superego, and it operates according to the reality principle, which fights against instant gratification. (C) is incorrect because the pleasure principle is the operating principle of the id, which seeks instant gratification.

46. A

Topic: Motivation, Emotion, and Personality

Research shows that emotions tend to be relatively short-lived phenomena, sometimes lasting for as little as a few minutes. Thus, **(A)** is correct because it is the best supported by research. (B) is incorrect because emotions often motivate people to act. (C) is incorrect because some emotions are ambivalent, containing both positive and negative elements. (D) is incorrect because emotions often have a profound effect on cognition. (E) is incorrect because emotions can vary widely in intensity.

47. D

Topic: Clinical Psychology

Dysthymia is a less severe form of depression. It is characterized by many of the same symptoms as major depressive disorder, but those symptoms are reduced in intensity or frequency. **(D)** is correct. (A) is incorrect because body dysmorphic disorder is in the category of obsessive-compulsive and related disorders. (B) is incorrect because depersonalization/derealization disorder is a dissociative disorder. Anorexia nervosa is a feeding and eating disorder, so (C) is incorrect. Cyclothymic disorder is in the category of bipolar and related disorders, so (E) is incorrect.

48. E

Topic: Motivation, Emotion, and Personality

Neuroticism, according to the Big Five model, varies on a continuum from anxious (high neuroticism) to stable (low neuroticism). **(E)** is thus correct. (A) is incorrect because it describes the range of agreeableness, (B) is incorrect because it pertains to conscientiousness, and (D) is incorrect because it describes openness to experience; these are three other factors in the Big Five model. (C) is incorrect because it pertains to psychoticism, a distinct factor in the Eysencks' PEN model.

49. D

Topic: Developmental Psychology

In the late 1960s, Diana Baumrind put forward a theory of child development that was based around parenting styles. The four parenting styles she identified were authoritative, authoritarian, permissive, and neglectful.

(D) is thus correct. Harry Harlow, Mary Ainsworth, and Konrad Lorenz all focused on attachment between parents and children, but not on differences in parenting styles; (A), (B), and (C) are incorrect. Albert Bandura developed social learning theory, which describes how people learn from one another through observation, imitation, and modeling; (E) is incorrect.

50. A

Topic: Clinical Psychology

In the DSM-5, attention deficit hyperactivity disorder, or ADHD, is classified as a neurodevelopmental disorder, which is the same category as disorders like autism spectrum disorder and specific learning disorders. **(A)** is thus correct. The remaining choices are other diagnostic categories in the DSM-5.

51. A

Topic: Motivation, Emotion, and Personality

According to Maslow's hierarchy of needs model, the need for safety must be satisfied before the need for love and belonging. **(A)** is thus correct, while (C) and (E) are incorrect. Family security must be satisfied before feelings of accomplishment, but after satisfying basic physiological needs such as shelter, so (B) and (D) are likewise incorrect.

52. D

Topic: Motivation, Emotion, and Personality

According to Hans Selye's model for stress, known as general adaptation syndrome, the body has a biological response to external stressors. After the first stage (alarm), in which the body produces stress hormones like adrenaline to deal with the stressor (called the fight-or-flight response), the body enters the resistance stage and begins to lower the production of stress hormones and regain equilibrium. Thus, **(D)** is correct and (B) is incorrect. Exhaustion is the third and final stage of general adaptation syndrome; in this stage, the body loses the ability to combat and adapt to persistent (long term) stress, leading to burnout and health issues. (A) is incorrect. Although recovery can refer to the body's return to good health after the exhaustion stage, it is not a formal stage of general adaptation syndrome, so (C) is incorrect. Homeostasis refers to a state of physiological and psychological equilibrium in the body; it is not a stage of general adaptation syndrome, so (E) is incorrect.

53. C

Topic: Scientific Foundations of Psychology

The median is the value in the middle of the data when it is arranged in increasing or decreasing order. When there is an even number of data points, it is equal to the average of the two points in the middle. Here, the two middle points are 7 and 9, and thus the median is $(7+9) \div 2 = 8$. **(C)** is correct. The other choices offer incorrect values: (A) gives the mode of the data set, (B) is too small, (D) gives the mean, and (E) is too large.

54. B

Topic: Clinical Psychology

Bipolar I disorder involves manic episodes with or without the presence of depressive episodes, while bipolar II disorder involves hypomanic episodes and at least one major depressive episode. Therefore, **(B)** is correct because depressive episodes are only a requirement for a bipolar II diagnosis. (A) is incorrect because bipolar disorders, such as bipolar I and II, are classified as mild, moderate, or severe according to the number and severity of symptoms. (C) is incorrect because dysthymic episodes are a diagnostic criterion for cyclothymic disorder, not bipolar I disorder. (D) is incorrect because periods of mania occur with both bipolar I and bipolar II. In bipolar II, however, these periods of mania are often shorter and less severe than in bipolar I. (E) is incorrect because medications and psychotherapy are often the first-line treatment for patients with bipolar I and bipolar II.

55. C

Topic: Cognitive Psychology

Michael suffers from retrograde amnesia, which is the loss of memories that happened prior to the accident. An adult patient with retrograde amnesia would be unable to recall details of events from their childhood; **(C)** is correct. Michael would remember how to ride a bike because patients with retrograde amnesia usually have an intact procedural memory, so (A) is incorrect. (B) and (D) are incorrect because patients with retrograde amnesia can remember events that occurred following their accident. Inability to form new memories is

anterograde, not retrograde, amnesia. If Michael could not remember his name or other aspects of his identity, as seen in (E), he would be suffering from dissociative amnesia. The onset of dissociative amnesia is typically correlated with emotional trauma, not neurological damage such as a traumatic brain injury.

56. D

Topic: Learning

The situation in the question stem actually describes the Little Albert experiment. The fact that the child started to become afraid of other white-furred animals is an example of stimulus generalization, making **(D)** correct. Acquisition is when a behavior, such as a conditioned response, has been learned, and stimulus discrimination is the ability to distinguish between similar but nonidentical stimuli, eliminating (A) and (B). Extinction is the cessation of a learned response, usually resulting from an end to conditioning, while spontaneous recovery is the reappearance of a learned response after its apparent extinction, making (C) and (E) incorrect.

57. B

Topic: Learning

The situation presented in the question is an example of operant conditioning. Because his action involves the removal of an aversive stimulus (one of the quizzes) in order to increase the frequency of a particular behavior (paying attention quietly), it counts as negative reinforcement; **(B)** is correct. This also eliminates (A), (C), and (D). Extinction is a term used in classical conditioning, and it refers to the cessation of a learned response, usually resulting from an end to conditioning; (E) is incorrect.

58. E

Topic: Sensation and Perception

As molecules enter the nose and get dissolved in the mucus found there, they eventually make their way to an olfactory receptor, which sends a chemical signal to the olfactory bulb. The olfactory bulb is where these chemical signals are turned into nerve impulses and sent to the limbic system and olfactory cortex, where the information is processed. **(E)** is correct. The remaining choices scramble the correct order.

because sensory adaptation occurs when constant sensation leads to not perceiving that sensation. (E) is incorrect because transduction is the conversion of sensations into nerve impulses.

59. C

Topic: Social Psychology

Tamara is experiencing a conflict between her belief that she doesn't require health insurance and the reality of catching a nasty flu. Thus, she would most likely be experiencing cognitive dissonance, an unpleasant mental state that arises from inconsistencies in beliefs and behaviors. **(C)** is correct. (A) and (B) are incorrect because there is no evidence that Tamara would respond to the situation with aggression, either toward family and friends or toward doctors and nurses. (D) is incorrect because there is no suggestion in the description that Tamara faces a conflict between the different roles she plays in her life. (E) is incorrect because the fundamental attribution error applies only to judgments of other people's behavior; it does not fit the scenario as described.

60. E

Topic: Scientific Foundations of Psychology

Internal validity is a measure of the extent to which a study measures what it is designed to measure. In a controlled experiment, for example, internal validity would indicate the extent to which changes measured in the dependent variable result from manipulations made to the independent variable. In contrast, external validity is a measure of the generalizability of research results. A study with high external validity could reach valid conclusions not just about the sample used, but also about the larger population it represents. Only **(E)** correctly characterizes both types of validity.

61. C

Topic: Sensation and Perception

Detecting differences in pitch or intensity of sound involves the sensation of sound. While an absolute threshold determines whether a stimulus can be perceived, the difference threshold is what determines whether a difference can be detected, which means that **(C)** is correct and (A) is incorrect. Difference thresholds are not constant and depend on the initial intensity of the stimulus, as proposed by Ernst Weber. (B) is incorrect because subliminal messages do not have to do with detecting differences in intensity, but rather with receiving messages at an intensity below conscious awareness. (D) is incorrect

62. C

Topic: Scientific Foundations of Psychology

The greatest strength of experimentation is its ability to offer insights into causality, or the presence of a cause-and-effect relationship between two variables. In particular, controlled experiments manipulate the experimental conditions, ensuring that the only differences between the control and experimental groups are the variables being studied. Therefore, only controlled experiments are capable of making determinations about causal relationships; **(C)** is correct. Longitudinal studies, cross-sectional studies, and naturalistic observations are types of observational studies in which variables tend not to be controlled; (A), (B), and (D) are incorrect. Despite being experiments, field experiments are conducted in more natural environments (not controlled ones), which limits the ability to control group differences and offer strong evidence of causality. Thus, (E) is incorrect.

63. B

Topic: Cognitive Psychology

Each half of the practice exam should have produced similar scores because the students answered the same number of questions each day. However, students did significantly better on the latter half of the questions, and thus this test had low levels of equivalent-form reliability. **(B)** is correct because equivalent-form reliability compares scores on two versions of the same test administered at separate times to the same group of people. Split-half reliability is similar to equivalent-form reliability because both require splitting test items into multiple groups. With split-half reliability, however, the two tests are given at the same time. Since the teacher gave half of the test to the students on one day and gave the other half of the same test to the same students on a different day, split-half reliability is not measured and (A) is incorrect. (C), (D), and (E) are incorrect because it is impossible to assess validity by comparing results on different parts of the same test; some external basis of comparison would be necessary to assess validity.

64. B

Topic: Developmental Psychology

In the healthiest type of attachment, secure attachment, the child uses the parent as a base to explore the environment of the room, but when the parent leaves, the child exhibits some kind of stress response and is happy when the parent returns. Since this is not happening in this situation, (A) is incorrect. If the child does not seem to react to the parent leaving or coming back, this is a sign that the child and parent have avoidant attachment. This can be caused by the parent not being attentive to the needs of the child, which means that secure attachment never develops. **(B)** describes the response of the child in the question stem, making it correct. (C) is incorrect because in ambivalent attachment, the child tends not to be comforted when the parent returns. (D) is incorrect because the child will tend to run away after the parent returns when there is disorganized attachment. (E) is incorrect because permissive attachment is not recognized terminology (permissive is a parenting style, not an attachment style).

65. D

Topic: Learning

The researcher who first developed the idea of the law of effect was Edward Thorndike, making **(D)** correct. The remaining choices are psychologists known for other research. Albert Bandura, (A), conducted the Bobo doll experiment, which demonstrated that aggression is learned by observing and modeling others. Edward Tolman, (B), was a behaviorist who developed the idea of latent learning by conducting experiments in which rats learned to run mazes even when reinforcement was withheld. Robert Rescorla, (C), studied cognitive processes in classical conditioning and maintained that an unconditioned stimulus is more effective if it surprises the learner. John Watson, (E), was the founder of the behaviorist school; he believed that psychology could only scientifically examine behavior, not unobservable mental processes, and he conducted the Little Albert experiment.

66. B

Topic: Cognitive Psychology

The primacy effect refers to the enhanced ability to recall items at the beginning of a sequence or list. In this context, participants would more easily recall the first things said than the details of the following dialogue. **(B)** is correct. (C) reflects the recency effect, which refers to enhanced memory of items at the end of a list or sequence. The remaining choices reflect neither of these effects.

67. E

Topic: Cognitive Psychology

Priming is the activation, often unconsciously, of particular associations that help with memory retrieval. There are different ways to use priming effectively. One method is to present the same or similar cues associated with the encoding process or the stimulus itself to the participants. Going to the location of the video would provide recall cues because participants could actually see the same environmental stimuli as they saw in the background of the video during their encoding process. Thus, **(E)** is correct. The remaining choices do not involve priming.

68. B

Topic: Cognitive Psychology

The misinformation effect is a phenomenon in which memories are altered by misleading information provided at the point of encoding or, as in this case, at the point of recall. In the study, the only difference between the two groups is that the robber was described as "yelling at" the clerk for the first group, but as "talking to" the clerk for the second group. "Yelling" is more commonly associated with aggression than "talking," so it is not surprising that the first group viewed the robber as being more aggressive due to the biased information supplied. **(B)** is correct. (A) is incorrect because proactive interference is the disruptive effect of old learning on the retrieval of new information, which doesn't apply here. Retroactive interference is the disruptive effect of new learning on the recall of old information; (C) is incorrect. Source amnesia is a memory construction error in which the context of how a memory was acquired is confused; (D) is incorrect. (E) is incorrect because repression is the unconscious stifling of particular memories, usually unpleasant ones, which doesn't apply in this context.

69. D

Topic: Cognitive Psychology

Elizabeth Loftus is best known for her work with false memory formation and the misinformation effect. **(D)** is thus correct. The other psychologists are known for other accomplishments. David Dunning is known for his work describing the Dunning-Kruger effect. While George A. Miller was one of the founders of cognitive psychology, he is most known for his work on human short-term memory. Howard Gardner is known for his development of the theory of multiple intelligences. Philip Zimbardo is known for his Stanford prison experiment and the Lucifer effect.

70. B

Topic: Biological Bases of Behavior

Darwin's theory depends on the concepts of variation, (C), the observation that individual organisms of the same species differ in their traits; inheritance, (E), the recognition that variations in traits can be passed down genetically; fitness, (A), the idea that some variations contribute more to an organism's survival than others; and natural selection, (D), the insight that organisms with better adaptive fitness outcompete less-fit organisms and have more offspring. These evolved traits are specifically known as adaptations because they adapt species to survive in their environments, making **(B)** correct.

71. B

Topic: Motivation, Emotion, and Personality

The incentive theory looks at motivation in terms of positive incentives (rewards) and negative incentives (punishments), so **(B)** is correct. (A) is actually a theory of emotion, not of motivation. (C), (D), and (E) are theories of motivation that focus on internal factors, rather than external factors such as gaining rewards and avoiding punishments.

72. E

Topic: Motivation, Emotion, and Personality

If psychological researchers want to generalize their findings from a sample of people to the larger population (e.g., with respect to which age group has, on average, more openness to experience), they typically use inventories and other surveys that ask close-ended questions (e.g., "Do you like trying new foods—yes or no?"). Thus, **(E)** is correct. (A) is incorrect because open-ended surveys are more difficult to generalize from, given the open-ended nature of the questions. (B), (C), and (D) would be more appropriate for studying one or a small number of subjects, not an entire population.

73. A

Topic: Motivation, Emotion, and Personality

According to Paul Ekman, there are seven basic emotions that are recognized across cultures: happiness, sadness, anger, contempt, disgust, fear, and surprise. Of the answer choices, only **(A)** provides an example of a basic emotion, namely, disgust. The remaining choices are incorrect because they describe non-basic emotions: excitement, jealousy, tiredness, and boredom.

74. C

Topic: Clinical Psychology

Cluster C personality disorders are characterized by anxious and fearful behavior and include the avoidant, dependent, and obsessive-compulsive personality disorders; **(C)** is correct. (D) may be tempting, given the similarities between obsessive-compulsive disorder (OCD) and OCPD. However, individuals with OCD view their obsessions and compulsions as a problem, while those with OCPD view their behavior as normal. (A) is incorrect because Cluster A personality disorders are characterized by odd or eccentric behavior and include the paranoid, schizotypal, and schizoid personality disorders. (B) is incorrect because Cluster B personality disorders are characterized by dramatic or eccentric behaviors and include the antisocial, borderline, histrionic, and narcissistic personality disorders. (E) is incorrect because anxiety disorders do not include personality disorders; individuals with these disorders view their anxiety as a problem.

75. B

Topic: Clinical Psychology

Primary prevention aims to avoid the occurrence of a problem altogether. In this case, advertising that highlights the connection between smoking and lung cancer might stop teens from smoking in the first place. **(B)** is thus correct. The other choices are not primary prevention because they focus on identifying or reducing adolescent nicotine use, rather than preventing it from starting.

76. D

Topic: Biological Bases of Behavior

The pons is a bulge-like structure at the front of the brainstem. The pons brings vital information from the two hemispheres to the cerebellum. The arrow in the figure is pointing to the pons; **(D)** is correct. (A) is incorrect because the parietal lobe is located above the temporal lobe and behind the frontal lobe. (B) is incorrect because the corpus callosum is a thick bundle of nerves in the middle of the brain that connects the two hemispheres. The midbrain is the top portion of the brainstem located above the pons; (C) is incorrect. (E) is incorrect because the cerebral cortex is a thin layer covering the entire cerebrum.

77. B

Topic: Clinical Psychology

Compared to white patients, black patients are more likely to terminate therapeutic relationships prematurely. Since this discrepancy may be due to barriers to accessing services or racially insensitive attitudes, (A) and (E) would likely be helpful strategies. Research has found that using multiculturally sensitive interventions like (C) and (D) also improve outcomes for patients of color. **(B)** is correct because there is no evidence that using cognitive therapy in particular would help improve therapy attendance for black patients.

78. D

Topic: Biological Bases of Behavior

A CT (computed tomography) scan uses X-ray technology to produce a highly detailed, three-dimensional neural image. Thus, it would be the ideal choice for visualizing a complex tumor, making **(D)** correct. A PET scan is commonly used to locate and record brain activity, making it most appropriate for (A). An fMRI measures brain activity by detecting changes in blood flow, making it most appropriate for (B). An MRI produces a detailed, high-resolution image of brain structures and

is especially useful for visualizing soft tissue that cannot be seen on a CT scan; (C) is incorrect. An EEG detects and records electrical brain activity, making it most appropriate for (E).

79. C

Topic: Developmental Psychology

Height in adolescents is influenced by a number of factors from both nature and nurture. (A) is incorrect because malnutrition could lead to lower than normal height in adolescents. (B) is incorrect because severe medical conditions during childhood can also cause stunted height. (D) is incorrect because biological sex influences the onset of puberty, which affects the timing of growth spurts that can greatly increase height; in addition, adult men tend to be taller than adult women. (E) is incorrect because height has a genetic basis, so children are likely to be taller if they have tall parents. That just leaves parenting style, for which there is no evidence that it influences height. **(C)** is thus correct.

80. B

Topic: Social Psychology

Zimbardo is well known for conducting the controversial Stanford Prison experiment, in which student participants were divided into groups to play the role of guard or prisoner. **(B)** is thus correct. The remaining choices summarize other famous experiments, ones not conducted by Zimbardo. (A) refers to the Milgram obedience experiments. (C) is Muzafer Sherif's Robbers Cave experiment. (D) describes research on stereotype threat. (E) is the Asch conformity experiment.

81. B

Topic: Scientific Foundations of Psychology

In John B. Watson's infamous Little Albert study, Watson conditioned a nine-month old child to be afraid of furry stuffed animals by startling him with loud noises in the presence of a white rat. Similar to Pavlov's experiment with dogs, the Little Albert study became a well-known example of classical conditioning and the behaviorist approach to psychology. **(B)** is correct and the remaining choices are incorrect.

82. A

Topic: Sensation and Perception

The fovea is a small indentation in the back of the eye that contains cone cells and helps facilitate color vision. Thus, **(A)** is correct. The iris controls the size of the pupil, which is where light enters the eye; (B) is incorrect. The pupil is the opening that allows light to enter into the eye; (C) is incorrect. The lens helps focus light onto the photoreceptor cells in the eye and is a clear, curved structure; (D) is incorrect. The cornea is a clear barrier between the structures of the eye and the outside world; (E) is incorrect.

83. A

Topic: Social Psychology

Ethnocentrism refers to judging other cultures on the basis of the values of your own culture. **(A)** best reflects this phenomenon because the tourist perceived another culture's culinary habits as disgusting on the basis of American culture's expectations about guinea pigs. (B) is incorrect because it involves the judgment of a consumer product that is common to both cultures. (C) is incorrect because there is no indication of a difference in cultures. (D) is incorrect because the corporation is simply following a particular cultural trend. (E) is incorrect because there is no indication of a clash between two distinct cultures.

84. C

Topic: Scientific Foundations of Psychology

Humanistic psychology emphasizes individual free will and the importance of self-development. A humanist would argue that in the face of difficult struggles, a person is free to choose how to manage the situation. Thus, **(C)** is correct. (A) is incorrect because it better reflects the sociocultural approach, which argues that people in a child's environment, including parents, teachers, and peers, play an important role in behavioral and psychological development. The biological approach focuses on studying the neurological bases behind psychological phenomena; (B) reflects this approach and is thus incorrect. (D) is incorrect because it reflects the behavioral approach, which argues that people are shaped through learning from previous experience. (E) is incorrect because it represents a psychoanalytic perspective with its focus on the unconscious.

85. A

Topic: Clinical Psychology

Eclectic therapy is when a therapist intentionally draws from a variety of approaches. **(A)** is correct because focusing on childhood experiences is a technique from psychodynamic therapy, cognitive restructuring is a technique from cognitive therapy, and unconditional positive regard is a technique from humanistic therapy. (B), (C), and (D) are incorrect because each describes only one element in the therapist's multifaceted approach. (E) is incorrect because "mixed" is not a term used to describe any therapeutic approach.

86. A

Topic: Scientific Foundations of Psychology

Biological psychologists investigate the interactions between the nervous system and behavior. In the question stem, the subject of study is the ratio of time spent in two distinctive neurological states (REM sleep to NREM sleep) and its effect on depressive behavior; **(A)** is correct. The other choices incorrectly characterize the perspective of the research as described.

87. B

Topic: Scientific Foundations of Psychology

Measures of spread describe the distribution of data, or how spread out the values are. The most common measures of spread are the range, variance, and standard deviation of a dataset. **(B)** is thus correct. (A) is incorrect because the correlation coefficient is a measure of how closely two variables are associated; it gives no indication of the dispersion of the data. (C) and (D) are incorrect because the mean and median are measures of central tendency, not spread. A confidence interval is a range of values that likely contains a parameter's true value (often with a 95% probability); though the range of values may vary in breadth, a confidence interval is not a direct measure of dispersion, making (E) incorrect.

88. D

Topic: Sensation and Perception

Binocular disparity is a binocular clue that allows humans to place objects in space. Because each eye sees a slightly different picture, the brain is able to process images coming from both eyes and determine depth, which means that **(D)** is correct. (A) is incorrect because it describes linear perspective, which is a monocular cue. (B) is incorrect because it describes opponent-process theory, which has to do with color processing and not with depth perception or binocular cues. (C) is incorrect because it describes interaural level difference, which has to do with hearing and not sight. (E) is incorrect because it describes monaural cues, which have to do with hearing and not sight.

89. B

Topic: Learning

A high-level process that involves thinking, anticipating, and other complex mental processes is cognitive learning, making **(B)** correct. Latent learning occurs without any obvious reinforcement and remains unexpressed until reinforcement is provided, while insight learning is a type of learning that occurs by suddenly understanding how to solve a problem rather than by trial and error, eliminating (A) and (C). (D) and (E) are incorrect because emotional learning addresses how emotions and emotional state affect cognitive processes, including memory formation and retrieval, and biofeedback uses electronic monitoring of autonomic functions (such as heart rate, blood pressure, or stress responses) for the purpose of bringing those functions under partially voluntary control.

90. E

Topic: Cognitive Psychology

A typical IQ test has a mean of 100 and a standard deviation of 15. People are considered intellectually disabled if they score two standard deviations or more below the mean. Conversely, gifted people have IQ scores two standard deviations or more above the mean, which corresponds to a score of 130 or above. **(E)** is correct because it is the only score among the choices in this range. The other choices correspond to scores within two standard deviations of the mean, which would be considered about average for IQ.

91. C

Topic: Learning

In classical conditioning, extinction is the cessation of a learned response after a conditioned stimulus stops being paired with an unconditioned stimulus. **(C)** best captures this definition. The remaining choices are definitions of other terms. (A) describes escape conditioning, (B) describes stimulus generalization, (D) describes shaping, and (E) describes learned helplessness.

92. D

Topic: Sensation and Perception

As a sound enters the ear through the auditory canal, it vibrates the tympanic membrane. This membrane is the beginning of the middle ear. Within the middle ear, there are small bones called ossicles (the malleus, incus, and stapes) that rest on the tympanic membrane and shake when the tympanic membrane shakes. The stapes rests on the oval window of the inner ear and transmits these vibrations to the fluid within the inner ear. The cochlea, part of the inner ear, contains specialized cells that turn these vibrations into nerve impulses. This pathway is described correctly by **(D)**, making it correct. The remaining choices describe the pathway incorrectly.

93. E

Topic: Developmental Psychology

In this case, the pieces of cake are the same size, but that does not stop Carlos from thinking that his brother got more than him. This is likely because Carlos has not yet developed an understanding of conservation. If Carlos understood conservation, he would know that changing the appearance (the number of pieces) did not change the amount of cake each child was given. However, since he is in the preoperational stage, which is the stage for children between ages two and seven, he does not understand the notion of conservation, so **(E)** is correct. (A) is incorrect because egocentrism is the self-centered perspective characteristic of young children. A lack of stranger anxiety would not explain Carlos' reaction since that principle has to do with being uncomfortable around strangers; (B) is incorrect. A lack of abstract reasoning is not at play since Carlos is not trying to solve an abstract problem; (C) is incorrect. Object permanence usually develops in the sensorimotor stage and does not have to do with the amount of cake each boy gets; (D) is incorrect.

94. B
Topic: Developmental Psychology

As adults age, they tend to reduce the number of social contacts and friendships that they have. However, the ties that remain typically become stronger and closer than previous relationships. This phenomenon is described by the socioemotional selectivity theory, and **(B)** is correct. (A) is the opposite of what socioemotional selectivity theory would predict. (C) is associated with Erikson's view of the psychosocial development of adolescents, so it is incorrect. (D) does happen with aging, but it is not associated with socioemotional selectivity theory and is thus incorrect. (E) is a normal part of the psychosocial development of adults but does not have to do with socioemotional selectivity.

95. C
Topic: Clinical Psychology

The two important factors to consider in this scenario are that Mary regularly purges her meals and that she has a normal BMI. Both of these facts point to bulimia nervosa, making **(C)** correct. (A) is a tempting answer, but anorexia nervosa is a disorder characterized by a strong desire to lose weight, a low BMI, and habitually restrictive eating, making it incorrect. (B) is eliminated because binge eating disorder is characterized by a tendency to consume large quantities of food and an inability to regulate consumption. (D) and (E) are incorrect because somatic symptom disorder is defined by the presence of bodily symptoms that lack physiological causes, and conversion disorder is characterized by the unexplained inhibition of voluntary functions.

96. D
Topic: Clinical Psychology

Schizotypal personality disorder is defined by having extreme superstitions and similar strange thinking patterns, making **(D)** correct. (A) is eliminated because schizoid personality disorder is characterized by emotional detachment and poor social skills. (B) is incorrect because cyclothymic disorder is defined by hypomanic and dysthymic episodes. Histrionic personality disorder is characterized by extreme extraversion and attention-seeking behavior, eliminating (C). Lastly, avoidant personality disorder is characterized by extreme shyness and intense fear of rejection, making (E) incorrect.

97. E
Topic: Learning

Classical conditioning occurs when a neutral stimulus is conditioned to elicit a response by being paired with a stimulus that elicits a natural, unconditioned response. (A) is incorrect because it describes the Little Albert experiment, a famous example of classical conditioning. (B) is incorrect because it describes an experiment similar to those that Ivan Pavlov conducted on dogs. (C) is incorrect because the unconditioned stimulus (the shock) is paired with the conditioned stimulus (pressing an elevator button) to cause a conditioned fear response. (D) is incorrect because it offers an example of taste aversion, a particular variation of classical conditioning that can occur after only a single experience. By process of elimination, **(E)** must be correct, and indeed this is an example of observational learning similar to the Bobo doll experiment conducted by Albert Bandura.

98. D
Topic: Motivation, Emotion, and Personality

The social cognitive perspective includes the idea of reciprocal determinism, that human beings both shape and are shaped by their environments. **(D)** is thus correct. (A) is incorrect because the biopsychological perspective emphasizes the influence of genes on personality. (B) and (E) are incorrect because they are two names for a perspective that emphasizes the role of the unconscious. (C) is incorrect because the behaviorist perspective would only acknowledge that human beings are shaped by their environments, but not that they shape those environments in turn.

99. A

Topic: Developmental Psychology

Erikson laid out eight stages of psychosocial development. He described adolescence, approximately between the ages of 12 and 18, as a time when teenagers experiment with their identities and the roles that they play. This is sometimes characterized by adolescents rejecting the identity that parents have set forth for them and trying on a variety of different roles and identities as they try to find one that fits them. Erikson described the developmental conflict as identity vs. role confusion, which means that **(A)** is correct. The remaining choices are other stages in Erikson's theory encountered at other times of life. (B) is the seventh stage, typically encountered during middle age. (C) is the first stage, which lasts until about a year-and-a-half of age. (D) is the third stage, typically encountered between ages three and six. (E) is the sixth stage, typically encountered during young adulthood.

100. E

Topic: Social Psychology

Research on attraction suggests that a number of factors influence its development and persistence. Geographical proximity increases the likelihood of attraction, which eliminates (A). Physical attractiveness is also important for attraction, so (B) is incorrect. (C) is incorrect because it describes the matching hypothesis, which has also been supported by research. (D) is incorrect because it is consistent with the phenomenon of reciprocal liking, in which people are more attracted to those who seem to like them back. That leaves **(E)**, which is correct because it contradicts the finding that people are more likely to be attracted to those who are fundamentally similar to them, not to those who are fundamentally different.

Section II

1. This question is worth 7 points, 1 point for each explanation and correct application to the situation. The following is a sample student response that would receive full credit, with indications of where points would be awarded in parentheses:

Conformity occurs when individuals in a group modify their behaviors to match others in the group, even if they do not agree with the group as a whole. When Jakub's friends started shunning Samir, they were participating in conformity. They did not participate in the situation that caused the disagreement between Jakub and Samir, but nevertheless followed Jakub's example and conformed to the group behavior of shunning Samir. (**1 POINT**)

Observational learning is learning based on watching the experience of others. Stefan served as a model for Jakub's behavior because Jakub learned his shunning behavior through observational learning. Jakub observed his father ignoring Olivia because of their disagreement, and despite the fact that he refused to shun Olivia himself, he nevertheless modeled this behavior in the way that he responded to Samir after the two of them had a disagreement. (**1 POINT**)

The fundamental attribution error is the tendency to attribute other people's actions to dispositional, rather than situational, factors. Stefan is likely falling prey to the fundamental attribution error because of how he interprets Olivia's behavior. When he talks to Jakub about it, he frames their disagreement as arising from something that is inherent to Olivia—namely, that she is a bad person. He attributes their disagreement to Olivia's disposition, not to the unique circumstances of the situation. (**1 POINT**)

Instead of confronting the problem or resolving the disagreement, Stefan is repressing his feelings about Olivia by not speaking with or about her. He could be in denial in some way, which is why he does not want to discuss Olivia with Jakub or anyone else in the family. These are both defense mechanisms, methods that the ego uses to protect itself from anxiety, that were characterized by Sigmund Freud. (**1 POINT**)

Jakub is showing signs of post-conventional morality according to Lawrence Kohlberg. Instead of accepting that his aunt is a bad person as dictated by his father, he violates his father's wishes and still contacts her. This means that he does not accept that morality is simply a matter of following rules given by authorities. He may be starting to question what moral principles are truly important to him. (**1 POINT**)

Based on his age and behavior, Jakub is likely in stage 5 of Erik Erikson's stages of psychosocial development, the conflict known as identity vs. role confusion. In this stage, he is developing his own identity and choosing the roles he will play in his life. This might be a contributing factor as to why he does not blindly accept his father's judgment of his aunt and still contacts her. (**1 POINT**)

According to Vygotsky, a more knowledgeable other (MKO) is someone with a better understanding of a task who is able to help learners learn that task if it's in their zone of proximal development. In this case, Olivia was acting as an MKO for Jakub with math. Because Olivia had more expertise in this area after going to college for mathematics, she was able to introduce Jakub to new ways of thinking about the content and new approaches to tackling his math problems. (**1 POINT**)

2. This question is worth 7 points: 2 for Part A, 2 for Part B, and 3 for Part C. The following is a sample student response that would receive full credit, with indications of where points would be awarded in parentheses:

In this experiment, the independent variable was the type of dance that the Parkinson's patients received lessons for, either tango or swing. (**1 POINT**) The dependent variable is the incidence of Parkinson's symptoms, as measured by the questionnaires. (**1 POINT**)

One way to improve the internal validity of the study would be to include an actual control group, one that received neither tango nor swing lessons. Without a proper control group, it is impossible to compare the results with a baseline state. (**1 POINT**) Another way to improve the internal validity would be to use random assignment for the experimental groups, rather than simply dividing people by last name. Non-random assignment can lead to systematic differences between experimental groups that can distort results. (**1 POINT**)

Dopamine is a neurotransmitter involved in mood, movement, attention, and learning. While too little dopamine can lead to Parkinson's disease, too much dopamine can result in schizophrenia. (**1 POINT**)

The parts of the brain responsible for fine motor control are the basal ganglia, which are located in the midbrain region. (**1 POINT**) The cerebellum, part of the hindbrain, is the area of the brain that most directly controls balance, but the vestibular system, located in the middle ear, plays a crucial role as well. (**1 POINT**)